The British Polity

Fifth Edition

Philip Norton

The University of Hull

Longman
Boston Columbus Indianapolis New York San Francisco Upper Saddle River
Amsterdam Cape Town Dubai London Madrid Milan Munich Paris Montreal Toronto
Delhi Mexico City São Paulo Sydney Hong Kong Seoul Singapore Taipei Tokyo

Acquisitions Editor: Vikram Mukhija
Editorial Assistant: Toni Magyar
Marketing Manager: Lindsey Prudhomme
Production Manager: Renata Butera
Project Coordination, Text Design, and Electronic Page Makeup: GGS Higher Education
  Resources, PMG
Creative Design Director: Jayne Conte
Cover Designer: Mary Siener
Cover Illustration/Photo: Andy Rain/Corbis
Manufacturing Buyer: Renata Butera
Printer and Binder: Courier, Stoughton
Cover Printer: Courier, Stoughton

Library of Congress Cataloging-in-Publication Data

Norton, Philip.
  The British polity / Philip Norton. — 5th ed.
    p. cm.
  Includes bibliographical references and index.
  ISBN-13: 978-0-321-21666-3 (alk. paper)
  ISBN-10: 0-321-21666-0 (alk. paper)
  1. Great Britain—Politics and government.   I. Title.
  JN231.N669 2011
  320.941–dc22
                            2009038695

Longman
is an imprint of

www.pearsonhighered.com

1 2 3 4 5 6 7 8 9 10—CRS—13 12 11 10

ISBN-13: 978-0-321-21666-3
ISBN-10:   0-321-21666-0

BRIEF CONTENTS

DETAILED CONTENTS

PREFACE

The theme of previous editions of *The British Polity* has been that of continuity and change in British politics. The theme is one that applies to the content of this edition. I have maintained the basic structure of the book, providing for continuity with previous editions. However, within the basic framework, there has been substantial change. This has been necessitated by the sheer scale of change in British politics over the past decade. The last edition was published in 2001. Since then, there has been significant constitutional, political, economic, and social change within the United Kingdom. In 2001, a Labour government under Prime Minister Tony Blair was elected for a second term of office with a large parliamentary majority; the Conservative opposition appeared to be destined for a lengthy stay in the political wilderness; the country was enjoying continued, indeed unparalleled, economic growth; and the constitutional reforms introduced by the Government—not least devolution of power to elected assemblies in Scotland and Wales—appeared to be bedding in effectively. It appeared to be an era of stability and growth. By the end of the decade, the situation was transformed. A Labour government under a new Prime Minister, Gordon Brown, faced economic turmoil and the legacy of an unpopular war with Iraq; the Conservative opposition looked likely to form the next government; and many of the constitutional reforms were not working out as intended. The British constitution was unsettled or, in the words of one distinguished political scientist, "a mess." The constitutional framework lacked coherence. There was no clear sense of direction.

NEW TO THIS EDITION

The extent of change is covered in this volume. It has necessitated extensive revision and the inclusion of much new data. I have also introduced material or reworked analyses in response to suggestions made by readers. Every chapter has been subject to some change. The principal features new to this edition include:

- more comparative material, not least in locating British society in relation to European and U.S. society (especially in Chapter 1).
- a sharper delineation of the legacies of empire, war, class, and political structures in shaping the contemporary British polity (Chapter 3).
- coverage of constitutional change (Chapter 4), including a settlement to the conflict in Northern Ireland (Chapter 10), and the introduction of a Supreme Court (Chapter 14).
- greater opportunities for lobbying by interest groups as a consequence of the dispersal of power to different decision-making bodies (Chapter 7).

- the results and consequences of elections to the U.K. Parliament (2001, 2005), the European Parliament (2004, 2009), and the devolved assemblies (2003, 2007) (Chapters 6, 9, 10).
- the scale and nature of political change, not least in relation to the fortunes of the political parties and the growth of support for third parties (Chapter 6).
- explanations not only of decline in support for a two-party system but also decline in support for political parties (Chapter 6).
- the changing face, fragmentation, and uncertain future of local government in England and Wales (Chapter 11).
- changes in the U.K. Parliament, the collapse in confidence as a result of the expenses scandal of 2009, and explanations of parliamentary power (Chapter 12).
- the changing nature and fragmentation of the mass media (Chapter 15).
- greater clarity in terms of theoretical approaches to constitutional change and the challenges facing the parties as they determine their stances on the future of the British constitution (Chapter 16).

Every chapter has been brought up to date, with the employment wherever possible of the most recent available data. Events as disparate as the decision by the British government in 2009 to provide some funding to charities to mount campaigns (Chapter 7) through to the *New Statesman* magazine the same year adding its (relatively isolated) voice to calls for the abolition of the monarchy (Chapter 13) have been included.

Since the previous edition, exchange rates have fluctuated, sometimes quite markedly. In this edition, dollar equivalents are calculated on an exchange rate of £1 = \$1.64.

FEATURES

The volume has three distinctive features, relating to structure, content, and theme.

The book is structured in order to provide a clear conceptual framework for the understanding of British politics, influenced in broad terms by a systems approach to public policy. As a result, it departs from a fairly common practice of considering the executive and legislature in tandem and focuses in the main section (Part III) on the bodies that determine public policy.

Part I establishes the cultural and historical framework for understanding contemporary British politics. Part II analyses the constitutional and political environment that shapes the making of public policy: the constitution, the electoral system, political parties, and interest groups. Part III examines the bodies that now make public policy: the U.K. government, the institutions of the European Union, the executives in Scotland, Wales, and

Northern Ireland, and local government in the United Kingdom. Part IV considers the bodies responsible for scrutinizing and legitimizing the policies of the U.K. government: Parliament and the monarchy. Part V looks at the bodies responsible for enforcing public policy (the courts and the police) and for communicating the actions of politicians and others (the mass media). Part VI examines the different approaches to constitutional change, the basic conflict between what have emerged as the two principal approaches, and the problems facing the political parties in determining a coherent approach to the type of constitution they favor for the United Kingdom. The book is thus designed to offer a comprehensive overview of the contemporary political system of the United Kingdom.

In terms of content, each chapter has been written as far as possible as a self-contained study. This is designed to have pedagogic utility, enabling instructors to select specific chapters for use in thematic as well as country-based courses. I have employed cross-referencing but, in order to maintain the internal coherence of a chapter it has sometimes been necessary to include a brief summation of material that can be found in the relevant core chapter. This also reduces the need for students to keep checking other parts of the book as they study a particular chapter. Also for pedagogic reasons, the chapters addressing institutions and processes seek not only to identify and explain the nature and operation of the body or process but also to draw out the debate surrounding it. Few aspects of the political process are free of controversy: Each has its supporters and critics. I seek to provide both sides of the argument.

In terms of approach, the key theme is that of continuity and change. Continuity is a clear and obvious feature of British politics. Much of the basic constitutional framework has been in place for centuries. A monarch and parliament were well established before Christopher Columbus sailed for the New World. The basic relationship between Crown and Parliament was established by constitutional changes introduced in the seventeenth century. However, continuity in terms of form has often masked substantial change in substance. Those changes have been especially marked in the past forty years, not least as a result of the United Kingdom's membership of the European Community (now the European Union) and the reforms introduced by a Labour government after 1997.

In looking at change, there are essentially two underlying and related themes. The first is the extent to which policy-making power has been fragmented. Power used to be heavily centralized within the government of the United Kingdom. In recent decades, some policy-making power has passed upward to the institutions of the European Union, some downward to elected bodies in Scotland, Wales, Northern Ireland, and London, and some sideways to the courts. This fragmentation has been the result of disparate changes to the constitution rather than the result of a single coherent approach to constitutional change. This creates problems for the political parties in addressing the future shape of the British constitution.

The related theme is that of the "Americanization" of British politics. Changes of recent decades will resonate with Americans: the dispersal of power among a range of elected and judicial bodies, the creation of a Supreme Court, the (relatively greater) willingness of legislators not to be dictated to by their parties. This resonance is variously addressed, though the theme itself is not drawn out explicitly or developed in depth. The reason for this is simple. Though there have been changes that will be recognizable in American eyes, the most significant feature of the British polity is its continuing dissimilarity to the U.S. polity rather than its similarity. The differences between the two may not be as marked as they were some decades ago, but they remain great and essentially unbridgeable. The reasons for this I seek to explain in the opening chapters.

SUPPLEMENTS

Longman is pleased to offer several resources to qualified adopters of *The British Polity* and their students that will make teaching and learning from this book even more effective and enjoyable.

For Instructors and Students

MYPOLISCIKIT VIDEO CASE STUDIES. Featuring video from major news sources and providing reporting and insight on recent world affairs, this DVD series helps instructors integrate current events into their courses by letting them use the clips as lecture launchers or discussion starters.

For Students

MYSEARCHLAB. Need help with a paper? MySearchLab saves time and improves results by offering start-to-finish guidance on the research/writing process and full-text access to academic journals and periodicals. Order MySearchLab with this book and receive a 15 percent discount. To learn more, please visit www.mysearchlab.com <http://www.mypoliscikit.com/> or contact your Pearson representative. To order MySearchLab with this book, use ISBN 0205719333.

ACKNOWLEDGMENTS

In writing this new edition, I have incurred a number of debts. I am especially grateful to Vik Mukhija at Pearson Longman for his encouragement and prodding, which has ensured the completion of this edition. I am also grateful to various readers who reviewed and commented on the previous edition and made some valuable suggestions. My thanks are also due to Peter Just, who has assisted with researching some data, and my colleague at the University of Hull, James Connelly, for reading part of Chapter 6.

As I have indicated, a number of changes have been made in succeeding editions as a result of comments from readers. I thank the following reviewers for their feedback: Jim Alt, Harvard University; Marat Akopian, Rutgers University; David Coates, Wake Forest University; and Bruce Wilson, University of Central Florida. I am again happy to invite comments; those from colleagues and readers have been extremely helpful. I alone, though, remain responsible for any errors, omissions, or misinterpretations that remain.

Philip Norton

PART

I

INTRODUCTION

CHAPTER

1

The Contemporary Landscape

ontinuity and change are features of every political system. What
makes each system significant is the nature and the extent of that
change. Some systems are characterized by rapid and sometimes
revolutionary change. Others are noted for continuity with past experience
and structures. The task of the student of politics is to discern the distinctive
features of that continuity and change; to generate concepts; and, if possible,
to construct models and theories that will aid understanding of and serve to
explain those distinctive features and the relationship among them.

The distinctive features of a political system can be recognized by comparing that system with another or, better still, with many others. In discussing the merits of comparative politics, a student in a class of mine once
objected to the whole exercise. "There's no point in comparing one country
with another," he argued. "Every country is unique." As others in the class
were quick to respond, the only way by which one knows that a country is
unique is by comparing it with others. Comparison is a fundamental tool of
understanding. Comparing one system or body with another enables one to
move beyond description and to consider relationships and what may be the
cause of those relationships. It also provides the means of establishing the
best, or a more desirable, way of organizing the system and enabling it to
operate more effectively and efficiently.

Space and resources preclude an exhaustive or even an extensive comparative study in this work. Instead, I will illustrate the distinctive nature of the
British polity by comparing it, principally though not exclusively, with the
American. They are similar in many respects, with a shared language; advanced
industrial economies; similar but not always identical political, social, and
economic values; and some mutual needs. Each has a sense of affinity with the
other. As we shall see, however, there are significant dissimilarities, which make

a comparative exercise useful. Such an exercise will serve not only to sensitize the American reader to the distinctive features of the British polity but also to make readers more aware of the features of their own polity.

However, if the United States and the United Kingdom are notably different, which one is closer to the international norm? If they are similar, are they alone in the world in sharing such similarities? To offer a wider perspective, the position of the United States and the United Kingdom will, where space and data permit, be put in a wider international context.

To help the reader understand continuity and change within the British polity, I will stress the significance of the political culture. Before we proceed to an analysis of that culture, a brief sketch of the salient features of contemporary Britain is necessary. This outline is especially pertinent for comparative purposes. There are important dissimilarities between the United States and Britain (and indeed between Britain and many other countries) in terms of geography, demography, and social history. Britain is a small, crowded island, largely oriented in terms of industry and population to England (and especially the southeast of England), with a class-based society that has superseded, but by no means discarded altogether the characteristics of, a feudal society. The purpose of this chapter is to highlight those features. Such a study is a prerequisite for a consideration of the political culture and the institutions and processes that culture nurtures.

LAND AND POPULATION

In terms of land distribution and usage, Great Britain is a predominantly agricultural kingdom, based on the three countries of England, Scotland, and Wales. (The United Kingdom comprises these three countries plus Northern Ireland: See Map 1.1.) However, in terms of the distribution and activities of the population, it is predominantly English, nonagricultural, and urban.

Great Britain occupies a total area of 88,798 square miles. This compares with an area of 3,615,123 square miles for the United States. Within the United States, ten states each have a greater land area than Britain. Alaska (586,412 square miles), Texas (267,339), and California (158,693) are the most notable. England has approximately the same land area as New York State, Scotland the same as South Carolina, and Wales the same as Massachusetts.

The disparity in population size is also substantial, though not quite so extreme. In 2008, the U.K. population was estimated to be 60.9 million, up from 38.2 million at the beginning of the twentieth century. The U.S. population in 2008 was estimated to be 303.8 million, up from 76 million in 1900. There is also a significant difference in population growth, as reflected in these figures. In 2008, the yearly growth rate in the United States was estimated to be 0.88 percent, compared to 0.28 percent in the United Kingdom. In terms of growth rates, Britain is a typical West European country. The largest growth rates are to be found in Africa and the Middle East, with many countries having a growth rate of more than 2 and sometimes 3 percent.

N

W ← → E

S

ATLANTIC
OCEAN

SCOTLAND

NORTH
SEA

Glasgow ● ● Edinburgh

NORTHERN
IRELAND ● Belfast

Leeds ●

Bradford ●
Manchester ●
Liverpool ● ● Sheffield

ENGLAND

● Birmingham

WALES

Cardiff ●
Bristol ●

LONDON

ENGLISH
CHANNEL

MAP 1.1
The United Kingdom

When the population is put in the context of land size, Britain emerges as a crowded island. The number of people per square mile in 2006 was just under 640 (or just over 246 per square kilometer). By European standards, this is high but not exceptional: The Netherlands and Belgium are even more densely populated and Germany is almost as densely populated. Globally, the United Kingdom is the 32nd most densely populated country (out of 192). The number of people per square mile in the United States in 2006 was just under 80. By worldwide standards, this is a low but not exceptional figure: It puts the United States in 142nd place. Russia, Brazil, New Zealand, Australia, and Canada are among the nations with lower population density.

Within the United Kingdom, the population is heavily concentrated in one country. In 2006, 50.7 million people were estimated to live in England (84 percent of the U.K. population), compared with a little over 5 million in Scotland (8 percent), just under 3 million in Wales (5 percent), and 1.7 million in Northern Ireland (3 percent). Within England, the greatest concentration of inhabitants is in the southeast of the country (that is, Greater London and the surrounding counties); just under one-third of the population of the United Kingdom resides there.

The population resides predominantly in areas classified, for local government purposes, as urban. Over 80 percent of the population in England, and more than 70 percent in Scotland and Wales, live in urban areas. Of people living in urban areas, 41 percent live in the ten most populous urban areas (Table 1.1), accounting for approximately one-third of the nation's population. The shift from rural to urban areas has been

TABLE 1.1

MOST POPULOUS URBAN AREAS IN THE UNITED KINGDOM, 2001

Urban area	Population (thousands)
Greater London	8,278
West Midlands[1]	2,284
Greater Manchester	2,240
West Yorkshire[2]	1,499
Greater Glasgow	1,168
Tyneside[3]	880
Liverpool	816
Nottingham	666
Sheffield	640
Bristol	551

[1]Includes Birmingham, the nation's second largest city
[2]Includes Leeds and Bradford
[3]Includes Newcastle upon Tyne
Source: Census 2001, Office for National Statistics

marked in England, the proportion of the population living in nonurban areas declining from a little over 35 percent in 1951 to not much more than 20 percent twenty years later.

Although approximately three-quarters of the land surface is used for agriculture, very few people are employed in the agricultural industry. There has been a persistent drift from land work since industrialization in the eighteenth and nineteenth centuries, a trend that continues. In the latter half of the twentieth century, the number of people employed in agriculture, forestry, and fishing had more than halved. Increased efficiency and greater mechanization have in part facilitated this development. (Britain has one of the heaviest tractor densities in the world.) By 2007, the number of employees in agriculture was down to 166,000; of these, almost 60,000 were seasonal or casual workers.[1] Just over half of the land on agricultural holdings is considered to be croppable, though three-fifths of the full-time farms are devoted mainly to dairying or beef cattle and sheep. Farms devoted to arable crops are predominant in the eastern part of England. Sheep and cattle rearing is a feature of the hills and moorland areas of Scotland, Wales, and northern and southwestern England.

Although Britain exports agrochemicals, agricultural equipment, and some agricultural produce and food products, it nonetheless has to import a substantial portion of its food supply. Indeed, Britain is heavily dependent on imports of raw materials. Compared with other large industrialized (and some developing) nations, Britain is notably lacking in natural resources. The exception is energy resources: It is a producer of oil and natural gas, though production peaked at the end of the twentieth century and is not adequate for the purposes of self-sufficiency. The United Kingdom is largely dependent on other nations either wholly or in part for products such as cotton, rubber, lead, tin, phosphates, rice, corn, silk, coffee, and tobacco. The list is by no means exhaustive. The United States, by contrast, is self-sufficient in most of these products, with surplus supply in several cases. Among other things, the United States is the world's largest producer, and consumer, of lead. France, Germany, Canada, Japan, and India are also more self-sufficient than Britain. This lack of raw materials is important not only for an understanding of contemporary Britain but also in providing a partial explanation of Britain's internationalist and imperialist history.

LINGUISTIC AND RACIAL DIFFERENCES

The population is predominantly English in birth as well as residence. It is also predominantly white and English-speaking. It is not, however, totally homogeneous. Not only is there a division in Britain between the English, the Scots, and the Welsh; there is also a division in Scotland between those who do and do not speak Gaelic, and in Wales between those who do and do not speak Welsh. In both cases, those who speak the traditional native languages are in a small minority. In Wales, only about one in five inhabitants can speak Welsh (down from one in two at the beginning of the twentieth century), though the number of people learning the language has shown an increase in recent years. The 2001 census revealed that in Scotland just over 92,000 people (under 2 percent of the population) had some Gaelic language ability; the number who could speak the language had fallen, though the number who could read it had increased. Most of those able to speak Gaelic are concentrated in the Scottish highlands and islands. Looking beyond Britain to Northern Ireland, a few families in the province still speak the Irish form of Gaelic. However, as we shall see in Chapter 10, the absence of homogeneity in the province extends far beyond linguistic differences.

The influx of immigrants into Britain, especially in the 1950s and early 1960s (numbers have been limited since the passage of the Commonwealth Immigrants Act of 1962), has also added to the diversity of the population and to linguistic differences. Immigration has resulted in a significant increase in the number of nonwhite citizens, though they constitute a small proportion of the population. The number of nonwhite people in Britain at the beginning of the twenty-first century (the 2001 Census) was 4.6 million—up from more than 1 million in 1968—with the largest single nonwhite community being the Indian (see Table 1.2). Of the ethnic minority population, just over half is U.K.-born. The nonwhite community constitutes 7.2 percent of the population. It is, though, relatively heavily concentrated—a factor often claimed to exacerbate racial tension—in a number of urban areas, notably London, Leicester, Birmingham, Bradford, and various other towns in the West Midlands and Yorkshire.

TABLE 1.2

POPULATION BY ETHNICITY, 2001

Ethnic Group	Population (thousands)	Minority ethnic population %
White	541,153 (92.1)	n/a
Mixed	677 (1.2)	14.6
Indian	1053 (1.8)	22.7
Pakistani	747 (1.3)	16.1
Bangladeshi	283 (0.5)	6.1
Other Asian	247 (0.4)	5.3
Black Caribbean	565 (1.0)	12.2
Black African	485 (0.8)	10.5
Other Black	97 (0.2)	2.1
Chinese	247 (0.4)	5.3
Other	230 (0.4)	5.0
Total minority ethnic population 4635 (7.9)		100

Source: Census 2001, Office for National Statistics

The United States has experienced analogous problems of concentration but has a much larger nonwhite population, African Americans accounting for more than 12 percent of the population. (There are also more than 7 million other nonwhite Americans.) There is also another significant difference. The African American population is as indigenous as the white. (Native Americans now account for well under 1 percent of the population.) As such, it is unusual for a black American to be asked, "Where do you come from?"—meaning, "What is your country of origin?"—whereas such a question is often asked of nonwhite Britons. The United States also has a far greater ethnic mix than the United Kingdom. The combined noun is common in discussions of that mix (German Americans, Polish Americans); there is no equivalent use in the United Kingdom.

RELIGION

Britain, like the United States, is a predominantly Protestant country. There the similarity largely ends. Britain has an established church, the United States does not. There is no separation of church and state in the United Kingdom. Religious assemblies are held in schools, mangers are displayed on public land at Christmas, and various official occasions—such as the enthronement of a new monarch—are held in church. Disputes over prayers in school occur but are unrelated to the principle of whether or not prayers should be held: The dispute is over whether they have to be predominantly Christian. (Some schools have a majority of non-Christian pupils.) Of publicly funded secondary schools, about one-third are "faith schools," that is, have a religious character; of these, the overwhelming majority are Christian.

Such a link between church and state says little, however, about religious dedication. Though most Britons identify themselves as Christians (just over 71 percent in the 2001 Census: Table 1.3), few are regular churchgoers and only about one-third actually believe in God or any type of Supreme Being. A 2006 survey found that only 10 percent of the population attend a place of worship once a week or more; 59 percent never or practically never go to church.[2] According to a Eurobarometer poll in 2005, only 38 percent of Britons believed in God. This put the United Kingdom in the lower half of EU countries. Most of those in the top half (mostly Roman Catholic countries) believed in God, whereas most citizens in the other half did not. The United Kingdom ranked 19th out of the 27 countries.[3] Whereas Britain is becoming a notably more secular nation, the United States remains a highly religious one. A *Financial Times*/Harris poll in 2006 found that the percentage of Americans believing in any form of God was 73 percent, almost twice the percentage of believers in the United Kingdom.[4]

Membership of a religion in the United Kingdom has shown a marked decline in recent decades. According to the British Social Attitudes Survey 2006/07, in 1964 almost three-quarters of Britons (74 percent) belonged to a religion and attended services; by 2005, the figure was only 31 percent.[5] The principal Christian churches have all suffered a marked decline in membership.

TABLE 1.3

RELIGION IN THE UNITED KINGDOM, 2001

	Religious affiliation	
	Thousands	Percentage
Christian	42079	71.6
Buddhist	152	0.3
Hindu	559	1.0
Jewish	267	0.5
Muslim	1591	2.7
Sikh	336	0.6
Other religion	179	0.3
No religion	9104	15.6
Not stated	4289	7.3

Source: Census 2001, Office for National Statistics

The Anglican Church of England is "by law established" the official church in England. (The Presbyterian Church of Scotland is the established church there.) As such, it is variously involved in the affairs of state. The monarch is the supreme governor (temporal head) of the church, and arch-bishops, bishops, and deans are appointed formally by the queen. The corona-tion of a new monarch is conducted by the senior churchman in the Anglican faith (the archbishop of Canterbury), and services of national celebration, or grief, are conducted in one of the principal Anglican churches, usually West-minster Abbey or St. Paul's Cathedral in London. The monarch is required by statute to be a member of the Church of England and must promise to uphold the faith. The most senior figures in the church—2 archbishops and 24 of the bishops—sit in the House of Lords. Various measures affecting the governing principles of the church require parliamentary approval.

A broad Protestant church, the Church of England was founded by King Henry VIII in the sixteenth century following his break with the Roman Catholic Church.[6] It comprises two provinces: Canterbury, headed by the archbishop of Canterbury (titled primate of all England), with 30 dioceses, and York, headed by the archbishop of York (primate of England), with 14 dioceses. Within the dioceses, there are more than 13,000 parishes. Though just over half of the population claim to be Anglicans, fewer than 2 million are actually members of the church and the figure continues to decline. The membership is lower than that of the Roman Catholic church and—in com-mon with most, though not all, Christian churches—is declining. In recent years the church has faced a schism on the issue of women priests. In 1992, the General Synod (the central governing body, comprising bishops, clergy, and lay members) voted to admit women to the priesthood, a move bitterly opposed by traditionalists, some of whom—clergy included—left the church. The division was reinforced in 2008 with a decision to ordain women bishops. A further split took place, not just in the Church of England but in the worldwide Anglican communion, over the issue of whether known homosexuals could be ordained.

The Roman Catholic church, the "out" and often legally discriminated-against church for most of the period since the Reformation in the sixteenth century, now enjoys the same freedoms as other religions. It is divided into seven provinces in Britain, each headed by an archbishop; the premier archbishop is the archbishop of Westminster. There are 30 episcopal dioceses, and 6 more in Northern Ireland. The church places particular emphasis on religious education as well as devotion, though the proportion of church members who attend services on a typical Sunday is not much different from the proportion of Anglican church members. As with the Church of England, membership is declining, though attendance at services showed some improvement in the first decade of the twenty-first century with the influx of predominantly Roman Catholic workers from eastern Europe.

Membership of other trinitarian churches (those believing in the union of the Holy Trinity under one Godhead) also has fallen in recent years. Increases have come in membership of the nontrinitarian churches and, more significantly, in the Sikh and Muslim religions. Both the Jewish and Muslim faiths are large communities by European standards. Most Jews are Orthodox Jews, with about 20 percent being members of the Reform or Liberal and Progressive movements. There are about 300 Jewish congregations in the country. Muslims are served by over a thousand mosques and prayer centers. The Islamic Cultural Center (and London Central Mosque) on the edge of London's Regent's Park constitutes the most important Muslim institution in the Western world.

Though religion remains politically and socially central to the life of Northern Ireland, its importance in Britain declined throughout the twentieth century. In the nineteenth century, it was an important influence in the politics of the nation: Tories were more likely to be Anglicans and Nonconformists, such as the Methodists, more likely to be Liberals. In significance, it has been displaced by class. That has since been fundamental in explaining British society and its politics.

CLASS

The United States does not have a feudal history. The significance of this fact was well described by Louis Hartz in his incisive work on the Lockean basis of U.S. society.[7] Britain, by contrast, does have a feudal past. Furthermore, unlike some of its European neighbors, it has witnessed no revolutionary break with past experience. As a result, the class patterns of a capitalist society have been superimposed on the hierarchical social structure of a departing feudal society.

Status derives from the tendency of people to accord positive and negative values to human attributes and to distribute respect accordingly. In feudal society, a superior status was accorded to the landowning aristocracy and gentry. They were deemed to have breeding and to be the best people to govern the land. They were deferred to as a socially superior body. It was a status that was passed on by inheritance, not one that could be acquired by merit or work.

Whereas status is essentially the product of a social system, class is the product of the economic.[8] Class grew out of industrialization and the development of a capitalist economy. It did not displace status; it usurped it. In the nineteenth century, the upper echelon of society comprised the traditional landed aristocracy, but it was an aristocracy that had absorbed largely, if not wholly, the new men of wealth who had made their money from trade and industry. These new men were drawn into this body until, eventually, they overwhelmed it.[9]

Class is generally recognized as a key feature of British society, yet it is difficult to define. In the United Kingdom, the term is employed in different senses. As the historian David Cannadine has argued, it can be used to denote social attitudes ("us" versus "them"), groupings in society based on occupation (upper, middle, and working), and hierarchy (in effect, status but not necessarily inherited, but rather earned or acquired, status).[10] These distinctions are useful in making sense of how class has developed in the United Kingdom.

Of these distinctions, the one most frequently employed is that based on occupation. However, even here there are problems. There is no agreement on how many classes exist or on how to measure class. Some studies identify the trinity, referred to by Cannadine, of upper, middle, and working class. However, there are few upper-class occupations (other than perhaps running great estates, occupations that are in effect often inherited) and it is more common—and, as A. H. Halsey has observed, characteristically British—to refer simply to two classes, the middle and the working.[11] Within each of the two classes, there are further divisions. Table 1.4 provides what has generally been employed as a basic delineation of them; this classification is still variously employed (not least by marketing companies), though since 2001 a more sophisticated eight-point classification has been utilized by the Office for National Statistics.

The problem with identifying class is compounded by the fact that there is a difference between attempts at objective measurement and self-assessment. In other words, how social scientists measure class and how others perceive it (particularly in terms of self-ascription) often are far from congruent. Social scientists may classify one particular occupation as upper-working class while some people in that occupation may regard themselves as middle class.

Membership of a class is not necessarily static. Some of the features of a status society, such as certain titles (Earl or Duke for example), can be passed from father to son: It is an inheritance based on law. Class can be inherited but it is an inheritance based on the market, which is less predictable than the law. Recent years have witnessed a growing social mobility. The children of many working-class parents have been upwardly mobile socially. The children of some middle-class parents have taken up working-class occupations.

TABLE 1.4

SOCIAL CLASSES IN BRITAIN

Class	Market research Designation	Encompassing
Middle class		
Upper-middle	A	Higher managerial and professional
Middle	B	Lower managerial and administrative
Lower-middle	C1	Skilled or supervisory nonmanual, lower nonmanual
Working class		
Upper-working	C2	Skilled manual
Working	D	Unskilled manual
	E	Residual, pensioners

As Halsey has recorded, "Men and women, moving and marrying between different occupational levels, both over the generations and also within their own working lives or careers, have become an increasingly common feature of British social life in the past half century."[12]

There are thus two features that are significant: the existence of class and greater class mobility. The importance of class has been highlighted consistently in surveys. Though increased social mobility and changes in the occupational profile of the nation appear to have reduced the significance (or, perhaps more accurately, the measurability) of class, most citizens continue to consider themselves members of a particular class. Surveys regularly find that over 90 percent of respondents ascribe themselves to the working or middle class (Table 1.5).[13] Awareness of class also remains a feature of contemporary society.

TABLE 1.5

SOCIAL CLASS BY SELF-ASCRIPTION, 1981–2008

Most people say they belong to the middle class or the working class. Which of these best describes you, middle class or working class?

	May 1981 (%)	August 1991 (%)	March 2008 (%)
Working class	63	61	52
Middle class*	28	30	44
Don't know	9	9	3
Refused	–	–	1

*In 1981 and 1991, asked as "middle/upper class"

Source: Ipsos MORI poll, March 2008, http://www.ipsos-mori.com/researchpublications/researcharchive/poll.aspx?oItemId=160

Indeed, survey data suggest that, if anything, awareness is increasing, not diminishing. A Gallup poll at the end of 1996 found that 72 percent of respondents thought that people were "very" or "quite" aware of social differences in Britain today—compared to 63 percent giving those responses in 1982. Awareness of a class system remains a marked feature of the twenty-first century. In 2008, 88 percent agreed that there was a class system in Britain; only 10 percent disagreed.[14]

The general pattern of change has been one of upward mobility. The change has been marked in the period between 1991 and 2008. Whereas in 1981 and 1991, 30 percent or less of people claimed to be middle class, by 2008 the percentage had increased to 44 percent (see Table 1.5). Greater mobility and affluence have eroded the claims to status. Mobility deprives one of claims to breeding. Acceptance of the principle of meritocracy is discordant with claims of inherited worth. Status remains important but it is no longer the central feature of British society that it was in preceding centuries.

Though measured principally in terms of occupation, class also connotes significant differences in lifestyles.[15] A whole range of interests and pursuits is associated with each particular class. The middle class, bolstered traditionally by higher incomes, have been able to afford their own homes—usually semi-detached or detached houses—and to take holidays in exotic climes. They have encouraged children to do well educationally and to go to university. They have pursued a range of leisure interests such as golf, tennis, squash, and skiing. They belong to country clubs and chambers of commerce. They are more likely than working-class families to be theater-goers and to be joiners of civic organizations and pressure groups. Working-class families traditionally have lived in often rented row houses; taken holidays—when they can afford them—at seaside resorts in the United Kingdom and, more recently, in Spain and the Mediterranean islands. They have also been less able to provide a supportive environment for children to pursue education to degree level and been more likely than the middle class to pursue interests such as football and snooker and more inclined to spend more time drinking in the local public house, or "pub." These are crude generalizations, but they point to the very real differences of lifestyles that are essentially ingrained and that often remain unaffected by significant changes in income. They are also differences generally recognized by Britons themselves. A 2008 survey found a range of activities associated with one class rather than another. Even the choice of supermarket was seen in class terms: Most people thought working-class people were more likely to shop at ASDA (a chain owned by the U.S. supermarket giant Wal-Mart) and middle-class people at Sainsbury's or Waitrose.[16]

The importance of class is political as well as social. Since the first half of the twentieth century, there has been a significant relationship between class and politics. The Labour party has attracted largely but not wholly the support of the working class, and the Conservative party that of the middle class. The significance of the class-party nexus will be explored in more detail later. There is recent evidence of a decline in class identification and in the correlation between class and party. Such decline, though, has been relative. Class

remains a feature of British society. Most Britons continue to ascribe themselves to a particular class. Politicians still employ the concept of class (if only
now to decry it) and sociologists would be lost without it.

EDUCATION

All children receive a primary and secondary school education but not all
proceed to higher education. After entering primary school at the age of 5,
children in England receive a common education until the age of 11, when
they enter secondary schools. In the two decades following the passage of the
1944 Education Act, secondary schools were divided into grammar and secondary modern schools. The former were essentially academic institutions,
oriented to scholastic skills, with a large proportion of pupils achieving university entrance. The latter taught more practical skills, some pupils going on
to a technical college and a very few achieving admission to university. Selection for entry to grammar schools was made by examination taken at age 11.
Labour politicians came to view the bifurcation of grammar and secondary
modern schools as socially divisive, with those attending secondary modern
schools being unable to shake off the perception of being failures and unable
to achieve the occupational opportunities of grammar school pupils. Following the return of a Labour government in 1964, a new scheme of education
was introduced, with selection and the dual school system being replaced
by a nonselective, all-encompassing system of comprehensive education.
Comprehensive schools were introduced over the next twenty years, under
both Conservative and Labour governments. In 1971, 38 percent of secondary schoolchildren in England attended comprehensive schools; by 1990, the
proportion had reached 92 percent. In Wales and Scotland, it was 99 percent
and 100 percent, respectively. A few grammar schools remained, and continue to remain, largely concentrated in certain counties, notably Kent and
Lincolnshire.

From the mid-1980s onward, Conservative governments introduced
other changes, largely designed to ensure that basic subjects were not
ignored and that parents had a greater influence over their children's
schools. The reforms included the introduction of a national curriculum,
with three core subjects (English, science, and mathematics) and seven foundation subjects, each with attainment targets and assessment arrangements.
Greater powers were also given to school governors. Funding remained
publicly provided, but school governing-bodies were given power to determine the spending priorities for most of their budget. Also, a school could
seek to take full control of its own budget and admissions policy through
opting out of the existing framework of control. Many of these changes—
especially the power for schools to opt out—proved contentious, the Conservatives seeing them as means of raising educational standards and critics
claiming they were attempts to restore some of the features of the system
that existed in the 1950s. When a new Labour government was elected in

1997, some changes were made to the status of those schools that had opted out, but otherwise most of the changes introduced in recent years were kept in place. The government also introduced academy schools, state-maintained independent schools set up with the help of outside sponsors and run by those sponsors, although operating within national requirements for curriculum and standards. By the end of 2008, there were over 100 academies in existence.

Although secondary education is compulsory, parents are not required to send their children to state schools but can choose instead to send them to private schools. Private schools tend to stress academic achievement and concentrate on developing the ability to pass examinations and on building self-confidence. Believing that their children will receive a better and more disciplined education, with a greater prospect of university entry than from a state school, many parents who can afford it send their children to such private institutions, known (confusingly) as "public schools." Fees at such schools vary. Popular boarding schools may charge anything between £10,000 ($16,400) and £20,000 ($32,800) a year, though the more prestigious schools, such as Eton, Harrow, and Winchester, can afford to charge considerably higher fees; in 2009, the fees at Eton were closer to £30,000 ($49,200). About 7 percent of children attend private schools, though more than one-quarter of entrants to the older universities are drawn from such schools.

From secondary school, students may proceed to institutions of further and higher education. *Further education* allows students to pursue especially work-related or vocational courses, or to study for qualifications not already gained in secondary school. Of students who proceed to study beyond secondary school, most do so in colleges of further education. *Higher education* comprises primarily the university sector. Recent years have seen both a change in the structure of higher education and an increase in the proportion of those going on to study beyond secondary school. Until 1992, institutions of higher education were divided into universities and polytechnics. The former were more academic, whereas the latter—first established in 1967—were more vocationally oriented, often providing "sandwich" courses (part study, part practical job experience) for their students. In 1992, the formal dividing line, known as the binary line, between universities and polytechnics was abolished, allowing polytechnics to acquire university titles, and a common funding agency was established.

At the beginning of the twentieth century, England had only seven universities, Scotland had four, and Wales had one. Relatively few were founded in the first few decades of the century. The main growth has been in the period since 1945, with a marked increase at the start of the twenty-first century. Of the 46 universities that existed before 1992, 28 were founded after 1945. As we have seen, polytechnics were first created in 1967. By the time the binary line was abolished, there were 30. (The 1960s also saw the creation of the "open university," a nonresidential university requiring no formal academic qualifications for admission and offering tuition by correspondence and through special radio and television programs.) Since 1992, a number of colleges (including some highly specialized colleges) have been awarded university status, with the result that by 2008 there were 126 universities in the United Kingdom. The expansion was designed to accommodate the target set by the Labour government that by 2010 there should be 50 percent of those in the 18–30 age range participating in some form of tertiary education. At the end of the 1980s, one in six young people continued education beyond secondary school. By 1996, the figure was one in three. By 2008 it was nearing the figure of one in two: About 44 percent of young people were in some form of tertiary education.

Within universities there is something of a hierarchy. The oldest universities, led by Oxford and Cambridge, have traditionally been viewed as the most prestigious, and again there is a social element to the prestige. Students from leading private schools will try to get a place at Oxford or Cambridge (commonly described collectively as "Oxbridge"), as will the more academically gifted pupils from state schools. Universities founded in the nineteenth century and first half of the twentieth are commonly referred to as "redbrick" universities (after the color of the brickwork), and universities founded in the latter half of the century are frequently dubbed "new universities." All these universities are distinguished from the former polytechnics that have achieved university status, the latter being referred to by various names, the most common simply being "post-1992 universities." This hierarchy has its parallel in the United States, the Ivy League universities constituting the equivalent of Oxbridge, though the United Kingdom lacks the significant divide that exists in the United States between private and state universities. The United Kingdom has only one private university, the University of Buckingham.

A university education continues to provide occupational advantage. More than 80 percent of graduates have ended up in the professional and managerial classes. They constitute less than one-third of those in these classes, but it is these classes that will provide proportionally more children than any other for university entry. The likelihood that a person will go to university, especially the older pre-1992 universities, remains strongly linked to social class.

British universities are notably strong internationally in terms of their research, being outranked in international tables usually only by American universities. Both countries maintain leading universities despite not heading the league table in terms of spending. Although the higher education sector in the United Kingdom is expanding, spending on higher education remains low by international standards.[17] In 2002, public spending on tertiary education institutions in the United Kingdom accounted for 0.8 percent of the gross domestic product (GDP). This put the nation at the lower end of the scale among advanced industrialized nations. The Organization for Economic Cooperation and Development (OECD) average was 1.1 percent; the figure for the United States was 1.2 percent. The table was topped by Scandinavian countries: Denmark (1.9 percent), Finland (1.7 percent),

Sweden (1.6 percent), and Norway (1.4 percent). Among the United Kingdom's leading competitor nations, only Japan devoted less of its GDP (0.4 percent) to tertiary education.

MARRIAGE, FAMILY, AND SOCIAL DEMOGRAPHY

Although much emphasis is placed on the individual, the family is still the most important social unit in Britain. There remains strong attachment to the ideal of marriage and having children. Despite a high divorce rate, marriage—and remarriage—remains popular. Most Britons (69 percent in 2007) believe that marriage is very important to bringing up children.[18] It remains the most common form of partnership for men and women.

Nonetheless, there have been important changes in recent years. There has been a decrease since the 1970s in the number of marriages. In 1972, the number peaked at 480,000. This is partly attributable to an increase in the number of people reaching marriageable age (a consequence of a post-war "baby boom"). By 2005, the number of marriages was just under 248,000. This still left the United Kingdom with one of the higher marriage rates among EU countries. (In 2005, it ranked 10th out of the 27 member states.) Men and women are also leaving it until later in life to get married. Most marriages are solemnized with a civil ceremony.

Divorce rates have increased since the 1960s, facilitated by various changes in the divorce laws. In 1958, there were around 24,000 divorces; in 1972 there were 125,000; and in 1993 there were 180,000—an all-time high. Numbers since have fluctuated, but they have been below the 1993 figure. In 2005, for example, there were 155,000 divorces (13.1 per 1,000 married population),[19] nonetheless making it one of the higher rates in the European Union (EU): Only seven EU member states had a higher divorce rate. It remains below the divorce rate in the United States.

There has been a notable increase in the number of unmarried couples cohabiting—and consequently in the number of children born out of wedlock—as well as in the number of people living on their own. From 1986 to 2004, the percentage of nonmarried people under 60 who cohabited rose from 11 percent to 24 percent among men and from 13 percent to 24 percent for women. There was also a marked increase in the number of children born outside marriage. The figure rose from 12 percent of births in 1980 to 43.7 percent in 2006: Only seven other EU states had a higher rate.

Households have also been getting smaller. In 1971, 18 percent of households in Britain comprised one person. By 1995 the figure was 28 percent and since then has not changed markedly: By 2007, the percentage was 29 percent. In 1961, the average household size was 3.1 people. By 1971, the number had fallen to 2.9 and by 1995 it was 2.4, again showing something of a plateau effect thereafter: In 2007, it was still 2.4.[20]

The decrease in the number of families with children reflects a fall in the birthrate, a feature common to all EU countries. In 2008, for the first time the number of people in the United Kingdom aged over 65 exceeded the number of people aged under 16. The increase in the number of one-person households is in part explicable by the increase in the size of the elderly population, especially older women, who tend to live longer than men. However, the largest increase in the two decades up to 2006 was among people in the age range 25 to 44 (and men in the age range of 45 to 64). Young people are choosing increasingly either to live on their own or, especially in the case of men, to live with their parents: In 2005, 57 percent of men aged 20 to 24 lived with their parents—up from 50 percent in 1990. The figures for women were 38 percent and 32 percent, respectively.[21]

Within these trends, there also are some variations correlated to region and class. In terms of births outside marriage, the percentage is greater in the northern regions of England (north, northwest, Yorkshire) than in southern regions. There is some correlation between household size and socioeconomic grouping. Households headed by someone in a skilled or semi-skilled job are more likely to have more young children than those headed by someone in a professional or managerial position.[22]

The traditional attachment to marriage remains a feature of British society, even if a substantial proportion of those marriages fail. The attachment to creating a family unit appears even stronger, reflected in the number of couples cohabiting increasing. This reflects a change in social attitudes. There is no longer a social stigma attached to cohabiting. There is also a greater willingness to accept cohabitation by same-sex couples. By the beginning of the twenty-first century, most people considered that sexual relations between two people of the same sex were not at all wrong. An unpublished Ipsos MORI poll in 2007 found that 68 percent of British adults believed that gay couples should be allowed to get married,[23] double the proportion of those holding such a view in the United States.[24] This followed the introduction in 2005 of civil partnerships for same-sex couples and some high profile partnerships of public figures, such as the singer Elton John and his partner David Furnish. The issue has been far less contentious than in the United States, where attempts have been made to introduce a constitutional amendment to ban same-sex marriage.

EMPLOYMENT

Britain was the first major nation to experience industrialization. Most of the population in the nineteenth century moved from the land to find jobs in manufacturing industries in the towns and cities. The north of England in particular witnessed the growth of major industrial conurbations. "Mill towns" became common features. So, too, did mining communities. Most of the economically active population came to be employed in primary industries and manufacturing. In the twentieth century, especially in the period since 1945, more and more workers moved into service industries. In 1955, 42 percent of those in employment had jobs in manufacturing. In 1978, the figure was 29 percent.

By 1997, the figure had declined to 17 percent. The trend continued in the twenty-first century. By 2007 it was down to 11 percent.

The biggest increases in the past thirty years have been in financial and business services—doubling from 2.5 million workers to 5.7 million between 1978 and 2007—and in public administration, education, and health.[25] The growth of service industries has been particularly marked in London and the southeast, where almost 75 percent of employees are now in the service sector. There has been a corresponding decline in employment in manufacturing, especially in the north. The closure of local factories, mills, and coal mines has been met in some cases by diversification and attracting new firms, but otherwise by migration and higher levels of unemployment than elsewhere. Today, Britain can be described as having a predominantly service economy with the southeast of England enjoying a preeminent position in that economy. That preeminence is now consolidated by British membership in the European Union and the increased trade with EU countries. The southeast of England forms part of a "golden triangle" within the Union, with access to the continent not enjoyed by more distant parts of the United Kingdom.

Within employment, recent years have seen a growth in the number of female workers and in the number of self-employed. In all categories other than service industries, male employees outnumber females. The extractive industries have been traditionally male preserves. In the service industries, more than half the workers are women. There have also been some significant changes in the type of employment on offer. Part-time jobs are now a significant feature of the British economy. In 2007, almost a quarter of those in employment worked part-time. This type of employment is marked among female employees: Almost 40 percent of the females in employment in 2007 worked part-time, compared to 8 percent of males in employment.[26] Part-time employment is marked in certain sectors, most notably distribution. Self-employment is highest in craft and related industries, followed by managers and administrators. The self-employed also constitute one of the categories most vulnerable to recessions in economic performance.

Employment rates have been high at times of economic growth but fallen markedly during recessions. Unemployment rates increased from the mid-1970s and the United Kingdom had the worst unemployment figures of the seven major countries of the OECD. Unemployment rates peaked in 1986, when just over 3 million people—11 percent of the work force—were out of work. With economic recovery, unemployment rates fell and were below 6 percent by 1990. Recession then pushed the numbers up again and they reached a peak in 1993 (10.4 percent); after that, the figures fell and in 2004–05 were down to 4.7 percent, their lowest levels since 1975. The rate increased slightly in 2006, fell early in 2007, and then increased markedly from 2008 onward: By May 2009, the figure exceeded 2 million (7.6 percent) and was expected to continue rising. Within the United Kingdom, the highest unemployment rate remains in Northern Ireland, where the percentage of people unemployed is consistently above 10 percent. Most EU countries (in 2006, 20 out the 27 members) have higher unemployment rates than in the United Kingdom.

PERSONAL WEALTH AND TAXATION

As we have seen, the country has witnessed some notable shifts in social behavior as well as in patterns of employment. There has been less significant change in the distribution of wealth.

The distribution of marketable wealth is skewed in favor of a minority. Marketable wealth comprises stocks and shares, cash, bank deposits, consumer durables, buildings, trade assets, land, and dwellings net of mortgage debt. In 1976, the total marketable wealth of the country was estimated to be £280 billion ($458.4 billion) and in 2003 it was estimated at £3,783 billion ($6.2 billion) (Table 1.6). The wealthiest 1 percent of the population own more than 20 percent of the marketable wealth; the wealthiest 10 percent of the population own more than half of the wealth. The least wealthy half of the population owns only 7 percent of the country's marketable wealth.

Net personal wealth showed a marked increase in the period from 1996 to 2006, in large part because of significant increases in house prices in a nation geared to house-ownership. In 2007, the Halifax Bank estimated that in the decade net personal wealth had more than doubled, to just over £6 trillion ($9.8 trillion).[27] Houses were estimated to account for 43 percent of the total personal wealth, compared to 26 percent in 1996. The figures for 2007 proved a high point, with a notable decline in 2008–09 at a time of recession, with a notable drop in the value of house prices.

However, there remained a notable divide between rich and poor, not just in terms of household wealth but also in location. A 2007 study found that already rich areas—notably the south-east of England—had become disproportionately wealthy over four decades. In contrast, in parts of some cities more than half of all households were classified as "breadline poor," meaning the members of the household had enough just to live on but could not indulge in other expenditure enjoyed by other members of society. However, the number of people defined as being in absolute poverty ("core poor") declined, from 14 percent of households to 11 percent. There was reported to

TABLE 1.6

Distribution of Marketable Wealth, 1976–2003

Percentage of population	Percentage of marketable wealth owned		
	1976	1996	2003
1	21	20	21
5	38	40	40
10	50	52	53
25	71	74	72
50	92	93	93

Source: Inland Revenue personal wealth, National Statistics Online, http://www.statistics.gov.uk/cci/nugget.asp?id=2

be a clustering of poverty in urban areas, with wealthy households concentrating on the outskirts of cities.[28]

Taxation is progressive, though the various rates have been reduced to two: a basic rate of 20 percent and a top rate of 40 percent. (At one stage there was a maximum rate of 83 percent.) The reduction—with a shift of emphasis from direct to indirect taxation—also has resulted in income tax constituting a smaller proportion of the GDP: In 2005 it constituted just over 10 percent, marginally above the EU average.

In terms of earned income, there are some notable, but predictable, differences in terms of family type. In terms of the distribution of household disposable income, single people with children are disproportionately to be found in the bottom fifth, whereas the position is reversed with a couple under state-pension age without children. In 2005–06, retired people, especially those living on their own were also more likely to figure disproportionately in the bottom fifth.[29]

CONCLUSION

Britain constitutes a small and crowded island with relatively few natural resources, with wealth and population heavily concentrated in the southeast of England. It is a largely secular society and one in which class remains important. These features distinguish it from the United States, which shares none of them. Though some of these features are shared with other European countries, in combination they render Britain distinct from its neighbors.

Compared with the United States and most European countries, Britain is notable for the absence—certainly since the seventeenth century—of invasion, civil war, or revolution. Continuity in both institutions and many social traditions is a feature that underpins many of the structures and political relationships that form the basis of discussion in later chapters. Nonetheless, some change has taken place. That is apparent from the brief description offered in this chapter. We have touched upon some of the social changes that have occurred. We will later draw out the extent of political change. Some of that change has been significant and dramatic, especially in recent decades. Observing change can nonetheless obscure the extent of continuity. This volume is designed to ignore neither. It seeks to explain both. Hence our theme of the two C's: continuity and change.

NOTES

1. Office for National Statistics, *Monthly Digest of Statistics 751*, Summer 2008 (Palgrave Macmillan, 2008), p. 31.
2. Tearfund, "Churchgoing in the UK," 2007.
3. European Commission, Special Eurobarometer 225, *Social Values, Science and Technology*, June 2005, p. 9.
4. *Financial Times*/Harris survey carried out December 2006. Harris Interactive. http://www.harrisinteractive.com.

5. A. Park *et al.* (eds.), *British Social Attitudes: The 23rd Report, 2006/2007* (Sage, 2006), p. 9.

6. Henry VIII was excommunicated by the pope in 1533, following the crowning of Anne Boleyn as queen, the pope having refused to annul Henry's previous marriage to Catherine of Aragon. Parliament responded with various acts establishing Henry's position as head of the church. By the Act of Supremacy of 1534, the king was recognized as "the only supreme head of the Church of England, called Anglicana Ecclesia."

7. L. Hartz, *The Liberal Tradition in America* (Harcourt, Brace & World, 1955).

8. See A. H. Halsey, *Change in British Society,* 2nd ed. (Oxford University Press, 1981).

9. Ibid., p. 47.

10. D. Cannadine, *Making History Now and Then* (Palgrave Macmillan, 2008).

11. A. H. Halsey, *Change in British Society,* 2nd ed. (Oxford University Press, 1981).

12. Ibid., pp. 53–54.

13. R. Jowell, S. Witherspoon, and L. Brook, *British Social Attitudes: The Fifth Report, 1988–89* (Gower, 1988), p. 227; E. Jacobs and R. Worcester, *We British* (Weidenfeld & Nicolson, 1990), pp. 138–139.

14. *Gallup Political and Economic Index,* January 1997, p. 26.

15. See A. Adonis and S. Pollard, *A Class Act: The Myth of Britain's Classless Society* (Hamish Hamilton, 1997).

16. Ipsos MORI, Survey on Class, March 2008, http://www.ipsos-MORI.com/content/survey-on-class.ashx.

17. Organisation for Economic Co-operation and Development (OECD), *Education at a Glance: OECD Indicators 2005* (OECD, 2005), Table B2.1b.

18. Ipsos MORI poll conducted in March 2007. B. Marshall *et al.*, *Blair's Britain: The Social and Cultural Legacy* (Ipsos MORI, 2007), p. 37.

19. Office for National Statistics, *Population Trends 132*, Summer 2008 (Palgrave Macmillan, 2008), p. 75.

20. *Social Trends 27* (The Stationery Office, 1997), p. 40; *Social Trends 38*, Office for National Statistics (Palgrave Macmillan, 2008), p. 16.

21. BBC News Online, 21 February, 2006, http://news.bbc.co.uk/1/hi/uk/4733330.stm.

22. *Social Trends 22* (Her Majesty's Stationery Office, 1992), p. 41.

23. B. Marshall *et al.*, *Blair's Britain: The Social and Cultural Legacy* (Ipsos MORI, 2007), p. 39.

24. CBS News poll, August 2008: *The New York Times,* 1 September 2008.

25. *Social Trends 38,* Office for National Statistics (Palgrave Macmillan, 2008), p. 52.

26. Ibid.

27. BBC News Online, 27 September 2007, http://news.bbc.co.uk/1/hi/business/7018253.stm.

28. Joseph Rowntree Foundation, *Poverty, Wealth and Place in Britain, 1968 to 2005,* reported in *The Guardian,* 17 July 2007.

29. *Social Trends 38,* Office for National Statistics (Palgrave Macmillan, 2008), p. 72.

CHAPTER

2

The Political Culture

Political culture is a vague, abstract concept that has been subject to various definitions.[1] In its simplest form, it may be described as denoting the emotional and attitudinal environment within which a political system operates. If we are to understand how a political system is formed and operates, we have to understand the environment that produced and nurtures it.

The focus of this chapter is the political culture of Britain and the means through which individuals are socialized into that culture. As I shall seek to show, that culture cannot be divorced from the constraints of history and of physical and spatial resources. Each has had a significant impact on the other. The collection of emotions and attitudes that form the political culture has served to shape actions and hence affect the nation's history. Conversely, those actions, as well as the country's geographic location and limited resources, have had consequences that have affected elite and mass attitudes.

A number of problems have to be borne in mind. There is the danger especially of tautology and, as may be inferred from the preceding paragraph, the "chicken and egg" problem—which came first?—in attempting to discern the cause-and-effect relationships among culture, history, and resources. The existence of a stable political culture in Britain has been ascribed by some to the effectiveness of government in being able to implement programs of public policy. But what has enabled government to be effective? Has it been a distinctive political culture, citizens accepting the legitimacy of government to act in the way that it does? If so, what explains the existence of such a culture? Is not a partial explanation the effectiveness of government? The problem is an acute one in Britain given the absence of any clear point of departure. Where do English, Scottish, and Welsh history begin? At what point is a political culture discernible? The basic conundrum is insoluble. It is important, though, to bear it in mind, with an awareness of it informing our study.

What, then, are the basic components of the British political culture? And by what process are the values and attitudes that form that culture imbued by Britons?

POLITICAL SOCIALIZATION

The various values and beliefs that coalesce to create, maintain, and variously modify the political culture are not generated in a vacuum; they are acquired through a process of socialization. In that process, the most important influences usually are family, education, occupation, geographic location, and, to a lesser extent, the mass media. For illustrative purposes, we shall consider their impact in shaping class and partisanship, before considering the basic underlying values that form the political culture.

Family

It is primarily from parents that children acquire particular values and habits. It is largely the parents who shape the child's view of society, including one's status in that society. It is also parents who significantly influence political perceptions and partisan support.

Perceptions of social class are derived not only from objective position but also often from inherited class orientations. Most children ascribe themselves to the same social class as their parents. The self-ascription is important and, as we have seen (Chapter 1), does not always correlate with objective assessments derived from socioeconomic conditions. A study by Jacobs and Worcester also found a relationship between those who were upwardly mobile and those who believed their parents were upwardly mobile. Their survey found that "46% of those who described themselves as upwardly mobile middle-class described their parents in the same terms and so did 44% of those who called themselves upwardly mobile working-class."[3] As they note, the claim to upward mobility may be an inherited characteristic.

Political habits and values are passed from parent to child. Children tend to inherit their parents' interest in politics (or, as appropriate, lack of it) and their partisan preferences. The influence is strongest when both parents share the same preference and that preference is known to the child.[4] There is evidence of decline in the class-party nexus,[5] but parents' preferences remain an important influence on partisan preference.

The influence of parents on partisanship is relevant for our study in later chapters. Of more immediate relevance for the political culture is the wider impact of parents: The fact that, whatever divergent influences may serve to modify or undermine particular values, it is the mother and father who remain the first and foremost points of reference in defining the political and social environment.

Education

Formal education is important in political socialization, less for its effect on partisan support (family remains the predominant influence) than for helping shape awareness of the political system and explicitly or, more often, implicitly the values that underpin it. In their classic but now dated study of the civic culture, Almond and Verba found that there were differences in attitude toward government between those with different levels of education, and between those who had received some formal education and those who had received none. The more extensive the education, up to university level, the greater the perceived significance of government action.[6] Nonetheless, the overwhelming majority of those with some formal education, primary or above, considered that national government had some effect.

Various studies in the United Kingdom have uncovered a relationship between education and levels of political activity. A 2008 survey found that among groups far less likely to be political activists were "people without formal qualifications (3% compared to 26% of those with postgraduate degrees)."[7] The study also found that graduates were more likely to discuss politics with friends or family (66 percent of graduates, compared to 21 percent of people with no qualifications).[8] It also found a relationship between political activity and a belief in being able to change the way the country is run.

Types of education may also serve to reinforce values and behavior. Public schools tend to reinforce middle- and upper-middle–class norms and expectations. Conservative members of Parliament, for example, have been drawn disproportionately from public schools and the universities of Oxford and Cambridge. At such schools, leading public figures are frequently invited to speak and pupils are encouraged to engage in activities appropriate for later public service (e.g., taking part in school debates), an environment maintained at Oxford and Cambridge. No such environment or traditions are normally provided in state comprehensive schools. In most cases, the school environment tends to reinforce the influence of the home background.

Occupation

Occupation and class, as we have seen (Chapter 1), are closely related. The former usually is employed as the primary criterion for determining the latter. Both are important in the context of political socialization. The nature of the occupation can affect values and perceptions of society. Having a poorly paid, mundane, and personally unrewarding job or, indeed, having no job at all is likely to invoke a greater sense of alienation than pursuing a well-paid and satisfying position. It would seem plausible to assume a broad correlation between these two positions and class, with those in the working class more likely to have more mundane, less-well-paid jobs and the middle class to have better-paid and probably more varied jobs. There also appears to be a broad correlation with perceptions of political knowledge and interest. The 2008 Audit of Political Engagement found that groups that were disproportionately less interested in politics were those from the lower social grades (see Table 1.4): Only 28 percent of those in social classes D and E (as defined in Table 1.4) expressed an interest in politics, compared with 68 percent in the A and B categories[9] There was a similar disparity in claimed knowledge of politics.

There also is a significant, and much charted, relationship between class and partisan support: The middle class has traditionally preferred the Conservative party and the working class the Labour party. The relationship is not exact and is declining, but—as we shall see in later chapters—remains important. The relationship is not that surprising, given that those in the middle class are more likely to occupy better-paid jobs and consequently able to pursue a preferred lifestyle than those in working-class positions. Hence, as the "haves" in society, the middle class is more likely to prefer the party that is more oriented to maintaining the status quo. The "have-nots" are more likely to support a party favoring a change to the existing system. This hypothesis has largely been borne out by the empirical evidence,[10] though the relationship—as we shall see—is no longer as strong as it once was.

The nature of particular jobs also may influence other values. Those who are employed as part of a large factory workforce are more likely to imbue values of social and political solidarity than those who occupy isolated positions, with little group contact, such as farm workers and people working from home. Those employed in the armed services are taught the importance of discipline. Those employed in the private sector are more likely to acquire an attachment to private enterprise than those employed in the public sector.

In many, if not most, cases the experience of occupation serves to reinforce values acquired through family, children seeing themselves occupying the same social stratum as their parents and taking up jobs that maintain them in that same social stratum. Again, though, as we have noted in Chapter 1 (see Table 1.5), there is some change, with a degree of class mobility, especially upward mobility.

Location

Location also can be important in the process of political socialization. Living in an area of expensive detached houses can serve to reinforce one's sense of being middle class. The area provides a social milieu that reinforces that awareness. Conversely, living in an area of terraced public accommodation can reinforce one's identification with the working class. Within such areas, there is often a particular lifestyle.

The independent influence of location is borne out when correlated with partisan support. As Miller found: "At a minimum, the class characteristics of the social environment have more effect on constituency partisanship than class differences themselves, perhaps much more. The partisanship of individuals is influenced more by where they live than what they do."[11] As we shall see in Chapter 5, there also is a correlation between party support and urban and rural locations and between party and region.

The values that may be reinforced or shaped by location are not confined to political partisanship and class. People living in small, self-sufficient rural communities are likely to have different values than those confined to overcrowded and largely transient urban areas. Those who live in small, tightly knit communities for decades are more likely to have a different view of life than those who lead a peripatetic existence. Britain, as we have seen, occupies a relatively small land area but nonetheless exhibits a number of significant regional variations.

Mass Media

The mass media of communication—principally television, radio, and newspapers—also are important agents of socialization. They constitute the most-used sources for acquiring knowledge of what is going on in society. Among the various media, radio and television tend to be the most trusted source in the Western world. In 2008, 55 percent of Britons expressed trust in information received from radio; 51 percent expressed trust in television.[12] For the European Union as a whole the figures were 62 percent and 53 percent, respectively. Britons were less trusting of the press: only 19 percent, the lowest among EU nations.

The media can serve, deliberately or otherwise, to reinforce, and possibly even change, values. Reinforcement is more likely given evidence that readers and viewers are likely to engage in a process of selective retention, selecting those items that reinforce existing beliefs (see Chapter 14). That reinforcement also can take the form of bolstering the legitimacy of existing institutions and processes. As we shall see, media exposure also can serve to have a "magnetizing" effect on partisan preferences. Most newspaper readers choose a paper whose partisan stance is in line with their own partisanship or, for young people, with that of their parents.

These media are also complemented now by the Internet. In 2008, 63 percent of U.K. homes were found to have Internet connection. Newspapers can be accessed online. The BBC has an award-winning Web site. Many other organizations, as well as individuals, can disseminate material via the Internet. The effect of this particular mode of communication on socialization is not yet clear. It opens up a far greater range of sources of information and comment than could previously be accessed by the average citizen. By being open access, it is also indiscriminate. Material may be put online that is rigorously researched or which constitutes the ramblings of a deranged mind. Eurobarometer data in 2008 revealed that only 36 percent of people in the European Union trusted the Internet.[13]

A Complex Mix

The process of socialization is a complex and continuous one. The influences just outlined are the most important, but they are not the only influences, nor are they mutually exclusive. Usually the reverse: They clearly interact and, more often than not, will reinforce one another. Parents remain the most important influence. Parental influence usually will be reinforced by the choice of newspaper and often by the choice of school and job. However, the influences are not always reinforcing. Pressure from peers at school may challenge values instilled at home. Social mobility, marriage into a family with different values, and exposure to certain programs or stories in the media may challenge received parental wisdom. Parental values may conflict with prevailing social norms: The belief in arranged marriages in traditional Indian families, for example, in a society where the belief in free choice for individuals prevails. Nor are the influences themselves necessarily static. Educational opportunities have changed over the past century, economic conditions have changed, and the mass media have developed, with the broadcast media assuming a new and central significance. And, in more recent years, more and more people are making greater use of the Internet for recreation and for acquiring information.

The importance of some of these changes, especially for partisan support, will be touched upon later in this volume. However, the changes we have mentioned are relative. In terms of the basic values being transmitted, the most significant feature is not change but continuity. There are differences in social and political values. We have illustrated the media of socialization in terms particularly of structuring social class and partisanship. There is, though, some convergence on a number of basic values. It is that convergence that provides the essential British political culture. In identifying the media of socialization, we have not identified those basic values. To know the media through which values and beliefs that coalesce to form the political culture are transmitted is useful, but does not serve to identify the culture itself.

THE POLITICAL CULTURE

In his work on political oppositions in Western democracies, Robert Dahl observed that patterns of opposition may have something to do with widely shared cultural premises. He noted that four kinds of culturally derived orientations toward politics seem to have a bearing on the pattern of opposition.[14] Those four orientations can usefully be employed not only to help one understand and explain attitudes toward political opposition in Britain but also to identify the fundamental characteristics of the political culture. They enable one to draw out the distinctive features of that culture and to consider the impact of both history and resources. Those four orientations, listed not in the order provided by Dahl but in the order I believe to be most significant to an understanding of the British political culture, are toward (1) problem solving, (2) the political system, (3) cooperation and individuality, and (4) other people.

Orientation toward Problem Solving

Giovanni Sartori has distinguished two approaches to problem solving: the empirical and the rational.[15] The empirical approach is concerned with what is and what can be seen and touched, proceeding on the basis of testing and retesting and largely rejecting dogma and abstract or coherent grand designs for change. The rationalist approach, by contrast, is concerned with abstraction rather than facts, stressing the need for deductive consistency and tending to be dogmatic and definitive. According to Dahl, "While the empirical approach takes the attitude that if a program does not work in practice there must be something wrong about the theory, the rationalist will retort that what is true in theory must also be true in practice—that it is the practice, not the theory, that is wrong."[16]

France has been identified as employing a rationalist approach. Germany and Italy, to some extent, also tend to find such an approach useful. Britain and the United States, by contrast, are seen as the exemplars of an empirical approach. Indeed, it is my contention that this approach is *most* marked in the British case and that it constitutes the most significant aspect of British political culture.

Although oriented more toward an empirical approach, the United States has exhibited some elements of the rationalist. The framers of the U.S. Constitution, although tempered by experience and (according to Charles Beard) self-interest, were infused with values articulated by the English philosopher John Locke and sought to impose a political framework in line with a Lockean conception of society.[17] Those values, expressed succinctly in the second paragraph of the Declaration of Rights (encompassing inalienable rights such as life, liberty, and the pursuit of happiness), and that conception of society have permeated the American consciousness, so much so that they have largely gone unstated. They have been so pervasive and so self-evident that there has been little point in articulating them.[18] Because they are seen as universal, there has been a tendency to wish to impart them to other countries.

Britain, by contrast, has a distinct orientation toward the empirical approach. Even the political system, however strong the attachment to it, tends to be justified in pragmatic terms. Democracy, having been implemented in largely pragmatic fashion, has been lauded on the grounds that "it works." The point has been well put by Vivien Hart in comparing U.S. and British approaches: "In America the emphasis has been on what democracy is and *should* be, while Britain has been characterized by a more pragmatic and less urgent emphasis on what democracy is and *can* be."[19] Empiricism seems appropriate to the English consciousness. Instinct, trial and error, and incremental change are the essence of the English approach to problem solving.

Such an orientation to problem solving has been a distinctive feature of English political culture for many centuries, discernible, I would suggest, since at least the thirteenth century. It is an approach that has informed political actions and hence the political history of the country. It is an approach that has informed actions in foreign as well as domestic policy. As a nation founded on maritime trade, Britain has historically been both more outward looking than the United States and empirical in its approach to events in the rest of the world. As Sir Christopher Meyer, a former British Ambassador to the United States, expressed it in 2008: "The supreme fallacy in foreign policy is to take the world as we would wish it to be and not as it actually is."[20]

An empirical orientation in turn has been reinforced by the experience of history—it is the approach that has always been employed, and no external constraints have managed to force themselves on the nation to generate conditions in which a rationalist approach would be possible. In the wake of the War of Independence, Americans were able to sit down and generate a political system from first principles. Invasions by foreign powers and liberations from foreign powers have put other states in similar positions. England, by contrast, never has been faced with or sought such an opportunity. The closest it came was during the Protectorate of Oliver Cromwell in the seventeenth century. When that failed, the country resorted as far as possible to the conditions prevailing prior to its creation. English history is scattered with philosophers generating theories that have failed to find congenial soil in the nation's consciousness. Ideologies have been either discarded or else molded to fit with the experience of history. Prevailing theories, once they no longer seem appropriate, have been dispensed with. The act of dispensing with them has not always met with common assent nor has it always been smooth—the English historical landscape is scattered with periods of violence and upheaval—but once the dispensing process is achieved, it has largely been accepted. Hankering after the old order is congenial to some minds, but seeking to revert by force or civil unrest to the *status quo ante* is not. In the English perception, empiricism is both a descriptive and a prescriptive term. To the Briton, it is both what should be and what he or she believes always has been.

Orientation toward the Political System

Orientation toward the political system may be classified as allegiant when attitudes, feelings, and evaluations are favorable to the political system; apathetic or detached when feelings and evaluations are neutral; and alienated when such feelings and evaluations are unfavorable.[21] Italy and France have been cited as examples of political cultures that generate alienation and a large measure of apathy. The former West Germany has been put forward as having a culture that generated detachment. In contrast, Britain and the United States are among those countries cited as exhibiting a strong allegiant orientation.[22]

Identifying the extent of allegiant attitudes is problematic in that differentiating diffuse and ingrained attachment toward a system from transient views of how the system operates can be difficult. Criticism of the operation of a political system may not indicate support for an alternative system. Indeed, citizens may be fiercely protective of their system relative to others while at the same time expressing a lack of trust in the way that the political elite operate in managing the system. I have previously argued that many values of the British political system are effectively protected, not by a formal constitutional construct, but by the political culture.[23] Some critics have argued that they were not protected, calling in aid opinion polls on the operation of the political system.[24] That, though, is to misunderstand the nature of the diffuse support for the basics, and especially the values, of the British political system.

The situation can be illustrated by reference to the United States. There is little evidence of demand for a fundamental change in the constitution of the United States. Some organizations, such as the Black Muslims, have advocated radical change, but such advocacy has not taken root. There is an attachment to the basics—the foundations—of the American system of government and that attachment remains despite a decline, indeed a collapse, in trust in some of the institutions of government. Trust in the executive in the United States fell to remarkably low levels in the first decade of the twenty-first century, surpassed only by the lack of trust in Congress: The percentage of Americans trusting Congress fell to below 10 percent. If such a lack of trust is maintained in the long term, it may serve to undermine the foundations of the system. In the short term, the fact that there is no burgeoning demand for systemic change points to the enduring strength of the system.

A similar position can be identified in the United Kingdom. There is criticism of the way the system of government operates, and in this case some demands for structural change, but the basics of the system appear to be embraced by the people of the United Kingdom. There is an attachment both to the parliamentary process and the constituency system on which Parliament is based. More than 70 percent of people questioned in a 2007 Ipsos MORI poll agreed or agreed strongly that a strong Parliament is good for democracy (only 5 percent disagreed) and that MPs are essential in representing the views of their constituents (only 10 percent disagreed). Most people questioned (60 percent) also agreed or strongly agreed with the statement that Governments are elected on a mandate and should have powers to act on it (only 7 percent disagreed).[25] Most also took the view that MPs needed sufficient resources to properly represent and inform constituents.

Such attachment to the political system though is contingent and not certain. If the system does not deliver what people expect of it, they are willing to express their dissent. Polls from the 1970s onward tapped a feeling that the system of government could be improved. More than 60 percent of respondents in the 2007 Ipsos MORI poll believed that the system of governing Britain could be improved quite a lot (38 percent) or needed a great deal of improvement (24 percent). However, changes over the preceding years had been gradual: The high point for dissatisfaction appeared to be 1995. Views also appeared to be affected by which party was in government: There was also a correlation between dissatisfaction and support for the main opposition party. Also, in terms of proposals for change the fundamentals of the system were not at the top of the list. Very few people expressed dissatisfaction with Britain's unwritten constitution (most either had no view or were neither satisfied nor dissatisfied) or how votes cast in a general election were translated into seats in the House of Commons. In terms of aspects of the system deemed most urgently in need of change, none was an embedded feature of the system. Instead, respondents favored changes to how the 1998 Human Rights Act worked and how political parties were funded. Only 9 percent thought that Britain's unwritten constitution was urgently in need of change.[26]

Almond and Verba found that evaluation of the political system in Britain was the product of a mix of participant and deferential orientations. A participant orientation developed in Britain (citizens being oriented to the input as well as the output side of the political system, believing that they enjoyed access to it), but it was one adapted to the existing deference to the independent authority of government. The participant orientation did not displace the deferential;[27] deference remained important.

The participant orientation finds expression in citizens' beliefs that they can influence government at both national and local levels. Although Almond and Verba found few people in their survey who actually sought to exert such influence, the proportion who believed they *could* do so was significant. Of British respondents, approximately three out of five believed they could influence government. (Only the United States managed to produce a higher proportion.) The proportion believing they had no influence was only one in five. Though subsequent surveys found that there were high levels of political efficacy, and some increase in participation in political activity, Almond and Verba may have tapped a participant attitude at an historical high point.

More recent surveys have suggested that the proportion of those believing that they can influence government has declined. The 2008 Audit of Political Engagement found that only about one in three of those questioned believed that when they got involved in politics they could change the way the country is run. There had been a slight drop since 2004. However, as the report noted, "while the public is less confident of the efficacy of political involvement than four years ago, there has not been a correspondingly large increase in the proportion professing a sense of powerless."[28] Despite a decline in turnout at general elections, most people engaged in some form of political or civic activity, including voting in local elections, signing a petition, doing voluntary work, or expressing political opinions online. Only 20 percent had not undertaken some form of such activity.[29] Furthermore, the form of participation in Britain is usually of peaceful activity within the established political framework. The 2008 Audit found that 40 percent of those questioned had signed a petition, but only 4 percent had taken part in a demonstration, picket, or march.

Deference remains important, but it is contingent and is most marked in terms of respect for law and those who operate above the political fray. Deference to authority has found expression in a number of ways. It is shown in the attachment to the autonomy of the state. Government is expected to be autonomous in resolving conflict and not be in hock to particular interests. An attempt in 1976 by the Chancellor of the Exchequer, Denis Healey, to make a reduction in income tax conditional on pay restraint by trade unions was attacked as a constitutional outrage, giving power to accept or reject a tax increase to a body other than Parliament. It can be shown in the extent to which Britons trust the state and the extent to which they comply voluntarily with laws passed by Parliament.

Criminal acts tend to be antisocial rather than conscious acts against the state.[30] A general strike by trade unions in 1926 failed in the face of government and popular resistance; the unions themselves were reluctant to be seen to be challenging the authority of the state. "Paradoxically," as A. H. Halsey wrote, "the General Strike of 1926, which may reasonably be described as a moment of tense confrontation between the two main classes . . . provides unmistakable evidence of a consensual political culture."[31] When trade unions, especially the National Union of Miners, were perceived to be exercising excessive political power in the 1970s and 1980s, the response was to curb trade union powers. This entailed the extensive use of police powers against striking miners, but the authority of government to take such action was not subject to popular challenge. When government authority has been challenged, citizens have expressed themselves in favor of maintaining that authority.

Such deference has been seen as allied with a social deference, citizens according certain skills of government to those drawn from a particular group. Walter Bagehot, in his classic work *The English Constitution*, identified England as a "deferential nation," one that had a structure of its own. "Certain persons," he wrote, "are by common consent agreed to be wiser than others, and their opinion is, by consent, to rank for much more than its numerical value."[32] Such deference, though in diluted form, survived into the era of mass suffrage and the democratic ideal. It has, though, been built on reciprocity between governors and governed. The populace has deferred to the independent authority of government and to those who occupy government in return for the satisfaction of expectations. Those expectations have covered the substance of policies as well as the conduct of government. If the governing regime fails to satisfy expectations, in terms of either policy or conduct, then deference is withdrawn. In terms of policy, this may lead to popular dissent, as happened with rioting over the introduction of a poll tax in 1990. In terms of the conduct of government, it led historically to overthrowing the regime, as happened in the 1640s and 1660s; the system of government that has evolved since then has militated against such extreme measures being considered. At the heart of the withdrawal of popular consent is the belief that the system has not been fair and that the interests of the people have been neglected. It is an underlying axiom that can be traced from Magna Carta in the thirteenth century.

Conversely, those to whom citizens accord deference have been characterized as having a sense of duty and as recognizing their responsibility to others. A stress on responsibilities as well as rights has been seen as a significant characteristic of the British political elite, and has been associated with a particular and often predominant tradition within the party that dominated government for most of the past century, the Conservative party (Chapter 6). If that responsibility has not been exercised, then popular support has been withdrawn.

The greater the perception of public service, exercised impartially, the greater the level of public trust. Confidence traditionally has been—and remains—high in the armed services and the police force, with levels of confidence above the average in EU countries.[33] In 2007, an Ipsos MORI poll found high levels of trust in a range of professions. Most people expressed trust in doctors (90 percent), teachers (86 percent), professors (78 percent), judges (78 percent), clergymen/priests (73 percent), scientists (65 percent), television newsreaders (61 percent), and the police (59 percent).[34] There are two additional noteworthy features. First, the figures represent a slight decline in trust from earlier surveys. Second, and perhaps counter-intuitively, younger people are more likely than older people to trust professionals. Older people are more likely to trust priests and clergymen.[35] Figures for trust in bureaucrats and politicians are less positive. Civil servants were trusted by 44 percent. Politicians are generally not well regarded and, historically, never have been. The institutions in which they serve attract mixed notices. In the 2007 poll, only 22 percent trusted government ministers to tell the truth and only 18 percent expressed trust in politicians generally. Parliamentarians attract a more mixed picture: As in the United States, there tends to be a difference in the evaluation of the legislature as opposed to the individual members. Perceptions that Parliament is doing a good job tend to vary over time, whereas a belief that the "local MP" is doing a good job tends to be consistent and positive.

Orientation toward Cooperation and Individuality

Some cultures emphasize the values of cooperating with others, conciliating opposing views, and being prepared to compromise and submerge personal ideas in a broader and more popularly acceptable solution. Others, by contrast, stress the virtues of maintaining the distinctiveness, ideas, and integrity of the group or the individual, such virtues being considered superior to those of compromise and cooperation.[36]

Various countries and regions have been cited as exhibiting a non-cooperative orientation, with the maintenance of group and individual integrity being stressed in both the general culture and political life. Dahl, for example, cited France and Italy.[37] Highly visible contemporary examples include large parts of the Middle East, the Balkans, and, indeed, one part of the United Kingdom: Northern Ireland. Northern Ireland stands out as an atypical part of the United Kingdom. Britain, along with the United States, is among those countries in which the political culture emphasizes the virtues of compromise and conciliation, without threatening personal integrity. The Anglo-American perception was well expressed by Edmund Burke in 1775. "All government, indeed every human benefit and enjoyment, every virtue, and every prudent act," he declared, "is founded on compromise and barter."[38]

This orientation in large measure underpins the stability of the political system. It explains how the elite has adapted to popular demands. As we have touched upon, and will detail in Chapter 3, there have been occasions when the monarch has effectively been deposed. However, both occasions in the seventeenth century could have been avoided had the monarchs (Charles I and James II) not been obdurate in asserting their divine right to rule. Compromise could have kept them on the throne. Since then, the political elite has proved able to adapt to changing conditions. The system has been modified to keep abreast of popular demands; change at times has been slow or encouraged by mass pressure but the basics of the system, certainly the form, have been maintained. As a result, democracy has been introduced and maintained within a system that has been both monarchical and aristocratic. The elite has conceded to the realities of political life, the monarch moving from being the principal political actor to a national and neutral figurehead. By being willing to adapt and compromise, the elite has avoided the revolutionary pressures exhibited in other countries, including its neighbor across the English Channel. Whereas the French overthrew their aristocracy, the British exhibited no equivalent tendency. Though there were some movements in Britain that took up the revolutionary cause, they failed to find fertile soil.

The system itself has also provided the means for achieving change. There is an acceptance of the parliamentary process and through that process change can be agreed and legitimized. An adversarial relationship between political parties has tended to mask a general acceptance of the rules of the game under which that relationship operates. At an elite level, partisanship influences the stance taken on the rules of the game, but the rules are generally accepted[39] and, indeed, the basic rules of parliamentary procedure have been notable for remaining in place despite the capacity of government, secure in a parliamentary majority, to change them.[40] Those procedures are premised on the belief that the government is entitled to get its business but the opposition is entitled to be heard.

The desire to compromise underpins the whole process of policy making. The relationship between bureaucrats and representatives of organized interests has been characterized as one of accommodation.[41] Though industrial relations often have been marked by an adversarial relationship, resolving disputes through bargaining has generally formed part of the culture of industrial life. There is almost a penchant for resolving disputes by discussion, by sitting around a table and ironing out differences. It is an orientation compatible with the others we have identified and is congenial to a society that stresses the responsibilities as well as the rights of the citizen. It is a predominant orientation: There are certainly exceptions, not least—as we have mentioned—in a particular part of the United Kingdom, namely Northern Ireland, but even there negotiations bore fruit in bringing different communities together in 2007 (see Chapter 10). It is an orientation that remains a feature of British society.

Equally a feature of British society is the attachment to the integrity of the individual. Britons accept the autonomy of the state and accord a similar status to the individual. There is a strong belief in individual liberty. The emphasis historically has been on liberties rather than rights. The individual has been deemed to be free to do whatever he or she wishes as long as it is not proscribed by law. Government has sought to act in the interests of all, not least historically in defending the realm and maintaining peace at home, but it has faced opposition in seeking to limit the capacity of the individual to determine his (and more recently her) own actions. Various restrictions have been imposed over time—from the imposition of an income tax through to a requirement to wear a seat belt in a car—but they have variously been opposed and accepted only after being agreed by Parliament. The belief in individual liberty has limited what government is prepared to do. When there are restrictions imposed, there is a strong attachment to due process. The restrictions have to be legitimized and, if an individual is taken to court, he or she is entitled to a fair hearing. An attachment to jury trials and *habeas corpus,* providing for a writ to be issued against unlawful detention, is a long-standing feature of the legal system. (*Habeas corpus* can be traced back beyond Magna Carta in 1215, but took its modern form in the thirteenth century. It has since been effectively superseded by statute.) The attachment remains pronounced in the twenty-first century. Attempts to limit jury trials, or to extend the period which terrorist suspects can be detained without being charged, have faced effective parliamentary opposition.

Orientation toward Other People

A belief that one can have confidence in others has been put forward as a culturally rooted phenomenon, with potentially important implications for political life. Research in the 1950s by Morris Rosenberg found that "faith in people" was related to democratic and internationalist values and attitudes.[42] In their study, Almond and Verba found that Americans and Britons "tend to be consistently more positive about the safety and responsiveness of the human environment."[43] The Germans and the Italians, by contrast, were found to be more negative, and the Mexicans inconsistent.

Faith in others can take various forms and one of the most significant aspects of British culture is that of tolerance. In a major BBC television series in 2008, *Britain from Above*, based on an aerial analysis of what, as we have seen (Chapter 1), is a densely crowded island, the presenter—journalist and former BBC political editor Andrew Marr—commented: "Everyone's crowded and jostled. And it works only because people are somehow quite nice to each other."[44] After Gordon Brown became prime minister in 2007, he initiated a national debate on Britishness and its core components. One that was offered was tolerance. This was criticized on the grounds that it was hardly unique to Britain. It is not exclusive but there is a plausible case to be made that it is a distinctive feature. Though the country over time has witnessed racial and religious discrimination, it has proved willing to accept and accommodate different groupings within society. That has encompassed providing political emancipation for Catholics and Jews in the nineteenth century through to decriminalizing homosexual behavior in the twentieth. Some could argue that many changes could have come sooner, and many of these changes were achieved in the face of intense opposition, but—once approved by Parliament—they came to enjoy acceptance.

If anything, this tolerance has become more rather than less marked in the twenty-first century. One telling example is the attitude toward Muslims. A Pew survey in 2005 found that the proportion of Britons having an unfavorable view of Muslims was 14 percent, compared to 22 percent in the United States and a number of other countries where such unfavorable views were notably pronounced: 50 percent in the case of China and 51 percent in the Netherlands (Table 2.1). It is also reflected, as we have seen (Chapter 1), in attitudes toward homosexual behavior. Homosexual behavior between males was decriminalized in 1967. (It was never an offence between females.) An Ipsos MORI poll in 2000 found that 46 percent of those questioned supported gay marriage. By 2007 the percentage had increased to 68 percent.[45]

This tolerance of others was also tapped by other surveys carried out by Ipsos MORI. In a report on Britain in the decade from 1997 to 2007, it found that: "Britons are also relatively supportive of living in racially mixed

TABLE 2.1

Views of Muslims

Unfavorable view of Muslims (%)	
Country	Percentage holding unfavorable view
Netherlands	51
China	50
Germany	47
India	43
Spain	37
Russia	36
France	34
Poland	30
Canada	26
United States	22
Great Britain	14

Source: Pew Survey, GB data from April/May 2005, reproduced in B. Marshall *et al.*, *Blair's Britain: The Social and Cultural Legacy* (Ipsos MORI, 2007), p. 40.

areas and opposed to the banning of wearing head scarves by Muslim women, while the qualitative research we do on the subject finds a strong sentiment of live and let live."[46] More than 60 percent thought that multiculturalism had made Britain a better place to live.

Surveys in recent years have shown that Britons retain a fairly positive view of themselves. The British—and European—Social Attitudes survey in 1998 of four European countries found that the highest level of national pride was to be found in Britain.[47] "Not surprisingly, national pride is related to attachment to one's country. In general, those who feel 'close' to their country display higher levels of national pride than those who do not feel as close."[48] Eurobarometer data in 2008 also showed that Britons tend to be satisfied with the lives they lead. An overwhelming majority of Britons (87 percent) were satisfied with the lives they lead, compared with 77 percent of citizens in the European Union as a whole.[49] The high percentage found in Britain was also a feature of Benelux and Scandinavian countries. Various surveys have found that Britons tend to regard other Britons as fairly trustworthy,[50] though trust in one's own nationality also tends to be a feature of most countries of western Europe.[51]

There are, though, some differences in levels of trust in other nationalities, though again a similar feature exists in other European countries. Though attitudes fluctuate, Britons tend to be more trusting of Americans than of other Europeans (Table 2.2). Distrust tends to be greatest in relation to Britain's old historical enemy, the French. There are strong emotional ties to old Commonwealth countries such as Canada, New Zealand, and Australia. The positive orientation toward the United States and a number of Commonwealth countries

TABLE 2.2

TRUST IN COUNTRIES, 2003

How much do you trust or distrust the following countries?

	Trust		Distrust		Trust over
	A lot (%)	A bit (%)	A lot (%)	A bit (%)	distrust
France	8	24	38	25	−31
Germany	9	32	26	27	−12
Russia	5	32	24	30	−17
Italy	11	43	12	23	+19
Spain	20	47	8	16	+43
America	26	30	24	15	+17

Source: Populus Ltd., poll archive, www.populuslimited.com/the-sun-the-eu-european-constitution-110503.html

is hardly surprising, partly for reasons of history and partly for reasons of language. Britons have tended to look toward the English-speaking world rather than to countries whose languages they have been reluctant to learn. The English and the Scots, as Anthony King has observed, have tended not to think like Europeans nor to think of themselves as Europeans.[52] This is relevant for understanding both the British political culture and the difficulties of Britain in adjusting to membership in the European Union. As we shall see (Chapter 9), the United Kingdom has at times looked more like a semidetached member of that union than a fully integrated one. It also has a broader relevance for understanding Britain's approach to world affairs.

Britons thus tend to have faith in themselves and a relatively discriminating faith in others. This is an important component of the political culture, though not one that renders Britain distinctive. It is the combination of orientations that renders the country distinct from the United States and from its European allies.

ADAPTING OR DECLINING?

The political culture of Britain may then be characterized, in broad terms, as having the four orientations identified: empirical in terms of problem solving and change, allegiant in terms of the political system, cooperative in making decisions, and trusting in relation to fellow citizens and allies.

The strength of the culture may be said to lie in the convergence of these orientations—that is, they are compatible with and reinforce one another, and similarly are compatible with and are reinforced by the experience of history. The stress on cooperation and compromise—on being tolerant and fair—has facilitated the integration of groups and individuals into the political system.

Such integration may be seen as reinforcing an allegiant rather than a neutral or alienated orientation to the political system. History has been kind: The country has staved off invasion by its enemies, and the resources have usually been available for government to make and meet commitments in response to changing demands and expectations. As a result, it has been possible to interpret the experience of history as justifying or reinforcing an attachment to empirical problem solving and to the virtues of cooperation and trust. Indeed, the interplay of these variables generated what Almond and Verba characterized as "the civic culture," "a pluralistic culture based on communication and persuasion, a culture of consensus and diversity, a culture that permitted change but moderated it."[53]

No culture, though, is necessarily inherently consistent or static. People may have attitudes that are not compatible with one another. Not everyone may be part of the dominant culture (if there is one). Societal values may change over time. Actions may be shaped by the culture but the culture itself may be affected, subtly or paradigmatically, by particular events or by developments over a period of time. British political culture exhibits tensions and has been subject to some changes in recent decades. For some, what we are witnessing is the political system adapting to pressures from within and beyond the shores of the United Kingdom. Others see the changes as challenging fundamentally the capacity of the existing system to meet the challenges. They see in particular a divergence between elite and popular behavior.

There are tensions that can be identified within the political culture. How far can a tolerant society cope with those who are intolerant? Should tolerance of whatever views people wish to express take priority over protecting the safety and well-being of minorities and individuals or indeed the general public? To what extent can suspected terrorists have their freedom of movement curtailed? These are real tensions within the United Kingdom. Adherence to the integrity of the individual underpinned the incorporation of the European Convention on Human Rights into U.K. law, through the Human Rights Act 1998. Attempts by government to restrict the movement of people suspected of supporting terrorism have fallen foul of judicial interpretations of the provisions of that Act. In 2008, the government sought to extend the period in which suspected terrorists could be detained without being charged with an offence. The measure enjoyed popular support but was opposed by many parliamentarians on grounds of infringing the rights of the individual.

Also adherence to particular cultural values may be more marked within one section of society than another. Though the orientations we have identified are widespread, some are more strongly held by some sections of the population than by others. Some of the distinctions can be related to the media of political socialization that we have identified. Support for established institutions, and especially the belief that they work well, is more pronounced among the better educated and the middle class. Political activism is also more marked among those who are better educated, read quality newspapers, and are middle class. There are also distinctions related to location. Those living in Scotland, Wales, and the north of England have tended to exhibit greater disaffection with the political system than those living closer to London. As we shall see (Chapter 10), nationalism has been a growing feature in both Scotland and Wales and pressures for self-government led to the creation in 1998 of elected assemblies in both, an example of adaptation to burgeoning popular demands.

The characteristics of the political culture may be shared by most, to a greater or lesser extent, but there may also be sub-cultures or those who do not share the dominant values. Some particular religious or ethnic groups may reject part or all of the culture. Historically, certain parts of the population of Northern Ireland have rejected the political culture of the United Kingdom and have not been prepared to resolve differences by compromise and negotiation (Chapter 10). There has also been identification of a social underclass that has little understanding of and adherence to the political institutions of the United Kingdom and little respect for authority. Those in this underclass do not share the tolerance of others that is a characteristic of British society: If they express any political allegiance it is to extreme political groups. They too embody a paradox: They claim to defend Britain by adopting un-British attitudes.

There is also perceived by some commentators to be a wider and growing divide between elite and popular behavior. Some, including a noted American academic, Samuel Beer, have argued that there has been a decline of the civil culture. Indeed, Beer has claimed that "it is no exaggeration to speak of a decline in the civic culture as a 'collapse.'"[54] The orientations of the culture—the positive orientation toward institutions and cooperation—he contended were diminishing, reflected in a conflict between elite and popular behavior. For Beer, as for constitutional reformers, a dysfunctional constitutional system was both cause and effect of this decline. Old institutions have been unable to meet expectations and to harness popular support. As institutions fail to meet those expectations, so trust in the effectiveness and equity of government diminishes. The greater the lack of trust, the greater the lack of cooperation, and hence the more government has to centralize power in order to meet its policy goals.

Empirical support for this thesis is found in a decline in voter turnout, a belief that the system of government is in need of change, and in the perceived centralization of government. Membership of political parties has declined and voter turnout has fallen, as has the percentage of the population voting for the two main parties. Single-party governments have been elected on smaller percentages of the poll than before, sometimes no more, and on occasion even less, than 40 percent. The existing system, according to the constitutional reform body, Charter88—founded, as its name implies, in 1988 and now part of a wider body, Unlock Democracy—was locked into a spiral of decline. The civic culture, on this argument, could be restored only through a new constitutional settlement, with existing structures swept away and replaced by a political system that engages the participatory energies of citizens.[55] Even if more people were taking part in political activity, that activity could be argued to be the product of an unresponsive political system.

Others would argue that what we are witnessing are tensions to which the system can adapt and is adapting. Those who identify a collapse in the civic culture base their thesis of decline on an atypical period. The civic culture tapped by Almond and Verba was, as we have mentioned, a high point in political participation and adherence to political institutions. What we have witnessed since is a reversion to the types of pressures and tensions that have characterized British history and to which the system, by its nature, has adapted. Debating and questioning the efficacy of the political system is something that has occurred throughout British history. The quarter-century after the Second World War was unusual in that the habit of discussing the nation's constitutional arrangements was lost and has only recently been regained. Identification of disaffection with the political system among particular groups, and the existence of an underclass, is again nothing new. There was an underclass that was no respecter of authority in the nineteenth century and indeed in the twentieth. Unrest among the populace was also more marked in the early years of the twentieth century, requiring on occasion troops being called out to support the police. There were race riots in Wales, London, and Liverpool. More recent examples of unrest are somewhat pale by comparison. Furthermore, as we have already noted, dissatisfaction with the system appears not to be with the fundamentals. Insofar as institutional change can address some of the problems, such as demands for self-government in different parts of the United Kingdom, then the political system has been modified to accommodate those demands.

Also undermining the thesis is that many of the changes in attitude among Britons toward the political system, manifested in declining support for political parties and trust in institutions, are to be found in other European countries.[56] What is relevant for the purposes of this argument is that many of these countries employ political structures and processes that reformers argue would address the problems identified in the United Kingdom. If they do not appear to be the solution to the problems of declining trust and participation in the countries where they are utilized, it is not clear why they will generate or regenerate a more participant attitude among Britons.

These competing analyses are basic to any study of contemporary British politics. They represent the two elements of change and continuity; the "decline" proponents identifying significant change in the civic culture, and the opponents of the decline thesis emphasizing continuity. They underpin, respectively, calls for—and a rejection of—a new constitutional settlement for the United Kingdom. We will variously have cause to refer to them in later chapters and they will form the basis of the concluding chapter in which we explore the debate as to the future direction of the British Constitution. Are current constitutional arrangements fit for purpose? Or are they in need of radical surgery?

NOTES

1. See D. Kavanagh, *Political Culture* (Macmillan, 1972), pp. 10–11.
2. Ibid., p. 10.

3. E. Jacobs and R. Worcester, *We British* (Weidenfeld & Nicolson, 1990), pp. 143–144.
4. See especially M. Franklin, *The Decline in Class Voting in Britain* (Oxford University Press, 1985), pp. 69–71, 78–79.
5. R. Rose and I. McAllister, *Voters Begin to Choose* (Sage, 1986), pp. 104–106.
6. G. Almond and S. Verba, *The Civic Culture* (Princeton University Press, 1963), pp. 86–87.
7. Hansard Society, *Audit of Political Engagement 5: The 2008 Report* (Hansard Society, 2008), p. 20.
8. Ibid., p. 16.
9. Ibid., p. 14.
10. R. J. Johnston, C. J. Pattie, and J. G. Allsopp, *A Nation Dividing?* (Longman, 1988), p. 49.
11. W. L. Miller, *Electoral Dynamics* (Macmillan, 1977). See also Johnston, Pattie, and Allsopp, pp. 61–63.
12. *Eurobarometer 69: Public Opinion in the European Union*, Spring 2008: National Report: United Kingdom (EU Directorate General Communication, 2008), pp. 18–19.
13. Ibid., p. 19.
14. R. A. Dahl (ed.), *Political Opposition in Western Democracies* (Yale University Press, 1966), p. 353.
15. G. Sartori, *Democratic Theory* (Wayne State University Press, 1962), p. 233, cited in Dahl, p. 354.
16. Dahl, p. 355.
17. L. Hartz, *The Liberal Tradition in America* (Harcourt, Brace & World, 1955). For the analysis by Charles Beard, see C. Beard, *An Economic Interpretation of the Constitution* (Macmillan, 1913).
18. Indeed, they have been so pervasive that Americans will not necessarily accept that there is such a pervasive consciousness. It can only be appreciated by being outside it.
19. V. Hart, *Distrust and Democracy* (Cambridge University Press, 1978), pp. 202–203.
20. Sir Christopher Meyer, "A Return to 1815 is the Way Forward for Europe," *The Times,* 2 September 2008.
21. Dahl, p. 353.
22. Almond and Verba, Ch. 14.
23. P. Norton, "In Defence of the Constitution," in P. Norton (ed.), *New Directions in British Politics?* (Edward Elgar, 1991), pp. 145–172.
24. F. Klug, K. Starmer, and S. Weir, *The Three Pillars of Liberty* (Routledge, 1996), Ch. 4.
25. Hansard Society, *Audit of Political Engagement 5: The 2008 Report* (Hansard Society, 2008), p. 33.
26. Ibid., p. 31.
27. Almond and Verba, pp. 455–456.
28. Hansard Society, *Audit of Political Engagement 5: The 2008 Report* (Hansard Society, 2008), p. 20.
29. Ibid., p. 50.
30. See R. N. Berki, *Security and Society* (Dent, 1986). Even though people trust the state, the concept of the state is not that well entrenched in English consciousness. It is, though, important to stress *English* consciousness: A proportion of the citizenry in Scotland and Wales have variously expressed resentment toward what is

seen as an "English" state, and in Northern Ireland some inhabitants have engaged in explicit and violent anti-state activity (see Chapter 9).

31. A. H. Halsey, *Change in British Society*, 2nd ed. (Oxford University Press, 1981), p. 70.

32. W. Bagehot, *The English Constitution* (first published 1867; Fontana, 1963 edition).

33. *Eurobarometer 69: Public Opinion in the European Union*, Spring 2008: National Report: United Kingdom, (EU Directorate General Communication, 2008), p. 20.

34. Royal College of Physicians, *Trust in Professions 2007: Public Awareness of Physicians and Trust in Professionals* (Royal College of Physicians, 2007), p. 7.

35. Ibid., p. 9.

36. Dahl, p. 354.

37. Ibid.

38. Speech on conciliation with the American Colonies, 22 March 1775.

39. See D. D. Searing, "Rules of the Game in Britain: Can the Politicians be Trusted?," *American Political Science Review*, 76, 1982, pp. 239–258.

40. See P. Norton, "Playing by the Rules: The Constraining Hand of Parliamentary Procedure," *The Journal of Legislative Studies*, 7 (3), 2001, pp. 13–33.

41. J. Richardson (ed.), *Policy Styles in Western Europe* (George Allen & Unwin, 1982).

42. M. Rosenberg, "Misanthropy and Political Ideology," *American Sociological Review*, 21, pp. 690–695; and "Misanthropy and Attitudes towards International Affairs," *Journal of Conflict Resolution*, 1, 1957, pp. 340–345, cited in Almond and Verba, p. 266.

43. Almond and Verba, p. 268.

44. "Talking Television with Andrew Marr," *The Sunday Telegraph: Seven* magazine, 10 August 2008, p. 51.

45. B. Marshall *et al.*, *Blair's Britain: The Social and Cultural Legacy* (Ipsos MORI, 2007), p. 39.

46. Ibid., p. 40.

47. *British—and European—Social Attitudes* (Ashgate, 1998), p. 8.

48. Ibid., pp. 8–9.

49. *Eurobarometer 69: Public Opinion in the European Union*, Spring 2008: National Report: United Kingdom (EU Directorate General Communication, 2008), p. 4.

50. *Eurobarometer, No. 33*, June 1990, Table 14.

51. N. Webb and R. Wybrow, pp. 103–104; *Eurobarometer, No. 33*, June 1990, Table 14.

52. A. King, *Britain Says Yes* (American Enterprise Institute, 1977), p. 6. See also L. Barzini, *The Impossible Europeans* (Weidenfeld & Nicolson, 1983).

53. Almond and Verba, p. 8.

54. S. H. Beer, *Britain against Itself* (Faber, 1982), p. 119.

55. See especially D. Marquand, *The Unprincipled Society* (Fontana, 1988).

56. See *Eurobarometer 69: Public Opinion in the European Union*, Spring 2008: National Report: United Kingdom (EU Directorate General Communication, 2008).

CHAPTER

3

Past and Present
Historical Perspective and Legacies

A number of introductory texts on British politics do not have chapters devoted specifically to political history. The omission is a surprising one. When the proposal for this book was under consideration by the publishers, a number of American professors were asked for their comments. One responded with this advice: "Make sure you incorporate as much historical detail as possible. American students don't know much about British history." The need for historical detail, however, is not confined to Americans interested in the subject; it encompasses all those who seek to make some sense of the institutions and complex relationships that form the British polity.

The country has witnessed continuous and sometimes dramatic change. In the past three hundred years alone, the nation has experienced industrialization, the advent of democracy, and the introduction and growth of the welfare state—yet the changes have been built upon and have adapted that which already existed. The body politic may have undergone radical surgery and it may have aged considerably, but it has continued to endure.

What, then, are the significant features of British history that help us understand the contemporary political system and the political culture? Limitations of space preclude a lengthy dissertation on what is a vast subject. That vastness is apparent when put in comparative perspective. The Magna Carta, for instance, was signed more than two centuries before Christopher Columbus set sail. A parliament was summoned more than five hundred years before the U.S. Congress first assembled. And a U.S. president, unlike a British monarch, cannot trace his forebears in office back more than a thousand years. Nonetheless, it is possible to provide a brief but structured sketch that furthers our understanding of contemporary British politics. This can be done under three headings: the emergence of parliamentary government, the development of the welfare state and managed economy, and the politics of Thatcher and Blair.

HISTORICAL PERSPECTIVE

The Emergence of Parliamentary Government

One of the essential features of the British constitution is a parliamentary government under a limited, or symbolic, monarchy. The formal elements of this type of government will be more fully outlined in the next chapter. For the moment, what concerns us is that this government is the product of change extending over several centuries, coming to fruition only in the past century. Its development sometimes has been characterized as being evolutionary, but in practice it is the outgrowth of piecemeal change.

Let us begin in the thirteenth century. Traditionally, the sovereign power in England resided in the monarch. Nonetheless, the king was expected to consult with his tenants-in-chief (the leading churchmen and the barons) in order to discover and declare the law and to have their counsel before any levies of extraordinary taxation were made. This expectation was to find documented expression in the Great Charter (*Magna Carta*) of 1215, by which the king recognized it as a right of his subjects "to have the Common Council of the Kingdom" for the assessment of extraordinary aids—that is, taxation. Such consultation was undertaken through a Great Council, from which evolved what was to be recognized as a *parlement* or Parliament. The Great Council itself was the precursor of the House of Lords. The House of Commons evolved from the summoning to council, in the latter half of the thirteenth century on a sporadic basis, of knights and burgesses from the counties and towns. At various times in the fourteenth century the Commons deliberated separately from the Lords, and there developed a formal separation of the two bodies.

During the period of the Tudor monarchs in the sixteenth century, Parliament acquired enhanced status. It was generally supportive of the monarch but became more powerful because the monarchs depended upon it for that support, especially during the reign of Elizabeth I. The relationship between Crown and Parliament under the subsequent Stuart dynasty was one of conflict. The early Stuart kings—James I and Charles I—sought to assert the doctrine of the divine right of kings and to deny many of the privileges acquired or asserted by Parliament. This conflict was to lead to the civil war and the beheading of Charles I in 1649. With the abolition of the monarchy came a brief period of rule by a Council of State elected by what was termed the Rump Parliament. (Some attempts were actually made to formulate what amounted to a written constitution, but they came to nothing.)[1] Rule by the Council of State was succeeded by Oliver Cromwell's unsuccessful military dictatorship, and in 1660 Charles's eldest son returned to assume the throne as Charles II. The period between 1642 and 1660 proved an aberration in British history. The Restoration witnessed an attempt to return, unconditionally, to the country's position as it was at the beginning of 1642.[2] Through this attempt, the Restoration lent itself to a repetition of the earlier struggle between the king and Commons. Relations between the two gradually deteriorated during the reign of Charles II and became severe in the reign of his successor, James II. James sought to reassert the divine right of kings, and Parliament combined against him. In 1688 James fled the country. At the invitation of Parliament, the throne was taken by William and Mary of Orange, James's son-in-law and daughter. Though the change represented a fundamental upheaval in the politics of Britain—and was to be characterized as the Glorious Revolution—it was nonetheless couched in terms of continuity. The king was deemed to have abdicated and the throne offered to his daughter and her husband, thus maintaining the family line.

The new occupants of the throne owed their position to Parliament, and the new relationship between them was asserted by statute in the Bill of Rights. Although the Bill of Rights was important for enumerating various "Liberties of this Kingdom" (some of which were to be similarly expressed during the following century in the Bill of Rights embodied in the United States Constitution),[3] its essential purpose was to assert the position of Parliament in relation to the Crown. The raising of taxes or the dispensing of laws without the assent of Parliament was declared to be illegal. The monarch was expected to govern, but to do so only with the consent of Parliament. The Act of Settlement of 1701, which determined the succession to the throne, affirmed that the laws of England "are the Birthright of the People thereof and all the Kings and Queens who shall ascend the Throne of this Realm ought to administer the Government of the same according to the said Laws and all their Officers and Ministers ought to serve them respectively according to the same."

The monarch thus became formally dependent on Parliament for consent to the raising of taxes and for the passage of legislation. In practice, he or she became increasingly dependent also on ministers for advice. The importance of ministers grew, especially in the eighteenth century. Following the death of Queen Anne, who outlived all her children, the throne passed to George, the Elector of Hanover, who spoke little or no English. The Hanoverian kings were not uninterested in political life, but they had difficulty comprehending the complexities of domestic and foreign affairs. According to the historian J. H. Plumb, both George I and George II were "crassly stupid" and "incapable, totally incapable, of forming a policy."[4] During the period of their reigns, the leading body of the king's ministers, generally known as the cabinet, began to meet without the king being present.[5] The period also witnessed the emergence of a minister who was to become popularly known as the prime minister. (Not until the twentieth century, though, was the office of prime minister to be mentioned in a statute.) The relationship among Crown, ministers, and Parliament in the century was one in which the king relied on his ministers to help formulate policy. Those ministers were chosen by the king on the basis of his personal confidence in them, and they remained responsible to him. They also were responsible to Parliament in order to achieve their ends, a fact recognized by both the king and his ministers. Nonetheless, parliamentary support was not difficult to obtain; the king and his ministers had sufficient patronage and position usually to ensure such support. A ministry that enjoyed royal confidence could generally take the House of Lords for granted, and provided it did not prove incompetent or seek to impose excessive taxation, "its position was unassailable in the Commons."[6] The position was to change significantly in the nineteenth century.

Britain underwent what has been popularly referred to as an industrial revolution from the middle of the eighteenth century to the middle of the nineteenth. Seymour Martin Lipset has characterized the United States as the "first new nation," but Britain has been described as "the first industrial nation."[7] Industry became more mechanized, improvements took place in agricultural production techniques, and there were improvements in transport and the organization of trade and banking. There was a notable growth in the size of cities, particularly in the early part of the nineteenth century. Men of industry and commerce began to emerge as men of some wealth. In 1813 Robert Owen referred to the "working class," a term brought into common speech by Lord Brougham.[8] By the 1830s, a non-landed middle class, artisans, and an industrial workforce were important constituents of the country's population.

Parliament remained dominated by the aristocracy and by the landed gentry. Representation in the House of Commons was heavily weighted in favor of the rural counties. Some parliamentary constituencies had only a handful of electors: Known as "rotten boroughs," these areas were often in the pocket of an aristocrat or local landowner.[9] Pressure for some parliamentary reform, with a redistribution of seats and a widening of the franchise, began to develop. It was argued that a Parliament full of men of wealth and property was unlikely to view industry, trade, and agriculture from the point of view of the laboring classes. Rotten boroughs were criticized as being used by the ministry to help maintain a majority. Unrest in a number of areas, both agricultural and industrial, and the French Revolution of 1830 (a spur to radical action) increased the pressure for change. One political group in particular, the Whigs, who had been the "outs" in politics for twenty-five years prior to 1830, began to see the need for some response to this pressure. The concession of some parliamentary reform was seen as necessary in order to prevent worse happening. The result, following the return of the Whigs to power, was to be the Reform Act of 1832.

The Reform Act, introduced, ironically, by the most aristocratic government of the century, reorganized parliamentary constituencies and extended the franchise. The electorate increased in size from a little under 500,000 to 813,000 electors.[10] Much remained the same as before—the new electorate constituted but one-thirtieth of the population, 31 boroughs still had fewer than 300 electors in each, voting remained by open ballot (secret ballots were considered rather un-English), and the aristocracy still held great sway politically. But the act precipitated important changes both within and outside the House of Commons.

The redistribution of seats and the extension of the franchise helped loosen the grip of the aristocracy and of ministers on the House of Commons. The size of the new electorate encouraged the embryonic development of political organizations. Members of Parliament (MPs) became less dependent on aristocratic patrons without acquiring too great a dependence on the growing party organizations. The result was to be a House of Commons with a greater legitimacy in the eyes of MPs and electors and with an ability to assert itself in its relationship with government. There was relatively little legislation—the domain of public policy was not great[11]—but what there was, the House proved willing to amend or reject. The House on occasion forced individual ministers to resign and sometimes even the whole government. In his classic work on the constitution, Walter Bagehot attached much importance to this "elective function"; the House of Commons, he declared, was "a real choosing body: it elects the people it likes. And it dismisses whom it likes too."[12] Debates in the House counted for something and, with the exception of the period from 1841 to 1846, party cohesion was almost unknown. The House of Commons did not itself govern, but government was carried on within the confines of its guidance and approval.

The period after 1832 also witnessed important changes in the relationships within and among the different elements of Crown, government, and Parliament. The monarch retained the formal prerogative power to appoint the prime minister, but the changed political circumstances essentially dictated that the person chosen should be able to command a majority in the House of Commons. Royal favor ceased to be an essential condition for forming the government. Within Parliament, the relationship between the two houses also changed. Members of the House of Lords sat by virtue of birth, holding hereditary peerages. The acceptance of the Commons as the "representative" chamber undermined the authority of the peers to challenge or negate the wishes of the other house. After the 1830s, the Lords tended to be somewhat restrained in their attacks on government measures. "This," as Mackintosh noted, "followed from the view that while a ministry retained the confidence of the elected representatives it was entitled to remain in office. The peers on the whole accepted these assumptions, though many found the explicit recognition of the situation hard to bear."[13] The remaining authority of the House of Lords was in practice to be removed in consequence of the 1867 Reform Act, though not until the twentieth century was the House forced formally to accept its diminished status.

Whereas the 1832 act helped ensure the dominance of the House of Commons within the formal political process, the passage of the Reform Act of 1867 began a process of the transfer of power from Parliament to ministers. The act itself was the product of demands for change because of the limited impact of the 1832 act and because of more immediate political considerations.[14] Its effect was to increase the size of the electorate from 1,358,000 to 2,477,000. (The number had grown since 1832 because of increased wealth and population.) Other significant measures followed in its wake. Secret voting was introduced by the Ballot Act of 1872. Other acts sought to prohibit as far as possible corrupt practices and limited the amount of money a candidate could spend on election expenses. Single-member districts (known in Britain as constituencies) of roughly equal electoral size were prescribed as the norm.[15] The 1884 Representation of the People Act extended the franchise to householders and tenants and to all those who occupied land or tenements with an annual value of not less than ten pounds. The effect of the act was to bring into being an electorate in which working men were in a majority. The consequence of these developments was to be party government.

The size of the new electorate meant that the voters could be reached only through some well-developed organization, and the result was to be the growth of organized and mass-membership political parties. The Conservative National Union and the National Liberal Federation were formed to facilitate and encourage the support of the new electors. However, contact with the voters was insufficient in itself to entice their support. Not only had a large section of the population been enfranchised, but also it was a notably different electorate from that which had existed previously. The new class of electors had different and greater demands than those of the existing middle-class electors. If the votes of working men were to be obtained, the parties had to offer them something. And the parties could govern effectively only if they presented a uniform face to the electorate and achieved a cohesive majority in the House of Commons to carry through their policies. What this was to produce was a shift of power away from the House of Commons to the cabinet and the electorate, with political parties serving as the conduit for this transfer.

The electorate proved too large and too politically unsophisticated to evaluate the merits of an individual MP's behavior. Political parties provided the labels with which electors could identify, and elections became gladiatorial contests between parties rather than between individual candidates. The all-or-nothing spoils of an election victory and the method of election encouraged (if not always produced) a contest between two major parties.[16] And having voted for party candidates, the electors expected the members returned to Parliament to support the program offered by their leaders at the election. Party cohesion soon became a feature of parliamentary life.[17] The House of Commons in effect lost two of the most important functions ascribed to it by Bagehot, those of legislation and of choosing the government: the former passed to the cabinet and the latter to the electorate. The cabinet constituted the leaders of the party enjoying a parliamentary majority. It assumed the initiative for the formulation and introduction of measures of national policy and became increasingly reluctant to be overruled by the House. The growth in the number and complexity of bills further limited the influence of the individual MP. Increasingly, his role (the House was still all-male) became one of supporting his leaders. The cabinet previously had rested its authority on the support of the House; now it derived its authority from the electors. As Mackintosh states, "The task of the House of Commons became one of supporting the Cabinet chosen at the polls and passing its legislation. By the 1900s, the Cabinet dominated British government."[18]

Further modifications and addenda took place in the first half of the twentieth century. The House of Lords was forced by statute in 1911 to accept its diminished status. The franchise was variously extended, most notably to half the population previously excluded because of their sex. The vote was extended to women aged 30 and over in 1918 and to women aged 21 and over (thus bringing them into line with male voters) in 1928. The first female MP to take her seat—the American-born Nancy Astor—did so in 1919.[19] The monarch's political influence further receded. The growth and increasing economic weight of groups generated more extensive and complex demands of government. And the size of government grew as its responsibility expanded.

Basically, though, the essential features of the political system were those established in the preceding century. The responsibility for making public policy rested with the government, a government derived from and resting its support upon a political party. That same party's majority in the House of Commons ensured that the government's measures were approved. Formal and political constraints limited the effect of any opposition from the House of Lords. The monarch gave formal assent to any legislative measure approved by the two houses. Thus, within the formal framework of deciding public policy, the government was dominant. The role of Parliament became largely but not wholly one of legitimating the measures put before it. For the monarch, that became the exclusive role (that is, in respect of legislation). Government, as we shall see, operated within a political environment that imposed important constraints, but the limitations imposed formerly by Parliament and the monarch were largely eroded. Britain retained a parliamentary form of government, but what that meant was not government by Parliament but government through Parliament.

The Welfare State and the Managed Economy

To comprehend some of the problems faced by contemporary British government, it is necessary to know not only the structure and relationships of the political system but also the popular expectations and the burden of responsibilities borne by government. Those expectations and responsibilities have not been static. Just as the governmental structure has been modified in response to political demands, so the responsibilities of government have grown as greater social and economic demands have been made of it.

Toward the end of the nineteenth century and more so in the twentieth, the responsibilities of government expanded. In part this expansion was attributable to the growth of the empire. (As prime minister in the 1870s, Benjamin Disraeli had played the "imperial card," the British empire expanding rapidly: By 1900 it covered virtually a quarter of the globe.) It was also attributable to the increasing demands and expectations of the newly enfranchised working population. Government began to conceive its duties as extending beyond those of maintaining law and order and of defending the realm. The statute book began to expand, with the addition of measures of social reform. Various such measures were enacted prior to 1867, though the most notable were to be enacted in the remaining decades of the century. They included measures to limit working hours for women and children, to improve housing and public health, to make education for children compulsory, to provide for the safety of workers (including the payment of compensation by employers in the event of accidents at work), and even to extend the right to strike.[20] Such measures, exploited for electoral advantage, were within the capabilities of the government to provide. They did not create too great an economic burden; they were not themselves economic measures.

The growth of expectations and the greater willingness of government to intervene in areas previously considered inviolate was to be continued and became more marked in the twentieth century. The general election of 1906 was a watershed in British politics. It was the first election to be fought essentially on national issues and it witnessed the return not only of a reforming Liberal government but also, and in some respects more significantly, of 27 Labour MPs. The Labour party had been created for the purpose of ensuring working-class representation in Parliament, and from 1906 onward class became a significant influence in voting behavior. The nature of electoral conflict changed as the Labour party succeeded the Liberal as the main opposition party to the Conservatives. The franchise was further extended, notably in 1918 and 1928, and new expectations were generated by the experience of the two world wars.

During the First World War (1914–18), socialists within the Labour party argued the case for the conscription of wealth (public ownership) to accompany the conscription of labor (the drafting of men into the armed forces). Politicians fueled rather than played down the belief that Britain should become, in the words of one politician, "a land fit for heroes" once "the war to end all wars" was won—in other words, that provision should be made for those who had fought for king and country. The period of the Second World War (1939–45) witnessed a significant shift of attitudes by a sizable fraction of the electorate. One informed estimate was that by December 1942, about two out of five people had changed their political outlook since the beginning of the war.[21] Opinion was moving toward the left of the political spectrum. There was a reaction against (Conservative) government unpreparedness for war in the 1930s and against those who had not done more to solve the nation's problems during the depression. There was support for calls for equality of sacrifice. There was some degree of goodwill toward the Soviet Union as a wartime ally. There was also, very importantly, the enhanced position of the Labour party. It had entered into coalition in 1940 (its leader, Clement Attlee, became deputy prime minister to Prime Minister Winston Churchill) and had demonstrated its claim to be a capable partner in government. As the 1940s progressed, there developed a notable movement, including within the Conservative party, for a greater degree of social and economic intervention by government. This was to find some authoritative expression during the war years themselves and especially in the years after 1945, when a general election resulted in the return of the first Labour government with a clear working majority in the House of Commons. The 1940s and the 1950s were to produce what Samuel Beer has referred to as the welfare state and the managed economy, or what some commentators have referred to as the period of the social democratic consensus.

The welfare state and the managed economy did not suddenly emerge full-blown in this period. The preceding decades had not witnessed governments unresponsive to electoral expectations and the nation's problems. The Liberal government before the First World War had made the first tentative steps in the introduction of old-age pensions (1908) and national health and unemployment insurance (1911). The interwar years had seen the introduction of a number of significant measures of social reform, especially those associated with a

Conservative, Neville Chamberlain, as minister of health. He proposed to the cabinet 25 measures and secured the enactment of 21 of them. These included unemployment insurance, public health and housing, and the extension of old-age pensions. Much of this legislation, as one biographer noted, "has an important place in the development of the Welfare State."[22] The Conservative government also began to engage in certain measures of economic management. It embarked on a protectionist policy and, in return for the grant of a tariff to an industry, demanded that its major producers reorganize themselves. Such producers were encouraged to reduce capacity and maintain prices. The gold standard was abandoned, the pound was devalued, and interest rates were lowered. The government even proved willing to take certain industries into public ownership: broadcasting, overseas airways, and the electricity-generating industry. By indulging in such policies, Beer has contended, government was beginning to move in the direction of a managed economy.[23] The movement, though, was modest. Government adhered to the prevailing orthodoxy that balanced budgets were necessary and desirable and that deficit financing was neither. Ministers showed little desire to emulate the extensive public works programs implemented in the United States by Franklin Roosevelt during the period of the first New Deal. (Indeed, Conservative leader Stanley Baldwin commented at one point that the U.S. Constitution had broken down and was giving way to dictatorship.)[24] Britain and the United States were similar, though, in that both were to be brought out of the depression of the 1930s not by government economic policies but by rearmament and the Second World War.

Two major documents published in the war years provided the planks for the final emergence of the welfare state and managed economy. These were the Report on Social Insurance and Allied Services by Sir William Beveridge (the Beveridge Report), published in November 1942, and the White Paper on Full Employment, published in 1944. The former proposed a comprehensive scheme of social security, one to provide "social insurance against interruption and destruction of earning power and for special expenditure arising at birth, marriage or death."[25] The latter was significant because of its opening pledge: "The Government accepts as one of their primary aims and responsibilities the maintenance of a high and stable level of employment after the war." There was also one particularly significant measure of social reform enacted during wartime: the 1944 Education Act, pioneered by R. A. Butler. It provided for the division among primary, secondary, and higher education—and, within secondary education, between secondary modern and grammar schools—that was to form the basis of the educational system for almost a generation.

The welfare state was brought to fruition by the passage of the 1945 Family Allowance Act, the 1946 National Insurance Act, the 1948 National Assistance Act, and by the establishment of the National Health Service (NHS) in 1948, entailing the nationalization of hospitals and the provision of free medical treatment. The principle enunciated by the Beveridge Report was largely put into practice. National insurance ensured a certain level of benefit in the event of unemployment or sickness. For those who required special help there was "national assistance," the provision of noncontributory benefits dispensed on the basis of means-testing. There were family allowances for those with children. The state now provided something of a protective safety net from the cradle to the grave. It was still possible to pay for private treatment in the health service, but for most people it was a case of having treatment "on the national health." The NHS became a feature of some pride at home and of considerable interest abroad.

Acceptance and usage of techniques pioneered by the economist John Maynard Keynes ushered in the managed economy. Government accepted responsibility for keeping aggregate monetary demand at a level sufficient to ensure full employment or what was considered as far as possible to constitute full employment (an unemployment rate of 1 percent or 2 percent was considered acceptable), and the annual budget was to be used as the main instrument of economic policy. The Labour government proved unwilling to pursue a more overtly socialist approach; physical controls acquired during wartime were eventually discarded and those industries that were nationalized, such as steel, the mines, and the railways, were basically essential and loss-making concerns. Government was prepared to pursue a managed rather than a controlled economy.

The Conservative party was returned to office in 1951 and was to remain there until 1964. It accepted, or appeared to accept, both the welfare state and Keynesian models of demand management. Indeed, it gave the impression of making a success of both. As heir to the Disraelian belief in elevating the condition of the people and as a party seeking to enhance its image among working-class voters, the Conservative party could claim both a principled and a practical motive for maintaining the innovations of its predecessor. At the same time, it was reluctant to pursue policies that would increase the tax burden on the public sector of the economy. Good fortune was with the government: World economic conditions improved and heralded a period of sustained growth in industrial output and trade. Government revenue was such that not only was it possible to sustain and indeed expand expenditure on the NHS but it was also possible to do so without substantial increases in taxation. Indeed, reductions rather than increases in tax rates were a feature of the period. There was an extensive and successful house-building program. Economic prosperity allowed government to maintain peace with the labor unions by allowing high wage settlements. It was also possible finally to abandon many of the controls maintained since wartime. Government was able to claim to have maintained full employment, an expanding economy, stable prices, and a strong pound. Despite the agonies of withdrawing from the imperial period of empire and various undulations in economic performance, the 1950s was seen more than anything as "an age of affluence."[26] In July 1957 Prime Minister Harold Macmillan was able to declare that, for most of the people, "You've never had it so good."

The 1960s witnessed a downturn in economic performance and a growing realization that, in comparative terms, Britain was faring less well than many of her continental neighbors. The Conservative government of Harold Macmillan responded with various novel proposals, including indicative economic planning and an application to join the European Economic Community. The succeeding Labour government of Harold Wilson, returned to office in 1964, sought a more comprehensive method of national economic planning as part of its grand design of modernization. Inflation and unemployment became more visible problems.

Despite the economic problems and some unrelated political problems of the 1960s, the country remained a relatively prosperous one. Living conditions continued to improve. The rise in wages exceeded the rise in inflation. Where economic conditions impinged on the ability to maintain the welfare state, it was essentially at the margin: Government imposed nominal charges for medicines obtained on NHS prescriptions. Parties tended to argue more about means rather than ends. The consensus that developed in the 1950s remained intact.

The Politics of Thatcher and Blair

The first attempt to break away from that consensus was made by the Conservative government of Edward Heath, which was returned to office in 1970. There was an emphasis on the withdrawal of government from economic activity and an attempt, ultimately unsuccessful, to curb trade union power. The aim was to force British industry to be more competitive. This goal also provided some of the motivation for British membership in the European Community, which Heath achieved in 1972. (Britain became a member of the Community on January 1, 1973.) However, the government's measures failed to stem a rise in inflation, and when unemployment reached record levels, the government embarked on a new interventionist policy, including the imposition of a pay and prices policy. The government lost office in 1974.

The return of another Conservative government five years later saw a more determined effort by Heath's successor as party leader, Margaret Thatcher, to achieve a free-market economy and to move away from, indeed dismantle, the postwar consensus. The Thatcher government heralded a break with its predecessors both in terms of style and substance. The prime minister in particular adopted a combative style of government in pursuit of her goal: a rolling back of the frontiers of the state. Government intervention was seen as economically harmful, stifling initiative and the creative forces of the market. "The public had to be persuaded to lower its expectations of, and dependence on, the state; the social democratic consensus had to be replaced by a new neoliberal consensus."[27] Various policies were pursued in an attempt to achieve this goal.

The Thatcher government was to make a notable difference to British economic and political life. The change was not as great as Margaret Thatcher wanted. Politically, despite periods of tremendous strength during her eleven and a half years as prime minister, Thatcher was never able to mold a party and a cabinet completely committed to her neoliberal philosophy (see Chapter 6). Many of the government's policies were not as radical as she wanted. Subsidies to public-sector industries were maintained. Mechanisms for controlling the money supply were less than adequate to the task. When the economy went into recession, the Conservative government under Thatcher's successor opted for budget deficits and a shift of emphasis from fighting inflation to pursuing growth.

There was no social revolution that could have resulted in established social position being displaced by a new meritocracy, nor was there a paradigmatic shift of attitudes. A survey by the *Economist* in 1992 found little change, compared with the position twenty years before, in the dominant position of public (i.e., private) school and Oxbridge graduates in the top posts in business, the arts, and the professions. In some areas, a number of people had made it to the top from humble backgrounds, including Prime Minister John Major. "But change has not just been slow. It has been almost non-existent."[28]

There was similarly little move toward values espoused by Margaret Thatcher. Ten years after Mrs. Thatcher came to power, a survey of popular attitudes found that, asked to choose between a Thatcherite and a "socialist" society, respondents opted for the Thatcherite model on only two out of five dimensions, and then only by slender majorities. Indeed, over the decade, opinion on some issues had moved away from a Thatcherite position: Asked to choose between cutting taxes and extending public services, opinion in 1979 was equally divided; ten years later, those favoring extending services outnumbered tax cutters by a margin of seven to one.[29] Where Margaret Thatcher carried, and sometimes increased, support was on issues on which she already had prevailing public support when she entered office.

Yet the Thatcher era did witness major changes, some of the most significant being continued or sustained by her successors. In terms of substantive changes, the most significant was the reduction in the size of the public sector. Various utilities and companies previously taken into public ownership were privatized (that is, sold back to the private sector), a policy also pursued by the government of Thatcher's successor, John Major. In the period of Conservative government from 1979 to 1997, almost 50 major companies were privatized, including the telephone, gas, water, steel, coal, and electricity utilities. Among them, the companies employed almost one million workers. By 1996 there were only seven major nationalized industries remaining. These were run by management boards, with government expecting them to be run as commercial enterprises. The size of the public sector thus contracted.

The emphasis on a market economy also led to reductions in income tax; to curbs on trade union power; to the ensuring of wider private ownership (not only of shares but also of housing); to the introduction of a greater market orientation for bodies remaining in the public sector, including local government and the NHS; and to greater autonomy in policy making by government. Organized economic interests that previously had been effectively co-opted in economic policy making were kept at arm's length. By the end of Margaret Thatcher's tenure of office in 1990, the nature of government and of public debate and the division between public and private sectors had changed significantly. Political parties were forced to work on the basis of a new political agenda.

Her successor as Conservative prime minister, John Major, continued a number of her innovative policies, including those on privatization, but sought neither to emulate her style nor to pursue her particular vision of future society. Rather, he consolidated the changes of the Thatcher era. The biggest impact of the Thatcher government was remarkably not so much on Thatcher's Conservative successor as prime minister, but rather upon her successor's successor—Labour prime minister Tony Blair, elected to office in 1997.

Richard Rose, in a seminal work entitled *Do Parties Make a Difference?* argued that political parties make some difference in British politics, but not as much as is commonly believed, and not as much as suggested by the "adversary politics" approach.[30] The latter contends that one party elected to office reverses the policies of the party previously in government and so one has almost a ping-pong effect in policy terms. Rose argues that British politics is characterized instead by a rolling consensus, one party making some difference, the opposition party then adapting to the changes made and, when it comes to office, accepting those changes and making some change of its own. The governments of Tony Blair and Gordon Brown appeared to validate Rose's thesis.

> The Thatcher influence was seen in Labour's gradual acceptance of so many policies that they had once opposed—privatisation, levels of direct taxation, the use of the free market in public services and changes in industrial relations laws. Indeed the consolidation of the reforms led Simon Jenkins to call Blair and Brown "Sons of Thatcher."[31]

Tony Blair and Gordon Brown did make some changes of their own. In Blair's case, as we shall see in Chapter 4, this was most pronounced with the implementation of significant measures of constitutional change. And vindicating the Rose thesis was the Conservative response to that change. Though the Conservative opposition voted against the measures of constitutional change introduced by the Blair government, the new leader of the Conservative party, William Hague, announced in 1998 that a future Conservative government would not seek simply to reverse them. Devolution, he acknowledged, would not be reversed and his party would compete to gain office in the new devolved assemblies.

After Tony Blair retired as prime minister in 2007, his policies were maintained by his successor, Gordon Brown. Though there were some differences of emphasis, not least in respect of constitutional reform and in the United Kingdom's relations with America (Brown took a more detached approach than Blair), there was no fundamental deviation from Labour's policies of the past decade. When Brown entered 10 Downing Street, the political and economic landscape of Britain was very different from that of fifty, and indeed twenty-five, years before. Much was still the same. Most traditional structures remained in place, as did many popular attitudes: The popular attachment to the NHS, for instance, remained strong. Government spending as a proportion of the GDP continued to grow. Continuity in many areas was marked, but so too was change. The economy was now a service economy with a greater emphasis on efficiency and global competition. Major utilities were operating in the private sector. Trade unions were no longer the significant political players they once had been. And political structures had undergone some significant changes.

GREAT BRITAIN OR LITTLE ENGLAND?

Let us move from narrative to thematic analysis. At the start of the twenty-first century, the United Kingdom remained a major economic and political power. It was a member of the G8, the eight economically most powerful countries in the world. It retained a permanent seat on the UN Security Council. It was the principal ally of the United States in the invasion of Iraq in 2003. It was also experiencing its longest period of economic growth in one hundred and fifty years. Every year since 1992 through to 2008 had witnessed growth.

On the face of it, the United Kingdom was proving a highly successful nation, both economically and politically. This was in sharp contrast to twenty-five years earlier, when it was often portrayed as "the sick man of Europe," with a weak economy—the nation having to seek help from the International Monetary Fund—and poor industrial relations. The political system also appeared unable to deliver strong government and to deal with inter-community armed conflict in Northern Ireland.

The change, though, masked uncertainty as to Britain's future and underlying tensions and weaknesses in its economic and political infrastructure. At a speech at West Point military academy in 1962, the American statesman Dean Acheson made the memorable comment that "Great Britain has lost an empire but has yet to find a role." According to some commentators, the attachment to empire has not completely been lost. Britain has had to adapt to a historical legacy and, for some, that adaptation—as in the changes brought about by Thatcher and Blair—has been late and, in other cases, has yet to be fully achieved. What made Britain great is seen also as limiting its potential. The nation, according to various analyses, has been held back by the legacy of *empire, war, class* and *political structures*. Though some of the effects of these legacies have been vitiated, they remain important for understanding both what has happened in British politics and society in the past half-century and the challenges that the nation faces.

Legacy of Empire

A consequence of empire has been that Britain has tended to retain a number of overseas commitments beyond what some regard as being within its financial capacity to do so. The policy of funding overseas military commitments and foreign investments has been pursued, according to some economists, at the expense of economic growth.[32] Political and economic pressures have resulted in Britain shedding most of its colonial territories, but it still retains interests beyond those of the North Atlantic alliance. It retains some dependencies and has sought to maintain an involvement in resolving conflicts in different parts of the globe. These interests have resulted on various occasions in the committal of troops: most notably in the Falkland Islands (1982), the first Gulf War (1991), Bosnia (1992), Kosovo (1999), East Timor (1999), and, most significantly in recent years, Afghanistan (2001), and Iraq (2003).

The attachment to Britain retaining a role on the world stage has been a feature of successive governments. It has underpinned a commitment to retaining a nuclear deterrent. Though Margaret Thatcher as prime minister sought to address the consequences of some other of the legacies we have identified, she was a believer in British strength abroad. Her reputation as the "Iron Maiden" rested in large part in her willingness in 1982 to commit British forces to re-take the Falklands Islands, a British dependency, after their invasion by Argentine forces. Tony Blair as prime minister proved an equally avid adherent to Britain's world role, committing troops to Afghanistan and Iraq and engaging in various acts of international diplomacy. After he ceased to be premier, he was appointed a middle east peace envoy. Both premiers reflected an enduring and widespread attachment to Britain as a global actor. When attempts were made, following the collapse of the Iron Curtain, to reap the "peace dividend" by reducing the size of Britain's armed services, there was sustained opposition from many politicians who believed the cuts threatened Britain's capacity to maintain its global influence.

Legacy of War

The Second World War sealed the fate of the British empire—the nation could no longer afford to sustain its colonial role—but had two other consequences for economic and political development.

First, there is a popular view that the Second World War was, for Britain, a military success but an economic disaster. The country was left in serious debt, primarily to the United States,[33] and with some of its industrial plant still intact. There was neither the capacity nor the incentive to start afresh; a number of other countries had no option but to begin anew, both politically and economically. Britain continued to produce in markets with low skill requirements. Companies and financial institutions remained more interested in profits than in long-term investment. Britain has thus had difficulty in keeping pace with the development of new, science-based industries.[34] Profit-maximization continues to characterize the approach of major companies and city institutions. British companies lag behind foreign competitors in terms of skills training and investment in research and development.

Second, the war had a profound impact on popular attitudes, not least to the role of government. As we have seen, there was a growing commitment to the role of government in providing for the welfare of the people. The downside, according to some analysts, is that the economic policies pursued by post-war governments created a dependency culture as well as maintained, indeed strengthened, vested interests and restrictive practices. Attempts by government to ensure industrial harmony proved expensive to the nation's capacity to compete. Industry was dogged by practices designed to maintain wage levels and employment even if those practices were manifestly inefficient and made the firm uncompetitive in international markets. Under this analysis, government in the quarter-century after the war often proved to be not so much part of the solution but rather part of the problem. It was this more short-term legacy that Margaret Thatcher sought to combat by pursuing a market economy. Though the emphasis under and since the Thatcher government has been to reduce dependency on the state, the commitment to public services, especially the NHS (providing services free at the point of delivery), remains strong.

Legacy of Class

As we have seen in Chapter 1, class did not displace status in British society. Preindustrial aristocratic attitudes were carried over into an industrial age. These attitudes included looking down on the pursuit of "trade" as somewhat socially inferior. Low priority was given to industry and science and, so this analysis goes, a tendency grew for those with wealth to favor professions such as the law.[35] Such attitudes are less pronounced but still apparent today. An allied perception, one that still exists, is that breeding—meaning principally status by inheritance—and a good general education constitute the basis for positions of eminence. The top positions in business and government are still likely to be held by men (rarely women) with a public school and Oxbridge education—or, indeed, no university education. Though the picture is changing, those in top managerial posts in the United Kingdom are less likely to be graduates than are those holding equivalent positions in the United States. Top management has often been notable for having no particular training for the task, the "old school tie" or family connections proving more valuable than a particular degree for advancing up the career ladder.

Some blame for economic under-performance has also been imputed to the egalitarianism of the labor movement, which harbors dislike of profits, risk taking, and management.[36] "There have been constant complaints of poor motivation of the labor force and lack of readiness to co-operate in changes of organization, equipment and productive methods (or, put differently, bloody-mindedness and militancy). Nor are such complaints new."[37] Unlike the case in the United States, there is no culture in the United Kingdom that favors ambition among blue-collar workers to achieve a junior managerial post and then a post above that. In some industries, it is not just management positions that traditionally have been seen as having passed from father to son, but the manual jobs as well.

Although the position is changing, the history of an "us" and "them" mentality in industrial relations has been argued to hinder economic growth.[38] The changes wrought in the Thatcher years were designed to rid the nation of such entrenched practices and mentalities. Industries, such as mining, where jobs passed from father to son have largely died out and merit is more to the fore in generating business leaders. Market forces now shape recruitment and industrial relations, delivering greater flexibility than was possible in postwar decades.

Legacy of Political Institutions

Some commentators have also argued that the effect of a political system, characterized by partisanship and centralization, has also been debilitating for the economy and political participation.

The adversary politics thesis contends that attempts to generate long-term solutions to problems are thwarted by a system that encourages an adversary relationship between the two main political parties, with those parties vying with one another for the all-or-nothing spoils of a general election victory.[39] Investors and managers are unable to plan ahead because they are uncertain as to what a future government may do. A party in opposition will say that it will reverse a policy brought forward by government: in the event it may not do so, but its threat to do so leaves markets uncertain. Furthermore, an adversary relationship has meant that government, despite large parliamentary majorities such as those enjoyed by Margaret Thatcher and Tony Blair, has been unable to mobilize a consensus in support of its policies. For those who advance this thesis, the political system does not offer the means of resolving the nation's problems; rather the way the system is structured is seen as part—a very central part—of the problem.

The thesis of centralization dovetails to some extent with that of adversary politics. As government responsibilities in the twentieth century expanded, so government power became increasingly centralized. The problem, according to a number of observers, was exacerbated by the election in 1979 of a Conservative government under Margaret Thatcher. To implement the goal of a free-market economy, the government had to strengthen its own powers, creating what Andrew Gamble termed "the Strong State."[40] Many commentators argued that that concentration of power was maintained, if anything enhanced, under the "presidential" leadership of Tony Blair. "At its heart the government has clung to the doctrine of parliamentary sovereignty – the seat of the central executive's political and administrative power."[41] Although powers were devolved to elected assemblies in Scotland and Wales, power over central economic and political issues remained firmly entrenched in Downing Street.

A centralization of power is seen as part of a vicious circle. The government, by virtue of a political system that (through a parliamentary majority) allows it largely unfettered lawmaking power, is able to extend its formal powers. However, the adversarial nature of that same system militates against its mobilizing the support of disparate groups—and the population generally—to tackle economic problems. Consequently, to tackle these problems, the government takes more powers. The more powers it takes, the more distant it becomes from those groups it needs to mobilize; hence a government with strong legal powers vested by Parliament but an increasingly limited capacity to mobilize support.

The thesis of pluralist stagnation asserts that the problem lies with the growth of groups in Britain, each group pursuing its own interests and bringing pressure to bear on government to provide resources or pursue policies to the benefit of its members. Government for its part has been unwilling to pursue policies that would arouse opposition from well-entrenched groups, resulting in inertia.[42] The problem has been exacerbated by the growth in the number of organized groups. Because there are so many, self-restraint would bring no discernible benefit to any particular group. As a result, even though recognizing the need for restraint, a group is tempted to maintain or increase existing demands. Other groups then compete by raising their demands. Government is then overwhelmed by the multiplicity of self-serving demands.

Identifying these legacies helps explain the distinctive place of the United Kingdom among Western nations—in combination they render it unique—and the nature of the challenges it faces. It also has relevance for our later analysis of the political system. The pursuit of particular economic policies and the structure of the political system constitute two principal, and competing, explanations for the decline in support for the two main political parties in recent years (Chapter 6). Pluralist stagnation is important for explaining the activity of pressure groups in recent decades (Chapter 7). Analyses of structure and class underpin debate on government and the civil service (Chapter 8) and, most important of all, the combination of adversary politics and centralization of power have been at the heart of demands for new constitutional arrangements in the United Kingdom. The debate about those constitutional arrangements features throughout subsequent chapters and forms the basis of our concluding chapter. The United Kingdom is witnessing some constitutional change, but is that change based on an accurate analysis of the problem?

NOTES

1. See A. H. Dodd, *The Growth of Responsible Government* (Routledge & Kegan Paul, 1956), pp. 43–44.
2. B. Kemp, *King and Commons 1600–1832* (Macmillan, 1957), p. 3.
3. Its provisions included, for example, "That excessive Baile ought not to be required nor excessive Fines imposed nor cruell and unusuall Punishments inflicted." Compare this with the Eighth Amendment to the United States Constitution, which prescribes that "Excessive bail shall not be required, nor excessive fines imposed, nor cruel and unusual punishments inflicted."
4. J. H. Plumb, *England in the Eighteenth Century* (Penguin, 1950), p. 5.
5. J. Mackintosh, *The British Cabinet*, 3rd ed. (Stevens, 1977), pp. 50–51.
6. Ibid., p. 64.
7. S. M. Lipset, *The First New Nation* (Heinemann, 1964); P. Mathias, *The First Industrial Nation* (Methuen, 1969).
8. Sir L. Woodward, *The Age of Reform 1815–1870*, 2nd ed. (Oxford University Press, 1962), p. 3.
9. A table compiled in 1815 revealed that 144 peers, along with 123 commoners, controlled 471 seats (more than two-thirds of the total number) in the House of Commons. M. Ostrogorski, *Democracy and the Organisation of Political Parties, Vol. 1: England* (Macmillan, 1902), p. 20.
10. J. B. Conacher (ed.), *The Emergence of British Parliamentary Democracy in the Nineteenth Century* (Wiley, 1971), p. 10. Different authors cite different figures.
11. Most measures placed before Parliament were usually small measures affecting private interests, for example giving the power necessary to enclose land or build a new railway line.
12. W. Bagehot, *The English Constitution* (first published 1867; Fontana, 1963 edition), p. 150.
13. Mackintosh, p. 113.
14. See Conacher, pp. 68–69, for a summary.
15. See H. J. Hanham, *Elections and Party Management*, 3rd ed. (Harvester Press, 1978), p. xii.

16. Similarly, in the United States the all-or-nothing spoils of presidential victory have encouraged two rather than many parties.
17. A. L. Lowell, *The Government of England*, Vol. 2 (Macmillan, 1924), pp. 76–78.
18. Mackintosh, p. 174.
19. Astor was not the first woman to be elected: Countess Markiewicz was elected in 1918 but, as a member of Sinn Fein, refused to take her seat. See P. Norton, *Parliament in British Politics* (Palgrave Macmillan, 2005), p. 171.
20. Reforms were introduced by Conservative as well as Liberal governments. On the Conservative reforms, see P. Norton (ed.), *The Conservative Party* (Prentice Hall/Harvester Wheatsheaf, 1996), p. 29.
21. P. Addison, *The Road to 1945* (Quartet, 1977), p. 127.
22. I. Macleod, *Neville Chamberlain* (Muller, 1961), p. 123.
23. S. H. Beer, *Modern British Politics* (Faber, 1969 edition), pp. 278–287.
24. Addison, *The Road to 1945*, p. 29.
25. *Social Insurance and Allied Services—Report by Sir William Beveridge*, Cmnd. 6404 (Her Majesty's Stationery Office, 1942), para. 17, p. 9.
26. Based on the title of Vernon Bogdanor and Robert Skidelsky (eds.), *The Age of Affluence 1951–1964* (Macmillan, 1970).
27. I. Crewe, "The Thatcher Legacy," in A. King (ed.), *Britain at the Polls 1992* (Chatham House, 1993), p. 18.
28. "The Ascent of British Man," *Economist,* 19 December 1992, p. 21.
29. Crewe, pp. 19–22. See also P. Norton, "The Conservative Party from Thatcher to Major," in A. King (ed.), *Britain at the Polls 1992* (Chatham House, 1993), pp. 32–33.
30. R. Rose, *Do Parties Make a Difference?* 2nd ed. (Macmillan, 1984). The "adversary politics" thesis is discussed in the next section.
31. D. Kavanagh, "The Blair Premiership," in A. Seldon (ed.), *Blair's Britain 1997–2007* (Cambridge University Press, 2007), p. 14.
32. See, for example, A. W. Manser, *Britain in Balance* (Penguin, 1973).
33. This fact is resented by part of the political elite in Britain. This was reinforced in 1945 by the terms of the loan to Britain by the United States. Some Conservative members of Parliament saw the terms as part of an attempt to open up world markets to the benefit of the United States, and some Labour members feared that it would, in the words of one of them, hitch the nation "to the American bandwagon." Further resentment was caused by the active opposition of the U.S. government to Britain's attempt to occupy the Suez Canal zone by force in 1956.
34. W. Grant, *The Politics of Economic Policy* (Harvester Wheatsheaf, 1993), pp. 16–17, 20.
35. See, for example, M. Postan, *An Economic History of Western Europe 1945–64* (Methuen, 1967).
36. See, for example, K. Joseph, *Stranded on the Middle Ground* (Centre for Policy Studies, 1976).
37. A. Cairncross, *The British Economy Since 1945*, 2nd ed. (Blackwell, 1995), p. 26.
38. See Cairncross, pp. 26–27.
39. A. King, *The British Constitution* (Oxford University Press, 2007), p. 78.
40. A. Gamble, *The Free Economy and the Strong State* (Macmillan, 1988).
41. D. Beetham, I. Byrne, P. Ngan, and S. Weir (eds.), *Democracy Under Blair: A Democratic Audit of the United Kingdom* (Politico's, 2002), p. 305.
42. See I. Gilmour, *The Body Politic,* rev. ed. (Hutchinson, 1971); and J. E. S. Hayward, *Political Inertia* (University of Hull Press, 1975).

PART II

THE POLITICAL ENVIRONMENT

CHAPTER

4

The Uncodified Constitution

A constitution may be defined as the body of laws, customs, and conventions that define the composition and powers of organs of the state and that regulate the relations of the various state organs to one another and to the private citizen.[1]

The United States has a constitution; so does the United Kingdom. Expressed in purely formal terms (Table 4.1) there is very little similarity between them. Indeed, the differences are such that to the student weaned on a study of the U.S. Constitution, the British Constitution is nearly incomprehensible. Even to the student of British politics it is not well understood. Nonetheless, the differences should not be emphasized to the exclusion of certain common features. Both Constitutions are strong in that they reflect their respective political cultures.

The U.S. Constitution is considered by Americans to embody the principles of a higher law, to constitute "in fact imperfect man's most perfect rendering of what Blackstone saluted as 'the eternal immutable laws of good and evil, to which the creator himself in all his dispensations conforms: and which he has enabled human reason to discover, so far as they are necessary for the conduct of human actions.'"[2] As the embodiment of a higher law, it thus not only needs to be distinguished from ordinary law, but also needs to be protected from the passing whims of politicians—hence the existence of extraordinary procedures for its amendment.

By contrast, the British Constitution has been admired by Britons for reflecting the wisdom of past generations, as the product of experience—in short, a constitution that stipulates what should be on the basis of what has proved to work, rather than on abstract first principles. The empirical orientation to change that underpins such a constitution also favors flexibility in amendment: As conditions change, so some amendment may be necessary. Formal extraordinary procedures for its amendment have not been found necessary.

TABLE 4.1

U.S. AND BRITISH CONSTITUTIONS

| | Constitutions | |
Characteristics	United States	United Kingdom
Form of expression	Codified	Uncodified
Date and manner of formulation	1787 by a constitutional convention	No one date of formulation, no precise manner of formulation
Means of formal amendment	By two-thirds majorities in both houses of Congress and by ratification of three-quarters of the states, or by conventions	No extraordinary provisions for amendment
Location of its provisions	The written document (also judicial decisions, custom usage, works of authority)	Statute law, common law conventions, works of authority
Bodies responsible for interpretation of its provisions	The judiciary primarily (can be overridden by constitutional amendment)	The judiciary (statute and common law), scholars, politicians (conventions)
Main provisions	Document as "supreme law," judicial review, separation and overlap of powers, federal system, bill of rights, republican form of government	Parliamentary sovereignty, "rule of law," unitary (union) state, parliamentary government under a constitutional monarchy
Public promulgation of its provisions (in textbooks, etc.)	Extensive	Infrequent

The differences in political culture have thus produced somewhat different constitutions, but the attachment to them is similar in the two countries. Also, as we shall see, there are certain similarities in sources and in the means of interpretation. The similarities are also somewhat greater as a result of constitutional changes in the United Kingdom in recent years. Indeed, we can distinguish between what may be termed the "traditional"—or Westminster—Constitution and what may, with some justice, be characterized as a modified Westminster Constitution that is developing in the United Kingdom. Let us consider first the essential features of the traditional constitution.

FORMS OF EXPRESSION

New nations from the eighteenth century onward have found it both necessary and useful to codify their constitutions. At the time that the founding fathers promulgated the U.S. Constitution in Philadelphia, a written constitution was exceptional. Today it is the norm. Having lacked the opportunity to create a new constitutional framework from first principles, Britain now stands out as one of only three nations lacking such a document.

The absence of a written constitution similar to that of the United States and other nations has led to the British Constitution being described as unwritten, but such a description is misleading. As we shall see, various elements of the Constitution find expression in formal, written enactments. What distinguishes the British Constitution from others is not that it is unwritten, but rather that it is uncodified. The lack of codification is of special importance. It makes it difficult to identify clearly and authoritatively what constitute the provisions of the Constitution. As Madgwick and Woodhouse have noted, "it is easier to say what the British constitution is not than to say what it is."[3] Nonetheless, certain principles clearly are at the heart of the Constitution, parliamentary sovereignty being the prime example, but there are many provisions, be they expressed through statute law or the writings of constitutional experts, that are of constitutional significance but on which there is no clear agreement that they are core provisions of the British Constitution. It is this lack of codified certainty that makes a study of the constitution so fraught with difficulty.

SOURCES

Because one cannot have recourse to one simple authoritative document to discover the provisions of the British Constitution, one has instead to research four separate sources: statute law, common law, conventions, and works of authority. Such sources are also relevant in analyses of the U.S. Constitution. Congress may pass measures of constitutional significance, such as certain stipulations of electoral law or the War Powers Act. Provisions of the Constitution are developed and molded by judicial decisions. In seeking to interpret the Constitution, the courts may have recourse to works by constitutional experts. The difference between the two countries is that whereas in the United States these are secondary sources, in Britain they are primary sources. In the United States the primary source is the written document.

Of the four sources, statute law is perhaps the best understood and, nowadays, the most extensive. It provides the main source for the part-written element of the British Constitution. It comprises acts of Parliament and subordinate legislation made under the authority of the parent act. Many acts of Parliament that have been passed clearly merit the title of constitutional law. Acts that define the powers of the various state organs (for example, the Parliament Acts of 1911 and 1949) and acts that define the relationship between Crown and Parliament (notably the Bill of Rights of 1689), between the component elements of the nation (the Act of Union with Scotland of

1707, for example, and the Scotland Act 1998), between the United Kingdom and the European Union (notably the European Communities Act 1972), and between the state and the individual (as with the Human Rights Act 1998) clearly constitute important provisions of the Constitution. They are published in authoritative, written form and, as acts of Parliament, are interpreted by the courts. This is the most important of the four sources both in quantitative and qualitative terms. It has increasingly displaced common law as the most extensive form of law in Britain and it is the most definitive of the four. It takes precedence over any conflicting common law and is superior to the conventions of the Constitution and to works of authority. Its precedence derives from the concept of parliamentary sovereignty. It has, as we shall see, also made possible the introduction of what amounts in effect to a "higher law" in the form of certain international treaties.

Common law constitutes legal principles developed by the courts and rules and customs of ancient lineage that are so well established that they have been upheld as law by the courts in cases decided before them. Once a court has upheld a provision as being part of common law, it creates a precedent to be followed by other courts. In past centuries, when few statutes were enacted, common law constituted the main body of English law; today, it has been largely but certainly not wholly displaced by statute law. Certain principles derived from common law remain fundamental to the Constitution, and these include the principle of parliamentary sovereignty.

Under the heading of common law come also prerogative powers—the powers and privileges recognized by common law as belonging to the Crown. Although many prerogative powers have been displaced by statute, many matters at the heart of government are still determined under the authority of the prerogative. By convention, such powers are normally exercised formally by the monarch on the advice of ministers, especially the prime minister. Historically, these have included making treaties, the appointment and dismissal of ministers, dispensing honors and declaring war. In 1972 the Treaty of Accession to the European Community (EC) was signed under prerogative powers. In 1982 a naval task force was dispatched to the Falkland Islands under the same authority. After he became prime minister in 2007, Gordon Brown sought to transfer certain of these powers to Parliament, proposing that MPs have the power to ratify treaties and also to assent to decisions to commit troops to action abroad. Although diminishing in number, prerogative powers remain of great importance, ministers taking decisions in the name of the Crown.

Generally included under the generic heading of common law is the judicial interpretation of statute law. Unlike those in the United States, British courts have no power to hold a measure unconstitutional. They are limited to the interpretation of provisions of acts of Parliament. Even in exercising their power of interpretation, they are limited by rules of interpretation and by precedent. (The exception is the highest domestic court of appeal—the House of Lords, succeeded in 2009 by a supreme court—which is not bound by its previous decisions.) Nonetheless, judges retain the power to distinguish cases, and by their interpretation they can develop a substantial body of case law. In interpreting acts of Parliament, they traditionally have assumed Parliament to have meant what, on the face of it, the words of an act appear to mean. However, following a decision of the House of Lords (in its judicial capacity) in 1992, it is now possible for courts, where they consider it necessary, to look at the proceedings of Parliament in order to determine what Parliament really meant. The courts have also assumed a new role as a consequence of British membership in the European Union—changing fundamentally the traditional constitution—but this role, as we shall see, derives from the provisions of an act of Parliament.

The third and least tangible source of the Constitution is that of convention. Conventions of the British Constitution are most aptly described as rules of behavior that are considered binding by and upon those who are responsible for making the Constitution work, but rules that are not enforced by the courts or by the presiding officers in either house of Parliament.[4] They derive their strength from the realization that not to abide by them would make for an unworkable Constitution. They are, so to speak, the oil in the formal machinery of the Constitution. They help fill the gap between the constitutional formality and the political reality. For example, ministers are responsible formally to the monarch. Because of the political changes wrought in the nineteenth century, they are by convention responsible now also to Parliament. By convention, the government of the day resigns or requests a dissolution of Parliament if a motion of no confidence is carried against it in the House of Commons. By convention, the monarch gives the Royal Assent to all legislative measures approved by Parliament. The last time a monarch refused assent was in 1707, when Queen Anne vetoed a Scottish Militia Bill. Queen Victoria in the nineteenth century contemplated refusing her assent to a measure, but wiser counsels prevailed.

No formal, authoritative documents establish these rules, and they find no embodiment in statute law. The courts may recognize them but have no power to enforce them. They are complied with because of the recognition of what would happen if they were not complied with. For the queen to refuse her assent to a measure passed by the two houses of Parliament would draw her into the realms of political controversy, hence jeopardizing the claim of the monarch to be above politics. A government that sought to remain in office after losing a vote of confidence in the House of Commons would find its position politically untenable: It would lack the political authority to govern. For ministers to ignore Parliament completely would prove equally untenable.

Some conventions may be described as being stronger than others. Some on occasion are breached, whereas others are adhered to without exception. On three occasions in the past century, the convention of collective ministerial responsibility has been suspended temporarily by the prime minister of the day. In contrast, no government has sought to remain in office after losing a parliamentary vote of confidence. The point at which a useful and necessary practice is accorded the status of a constitutional convention is not clear. Once a practice has become well established in terms of the relationship within or between different organs of the state and has found recognition in works of authority and by those involved in its operation, then it may be said to have reached the status of a convention. At any one time, though, a number of relationships may be said to be in a constitutional haze.

The fourth and final source of the Constitution is that of works of authority. These have persuasive authority only. What constitutes a "work of authority" is rarely defined. Various early works are accorded particular standing by virtue of the absence of statutes or other written sources covering a particular area. The statements of their writers are presumed to be evidence of judicial decisions that have been lost and are therefore accepted if not contrary to reason.[5] Among the most important early sources are Fitzherbert's *Abridgment* (1516) and Coke's *Institutes of the Law of England* (1628–44). More recent works have been called into aid on those occasions when jurists and others have sought to delineate features of the contemporary Constitution; this has been the case especially in determining the existence or otherwise of conventions. Given that conventions are prescribed neither by statute nor by judicial interpretation, one must study instead scholarly interpretations of political behavior and practice. Especially important authoritative works in the nineteenth century were those by John Austin and A. V. Dicey. Important names in the twentieth century included constitutional lawyers and academics such as Sir Ivor Jennings, Sir Kenneth Wheare, Geoffrey Marshall, O. Hood Phillips, and E. C. S. Wade[6] and in the twenty-first century include Vernon Bogdanor, Rodney Brazier, and Peter Hennessy.[7]

Given the disparate sources of the British Constitution and the fact that important relationships within and between organs of the state are not laid down in any one formal or binding document, it is not surprising that one must have recourse to books by constitutional scholars to discover the extent and nature of those relationships. Works of authority tend to be consulted more frequently in the field of constitutional law than in any other branch of English law.

MEANS OF AMENDMENT

Given the disparate primary sources of the British Constitution and the difficulty in determining where the Constitution begins and ends, it is perhaps not surprising that there are no extraordinary procedures for its amendment. Statute and common law of constitutional significance are subject to amendment by the same process as that employed for other legislative enactments. Conventions can be modified by changes in behavior or by reinterpretations of the significance of certain behavior. Works of authority can be rewritten or subjected to different interpretations in the same way as can other texts.

Much the same can be said about constitutionally significant statute law, judicial decisions, and works of authority in the United States. Even the provisions of the formal document, the U.S. Constitution, may be amended by judicial decisions and custom usage. The difference between the two countries is that the formal wording of the U.S. Constitution can be amended only by an extraordinary process, that is, one that goes beyond the provisions employed for amending the ordinary law. (Because of the extraordinary procedures necessary for amendment, the provisions of the Constitution are commonly referred to as "entrenched.") No such formal amending procedures exist in Britain, where there is no formal document.

INTERPRETATION

As may be surmised from the foregoing, there is no single body endowed with responsibility for interpreting the provisions of the Constitution. As in the United States, statute and common law are subject to judicial interpretation, but there is no power of judicial review, at least not as the term is understood in the United States. The courts can influence and to some extent mold certain provisions through their interpretation of statute and common law. Indeed, their use of common law has been of special importance in outlining and protecting certain rights of the individual. However, at the end of the day, they are subject to the wishes of Parliament. Judicial interpretation of statute law can, under the traditional constitution, be overridden by a new act of Parliament.

Identification and interpretation of conventions have little to do with the courts. Conventions arise as a result of changes in the relationships within and between different organs of the state. Their delineation rests with scholars, and their enforcement rests with those at whom they are aimed.

MAIN PROVISIONS

The central provisions of the traditional, or Westminster, British Constitution are listed in Table 4.1: parliamentary sovereignty, the rule of law, a unitary (as opposed to a federal) system, and parliamentary government under a constitutional monarchy. The notable characteristic of this constitution is that it facilitated strong government in the United Kingdom. Under it, power has been concentrated both politically (Whitehall as the center of the executive) and geographically (Whitehall being at the center of the nation's capital). The constitution derived from the Glorious Revolution of 1688–89 and events subsequent to that, especially—as we shall see—in the nineteenth century. Formally, the Westminster Constitution still exists—the four components remain in place—but it has changed dramatically in the last three decades. What the United Kingdom now has, insofar as it can be characterized, is a modified Westminster Constitution. It no longer facilitates, to the extent that it did in the period from the late nineteenth century to the 1970s, strong, central government. The reasons for this change are to be found in two developments. The first is British membership in the EC, now the European Union. Membership has added a new dimension to the British constitution (see later, Table 4.2) and forms, in effect, a fifth central component. The second development comprises various constitutional changes introduced after 1997 by the Labour governments of

TABLE 4.2
CONSTITUTIONAL IMPLICATIONS OF MEMBERSHIP IN THE EUROPEAN COMMUNITY
The effect of U.K. membership of the European Community was to: [1] Give the force of law in the United Kingdom to existing and (under the terms of the 1972 European Communities Act) to *future* European legislation.   *[Thus when law is made within the institutions of the European Community, the assent of Parliament is not required: Parliament has given its assent in advance under the terms of the 1972 Act.]*   [2] Give European law precedence over U.K. law.   [3] Give the power to determine disputes to the courts.   *[Thus the courts are the final arbiters of the provisions of the European treaties. The ultimate arbiter is the European Court of Justice.]*

Tony Blair and Gordon Brown (see later, Table 4.3). Foremost among these is devolution—the devolving of powers to elected assemblies in Scotland, Wales, and Northern Ireland—and the passage of a Human Rights Act. None destroys, at least not formally, any of the existing core components of the Constitution, but they serve variously to weaken or strengthen them.

Parliamentary Sovereignty

Parliamentary sovereignty was identified by the great nineteenth century constitutional lawyer, A. V. Dicey, as one of the twin pillars of the British Constitution.[8] (The other was the rule of law.) Dicey also offered the most succinct definition of parliamentary sovereignty, one that has been highly influential ever since. Parliamentary sovereignty, he wrote, means that Parliament has "the right to make or unmake any law whatever; and, further, that no person or body is recognized by the law of England as having a right to override or set aside the legislation of Parliament."[9] An act passed by Parliament will be enforced by the courts, the courts recognizing no body other than Parliament as having authority to override such an act. Parliament itself can substitute an act for an earlier one. One of the precepts derived from the principle is that Parliament is not bound by its predecessors. Once Parliament has passed an act, it becomes the law of the land. It is not open to challenge before the courts on the grounds of being unconstitutional.

Although Dicey claimed more ancient lineage for it, the principle of parliamentary sovereignty became established as a judicial rule in consequence of the Glorious Revolution of 1688 and subsequent Bill of Rights, which established the relationship between the Crown and Parliament (see Chapter 3). It was the product of an alliance between Parliament and common lawyers and of the intimidation of judges by the House of Commons. Assertion of the principle served to do away with the monarch's previously claimed powers to suspend or dispense with acts of Parliament and it served to deny judges the

TABLE 4.3

CONSTITUTIONAL CHANGES INTRODUCED BY LABOUR GOVERNMENTS SINCE 1997

Use of Referendums
Use of referendums in Scotland (1997), Wales (1997), and Northern Ireland (1998) to approve the creation of elected assemblies and in London (1988) to approve the establishment of an elected mayor and authority. Promised referendum on a new electoral system for parliamentary elections and in the event of the government recommending that the United Kingdom should join a single European currency.

Devolution of Powers to Elected Assemblies
Creation of elected assemblies in Scotland, Wales, and Northern Ireland and of an elected mayor and authority in London.

Human Rights Legislation
Passage of an act—the Human Rights Act 1998—incorporating most of the provisions of the European Convention on Human Rights into British law. The main provisions took effect in 2000. The courts are empowered to issue declarations of incompatibility where provisions of U.K. law are found to be incompatible with provisions of the Convention.

Introduction of New Electoral Systems
Introduction of systems of proportional representation, of different sorts, for elections to the European Parliament, the Scottish Parliament, the Welsh Assembly, the Northern Ireland Assembly, and the London Assembly.

Freedom of Information Legislation
Passage of the Freedom of Information Act 2000, covering not only government departments but also several thousand bodies fulfilling public functions. The Act took effect in 2005.

Reform of the House of Lords
Passage of an act—the House of Lords Act 1999—removing most hereditary peers from membership of the House of Lords.

Creation of a Supreme Court
Passage of an act—the Constitutional Reform Act 2005—creating a new Supreme Court as the highest court of appeal. The new court came into being in October 2009, succeeding the House of Lords. The act also made the Lord Chief Justice (a judicial appointment) the head of the judiciary, in place of the Lord Chancellor (a political appointee).

Transfer of Prerogative Powers to Parliament
Power to ratify treaties was given to Parliament under a measure introduced in 2009 and the need for the House of Commons to assent to the commitment of forces abroad (the war-making power) embodied in a parliamentary resolution.

power to strike down measures. If the king was bound by the will of Parliament, then so too were the king's courts. It came to occupy a unique place in constitutional law. The principle finds no expression in statute or any other formal enactment. It exists in common law but enjoys a special status beyond that enjoyed by other principles of common law. Its underpinnings are not only legal but also political and historical. Judicial obedience to it constitutes what H. W. R. Wade referred to as "the ultimate political fact upon which the whole system of legislation hangs."[10] No statute can confer the power of parliamentary sovereignty, for that would be to confer the very power being acted upon. It is therefore considered to be unique. As Hood Phillips states, "It may indeed be called the one fundamental law of the British Constitution."[11]

However, as we shall see, this "one fundamental law" is challenged, in effect, by the consequences of British membership of the European Union and by devolution. The use of referendums—to approve, for example, devolution in Scotland, Wales, and Northern Ireland—has also been argued to limit parliamentary sovereignty: Though the results of the referendums are advisory, it would appear perverse for Parliament to then go against them. The doctrine remains extant—Acts of Parliament remain omnicompetent—but the capacity of Parliament to make or unmake any law whatsoever, with no body other than Parliament being able to set aside that law, is now limited, and limited by Parliament's own actions.

The Rule of Law

The second pillar identified by Dicey was that of "the rule of law." Few students of the Constitution would deny the importance of the tenet. However, it is a concept that has labored under two limitations. One limitation has been that there is no agreed definition of the term. Dicey himself argued that it comprised "at least three distinct though kindred conceptions": "that no man is punishable or can be lawfully made to suffer in body or goods except for a distinct breach of law established in the ordinary legal manner before the ordinary courts of the land"; that "no man is above the law [and] every man, whatever be his rank or condition, is subject to the ordinary law of the realm and amenable to the jurisdiction of the ordinary tribunals"; and that "the general principles of the constitution [are] the result of judicial decisions determining the rights of private persons in particular cases brought before the courts." These three conceptions have been subject to various criticisms: among them, that many discretionary powers are vested in officials and public bodies, that many officials and bodies have immunities that the ordinary citizen does not have, and that certain rights have been modified by or enacted in statute. Furthermore, it is not clear why Dicey's third conception should be considered "kindred" to the other two. Some students of the Constitution find Dicey's analysis useful, and others tend to be dismissive; even Dicey later revised his own definition.

The rule of law, then, stands as a central element of the British Constitution, but no one is sure precisely what it means. It remains "one of the most elusive of all political concepts."[12] Some writers, especially in recent years, have tended to accord it a wide definition, encompassing substantive rights. On their argument, the rule of law cannot be said to exist unless basic human rights are protected. Others have adopted a narrow and more long-standing definition, contending that the concept entails certain procedural (or "due process") rights, that government must be subject to the law, and that the judiciary must be independent. The problem is one of determining what those rights are, how they are to be protected, and how the independence of the judiciary is to be maintained.

The second limitation is that the rule of law is not logically compatible with that of parliamentary sovereignty. Parliament could, if it so wished, confer arbitrary powers upon government. It could fetter the independence of the judiciary. It could limit or remove altogether certain rights presumed to exist at common law. The rule of law, in short, could be threatened or even dispensed with by parliamentary enactment. Dicey himself recognized this problem and sought to resolve it. He argued, in essence, that the rule of law prevented government from exercising arbitrary powers. If government wanted such powers, it could obtain them only through Parliament (Parliament itself has never sought to exercise executive powers) and the granting of them could take place only after deliberation and approval by the triumvirate of monarch, Lords, and Commons.[13]

Such an argument serves to explain potential impediments to a government intent on acquiring arbitrary powers. It does not deny the truth of the assertion that Parliament could, if it wished, confer such powers upon government. Critics of the Westminster Constitution have variously sought to provide some means of protecting rights from a powerful executive. For many years they advocated an entrenched Bill of Rights or, at least, the incorporation into British law of the European Convention on Human Rights (see Chapter 14). With the return of a Labour government in 1997, they achieved the latter. The Human Rights Act 1998 brought the provisions of the Convention into British law. Parliamentary sovereignty remains in place—the courts are not empowered to strike down laws that contravene the Convention, and Parliament could repeal or amend the 1998 Act. But the Act creates a legal environment that makes it difficult for Parliament and government to consider overriding its provisions, or not to act when the courts declare a measure in breach of the Convention.

Unitary (or Union) State

The third feature of the Constitution that I have listed—that the United Kingdom is a unitary state—is a less difficult one to comprehend. The United States is a federal nation. The power vested in the federal government is that delegated in the U.S. Constitution: All other powers not delegated rest with the states or the people. The U.S. Congress cannot abolish the states nor legislate to remove those powers. In the United Kingdom, Parliament exercises legal sovereignty. It can create regional and local units of government and confer powers and responsibilities on them. It can also remove those units of government and their powers.

The unitary nation is that of the United Kingdom of Great Britain and Northern Ireland. Wales was integrated with England in 1536 by act of Parliament (the Laws in Wales Act), and Scotland and England were incorporated in 1707 by the Treaty of Union and by the Act of Union with Scotland. Ireland entered into legislative union in 1801. Following an armed uprising, the emergence of the Irish Free State was recognized in 1922 and given the status of a self-governing dominion. (The Irish Constitution of 1937 declared the country to be a sovereign independent state, a position recognized by the Westminster Parliament in 1949.) Excluded from the Irish Free State were the northern six counties of Ireland, forming part of the traditional region of Ulster. The Protestant majority in Ulster wished to remain part of the United Kingdom, and the province of Northern Ireland has so remained.

Though power remains centralized, the different parts of the United Kingdom have retained their distinctive identities and, in the case of Scotland, retained a legal and educational system different from that of the rest of the United Kingdom. It is because of these distinct identities that the United Kingdom has sometimes been characterized as a union state, several countries coming together in one union. Recent years have seen a greater emphasis on this element, with some political powers now being devolved to elected assemblies in Scotland, Wales, and Northern Ireland (Chapter 10). (There is also some pressure for more powers to be devolved and for the creation of elected regional assemblies in England or an English parliament.) Again, parliamentary sovereignty remains in place—Parliament can repeal or amend the acts setting up the elected assemblies (as it did with an earlier act creating a parliament in Northern Ireland)—but political pressures may make it difficult to change the arrangements. Some commentators have also argued that the basis on which a Northern Ireland parliament and related bodies were created in 1998, involving agreement and cooperation with another country (the Republic of Ireland), makes it difficult for Parliament unilaterally to alter the arrangements.

Parliamentary Government under a Constitutional Monarchy

The fourth element of the Constitution is one that I have described as a parliamentary government under a constitutional monarchy. It is this element that is especially important in terms of the current relationships among the different organs of the state and the one in which conventions of the Constitution are predominant. It constitutes an assembly of different relationships and powers, the product of traditional institutions being adapted to meet changing circumstances. The developments producing this form of government were sketched in Chapter 3. The result, as we have seen, was parliamentary government in the sense of government *through* Parliament rather than government *by* Parliament, with a largely ceremonial head of state. The essentials of this form of government may be outlined as follows.

In the relationship among government, Parliament, and the monarch, the government dominates. Although lacking formal powers, the cabinet is recognized by convention as being at the heart of government. It is responsible for the final determination of policy to be submitted to Parliament, for the supreme control of the national executive in accordance with the policy pre-scribed by Parliament, and for continuous coordination and delimitation of the interests of the several departments of state.[14] It is presided over by the prime minister. The prime minister is appointed by the monarch. By conven-tion, the monarch summons the leader of the party with a majority of seats in the House of Commons. (In the event of a party having no overall majority, the monarch summons whomever he or she believes may be able to form an administration.) The prime minister then selects the members of his or her cabinet and other government ministers and submits their names to the monarch who, by convention, does not deny the prime minister's choice. By convention, ministers are drawn from Parliament and, again by convention, predominantly from the elected house, the House of Commons. Although the government no longer is chosen by the Commons, it nonetheless is elected through the House of Commons: There is no separate election of the execu-tive. There is a separation and overlap of powers between the government and the House of Commons in Britain but no equivalent separation of personnel. Government ministers are drawn from, and remain within, Parliament.

Legally, ministers are responsible to the monarch. Politically, they are responsible for their policies and actions to Parliament. Ministers are respon-sible to Parliament through the convention of individual ministerial responsi-bility, which assigns to them control of their departments, for which they are answerable to Parliament. The cabinet is similarly responsible to Parliament through the convention of collective ministerial responsibility. This conven-tion, one scholar writes, "implies that all cabinet ministers assume responsi-bility for cabinet decisions and actions taken to implement those decisions."[15] It also has begotten two other conventions. It is a corollary of collective responsibility that any minister who disagrees publicly with a cabinet deci-sion should resign and that a government defeat in the House of Commons on a vote of confidence necessitates either the resignation of the government or a request for a dissolution of Parliament. (There is no convention as to which of these alternatives the government should select.) Party cohesion ensures that the cabinet usually enjoys a parliamentary majority, so the chances of losing a vote of confidence are slim, though not non-existent: The last time a government lost a vote of confidence was in 1979.

The cabinet approves government bills to be presented to Parliament. (In drawing up measures, it is aided primarily by its officials—that is, civil servants—and will frequently consult with interested bodies: Such consultation, though, enjoys no formal recognition in constitutional terms.) Within Parlia-ment, the most important house is the Commons. It is expected to submit bills to sustained scrutiny and debate before giving its assent to them (or not giving its assent to them, but the influence of party usually precludes such an out-come). Formally, the Commons is free to pass or reject bills as it wishes. The House of Lords is more constrained (see Chapter 3); it was forced to accept restricted powers under the terms of the 1911 and 1949 Parliament Acts. Under the provisions of the 1911 act (a measure to which the Lords acquiesced under threat of being swamped with a mass of new Liberal pro-reform peers), the Lords could delay passage of non-money bills for only two successive sessions. Such bills were then enacted if passed by the Commons again in the succeeding session. Money bills, those certified as such by the speaker of the House of Commons, were to receive the Royal Assent one month after leaving the Commons, whether assented to by the House of Lords or not. The only significant power of veto retained was that over bills to prolong the life of a Parliament. (The delaying power over non-money bills was reduced by a further session under the terms of the 1949 Parliament Act, itself passed under the provisions of the 1911 act.) There is an agreement among the parties in the House, dating from the Parliament of 1945–50, that a bill promised in a government's election manifesto—and by extension, the government's legislative program—should be given an unopposed second reading (see Chapter 12). Though the House of Lords may (and frequently does) amend a government bill, it does not normally reject it. In 1999, an act was passed changing the composition of the House of Lords (see Chapter 12), though not its powers.

Once a bill has received the assent of both houses, it goes to the monarch for the Royal Assent. By convention, this assent is always forthcoming. As was already mentioned, not since Queen Anne's reign has a monarch refused assent. Queen Victoria contemplated such refusal but was persuaded otherwise. By convention, the queen exercises her powers on the advice of her ministers. In certain extreme circumstances, Her Majesty may find herself in a position in which she is called on to use her discretion in making a political decision. Such cases are rare, though the queen would probably prefer them to be nonexistent. The strength and the value of the contemporary monarchy derives from being above and avoiding political decisions.

The moment a bill receives the Royal Assent it becomes an act of Parliament. It is then enforced and upheld by the agencies of the state. The development of a form of representative democracy in the nineteenth century led Dicey to distinguish between legal sovereignty, which continued to reside with the triumvirate of the monarch, Lords, and Commons, and political sovereignty, which he deemed to rest with the electorate. This somewhat clumsy distinction has a certain utility. The electorate may have the power to choose the members of the House of Commons, but the will of the electorate is not something formally recognized by the courts. The courts recognize and will enforce only acts of Parliament.

Under the provisions of the 1911 Parliament Act, the maximum life of a Parliament is five years. (Previously, the period was seven years.) Within that period, the prime minister is free to recommend to the monarch a dissolution—in effect, to call a general election. Unlike the United States, Britain has no fixed-term elections at a national level. The ability of a prime minister effectively to call a general election has been regarded by some writers as the most important weapon in ensuring parliamentary support. The prime minister can threaten to recommend a dissolution if he or she does not receive the necessary support to get a measure through. Such a threat may constitute a bluff in that the prime minister is unlikely to want to run the risk of losing office, but nonetheless it has proved a potent influence in determining parliamentary behavior. It would be exceptional, albeit not unknown, for MPs of the government party to vote against their own side on a vote of confidence. No government since the nineteenth century has lost a vote of confidence as a result of dissent by its own supporters[16]—hence the dominance of government.

In summary, then, the fourth element of the Constitution—parliamentary government under a constitutional monarchy—may be seen to comprise different relationships and powers, which are the product of traditional institutions being adapted to meet changing circumstances and are prescribed by a variety of measures of statute and common law and by convention. The working of the various relationships within the framework established by law and convention is made possible by the operation of political parties. To understand contemporary British politics, one has to understand this framework.

THE CHANGING CONSTITUTION

To understand British politics fully, one also has to go beyond this framework. This brings us to two periods, or waves, of major constitutional change in the United Kingdom They can be characterized as waves of change because they continue to flow, almost tide-like, over a period of time. The first wave of change has been membership of the European Community—now the European Union—and the changes brought about by amendments to the treaties creating the Community. The second wave has comprised the various changes to the constitutional framework introduced since 1997 by Labour governments under Prime Minister Tony Blair and his successor Gordon Brown.

European Union Membership

What now constitutes in effect the fifth core element of the British Constitution is something for which there is no parallel in North America: That is, membership in a supranational body.[17] The United Kingdom became a member of what was then the EC on January 1, 1973. Under the Treaty on European Union (the Maastricht Treaty) in 1993, the EC became one of three pillars in a new European Union. The effect of membership in the EC, now the EU, has been to add a new dimension to the formulation, approval, and enforcement of measures of public policy.

By virtue of membership, decision-making competence in a number of sectors has passed from the British government to the principal executive institutions of the European Union: the Council of Ministers, comprising the relevant ministers drawn from the member states, and the Commission, the permanent bureaucracy headed by a College of Commissioners. (The commissioners are nominated by, but required to be independent of, the member states.) The Council is the ultimate decision-making body; the Commission in most spheres has the exclusive power to propose legislation.

British ministers thus form part of a wider, collective decision-making body. Under the terms of the international treaties creating the bodies, the council and Commission can issue different forms of legislation (see Chapter 9). Under the terms of the European Communities Act of 1972, which provides the legal basis necessary for membership, the force of law is given in the United Kingdom to European regulations. Such legislation has immediate and general applicability. The assent of Parliament is not required: It has, in effect, been given in advance under the provisions of the 1972 act. In the event of any conflict between domestic (known as municipal) law and European law, the latter is to prevail. Disputes concerning European law are to be treated by British courts as matters of law, and cases that reach the highest domestic court of appeal must, under the provisions of the Treaty of Rome, be referred to the European Court of Justice for a definitive ruling. Requests also may be made from lower courts to the Court of Justice for a ruling on the meaning and interpretation of the treaties.

Membership has thus had profound constitutional implications for the United Kingdom. These implications are even more pronounced now as a result of the implementation of new treaties and treaty amendments since 1972. One of the most significant was the Single European Act, which came into force on July 1, 1987. The effect of the treaty was to change the power relationship *between* the institutions of the Community and the member states, and *within* the Community among the different institutions. The treaty extended the provision for qualified majority voting (QMV) in the Council of Ministers: This means one or more ministers can be outvoted by the ministers from the other countries. (Each minister enjoys a stipulated number of votes, depending on the size of the country.) A measure thus can be opposed by the British government and Parliament and yet, if it achieves the necessary number of votes in the council, be enforced as law in the United Kingdom. The treaty also accorded a stronger role to the directly elected European Parliament; it now is more directly involved in the discussion and amendment of council proposals and, in certain circumstances, can fulfill a significant blocking role. Its powers have been further strengthened under the Maastricht and Amsterdam Treaties (see Chapter 9). The Lisbon Treaty, ratified in 2009, constituted a further step change through creating new leadership positions within the EU and removing the pillar structure of the EU.

Membership in the European Union has been added on and, as far as possible, integrated with the existing provisions of the Westminster Constitution. The "fit," as we have already had cause to note, has not necessarily been complete. The British government retains its autonomy in several significant sectors of public policy, though the number is diminishing. There is a capacity for tension between the established national institutions and those grafted on at a supranational level. Various provisions of statute law—the European Communities Act of 1972 and the subsequent amending Acts—may be seen as constituting a Trojan horse, allowing the introduction of a new layer to the British Constitution. Existing institutions and procedures have not yet become fully accommodated to this new dimension.

The most fundamental lack of "fit" exists in relation to the doctrine of parliamentary sovereignty. The doctrine has been undermined, especially as a result of a rulings by the European Court of Justice and by the House of Lords—notably in the 1994 case of *Ex Parte EOC,* in which the House of Lords held provisions of an Act of Parliament to be incompatible with EC law—but remains intact in that Parliament retains the power to repeal the original European Communities Act of 1972. Although withdrawal would create enormous difficulties—an event for which there is no precedent—the British courts would, under the doctrine of parliamentary sovereignty, enforce the act of repeal. However, repeal is not regarded as likely and the longer the period of membership in the European Union the more likely the prospect of the doctrine falling away, the provisions of the European treaties forming some form of "written" constitution for the United Kingdom.

Constitutional Reform under a Labour Government

Constitutional changes introduced under Labour governments since 1997 have further served to modify the contours of the British Constitution.[18] Some of these changes we have touched upon already. They are summarized in Table 4.3. [Some have had a limited impact on the basic features of the traditional, Westminster Constitution; others have had a significant impact.]

The doctrine of parliamentary sovereignty has, as we have seen, been challenged by the consequences of membership in the European Union. It has also been challenged—albeit, at least formally, to a lesser extent—by the incorporation of the European Convention on Human Rights into British law. The Convention is an international treaty that seeks to protect basic human rights. (Among its provisions: a right to life, liberty, and respect for private and family life, and freedom from torture and discrimination.) It was ratified by the United Kingdom in 1951 but never incorporated into British law. In 1965 British citizens were given the right to petition the European Court on Human Rights if their rights were infringed. If the United Kingdom lost a case in the Court, the government brought forward legislation to bring U.K. law into line with the judgment of the Court. However, it was not legally obliged to do so. Cases brought before the European Court also usually took several years to resolve. In 1998, the Labour government achieved passage of an act incorporating the Convention into British law. The act maintains the doctrine of parliamentary sovereignty. The courts cannot strike a British law as being contrary to the provisions of the Convention. All they can do is issue declarations of incompatibility, declaring a provision to be in breach of the Convention. It is then up to Parliament as to whether or not it changes the law to bring it into line with the provisions of the Convention. In practice, whenever the courts declare a provision of British law in breach of the Convention, the government will bring legislation forward, or take appropriate action, to bring it into line with the decision of the courts. Thus, although formally the doctrine of parliamentary sovereignty remains intact, in practice it is being undermined: The courts will, in effect, be deciding whether a provision of British law is in conflict with some higher law and should be set aside. Parliament retains the power to amend or repeal the Human Rights Act, but it is unlikely to exercise that power. The longer the Act remains in force then, as with the European Communities Act, the greater the prospect of the doctrine of parliamentary sovereignty falling away.

The effect of the Human Rights Act has been to undermine one pillar of the Constitution while strengthening another: that of the rule of law. As we have noted, under the traditional Constitution the rule of law is logically subordinate to the doctrine of parliamentary sovereignty. The enactment of the Human Rights Act gives a greater protection to the second pillar, though not formally destroying the first pillar. The rights of citizens have also been extended by freedom of information legislation (the Freedom of Information Act 2000, its provisions taking effect in 2005). The effect of membership of the European Union and the passage of the Human Rights Act has been to create a major new judicial dimension to the British Constitution, giving the citizen far greater opportunities than ever before to pursue through the court's claims against the government or another public body.

The unitary state remains formally intact but has been modified in practice by the creation of elected assemblies in different parts of the United Kingdom. Ultimate power to modify the powers of these assemblies and, indeed, to abolish them, remains with Parliament. That is the formal constitutional position. The political reality is very different. There is little prospect of Parliament repealing the devolution legislation (see Chapter 10). The Scottish parliament, in particular, has been vested with a wide range of legislative and executive powers, including a power to vary the standard rate of income tax. So long as the new assemblies remain in place, the United Kingdom has an unusual constitutional structure, with elected assemblies in different parts of the kingdom but not in the part in which the vast majority of Britons live: that is, England. The United Kingdom thus has what has been termed asymmetrical devolution: a U.K. Parliament and elected assemblies in Scotland, Wales, and Northern Ireland, but not in England. Formally, it remains a unitary state but with power dispersed in a skewed manner.

Parliamentary government has been affected in different ways by changes since 1997. Constitutional changes under the Blair Government constrained Parliament's position in the constitutional framework of the United Kingdom, through transferring powers to other bodies. Legislative and other changes introduced under the premiership of Gordon Brown sought instead to strengthen Parliament. The challenges to Parliament that arose under the Blair Government are several. They included the use of referendums, new electoral systems for devolved bodies, and reform of the House of Lords.

Parliamentary government is challenged by the use of referendums. Again, the formality is retained in that referendums are advisory only. Parliament is the body that deliberates and ultimately decides. However, referendums represent, in practice, particular issues being handed over for determination by the electorate. Though a referendum is formally advisory rather than binding, it would be perverse for Parliament to authorize a referendum and then to enact legislation contrary to the outcome of the referendum. Referendums have been a notable feature of the period since the election of a Labour government in 1997, with more promised. The use of forms of proportional representation (PR) for elections to the different assemblies, as well as for the election of the mayor of London, also has potential implications for this feature of the traditional constitution. The use of PR systems for other elected bodies[19] adds pressure for the use of PR in elections to the House of Commons: Its use would, according to critics, undermine the accountability of the present parliamentary system (see Chapter 5). The removal of most hereditary peers from the House of Lords, under the provisions of the 1999 House of Lords Act, does not formally affect the basic relationships of the traditional Constitution. However, any second stage reform—the removal of hereditary peers constituting a first stage—may involve a change in form and powers, with important consequences for the relationship between the two chambers of Parliament.

Changes introduced under the Brown premiership have operated in a countervailing direction. Whereas the Blair Government introduced reforms that were external to Parliament, and had the effect of constraining it, Gordon Brown as prime minister initiated reforms designed to strengthen Parliament in the political system. At the heart of a program of reform, titled *The Governance of Britain,* was giving powers to Parliament. In particular, Brown sought to transfer a range of prerogative powers, including most notably those to ratify treaties and to assent to the use of armed forces abroad (the war-making power) to Parliament. The power to ratify treaties was embodied in a Bill introduced in Parliament in the 2008–09 session of Parliament and the need to gain the assent of the House of Commons to the commitment of forces abroad embodied in a parliamentary resolution.

Parliamentary government under a constitutional monarchy thus remains a central feature of the Constitution, but one that, like other features, is being modified and may be under further threat in the future.

CONCLUSION

The shifting and complex web of relationships and powers that forms the British Constitution is not an easily discernible one. Some powers and relationships recognizably fall within the rubric of the Constitution. Others are less easy to classify. Sometimes a feature of the Constitution is discerned as such only at the time when it has just ceased to have much relevance. Walter Bagehot's *The English Constitution,* published in 1867, constituted a classic description of a Constitution that had not previously been so well sketched, yet a Constitution that was to undergo significant modifications as a result of the passage that very same year of the Second Reform Act. Bagehot's work continued to be regarded as an authoritative work long after the Constitution had undergone fundamental change. A description of the Westminster Constitution penned in 1970 would be in need of significant amendment within two years, as would a description penned just before the general election of 1997.

Grasping the essentials of the Constitution at any given moment is clearly a demanding and confusing task. Dicey claimed that, as a result of his work, the constitution no longer appeared as a "sort of maze." According to one critic, "it stills feel like a maze when you seek to leave it."[20] It is confusing even to those charged with its interpretation and to those who seek to make it work. To the student of the subject, the British Constitution appears complex, confusing, ill-defined, and, in many respects, amorphous. Such a reaction is both natural and understandable: The Constitution does exhibit those very characteristics.

At the heart of the difficulty of delineating clearly the essential features of the Constitution is its ever-changing nature.[21] Statute law, as we have seen in the case of membership in the European Union and devolution, can introduce new bodies of government. Constitutional norms serve to influence and mold political behavior. Conversely, political behavior helps influence the contours of the Constitution. As we have seen, such changes are made possible by the assimilating influence of conventions. "The conventions of the constitution," as LeMay observed, "have meaning only when they are looked at against a background of continuous political change. It is very difficult to say with certainty what they were at any particular moment. Above all, they cannot be understood 'with the politics left out.'"[22]

The Constitution has proved adaptable to changing political conditions. That adaptation, though, has not been smooth or seamless. The Westminster Constitution has variously encountered criticism and has been on the agenda of political debate for more than a quarter of a century. As we shall see in the Conclusion, there have been calls for a radical overhaul, some reform bodies arguing for a new constitutional settlement to replace that of 1688–89. Several different intellectually coherent approaches to constitutional change have emerged, each positing a particular type of constitutional framework for the United Kingdom. The Labour Government of Tony Blair embarked on a substantial program of constitutional reform—collectively the most radical since the late seventeenth and early eighteenth centuries, according to one leading American observer[23]—but one that fell short of replacing the Westminster model. Each reform was justified on its own merits and not related to any clear view of what type of constitution should exist.[24] The reforms of the Blair era were essentially disparate and discrete, with no attempt to relate them to one another or to a particular constitutional vision. When Gordon Brown became prime minister, he took the constitution in a different direction, but like Blair lacked any clear constitutional end-point.[25] What we have, in effect, is a modified Westminster Constitution. Some critics would argue that the changes have gone too far, and that what the United Kingdom has is a fairly shapeless Constitution. Others—advocates of a new Constitution—argue that it has not gone far enough. And some, as we shall see (Chapter 16), continue to make the case for the fundamentals of the Westminster system.

NOTES

1. O. Hood Phillips, *Constitutional and Administrative Law*, 6th ed. (Sweet & Maxwell, 1978), p. 5.
2. C. Rossiter, prefatory note to E. S. Corwin, *The "Higher Law" Background of American Constitutional Law* (Cornell University Press, 1979 ed.), p. vi.
3. P. Madgwick and D. Woodhouse, *The Law and Politics of the Constitution* (Harvester Wheatsheaf, 1995), p. 11.
4. See G. Marshall and G. Moodie, *Some Problems of the Constitution*, 4th rev. ed. (Hutchinson, 1967), p. 26.
5. Phillips, p. 25.
6. See P. Norton, *The Constitution in Flux* (Basil Blackwell, 1982), p. 9.
7. Their works include R. Brazier, *Constitutional Practice*, 2nd ed. (Clarendon Press, 1994), P. Hennessy, *The Hidden Wiring* (Gollancz, 1995), and V. Bogdanor, *The Monarchy under the Constitution* (Clarendon Press, 1995).
8. A. V. Dicey, *An Introduction to the Study of the Law of the Constitution*, 10th ed. (first published 1885; Macmillan, 1959).
9. Ibid., pp. 39–40.
10. H. W. R. Wade, "The Basis of Legal Sovereignty," *Common Law Journal*, 1955, cited by E. C. S. Wade in his introduction to the 10th ed. of Dicey, p. lvi.
11. Phillips, p. 46.
12. "The Rule of Law in Britain Today," *Constitutional Reform Centre: Politics Briefing No. 6* (Constitutional Reform Centre, 1989), p. 1.
13. See Norton, pp. 16–17.
14. As listed by *The Report of the Machinery of Government Committee* (His Majesty's Stationery Office, 1918).
15. S. A. de Smith, *Constitutional and Administrative Law* (Penguin, 1971), p. 176.
16. The government of Neville Chamberlain effectively fell in 1940 because of dissent by its own backbenchers, though it retained a majority in the parliamentary vote that took place. The government, in effect, got the message without having to be defeated formally. On three occasions in this century, government has actually lost a vote of confidence—in 1924 (twice) and 1979—but in each instance the government party did not enjoy an overall parliamentary majority.
17. In a North American context, the closest equivalent is the North American Free Trade Agreement (NAFTA), but that does not have the governmental element of the European Union.
18. See A. King, *The British Constitution* (Oxford University Press, 2007) and V. Bogdanor, *The New British Constitution* (Hart Publishing, 2009).
19. See Ministry of Justice, *Review of Voting Systems: The Experience of New Voting Systems in the United Kingdom since 1997*, Cm 7304 (The Stationery Office, 2008).
20. A. Barnett, *This Time: Our Constitutional Revolution* (Vintage, 1997), p. 281.
21. See, for example, V. Bogdanor (ed.), *The British Constitution in the Twentieth Century* (Oxford University Press, 2003) and J. Jowell and D. Oliver (eds.), *The Changing Constitution*, 6th ed. (Oxford University Press, 2007).
22. G. LeMay, *The Victorian Constitution* (Duckworth, 1979), p. 21.
23. R. Stevens, *The English Judges* (Hart, 2002), p. xiii.
24. See P. Norton, "The Constitution," in A. Seldon (ed.), *Blair's Britain 1997–2007* (Cambridge University Press, 2007), pp. 119–120.
25. P. Norton "The Constitution under Gordon Brown," *Politics Review*, 17 (3), 2008, pp. 26–29.

5

The Electoral System
Campaigns, Voting, and Voters

In the United States, citizens are presented with the opportunity to go to the polls at frequent and fixed intervals to elect at national, state, and local levels a host of legislators, executive heads, councilpersons, officials, and even, in some states, judges. Before polling day, the citizen is faced with a lengthy election campaign: There are primary campaigns, the primary elections, the general election campaign, and the general election itself. The presidential election campaign lasts for nearly a year; with all the preplanning, advance publicity, and fund-raising, it lasts for much longer. Given the short interval between elections, campaigns for the U.S. House of Representatives are virtually continuous. Candidates spend much of their time raising funds to fight the next election. In financial terms, elections are big business. Once in the polling booth, the voter is faced with a daunting array of candidates: Given the number of offices to be filled and the number of people seeking to fill them, the number of names may be a three-figure one. Voting and its subsequent tabulation are much eased by the use of voting machines. With more than one office usually to be filled in an election, voters can—and do—split their tickets between parties. Once elected, there is a gap of over two months before officeholders take up their posts.

How do such characteristics compare with elections in the United Kingdom? For most of the past century, the two electoral systems have been marked by their differences rather than by their similarities. In the United Kingdom, a citizen may have the opportunity to vote in the election of a national body only once every five years. That election is for the House of Commons and the House of Commons alone. As we shall see (Chapter 12) the members of the House of Lords are not elected. There is no separate election of the executive: The leader of the party with a majority of seats in the House of Commons is invited to form a government. (The choice of party leaders is a matter for the parties themselves.) The date of an election is not known until approximately four weeks before the event, when the prime minister recommends to the queen a dissolution of Parliament. Although there is much anticipatory planning, the election campaign proper extends over approximately three weeks. There are no primaries: Candidate selection is an internal matter for the parties. The campaign is fought on a national, and party, basis. It is funded and organized by the established parties, not by individual candidates or campaign organizations created by the candidates. There are statutory limits on the amount that can be spent during election campaigns. On polling day the elector is faced with a small ballot slip on which are printed the names usually of about five or six candidates. (Six or more candidates standing in any one constituency would be unusual.) The voter places a cross next to the name of only one of them. With each elector having only one vote to cast for only one candidate, there is no such thing as ticket splitting. At the close of polling, the votes are collected in one central area in each constituency and counted by hand. A sufficient number of results is usually announced within a few hours of the close of the polls to know which party has won the election. If the party in office has lost, the prime minister goes to Buckingham Palace to tender his or her resignation. The leader of the party newly returned with a majority of seats is then summoned. The new cabinet and other ministerial appointments are announced within a matter of days, sometimes within a matter of hours. Within a month of an election being called, Britain may find itself with a new government.

These features of the British system remain in place. However, there have been changes in recent years that mean that, in quantitative terms, there are features of elections in Britain that now bring Britain closer to the American experience. However, those very same changes have meant that, in qualitative terms, the differences between the two systems are even more pronounced. In quantitative terms, there are now more elections in the United Kingdom. Until 1979, voters in Britain were able to vote for members of local councils and for members of the House of Commons. In 1979, direct elections to the European Parliament were introduced, giving British voters the opportunity to elect British Members of the European Parliament (MEPs). In 1998, Parliament in Britain approved legislation setting up elected assemblies in Scotland, Wales, Northern Ireland, and London. In all these places, electors have acquired the right to elect members of bodies that exist between local and national level. A voter in Scotland, for example, is thus now entitled to vote in elections to a local council, the Scottish Parliament, the House of Commons, and the European Parliament. The extension in the number of elections is thus substantial, relative to past experience, but is still limited. Voters in England, other than in London, have no intermediate layer of government to elect. The qualitative change is in terms of the type of voting systems employed. For most local elections and elections to the House of Commons, the system employed is the same as that in the United States: the first-past-the-post system, the candidate with a plurality of votes being declared elected. However, for elections to other bodies, different systems of proportional representation (PR) have been introduced.[1] The additional member system (AMS) has been introduced in Scotland and Wales, as well as for elections to the Greater London Assembly.

The regional list system is employed for elections to the European Parliament, except in Northern Ireland, where the single transferable vote (STV) system is used. The STV system is also now used for Scottish local elections, being employed for the first time in 2007. And a system known as the supplementary vote (SV) is used for the election of directly elected mayors, including the mayor of London. Voters in the United Kingdom are now thus called upon to (1) vote more often than before and to (2) do so using different voting systems. In the former case, they are coming closer to the experience of U.S. voters. In the latter, they are moving further away.

In this chapter, the focus is national elections. That means elections to the House of Commons. It is these elections that determine which party forms the government of the United Kingdom. Elections to the European Parliament will be discussed in Chapter 9 and to the Scottish, Welsh, Northern Ireland, and London assemblies in Chapter 10. Given that our focus here *is* national elections, the American and British systems remain notable for their differences.

The essential characteristics of national elections in the United States and the United Kingdom are contrasted in Table 5.1. Let us consider in a little more detail some of the main features of national elections in Britain and of electoral behavior before proceeding to a consideration of the current controversy surrounding the electoral system.

THE ELECTORAL STRUCTURE
Electors

As we have seen (Chapter 3), the franchise was variously extended in the nineteenth century. The basis on which the vote was given was that of property. Not until 1918 was universal manhood suffrage introduced on the basis of (six months') residence. In the same year, women aged 30 and over, if already local government electors or married to such electors, were given a vote in general elections. The vote was extended to all women aged 21 and over in 1928. It was extended to 18- to 20-year-olds in 1969. The various extensions of the franchise during the course of the twentieth century, much more radical in numerical terms than the various extensions of the previous century, and the growth in population have resulted in the electorate growing from 6,730,935 in 1900 to 44,245,939 in 2005. The 1949 Representation of the People Act, which abolished plural voting, effectively brought to final fruition the principle of "one person, one vote."[2] The only people excluded now from the franchise are members of the House of Lords (given that they have their own house), imprisoned criminals, people convicted of certain election offences, and aliens. Historically, those of "unsound mind" have been excluded, but in 2008 it was announced that the Government intended to remove the prohibition. It was also reviewing the blanket prohibition on imprisoned criminals. The prohibition on aliens is not as restrictive as it may sound: Commonwealth citizens resident in the United Kingdom are entitled to

TABLE 5.1

United States and United Kingdom National Elections

Characteristics	United States	United Kingdom
Bodies elected	President and vice president Senate House of Representatives	House of Commons
Constituencies	President: national Senate: state House: single-member districts (435)	Single-member districts (constituencies) (646)
Terms of Office	President: four years (two-term maximum) Senate: six years (one-third elected every two years) Representative: two years (limits to seeking reelection by senators or representatives vary by state)	Maximum of five years (no limit to seeking reelection)
Eligibility for candidature	President: native-born citizen, age 35 or over, 14 years resident in U.S. Senator: age 30 or over, 9 years a citizen, inhabitant of state Representative: age 25 or over, 7 years a citizen, inhabitant of state	Citizen age 18 or over (certain exceptions)
Fixed-term or irregular elections	Fixed term	Irregular (but must not go beyond five-year intervals)
Mode of election	Plurality vote for Senate and House, popular vote and electoral college for president	Plurality vote
Date of election determined by	Acts of Congress	Recommendation of prime minister to monarch (within five-year limit and subject to certain qualifications)

(continued)

TABLE 5.1 (continued)		
Characteristics	United States	United Kingdom
Franchise	Citizens age 18 and over (certain exceptions)	Citizens age 18 and over (certain exceptions)
Registration procedures	Varies by state: historically, required to register in person	Head of household by law completes annual registration form, submitted by mail

vote as are citizens of the Republic of Ireland. EU citizens living in the United Kingdom are entitled to vote in European Parliament and local elections.

To exercise one's right to vote, it is necessary to be on the electoral register, which is compiled annually. Each year every household receives an electoral registration form. The head of the household is required to complete it and to list all those who are resident in the dwelling on a particular date—October 10 in Great Britain and September 15 in Northern Ireland—and are eligible for inclusion. This includes those who will attain the age of 18 years during the period that the new register comes into effect. These forms are returned by mail to the registration officer for the constituency. About a third of households fail to respond and have to be chased up by mail and, if that fails, in person.[3] Once the register is compiled, it is open for inspection; it takes effect the following February, and is in force for one year. A voter is entitled to apply to vote by post. Previously a reason had to be given, but each elector is now automatically entitled to have a postal vote.

Compared with registration procedures adopted previously in most U.S. states,[4] the British practice is efficient and effective. Completing the registration forms is a legal requirement. Supplementary registers are published every month to allow registration officers to include people wrongly omitted. Even so, it has been estimated that anywhere between 5 and 10 percent of adults fail to register. Some voters fill in registration forms incorrectly or, for a variety of reasons, fail to complete them.[5] There is no procedure analogous to the U.S. practice of registering as a Republican, Democrat, or Independent; given the absence of primary elections in Britain, there is no logical reason that one should exist.

Constituencies

The United Kingdom is divided into single-member constituencies, though the number can and does vary. At one time earlier in the twentieth century, when the whole of Ireland was still part of the United Kingdom, there were over 700. Since then, the figure has varied between 600 and 700, usually in the lower half of the range. In 1950 there were 625 seats, the figure rising at several general elections until it reached 659 in 1997 (see Table 5.2). The number was reduced in 2005 to 646 because of a reduction in the number of seats

TABLE 5.2

GENERAL ELECTION RESULTS, 1945–2005

General Election (Winning party in capital letters)	Votes cast[1]		Seats won[2]	
July 1945				
LABOUR	11,995,152	(47.8)	393	(61.4)
Conservative	9,988,306	(39.8)	213	(33.3)
Liberal	2,248,226	(9.0)	12	(1.9)
Others	854,294	(2.8)	22	(3.4)
Turnout: 72.7%	25,085,978	(99.4%)	640	(100.0%)
February 1950				
LABOUR	13,266,592	(46.1)	315	(50.4)
Conservative	12,502,567	(43.5)	298	(47.7)
Liberal	2,621,548	(9.1)	9	(1.4)
Others	381,964	(1.3)	3	(0.5)
Turnout: 84.0%	28,772,671	(100.0%)	625	(100.0%)
October 1951				
CONSERVATIVE	13,717,538	(48.0)	321	(51.4)
Labour	13,948,605	(48.8)	295	(47.2)
Liberal	730,556	(2.5)	6	(1.0)
Others	198,969	(0.7)	3	(0.5)
Turnout: 82.5%	28,595,668	(100.0%)	625	(100.1%)
May 1955				
CONSERVATIVE	13,286,569	(49.7)	344	(54.6)
Labour	12,404,970	(46.4)	277	(44.0)
Liberal	722,405	(2.7)	6	(0.9)
Others	346,554	(1.2)	3	(0.5)
Turnout: 76.7%	26,760,498	(100.0%)	630	(100.0%)
October 1959				
CONSERVATIVE	13,749,830	(49.4)	365	(57.9)
Labour	12,215,538	(43.8)	258	(40.9)
Liberal	1,638,571	(5.9)	6	(0.9)
Others	142,670	(0.8)	1	(0.2)
Turnout: 78.8%	27,746,609	(99.9%)	630	(99.9%)
October 1964				
LABOUR	12,205,814	(44.1)	317	(50.3)
Conservative	12,001,396	(43.4)	304	(48.2)
Liberal	3,092,878	(11.2)	9	(1.4)
Others	347,905	(1.3)	0	(0.0)
Turnout: 77.1%	27,647,993	(100.0%)	630	(99.9%)

(continued)

TABLE 5.2 (continued)

General Election (Winning party in capital letters)	Votes cast[1]		Seats won[2]	
March 1966				
LABOUR	13,064,951	(47.9)	363	(57.6)
Conservative	11,418,433	(41.9)	253	(40.2)
Liberal	2,327,533	(8.5)	12	(1.9)
Others	422,226	(1.2)	2	(0.3)
Turnout: 75.8%	27,233,143	(99.5%)	630	(100.0%)
June 1970				
CONSERVATIVE	13,145,123	(46.4)	330	(52.4)
Labour	12,179,341	(43.0)	287	(45.6)
Liberal	2,117,035	(7.5)	6	(0.9)
Others	903,299	(3.2)	7	(1.1)
Turnout: 72.0%	28,344,798	(100.1%)	630	(100.0%)
February 1974				
LABOUR	11,639,243	(37.1)	301	(47.4)
Conservative	11,868,906	(37.9)	297	(46.8)
Liberal	6,063,470	(19.3)	14	(2.2)
Others (Great Britain)	1,044,061	(3.4)	11	(1.7)
Others (Northern Ireland)[3]	717,986	(2.3)	12	(1.9)
Turnout: 78.7%	31,333,666	(100.0%)	635	(100.0%)
October 1974				
LABOUR	11,457,079	(39.2)	319	(50.2)
Conservative	10,464,817	(35.8)	277	(43.6)
Liberal	5,346,754	(18.3)	13	(2.0)
Scottish National Party	839,617	(2.9)	11	(1.7)
Plaid Cymru	166,321	(0.6)	3	(0.5)
Others (Great Britain)	212,496	(0.8)	0	(0.0)
Others (Northern Ireland)	702,904	(2.4)	12	(1.9)
Turnout: 72.8%	29,189,178	(100.0%)	635	(99.9%)
May 1979				
CONSERVATIVE	13,697,690	(43.9)	339	(53.4)
Labour	11,532,148	(36.9)	269	(42.4)
Liberal	4,313,811	(13.8)	11	(1.7)
Scottish National Party	504,259	(1.6)	2	(0.3)
Plaid Cymru	132,544	(0.4)	2	(0.3)
Others (Great Britain)	343,674	(1.2)	0	(0.0)
Others (Northern Ireland)	695,889	(2.2)	12	(1.9)
Turnout: 76.0%	31,184,015	(100.0%)	635	(100.0%)

(continued)

TABLE 5.2 (continued)

General Election (Winning party in capital letters)	Votes cast[1]		Seats won[2]	
June 1983				
CONSERVATIVE	13,012,602	(42.4)	397	(61.1)
Labour	8,457,124	(27.6)	209	(32.1)
SDP/Liberal Alliance	7,780,577	(25.4)	23	(3.5)
Scottish National Party	331,975	(1.1)	2	(0.3)
Plaid Cymru	125,309	(0.4)	2	(0.3)
Others (Great Britain)	198,834	(0.6)	0	(0.0)
Others (Northern Ireland)	764,474	(2.5)	17	(2.6)
Turnout: 72.7%	30,670,895	(100.0%)	650	(99.9%)
June 1987				
CONSERVATIVE	13,760,525	(42.3)	376	(57.8)
Labour	10,029,944	(30.8)	292	(35.2)
SDP/Liberal Alliance	7,341,152	(22.6)	22	(3.4)
Scottish National Party	416,873	(1.3)	3	(0.5)
Plaid Cymru	123,589	(0.4)	3	(0.5)
Others (Great Britain)	127,329	(0.4)	0	(0.0)
Others (Northern Ireland)	730,152	(2.2)	17	(2.6)
Turnout: 75.3%	32,529,564	(100.0%)	650	(100.0%)
April 1992				
CONSERVATIVE	14,092,235	(41.9)	336	(51.6)
Labour	11,559,735	(34.4)	271	(41.6)
Liberal Democrat	5,999,384	(17.8)	20	(3.1)
Scottish National Party	629,555	(1.9)	3	(0.5)
Plaid Cymru	154,390	(0.5)	4	(0.6)
Others (Great Britain)	445,612	(1.3)	0	(0.0)
Others (Northern Ireland)	731,782	(2.2)	17	(2.6)
Turnout: 77.7%	33,612,693	(100.0%)	651	(100.0%)
May 1997				
LABOUR	13,518,167	(43.2)	419	(63.6)
Conservative	9,600,943	(30.7)	165	(25.0)
Liberal Democrat	5,242,947	(16.8)	46	(7.0)
Scottish National	621,550	(2.0)	6	(0.9)
Plaid Cymru	161,030	(0.5)	4	(0.6)
Others (Great Britain)[4]	1,362,661	(4.3)	1	(0.2)
Others (Northern Ireland)	790,762	(2.5)	18	(2.7)
Turnout 71.5%	31,298,060	(100.0%)	659	(100.0%)

(*continued*)

TABLE 5.2 (continued)				
General Election (Winning party in capital letters)	**Votes cast[1]**		**Seats won[2]**	
June 2001				
LABOUR	10,724,953	(40.7)	412	(62.5)
Conservative	8,357,615	(31.7)	166	(25.1)
Liberal Democrat	4,814,321	(18.3)	52	(7.7)
Scottish National	464,314	(1.8)	5	(0.7)
Plaid Cyrmru	195,893	(0.7)	4	(0.6)
Other (Great Britain)	989,611	(3.9)	2	(0.3)
Other (Northern Ireland)	810,374	(2.9)	18	(2.7)
Turnout 59.4%	26,367,383	(100.0%)	659	(99.7%)
May 2005				
LABOUR	9,552,436	(35.2)	355	(55.0)
Conservative	8,784,915	(32.4)	198	(30.6)
Liberal Democrat	5,981,874	(22.0)	62	(9.6)
Scottish National	412,267	(1.5)	6	(0.9)
Plaid Cyrmru	174,838	(0.6)	3	(0.5)
Other (Great Britain)[5]	1,524,578	(5.7)	4	(0.6)
Other (Northern Ireland)	717,602	(2.6)	18	(2.7)
Turnout 61.4%	27,148,510	(100.0%)	646	(99.9%)

[1]Percentages do not always add up to 100 because of rounding.

[2]The Speaker, where seeking reelection, is included with original party.

[3]Prior to 1974, UUs were affiliated with the Conservative party. Thereafter they sat as a separate parliamentary party.

[4]Includes the Referendum party, which won 811,827 votes.

[5]Includes UK Independence Party (UKIP) which won 605,973 votes.

in Scotland (Scots having now their own parliament) but will increase at the next general election to 650 as a result of boundary changes in England.

The drawing of boundaries is the responsibility of bodies known as boundary commissions: There is a commission each for England, Scotland, Wales, and Northern Ireland. Each commission is chaired by the speaker of the House of Commons (a nonparty figure who, in practice, never participates) and each has a judge as deputy chairman. Assistant commissioners, usually lawyers, are appointed to supervise local inquiries, and the staff of the commissions includes the country's main officials dealing with population and geographic surveys.

In redrawing boundaries the commissions are guided by rules laid down by act of Parliament. They are supposed to ensure that constituencies are as equal as possible in the size of their electorates. However, they are permitted to deviate from this equality if special geographic considerations (for example, the size, shape, and accessibility of a constituency) appear to render such a deviation desirable. Other rules further complicate the position. The commissioners are enjoined not to cross local authority boundaries in creating parliamentary constituencies. As a result, the number of electors can and does differ between constituencies and also between countries. The electoral quota (the national electorate divided by the number of seats) is greater in England, for example, than in the sparsely populated Wales.

The frequency of reviews has varied. Under legislation passed in 1992, there must now be a review every eight to twelve years (previously it was every ten to fifteen years) though a commission may issue an interim report. Before making their recommendations, the commissioners consider submissions from interested bodies, primarily the local political parties. If a proposed change has the support of the local parties, it is usual for the commissioners to accept it. Once they have completed their work, their recommendations are presented to a government minister, the home secretary, who is then required to lay them before the House of Commons for approval. The recommendations can prove controversial. Boundary reviews in 1948 and 1955 were the subject of protests, and in 1969 the Labour home secretary advised his supporters in the House to vote against the commission's recommendations, which they did. As a result, the 1970 general election was fought on the basis of the old boundaries. The commission's recommendations were implemented in the new Parliament. The next review by the commission was completed in 1982 and challenged unsuccessfully in the courts by the Labour party. The most recent review was completed for Scotland prior to the 2005 general election and took effect in that election; the reviews for Wales, England, and Northern Ireland were completed after 2005 and will take effect at the next general election.

Between reviews, there is also considerable movement of population: About three-quarters of a million people move each year. Given the period between reviews, disparities in constituency size can become marked. For example, before the boundary revisions made in 1983, 39 percent of seats deviated from the electoral quota by + or – 20 percent. Even after the revisions, 5 percent of the seats still deviated from the quota by the same margin. At the 2005 general election, two constituencies each had more than 100,000 electors (Falkirk with 110,833 and the Isle of Wight with 107,737). At the other end of the scale, the constituency of Na H-Eileanan An Iar (the Western Isles) had an electorate of 21,169 and the constituency of Orkney and Shetland one of 32,639. The Welsh constituency of Meirionnydd Nant Conwy had 33,472 electors.

Campaigns

An election campaign extends formally over a period of three to four weeks, though if a Parliament goes beyond four years in duration there is a tendency for parties to start campaigning de facto in anticipation of an election being called. Both the 1992 and 1997 elections took place at the end of Parliaments that had lasted five years and both were preceded by what were, in effect, lengthy campaigns by the main parties. However, the formal campaign gets under way only after Parliament has been dissolved and candidates formally nominated. For U.S. politicians, there are essentially four stages in an election campaign: profile raising, fund-raising, the primary campaign, and the general election. For British politicians, only the first and the last stages apply. Incumbents and challengers in Britain do not have to contest primary campaigns, and fund-raising is the task of the party organizations. Activity in the constituency—and, for the incumbent, in the House of Commons—is important for gaining visibility with electors. However, only in the event of a formal election campaign are the resources of the local party mobilized on an extensive scale.

In British elections, unlike those in the United States, the personalities of candidates (except for national leaders) and their personal wealth play only a marginal role. There is some evidence that incumbency can make some difference, affecting the outcome in tight contests,[6] but the impact of the candidate is usually overwhelmed by the impact of party. The campaign is fought in practice on a national level between the two main parties, the candidates and the local campaigns serving to reinforce the national campaigns of their leaders. Candidates are selected locally by the parties, and the parties provide the finance and the organization for the campaign.

Election expenses in each constituency are limited by statute and have been since 1883. Expenditure is permitted only where authorized by the candidate, the candidate's election agent, or a person authorized in writing by the agent. The maximum permitted expenditure is calculated on the basis of a fixed sum plus a limited amount based on the number of electors. In 2005 the limit was £7,150 ($11,726) plus 7p pence per voter in each county (predominantly rural) constituency and £7,150 ($11,726) plus 5p per voter in borough (urban, and smaller in area) constituencies. Certain types of expenditure are illegal, such as paying an elector to exhibit a poster or paying for voters to be taken to and from the polling booths. Other bodies, such as interest groups, may also engage in the campaign, up to a limit of £500 ($820) each.

Even with the modest expenditure that is permitted, most candidates fail to spend the maximum allowed.[7] Some devices for keeping costs low are employed and these can, where required, provide up to an extra 20 percent of expenditure:[8] A popular ploy is to purchase stationery in advance and then resell it cheaply to the candidate as secondhand stock. In 1997, telephone canvassing was variously employed "although its costs seldom appeared in expense returns."[9] Few candidates, though, are prepared to run too many risks for fear of having their elections challenged and declared void: Expenses have to be declared and opponents keep a wary eye open for any infringements of election law. There is, in any event, a major practical constraint: The parties have difficulty raising sufficient money to fight campaigns.

Each candidate is permitted one postage-free mailing of one piece of election literature. Other literature is distributed, door-to-door or in the street, by unpaid party activists. The main item of literature is the candidate's election address. This will usually incorporate a summary of the main points of the party's national election manifesto. After the 2005 election, 89 percent of respondents in a MORI poll remembered getting leaflets delivered through the door.[10] Candidates have traditionally spent a good part of their time making speeches throughout the constituency, not infrequently at thinly attended meetings, and canvassing door to door where possible. Attendance at meetings is nowadays so thin that candidates organize few if any meetings, preferring in some cases to attend meetings for all candidates organized by local bodies, such as churches, and to get out on the streets canvassing. The candidate will be aided by volunteers who help in the campaign office—much use being made nowadays of computer-generated literature—and who canvas door-to-door to try to determine where supporters live. On polling day they will keep a running tab on who has voted in order to ensure that support is maximized. Since 1997, there has been something of a shift, with leafleting and door-to-door campaigning being supplemented by telephone canvassing, especially in key seats and with the campaigning being more directly organized by the national party headquarters.[11] The 2001 election was also seen as the first "Internet election," with the parties making use of websites to promote their campaigns, though the effect has been limited.[12] The 2005 campaign saw a greater use of websites by individual candidates—about 1,300 candidates (37 percent of the total) had them—but they received few visits by electors during the campaign. Electors seeking election information online were more likely to visit the BBC website. "As for the party campaigns online, only around 3 per cent of people with access had visited a party website and 1 per cent had visited candidate suites during the election."[13] Conservative candidates were most prominent in employing websites. The party also borrowed from the successful George Bush campaign in the United States by employing Voter Vault database software, which focused on individual-level, rather than ward, targeting.

The main focus of the campaign is national. The party leaders make regular and well-publicized appearances throughout the country, ensuring that the national press and television reporters follow in their wake, as well as hold daily press conferences. The press conferences are usually held early in the morning in an attempt to set the day's political agenda. The national party organizations also increasingly make use of press advertising. It used to be the case, up to the 2001 election, that as long as expenditure could not be said to apply in support of specific candidates, national party campaigns did not fall foul of the election finance restrictions. Under legislation enacted in 2000, there is now a limit on how much each party may spend. During the 2005 election campaign, the Conservative, Labour, and Liberal Democratic parties spent £40 million ($65.6 million) centrally. The combined Conservative and Labour expenditure accounted for just over 80 percent of all party expenditure. The Labour party spent £17.9 million ($29.4m), the Conservatives £17.8 million ($29.2m), and the Liberal Democrats £4.3 million ($7.1m).[14] The largest single item of expenditure was advertising. The parties also enjoyed the benefit of free but limited television time. Paid political advertising on television is not allowed: Each party is allocated a set number of party election broadcasts that are transmitted on all television channels. These broadcasts, though short (no more than 5 minutes in duration), "lack credibility and quickly lose viewers,"[15] the parties relying instead on television news coverage to try to shape the agenda and get their message over to viewers. In television coverage, the party leaders tend to attract the lion's share of attention.

The basis of the parties' appeal to the country is the election manifestos that they issue. In recent elections these have become increasingly lengthy and specific documents, detailing the intended policies and measures to be pursued by a party if returned to office. They constitute a topic of some controversy. It has been argued that very few electors actually read them. Though available for sale at bookshops, the manifesto of a party will be purchased by fewer than 1 in every 200 voters.[16] Though now available online, few electors—as we have seen—visit the party websites. It has also been argued that in voting for a party not all voters will be endorsing the policies put forward in the manifesto.[17] They also are viewed as hostages for the future, parties in office being open to attack when promises are not fulfilled, even if conditions no longer make the proposal viable. In practice, they constitute something of a guide to interested bodies and provide a framework for the main items of legislation introduced by an incoming government in the first session or two of a new Parliament: Most manifesto promises are usually implemented.[18] A more relevant criticism is that manifesto promises may not address themselves to the country's real problems. Some would argue that, by virtue of the manner of their compilation and their utilization as a means furthering the adversary relationship between the parties, manifestos add to those problems rather than offering solutions.[19]

Candidates

Any citizen aged 18 years or over is eligible to be a candidate for election to the House of Commons. There are certain limited exceptions. Precluded from serving in the House of Commons are those who are disqualified from voting, as well as policemen, civil servants, judges, members of certain public bodies, undischarged bankrupts, members of the armed services, and certain holders of other offices. Clergy also used to be barred but the prohibition was lifted in 2001. To be a candidate one has to obtain the signature of ten electors in the constituency and—a practice unknown in the United States—submit a deposit of £500 ($820), returnable in the event of receiving 5 percent of the votes cast. (From 1918 to 1985 the deposit was £150 ($246), returnable in the event of receiving one-eighth of the votes cast.) Unlike in the United States, there are no residence requirements: Hence, parties enjoy a wider range of choice in the selection of candidates.

In practice, candidates are party candidates. Since 1969, candidates have been able to include their party designation on the ballot paper. Parties themselves are now legally recognized and have to be registered for the purpose of promoting candidates. In some recent general elections there have been examples of locally popular candidates holding their marginal seats against the national swing (even in some instances increasing their majorities). As we have noted, some research has suggested that the "personal vote" achieved by candidates may be higher than was previously assumed. However, party remains the primary and almost exclusive influence on voting behavior. Since 1950, only five MPs have been elected in Britain (excluding Northern Ireland) without the support of a major party, and four of these were incumbent party members who had broken with their parties. In 1997, one Independent candidate, Martin Bell, was elected, but he was fighting a seat in which both the Labour and Liberal Democratic candidates had stood down in his favor. The only Independent to be elected against opposition from Labour and Conservative candidates was Dr Richard Taylor (standing under the banner of Independent Kidderminster Hospital and Health Concern, to save a local hospital) who was elected for Wyre Forest in 2001 and re-elected in 2005.

All constituencies in Great Britain are contested usually by Conservative and Labour candidates (the exception in 1997 was the seat in which Martin Bell was elected, where the contest was between Bell and the incumbent Conservative) as well nowadays as by Liberal Democrats. In English seats, candidates from these three main parties will usually occupy the top three places. In the other parts of the United Kingdom, the picture is more complicated.

In Scotland, the Scottish National Party (SNP) is a significant electoral force. Its parliamentary representation has fluctuated. In October 1974 it won 11 seats, but only 2 in the following Parliament. In 1997, it won 6 of the 72 seats in Scotland. However, it has established itself as the main challenger to the Labour party, which is the dominant party in Scotland. In 1997, the SNP won 22 percent of the votes cast in Scotland, ahead of both the Conservatives and the Liberal Democrats. In 1999, it consolidated its position as the second largest party, winning 35 seats in the new 129-member Scottish parliament, against 56 won by Labour. The same year it also won two seats in the European Parliament; it maintained both in 2004. In the 2001 general election it won five seats and increased the number to six in 2005. More significantly, it emerged as the largest single party in the elections to the Scottish Parliament in 2007, winning 47 seats, one more than Labour (Chapter 10).

In Wales, the nationalist party is Plaid Cymru (the Party of Wales) which, between 1974 and 1997, has won between two and four seats in the province. In 1997, it held 4 of the 40 seats in Wales, against 34 won by Labour. In the elections to the new Welsh assembly in 1999, the party won 17 seats, a number in excess of the combined total won by the Conservatives and the Liberal Democrats. It won two seats in the European Parliament, though lost one in 2004. In 2007, it won 15 seats in the Welsh Assembly—Labour won 26—and formed a coalition government with Labour (Chapter 10).

In Northern Ireland, the principal parties are specific to the province, comprising two main Unionist parties (the Ulster Unionists and the Democratic Unionists) and two nationalist parties (the Social Democratic and Labour Party and Sinn Fein, the latter being the political wing of the Provisional IRA). There is also a nonsectarian Alliance party. The Ulster Unionist (UU) party used to be the dominant unionist party, but was displaced—both in Westminster and the Northern Ireland Assembly—in the first decade of the new century by the Democratic Unionist Party (DUP) under its longstanding leader Ian Paisley. In the 2005 general election, the DUP won 9 of the 18 seats in the province; the UUs won one. In the 2007 elections to the 108-seat Northern Ireland Assembly, the DUP won 36 seats and the UUs 17. In the 2005 general election, Sinn Fein won five seats and the SDLP won three. In the 2007 Assembly elections, Sinn Fein won 28 seats and the SDLP 16. The Alliance party won seven seats. As we shall see (Chapter 10), a power-sharing executive in the province was created from four parties in 2007. Traditionally, the main British parties have steered clear of campaigning in the province. The UUs used to be part of the Conservative party but severed their links following the introduction of direct rule in the province in 1972. More recently, the Conservative party has sought to organize in the province, but it has had little appreciable impact. In 2008 it sought to renew its links with the UU party.

The election of candidates representing regionally based parties has meant that there are ten parties, plus the Independent MP Dr Richard Taylor, represented in the House of Commons. Of the three main parties, the Labour party is strongest in northern England, Scotland, and Wales. The Conservative party is strongest in southern England; in recent elections it has struggled to gain any seats in Scotland (it had none in 1997 and only one in 2001 and 2005). The Liberal Democrat party traditionally is strongest in what is known as the "Celtic fringe" of southwest England, Scotland, and Wales, though it has also picked up some seats in the south of England at the expense of the Conservatives and some urban seats at the expense of Labour.

Other parties also ostensibly are keen to be represented in the House of Commons. Recent decades have seen a growth in the number of candidates contesting seats. The 1951 general election was fought by 1,376 candidates, that of 1983 by 2,579, an average of four per seat. It was in order to deter supposedly frivolous candidates that the deposit for candidature was raised to £500 in 1985, but the deterrent effect was short-lived and modest. In 1987, the number of candidates was not much fewer than in 1983: a total of 2,325. In 1997 it reached a record 3,724 candidates (5.6 candidates per constituency). In 2001 the number was 3,319 and in 2005 3,554. The large number is the result principally of fringe candidates supplemented by candidates from well-organized minor parties. In the 2005 election, 119 parties fielded candidates. Six of these fielded 50 or more candidates. The United Kingdom Independence party (UKIP), favoring the United Kingdom's withdrawal from the European Union, fielded 496 candidates. The environmentalist Green Party put up 183 candidates. The British National Party (BNP), a far-right nationalist party, fielded a total of 118 candidates; Veritas, a break-away party from UKIP, led by a former television presenter, put up 65 candidates; and the Socialist Labour party had 50. The colorful Monster Raving Loony Party, renowned for having candidates with bizarre names and costumes, fielded 19 candidates. None won any seats. UKIP was the only party to achieve more than 1 percent of the vote nationally: It won 2.3 percent of the vote; the Green party won 1 percent. The experience of the fringe candidates in the seats shown in Table 5.3 is typical of how they fared.

TABLE 5.3

SELECTED CONSTITUENCY RESULTS, 2005

Watford

Electorate: 76,034

C. Ward (Labour)	16,575	(33.5%)
S. Brinton (Liberal Democrat)	15,427	(31.2%)
A. Miraj (Conservative)	14,634	(29.5%)
S. Rackett (Green)	1,466	(3.0%)
K. Wright (UKIP)	1,292	(2.6%)
LABOUR MAJORITY	1,148	(2.32%)

Total vote: 49,532

Turnout: 65.14%

A seat in Hertfordshire, north of London; A conservative-held seat prior to 1997.

Ceredigion

Electorate: 53,776

M. Williams (Liberal Democrat)	13,130	(36.5%)
S. Thomas (PC)	12,911	(35.9%)
J. Harrison (Conservative)	4,455	(12.4%)
A. Davies (Labour)	4,337	(12.0%)
D. Bradney (Green)	846	(2.4%)
I. Sheldon (Veritas)	268	(0.7%)
LIBERAL DEMOCRAT MAJORITY	219	(0.61%)

Total vote: 36,016

Turnout: 66.97

A Welsh seat, previously held by Plaid Cymru. This was one of the seats gained by the Liberal Democrats in 2005.

Rhondda

Electorate: 50,461

C. Bryant (Labour)	21,198	(67.8%)
L. Jones (PC)	4,956	(15.9%)
K. Roberts (Liberal Democrat)	3,264	(10.4%)
P. Stuart-Smith (Con)	1,730	(5.5%)
LABOUR MAJORITY	16,242	(51.94%)

Total vote: 31,270

Turnout: 61.96

A safe Labour seat in the mining valleys of Wales.

Richmond (Yorkshire)

Electorate: 69,367

W. Hague (Conservative)	26,722	(58.9%)
N. Foster (Lab)	8,915	(19.7%)

(continued)

TABLE 5.3 (continued)		
J. Bell (Liberal Democrat)	7,982	(17.6%)
L. Rowe (Green)	1,581	(3.5%)
CONSERVATIVE MAJORITY	17,807	(39.26%)
Total vote: 45,359		
Turnout: 65.39%		
A safe Conservative seat in rural North Yorkshire, held by William Hague, Leader of the Conservative Party from 1997 to 2001.		

Candidate Selection

Candidate selection is undertaken locally, though with the national party organizations exercising some degree of control. In Britain, unlike in the United States, there are no primary elections and the selection of a candidate is in practice determined by the party activists. Where a seat is a "safe" seat for a party, this selection is usually tantamount to election.

In the Conservative party, aspiring candidates have to be on the party's Approved List of Parliamentary Candidates maintained by the party's national headquarters. (Local parties may choose someone not on the list, but the candidate then has to be approved by the party nationally.) Achieving a place on the list was previously done through an interview with the party vice-chairman and the national committee responsible for candidates. In recent years, the procedure has been extended and more professional methods of selection employed. The first step is an interview with a regional director. If that proves successful, the aspiring candidate then completes an application form and, following inquiries based on the application, is interviewed by a Parliamentary Assessment Board: This comprises a day-long course where the suitability of the candidate is addressed.[20] If the applicant passes the Board, and not all do, he or she then goes on the Approved List and can start applying when constituency vacancies arise. David Cameron as party leader also introduced a priority list (an "A-list") of candidates—candidates that the party was especially keen to get adopted, including female candidates and from ethnic backgrounds: The list proved controversial but nonetheless had some effect in broadening the backgrounds from which Conservative candidates were drawn. More Asian and women candidates were adopted: The media highlighted the adoption of a high-flying lesbian businesswoman for a winnable seat.

A local Conservative association seeking a candidate will invite applicants and will be sent the names of those on the Approved List wishing to be considered for the seat. The association will appoint a selection committee, usually comprising the association officers and representatives from its different branches and associated groups, to draw up a short list and then recommend three or more names to the executive council, the main decision-making body of the association. The council may then recommend one name for approval to a general meeting of the association or it may put forward more than one name and leave it to the general meeting to decide. In recent years, some local parties have adopted primaries or open meetings to select a candidate: not only have party members been invited but also in some cases non-party members.

Traditionally, Conservative selection committees have been less concerned with the political views of applicants than have Labour committees.[21] The Parliamentary Assessment Board looks at such things as the ability to relate to people, campaigning and communication skills, resilience and drive, intellect, and conviction. Selection committees have tended to be influenced by an applicant's knowledge of the constituency, and whether or not he or she has the makings of a good constituency member or, in some cases, a national figure. (On occasion, more esoteric considerations may apply.)[22] Other influences can include, in some areas, religion and quite often age and sex. Local parties have historically tended to adopt white, male middle-class professionals. The party has made some inroads in broadening the base of candidates. In 2005, the party achieved the election of a black and an Asian MP; a leading MP who had come out as gay also achieved re-election.

It is rare for local Conservative parties to oust sitting MPs—they are normally automatically re-adopted as candidates. Occasionally, an MP has been quietly persuaded—sometimes not so quietly—to stand down because of some personal problem (drink or divorce), though rarely on policy grounds. In 2009, a number were told or persuaded to announce they would not seek re-election in the light of a scandal about expenses claimed by MPs (see Chapter 12). They included a long-serving MP who had tried to claim on expenses the cost of a duck-house for his pond and another who claimed for cleaning out his moat.

Although the Labour candidates selected are increasingly similar in background to Conservative candidates, the selection procedure in the Labour party differs from that of the Conservatives. It also has undergone a number of recent changes. A local Labour party will seek a candidate by inviting nominations. Nominations may be made by local ward committees, party groups such as the women's section, and affiliated organizations, principally trade unions. (An aspiring candidate can approach such groups to solicit a nomination.) Once nominations are received, the executive committee, responsible for the day-to-day running of the party, will draw up a short list. Until 1989, the selection was made by the General Management Committee, comprising representatives from the different ward committees and affiliated organizations. From 1989 until 1993, the selection was made by an electoral college in which at least 60 percent of the votes were allocated to local party members and up to 40 percent to affiliated organizations. In 1993 the party conference voted to approve selection on the basis of one member, one vote (OMOV). The conference also voted to introduce all-women shortlists in 50 percent of the most winnable seats and 50 percent of those where Labour MPs were retiring. This policy was in place until 1996, when an industrial tribunal held it to be unlawful. The policy nonetheless resulted in a record number of women being selected as women candidates.

The successful candidate has to be endorsed by the party's National Executive Committee (NEC). The NEC has also acquired more direct powers to influence outcomes in certain cases. It now has the power to determine the shortlist for candidates in by-elections (a power acquired following some highly controversial choices as candidates by local parties) and in seats where the incumbents retire after an election has been called. Some MPs have delayed announcing their retirement until after an election has been called so that the NEC can select candidates supported by the party leadership, usually people seen as future ministerial material. On occasion, the NEC has also used its power to refuse endorsement to candidates and to block attempts by local parties to replace incumbent MPs.

Candidate selection was a controversial issue in the 1980s, leftwing activists persuading the party conference in 1981 to change the party rules in order to make it easier for local activists to oust sitting Labour MPs. By 1986, a total of 14 MPs had been deselected. The changes in the method of local selection from 1989 onward were designed to limit the influence of leftwing activists. In the 1987–92 Parliament, only two Labour MPs were deselected, and in the 1992–97 Parliament, only one. In 1998, the party NEC approved changes that provide for automatic reselection of sitting MPs, unless opponents can trigger and win a ballot requiring a reselection contest. It also approved the introduction of an approved candidates' list, similar to the practice of the Conservatives. In addition, it agreed that local parties should in future be sent reports on their MPs' parliamentary performance. According to party leaders, this was in order that local parties could decide if any action should be taken against MPs who were not applying themselves to their parliamentary duties. In the eyes of leftwing Labour MPs, it was a means of using local parties to discipline them if their voting records revealed they were disloyal to the leadership. As on the Conservative side, the scandal in 2009 regarding MPs' expenses led to a number of Labour MPs announcing they would not seek re-election, including two who faced possible criminal charges.

The principle of local selection is also a feature of the other national parties in Britain with parliamentary representation. In the Liberal Democrat party, for example, the executive of the local party (or a sub-committee) draws up a shortlist and the candidate is picked following hustings: All party members in the constituency have the right to vote. However, there is a difference in that whereas Conservative and Labour local parties usually have to choose from many eager applicants, other parties often have difficulty in recruiting candidates. This is reflected in the wording of the Liberal Democrat constitution. It provides that "subject to there being a sufficient number of applicants of each sex," short lists of two to four must include at least one member of each sex and short lists of five or more must include at least two members of each sex.[23]

It is not just the Conservative Party that has tended to adopt candidates who are middle class, middle aged, male, and white: It has been a feature of all the main parties. Female and nonwhite candidates are exceptional, but not as exceptional as they used to be. In the 1997 election, a record number of women were elected to the House of Commons—120 (18 percent of the House), double the number elected in 1992. The number fell to 118 in 2001 but reached 127 (19 percent of MPs) in 2005. The 1997 election also saw the election of nine black and Asian MPs, compared with six in 1992, four in 1987, and none before 1987. In 2001 the number increased to 12: In 2005 it was 15 (2.3 percent of the membership).

The successful candidates more than the unsuccessful ones tend to be middle-aged, university educated (and, in the case of Conservative MPs, products of public schools), and drawn from business and the professions (see Chapter 12). In postwar years, there has been a tendency for MPs to be even more middle class than previously.[24] Recent decades also have seen the emergence of more career-oriented MPs, devoted to politics and a lifetime of service in the House of Commons.[25]

Elections

In each of the 646 single-member constituencies, the method of election employed is the plurality or "first-past-the-post" method, with the candidate who wins the largest single number of votes—even though it may not be an absolute majority—being declared the winner. It is the same method as that employed in the Senate and House elections in the United States. However, most contests in the United States are straight fights between Democrats and Republican candidates, thus producing a victor with more than 50 percent of the votes cast. In the United Kingdom, three- or four-way fight are now common and can result in the winning candidate achieving way below 50 percent of the vote. Indeed, in hotly contested four-way fights it is actually possible to win with less than 30 percent of the vote, as happened in the constituency of Inverness, Nairn, and Lochabar in the 1992 election, when the victorious candidate won with 26.7 percent of the vote. The result in the constituency was exceptional, though not unique. In the 2005 general election, the SDLP candidate won the seat of Belfast South with 32.1 percent of the vote. In the Watford constituency (Table 5.3), there was a close three-way contest, the Labour candidate winning with 33.5 percent of the vote. The Welsh seat of Ceredigion (Table 5.3) illustrates a two-way contest, with other candidates amassing more than a quarter of the vote, the Liberal Democrat candidate winning the seat with 36.5 percent of the vote.

Most seats are usually considered safe seats for one or the other of the two main parties, that is, the winning candidate has achieved a margin that constitutes 10 percent or more of the total poll. The election battle takes place, in effect, in the minority of seats that are considered "marginals." In the 1980s and early 1990s, more than 70 percent of seats fell in the category of safe seats. Some were deemed to be very safe. The effect of the 1997 election (Table 5.2), in which the Conservatives lost more than half the seats they were defending—including a great many "safe" seats—was to change perceptions of safe and marginal seats. In 2008 and 2009, with the Labour party trailing significantly behind the Conservatives in the opinion polls, there was the prospect of the next general election producing a 1997-effect in reverse.

The electoral system, as we shall see, has facilitated the return of governments enjoying an overall majority of seats in the House of Commons. In all but one of the general elections since (and including) 1945, one party has won an absolute majority of seats. The Labour party has achieved an overall majority in eight elections, on three occasions by slim margins (in 1950, 1964, and October 1974). The party also formed the government following the February 1974 election, in which it won more seats than any other party but did not obtain an overall majority (see Table 5.4). Its best result was in 1997, winning 418 seats in the then 659-member House. Conservatives have won overall majorities by clear margins in eight elections since 1945, four of them consecutively in the period after 1979.

TABLE 5.4

PARLIAMENTARY MAJORITIES, 1945–2005

Parliament	Party returned to office	Overall majority*
1945–50	Labour	146
1950–51	Labour	5
1951–55	Conservative	17
1955–59	Conservative	60
1959–64	Conservative	100
1964–66	Labour	4
1966–70	Labour	98
1970–74	Conservative	30
1974	Labour	−33
1974–79	Labour	3
1979–83	Conservative	43
1983–87	Conservative	144
1987–92	Conservative	101
1992–97	Conservative	21
1997–2001	Labour	179
2001–05	Labour	167
2005–	Labour	66

*Overall majority following general election. The speaker, where seeking reelection, is included in the original party. A negative number indicates that a minority government was returned to office.

VOTING BEHAVIOR

Recent decades have seen some significant shifts in the nature and pattern of electoral support for British political parties. In the quarter century after the Second World War, Britain displayed the characteristics of a stable two-party system.[26] During that period:

1. There was a high turnout of electors.
2. Of those who voted, virtually all voted for either the Conservative or the Labour party.
3. The most significant predictor of party voting was class.
4. The class base of voting produced stable blocks of voting support, with changes in government being determined by small shifts of voting support from one party to another.

The first two generalizations are borne out by the data in Table 5.2. In every general election held from 1950 to 1966 inclusively, more than three-quarters of those on the electoral register turned out to vote and, of those who did so, 87 percent or more voted for either the Conservative or Labour candidates. In the 1950 election, turnout reached 84 percent. In the election of the following year, almost 97 percent of those who voted cast their ballots for one of the two main parties.

The third generalization is drawn from survey data, which demonstrate the close relationship of class and party in this period. In the general elections held in the 1950s, 70 percent or more of middle-class voters cast their votes for the Conservative party. In the 1960s, 60 percent or more of working-class voters cast their votes for the Labour party.[27] Party support was most marked at the two extremes of the social scale. In 1951, 90 percent of the upper-middle class voted Conservative. In 1966, 72 percent of the "very poor" voted Labour.[28] Class was not an exclusive predictor of voting behavior, nor was the relationship between class and party symmetrical: The middle class was more Conservative than the working class was Labour. One-third of working-class voters regularly voted Conservative. Nonetheless, class remained the most important predictor of how an elector might vote—so much so that one writer, Peter Pulzer, was to declare in 1967 that "class is the basis of British party politics: all else is embellishment and detail."[29]

The class basis of electoral behavior provided each party with a substantial base of support. Small shifts in support could turn one party out of government at an election and replace it with another, but the period of the 1950s in particular did not witness major shifts in voting intentions between elections. This was reflected in by-election results. In the period from 1945 to 1959, there were 168 by-elections: Only ten of them resulted in losses by the incumbent party. Stability seemed a feature of the two-party system.

The period since the end of the 1960s has produced a very different picture. Turnout since 1966 has been more variable and, in recent elections, notably low. In the four general elections held from 1950 to 1959, the average turnout was just over 80 percent. In the nine elections from 1964 to *voter turnout = y = decline in class-party*

1992, the average was just over 75 percent, almost 5 percent lower. In the three elections of 1997, 2001, and 2005, the average has been 64.1 percent (Table 5.5). In the period from 1964 to 1992, the percentage casting ballots for either Conservative or Labour candidates averaged 79.6 percent. In the three elections since 1997 it has averaged 71.3 percent. The general elections of 2001 and 2005 have marked the low point in terms of the combination of turnout and two-party support.

The explanation for this change generally has been ascribed to a decline in the class-party nexus. The two main parties can no longer rely on their "natural" class support. The relative decline in this support is borne out by survey data from recent general elections (Tables 5.6 and 5.7). The figures in Table 5.6 show the extent to which Labour could not rely on its traditional class support in the 1992 election—not even mustering the support of a majority of working-class voters—and the failure of the Conservatives to hold on to their traditional middle-class support in 1997. The figures for the two elections reveal the remarkable volatility in voting behavior. Labour made remarkable gains in 1997 but the improvement took place across all social classes.[30] Although social class continues to structure party choice, it is no longer the predictor of party choice that it once was.

TABLE 5.5

TURNOUT AND TWO-PARTY VOTING, 1945–2005

General election	Percentage turnout	Of those voting, percentage Voting Con. or Lab.
1945	72.7	87.6
1950	84.0	89.6
1951	82.5	96.8
1955	76.7	96.1
1959	78.7	93.2
1964	77.1	87.5
1966	75.8	89.8
1970	72.0	89.4
1974 (Feb.)	78.7	75.0
1974 (Oct.)	72.8	75.0
1979	76.0	80.8
1983	72.7	70.0
1987	75.3	73.0
1992	77.7	76.3
1997	71.5	73.9
2001	59.4	72.4
2005	61.4	67.6

TABLE 5.6

VOTE BY SOCIAL CLASS, 1997

Party	Professional and managerial (AB) %	Office and clerical (C1) %	Skilled manual (C2) %	Semiskilled, unskilled, residual (DE) %
Conservative	42 (57)*	26 (41)	25 (38)	21 (37)
Labour	31 (20)	47 (33)	54 (41)	61 (47)
Liberal Democrat	21 (21)	19 (14)	14 (18)	13 (15)

*1992 percentages in parentheses.
Source: NOP/BBC exit polls; J. Curtice, "Anatomy of a Landslide," Politics Review, 7 (1), 1997.

Also of declining significance have been the variables of gender, age, and religion. Traditionally, women have been somewhat more likely to vote Conservative than men. In most postwar elections, more men have voted Labour than have voted Conservative, whereas more women have voted Conservative than voted Labour. However, the bias was a slight one. According to Gallup, the bias disappeared in 1983 and according to MORI it disappeared in 1987. There was a slight bias in 1992 but again it disappeared in 1997 and 2001. In 2005, the bias was in favor of Labour, with more women (38 percent) than men (34 percent) voting Labour.[31]

Age also shows some variation, but again, as a predictor of voting behavior, is of limited utility. The older the voter, the greater the likelihood of voting Conservative (Table 5.8). As is apparent from the data in Table 5.8, there is no distinctive pattern of support among the different age groups. Labour gained more support from younger voters than older voters in 2001 but did

TABLE 5.7

VOTE BY SOCIAL CLASS, 2005

Party	Professional and managerial (AB) %	Office and clerical (C1) %	Skilled manual (C2) %	Semiskilled, unskilled, residual (DE) %
Conservative	37 (39)*	37 (36)	33 (29)	25 (24)
Labour	28 (30)	32 (38)	40 (49)	48 (55)
Liberal Democrat	29 (25)	23 (20)	19 (15)	18 (13)

* 2001 percentages in parentheses.
Source: MORI, A. King, "Why Labour Won—Yet Again," in J. Bartle and A. King (eds.), Britain at the Polls 2005 (CQ Press, 2006), p. 176.

TABLE 5.8

Party Support by Age, 2005

	Age					
	18–24 %	25–34 %	35–44 %	45–54 %	55–64 %	65+ %
Cons	28 (27)*	25 (24)	27 (28)	31 (32)	39 (39)	41 (40)
Lab	38 (41)	38 (51)	41 (45)	35 (41)	31 (37)	35 (39)
LibDem	26 (24)	27 (19)	23 (19)	25 (20)	22 (17)	18 (17)

* 2001 percentages in parentheses.

Source: MORI, A. King, "Why Labour Won—Yet Again," in J. Bartle and A. King (eds.), *Britain at the Polls 2005* (CQ Press, 2006), p. 176.

less well among the 25–34 age range in 2005. It is possible that this reflects a generational cohort change; Butler and Stokes found in their survey that it is not age as such that influences voting behavior but rather the period at which one becomes politically aware. Once one has built up a pattern of voting for a particular party, one is not likely to change.

Religion, once an important variable in explaining voting behavior, is no longer the force it was. It was a significant influence in the nineteenth century, but declined rapidly in the twentieth as class became more important. Butler and Stokes found the relationship between religion and party of declining relevance with each generation. In some areas where religious loyalties remain strong, such loyalties can still alter the pattern of class voting. An obvious example is Northern Ireland (see Chapter 10), though mainland examples can be found in certain cities, notably Glasgow and Liverpool. In such cities, there is a sizable Irish Catholic vote, and that swells the Labour vote in elections.[32] Liberal Democrats also tend to maintain support in areas of traditional strength of nonconformist religions. Overall, though, the impact of religion is marginal and that marginality is reflected in the fact that it no longer figures in analyses of general elections.

Class, then, is of declining relevance as a predictor of voting behavior, and it has not been displaced by the other variables we have identified. The waning of the class-party nexus would appear to explain a greater volatility in voting intentions. Though the Conservative party won four consecutive general elections from 1979 onward, each time with roughly the same share of the national poll, this did not reflect a stability in support among the electorate. Opinion polls showed some marked swings in opinion in between elections and the Conservative party had difficulty winning seats in by-elections: Indeed, during the prime ministership of John Major (1990–97), the party failed to hold on to any of the seats it was defending in by-elections. In late 1992 the party suffered a major loss of support in the polls and in 1997 suffered its worst defeat of the century. The extent of the massive swing of support from the Conservatives to Labour is apparent from the preceding tables. The extent of change is apparent if one compares the results of the general election of 1983 with those of 1997 (Table 5.2).

Electoral behavior has thus changed significantly. The class-party nexus has waned, though not disappeared. Both main parties have substantial bodies of committed supporters, but not to the same extent as before. Voters do not identify with parties to the same degree as in earlier decades.[33] The Conservative and Labour parties still dominate in the parliamentary arena, but in combination no longer enjoy the monopoly they once enjoyed.

Explanations of Voting Behavior

Is it possible, then, to provide any clear explanation of contemporary voting behavior? The analysis of electoral behavior has been a significant feature of British political science in recent years. Several, often competing, models of electoral behavior have been constructed. The class-based model held sway in postwar decades but has declined in significance since.

The different explanations can be grouped under two headings. There are those explanations that derive from the voter as part of a wider and usually enduring body, and those that derive from the voter exercising individual choice. The former encompasses class, consumption, and location and can help explain consistent patterns of party support. The latter encompass issues and performance evaluation and can help explain volatility in voting behavior.

CLASS   The class-party nexus, as we have seen, declined in the 1970s and 1980s. Class became a less useful predictor of voting behavior, apparently because of changing social patterns—rendering class itself less relevant—and because of class dealignment, or those within a class being less likely to vote for their "natural" class party. Class, nonetheless, has not ceased to be relevant. As can be seen from Tables 5.6 and 5.7, those at the top end of the social scale are more likely to vote Conservative than Labour. Those at the other end are more likely to vote Labour than Conservative. However, the figures in the tables also show now the limitations of trying to predict voting on the basis of class. In 1992, Labour received less than 50 percent of the votes of those in social classes DE. In 1997, the Conservatives failed to carry an absolute majority of those in classes AB. Among white-collar workers, the Conservatives had an 8 percent advantage in 1992. In 1997, that had switched to a 21 percent advantage to Labour. In the 2005 election, the Conservatives managed to make inroads into the C1 and C2 voters, compared with 1997, but did not increase notably their support in their traditional stronghold of AB voters.

As the class-party nexus appeared to decline, some students of electoral behavior sought to demonstrate that class remained of greater utility than critics claimed. They did so through a redefinition of class. Instead of relying on the occupation of the heads of households, they utilized more sophisticated criteria. Heath, Curtice, and Jowell, for example, took into account authority at work and those who were self-employed.[34] The problem with these new variables was that those with the greatest predictive value covered but a small proportion of the population. In the analysis of Heath and his associates, only about one in three voters were in categories where as many as half of the voters supported one party.[35] The explanatory value of this approach was thus extremely limited.

Another analysis suggested the continuing relevance of class polarization, but only in a particular part of the country. Political geographers Johnston and Pattie argued that class divisions had persisted in the north of England but declined substantially in the south.[36] Thus, even on the basis of more recent analyses that seek to utilize the concept, class has some continuing relevance, but not to the same extent as before. It is necessary to identify other influences that have become more salient. That is emphasized especially by the findings from the most recent general elections.

CONSUMPTION   One of the more controversial theses was that first advanced in 1979 by Patrick Dunleavy.[37] He contended that not only has there been a class dealignment but also that there has been a realignment: The cleavage based on production has been replaced by one based on consumption. In other words, class voting—derived from one's stance in relation to the means of production—has been replaced by voting based on public and private consumption. Those who rely on services provided by the state (housing, education, health, transport) are most likely to vote Labour; those who rely on services provided by the private sector are most likely to vote Conservative. The greater the degree of private-sector consumption, the greater the likelihood of voting Conservative. Thus, home-owning households with two cars were 4.39 times more likely to vote Conservative than those with no car who rent their homes from the local authority.

The problem with this particular analysis is the same as that with the redefinition of class: The ideal type (home-owning, car-owning, privately educated, buying private health care) is relatively small. One test of the consumption cleavage thesis found that it did not explain anything that could not be explained through existing approaches.[38]

LOCATION   Various studies have demonstrated the independent influence of location in voting behavior. A middle-class voter in an urban area is more likely to vote Labour than is a middle-class voter in a rural area. A trade unionist in a rural area is more likely to vote Conservative than is a trade unionist in an urban area. One explanation for this phenomenon is the process of socialization. Living for a long period of time in a particular locality, one begins to absorb the predominant values of that community.

Recent decades have witnessed a marked north–south polarization and an urban–rural polarization in party support. Research by Curtice and Steed found that the spatial divisions began to emerge after 1955. "A North-South cleavage began to emerge in the 1955–59 swing while the urban-rural cleavage became clearly more evident in the 1959–64 swing."[39] Conservative support has become more pronounced in the south of England, whereas Labour support has increased in the north and Scotland.

In each of the elections between and including 1979 and 1992, the Conservative party was carried to victory largely on the votes of the electorate in the southern half of England (see Map 5.1). Labour achieved a notable predominance in Scotland. The divide was exacerbated in the 1997 general election. In the general election of 1959, the Conservatives won 31 seats in Scotland and Labour won 38. In 1997, the Conservatives won no seats at all in Scotland; Labour won 56. Labour achieved a similar predominance in Wales: In 1997 it won 34 seats, the Conservatives won none at all. Conservative weakness remained pronounced in the elections of 2001 and 2005, winning only one seat in Scotland at each election: It had been displaced by the SNP as the main challenger to the Labour party.

In contrast, the Conservatives have tended to dominate in southern England. This dominance was pronounced in the 1980s and early 1990s, Labour seats in the southern half of the country outside Greater London virtually disappearing. Labour made significant inroads in the south in the 1997 election but it remained the base of Conservative strength, as demonstrated by the results in the 2005 election (see Map 5.1). The Conservative party, once a U.K.-wide party, has become very much an English party in terms of support.

The urban–rural divide has been equally pronounced. Conservative support in the larger cities has been declining for forty years. By 1983, the number of seats it was winning in the larger cities was half that achieved in 1959. The position became more pronounced in subsequent elections. In 1959, in the three large cities of Glasgow, Liverpool, and Manchester, the Conservatives won 15 seats. In 1983, they won just one, and none at all in the five subsequent general elections. Since 1997, the Conservative party has been essentially eliminated as an "urban" party.

The explanations for the spatial polarization are to be found in mobility and economic change. The north of England has continued to rely on many old traditional industries, characterized by mass unionized workforces and relatively little mobility. It has thus retained an environment conducive to established class politics, as identified by Johnston and Pattie. Economic decline in recent decades has hit the traditional manufacturing industries hardest, producing high unemployment. The area has thus been the one area in which Labour has been able to maintain a strong base. The south has been characterized by a growing service industry, less tied to traditional trade unionism than the north, and by greater mobility in the workforce. A similar development has characterized urban and suburban areas, inner cities being characterized often by economic decline, with the more prosperous white-collar workers moving to the suburbs. Other influences appear to have been at work in Scotland and Wales, where the Conservatives have suffered from perceptions of being an English party. There is thus a correlation between location and party support, with location being both an independent as well as a dependent variable in explaining that support. However, location can only offer a partial explanation. It cannot serve to explain Labour support in rural areas, nor can it serve to explain the dramatic swing in support to the Labour party in 1997, which occurred—albeit with some limited variations—across

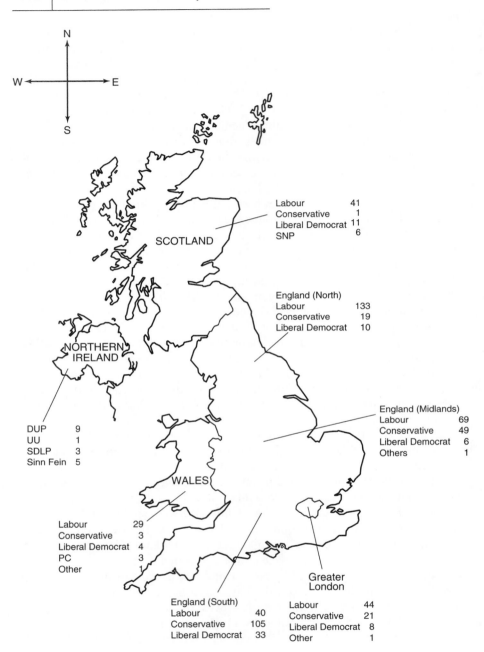

FIGURE 5.1
General election results by region, 2005

all parts of Great Britain and has been maintained since. Regional disparity between the parties also declined somewhat in the 2001 general election, when the swing to the Conservatives in Labour's heartland exceeded that in the south, "further reducing regional polarization."[40]

ISSUES   As class was perceived to have declined as a determinant of voting behaviour, various analysts asserted the increasing significance of issue-based voting. The most sophisticated analysis has been that offered by Mark Franklin in *The Decline of Class Voting in Britain*.[41] He charts the decline in class-voting since 1964, which he contends is a consequence of changing social structures and a reduced appeal of the Labour party to its traditional class groups. "The decline in the class basis of voting amounts to a weakening of constraints on volatility and self-expression and the consequence was to open the way to choice between parties on the basis of issue preferences."[42] As the constraint of class has declined, so attitudes—reevaluated in the light of changing conditions—have played a greater role in shaping voting choice. Voters have been more willing to vote on the basis of issue preference and that has generated greater volatility in electoral behavior. Preferences thus vary and can change over time. Issue voting, as Franklin recognized, makes for uncertainty in electoral outcomes.

The issue-voting approach has been the subject of both challenge and defense.[43] A study, based on the British Election Panel Survey (1997–2001), by Geoffrey Evans and Robert Anderson found that voters' positions on issues were heavily influenced by existing partisan orientations. Their research revealed "the dynamic reciprocal association between party identification and issue proximity is heavily weighted in favor of the former influencing the latter. Partisan effects are simply much more powerful than those of issue proximity."[44] Issues may prompt some electors to change their party support, but existing party support is a major influence in how electors view the issues. Furthermore, there is evidence that electors may support a party despite it taking stances on issues that they do not support. Were issue-voting the sole determinant of electoral behavior in Britain, then survey data suggest that Labour would have won the general election in 1992. "Sixty-three percent of those who considered unemployment important favored Labour's ability to handle it, yet only 47 percent of them actually voted Labour."[45] Similar disparities were found on other issues. Issues are important—not least, as we shall see, among voters with higher levels of knowledge—but by themselves insufficient to explain electoral outcomes.

PERFORMANCE EVALUATION   Class, however important as a variable in shaping voting behavior, has never been an exclusive influence. If it were, elections would have demonstrated a more consistent outcome. Other variables served to make the difference between success and failure in general elections. Various studies have reinforced the accepted wisdom that evaluation of performance in office has been crucial. With the decline in the class–party link, this instrumental variable becomes more important.

Evaluation takes different forms. Voters may evaluate a party in terms of retrospective and prospective performance, in other words, judging parties according to how they have performed in office or according to how they think they will perform in office. The evaluation may also be subjective or objective, that is, judging parties on the basis of what the voter thinks of the performance in office or on the basis of what the parties have actually delivered.

These distinctions were developed by Paul Whiteley. Utilizing data drawn from the 1979 Election Study, he concluded that subjective judgments were better predictors of voting behavior than objective factors, and that of retrospective and prospective evaluations, the former were more significant than the latter for explaining support—and the decline in that support—for the Labour party.[46] Though critics have questioned his thesis, doubting the extent to which Labour suffered in later elections from retrospective evaluation, there is substantial evidence to support the utility of performance evaluation. Sarah Butt, in an analysis of the data from the British Election Panel Study, found that:

> . . . the evidence supports the hypothesis that retrospective voting is an important heuristic for all voters, with the effects of evaluations of the national and vote choice being comparable across knowledge groups. This is in contrast to voting on the basis of issues, where successfully matching one's own position on taxation or privatization to party choice was a function of increased knowledge.[47]

Her research showed that knowledge may affect voting on some issues, such as Europe, less than others. Evaluations of the individual effect of policies were a significant predictor of party choice only among those with high knowledge. Performance evaluation was important across all groups.

Evaluation of performance emerges as a highly plausible explanation of both the Conservative victory in 1992 and the massive Labour victory in 1997. In terms of objective, retrospective evaluation, it could be argued that the Conservatives should have lost heavily in 1992. The election took place during the longest recession since the 1930s. Similarly, on the same criteria, the Conservatives should have won in 1997, when the economy was strong, with inflation and interest rates at low levels. However, voters judged the Conservatives in 1992 on a more subjective and prospective basis:

> In April 1992, notwithstanding objective economic conditions, most voters did not hold the Major government responsible for the length and depth of the recession, and many believed that their own economic circumstances were most likely to improve if the Conservatives continued in office.[48]

In 1997, the Conservatives were seen by electors to have destroyed their claim to be competent in handling the economic affairs of the nation. The withdrawal from the European exchange rate mechanism in September 1992 triggered a collapse in support from which the party never recovered. Other activities of government and of individual politicians reinforced the negative perception of the party's performance in office, resulting in the party's disastrous performance in the general election.[49]

These individual-level analyses are important for helping make sense of the growing volatility in electoral behavior. Recent decades have seen a growing electoral volatility in Britain, though no greater than the volatility in other West European countries. However, the 1997 election was remarkable for the extent of change, exhibiting a volatility unusual by European standards.[50]

However, none of these approaches is sufficient to provide an exclusive explanation of voting behavior. Class and location may enable one to predict that the owners of a mansion in a rural county in the south of England are likely to vote Conservative. They do not help predict or explain why some mansion owners do not vote Conservative or why, in 1997, many of them switched to vote Labour. Given a party's variable performance in office, performance evaluation does not help explain why millions of voters continue to vote for the same party, election after election. In 1997, the Conservative party went down to a massive defeat, yet still garnered 9.6 million votes.

Most of the explanations we have considered serve to explain some degree of behavioral change. Elections in Britain, to quote Rose and McAllister,[51] have become more open. As elections have become more open, the study of them has become more extensive and increasingly sophisticated. The old certainties of class-based voting no longer apply.

THE CURRENT DEBATE

Electoral behavior, then, has been the subject of extensive academic analysis. That behavior occurs within the context of a particular electoral system, and in recent years that system itself has been the subject of public debate. The debate became prominent in the latter half of the 1970s and has reemerged since as part of a wider discussion about Britain's constitutional arrangements. In 1997, a party was elected to government that was committed to holding a referendum on the electoral system. The electoral system, according to its critics, is a dysfunctional one, in need of replacement. The view is not one that enjoys universal support.

A Dysfunctional Electoral System?

Critics of Britain's first-past-the-post electoral system have grown in recent decades. They have leveled three principal objections.

The first is that it does not deliver the political goods so frequently claimed for it. The traditional strength of the system is argued to be that it facilitates the return of a single party to government, secure in a majority of seats in the House of Commons. In the February 1974 general election, no one party gained an overall majority. In the following Parliament, elected in October 1974, Labour was returned with a minute overall majority, and two years later slipped into minority status in the House. It survived in government for a year (1977–78) as a result of a pact with the parliamentary Liberal Party. In the Parliament elected in 1992, the government's majority fell as a result of by-election losses and defections, and by the end of the Parliament, the government was in a minority in the House. Given the increasing volatility of the election, and the increase in the number of third parties, critics argue that the chances of a hung Parliament—no one party enjoying an overall majority of seats—are greater than before.[52] The volatility may result in a massive majority for a party—as happened in 1983 and 1997—but equally it may result in no one party having an absolute majority and being able to form a government. The claimed "stability" of the existing system is thus not what it was.

The second and most powerful argument deployed by critics is that the existing system is unfair. There are four potential victims of this unfairness. The first is the voter. As can be seen from Table 5.2, the electoral system does not produce a precise correlation between the percentage of votes cast for a party and the percentage of seats the party wins in the House of Commons. One party gets into government, even though it has failed to win a majority of the votes cast. (Not since 1935 has a party been elected to office with more than 50 percent of the votes cast.) Thus, it is claimed, voters do not get the results they want. The second victim is a particular category of voter: those voting for candidates who lose. Only the votes cast for the winning candidate count. "Most people's votes," declared Professor Robin Blackburn in 2008, "don't actually count . . . and people are aware of that."[53] Thus, for example, in the 2005 general election, what was the point of voting Conservative or Liberal Democrat in the constituency of Rhondda or Labour or Liberal Democrat in Richmond (Table 5.3)? The votes cast for the Conservative and Liberal Democrat candidates are wasted. The third potential victim is one of the major parties. Because of the distribution of party support in constituencies, it is possible for one party to gain more votes than the other party, yet win fewer seats.[54] A similar phenomenon is apparent in the United States, where it is possible for a candidate for the presidency to win more popular votes than the other main candidate, yet end up with fewer votes in the Electoral College, as happened in presidential election in 2000. The phenomenon has been seen twice in Britain: As can be seen from Table 5.2, the Labour party gained more votes than the Conservatives in the 1951 general election, but the Conservatives won a majority of seats and formed the government. The situation was reversed in February 1974, when the Conservatives won more votes than Labour, but fewer seats. Labour went on to form the government. The fourth victim of unfairness is the Liberal Democratic party. As the third party, it has tended to suffer from its support being fairly consistently spread around the country. It is possible to win 20 percent of votes in most seats and not win any seats at all. The situation has not been quite that bad for the party, but it has not been that far from it. The disparity between the percentages of votes won and the seats in the House of Commons can be seen in Table 5.2. In 1983, the Liberal/Social Democratic Alliance won just over 25 percent of the votes cast—only 2 percent behind the Labour party—but got only 3.5 percent of the seats: Labour gained 32 percent of the seats. Even in 2005, with its best performance in terms of the number of seats won since 1924, the Liberal Democrats garnered 22 percent of the votes cast but held just under 10 percent of the seats in the House of Commons.

The third criticism of the electoral system is that it encourages adversarial politics in Britain, with consequent negative consequences for the nation's economic performance. The "adversary politics" thesis, first developed by a number of academics led by S. E. Finer[55] (see Chapter 3), is that the electoral system has encouraged a polarized contest between two parties for the winner-take-all spoils of a general election. One party is returned to office with an overall majority and implements its manifesto program, a program neither known nor supported by most electors and one drawn up on the basis more of party dogma than of a dispassionate and well-informed analysis of Britain's problems. If the other party then wins at a subsequent election, it implements its own distinctive program. There has thus been the potential for public policy to lurch from one position to another, the policy pursued by government never quite matching the wishes of the electoral center. The results, in short, have been unrepresentative governments—pursuing policies more politically extreme than those favored by the more centrist electorate—and policy discontinuity. Policy discontinuity has frustrated industrialists and investors who wished to engage in forward planning: They are not able to plan ahead on the basis of stability in government programs.

Indeed, the conditions created by the electoral system have been seen as being at the heart of Britain's problems. To win an election, a party makes extravagant promises, doing so to outbid the other party. In office, it finds it can no longer raise the resources to meet those promises. It therefore has to change track, further adding to confusion in governmental policy making. However, it also has to act in a way that does not jeopardize its chance of winning the next election. Hence it is reluctant to take the unpopular measures deemed by some to be necessary to tackle Britain's long-term problems, a charge leveled against Tony Blair in his first term of office. Even when a government gains reelection, the adversary relationship militates against its being able to mobilize popular support in order to achieve its goals. The response of the government, according to critics, is to strengthen its own power, thus further reducing its capacity to mobilize necessary, and voluntary, support. The result, in short, has been a vicious circle.[56]

The solution to the problem, or at least a partial one, was perceived by these critics as the introduction of a new electoral system, one that introduced a method of proportional representation. PR, it was argued, would be fairer than the existing electoral system, ensuring that a party received the share of parliamentary seats equivalent to its national vote. Furthermore, given existing voting behavior, it would deprive any one party of an overall majority of seats. Forming a government with an overall parliamentary majority would thus necessitate a coalition. This would likely involve one of the main parties having "to co-operate with a party or parties taking a more central stance," hence leading to greater moderation in policy.[57] Given that such a coalition would enjoy the support of more than 50 percent of electors and that the turnover of seats under PR is small, the coalition would likely remain in office for the foreseeable future and hence be in a position to ensure a degree of policy continuity. The overall effect of PR would thus be to put an end to the worst features of adversary politics and its unfortunate consequences.

An Effective Electoral System?

Supporters of the first-past-the-post electoral system have been active in recent years in defending the existing method of electing MPs. The principal justifications advanced for the existing electoral system have been fourfold. First, the system is coherent. The electoral system facilitates the return of a single party to government. Political power thus resides in one body (the party in government) and the rest of the political system revolves around that one central political fact. The system is perceptible and people know who is responsible for decisions that are made. In the 2008 Audit of Political Engagement, most of those questioned were satisfied or were neither satisfied nor dissatisfied with how votes cast in a general election were translated into seats in the House of Commons. The net satisfaction rate was +15.[58]

Second, and crucial to the defense of the existing arrangements, the electoral system helps ensure that the government is accountable. Electors know whom to hold accountable for decisions that are made and can remove them from office. There is one body—the party in government—that is responsible for making domestic public policy. That body cannot blame anyone else if electors find policy unpalatable. The distinguished political philosopher Sir Karl Popper argued that the most important attribute of an electoral system was not the ease by which a government could be elected, but rather the ease by which it could be removed.[59] If electors do not like what government is doing, they can sweep it out of office at the next election. Members of the government know that they are not going to be able to engage in post-election bargaining with other parties to stay in power. Thus, in Popper's words, election day constitutes "Judgment Day."

Third, the system is responsive. Because a government knows it may be swept out at the next election, it is responsive to public reaction to its policies. When the Conservative government under Margaret Thatcher introduced a new local tax (the community charge, popularly dubbed the poll tax) in place of the existing local tax, it proved widely unpopular. It resulted in demonstrations and even riots. Recognizing that it could lose the next election as a result, the party in government got rid of the tax, in the process getting rid of the party leader, who was committed to maintaining the tax.

Fourth, it is effective. The electoral system enables a single party to be returned to office and that party is then able to implement the program that it placed before voters during the election. Governments have a high success rate in implementing the commitments embodied in their party manifestos.[60] There may be some modification during the lifetime of the Parliament, but overall they implement what they have promised to implement. If electors then disapprove, they can turn out the government at the next election.

Defenders of the first-past-the-post system also challenge the basis of the claims for a new electoral system. The argument of "fairness" is contested.[61] The existing system may place disproportionate political power in the largest single party but that, it is argued, is fairer than placing disproportionate political power in the hands of the smallest, or one of the smallest, political parties. This, it is argued, would likely be the case under a PR system, a third party holding the balance of power. Ensuring a party with 15 percent of the votes had 15 percent of the seats could produce a highly unfair distribution of political power. The party holding 15 percent of the seats could, by holding the balance of power, exercise more than 15 percent of the negotiating power in the House of Commons. A more proportional system, it is argued, would also be unfair in that it would likely result in the choice of government resting not with electors exercising their judgment in the polling booths, but with party leaders engaging in post-election bargaining. The result of post-election bargaining could be a coalition for which not one elector has voted. Thus, for example, following the elections to the National Assembly for Wales in 2007, bargaining between the parties resulted in a Labour-Plaid Cymru coalition. Not one elector had cast a vote definitively for such a coalition. Far from being fair to voters, PR could deny them the opportunity to choose the government of the United Kingdom.

The adversary politics thesis developed by the reformers has also been challenged. Two mutually exclusive arguments are deployed against it. One line of argument accepts the notion of an adversary relationship between the parties but considers this a beneficial rather than a harmful process. The electorate is offered a clear choice and it results in one party with a mandate from the people getting on with the job of governing. PR, it is feared, would facilitate a blurring of choice and prevent a party from being returned with a mandate clearly approved by the people.

The other argument deployed against the adversary politics thesis calls into doubt the relevance of the notion itself. The rhetoric of adversary politics, it is argued, hides a more consensual substance. In terms of government legislation, empirical research has indicated that a consensual model is indeed more applicable.[62] In this view, parties are seen as being not quite as central to formulation of public policy as is believed by both reformers and politicians. The external demands are such that the government can often only act as arbiter between competing demands and respond, under guidance from civil servants, to international events and trends over which it has no direct influence. Whichever party is in power makes some, but not a great deal, of difference. This particular argument received reinforcement by a study undertaken by Richard Rose. He examined the relationship between electoral systems and economic performance in 21 advanced industrial nations and found that there was no consistent link. "Differences in economic performance," he wrote, "cannot be explained by differences in electoral systems."[63] His conclusion undermined a central tenet of the reformers' case.

For defenders of the first-past-the-post system, the alternatives threaten to undermine the advantages of the existing system, offering no tangible benefits in their place and threatening to undermine the stability and effectiveness of the political system.

A New Electoral System?

Supporters of electoral reform made much of the running in debate at the end of the twentieth century. They also grew in number. The Liberal Democrats were longstanding supporters of reform. A growing body of Labour supporters also came round to their point of view. Various bodies were created to make the case for change. An umbrella reform movement, Charter88, was formed in 1988, and included in its manifesto the introduction of a new electoral system. Labour leader Neil Kinnock in 1991 set up a commission to consider electoral reform and his successor, John Smith, committed the party to supporting a referendum on electoral reform. Smith's successor, Tony Blair, maintained that commitment. The Labour manifesto in the 1997 general election declared: "We are committed to a referendum on the voting system for the House of Commons. An independent Commission on voting systems will be appointed early to recommend a proportional alternative to the first-past-the-post system."[64] Shortly after the party was returned to power, Blair appointed a commission under a leading Liberal Democrat (and ex-Labour cabinet minister), Lord Jenkins of Hillhead, to propose an alternative to the existing system.

The various alternative systems on offer are listed in Box 5.1. The Liberal Democrats have favored the use of STV. Support for AMS has been more pronounced among Labour politicians. Some Labour MPs have tended to support the Alternative Vote (AV) or SV because it can be utilized within existing constituencies, and thus is the least disruptive. As we noted in the introduction to the chapter, most of the systems have now been used for elections to various positions in the United Kingdom. Each has its merits but also its demerits[65] and there is no agreement that any one of them should be employed for elections to the House of Commons. Though a regional list system has been introduced for elections to the European Parliament, there are no advocates of its use for elections to the House of Commons, principally because it destroys the need for constituencies. It also makes possible a concentration of power in the hands of party leaders in selecting and ranking candidates. The STV system cannot necessarily produce strict proportionality: It has been categorized as "contingently proportional."[66] In Ireland, its use has encouraged excessive localism on the part of members of the parliament. AMS can deliver proportionality, though that depends on the proportion of additional members (a 50-50 split between constituency members and additional members delivers proportionality) and on voters not splitting their votes between the constituency and the list. Critics also claim that it will result in two tiers of MPs, those elected by constituencies having to carry a massive and unnecessary burden of constituency work. They point now to the experience of the Scottish Parliament, elected by such a system, which has experienced clashes between constituency-elected members and list members over who represents people in a certain area.[67] The Alternative and Supplementary Vote are attacked because they are not proportional systems.

One variant that came on the agenda of debate in 1998 as a result of the work of the Jenkins Commission was termed "AV Plus" or "AV Top Up." This entailed utilizing AV—thus allowing constituencies to be retained, with a direct link between electors and a particular MP—but with additional Members being created to provide for some element of proportionality. This was seen as an attempt to square a circle, introducing a greater element of proportionality without losing the constituency link. Critics noted that had

BOX 5.1

Alternative Electoral Systems

List System

Electors vote for lists of candidates put forward by the parties and seats are allocated on the basis of the percentage of the votes won by each party. Under "closed" list systems, electors cannot influence the rank ordering of candidates; under "open list" systems they can (though in practice they rarely do). The system can be organized on a regional or national basis. A regional list system is used in Britain for the election of MEPs.

Single Transferable Vote (STV)

Under this system, there are multi-member constituencies, with each elector able to indicate a preference on the ballot paper, putting the number 1 beside the name of the candidate most preferred, 2 against the name of the elector's second choice, and so on. A quota is established by the formula of dividing the number of valid ballots cast by the number of seats, plus one: To the resulting figure, one is added. Thus in a five-member constituency in which 120,000 ballots are cast, the formula would be

$$\frac{120,000}{5+1} + 1$$

Hence the quota (the number of ballots required to elect one member) would be 20,001. Any candidate receiving this number of votes is declared elected. The second preferences of any of the candidate's surplus votes, plus those of the candidate at the bottom of the poll, are then redistributed, and so on until the necessary number of candidates reach the quota. There are different formulae employed to determine how the votes are redistributed. The STV system is employed in the United Kingdom for the elections to the Northern Ireland Assembly and for local government elections in Northern Ireland and Scotland.

Additional Member System (AMS)

Under this system, single-member constituencies are retained, with the first-past-the-post method of election retained in each. Additional seats are then allocated to parties on a regional basis, usually with a threshold requirement (a party has to obtain a specified percentage—say 5 percent—of the vote in any area of allocation in order to obtain additional seats). Additional seats go to the parties on the basis of the proportion of votes received in the region. The AMS is employed in the United Kingdom for elections to the Scottish parliament and the Welsh Assembly (See Chapter 9) and to the Greater London Assembly.

Alternative Vote (AV)

This is not a proportional system. It retains the single member constituency. Voters list their preferences against candidates' names. If a candidate receives an absolute majority of the votes cast, then he or she is declared elected. If no candidate receives an absolute majority, the candidate with the least number of votes is eliminated and the second preferences of that candidate are then redistributed; the process continues until a candidate has an absolute majority.

Supplementary Vote (SV)
This is a variant of the AV. A single member constituency is retained but each voter has only two votes—a principal and a supplementary vote. If one candidate achieves an absolute majority of the principal votes cast, then the candidate is declared elected. If no candidate achieves an absolute majority, all the candidates other than the top two are eliminated and the second preferences of the eliminated candidates are then redistributed. If the second vote is for an eliminated candidate, it is discarded. SV is used in Britain for the election of the London Mayor and for mayoral elections in those (relatively few) local councils that have directly elected mayors.

Alternative Vote Plus (AV Plus)
This utilizes the AV in individual constituencies but then provides for a "top up" of members from a list system. The number of members elected under a list system can be used to correct for the disproportionality that can result from the use of the AV. ■

the AV system been used in 1997, the results would have been more disproportional than they were under the first-past-the-post system. They also noted that seeking to introduce such a skewed system and then introducing an extra element to overcome the very defect that had been introduced was to employ rather warped and tortuous logic.

The debate over reform was especially intense in 1998. A campaigning organization called Make Votes Count was created, comprising a coalition of groups such as Charter88, the Electoral Reform Society, and the left-wing think tank the New Politics Network.[68] It was dedicated to making the case for a reform of the electoral system. In October of that year, the Jenkins Commission reported and recommended "AV Plus," though with the bulk of MPs being elected by constituencies.[69] By recommending that most MPs be elected by constituencies (rather than on the basis of a 50-50 split between constituency and "top-up" members), the potential of a single party being elected to government was retained.

The report was immediately attacked by supporters of the existing electoral system[70] and by some supporters of reform who favored other PR systems. Supporters of the existing system argued that it went too far: It was calculated that under this system most elections since 1945 would have produced "hung" Parliaments (i.e., no one party winning an overall majority). They also pointed out that no other country employed AV Plus. Supporters of other PR systems argued that it did not go far enough, since it did not provide for strict proportionality. The government was noncommittal on when the Commission's recommendation would be put to a referendum and it became increasingly clear that it would not be before the next general election. Various leading members of the cabinet were known to be opposed to the proposal and the prime minister did not appear enthusiastic to pursue it. At the 2001 general election, the promise of a referendum was omitted from the Labour party manifesto and it was not resurrected. As the Labour party was now the notable beneficiary of the existing electoral system, demand for change within the party was muted.

Opinion polls suggest that electoral reform elicits far less support than other items of constitutional reform. Support for change is broad but not particularly deep.[71] If asked if they favor electoral reform, respondents will tend to answer yes. If asked if they accord any priority to the issue they will tend to answer no. In the 2008 Audit of Political Engagement, only 14 percent of those questioned thought the way in which votes cast in a general election were translated into seats was one of constitutional arrangements most urgently in need of change. The option came 7th out of a list of 12 (excluding "don't know").[72] As the authors of the Audit wrote in their analysis of the survey data: "It is hard to see any public momentum behind calls for votes at 16, electoral reform or fixed-term parliaments. These are not the issues that are worrying even those who feel the system is unsatisfactory, and there is little or no correlation between attitudes to these issues and disconnection or non-participation."[73]

Though expressing support for the principle of electoral reform, surveys also tap the fact that electors do not favor the likely consequences of such a reform. Previous surveys have found that electors prefer single-party government over a coalition and the 2008 Audit of Political Engagement found that 60 percent of those questioned tended to agree or agreed strongly with the statement that "Governments are elected on a mandate and should have powers to act on it."

Though there is some intense pressure for change, this finds no replication among government or the public. The situation in which electoral reform for U.K. parliamentary elections is likely to come about is in the event of a "hung" parliament with the Liberal Democrats making electoral reform a condition of entering a coalition. So long as there is single-party government, the party in government is unlikely to be an enthusiast for changing the very system that has put it in power.

NOTES

1. See T. Lundberg, "A decade of electoral reform in the UK," *Politics Review*, 18 (1), 2008, pp. 27–29; and Ministry of Justice, *Review of Voting Systems: The Experience of New Voting Systems in the United Kingdom since 1997*, Cm 7304 (The Stationery Office, 2008).
2. Until then, some voters had two votes. There were 12 University seats, with the Members being elected by graduates. A graduate thus had a constituency vote and a University vote. The seats were abolished by the 1949 Act.
3. R. Blackburn, *The Electoral System in Britain* (Macmillan, 1995), p. 85.

4. Provisions for registration in the United States have improved as a consequence of the National Voter Registration Act 1993 but still leave the onus on the citizen to register. Before then, methods differed between states.

5. See Blackburn, pp. 84–86. Some people have no interest in voting, some may fail to register if there is no election in the offing, and in 1990 a notable decline in registration was attributed to people wanting to avoid paying the "poll tax" (see Chapter 9).

6. See P. Norton and D. M. Wood, *Back from Westminster* (University Press of Kentucky, 1993).

7. See D. Butler and D. Kavanagh, *The British General Election of 1997* (Macmillan, 1997), p. 223.

8. M. Pinto-Duschinsky, *British Political Finance* 1830–1980 (American Enterprise Institute, 1981), p. 249.

9. Butler and Kavanagh, *The British General Election of 1997*, p. 212.

10. D. Denver, "Modern election campaigning," *Politics Review*, 16 (4), 2007, p. 9.

11. Denver, "Modern election campaigning," pp. 9–10.

12. C. Ballinger, "The Local Battle, the Cyber Battle," in D. Butler and D. Kavanagh, *The British General Election of 2001* (Palgrave Macmillan, 2002), pp. 224–233.

13. S. Ward, "The Internet, E-Democracy and the Election: Virtually Irrelevant?" in A. Geddes and J. Tonge (eds.), *Britain Decides: The UK General Election 2005* (Palgrave Macmillan, 2006), p. 203.

14. Electoral Commission, *Election 2005: Campaign Spending* (Electoral Commission, 2006).

15. D. Kavanagh, *Election Campaigning* (Blackwell, 1995), p. 41.

16. According to the figures in Blackburn, p. 287, fewer than 200,000 copies of each party manifesto were printed and sold in 1992.

17. S. Weir and D. Beetham, *Political Power and Democratic Control in Britain* (Routledge, 1999), p. 105.

18. R. I. Hofferbert and I. Budge, "The Party Mandate and the Westminster Model: Election Programmes and Government Spending in Britain, 1945–85," *British Journal of Political Science*, 22, 1992, pp. 151–182; Weir and Beetham, p. 114.

19. For a thorough discussion, see D. Kavanagh, "The Politics of Manifestos," *Parliamentary Affairs*, 34 (1), 1981, pp. 7–27, and Weir and Beetham, pp. 100–115.

20. See Conservative Party, *How to Become a Conservative MP*, 2009, http://www.conservatives.com/pdf/howtomp.pdf.

21. See M. Rush, *The Selection of Parliamentary Candidates* (Longman, 1969) for the period of the 1950s and 1960s. No changes were reported in M. Rush, "The 'Selectorate' Revisited: Selecting Parliamentary Candidates in the 1980s," *Teaching Politics*, 15 (1), 1986, pp. 99–113.

22. When this author served on a selection committee many years ago, one question asked during the short-listing process was "Can't we interview him? He has a nice name." The response: a polite "no."

23. Liberal Democrat Party, *Constitution of the Federal Party* (Liberal Democrat Party, 2006), provision 11.5(g).

24. M. Rush, "The Members of Parliament," in M. Ryle and P. G. Richards (eds.), *The Commons under Scrutiny* (Routledge, 1988), pp. 26–27; B. Criddle, "MPs and Candidates," in Butler and Kavanagh, pp. 204–206.

25. A. King, "The Rise of the Career Politician in Britain—and Its Consequences," *British Journal of Political Science*, 2 (3), 1981, pp. 249–285; P. Riddell, *Honest Opportunism* (Hamish Hamilton, 1993).

26. See G. Sartori, *Parties and Party Systems: A Framework for Analysis* (Cambridge University Press, 1976), pp. 158–189; P. Norton, "Britain: Still a Two-Party System?" in S. Bartolini and P. Mair, *Party Politics in Contemporary Western Europe* (Frank Cass, 1984), pp. 27–45.

27. B. Sarlvik and I. Crewe, *Decade of Dealignment* (Cambridge University Press, 1983), p. 87.

28. The Gallup Poll, "Voting Behaviour in Britain," in R. Rose (ed.), *Studies in British Politics*, 3rd ed. (Macmillan, 1976), p. 206.

29. P. Pulzer, *Political Representation and Elections in Britain* (Macmillan, 1967), p. 98.

30. See J. Curtice, "Anatomy of a Landslide," *Politics Review*, 7 (1), 1997, pp. 2–8.

31. A. King, "Why Labour Won – Yet Again," in J. Bartle and A. King (eds.), *Britain at the Polls 2005* (CQ Press, 2006), p. 176.

32. R. Rose, *The Problem of Party Government* (Penguin, 1976), p. 43.

33. See Sarlvik and Crewe, pp. 334–336.

34. A. Heath, R. Jowell, and J. Curtice, *How Britain Votes* (Pergamon, 1985), pp. 22ff.

35. R. Rose and I. McAllister, *Voters Begin to Choose* (Sage, 1986), p. 46.

36. R. Johnston and C. J. Pattie, "Class Dealignment and the Regional Polarisation of Voting Patterns in Great Britain, 1964–1987," *Political Geography*, 11 (1), 1992, pp. 73–86.

37. P. Dunleavy, "The Urban Basis of Political Alignment: Social Class, Domestic Property Ownership and State Intervention in Consumption Processes," *British Journal of Political Science*, 9, 1979, pp. 409–444.

38. M. Franklin and E. Page, "A Critique of the Consumption Cleavage Approach in British Voting Studies," *Political Studies*, 32, 1984, pp. 521–536.

39. J. Curtice and M. Steed, "Electoral Choice and the Production of Government," *British Journal of Political Science*, 12, 1982, p. 256

40. J. Bartle, "Why Labour Won – Again," in A. King (ed.), *Britain at the Polls 2001* (Chatham House Publishers, 2002), p. 170.

41. M. Franklin, *The Decline of Class Voting in Britain* (Oxford University Press, 1985). See also H. Himmelweit, P. Humphreys, and M. Jaeger, *How Voters Decide* (Open University Press, 1985).

42. Franklin, p. 176.

43. See Rose and McAllister, p. 147; and R. J. Johnston, C. J. Pattie, and J. G. Allsop, *A Nation Dividing?* (Longman, 1988), p. 59.

44. G. Evans and R. Anderson, "Do Issues Decide? Partisan Conditioning and Perceptions of Party Issue Positions across the Electoral Cycle," in R. Scully, J. Fisher, P. Webb, and D. Broughton (eds.), *British Elections and Parties Review*, Vol. 14 (Taylor & Francis, 2004), p. 31.

45. D. Sanders, "Why the Conservative Party Won—Again," in A. King (ed.), *Britain at the Polls 1992* (Chatham House, 1993), p. 195.

46. P. Whiteley, *The Labour Party in Crisis* (Methuen, 1983), p. 106.

47. S. Butt, "Political Knowledge and Routes to Party Choice in the British General Election of 2001," in R. Scully, J. Fisher, P. Webb, and D. Broughton (eds.), *British Elections and Parties Review*, Vol. 14 (Taylor & Francis, 2004), pp. 14–15.

48. D. Sanders, "The New Electoral Battleground" in A. King (ed.), *New Labour Triumphs: Britain at the Polls* (Chatham House, 1997), p. 224.

49. See D. Denver, "The Government That Could Do No Right" and P. Norton, "The Conservative Party: 'In Office but Not in Power'" in King, *New Labour Triumphs*.

50. See Sanders, "The New Electoral Battleground," pp. 222–223.

51. Rose and McAllister, pp. 128–133.

52. J. Curtice and M. Steed, "Electoral Choice and the Production of Government," *British Journal of Political Science*, 12 (2), 1982, pp. 249–298.

53. R. Blackburn, Compass Conference, 2008, http://www.makemyvotecount.org.uk/opus26187/Compass_Conference_Summary.pdf

54. For example, Party A could win two marginal seats by the barest of margins while Party B won one seat with an overwhelming majority; the aggregate vote for Party B in the three seats could well exceed that of Party A, but Party A has won twice as many seats. The same phenomenon can be observed in state results in presidential elections in the United States, most notably so in the presidential election of 2000, resulting in one candidate gaining more electoral college votes than his opponent, but fewer votes.

55. S. E. Finer (ed.), *Adversary Politics and Electoral Reform* (Wigram, 1975), pp. 30–31.

56. See the comments of P. Jay, "Englanditis," in R. E. Tyrell, Jr. (ed.), *The Future That Doesn't Work* (Doubleday, 1977), p. 181; and S. E. Brittan, *The Economic Consequences of Democracy* (Temple Smith, 1977).

57. Finer, pp. 30–31.

58. Hansard Society, *Audit of Political Engagement 5: The 2008 Report* (Hansard Society, 2008), p. 28.

59. Sir K. Popper, " 'The Open Society and Its Enemies' Revisited," *Economist*, 23 April 1988.

60. R. Rose, *Do Parties Make a Difference?* 2nd ed. (Macmillan, 1984), pp. 64–67; R. I. Hofferbert and I. Budge, "The Party Mandate and the Westminster Model: Election Programmes and Government Spending in Britain, 1945–85," *British Journal of Political Science*, 22 (2), 1992, pp. 151–182.

61. See P. Norton, "The Case for First-Past-The-Post," *Representation*, 34 (2), 1997, pp. 84–88.

62. Rose, *Do Parties Make a Difference?*

63. R. Rose, *What Are the Economic Consequences of PR?* (Electoral Reform Society, 1992), p. 17.

64. Labour Party, *New Labour: Because Britain Deserves Better* (Labour Party, 1997), p. 33.

65. See R. Kelly, "Alternative electoral systems," *Politics Review*, 15 (4), 2006, pp. 30–33, and Ministry of Justice, *Review of Voting Systems: The Experience of New Voting Systems in the United Kingdom Since 1997*, Cm 7304 (The Stationery Office, 2008).

66. P. Dunleavy, H. Margetts, B. O'Duffy, and S. Weir, *Making Votes Count* (University of Essex, 1997), p. 28.

67. In November 1999 an investigation was ordered by the presiding officer after a clash between some constituency members and some elected from the party list as to who represented the people in a certain area.

68. Charter88 and New Politics Network merged in 2007.

69. *The Report of the Independent Commission on the Voting System* (The Stationery Office, 1998).

70. See, for example, P. Norton, *Power to the People* (Conservative Policy Forum, 1998).

71. MORI, *State of the Nation 1995* (MORI, 1995), p. 10.

72. Hansard Society, *Audit of Political Engagement 5: The 2008 Report* (Hansard Society, 2008), p. 31.

73. Ibid., p. 40.

CHAPTER

6

Political Parties
More or Less Than a
Two-Party System?

In the United States, political parties provide some measure of choice among candidates at election time. They offer a reference point for many electors. They usually do little else. Despite an increase in partisanship in recent decades,[1] U.S. parties remain comparatively weak bodies, characterized by faction rather than party.[2] Ideological and structural factors militate against them developing as coherent and programmatic bodies. They operate within a broad ideological consensus,[3] rendering differences between parties that are often largely differences of degree rather than kind. Elections, consequently, are often fought on the basis of trust, personality, or particular issues rather than competing programs. Even if the parties are able to present coherent and competing programs, the structure of the U.S. political system works against such a program being carried through successfully: A party needs to be cohesive to capture the White House and to achieve the return of a majority of its supporters in both houses as well as overcome internal procedural constraints within Congress. The occasions when the conditions of programmatic coherence, party unity, and control of executive and legislative branches have been present—as during the period of the first New Deal and the Great Society program—are notable for their rarity—and their brevity. It has proved impossible to sustain strong party government in the United States.

Britain lacks those features that have facilitated a weak party system in the United States. A unitary and parliamentary form of government has favored the development of centralized and cohesive parties geared to offering a programmatic choice to the electors and to carrying out that program once the all-or-nothing spoils of a general election have been gained. The executive dominance of the House of Commons ensures legislative approval of the party program: The doctrine of parliamentary sovereignty puts the program's implementation beyond challenge by the courts. It is, in short, the very model of a strong party government. It is a model that has been variously admired. It has variously found favor with U.S. scholars because of its apparent ability to ensure the realization of social reform.[4] It appeared to influence the report of the Committee on the Constitutional System in 1987, which recommended that members of Congress be permitted to sit in the Cabinet.[5] It is held up as an antidote to the brokered politics of the United States.

To stress the differences of the two systems is both important and necessary. However, it runs the risk of obscuring some important similarities. U.S. parties may be weak and British parties strong by comparison, but both the United States and Britain are notable for having systems dominated by two parties. The Republican and Democratic parties are dominant in U.S. elections, the Conservative and Labour parties (albeit to a lesser extent) dominate in British elections. There are also *some* similarities between the parties themselves. The Republican Party in the United States and the Conservative Party in Britain are essentially right-of-center parties that tend to attract support from similar constituencies, notably the middle class. In the 1980s, there was a notable empathy between President Ronald Reagan and Prime Minister Margaret Thatcher as well as between their successors, George Bush and John Major. The Democratic Party and the Labour Party are more left-of-center parties appealing to blue-collar workers. In the 1960s, Labour leader Harold Wilson is reputed to have wanted to model himself on John Kennedy and his party on the Democratic Party. The new Labour Prime Minister in 1997, Tony Blair, developed an affinity with President Clinton; both tried, with some success, to make their parties more attractive to a wider social spectrum, Blair to "middle England" and Clinton to "middle America." In recent decades, parties in both countries have witnessed similar but not identical falls in support and partisan identification among electors. These, though, are broad generalizations and should not be pushed too far. Some Conservative politicians support the Democrats. Tony Blair got on well with Clinton's Republican successor, George W. Bush. The correlation between U.S. and U.K. parties is far from exact, and those parties operate in political systems that are notable for their very sharp differences.

It is important first to consider the growth and the nature of the two main political parties. In their origin and growth, they are distinctly British and can be understood only within the context of British history and political culture.

THE PARTIES IN BRITAIN

The first principle of party, according to Edmund Burke in the eighteenth century, was "to put men who hold their opinions into such a condition as may enable them to carry their common plans into execution." At the time that he was writing, that "condition" meant gaining the confidence of the king. With the widening of the franchise in the nineteenth century, it came instead to depend on the confidence of the electors. As bodies that seek electoral success in order to form the government, political parties may be said to have developed in Britain following the Reform Act of 1832; as bodies seeking that success in order to fulfill particular programs—a stage arguably never reached by U.S. parties—they are more especially the product of the Reform Act of 1867.

The need for electoral support after 1832 and the difficulty of establishing direct personal contact with the enlarged electorate encouraged the development of embryonic political *organization*: Political clubs were formed, election funds were established, registration societies—to ensure that supporters were registered to vote—were brought into being, and in some parts of the country (notably Lancashire) constituency associations were formed. Nonetheless, as we have seen (Chapter 3), the differences between pre- and post-1832 days were not as marked as some might have supposed: The aristocracy remained politically eminent, voting was still by open ballot, and corrupt practices were still common. All this were to change as a result of the Reform Act of 1867 and the reforming measures of the next eighteen years. The electorate was now of such a size (2.5 million: See Chapter 3) and of such a nature that highly organized political parties became necessary both for facilitating contact and for aggregating the interests of voters through some form of party platform. Bribery and other corrupt practices, as well as the open ballot, were formally done away with by statute, though the size of the electorate alone did much to remove bribery as an effective weapon of influence. Organized corruption, as Richard Crossman observed, was gradually replaced by party organization,[6] and the two main parties of the day, to employ Maurice Duverger's terminology, were developed from cadre into mass-membership parties. The Liberal Party created the National Liberal Federation to widen its appeal to the newly enfranchised voter. The Conservative Party created the Conservative National Union in 1867 and Conservative Central Office in 1870, the latter to provide professional support to the voluntary wing of the party. Highly organized, mass-membership political parties became a feature of British political life.

In the latter half of the nineteenth century, the two dominant parties were the Conservatives and the Liberals.[7] Both adhered to a hierarchical conception of party structure and both had parliamentary parties that predated the creation of the extraparliamentary parties. The voluntary organizations were created primarily to mobilize support for the parliamentary leaders: They were not expected to formulate policies or to give instructions. The conventions of the Constitution also facilitated this form of "top-down" leadership within the parties. Although both parties began to appeal to the country on the basis of particular platforms, the notion of "the manifesto" was not well developed. The party leaders were expected to make an appeal to the country and, if elected, were expected to proceed with the task of governing.

Such approaches were to be modified in the twentieth century. One important influence was the development of the Labour Party. It was created to achieve the return to Parliament of representatives of the working classes and it adhered to the concept of intraparty democracy. Implementation of the party's election manifesto became the touchstone by which party activists could determine whether party leaders were adhering to the party's program. The party's internal norms were not altogether compatible with those of the Constitution. The party favored the election of party leaders, which in government would mean the members of the cabinet, whereas the Constitution conferred such power on the prime minister. Under the leadership of Ramsay MacDonald, the first Labour prime minister, this conflict was resolved largely in favor of the Constitution. Nonetheless, tension between a "top-down" form of political leadership, in which the party defers to the guidance given by its leaders, and a "bottom-up" form, in which leaders are bound by decisions taken by party members, has been a recurrent feature of Labour Party politics.

The Labour Party displaced the Liberal Party as one of the two main parties in Britain in the 1920s. In 1922 it was recognized as the main opposition party in Parliament. During the twentieth century, the Conservative Party tended to be the governing party, with the Labour Party as the challenger. The Conservatives dominated the interwar years, between 1918 and 1939, and then, in the fifty years following the end of the Second World War, held office for thirty-three of them. As we saw in Chapter 5 (Table 5.4), the Labour Party was returned to office with substantial majorities on only three occasions (1945, 1966, and 1997). However, although the century has been characterized as the Conservative Century,[8] the last election of the century saw a remarkable change of party fortunes. Labour won the 1997 general election with a stunning majority and the Conservatives suffered their worst defeat since 1906. At the beginning of the twenty-first century, the Labour Party appeared to have replaced the Conservative Party as the "in" party in British politics. In 2005, it was returned for a third consecutive term of office. There was also a notable increase in the parliamentary representation of the principal third party, the Liberal Democratic Party, successor to the Liberal Party. In 2005, it achieved its best result in a general election since 1924.

A number of other parties were also successful in getting candidates elected to the European Parliament and the new assemblies in the different parts of the United Kingdom. Indeed, so successful in fact that various parties—deemed minor at the level of competition for election to the House of Commons—have emerged in the twenty-first century as governing parties in Scotland, Wales, and Northern Ireland. The Labour and Conservative parties dominate at the level of the U.K. Parliament but not at the level of the different semi-autonomous parts of the United Kingdom.

The increasing volatility of the British electorate (Chapter 5) and the use of new electoral systems for elections to parliamentary bodies other than the House of Commons have meant that the fortunes of the parties have become less predictable than before.

The Conservative Party

Although British Conservatism can be traced back several centuries, indeed to Hooker in the sixteenth century, the emergence of a political party with the name Conservative took place in the fourth decade of the nineteenth century.

The name Conservative was first used by an anonymous writer in 1830, and the term was in common usage by 1832. The party set up an election fund in 1835.[9] It was the successor to the Tory Party, the party of the landowning gentry, which had largely disintegrated under the leadership of the duke of Wellington in the 1820s. The new party inherited both the base of Tory support and the party's central tenets.[10] Foremost among these was a belief in the organic nature of society. Society was seen as a historical product, a thing of slow and natural growth, an organic entity with unity and character. Concomitantly, the party inherited from the philosophy of Edmund Burke a belief in gradual change: Society was evolutionary, not static. Change, though, had to be evolutionary, not revolutionary. It had to improve, not destroy. Change had to take place without doing violence to the existing fabric of society. The party was committed to the defense of existing and worthwhile institutions: It stood for the defense of Constitution, Crown, and Church. If there was to be reform it should be to save the Constitution, not to subvert it. It was a corollary of such beliefs that the party adhered to an ordered society, one in which law, order, and authority were upheld. It stood for the defense of property. Private property, as Burke contended, was a bulwark against tyranny: Without private property, the overpowerful state could not be resisted. One could identify the party as adhering also to limited but not necessarily weak government. Government was perceived as having but a limited role to play in society, primarily that of defending the realm, but if strong government was on occasion necessary to maintain the king's government, then so be it. In short, then, the party stood basically for the existing order of things but was prepared to admit the need for occasional change, change not for the sake of change but in order to preserve.

The party's base of support initially was a restricted one. It was essentially a party of the landed interest. It had no national appeal and for the middle years of the century was very much the "out" party in politics. It was transformed into a national party under the leadership of Benjamin Disraeli. He had to devise an appeal that made the party relevant to the problems of the day. This he did: To the corpus of Conservative beliefs he added adherence to the notion of One Nation—that is, One Nation at Home and One Nation Abroad. Domestically, this meant that the party would not divide the nation in the interests of one class but would look after the interests of all classes. The party would balance social forces and establish common goals. Internationally, it meant the development and maintenance of the empire. This concept identified the party with the achievements of the nation; it provided an inspiring theme to unite in patriotic harmony all Englishmen, if not all Britons. As part of the theme of One Nation, Disraeli was to demonstrate concern for the welfare of the people—much of the social reform legislation of the latter half of the century was Conservative-inspired—while stressing the imperative of maintaining institutions and social stability. Coupled with this national appeal was the development of the party as a mass-membership organization, one that ensured that the party's message reached the new electors. By the time of Disraeli's death in 1881, the Conservative Party had laid claim to be a national party, one of responsibility and government. For the last quarter of the century and for most of the twentieth, the party was to dominate British politics.[11]

As the party developed to acquire its national status, so it acquired new support. It obtained the support of a substantial fraction of working-class voters, in large part because industrialists and mill owners—the employers of the workers—were associated with the Liberal Party. It acquired defectors from the ranks of the Liberals, notably the Liberal Unionists, toward the end of the nineteenth century. The influx of Liberals tended to move it more in the direction of a capitalist party, supporting the making of money by individual enterprise rather than looking down on it as a slightly degrading pursuit. By the twentieth century the Conservative Party was cohesive but constituted a coalescence of different strands of thought.

Within British Conservatism, there are two main strands: the "Tory" and the "Whig," each of which may be further subdivided.[12] The Tory strand of thought places emphasis on social discipline, on authority, on continuity, and on ensuring that change does not do violence to the essential fabric of society; it tends to adhere strongly to the Disraelian concept of One Nation. The Whig strain is more concerned with future goals and places emphasis on the creation of wealth and the most efficient form of economic organization. It is thus more concerned with economics, whereas the Tory strain is more concerned with morals. Within the party, there is the potential for tension between continuity and change, between those favoring change in more radical or rapid form and those favoring moderation, and also between the Tory emphasis on social unity and the Whig neoliberal element, which stresses creative tension and competitive struggle.[13] On occasion, such tension has been realized. In the 1840s and again in the first decade of the twentieth century, the party split on the issue of tariff reform (the liberal strain within the party favoring free trade, the Tory element favoring the erection of tariff barriers to protect British industry). In the 1970s and 1980s the party was divided on the issue of economic policy and in the 1990s on the issue of European integration. Such occasions, though, have been the exception rather than the rule. Cohesiveness has been a distinguishing feature of the party for most of its history.

The cohesiveness of the Conservative Party may be attributed largely to the fact that, unlike the Labour Party, it is a party of tendencies rather than of factions[14]—that is, it lacks permanent factions organized to promote a specific set of beliefs. Rather, it comprises a set of differing but not mutually exclusive stands of thought that are not aligned in consistent opposition to one another. On some issues there may be dissent within the party, but the composition of the dissenting body changes from issue to issue, almost like a chemical reaction. One may be a Tory on one issue and something of a Whig on another. In consequence, a party member may disagree with the party on one issue but agree with it on other issues. This is in contrast to the Labour Party, which throughout its history has tended to be divided on a factional basis, with a clear divide between left and right wings of the party.

The Conservative Party traditionally has been led by leaders drawn more from the Tory than the Whig strain within the party. The postwar leaders up to 1965—Winston Churchill, Sir Anthony Eden, Harold Macmillan, and Sir Alec Douglas-Home (see Table 6.1)—were men essentially in the Tory paternalist mold, more concerned with social harmony and order than with the intricacies of economic management. In the 1960s the party's fortunes took a turn for the worse. The economy began to falter, and the party suffered a bitter, public battle for the party leadership in 1963. It seemed unable to offer a young and dynamic leadership to match that which the Labour Party was providing. Sir Alec Douglas-Home was able to assume the office of prime minister only after renouncing his title as the 14th Earl of Home. (The prime minister, by convention, sits in the Commons, not the House of Lords.) The party seemed to be out of touch with the tenor of the times, and in 1964 it lost the general election.

In July 1965, Douglas-Home resigned the party leadership. Previously the leader had not been elected but had been allowed to "emerge" following private consultations within the party hierarchy. Following the struggle for the leadership in 1963, rules for the election of the leader were adopted in 1964 and first employed in 1965. The electorate was the parliamentary party, and the MPs chose as leader Edward Heath, who was seen by his supporters as a neoliberal and as capable of challenging the Labour Party under the leadership of Harold Wilson. Both Heath and Wilson came from relatively humble origins, were of similar age, and stressed the need for economic efficiency.

The first four years of Heath's leadership were inauspicious ones, but in 1970 he led his party to a largely unexpected election victory. As prime minister he pursued what appeared to be a free-market economic policy. The aim was to force British industry to be more efficient. This goal also provided part of the motivation for British membership in the EC, which Heath achieved in

TABLE 6.1

CONSERVATIVE PARTY LEADERS SINCE 1945

(1940)–55	Winston Churchill	[prime minister 1940–45, 1951–55]
1955–57	Sir Anthony Eden	[prime minister 1955–57]
1957–63	Harold Macmillan	[prime minister 1957–63]
1963–65	Sir Alec Douglas-Home	[prime minister 1963–64]
1965–75	Edward Heath	[prime minister 1970–74]
1975–90	Margaret Thatcher	[prime minister 1979–90]
1990–97	John Major	[prime minister 1990–97]
1997–2001	William Hague	
2001–03	Iain Duncan-Smith	
2003–05	Michael Howard	
2005–	David Cameron	

1972 (see Chapter 9). However, the government's economic policy failed to produce the desired results. Unemployment and inflation spiraled, and in 1972 Heath dramatically undertook U-turns in industrial and economic policies: Public money was made available to help regional development and a statutory pay-and-prices policy was introduced.[15] The government's strategy was dashed by a world energy crisis and by opposition at home from trade unions. Heath called an election in February 1974 and, although the Conservatives got more votes than Labour, they got fewer seats. After seeking unsuccessfully to arrange a deal with the parliamentary Liberal Party, Heath resigned. A minority Labour government took office. In October, another general election gave Labour more seats and a small overall majority.

Heath's U-turns had not been popular with a section of the Conservative Party, especially neoliberals who saw them as an abandonment of their cherished free-market doctrine. Pressure within the parliamentary party resulted in Heath agreeing to new rules providing for the annual election of the leader. Heath immediately offered himself for reelection. In the election, held in 1975, Heath's main challenger was Margaret Thatcher, a little-known figure who had served in his Cabinet as education minister. She espoused the rhetoric of the neoliberal wing of the party and offered a new style of leadership. In the first ballot, Thatcher got 130 votes to Heath's 119. (A third candidate got 16 votes.) Heath promptly resigned the leadership and in a second ballot—in which new challengers were able to stand—Thatcher easily beat her other rivals. The Conservative Party had acquired its first female leader, one who was more clearly identified with the neoliberal wing of the party than any of her male predecessors.

Thatcher led the party in opposition until 1979, when the Labour government—by that time in a minority in the House of Commons—was defeated in a vote of confidence. A general election ensued, in which the Conservatives capitalized on the unpopularity of the government, its tax policies, and its links with the unions. Margaret Thatcher led her party to victory and she entered Downing Street as Britain's first female prime minister. She was to remain in Downing Street longer than any other prime minister of the twentieth century, a total of eleven years and six months. Her premiership went through three distinct periods.

The first period was one of bitter conflict. Under her leadership, the government embarked on a rigorous policy of controlling the money supply, reducing direct taxation, and limiting public expenditure in order to combat inflation. The policy ran into trouble. Techniques for controlling the money supply proved inadequate for the purpose. Attempts to reduce public spending proved unpopular in the country and with sections of the Conservative Party. The Tory wing proved especially uneasy about the effects the policy was having. Thatcher dismissed her party critics as "wets."[16] (Her supporters were then dubbed "dries," though becoming more frequently known by the eponymous title of "Thatcherites.") However, some of those critics were in the Cabinet and, despite the dismissal of various "wets" from the Cabinet between 1981 and 1983, the prime minister failed to persuade her own government to adopt more stringent measures. Subsidies to nationalized industries were continued. Trade union reforms were radical, but not as radical as the prime minister wanted.

The effects of the government's economic policy at a time of recession, and splits within the party, resulted in the government becoming highly unpopular. The party trailed in the opinion polls. At one point in 1981, following the formation of the Social Democratic Party (SDP), the Conservative Party was actually third in the polls. Within the parliamentary party, there were threats of a candidate running against Thatcher for the party leadership. The threat was never carried out but it served to emphasize the leader's political vulnerability.

The second period was that of domination by the leader. It began in 1982. Economic indicators began to move in the government's favor. The government's response to the Argentinean invasion of the Falkland Islands—dispatching a military task force to expel the invaders—restored it to popular favor. Following the successful recapture of the islands, the Conservative lead in the opinion polls held until the 1983 general election, sustained by falls in inflation and interest rates and by disarray within the Labour Party. The Falklands campaign also transformed the image of the prime minister. Prior to the campaign, the percentage of electors satisfied with her leadership was less than 30 percent; afterward, it was nearly 60 percent.[17] In the 1983 election, the party was swept back to office with the largest majority achieved by any Conservative government since 1935.

Thatcher's ascendancy was maintained in the new Parliament. The government faced down a prolonged national miners' strike; after 11 months of bitter conflict, the strike collapsed. It undertook an extensive program of privatization, a range of public utilities and companies being sold off to the private sector. Some sales, such as those of British Petroleum (BP), proved particularly popular. The proportion of the population owning shares quoted on the stock exchange doubled. Economic conditions improved: Unemployment peaked in 1986 and began to drop; inflation continued its downward trend. Economic improvement generated greater optimism for the future.

During this period, the government suffered a number of setbacks, including a major dispute between senior ministers in 1986, when two clashed over the most appropriate rescue package for Britain's only remaining, and ailing, helicopter company (Westland). The clash resulted in the resignation of both ministers, and generated complaints of a directionless cabinet and of a cover-up over the leaking of certain documents.[18] Dubbed the Westland affair, it dented the government's popularity, but the unpopularity proved short-lived. The government recovered and was in a sufficiently strong position for Thatcher to lead it to election victory again in 1987. In so doing she achieved an event unprecedented in the history of mass politics in Britain: She was the first leader to take her party to victory in three consecutive elections. The party was returned to office with an overall parliamentary majority of 101. Margaret Thatcher was at the zenith of her power.

The third period was one of conflict and fall.[19] In the new Parliament, the government embarked on a number of radical legislative measures. These included the replacement of the domestic rates, a local property tax paid annually, with a community charge based not on property but on the number of residents. Popularly dubbed the "poll tax," it was the most unpopular of several unpopular measures. Economic indicators also began to worsen. In 1989, inflation began to rise and Thatcher got into what became a public dispute with her chancellor of the exchequer, Nigel Lawson, over economic policy. In October 1989, he resigned. The party also witnessed internal rifts over the issue of European union. In 1988, Thatcher delivered a speech putting the case against further moves toward political and economic union. The speech generated a clash between opponents (Euro-skeptics) and supporters (Euro-enthusiasts) of such union. The clash meant that the party faced the European Parliament elections in June 1989 in disarray. In those elections the party lost 13 of its 45 seats, all to Labour candidates. It was the first time Margaret Thatcher had led her party to an electoral defeat.

Thatcher's stance on Europe propelled one Euro-enthusiast in the parliamentary party to challenge her in 1989 for the party leadership. Sir Anthony Meyer, a 69-year-old backbencher with no ministerial experience, knew he had no chance of winning, but was keen to allow dissidents to make their opposition clear. In the December 5 ballot, 314 Conservative MPs (84 percent of the parliamentary party) voted for Thatcher, 33 (9 percent) voted for Meyer, and 27 (7 percent) spoiled their ballots or abstained from voting. Sixty MPs had withheld their support from the leader.

In the spring of 1990, the introduction of the poll tax in England and Wales resulted in a significant level of nonpayment and demonstrations, some of them violent; London witnessed its worst riot in recent history. Labour led the Conservatives in the opinion polls by more than 20 points. Some Conservative MPs pressed for a reform, or even abolition, of the tax. Thatcher made clear she was committed to it. In the fall, she reiterated her opposition to further European union: "No, no, no," she thundered in the House of Commons. Those words precipitated the resignation of a senior cabinet minister, Sir Geoffrey Howe. His resignation speech, delivered on November 13, offered a stunning indictment of the prime minister's leadership. The following day, Michael Heseltine—a former cabinet minister, out of office since the Westland affair—announced he would challenge Thatcher for the party leadership.

The first ballot in the leadership contest was held on Tuesday, November 20. The prime minister herself was in Paris at a European summit the day of the poll. To win, a candidate had to obtain an absolute majority and a majority that constituted 15 percent of those eligible to vote. In the event, Thatcher fell four votes short. Under the rules, a second ballot was necessary. Thatcher declared her intention to contest that ballot. However, after consulting members of her Cabinet, she decided against doing so. In so deciding, she brought her leadership of the Conservative Party—and hence her premiership—to an end.

In the second ballot, two new challengers emerged to contest the leadership against Heseltine: Foreign Secretary Douglas Hurd and Chancellor of the Exchequer John Major. Major was 48 and was little known outside Westminster. In the ballot, held on November 27, Major led the field: He got 185 votes,

Heseltine 131, and Hurd 56. The two other candidates immediately conceded defeat. John Major was the new party leader and was to serve as prime minister for seven years. There were two distinct periods to his leadership.

The first period was one of recovery. Major brought in a new leadership style as prime minister. Unlike his predecessor, he did not adopt a confrontational stance, either in the cabinet or on the public platform. He preferred private, face-to-face meetings to the public arena. It was an approach that proved politically effective. He was more popular than his party. Despite the country slipping deeper into recession, survey data showed that electors blamed global economic conditions and his predecessor rather than John Major. Though the Conservatives trailed Labour in the opinion polls for most of 1991 and early in 1992, Major nonetheless led the Conservatives to victory in a general election on April 9, 1992. His government had the appearance of newness—unlike the old Thatcher government—and electors' unwillingness to trust Labour outweighed their dislike of the government's handling of a range of issues. The Conservatives were returned to office with a reduced parliamentary majority (of 21), but a majority nonetheless.

The second period was one of dramatic decline and internal party warfare. The election victory proved to be the one bright spot for the Conservatives. In 1992, the party again split badly on the issue of Europe (see Chapter 9), and a pound sterling crisis in September forced the government to withdraw from the European exchange-rate mechanism. In the three months prior to Britain's withdrawal, the Conservatives trailed Labour in the opinion polls by an average of just over 2 percent: In the three months following it, they trailed by almost 18 percent and never really recovered during the rest of the Parliament. "Confidence in John Major, the government's overall record and the future of the economy collapsed in tandem."[20] The party had lost its claim to be the party of economic competence. In May 1993, the prime minister dismissed the much-criticized Chancellor of the Exchequer, Norman Lamont. In his resignation speech in the House of Commons, Lamont savaged the government, claiming it was in office but not in power. Two months later, John Major was the most unpopular prime minister since opinion polling began. The party continued to court unpopularity as its MPs squabbled over the issue of European integration—Major himself criticizing some members of his own cabinet—and was hit by claims of financial and sexual impropriety leveled against various ministers and backbenchers.[21] Major's leadership became an increasing topic of debate, with various claims that he would be challenged for it. In the summer of 1995, he decided to take on his critics. He resigned the party leadership, offered himself as a candidate, and dared his critics to stand against him. A member of his own cabinet, John Redwood, resigned in order to contest the leadership. Though Major won—by 218 votes to 89, with 8 abstentions and 12 spoiled ballot papers—more than a hundred MPs, a third of the party, failed to back him.[22] Major's reelection failed to stem the party in-fighting. The party continued to be hit with allegations of private misconduct by MPs and with clashes over the issue of European integration.

During Major's leadership, the party failed to hold on to any of the seats it defended in by-elections (in the 1992–97 Parliament, it defended eight seats and lost them all), and four Conservative MPs defected to other parties. On March 17, 1997, Major announced that the general election would be held on May 1. The result was a disaster for the party: It lost just over half of the seats it was defending. It was reduced to 165 members in a 659-member House. Labour achieved an overall majority that was bigger than the size of the Conservative parliamentary party. Seven members of the cabinet were among the casualties. Taking the party's share of the vote together with the number of seats it won, it was the party's worst defeat of the twentieth century.

Once the results of the election were known, Major resigned as prime minister. Rather than spend a lengthy period as leader of the opposition, he immediately announced his resignation as party leader. Five former cabinet ministers contested the leadership. Two did badly in the first ballot and dropped out. In the second ballot, former Chancellor Kenneth Clarke got 64 votes, former Welsh Secretary William Hague got 62, and John Redwood, who challenged Major in 1995, got 38. Clarke—a noted supporter of European integration—was the candidate of the party left, Hague was seen as the candidate of the party center and center-right, and Redwood represented the Euro-skeptic right. Under the party's rules, Redwood was eliminated from the contest. In the third ballot, Hague won with 92 votes to 70 for Clarke. Hague was carried to victory by the votes of party loyalists and Euro-skeptics.[23] Like John Major, his support was broad but not deep.

Hague was 36 years of age. He had first come to national attention when, as a 15-year-old schoolboy, he had addressed the party conference. He had entered Parliament in 1989—still in his twenties—and became the youngest member of the cabinet in 1995 at the age of 34. As soon as he was elected leader, he immediately set about reforming the party. He instituted a radical change in the structure and organization of the party. He introduced a new method of electing the party leader, involving the membership of the party. He apologized for various past mistakes the party had made. He began a campaign of "Listening to Britain," all in an attempt to dispel the perception that the party had been arrogant in power. Although he proved a particularly effective performer in the House of Commons, and the party achieved a remarkable success in the 1999 elections to the European Parliament—emerging, ahead of Labour, with the largest number of seats—the party continued to trail badly behind in the opinion polls. In the 2001 general election campaign, Hague adopted a strategy of appealing to the party's core vote, one that had the effect of alienating the voters the party needed to attract in order to stand any chance of winning. It failed to make any significant dent in Labour's majority, with the party making a net gain of only one seat. As can be seen from the data in Chapter 5 (Table 5.2), it was in essence a standstill election. Hague followed the precedent set by Major and promptly resigned.

Under rules introduced by Hague and endorsed by the party, the party leader was now to be elected by the party membership. Conservative MPs had to ballot to narrow the choice down to two candidates, but party members then voted on which one was to be leader. Five candidates declared themselves and the MPs narrowed the field to a little-known right-wing MP, former Army officer Iain Duncan-Smith, and the well-known and popular former Chancellor of the Exchequer, Ken Clarke, a noted Europhile.[24] Clarke's popularity in the country failed to offset party members' distrust of his pro-European approach and Duncan-Smith won by 155,933 votes (61 percent) to Clarke's 100,864 (39 percent). The results were announced on September 13, 2001, having been delayed by a day because of the attacks on the World Trade Center and the Pentagon in the United States on September 11.

Duncan-Smith had no ministerial experience and had no deep support in the parliamentary party (less than a third of Tory MPs had voted for him in the final parliamentary ballot)[25] or in the party as a whole: The membership was voting against Clarke rather than for Duncan-Smith. His leadership proved disastrous. Like his predecessor, he failed to convey a clear sense of direction but unlike Hague he was not a good speaker. He appeared inconsistent on issues. He clashed with different sections of the party, including Tory peers in the House of Lords (over reform of the Lords) and with social liberals in the party in the Commons (over adoption of children by gay couples). He also appeared prone to panic, perceiving plots against him.[26] In October 2002, a poll found that 53 percent of party members thought the party had made a mistake in electing him as leader. Conservative MPs began to agitate to remove him and later that month forced a ballot of the parliamentary party on his continued leadership. By 90 votes to 75, they voted him out of the leadership.

There was no ballot to elect a leader in succession to Duncan-Smith, as there was only one candidate nominated to succeed him, former Cabinet minister Michael Howard. Howard was on the right of the party and had been a fairly authoritarian Home Secretary. He was well known but not especially popular in the country—some cartoonists characterized him as a vampire—and he essentially followed the pattern of his predecessors. He failed to demonstrate a clear vision for the future, appeared inconsistent, and as the 2005 election approached—and with the party trailing in the opinion polls—resorted to appealing to the party's core vote. Whereas Hague had appealed on the issue of opposition to further European integration, Howard focused on immigration. Electors favored the party's stance on the issue but did not accord it priority over other issues that determined how they voted. Though gaining seats (see Table 5.2), the party nonetheless went down to a third consecutive defeat.

Howard followed the now-standard pattern and promptly resigned the leadership. Several candidates put their name forward: It was widely assumed that the contest would be between two former ministers, right-winger David Davis and Ken Clarke. However, after a bravura performance at the party conference, a relatively new and up-and-coming MP, David Cameron, emerged as a serious contender and Ken Clarke failed to make it to the final two. The contest was between Davis and Cameron. Cameron was drawn from what used to be seen as the traditional background for Tory leaders, having been educated at Eton and Oxford. Davis was seen as representing a new breed: The son of a single mother, brought up in public housing, he had been successful in business. Cameron was young (born in 1966) and viewed as on the liberal wing of the party. He was a good performer on the public platform: Davis was not. Cameron won the vote of party members by 134,446 votes (67.6 percent) to 64,398 (32.4 percent) for Davis.

Cameron set about transforming the image of the party. He avoided excessive policy commitments, set up policy groups to advise the party, and emphasized issues such as the environment. He proved a good communicator and stressed what the party was for (freedom, protecting the environment, family, public services) rather than what it was against. He was a social liberal and pragmatic in economic terms. Unlike his predecessors, he avoided short-term responses to issues and concentrated on the performance of the Labour government. As the fortunes of the government declined, support for the Conservative Party increased. Cameron was able to demonstrate the Conservative Party was again a party that was electable.[27] The party established a consistent lead in the opinion polls in 2008, at one point achieving a 20-point lead in the polls. Though the lead fluctuated, especially as voters rallied around the Labour government when the economic crisis of 2008 struck, it nonetheless maintained a lead and was widely expected to form the next government. There was the prospect of the party winning a general election for the first time in almost twenty years.

PARTY ORGANIZATION Until 1998, the party had three distinct elements. One was the parliamentary party. This stood as an essentially autonomous body within the party. Another was the professional organization, comprising full-time professionals who existed to service the rest of the party. Most were employed in the party's Central Office, though some were employed at a regional level. The third element was the voluntary wing of the party, comprising party members throughout the country. The voluntary wing was organized through the National Union of Conservative and Unionists Associations. As we have already noted, both the Central Office and the National Union were created as a response to the new political situation brought about by the Reform Act of 1867. The National Union brought together the essential components of the party: the constituency parties. Each constituency party elected its own officers, had its own branches, and enjoyed a large measure of autonomy in selecting parliamentary candidates. Each local party engaged in fund-raising and social activities as well as candidate selection and campaigning during elections. Each local party also undertook membership recruitment. Members were recruited on a dues-paying basis (though there was no fixed membership fee) and membership was of the local constituency party. Legally, there was no national Conservative Party that one could join, the party comprising an amalgam of the local parties.

At the head of the party was the leader, in whom was vested enormous power. The leader was the fount of all policy, and chose the chairman and other leading officers of the party organization as well as the members of the front bench in the House of Commons. The annual party conference and other bodies within the party had advisory roles only. The leader was not all-powerful, in that there was a mutual dependence of the leader and led on one another—the leader had to carry the party in order to ensure that the leader's goals were met—and the position of the leader was sometimes under threat.[28] Even so, the leader was a powerful figure and recognized as such: The party looked to the leader to lead.

The party organization was variously reformed. There were significant changes following the party's loss of power in 1945. New bodies, such as the Conservative Political Centre (to encourage two-way discussion between members and party leaders), were formed, the party's youth wing was reorganized as the Young Conservatives, and a major—and successful— membership drive was undertaken. Even so, the basic structure of the party remained intact. This was to change following the election of William Hague as party leader in 1997.

When Hague took over the leadership in 1997, the Conservative Party faced a situation where it had (by historical standards) a small parliamentary party, a declining party membership (some constituency parties virtually existed in name only), and difficulty in raising funds to maintain the level of activities normally undertaken by Central Office. To meet what was seen as a critical situation for the party, Hague immediately undertook to overhaul party organization. Under his leadership, the three elements of the party were integrated into one. At the head of the party organization was a governing board, with most of its members elected, drawn from each part of the party. In addition to the annual party conference, a national Conservative convention was created, meeting twice a year to act as a link between the party leadership and members. The essential components of the organization remained the constituency parties. Each local party now had a chair, plus one deputy chair responsible for political activity and campaigning and another responsible for finance and membership.

Among other changes, the party sought to create a national membership (and a national minimum subscription): Members now join "the" Conservative Party. The national membership—producing, for the first time, a centrally held list of members—also makes possible one other major change: the involvement of the party members—and not just MPs—in the election of the party leader. A leadership contest can only be triggered by MPs, with MPs balloting to narrow the field to two candidates, but, in the final ballot, the choice rests with party members, voting on the basis of OMOV. For the Conservative Party, this change represented a massive shift from past practice.

Though the party still places great emphasis on the role of the leader, and the leader still exercises many of the traditional powers of the leader (including the selection of the party chairman—who chairs the new governing board— and front benchers), there is a far greater emphasis on the party membership. Membership, however, has declined markedly over the years. By 1997, the membership—which in the early 1950s claimed to be almost 3 million—was, according to some calculations, 750,000, and according to others, around or below 500,000. Following the creation of the new party structure, there was some evidence of an increase in membership, but the initial increase was modest. By mid-2000, the membership was reported to be no more than 350,000 and by the end of 2008 was claimed to be no more than 250,000.[29] The membership is an ageing one—the average age is over 60—though there is evidence of some appeal to students. The youth section, Conservative Future, is the largest political youth movement in Britain.

PARTY FUNDING   Of the political parties, the Conservative has historically been the best financed and throughout the twentieth century regularly outspent its opponents. By the last quarter of the century, a declining membership was taking its toll, reinforced at the end of the century by unpopularity and ejection from office.

The party's principal income derives from membership fees, constituency associations, individual and corporate donations, and public funding. The income from membership fees and constituency associations has declined—largely attributable to the fall in membership—while dependence on donations, as well as public funding, has increased. It has been estimated that that for both main parties in the United Kingdom membership fees accounted for 49 percent of the parties' central income in 1975–79. This had declined to 25 percent in 1993–97. By 2005, membership fees accounted for only 3.5 percent of the Conservative Party's central income.[30] Reliance on individual donations, from individuals and companies, has been a longstanding feature of the party, and by 2001–05, high value donations (over £100,000 including aggregated donations) accounted for 43 percent of the party's donation income. Some of this has come from wealthy individuals. One of the main corporate givers was a company linked to the party's treasurer (later its deputy chairman), Lord Ashcroft, a multimillionaire. By 2008, the company (Bearwood Corporate Services) was the party's biggest corporate giver.[31] A further 29 percent of the party's income came from state funding in the form of money paid to opposition parties (known as Short money) to fulfill their parliamentary duties and policy development grants.[32] All parties have been subject to detailed reporting requirements since 2000 and the party, along with the other main parties, has been subject to criticism over its compliance with those requirements. The role played by Lord Ashcroft, who has significant overseas business interests (primarily in Belize) and whose tax status has been subject to speculation (critics query whether he is treated as a U.K. resident), has been the matter of extensive speculation.

In common with other parties, the party has had difficulty in recent years in raising funds to meet all its election and organizational commitments. Expenditure increases in election years. In the 2001 general election campaign, the party spent £12.8 million ($20m.) and in the 2005 campaign it spent £17.85 million ($29.3m.). Even with various attempts at streamlining, costs have continued to exceed income (see Table 6.2). About 80 percent of party expenditure is on routine expenditure. To reduce costs, there have been exercises in rationalization: In 2008, 10 percent of Central Office staff were made redundant. Despite such efforts, the party continues to rely on borrowing money and for many years has carried a significant deficit. In 1993, it had

TABLE 6.2

CONSERVATIVE PARTY INCOME AND EXPENDITURE 2001–05

	Year				
	2001	**2002**	**2003**	**2004**	**2005**
Income	£23.3m	£9.9m	£13.6m	£20.0m	£35.3m
Expenditure	£25.0m	£10.5m	£16.0m	£26.2m	£39.2m

Source: House of Commons, Constitutional Affairs Committee, Party Funding, First Report of Session 2006–07, HC 163-I (London: The Stationery Office, 2006), pp. 10, 17.

a deficit of £19 million ($31.2m.): Energetic fundraising helped bring the party back in balance, but by 1997 it again was in deficit—estimated to be in the region of £4 million ($6.6m.). By 2005, this had increased to £6.2 million ($10.2m.). The party's increased popularity after 2005 contributed to more money being donated, and by the end of 2009 it was reported that the party had largely cleared its debt.

The party has thus attempted to restore its status as a party competing for office while at the same time having regularly to reorganize and retrench in order to stay afloat financially. For most of the twentieth century, the party was in power and was a well-financed organization. By the beginning of the twenty-first century, its dilemma was that it was neither.

The Labour Party

The Labour Party is best described as a coalition of disparate interests. It was formed, in effect, on February 27, 1900, at a conference comprising representatives of the socialist Independent Labour Party (the ILP), the Marxist Social Democratic Federation (the SDF), the Fabian Society (which believed in socialism by gradual means), and 65 trade unions. It called for "establishing a distinct Labour Group in Parliament, who shall have their own whips and agree upon policy, which must embrace a readiness to cooperate with any party which for the time being may be engaged in promoting legislation in the direct interest of labour, and be equally ready to associate themselves with any party in opposing measures having an opposite tendency." The conference refused to accept an SDF motion linking it with socialism and the class war, and the SDF subsequently withdrew from the movement. An executive committee, the Labour Representation Committee, was set up, consisting of representatives from the different organizations, the trade union representatives being in the majority. There was thus witnessed, in Carl Brand's words, "an alliance between socialism and trade unionism"; he added, "It was done in characteristically British fashion: with scant regard for theory, the best tool possible under the circumstances was fashioned. In spite of the fact that for two decades the drive had come from the socialists, they did not insist upon their name or programme."[33] In the general election of 1906, 29 Labour MPs were elected and the Labour Representation Committee thereupon changed its name to the Labour Party. The Labour Party had established itself on the British political scene.

The next major event in the party's history was the adoption of a new Constitution in 1918. There was a strong socialist element within the party, notably represented by the ILP, and the First World War had appeared to make socialist principles more relevant than they had been previously. It has also been argued that adopting a socialist program served a functional purpose in differentiating the party from the Liberals.[34] In any event, the party adopted what has been termed a Socialist Commitment and, in Clause 4 of its new Constitution, committed itself to the common ownership of the means of production. (The words "distribution and exchange" were added in 1928.) At its subsequent conference it adopted a program, *Labour and the New Social Order*, incorporating four principles: the enforcement of a national minimum (in effect, a commitment to full employment and a national minimum wage); the democratic control of industry, essentially through public ownership; a revolution in national finance (financing of social services through greater taxation of high incomes); and surplus wealth for the common good, using the balance of the nation's wealth to expand opportunities in education and culture. The program was to form the basis of party policy for more than thirty years.[35] At the same time, however, the party amended its own procedures in a way that weakened the socialist element within its ranks: The trade unions, on whom the party depended for financial support, were given greater influence through the decision to elect members of the party's NEC at the party conference, where the unions dominated; and the ILP was weakened by the decision to allow individuals to join the Labour Party directly. Previously, membership was indirect, through membership of affiliated organizations, and the ILP had been the main recruiting agent for political activists. Socialists within the party were to become increasingly wary of the attitude adopted toward the party's program by those who dominated the party leadership.

At the 1918 general election 63 Labour MPs were returned. In 1922 the number rose to 142, making the party the second largest in the House of Commons. In the 1923 general election the Conservatives lost their overall majority and Labour, with Liberal acquiescence, formed a short-lived minority government under the leadership of Ramsay MacDonald. Given the political constraints, the government achieved little—its main domestic success was the passage of a housing bill—and lasted less than ten months. A second minority Labour government was formed following the 1929 general election. Its domestic program was largely crippled either by the Liberals in the Commons or the Conservatives in the Lords. In response to the depression, it sought international loans, but these were dependent on financial cutbacks at home. The cabinet was divided on the issue and MacDonald tendered the government's resignation, subsequently accepting the king's invitation to form a coalition, or "National," government incorporating Conservative and Liberal MPs. The new government, though led by MacDonald, was dominated by the Conservatives. Within the Labour Party, MacDonald's action was seen as a betrayal of the party's cause and only a handful of Labour MPs followed him into the new government. The majority of the parliamentary party, along with the trade unions, disavowed his action, and he and his supporters were subsequently expelled from the party. The National government, with Mac-Donald and his supporters standing as National Labour candidates, won a landslide victory in a quickly called general election. The Labour Party achieved the return of only 52 MPs and, though the number increased to 154 in the 1935 general election, spent the 1930s in a political wilderness.

The Second World War, as we have seen (Chapter 3), had a significant impact on the fortunes and the appeal of the party. There had been a shift in popular attitudes, conducive to some form of social welfare program, and the party had proved itself a responsible partner of government in the wartime coalition. In 1945 it was returned with a large overall majority. In office, it implemented its election manifesto *Let Us Face the Future*, bringing into public ownership various public utilities and introducing a comprehensive social security system and national health service. Much of its program was soon implemented, perhaps too soon. By the end of the Parliament, the party had begun to lose its impetus and there were growing doubts as to the direction in which it should be going. In the general election of 1950 "Labour's campaign looked as much to the past as to the future"[36] and it was returned with a bare overall majority; in the general election called the following year it lost that majority altogether (despite receiving more votes than any other party), the Conservatives being returned to office.

The 1950s proved to be a period of bitter dispute within the party. The left wing within the party continued to press for greater control of the economy and the taking into public ownership of important industries: It remained committed to Clause 4 of the party's constitution. Revisionists within the party, influenced by Anthony Crosland and his 1956 seminal work, *The Future of Socialism*, argued that public ownership was no longer necessary because of the absence of large-scale unemployment and primary poverty. Rather, they argued, one should accept the mixed economy and seek instead the goal of equality—equality of opportunity, especially in the sphere of education. Such a goal was possible in an affluent managerial society. Public ownership was seen as largely irrelevant. The dispute between the two sides culminated at the turn of the decade, when party leader Hugh Gaitskell sought to remove Clause 4 from the party constitution. The major unions swung against him at the party conference and he was forced to back down. "Clause IV was retained, though, as a face saver, supplemented by an additional, fuller (and rapidly forgotten) statement of principles."[37] Gaitskell then turned his attention to the issue of the British nuclear deterrent, vigorously opposing attempts to commit the party to a policy of unilateral nuclear disarmament, and in so doing faced another serious internal party dispute.

Conservative unpopularity in the early 1960s and the election of Harold Wilson as party leader in 1963 following the sudden death of Gaitskell helped restore unity to the Labour Party as it sensed electoral victory. The party was returned to office in 1964. However, its periods of office from 1964 to 1970 and later from 1974 to 1979 were not successful ones. The attempt at a national plan in the first Wilson government was effectively still-born, and both periods of government witnessed generally orthodox attempts to respond to economic crises. The period of Labour government from 1974 onward, in particular, appeared to lack any clear direction, being pushed in different directions by international pressures and the domestic problems associated with trying to stay in office while lacking an overall parliamentary majority. The period witnessed a growing tension within the party between those who adhered to a gradual approach to the achievement of socialist goals, recognizing the constraint imposed by prevailing conditions, and those on the left who pressed for more immediate action and the taking into public ownership of key industries such as the banks. This tension effectively emerged onto the political stage as open and violent political warfare following the election defeat of 1979. It was not only to take the form of a policy dispute but also to be fought largely and ostensibly on the question of the party's constitution.

The Left within the Labour Party argued that the social democratic consensus policies of the 1950s had been tried and had failed. What was needed was a socialist economic policy, one not seriously tried before by a Labour government. The Left sought to increase its influence within the party by arguing for the election of the party leader (Table 6.3) by a wider franchise than the Parliamentary Labour Party (PLP), the compulsory reselection of MPs, and the vesting of the responsibility for writing the election manifesto in the party's NEC, where the Left was strong, rather than jointly by the NEC and the parliamentary leadership. At the party's 1980 conference the Left was successful in achieving two of these three objectives: the widening of the franchise for electing the leader, and MPs being subject to compulsory reselection procedures. At a special conference in January 1981 the party adopted a formula for the election of the leader by an electoral college, the trade unions to have 40 percent of the votes, constituency parties 30 percent, and the PLP

TABLE 6.3

LABOUR PARTY LEADERS SINCE 1945

(1935)–55	Clement Attlee	[prime minister 1945–51]
1955–63	Hugh Gaitskell	
1963–76	Harold Wilson	[prime minister 1964–70, 1974–76]
1976–80	James Callaghan	[prime minister 1976–79]
1980–83	Michael Foot	
1983–92	Neil Kinnock	
1992–94	John Smith	
1994–2007	Tony Blair	[prime minister 1997–2007]
2007–	Gordon Brown	[prime minister 2007–]

30 percent. (This new method was employed for the first time in 1983 following the resignation of party leader Michael Foot.)

For a number of politicians on the right of the party, already bitterly opposed to the party's policy to withdraw from the EC, the constitutional changes constituted the final straw. They responded by creating a Council for Social Democracy and then, in March 1981, broke away from the party completely, forming a new party, the Social Democratic Party (the SDP). Others in sympathy with their views remained within the Labour Party to fight the battle there.

The next two years proved politically disastrous for the Labor Party. In the fall of 1981, there was a bitterly fought contest for the party deputy leadership between the incumbent, Denis Healey, and the candidate of the Left, Tony Benn. Healey won by a tiny margin. More and more Labour MPs defected to join the SDP. The party entered the 1983 general election campaign with a manifesto that called for withdrawal from the EC, a non-nuclear defense program, a "massive" rise in public expenditure, a wealth tax, and the return to public ownership of assets privatized by the Conservatives. The manifesto was described by one of the party's own leading figures as "the longest suicide note in history." The party faced both a Conservative government buoyed by the success of the 1982 Falklands campaign and the SDP, which was drawing away some of Labour's traditional supporters. The party had a disastrous campaign, with a leader (Michael Foot) whom the media refused to take seriously as a potential prime minister. On election day, Labour suffered its worst result since 1918 in terms of the percentage of the vote obtained. It got 28 percent of the votes cast, only marginally ahead of the share obtained by the alliance of Liberal and Social Democratic parties.

In the wake of the election defeat, Foot resigned the leadership and was succeeded by Neil Kinnock, a 41-year-old Welshman with no ministerial experience. Despite occasional effective speeches on the conference platform, Kinnock did not shine in the House of Commons and was no match for Margaret Thatcher. He did, however, achieve greater control than his predecessor over the party organization and began to mold it into a more effective body for fighting elections. His performance in the 1987 general election was recognized as highly professional—according to a Gallup poll, 43 percent of those questioned thought he had campaigned impressively, against 20 percent so rating Thatcher—and Labour mounted a more polished campaign than the Conservatives. The party's manifesto, however, remained an electoral liability, its defense policy in particular being exploited by its opponents. (It had committed itself to replacing nuclear defense with a conventional force.) In an exit poll on election day, 52 percent of those questioned said the party's defense policy had made them "less likely" to vote Labour. The party made some gains, especially in Scotland, but was still relegated to the political wasteland of opposition.

Immediately after the election, the party established seven policy groups to review policy. In 1988, the groups produced a broad review of policy and the following year produced specific policy recommendations. The recommendations shifted the party away from the policies that had proved an electoral liability. On defense, for example, it moved the party toward multilateral nuclear disarmament. Neil Kinnock was able to use his control of the party's NEC and an increasing body of support within the party to achieve endorsement by the party conference of the recommendations.

The party's new policy was embodied in a policy document, *Meet the Challenge, Make the Change* (1989), and in two subsequent documents, *Looking to the Future* (1990) and *Opportunity Britain* (1991). "Overall, two major themes emerged. . . . First, intraparty political debate over the extent of public and private ownership was outdated; and second, the quality of public service should be improved by putting the needs of the user before those of the producer."[38] The review established a new paradigm for the party, aided in the defense sector by the collapse of the Iron Curtain and the end of the Cold War. By 1990, Labour began to appear as a moderate and credible alternative to the increasingly unpopular Thatcher government.

Labour achieved a large lead in the opinion polls early in 1990. That lead receded later in the year and briefly disappeared altogether following the replacement of Margaret Thatcher with John Major as prime minister, and in the wake of the 1991 Gulf War. The party reestablished a lead in the polls later in 1991, which it retained into 1992 and the election campaign in March and April. However, the lead was not as large as might have been expected given the severity of the recession and, against general expectations that Labour would win more seats than the Conservatives, Labour failed to pull off an election victory. Though losing seats, the Conservatives held on to an overall majority in the House of Commons. Despite it being preferred over the Conservatives on most social issues, Labour had failed to shake off a lingering public distrust in its competence to handle the economy and in the qualities of its leader. Most voters believed the Conservatives were better able to handle the economy than Labour, that a Labour government would increase taxes, and that John Major was better qualified to be prime minister than Neil Kinnock.[39]

In the wake of the election defeat, Neil Kinnock resigned the leadership. In July, he was succeeded by a 53-year-old Scot, John Smith, who won the leadership contest decisively: He got 91 percent of the votes (winning easily in each of the three parts of the electoral college), his challenger, Bryan Gould, the candidate of the Left, picking up the remaining 9 percent. Smith was seen as a solid performer and got off to a good start, but thereafter failed to shine. Conservative unpopularity, however, ensured Labour maintained a strong lead in the opinion polls. Smith's leadership was short. On May 12, 1994, he suffered a massive and fatal heart attack. The leadership was then contested by three candidates: Tony Blair, John Prescott, and Margaret Beckett. Blair was 41 years of age, a lawyer by training, and represented a new, right-wing modernizing element in the party. "After eleven years in opposition, and after the success of both Bill Clinton and the Australian Labour Party, Blair had developed into a convinced modernizer believing that only a moderate, left-of-center, pro-European party, independent of the trade unions, would be elected to office."[40] Prescott and Beckett were both on the party's left wing and in parliamentary terms were long-serving Members. (Prescott had been elected to Parliament in 1970 and Beckett was first elected in 1974, whereas Blair was elected to the House in 1983.) Blair won a comfortable—but not overwhelming—victory, carrying each section of the electoral college (each now having equal weight in the contest, with the principle of OMOV being applied in each): He achieved just over 60 percent of the votes in the parliamentary section and just over 50 percent in each of the other two sections. Prescott was elected deputy leader.

Once elected as leader, Blair immediately set about creating what he termed—and what was to become in common parlance—"New Labour." One of his first acts was to get the party to jettison Clause 4 of the party constitution and replace it with a new clause entitled *"Labour's Aims and Values."* The change was approved by a special party conference in 1995. The new clause defined Labour as a "democratic socialist party" and committed the party to common endeavors and to work for a dynamic economy (joining

---

Clause 4: Labour's Aims and Values

1. The Labour Party is a democratic socialist party. It believes that by the strength of our common endeavour we achieve more than we achieve alone, so as to create for each of us the means to realise our true potential and for all of us a community in which power, wealth and opportunity are in the hands of the many not the few, where the rights we enjoy reflect the duties we owe, and where we live together, freely, in a spirit of solidarity, tolerance and respect.
2. To these ends we work for:
    A dynamic economy serving the public interest, in which the enterprise of the market and the rigour of competition are joined with the forces of partnership and co-operation to produce the wealth the nation needs and the opportunity for all to work and prosper, with a thriving private sector and high quality public services, where those undertakings essential to the common good are either owned by the public or accountable to them;
    A just society, which judges its strengths by the condition of the weak as much as the strong, provides security against fear, and justice at work; which nurtures families, promotes equality of opportunity and delivers people from the tyranny of poverty, prejudice and the abuse of power;
    An open democracy, in which the government is held to account by the people; decisions are taken as far as practicable by the community they effect; and where fundamental human rights are guaranteed;
    A healthy environment, which we protect, enhance and hold in trust for future generations.
3. Labour is committed to the defence and security of the British people, and to co-operating in European institutions, the United Nations, the Commonwealth and other international bodies to secure peace, freedom, democracy, economic security and environmental protection for all.
4. Labour will work in pursuit of these aims with trade unions, co-operative societies and other affiliated organisations, consumer groups and other representative bodies.
5. On the basis of these principles, Labour seeks the trust of the people to govern.

FIGURE 6.1
New Clause 4 of the Labour Party constitution

the enterprise of the market with the forces of partnership and cooperation), a just society, an open democracy, and a healthy environment. The new clause is reproduced in Figure 6.1. Blair also committed the party to five principal and specific aims if returned to office: cutting class sizes in junior schools, speeding up punishments for young offenders, cutting the waiting lists of those waiting for hospital treatment, taking 250,000 young people off welfare benefits, and setting tough rules on government borrowing and spending. In addition, a commitment was made to stick to Conservative spending plans during the first two years of a Labour government. In addition, there were to be no increases in the basic and top rates of income tax. "Moderation and caution were the essence of New Labour's appeal to the voters."[41]

This new moderate message was accompanied by a continuing utilization of new campaign techniques. The party threw off its old image as an old-fashioned organization and embraced new technology. It utilized the Internet to disseminate information; a "cyber cafe" was created at the party conference. It used telephone canvassing on an extensive basis. Focus groups were used to test reaction to policies. Key seats and key groups of voters—especially middle-income families—were targeted for special treatment. "New Labour" came across as a new party both in terms of what it stood for and in terms of how it was organized. It increasingly attracted back supporters who had defected in the 1980s to the SDP. It made inroads into traditional areas of Conservative strength and entered the 1997 election campaign with a massive lead in the opinion polls. That lead was translated into victory at the polls.

Labour was elected in 1997 with an overall majority of 179 in the House of Commons. As we have seen in Chapter 5 (Table 5.4), it was the largest majority achieved by a postwar government. The government set about implementing its election promises. At the forefront of these was its pledge to introduce constitutional change. As we have seen in Chapter 4, these promises encompassed, among other things, elected assemblies in Scotland and Wales, an elected mayor and authority for Greater London, the incorporation of the European Convention on Human Rights into British law, and reform of the House of Lords. There were also several measures passed covering education and law and order and another to introduce a national minimum wage.

Tony Blair also strengthened his hold on the party organization. The new methods of election to the European Parliament were seen as being used by the leadership to remove left-wing incumbents. The party conference was given a new format to squeeze out motions that challenged government policy. Stricter discipline was imposed in the parliamentary party, MPs being given instructions on how to vote and what to do via pagers. It was also decided to send to local parties each year a report on the activity of the local MP. At government level, the prime minister appointed in 1998 a new minister for the cabinet office—dubbed by the media as "the enforcer"—to ensure that departments carried out government policy. All such activity led various commentators to assert—as they had variously done under the prime ministership of Margaret Thatcher—the "presidentialization" of British politics.

Despite some electoral embarrassments—the party failed to win an absolute majority of seats in the new Scottish Parliament (it was forced to enter into coalition with the Liberal Democrats) and came in second to the Conservatives in elections to the European Parliament—the party nonetheless remained the "in" party in British politics. The Conservative Party had difficulty creating itself as an effective opposition and the economy entered an unprecedented period of sustained economic growth. Labour had turned the tables on the Conservative Party: Labour was now seen as the party of governance, more trusted than the Conservatives in handling the economic affairs of the nation. When Blair called an election in 2001, the result was not a surprise: Labour was returned to office with another large majority. The Conservatives gained only one seat extra in the election.

The 2001 Parliament was dominated by foreign policy: the decision to go to war in Afghanistan in 2001 and Iraq in 2003. The decision to join the United States in invading Iraq created a major rift within the party's ranks. When the House of Commons voted on the issue, it was carried by the votes of Tory MPs: Labour faced the biggest back-bench rebellion in its history: 143 Labour MPs voted against the government. The action undermined the government's unpopularity. The government also pursued a number of other domestic policies—including introducing top-up fees for university students (having said in its manifesto that it would do the opposite)—that generated dissent within its own ranks. Despite growing popular unease with the government, the Conservative Party was still not seen as a credible alternative. When Blair called an election in 2005, he achieved the unprecedented feat for a Labour prime minister of leading his party to a third consecutive election victory. Though the government's majority was reduced, it was still a substantial one.

In 2007, after ten years in office—and following pressure within the party's ranks (not least from Gordon Brown, the chancellor of the exchequer)—Blair stepped down and was succeeded by Brown. Brown was slightly older than Blair and was widely reported to have resented Blair standing for leader in 1994; he felt he should have been the candidate. Brown had been heir apparent since the party entered government and there were regular reports of his impatience to assume the mantle of the premiership. When he did so, he placed a greater emphasis on reform within government—he introduced a *Governance of Britain* agenda, which included transferring some prerogative powers to Parliament—and on social policy. However, he soon ran into problems. He was encouraged by some supporters to call a general election in the autumn of 2007: It was widely expected that he would so, but he then announced there would be no election. It suggested caution and poor political skills. Conservative support began to increase. In 2008, the Tory lead in the opinion polls at one point reached 20 points. The nation was then hit by the global "credit crunch," with government having to devote billions of pounds to saving leading banks. Brown's initial handling of the crisis attracted public support: He was seen as an experienced pair of hands. However, as the measures taken by government failed to have the desired effect, the Conservative lead in the polls increased. The lead was such as to convince commentators that—with a general election due by the summer of 2010—Labour would soon swap the role of the "in" party in British government to that of the "out" role. The party was also hit by a scandal surrounding MPs' expenses in 2009 (Chapter 12). In the same year it did disastrously in the local elections and in European Parliament elections it won only 13 seats (down from 19 in 2004 and 29 in 1999). Having been the dominant party in British politics for more than a decade, its opponents were able to exploit a feeling among electors that it was time for a change. Though surveys suggested that electors still had doubts about the Conservative Party, these were outweighed by their dislike of the Labour government, and especially Prime Minister Gordon Brown.

PARTY ORGANIZATION   Formally, the party stresses the concept of intraparty democracy. Historically, the two most important bodies in the party, according to the party's constitution, have been—and remain—the party conference and the NEC. The party conference, which meets each year in the autumn, is formally responsible for determining the party program. A proposal that receives two-thirds or more of the votes cast at conference is adopted as part of the program. Between conferences, the body responsible for party organization and policy discussion is the party's NEC, which will normally bring policy documents forward for approval by the conference.

In practice, the reality of power in the party is much more complicated. Under Neil Kinnock's leadership, the power of the NEC over local parties was increased. In 1997, reflecting the shift from Old Labour to New Labour, various policy forums were introduced. These were designed to give members some input into policy deliberations. A National Policy Forum (NPF)—with 175 members, meeting two or three times a year—was created and this oversees policy commissions, which send policy proposals to local parties and affiliated bodies. The local parties and affiliated bodies form policy forums to discuss the proposals and then report back to the policy commissions. The NPF, along with a Joint Policy Commission (JPP)—chaired by the party leader and including some ministers, MPs, MEPs, and party officials—consider the reports and prepare summaries for the party conference. Following debates at conference, the NPF and JPP prepare summaries and reports, which are sent to constituency parties and affiliated bodies. They respond and the NPF and JPP prepare proposals which are then presented to the party conference, which then determines whether to support them. Each report is voted on as a single entity: There is no scope for selecting particular parts for approval or rejection.

Though on the surface strengthening the position of party members, the whole process is claimed to be dominated by party officials, with the party conference in effect endorsing what the leadership wants. The development is seen as part of a long process in which the significance of the party conference has declined. At the conference, voting has historically been based on an organization's membership, not on the individual votes of those present. Thus the trade unions, with large affiliated memberships, have cast the most votes. In the 1950s, the unions' so-called block vote used to be cast regularly in support of the party leadership but became less predictable from the early 1960s onward. Under the leadership of Neil Kinnock, the unions generally supported his attempts to moderate the party in policy terms but were wary of attempts to reform their own role in party activities. Moves by Kinnock to reduce union influence at conference and in candidate selection in constituencies ran into some union criticism. "No say, no pay" was how one union leader responded to attempts to reform the block vote. At the 1992 conference, it was agreed to cut the union voting strength at conference from 87 percent to 70 percent. John Smith sought to limit the collective impact of the unions even further, again encountering opposition. A further reduction in the union vote was achieved under Blair's leadership. At the 1995 conference, the union's voting strength was reduced to 50 percent.

Traditionally, Labour conferences have differed from Conservative conferences in that the latter are advisory and often stage-managed affairs. Labour conferences have often been lively and unpredictable. However, they are now seen as resembling far more their Conservative counterparts. Indeed, under Blair's leadership, Labour conferences were molded for the purposes of media presentation. Labour activists have complained that the policy forums and the party conference are, in the words of one MP, "a smokescreen for autocratic decision making."[42] In 1997, the party manifesto was put to a ballot of party members. The practice was not repeated in 2001 and 2005. According to a former deputy leader of the party, the 2005 manifesto was "presented to the party *fait accompli*" with "no obvious sign that the membership had been heeded."[43]

The transformation of the party from an apparently old-fashioned, left-wing, union-dominated party to a modern, centrist party free of union control has also been reflected in changes in its membership. The party has a large, indirect membership deriving from trade unions and other affiliated organizations. Members of unions pay, as part of their union subscription, a "political levy" (unless they explicitly opt out of so doing) and thus become affiliated members of the party. This affiliated membership provides the party with most of its income as well as a large paper membership. The party has almost 5 million affiliated members. This affiliated membership has dwarfed the number of individuals who have joined the party directly, thus allowing the unions to dominate both the party conference and local parties. The direct membership of the party has traditionally been much lower than that of the Conservative Party. Even in the early 1990s, the Labour Party had fewer direct members than the Conservative Party. This changed initially under Blair's leadership: By 1997—the year of Labour's triumph at the polls—it topped the 400,000 mark, outstripping the declining membership of the Conservative Party. This proved a high point. As the years of Labour government progressed, membership declined. In a submission to the Electoral Commission in 2008, the party conceded that its membership at the end of 2007 stood at just under 177,000. It was believed to be the lowest since the party had a direct membership. Many local parties existed in name only and the party had difficulty bringing in new blood to revive its grassroots organization.

PARTY FUNDING   The upsurge in membership in the 1990s and the party's
dominance in the opinion polls—establishing it as the government in waiting—
also had one other effect. It helped the party's financial situation. By the end
of the 1980s, the party had a running deficit of more than £1 million ($1.64
million). This was exacerbated by the cost of the 1992 election campaign.
Under Blair's leadership, membership increased and the party became more
attractive to donors. The unions continued to provide the bulk of the party
finance—between 1992 and 1997, four unions gave donations of at least
£1 million a year each—but the proportion declined. Between 1986 and
1996 the proportion of party funds supplied by the unions declined from
two-thirds to one-half. Private business became increasingly important as a
source of funds, providing—according to one source—some £15 million
($24.6 m.) over a nine-month period from June 1996.[44] Some individuals are
known to have donated more than £1 million ($1.64m.) each. One donor
attracted particular controversy. Bernie Ecclestone, a leading figure in Formula One car racing, made a £1 million donation to the party. When the
Government subsequently decided, not long after the 1997 general election,
to extend the period for the phasing out of tobacco advertising in motor racing, there were accusations of a conflict of interest. As a result of the controversy, the party returned Ecclestone's donation to him.
     The 1997 election took its toll on party finances. It is estimated that the
party spent some £26 million ($42.6 m.) on the election. It had a staff of
some 250 in a new campaign headquarters (Millbank Tower). After the election, it had a deficit of some £2 million ($3.3 m.) and had to reduce the num-
ber of personnel. This was a recurring theme throughout the next decade, the
party building up debts and then having to rationalize. In the 2005 general
election, it spent £17.9 million ($29.4m.). By 2007, it had a debt of nearly
£25 million ($41m.). By reducing costs, including reducing the number of
staff, it managed to reduce this to just under £18 million ($29.5m.) the fol-
lowing year, but it owed £15 million ($24.6m.) to individual lenders. The
party's reliance on individual lenders proved highly controversial, especially
when allegations were made (and investigated by the police) that some
donors had been offered peerages in return for donations. Some nominees for
peerages who were leading donors had their nominations declined by the
House of Lords appointments commission.
     Most of the party's central income is spent on personnel and organiza-
tion. The same applies to money raised locally. Like the Conservatives,
Labour has local constituency parties. Income raised by local parties varies
considerably. Many—over 200—benefit from some funding from the unions.
The trades unions used to sponsor candidates but, in order to avoid claims of
a conflict of interest by MPs, Tony Blair persuaded the unions to sponsor the
local parties directly rather than the candidates. The sponsorship provides a
modest but very useful income. Historically, local Labour parties have not
been as well funded nor as well organized as Conservative constituency parties. The Conservatives have tended to have far more constituency agents
(full-time executive officers). But in recent years the gap has narrowed, if not

disappeared, in part because of improvements in Labour's organization, but more importantly, because of the decline in Conservative funding and organization. In the first decade of the twenty-first century, both parties had difficulty maintaining a credible grassroots organization.

THIRD PARTIES

In the postwar years from 1945 to 1970, the principal third party in Britain, and the only one to enjoy parliamentary representation throughout the period, was the Liberal Party. Its parliamentary strength was small, but as *the* third party it had no obvious competitors. That ceased to be the case in the last quarter of the century. In the twenty-first century, third parties are notable for their number and their presence in parliamentary bodies in the United Kingdom.

In the 1970s, the Scottish and Welsh Nationalist parties grew in strength: They had both gained a parliamentary toehold in the 1960s (one seat each) but that grew rapidly in 1974. In 1972, the Ulster Unionists in Northern Ireland, previously affiliated with and, in parliamentary terms, subsumed within the Conservative Party, broke away (in protest at the imposition of direct rule in the province) to sit as a separate parliamentary party. The Unionists witnessed divisions within their own ranks, resulting in the return of MPs representing different Unionist parties.

The situation became even more complicated in the 1980s. In 1981, the SDP, drawing its parliamentary strength from defecting Labour MPs (and one defecting Conservative), was formed. It then entered into an alliance with the Liberal Party. In 1988, the two parties voted to merge. They created the Social and Liberal Democratic Party, known popularly as the Liberal Democratic Party.

In 1987, the sole SDLP MP from Northern Ireland was joined by two more colleagues, thus establishing another new parliamentary party. A Sinn Féin MP, Gerry Adams, had been elected in 1983 and 1987 (though refusing to take his seat in the Commons). He lost his seat in 1992 but was elected again in 1997, along with another Sinn Féin candidate, Martin McGuiness. Both refused to take the oath and so were barred from the House. However, in terms of numbers, they were sufficient to form a parliamentary party.

Nine parties had members elected to the House of Commons in 2005. (Two independent MPs were also elected.) In 2008, one MP, having lost the Conservative whip, joined the UKIP, thus giving the party its first MP. The position has become even more complex in recent years with other parties gaining seats in the Scottish Parliament, the Northern Ireland assembly, the National Assembly for Wales, and the European Parliament (Table 6.4). As a result of elections to these bodies, the number of parties able to claim some form of parliamentary representation has increased substantially. Not only have third parties gained representation to these bodies, some have also become parties of government. The SNP, Plaid Cymru, the DUP, and Sinn Féin may each have a small number of members in the House of Commons, but they are in their respective devolved bodies parties of government.

TABLE 6.4

Party representation in parliamentary bodies

	Number of members elected to				
Party	House of Commons (2005)	Scottish Parliament (2007)	Welsh Assembly (2007)	Northern Ireland Assembly (2007)	European Parliament (2009)
Labour	355	46	26		13
Conservative	198	17	12		25
Liberal Democrat	62	16	6		11
Scottish National	6	47			2
Plaid Cymru	4		15		1
Ulster Unionist	1			18	1
Democratic Unionist	9			36	1
SDLP	3			16	
Sinn Féin	5			28	1
Green		2		1	2
UK Independence					13
British National Party					2
Alliance				7	
People's Voice			1		
Progressive Unionist				1	
Respect	1				
Independent	2	1			

The Liberal Democrats

The *Liberal Democratic Party* was formed in 1988 by the merger of the long-established Liberal Party and the relatively new SDP. By virtue of its age and parliamentary representation, the Liberal Party was the senior partner in the merger.

The Liberal Party had a relatively short history as a major political party, spanning less than sixty years. Succeeding the Whigs in the 1860s, it was a major force on the British political scene until the 1920s, when it went into rapid decline. Like the other parties, it is a coalition of interests. The main tenets of Gladstonian Liberalism in the nineteenth century were free trade, home rule for Ireland, economy wherever possible, and social reform where necessary. Within the party there was a radical wing, which placed more emphasis on social reform, as well as an imperialist wing.[45] Returned to government in 1906, the party enacted a number of social reforms, but it proceeded on the basis of no coherent program and was divided on a number of important issues. The second decade of the century proved a disastrous one. The party was beset by such problems as division in Ireland, the suffragettes, and the First World War.[46] It was also rent asunder by a rift between Herbert H. Asquith, the party leader until 1916, and Lloyd George, who successfully displaced him. The rift was never really healed successfully. The party's internal problems and its declining electoral appeal were to reduce its parliamentary numbers. In 1918 the election was won by a coalition consisting of Lloyd George Liberals and the Conservatives. The Conservatives were the dominant partner, though Lloyd George remained as premier. In 1922, Conservative MPs brought the coalition to an end. In the ensuing general election, 62 National Liberal and 54 Liberal MPs were returned. The position improved temporarily in 1923, when 159 Liberal MPs were returned. In 1924 the number returned was only 40. In subsequent elections the number returned was 59 (1929), 33 (1931, 41 Liberal National MPs also being returned),[47] and 20 (1935). In the general elections between 1945 and 1979 the number of Liberal MPs elected varied from 6 to 14. The only occasion in postwar years when it came close to government was during the period of the Liberal-Labour (known as the Lib-Lab) Pact from 1977 to 1978, when it achieved some concessions and the opportunity to consult in return for sustaining the minority Labour government in office.[48] The pact proved unpopular with party activists and was short-lived.

The fortunes of the party appeared to improve in 1981, when it entered into an alliance with the newly formed SDP. The SDP was formed in March 1981 when a number of Labour politicians broke away from the Labour Party. The new party was led by four former Labour Cabinet ministers, dubbed by newspapers as "the Gang of Four": Roy Jenkins, Shirley Williams, David Owen, and William Rodgers. The party was created with the ostensible aim of "breaking the mold" of British politics.[49] It wanted to get away from the adversary relationships that had characterized British politics, favoring instead consensus government that would represent the center ground of British politics. It favored decentralization, equality, electoral reform, a pay-and-prices policy, and European integration.

By the end of 1981, a total of 27 Labour MPs (and one Conservative) had defected to join the new party. It attracted over 70,000 members, and by December its support in the Gallup poll exceeded that of any other party. It formed an alliance with the Liberal Party, and alliance candidates began to score some notable victories in by-elections.[50] Within a year of its formation, it posed a threat to the two main traditional parties.

During 1982 it began to develop its internal organization and to formulate policies. It also witnessed a decline in support. The former may provide a partial explanation for the latter. As the party committed itself to specific policies and as it selected a leader with a distinctive leadership style and appeal, so it began to shed its "catchall" appeal. A contest for the party leadership and a dispute with the Liberals over the allocation of alliance candidatures produced some loss of support. The Falklands campaign also served to rob it of much-needed publicity.

A consequence of these developments was that the alliance entered the 1983 election campaign in third place in the opinion polls. As the campaign progressed and the Labour campaign faltered, alliance support increased. In the end, despite its worst share of the poll for almost seventy years, the Labour Party retained second place in the polls and benefited from the concentration of its support. The alliance obtained 26 percent of the votes but suffered from the broadness of its support: Only 23 alliance MPs were returned, 17 of them Liberals and 6 SDP.

The two parties remained in alliance but, with a limited parliamentary base, failed to make a dent in public consciousness during the new Parliament. In the general election of 1987, alliance candidates garnered just under 23 percent of the vote and 22 seats. Following the election, Liberal leader David Steel pressed for a merger of the two parties, believing that such a move was necessary if the alliance were to maximize its impact. Agreement was reached eventually on a merged party: The new party was formed with the support of all 17 Liberal MPs but only two SDP MPs; the remaining three SDP MPs refused to join.

The new party immediately encountered a problem of nomenclature: Liberals were insistent that the name "Liberal" should not be lost. Finally the party chose the name of the Social and Liberal Democratic Party. It was not a popular choice, especially with Liberal MPs, and the name was believed to contribute to confusion on the part of electors about the nature of the party. The party elected as leader a relatively new MP, Paddy Ashdown, a candidate with a reputation for dynamism and for occasionally being erratic. The combination of new name and leader appeared to leave electors confused as to what the party was and what it had to offer. The party did badly in local elections in 1988 and 1989 and trailed the Green Party in the 1989 European Parliament elections, in which the party got a little over 6 percent of the vote. That performance represented the nadir of the party's fortunes. The party then decided to be called by the name Liberal Democrats. In 1991, Paddy Ashdown had a "good Gulf War": The only ex-serviceman (he had served in the marines) among the party leaders, he appeared frequently on television to provide authoritative comments. Party fortunes appeared to improve. In the 1992 general election, the party got just under 18 percent of the vote: down on the alliance performance in 1983 and 1987 but better than might have been expected two or three years before. The party was overshadowed after 1992 by Labour's dominance in the opinion polls and, especially after Tony Blair became leader, by Labour's move toward the political center. Former Labour supporters who had defected to the SDP in the early 1980s returned to the fold. In 1997, the party failed to improve on its percentage share of the vote but, because of tactical voting (Labour supporters voting Liberal Democrat in seats in which the Liberal Democrats were the principal challengers to the incumbent Conservatives), the party achieved its best parliamentary representation for more than sixty years: 46 Liberal Democrats were elected to the House of Commons. For the first time in postwar history, the party had a notable presence in Parliament. Though the size of Labour's majority meant that the Liberal Democrats could not have an impact on the outcome of votes, the party shared some policy goals with Labour, especially on constitutional issues, and Prime Minister Blair set up a Cabinet committee, comprising ministers and some Liberal Democrat MPs, to consider constitutional change. The committee had no decision-making powers but it constituted a significant departure in terms of constitutional practice. In 1999, the party saw greater practical cooperation with the Labour Party: In Scotland, where it won 17 seats in the new parliament, it entered into coalition with Labour in order to form a Scottish administration. The leader of the Liberal Democrats in Scotland became deputy first minister (see Chapter 10) and various portfolios were given to the party. In 2000, it also formed a coalition with Labour in the National Assembly for Wales. At the same time, the party saw a change in leadership. Paddy Ashdown decided to retire in 1999. The party elected in his place a 39-year-old former SDP MP, Charles Kennedy. He proved popular with electors. In the 2001 election, the party saw the election of 52 MPs and in 2005 it achieved its best result since 1924 with the return of 62 MPs. The party picked up further seats in by-elections.

The fortunes of the party, however, started to decline thereafter. There were problems in terms of leadership and ideology. In 2006, persistent rumors of a drinking problem led to Kennedy being forced out of the leadership—he subsequently admitted to being an alcoholic. He was replaced by Sir Menzies Campbell, a much-respected 64-year-old MP. Menzies' age and an initially faltering parliamentary performance were used against him by critics and he resigned the following year. His successor was 40-year-old Nick Clegg, a former member of the European Parliament who had only been elected to the House of Commons in 2005. The changes in leadership did little to enhance political support for the party. It was overshadowed by the two larger parties—Conservative leader David Cameron appearing to siphon some support from Liberal Democrats and with Labour not pursuing close links; the Cabinet committee on constitutional change had been moribund for some years. In Scotland, following the 2007 elections, the party ceased to be a party of government. (It had ceased to be in coalition with Labour in Wales in 2003.) Nationally, the party trailed in third place in the opinion polls, showing little signs of picking up further support.

The party also suffered from internal ideological tensions. Members coming from an SDP background, such as Charles Kennedy, were inclined to accord a much greater role to the state than were members from a consistently Liberal background. Some of the latter pursued a free market theme in 2004 with the publication of a series of essays entitled *The Orange Book: Reclaiming Liberalism*. One of the contributors was Nick Clegg and, as leader, he moved the party toward a more neo-liberal approach. Critics were able to claim that this did little to carve out a distinct approach that differentiated the party from its two main rivals.[51]

Scottish and Welsh Nationalists

Prior to the 1960s the nationalist parties in Scotland and Wales had not proved to be politically important. Their main achievement had been "simply to survive."[52] In the 1960s, both parties—first *Plaid Cymru* (Party of Wales) and then the *Scottish National Party* (SNP)—achieved a parliamentary toehold (each won a seat in a by-election) and then became more significant forces in the 1970s. This was especially so in the case of the SNP.

Favoring independence for Scotland, though being prepared to accept an elected national assembly as a step on that path, the SNP was able to exploit dissatisfaction with Westminster government and to make use of an issue that became salient during this period: North Sea oil. It argued that the oil was Scottish oil and that revenue from it could make an independent Scottish government viable. In Wales, the Plaid argued more for self-government than for independence and was able to play on the fears of the indigenous Welsh population, which felt its heritage to be threatened by English encroachment.

In the October 1974 election, the SNP won 11 seats in Scotland and Plaid Cymru won three in Wales. As nationalist support increased in both countries, it began to constitute a threat to the dominant party in both: the Labour Party. The threat was especially strong in Scotland: In addition to winning 11 seats in October 1974, the SNP came second in 35 of 41 Labour-held seats. The Labour government introduced a scheme for elected assemblies in Scotland and Wales, but the proposal was rejected decisively in a referendum in Wales and failed in Scotland (see Chapter 10). The nationalist parties appeared less prominent during the period of Conservative government from 1979 to 1997, though both still maintained a parliamentary presence. Though its number of seats in the House declined, the SNP managed to maintain its share of the poll in Scotland and it had the bonus of winning, and retaining, a seat in the European Parliament. In the 1994 elections to the European Parliament, it doubled its representation. In the 1997 general election, it won six seats in the House of Commons—double the number elected in 1992—and, more significantly, took 22 percent of the vote in Scotland (slightly up on its 1992 percentage), establishing it as the second largest party in Scotland. The new Labour government's commitment to elected assemblies in Scotland and Wales resulted in legislation creating both bodies (Chapter 10). The SNP, under its leader Alex Salmond, mounted a strong challenge in elections to the new Scottish Parliament, emerging as the second party and denying the Labour Party an absolute majority of seats. The SNP won 35 seats—to Labour's 56—in the 129-member parliament. To stave off the SNP challenge, Labour members of the new parliament formed a coalition with the Liberal Democrats. However, Labour lacked decisive leadership and was overshadowed when Alex Salmond returned as SNP leader (having previously stepped down) and led an effective campaign for Scotland to have greater powers. In the 2007 Scottish elections the SNP emerged as the largest single party, winning one more seat than Labour, and formed a minority administration with Salmond as first minister. Support for the SNP continued to grow, though the economic crisis of 2008 dented its claims that Scotland could survive as an independent nation: Both the principal bank and building society in Scotland were unable to survive as independent entities. The SNP nonetheless remained a major player in Scottish politics, having gone from a minor party with no parliamentary representation to forming the party of government, its leader becoming first minister in Scotland.

Similarly, in Wales, Plaid Cymru—which won four seats in the 1997 general election—established itself as the second largest party in the National Assembly for Wales, winning 17 seats (to Labour's 28) in the 60-member body. It also achieved a notable success in the 1999 elections to the European Parliament, winning two seats in a body in which it previously had no representation. It failed in the 2003 Welsh elections to prevent Labour winning 30 of the 60 seats in the assembly and it lost one of its European seats in 2004. In the 2007 Welsh elections, it had only 15 members elected to the assembly. However, decline in support for Labour in 2007 meant that it had to seek a coalition partner to stay in office, and after protracted discussion it eventually formed a coalition with Plaid Cymru, its long-time enemy. Plaid Cymru thus, like its Scottish counterpart, became a party of government.

By the end of 2007, both nationalist parties thus enjoyed parliamentary representation at three levels—in their home assembly, in the U.K. Parliament, and in the European Parliament—and in their home assemblies had moved from being outsiders to being insiders. Though constituting opposition parties in Westminster, in their home territory they were part of government.

Northern Ireland Parties

In Northern Ireland the majority of voters vote Unionist, supporting the maintenance of the union with Britain. They have been represented, historically, by the Unionist Party. Originally a united party tied to the British Conservative Party, it disassociated itself (though in organizational terms not totally) from the Conservative Party following the imposition of direct rule in the province by a Conservative government in 1972. It also divided within itself, the two main Unionist parties being the *Ulster Unionists* and the *Democratic Unionists*. The UUs tend to be more middle class and Anglican and Methodist, whereas the Democratic Unionists, led for most of their existence by fundamentalist Protestant clergyman Ian Paisley, appeal more to working-class Protestants and are more heavily Presbyterian. Until the end of the twentieth century, the Ulster Unionist Party was the more dominant of the two: In 1997, it won 10 of the 18 seats in the province, while the Democratic Unionists were reduced from three to two seats. However, the situation changed dramatically in the new century, the more aggressive stance of the DUP appealing more to unionist voters than the more moderate and accommodating stance of the UUs. In 2005, the Democratic Unionists won 9 of the 18 seats in the province (the UUs won one) and in elections to the Northern Ireland Assembly in 2007 the DUP won 36 seats to 17 for the UUs. In 2007 an historic agreement was reached, with the Democratic Unionists and Sinn Féin—the two parties at opposite ends of the political spectrum—agreeing to form a power-sharing executive. Having been a party of opposition, and vehemently opposed to Sinn Féin, the Democratic Unionists were now a party of government in alliance with their previous enemy.

Within the province, there is also the predominantly Catholic party, the *Social Democratic and Labour Party* (the SDLP). In the general election of 2005, it won three parliamentary seats in the province. It was a party of government—in alliance with the UUs—in the period from 1998 to 2003 when the Northern Ireland assembly was in existence (it was variously suspended; see Chapter 10) but was then overshadowed by Sinn Féin. Though *Sinn Féin*, the nationalist party and political wing of the Provisional Irish Republican Army (IRA), won usually only two or three Westminster seats, in 2005 it won five seats and in 2007 agreed to enter a power-sharing alliance with the Democratic Unionists.

Of the nine parties represented in the House of Commons in the 2005 Parliament, four were thus from Northern Ireland (though the Sinn Féin MPs, as in previous parliaments, did not take their seats). The province also has other parties, which—though not gaining seats in the House of Commons— have achieved some representation in the Northern Ireland Assembly. The *Alliance Party*, unconnected to the former British SDP/Liberal alliance, is a nonsectarian party that seeks to bridge the gap between the two communities. Though never winning any seats in the House of Commons, it did achieve parliamentary representation in 1996 when its leader, John Alderdice, was created a life peer. It has won seats in the new Northern Ireland assembly. (Alderdice was among its assembly members and served as the presiding officer from 1998 to 2004.) In the 2007 elections to the 108-member assembly, the party won seven seats. In 2007, the Green Party won its first seats in the assembly. Another member was elected under the label of Progressive Unionist.

Other Parties

Various other parties contest parliamentary election in the United Kingdom. In 2005, no less than 47 parties contested more than one seat. The more successful are listed in Table 6.5. Most never achieve national prominence. A few do, but usually on a temporary basis. *The Liberal Party* is best described as the Continuing Liberal Party and was formed to represent Liberals opposed to the 1989 merger with the SDP. Despite the support of a former Liberal MP, it failed to make a mark. In elections to the European Parliament in 1999, it attracted 93,000 votes, less than 1 percent of the poll. Following the merger of the two parties, a *Continuing SDP* was also formed, including in its ranks three SDP MPs, but it faded at the 1992 election. The *Natural Law Party*, expounding the "vedic science" of Maharishi Mahesh Yogi, contested 309 seats in 1992 and 195 in 1997 but made no impact: It achieved an average of 155 votes per candidate in 1997. It fought no seats in 2001. The *Referendum Party* was formed by millionaire businessman Sir James Goldsmith to demand a referendum on Britain's future in the European Union. It was the

TABLE 6.5

MINOR PARTIES IN THE 2005 GENERAL ELECTION

Party	Votes	% share of poll	Average vote %	Candidates	Lost deposits
UK Independence	605,173	3.2	2.8	496	458
British National Party	192,706	0.7	4.3	119	85
Green	283,477	1.0	3.4	202	178
Respect	68,094	0.3	6.8	26	9
Scottish Socialist	43,514	0.2	2.0	62	56
Socialist Labour	20,192	0.1	0.8	50	49
Veritas	40,481	0.1	1.3	33	32

Source: D. Kavanagh and D. Butler, *The British General Election of 2005* (Palgrave Macmillan, 2005), p. 204.

only minor party in the 1997 election to win more than 2.5 percent of the votes cast and, as such, it established itself as the fourth party in England. Its prominence was short-lived: Goldsmith died shortly after the election and the party largely disappeared from view. The *Pro-Life Alliance*—an anti-abortion organization—decided to contest more than 50 seats in the 1997 election, thus giving it a free election broadcast but not many votes, an average of 350 votes per candidate. It lost its deposit in every seat it contested.

Other parties have proved more enduring. The *UK Independence Party*, favoring British withdrawal from the European Union, has failed to make much headway in elections to the House of Commons—in 2005 it fought 496 seats but won none—but has achieved prominence as a result of the elections to the European Parliament. In 1999, it won just under 700,000 votes—7 percent of the poll—and gained three seats. In 2004, it gained 16 percent of the votes, enabling it to win 12 seats—the same number as the Liberal Democrats. In 2009 it gained 13 seats, putting it ahead of the Liberal Democrats. Its representation gave it an electoral legitimacy and an important platform.

The *British National Party* represents the far right, constituting a breakaway movement from the National Front, a right-wing neofascist party that attracts support largely on the basis of opposition to immigration by nonwhites. The party, like the National Front before it, has attracted little support in general elections. It fielded 33 candidates in the 2001 election and 119 in 2005, but none coming close to winning and, in most cases, losing their deposit. However, the party has had greater success in elections to local councils and the European Parliament. It has picked up some council seats, attracting support in parts of Yorkshire, Lancashire, and London. In the 2004 elections to the European Parliament, it attracted 4.9 percent of the poll, but won no seats. In 2009, it won two seats—one in the north-west and one in Yorkshire and the Humber region—giving it a political platform and a much-craved legitimacy.

The *Green Party* was founded as the People's party in 1973, changed its name to the Ecology party in 1975, and took its present name in 1985. It made little impact until 1989, when it attracted 14.5 percent of the vote in elections to the European Parliament. Though not achieving similar levels of support in later elections, the introduction of a system of PR for elections to the parliament meant that in 1999, with 6 percent of the votes, it won two seats. It repeated the performance in 2004 and 2009. It has had less success in elections to the House of Commons. It fought 202 seats in the 2005 general election, achieving an average of 3.4 percent of the poll, but winning none of them.

The *Socialist Labour Party* was, like the Referendum Party, a new body created to contest the 1997 general election. It was set up by the leader of the national union of mine workers, Arthur Scargill. It represented the far left in British politics which, by itself, has never fared well in national elections.[53] Although one candidate was elected to the Scottish Parliament in 1999, the party failed to make a mark in other elections. It fought 114 seats in the 2001 general election and 50 in the 2005, but with no success.

The *Respect Party* was founded in 2004 by former Labour MP George Galloway. It was a far-left party formed to draw together left-wing groups and to express opposition to the Iraq war. It contested 26 constituencies in the 2005 general election, Galloway winning the constituency of Bethnal Green and Bow in an acrimonious contest with the incumbent Labour MP. It achieved on average 6.8 percent of the vote, doing best in constituencies with high Muslim populations.

These represent the more prominent of the minor parties. Elections in the United Kingdom are fought by several parties, but because of the electoral system for elections to the House of Commons, minor parties stand little chance of gaining seats at Westminster. Those that do tend to have concentrated support in particular parts of the United Kingdom, such as nationalist parties in Scotland, Wales, and Northern Ireland. Where they stand the greatest chance is in elections to elected assemblies in the United Kingdom and to the European Parliament.

DECLINE IN TWO-PARTY SUPPORT

The past three decades have witnessed major changes in electoral behavior and in support for the two main parties. One of the principal changes that has been variously identified has been a decline in support for the two main parties. What is the evidence for a decline in the two-party system? If there has been a decline, what explains it?

A decline in voting support for both parties has been sketched in Chapter 5. Ever since the peak of two-party support reached in the 1950s, electors have shown a relative desertion of both main parties. In every general election from 1983 onward, more than 20 percent of those who voted have cast their ballots for candidates other than Conservative and Labour candidates: In 1997, the Labour Party was swept to victory with 43.2 percent of the votes cast—a smaller percentage than it had achieved in the three general elections of the 1950s, when it lost to the Conservatives. In 2005, it won the general election with 35.2 per cent of the vote, the smallest poll achieved by any winning party in postwar history. In 1997, the Conservatives achieved their worst share of the poll since 1906, fewer than one in three of those who voted casting their ballot for the party.

Furthermore, these low percentages are in the context of a lower voter turnout than in earlier decades. If we take the votes cast as a proportion of the total eligible electorate, then the contrast is even more stark (Table 6.6). In the 1950 general election, three-quarters of the eligible electorate (75.2 percent) voted for one of the two main parties. In the 2005 general election, only 18.2 million out of 44 million electors—41 percent of the eligible electorate—voted Labour or Conservative. Labour won a majority on the votes of less than one-quarter of the electorate. More than half the electorate either stayed at home or voted for parties other than the Labour or Conservative parties.

Other indicators have also been employed to show a relative desertion of the two main parties. One has been in levels of party identification. There has been a long-term decline in partisan attachment. As Paul Whiteley has recorded, "In 1964, when the first surveys were done, close to 50 percent of all voters were strongly attached to a political party. In 2001 this was reduced to only 13 percent. To be fair, a majority of voters still have a partisan attachment, but it is much weaker than it used to be."[54]

Another indicator has been a decline in membership. The Conservative Party claimed a membership of 2.8 million in 1952. That was a high-water mark, but it was still able to claim a membership in excess of 2 million in 1958. By the mid-1990s, according to one survey, membership was down to around 500,000.[55] By the end of 2008, as we have noted, its membership was reported to be no more than 250,000. The Labour Party reached its peak in membership at about the same time as the Conservatives, claiming a membership of just

TABLE 6.6

Two-party support, 1950 and 2005

Party	Votes won as percentage of votes cast		Votes won as percentage of electorate	
	1950	2005	1950	2005
Labour	46.1	35.2	38.7	21.6
Conservative	43.5	32.4	36.5	19.8
Totals	89.6	67.6	75.2	41.4

over 1 million in 1952. By 1992, its membership was approximately 260,000, the lowest membership figure since 1929. It witnessed an increase in the 1990s—peaking, as we have noted already, at just over 400,000 in 1997—but decreased thereafter. As we have seen, by the end of 2007 it had a membership of less than 200,000. At the beginning of the 1950s, almost one in ten Britons belonged to one of the two main parties. By 2008, the figure was 1 in 120.

The principal explanations for decline in two-party support can be subsumed under three headings: *structural dealignment, policy orientation*, and *performance*. The first two explanations correlate closely with the partisan preferences of those who advance them. The structural analysis tends to be advanced by members of center parties and by a few within each of the main parties. The policy-orientation thesis is advanced predominantly by protagonists *within* the two main parties.

Structural Dealignment

The structural thesis is one we have touched upon already (Chapters 3 and 5). The contention is that the decline in support for the two main parties is the product of the structure of the two-party system. The two parties dominate the political agenda, taking positions that are not congruent with the wishes of most electors. Such a stance is dictated by the electoral system, forcing the parties to compete for the all-or-nothing spoils of electoral victory and, in so doing, to compete vigorously with one another in an adversary relationship. Once in office, a party often must modify or abandon its program when it discovers the resources do not exist to meet the more extravagant of its promises (made in order to outbid its opponent party). There is thus a poor fit between what electors want and what the parties actually provide. Britain, in short, has a dysfunctional party system. As the economic resources to meet manifesto promises have declined, in inverse relationship to the growth of such promises, so voter disenchantment with the two parties—one in government, the other forming the alternative government—has grown.

Given that the party system cannot be separated from the workings of the nation's electoral arrangements, it is not surprising that proponents of this thesis advance reform of the electoral system as a primary means of resolving the problem. A system of PR, it is argued, would ensure a fit between voters' wants and public policy as well as increase support for, and participation in, the political system.

The problem with this argument, as Nevil Johnson has observed, is that a decline in support for one or both of the two main parties does not of itself demonstrate a decline in support for the two-party system.[56] Voters may support a particular third party because they wish it to replace one of the existing major parties in a two-party framework. (Even Paddy Ashdown, when leader of the Liberal Democrats, spoke of his party replacing the Labour Party as the principal challenger to the Conservatives.) There are no objective data to suggest that electors wish to dispense with what supporters view as the fruits of a two-party system: a clear choice between parties, and a party government with an overall majority. Indeed, there are data that suggest the opposite. Survey data reveal broad, but not deep, support for some change in the electoral system, but not for the consequences such a change would have.[57] Electors dislike the prospects of a Parliament in which no one party has an overall majority. In a poll conducted in the final days of the 1992 general election campaign, 56 percent of those questioned were opposed to a "hung" Parliament.[58]

Policy Orientation

This thesis about the two-party decline takes different forms, largely dependent upon where one stands in the political milieu. One form, which may be described as the *consensus thesis*, attributes decline in party support to the consensus policies of postwar decades, when the two parties followed similar Keynesian economic policies. This was the era of the social democratic consensus, or what Samuel Beer termed the Collectivist era.[59] For socialists within the Labour Party and neoliberals within Conservative ranks, this consensus was responsible for the decline in support for their parties. It was responsible for that decline for two reasons. First, the policies themselves were deemed inadequate to meet Britain's fundamental problems. Socialists favored more state control; neoliberals wanted a free market economy. Second, the consensual stance of the parties robbed the electors of a clear choice between competing policies. A lack of partisan conflict generally has a deflating effect on turnout.[60] As one commentator noted in 2007, "A major incentive for loyalty to a political party is a commitment to the transformation of society; and with the main parties all tending to support society as it already is, one crucial motivation for membership has been removed."[61]

Those advancing this thesis could point to the decline in two-party support being most marked in the 1970s. For neoliberals in the Conservative Party, the pursuit of Thatcherite policies from 1979 onward ensured a clear choice and one that resulted in successive victories in four general elections. The loss of the election in 1997 was blamed on John Major and his failure to pursue distinctive Thatcherite policies. Socialists in the Labour Party attributed Labour's failure in 1970 and 1979 to the absence of a socialist program and its continuing failure in the 1980s to the retrospective evaluation by electors of earlier Labour governments. Voters were continuing to vote on their evaluation of past performance rather than on an evaluation of what was being offered for the future. As Paul Whiteley expressed it, "If centrist policies fail, as they have done for the most part during Labour's tenure in office, no amount of moderation will bring electoral success."[62]

This thesis is challenged by the *extremist thesis*. This contends that a decline in support for both parties was the result of extreme policies pursued by both of the parties. The left-wing programs of Labour in the 1980s, and especially in the 1983 election, resulted in a disastrous electoral performance, the party almost being squeezed into third place by the Liberal/Social Democratic alliance. The Conservative Party won three elections under

Margaret Thatcher's leadership, but did so despite Thatcherism and not because of it. Electors, on balance, preferred a Conservative government to a Labour one, but they did not support, nor did they move more in the direction of supporting, Thatcherite policies.[63] The policies, particularly the economic policies, pursued by the Thatcher government alienated many voters, resulting in disaffected Conservative supporters switching their support to center parties. Although the Conservative Party won the elections, it did so on a low share of the poll. Hence, Conservative victory over Labour masked an underlying decline in support. When both parties moved more toward the center ground, the support for the principal third party declined. A more moderate approach by the Major government, it is argued, helped keep the Conservatives in power in 1992, and a more moderate program helped Labour to a stunning victory in 1997 and re-election in 2001 and 2005, albeit on a low share of the poll.

Performance

In Chapter 5, we identified explanations for greater volatility in voting behavior. Explaining greater volatility is not necessarily to explain a *decline* in support for the two main parties. Voters may switch their votes more frequently but the switch could be from one of the two main parties to the other one. However, one of the explanations may have relevance: that of performance evaluation. Voters look to a party to be competent in governing the nation and especially in handling the nation's finances. Traditionally, the Conservatives have benefited from appearing to be a party of governance, that is, a party knowing how to govern the nation effectively. This is important in understanding Conservative success in the 1980s: Even though many of the policies pursued by the Conservative government were not popular, the Conservatives still led in the opinion polls. Electors favored the party because it looked as if it knew what it was doing and was able to deliver economic success.[64] In the eyes of electors, the Conservatives lost this claim to competence in 1992 and failed to recover it in succeeding years.

Performance is relevant to explaining a decline in two-party voting in that neither party may be able to deliver what voters want. Two-party voting was at its height at a time of relative economic prosperity for the United Kingdom. It has declined as the capacity of government to meet the economic expectations of citizens has declined. We have already touched upon this phenomenon (Chapter 3). As Richard Rose has argued in *Do Parties Make a Difference?* the party in government can make some difference to economic performance, but not much.[65] A globalization of markets and membership of the European Union further constrain the independent capacity of government to determine outcomes. "Even if governments wanted to pursue unorthodox economic policies, they would be prevented from doing so by the many 'veto players' which exist in the global political economy."[66] Thus, whichever party is in the power, it is not going to be able to buck international pressures and markets. If parties, when in office, are not able to deliver the goods expected of them then voters may desert those parties and either support third parties or no parties at all.

Supporters of this thesis argue that it has a better explanatory value than the other explanations. Significant shifts in public policy are notable between elections, as reactions to external developments rather than as a consequence of a change of party in office. The drop in two-party voting appears to bear little correlation to the shifts of parties to the center or the extreme. Two fairly centrist parties faced one another in 1992 and turnout and two-party voting increased; two even more centrist parties faced one another in 1997 and turnout and two-party voting declined.

This explanation does not suggest that what parties do in office is not important—a party may pursue social policies, for instance, that affect many millions of people—but that the impact governments can have on economic trends is limited and that it is competence, especially in handling economic affairs, that determines citizens' evaluations of government. As globalization limits what governments can do, the two parties may have to limit what they offer to electors and seek to limit expectations. This may prove difficult in a political environment in which others are suggesting that the problem is one of structural dealignment or bad policies.

DECLINE IN PARTY SUPPORT

Support for the two principal parties has declined over time. Fewer people are voting Conservative or Labour. However, as we have seen, fewer people are voting. Is this decline simply a consequence of dissatisfaction with the two main parties or a consequence of more general societal trends? Decline in support for political parties may be a consequence of *disillusionment, displacement,* or *disinterest.*

Disillusionment

Voters may be disillusioned with not only the two main political parties but parties, and political activity, in general. As we have seen, the parties compete to gain votes and may make promises which voters then perceive as not being delivered. Though parties have a good track record in government of delivering on specific manifesto promises, they are judged primarily on their capacity to manage the economy. The explanation of poor performance, discussed above, can affect attitudes toward parties as a whole. Negative perceptions can lead to a lack of trust. One author, Colin Hay, has argued that globalization has led to a popular fatalism about politics and criticism of the state has led to distrust of government and parties[67]. A lack of trust in political parties is a marked feature of politics in the United Kingdom, though it is not confined to the United Kingdom. Eurobarometer data for 2008 show that political parties are not trusted across the European Union, though the proportion of British citizens not trusting parties—81 percent—is above the EU average (76 percent).[68]

Lack of trust in political parties, however, does not necessarily denote a lack of interest in politics. Indeed, it could be hypothesized that a lack of trust in parties is greater among those interested in politics, since their awareness and expectations are likely to be greater than among those with no interest in politics.

Displacement

Electors may not have lost their interest in political activity but rather switched their activity from catch-all political parties to more highly targeted outlets. In some cases, there has been a switch within the ambit of political parties, people moving from a mainstream party to a third party. In other cases, they have moved their interest from political parties to interest groups. Interest groups channel their very specific interests in a way that broad-based political parties cannot.

Survey data reveal that levels of interest in politics have not fallen in recent decades. In 1973, 60 percent of people questioned said they were very or fairly interested in politics. That figure did not change much in subsequent decades and in 2005 stood at 61 percent.[69] However, despite this interest, membership of political parties has declined. Over the same period, there has been a significant growth in the number of interest groups, enabling the particular interests of people to be harnessed by organizations with a particular focus (Chapter 7). People devote their time and resources to such groups and seek to influence public policy through them, rather than through political parties. Money flows to such groups rather than parties. As the Ipsos/MORI polling organization recorded in 2008, "Britons are more than seven times as likely to have donated money to a charity or campaigning organisation than to a political party."[70] Political parties are not able to compete with what specific interest groups can offer. The Royal Society for the Protection of Birds (the RSPB) has more members than the three largest political parties combined.

Disinterest

A failure to engage with political parties—either joining them or voting for them—may be a consequence not of disillusionment but simply a lack of interest in what they are doing. Many people are believed to have joined political parties in earlier decades for social reasons. They were means of meeting other people, of socializing, and of engaging in civic activity. The Young Conservative movement, for example, was often portrayed as a marriage bureau. Over time, more competitors have emerged. The parties have been overtaken by a range of outlets for social engagement. Party membership has declined as ownership of televisions has increased and, in recent decades, as people have connected to the Internet. The parties are seeking to utilize the Internet, but having to do so against intense competition from others seeking the attention of a population increasingly geared to short-term stimulation. Young people are interested in voting, but it is voting for competitors in television talent contests rather than voting for political parties. People are more interested in sport and celebrity than in the activities of politicians. "There has been a boom in celebrity, gossip-based magazines with annual sales in 2006 hitting the £1billion ($1.64b.) mark for the first time. For the most part, this represented a continuation of a well-established trend. . . ."[71] Party politicians are generally not part of the celebrity culture.

CONCLUSION

At the parliamentary level, the United Kingdom remains a predominantly two-party political system. However, that dominance masks a decline in support for both main parties as well as a growth in the number of parties forming part of government in the devolved parts of the United Kingdom. Whereas competition for parliamentary elections in England is essentially between two (in some areas, three) parties, competition in Scotland, Wales, and Northern Ireland is essentially multi-party. There is a fragmentation of support for the two main parties, though they continue to dominate politics at Westminster. The political environment that they inhabit is, however, more crowded, and they operate against a backdrop of declining electoral support.

NOTES

1. L. M. Bartels, "Partisanship and Voting Behavior, 1952–1996," *American Journal of Political Science*, 44, 2000 pp. 35–50; D. Hayes, "Has Television Personalized Voting Behavior?" *Political Behavior*, 31 (2), 2009, 231–260.
2. See, for example, D. McSweeney and J. Zvesper, *American Political Parties* (Routledge, 1991) and M. P. Wattenberg, *The Decline of American Political Parties 1952–1992* (Harvard University Press, 1994).
3. See especially L. Hartz, *The Liberal Tradition in America* (Harcourt, Brace and World, 1955). Also S. M. Lipset, *American Exceptionalism* (Norton, 1996).
4. L. D. Epstein, "What Happened to the British Party Model?" *American Political Science Review*, 74 (1), 1980, pp. 9–22.
5. *A Bicentennial Analysis of the American Political Structure* (Committee on the Constitutional System, 1987).
6. R. H. S. Crossman, "Introduction" to W. Bagehot, *The English Constitution* (Fontana, 1963 edition), p. 39.
7. See J. Vincent, *The Formation of the British Liberal Party 1857–68* (Penguin, 1972).
8. A. Seldon and S. Ball (eds.), *Conservative Century* (Oxford University Press, 1994).
9. R. Blake, *The Conservative Party from Peel to Churchill* (Eyre and Spottiswoode, 1970), p. 2.
10. On the basic tenets, see P. Norton, "Conservatism," in M. Foley (ed.), *Ideas That Shape Politics* (Manchester University Press, 1994), pp. 39–45.
11. See P. Norton, "History of the Party I: Tory to Conservative" and P. Norton, "History of the Party II: From a Marquess to an Earl," in P. Norton (ed.), *The Conservative Party* (Prentice Hall/Harvester Wheatsheaf, 1996).

12. P. Norton and A. Aughey, *Conservatives and Conservatism* (Temple Smith, 1981), Ch. 2.
13. See Norton, "Conservatism," and A. Aughey, "Philosophy and Faction," in Norton, *The Conservative Party*.
14. See R. Rose, "Parties, Factions and Tendencies in British Politics," *Political Studies*, 12, 1964, pp. 33–46.
15. See P. Norton, *Conservative Dissidents* (Temple Smith, 1978), Ch. 4, and J. Campbell, *Edward Heath* (Jonathan Cape, 1993), Part 4.
16. The epithet *wet* has different meanings and uncertain origins. In the present context, it derived from Mrs. Thatcher's habit of annotating papers with the word when she wished to indicate that a particular proposal or comment was indecisive, bland, and poorly argued.
17. "The Thatcher Style," *The Economist*, 21 May 1983, p. 32.
18. See H. Young, *One of Us* (Macmillan, 1989), pp. 431–458.
19. See P. Norton, "The Conservative Party from Thatcher to Major," in A. King (ed.), *Britain at the Polls 1992* (Chatham House, 1993), pp. 29–69.
20. I. Crewe, "Electoral Behaviour," in D. Kavanagh and A. Seldon (eds.), *The Major Effect* (London: Macmillan, 1994), p. 109.
21. See D. Denver, "The Government That Could Do No Right," in A. King (ed.), *New Labour Triumphs: Britain at the Polls* (Chatham House, 1997), pp. 26–38.
22. P. Norton, "The Conservative Power: 'In Office but Not in Power,'" in King, *New Labour Triumphs*, pp. 99–103.
23. P. Norton, "Electing the Leader: The Conservative Leadership Contest," *Politics Review*, 7 (4), 1998, pp. 10–14.
24. See P. Norton, "The Conservative Party: The Politics of Panic," in J. Bartle and A. King (eds.), *Britain at the Polls 2005* (CQ Press, 2006), pp. 36–37.
25. In the final ballot among MPs, the result had been: K. Clarke 59, I. Duncan-Smith 54, and M. Portillo 53.
26. See Norton, "The Conservative Party: Politics of Panic," pp. 38–39.
27. See P. Norton, "David Cameron and Tory Success: Architect or By-stander?" in S. Lee and M. Beech (eds.), *The Conservatives under David Cameron* (Palgrave Macmillan, 2009), pp. 31–43.
28. See especially P. Norton, "The Party Leader," in Norton, *The Conservative Party*, pp. 142–156.
29. I. Kirby, "Gone-servative Party!," *News of the World*, 20 December 2008.
30. House of Commons, Constitutional Affairs Committee, *Party Funding*, First Report of Session 2006–07, HC 163-I (London: The Stationery Office, 2006), p. 11.
31. J. Ungoed-Thomas, "5,000-Mile Money Trail to Tory HQ," *The Sunday Times*, 14 September 2008.
32. House of Commons, Constitutional Affairs Committee, *Party Funding*, First Report of Session 2006–07, HC 163-I (London: The Stationery Office, 2006), p. 14. Short money is so-called after Edward Short, Leader of the House of Commons at the time that it was introduced.
33. C. F. Brand, *The British Labour Party* (Stanford University Press, 1965); see also F. Williams, *Fifty Years March* (Odham, n.d.), Part 1.
34. S. H. Beer, *Modern British Politics*, rev. ed. (Faber, 1969).
35. H. Pelling, *A Short History of the Labour Party*, 5th ed. (Macmillan, 1976), p. 44.
36. K. Jefferys, *The Labour Party since 1945* (Macmillan, 1993), p. 24.
37. E. Shaw, *The Labour Party since 1945* (Blackwell, 1996), p. 63.

38. P. Seyd, "Labour: The Great Transformation," in A. King (ed.), *Britain at the Polls 1992* (Chatham House, 1993), p. 76.
39. I. Crewe, "Why Did Labour Lose (Yet Again)?" *Politics Review,* 2 (1), September 1992, pp. 2–11.
40. P. Seyd, "Tony Blair and New Labour," in A. King (ed.), *New Labour Triumphs: Britain at the Polls* (Chatham House, 1997), p. 52.
41. Seyd, "Tony Blair and New Labour," p. 60.
42. Quoted in R. Kelly, "Making Party Policy," *Politics Review,* 15 (2), 2005, p. 3.
43. Roy Hattersley, *Guardian,* 7 April 2005, quoted in R. Kelly, "Making Party Policy," *Politics Review,* 15 (2), 2005, p. 3.
44. Butler and Kavanagh, *The British General Election of 1997,* p. 55.
45. P. Rowland, *The Last Liberal Governments* (Macmillan, 1969), p. 34.
46. See T. Wilson, *The Downfall of the Liberal Party 1914–1935* (Fontana, 1968), p. 20.
47. The Liberal National MPs became allied with and were eventually absorbed into the Conservative Party.
48. See A. Michie and S. Hoggart, *The Pact* (Quartet, 1978).
49. See I. Bradley, *Breaking the Mould?* (Martin Robertson, 1981) and I. Crewe and A. King, *SDP: The Birth, Life and Death of the Social Democratic Party* (Oxford University Press, 1995).
50. Within months of its creation, it achieved notable victories in Croydon North-West in October, Crosby in November (won by Shirley Williams), and Glasgow, Hillhead, the following March (won by Roy Jenkins).
51. M. Garnett, "Party Ideology after Blair," *Politics Review,* 17(4), 2008, pp. 11–12.
52. H. M. Drucker and G. Brown, *The Politics of Nationalism and Devolution* (Longman, 1980), p. 167.
53. The British Communist Party, founded in 1921, has had little impact in electoral terms. One Communist MP was elected in 1924, one in 1935, and two in 1945. Since then the party has achieved no parliamentary representation and has never come close to doing so. What power it had in the 1970s and 1980s was through some of its members holding office in certain trade unions. See R. Taylor, *The Fifth Estate* (Pan Books, 1980), p. 325.
54. P. Whiteley, "The State of Participation in Britain," *Politics Review,* 16 (1), 2006, p. 18.
55. *The Times,* 10 October 1994. See also Tether, "The Party in the Country II: Members and Organisation," in Norton, *The Conservative Party,* pp. 116–117.
56. N. Johnson, book review, *The Times Higher Education Supplement,* 22 July 1983.
57. See P. Norton, "Does Britain Need Proportional Representation?" in R. Blackburn (ed.), *Constitutional Studies* (Mansell, 1992).
58. *The Times,* 6 April 1992. When given a straight choice between PR or one-party government, or between majority or coalition government, a plurality has tended to favor the existing arrangements: In an exit poll during the 1987 election, 49 percent were for the existing system, 46 percent for PR (*The Independent,* 13 June 1987), and in a MORI poll in 1991, 38 percent were for majority government, 25 percent for coalition government (*The Independent,* 25 April 1991).
59. Beer, *Modern British Politics.*
60. See H. D. Clarke, D. Sanders, M. C. Stewart, and P. Whiteley, *Political Choice in Britain* (Oxford University Press, 2004).

61. M. Garnett, "British Political Parties and Democracy," *Politics Review,* 26 (3), 2007, p. 26.
62. P. Whiteley, "The Decline of Labour's Local Party Membership and Electoral Base, 1945–1979," in D. Kavanagh (ed.), *The Politics of the Labour Party* (Allen and Unwin, 1982), p. 132. See also P. Whiteley, *The Labour Party in Crisis* (Methuen, 1983).
63. See especially I. Crewe and D. Searing, "Ideological Change in the British Conservative Party," *American Political Science Review,* 82 (2), 1988; R. Jowell, S. Witherspoon, and L. Brook, *British Social Attitudes, Fifth Report* (Gower, 1988) and P. Norton, "The Conservative Party from Thatcher to Major," in King, *Britain at the Polls 1992.*
64. See Norton, "The Conservative Party: 'In Office But Not in Power,'" in King, *New Labour Triumphs.*
65. R. Rose, *Do Parties Make a Difference?* 2nd ed. (Macmillan, 1984).
66. P. Whiteley, "The State of Participation in Britain," *Politics Review,* 16 (1), 2006, p. 20.
67. C. Hay, *Why We Hate Politics* (Polity Press, 2007).
68. European Commission, *Eurobarometer 69, National Report: United Kingdom,* Spring 2008, (European Commission, 2008), p. 21.
69. B. Marshall, B. Duffy, J. Thompson, S. Castell, and S. Hall, *Blair's Britain: The Social & Cultural Legacy* (Ipsos/MORI, 2008), p. 49
70. *Blair's Britain: The Social & Cultural Legacy*, p. 49
71. Ibid., p. 55.

Interest Groups
Insiders or Outsiders?

Interest groups have commonly been defined as bodies that seek to influence government in the allocation of resources without themselves seeking to assume responsibility for government. This definition is usually employed to distinguish such groups from political parties, which do seek, through electoral success, to form the government. The distinction, though not watertight,[1] is nonetheless a useful one.

Interest group activity and the study of it have, historically, been more apparent in the United States than in Britain. This difference is explicable largely in terms of the different political systems. The United States has been characterized as enjoying a "multiple access" system. A group can seek to influence a particular department or bureau. If that attempt fails, it can lobby the White House. It can lobby Congress. The separation of powers and the relative weakness of political parties—in essence, depriving representatives and senators of a protective party shield to hide behind—make members of Congress worthwhile targets for group pressure. Such pressure is applied continuously on Capitol Hill; well over 34,000 registered lobbyists are retained by groups of some sort to lobby members of Congress.[2] If pressure in Washington fails, a group can always turn to the state or district to try to rouse support there. Rallies may be organized. A mass mailing to Congress may be instigated. Not surprisingly, such visible activity and its apparent effect have been the subject of serious study and academic debate. The United States has been the breeding ground of group and pluralist theory.

The position in the United Kingdom in terms of group activity has been different. For groups seeking to influence government decisions, the principal focus of activity is the executive: the ministers and officials occupying the government departments. Attempts to lobby Parliament or to maintain regular contact on a scale analogous to that maintained on Capitol Hill have been notable for their rarity. Many groups have maintained friendly contact with members of Parliament; as we shall see, an increasing number make use of professional lobbyists, but their number is relatively small. Lobbying of MPs has been viewed as an admission that attempts to influence ministers and their officials have failed. It is often an unprofitable exercise: Failure to influence ministers will frequently be replicated in a house dominated by those same ministers. Interest-group activity has thus tended to be less visible than in the United States.

The relative lack of visibility of group activity should nonetheless not be misconstrued. Group activity in Britain has been difficult to study because it has not been conducted as obviously and as openly as in the United States. And the lack of such obvious public conduct may be indicative of group influence, not weakness. Only if groups fail to influence ministers or officials do they need to go public and concentrate on Parliament and the media. For much of the postwar period, in which group pressure increased, government was able to satisfy the wants of those groups making demands of it as well as of consumers: There was little need for the more influential sectional groups to mount campaigns. In recent decades, important groups have become far more visible in their attempts to influence government. And as group activity has become more visible, the role played by particular groups in the political arena has become a topic of controversy, both academic and political.

TYPES OF INTEREST GROUPS
Sectional Interest and Promotional Groups

Interest groups have been variously subdivided for analytic purposes. One subdivision, the most common and longstanding, is that between *sectional interest* groups and *promotional* groups. The former, as the name implies, are formed to defend and pursue the interests of specific sections of the community, sections usually defined on an economic basis. (Indeed, to emphasize the point, some writers distinguish between economic or producer groups and promotional groups.) Promotional groups exist to promote particular causes, which may draw their support from disparate individuals and are not based on economic divisions within society. There are a number of recognizable interest groups that fall somewhere between the two categories (for example, the Automobile Association) and others that do not easily fall into either category.

Sectional interest groups are usually permanent bodies formed for a purpose primarily other than influencing government. Most are created to provide services of one form or another to their members: for example, negotiating on their behalf; providing legal, social, and insurance facilities; offering advice and information; and providing a forum in which matters of common interest can be discussed and policy determined. Such groups are numerous. They include, for example, trade unions, the Law Society, the National Farmers Union, the Royal College of Nursing, the Police Federation, the British

Medical Association, and various employers' associations. Membership in such bodies is normally exclusive, and actual membership is often close to the potential membership. In some instances, membership in a professional body is a requirement for pursuing a particular vocation. Many have their counterparts in the United States: The AFL-CIO (the American Federation of Labor–Congress of Industrial Organizations), for example, is the rough equivalent of the Trades Union Congress (TUC) in Britain, and the American Medical Association the equivalent of the British Medical Association.

Whereas sectional groups seek to promote the interests, normally the economic interests, of their membership, promotional groups seek to promote a cause or causes that are not usually of direct economic benefit to their members. The motivation for joining a sectional group is economic, and for joining a promotional group, often moral or ideological. Promotional groups may seek to promote and defend the interests of particular categories of individuals within society (for example, the National Society for the Prevention of Cruelty to Children), of particular rights (Liberty, formerly the National Council for Civil Liberties), or of shared beliefs (the Christian Institute). Some seek to achieve specific objectives, often reflected in their title (for example, the Abortion Law Reform Association). A number are essentially defensive groups formed to counter the campaigns mounted by reform movements: For example, the Society for the Protection of the Unborn Child (SPUC, now the Society for the Protection of Unborn Children) was formed to oppose the pro-abortion lobby, and the British Field Sports Society was created to defend hunting against the activities of the League against Cruel Sports. A number of such groups, by their nature, are little concerned with public policy and rarely engage in political activity. Others, by contrast, often exist for the purpose of pursuing a public campaign to achieve a modification of public policy and the enactment of legislation.

Insider and Outsider Groups

A second subdivision, developed by Wyn Grant, focuses on the relationship between groups and government. This distinguishes between *insider* and *outsider* groups.[3] Insider groups are regarded as legitimate by government and are consulted on a regular basis. They are deemed to be bodies that act responsibly and are prepared to engage in confidential negotiation. Outsider groups are groups that are not regarded by the government as legitimate bodies to consult on a regular basis or do not seek such status. They frequently resort to public protest.

When he first formulated these categories, Grant sought to refine them, offering various subdivisions of each. He subdivided insider groups into prisoner groups (dependent on government, not least for funding, and thus unable to break away), low-profile insiders (working behind the scenes), and high-profile insiders (cultivating public opinion to reinforce their contact with government). He subdivided outsider groups into potential insiders (working to gain insider status), outsiders by necessity (lacking the sophistication to gain insider status), and ideological outsiders (rejecting the existing political system and therefore not prepared to work within its rules and practices). Other commentators have since formulated alternative or similar distinctions.[4] One set of authors supplemented the insider/outsider dichotomy with a third category: that of thresholder groups.[5] These are groups that oscillate between insider and outsider strategies. Trades unions were offered as examples of thresholder groups, sometimes adopting an outsider approach—standing apart from government—and at other times seeking insider status, wanting to be consulted by government on issues that affected them.

There is a rough correlation between sectional interest and insider groups and between promotional and outsider groups. The sectional interest groups already mentioned, for example, would mostly fall into the insider category and most of the promotional groups into the outsider category. However, the correlation is not exact. Some sectional interest groups may not be consulted regularly by government. Given their concerns, they may not seek to be consulted. A number of promotional groups may have achieved such high public status or may have developed such a specialist knowledge in their field that they are treated as legitimate by government and thus have insider status.

The insider-outsider categorization not only has a political focus but also is dynamic. That is, it admits of a group moving from one category to another. An outsider group may become an insider group. An insider group may produce such poor information or engage in activities that result in government deciding not to consult it, thus consigning it to outsider status. Grant's work thus allows us to see movement in a way that the sectional interest–promotional categorization does not. However, it has a similar limitation. Just as some groups do not fall exclusively within the domain of a sectional interest or a promotional group, some do not fall squarely within the exclusive domain of an insider or outsider group: Both categories have their hybrids.

In this chapter, we shall treat the two sets of categorizations as being complementary rather than competing with one another, utilizing the established distinction between types of groups (sectional interest/promotional) and relating it to group status in relation to government (insider/outsider). For much of the past century, sectional interest groups have been recognized as having achieved, in the main, insider status. Conversely, most promotional groups have been accorded outsider status. However, what we have witnessed in recent years has been a change in the relationship to government. In terms of high policy—policy that is concerned with the economic well-being and security of the nation—sectional interest groups have, to some extent, joined promotional groups in being outsiders to the decision-making process. In terms of medium- and low-level policy, especially policy adjustments and detailed policy implementation, promotional groups have tended to join sectional interest groups in enjoying, in some measure, insider status.

THE DEVELOPMENT OF INTEREST GROUPS

Interest groups in one form or another have existed for many years. Some existed in the fifteenth and sixteenth centuries—for example, various merchant guilds. The earliest, according to R. M. Punnett, was the fourteenth-century Convention of Royal Burghs in Scotland.[6] In succeeding centuries, various groups were formed. Some we would now recognize as sectional interest groups and some as promotional groups. There were various groups established in the nineteenth century to press for parliamentary reform or, in the 1840s, to achieve a repeal of the corn laws. Later on in the century, trade unions and employers' organizations began to be formed. However, the phenomenon of a large and diverse body of permanent, well-organized groups making demands of government is a relatively recent one, largely associated with the growth of government activity, especially in the years after the Second World War. "This surely was inevitable," wrote Robert McKenzie. "Once it had been largely agreed by all parties that the government (national and local) should collect and spend over a third of the national income, tremendous pressures were bound to be brought to bear to influence the distribution of the burdens and benefits of public spending on this scale."[7] Those pressures were channeled especially through and articulated by sectional interest groups. Groups needed government in order to ensure that their members got the share of the economic cake that they desired. Conversely, government needed the groups—for advice, for information, and for cooperation. The relationship became one of mutual dependence. Hence sectional interest groups became, predominantly, insider groups.

As government extended its activities into the economic and social life of the nation, and especially as it began to utilize Keynesian techniques of economic management, it came to depend on information on which it could base both particular and macroeconomic policies. Such information often could be supplied only by sectional interest groups. The groups were also in a position to offer advice. The nearer the actual membership of a group came to its potential membership (all solicitors are members of the Law Society, for example), the closer the group came to enjoying a monopoly of the expertise and understanding peculiar to that section of society. "If doctors are powerful," writes one observer, "it is not just because of their characteristics as a pressure group but because of their functional monopoly of expertise."[8] Government also became dependent on such groups for cooperation in the implementation of policies. If groups are ill-disposed toward a government proposal that affects them, they have the sanction of withdrawing their support in the carrying out of that proposal. A policy of noncooperation may cause grave and sometimes insurmountable difficulties for government. The 1971 Industrial Relations Act, for example, failed largely because of the refusal of trade unions both to register under its provisions and to recognize the National Industrial Relations Court it created. The act was subsequently repealed. Such instances of noncooperation are rare, a sign not of group weakness but of political strength. Anticipation of opposition from affected groups will frequently induce government to refrain from pursuing a particular policy or, more likely, to seek some modification acceptable to the groups concerned; in 1989, for example, the Conservative government modified proposals for reform of legal services following opposition from the legal profession.

The growing interdependence of government and groups led some observers to view sectional groups as central to policy making. They saw the ideological gap between the parties as having narrowed, with government acting primarily as arbiter between competing group demands, seeking to meet the demands of groups while meeting the expectations of consumers. It was seen as the age of what Beer referred to as the "new group politics."[9] Whereas the electoral contest between parties may appear to emphasize an adversary relationship, the relationship between government and groups was perceived as a consensual one. To proceed with a given policy, government and the affected groups had to reach some measure of accord: One had to influence the other. In the formulation of public policy, government and groups could be seen increasingly as being inseparable.

The twentieth century witnessed a remarkable growth in the number of interest groups. The first half of the century witnessed especially the development of sectional interest groups. Insider groups were drawn principally from their ranks. The latter half of the century saw a notable expansion in the number of promotional groups, often single-issue groups. They have generally fallen into the category of outsider groups, though—as we have noted—the two are not synonymous, and some promotional groups have come to be treated as insider groups by government. There is, thus, a remarkable range of interest groups in existence. It is helpful, first, to flesh out the sheer diversity of such groups before addressing their relationship in recent years to government.

Sectional Interest Groups

There are at least several thousand bodies in Britain that constitute sectional interest groups. It is common to look at such groups under the three sectoral headings of labor, business, and agriculture. Although the business and labor sectors have "peak," or umbrella, organizations, they are notable for the number of groups that exist within them.

LABOR   The groups within the labor sector comprise primarily trade unions. Some are extremely small and specialized, whereas others are large and, increasingly, not confined to a particular industry or trade. Following various mergers, the two largest unions now account for nearly half of all union membership. Within the union movement, the older unions representing manual workers (such as miners) have suffered a dramatic decline in membership, and those representing white-collar workers (scientists, teachers, technicians, and other professional employees) have grown. The overall trend, though, has been one of decline. In the 1970s, over 40 percent of employed civilian workers were members of trade unions, the percentage reaching over 50 percent (in excess of 12 million workers) by the end of the decade. The period since has been one of decline: By 2006, the percentage had declined to 26 percent.[10] Unions have variously merged to remain viable entities.

The income of each union comes primarily from membership subscriptions and from interest on invested capital. (Union pension funds are among the major investors in Britain.) Unions provide a variety of services to members, such as insurance schemes, benevolent funds, discounts on purchases at certain stores, help with house purchases, strike funds, wage negotiations with employers, and the compiling and publishing of information useful to members. More than two-thirds of union expenditure is on working expenses (paying the salaries of full-time officials, rent, and running of headquarters), and most of the remaining one-third is spent on providing various benefits to members.

The "peak" organization for trade unions is the TUC. In 2009, 60 unions were affiliated with it, representing some 6.4 million out of just over 7 million unionized workers. It is a far more inclusive body in terms of the large and important unions than is its equivalent in the United States, the AFL-CIO. A number of the largest unions in the United States, such as the auto workers, are not affiliated with the U.S. body. In Britain, the largest unions are in the TUC. The two largest, Unite (formed in 2007 as a result of a merger between the Transport and General Workers Union and Amicus, itself the product of various mergers) with 1.9 million members, and Unison, a public sector union, with 1.3 million members, far outstrip other unions in terms of size. Most other unions affiliated to the TUC have fewer than 50,000 members.

The TUC coordinates the activities of its members and represents them in dealings with government. It has a number of specialist departments on topics such as economics and social affairs, and equality and rights; these departments research and compile data and help various specialist committees of the TUC to formulate policy. It provides a service of trade union education and it provides members to serve on various advisory and quasi-governmental bodies. It has an executive body, the General Council, which has 48 elected members and meets seven times a year. The chief executive officer is the General Secretary.

Three pertinent points can be made about trade unions. First, they are largely decentralized. The TUC annual congress constitutes at best a federal body. Individual unions are largely autonomous and often have difficulty in asserting their wishes over local branches. Most industrial work stoppages (over 90 percent) are unofficial, which means they take place without the official sanction of the union. Second, the trade unions have a close relationship with the Labour Party, much closer historically than has been the case between any union and party in the United States or in most other European countries. As we have seen (Chapter 6), the trade unions were the largest sponsoring element when the Labour Party was formed, and they continue to be its main provider in both income and affiliated membership. This relationship may in part help explain the third feature. Although unions may and do seek to influence government policy on such issues as employment and the economy, union militancy and strikes are used to pursue wage claims rather than political ends. Overtly political strikes or "days of action" are rare; unions rather have looked to the Labour Party to achieve their political goals.

BUSINESS   In the business sector, sectional groups are equally if not more diverse. Although there is a well-known peak body for firms in industry, the Confederation of British Industry (CBI), it is far from all-encompassing. According to Wyn Grant and David Marsh, "There is a large and complex system of associations which look after the interests of individual industries or, in some cases, the interests of manufacturers of particular products, and many large firms deal directly with government."[11] Finance and the retail sector have their own structures and arrangements with government that are separate from those of the industry sector. "The City," the name given to the interests and institutions that inhabit the square mile of the City of London (Bank of England, the Stock Exchange, the Discount Market, the London Bankers' Clearing House, the commodity markets, insurance companies, and the like), is essentially a separate interest with its own structures and concerns, the latter not always compatible with those of business organizations. Company directors have their own organization in the form of the Institute of Directors (IoD), a highly organized body, with headquarters in Pall Mall, London; it has a somewhat greater free-market orientation than the CBI. There are chambers of commerce throughout the country, though they tend to be most active and effective at regional and local levels rather than on a national scale. In addition, there is a host of trade associations, important ones being bodies such as the Society of Motor Manufacturers.

These examples give some flavor of the diversity of business organizations. The most visible body, that which receives most academic and media attention, is the CBI. It was formed in 1965 as a result of the amalgamation of the Federation of British Industries (known, confusingly to Americans, as the FBI), the British Employers' Confederation, and the National Association of British Manufacturers. It sought to bring together the resources of the amalgamated bodies to form a more efficient servicing body and a more effective representative of industry's needs in discussions with government. Indeed, its functions are not dissimilar to those of unions: It provides various services to its members and it seeks—its primary and explicit aim—to represent them in negotiations with government departments and with government generally. It provides advice and assistance on industrial problems; it provides information on such things as technical translation services, and conditions in foreign countries; it produces its own economic reports; and, in practice, it provides a medium through which firms and associations can make new and useful contacts. It seeks to act as a voice for the needs of industry: "We provide real value for our members: campaigning and lobbying, access to the most senior business and political networks, insights on where policy is heading, key statistics from our information teams, and more policy specialists than any other business organization."[12]

Membership in the confederation is broad, though industrial companies are predominant. It has 200,000 small and medium enterprises (SMEs), over

150 sectoral associations, and 80 of the top 100 companies as members. Of the SME members, over 90 percent of them have fewer than 200 employees. Most small firms, though, are not members; the smaller the firm, the less likely it is to be a member. (The Federation of Small Businesses, with 215,000 members, claims to speak for such firms.) More than half of the CBI's income comes from the companies with more than 1,000 members (subscriptions being based on a company's salary bill and its U.K. turnover), and more than three-quarters comes from industrial companies. Income is used primarily to finance its staff of just over 300, headquarters in London's Centre Point, 12 regional offices, and an office in Brussels.

The main body within the CBI is its council, which meets several times a year, but it has a chairman's committee that takes the lead position in setting the organization's position on policy matters, and a board that deals with organizational and financial matters. It also has 13 elected regional councils and 16 standing committees. Within the council, the two most prominent and influential figures are the president, usually an industrialist drawn from one of the major companies, and the director-general, the full-time chief executive, usually drawn from a senior position in industry. As a result of the work of the council, the standing committees, and its regional councils, it claims that more than 2,500 people are involved in the CBI policy-making process.

Politically, the CBI has no formal link with any political party, but it has tended to be closely associated with the Conservative Party, the party most closely associated with business. Although the CBI itself has never made any contribution to Conservative Party funds, a number of its members are or have been contributors to party funds. However, the links are now not as strong as they were.

AGRICULTURE   Although not an inclusive peak organization, the CBI nonetheless is more extensive than any similar body in the United States. Similarly, in the agriculture sector the National Farmers Union of England and Wales (NFU) is the predominant body; in the United States there are more obviously competing bodies in the form of the Farmers' Union, the National Grange, and the American Farm Bureau Federation. The NFU in 2009 had a membership of 55,000 farmers and growers in England and Wales. (There are separate NFUs in Scotland and Northern Ireland.) It also has more than 60,000 countryside members, comprising people who do not rely on farming for their main income but have an interest in the land (such as smallholders). Each member of the NFU pays an annual subscription (for farmers and growers, a payment based on the size of the enterprise and a flat fee for others) and in 2008 the Union's income from subscriptions was £28.4 million ($46.4m.). The money is used to fund its staff and services as well as education campaigns designed to increase popular understanding of farming. Like its union and business counterparts, the NFU provides various services to members (including advice on legal, planning, and taxation matters) and also represents the interests of members in discussions with government.

The NFU is by no means the only body seeking to represent farming interests. The Farmers' Union of Wales, for example, is recognized by government as a representative body for the purposes of discussing agricultural matters. There are also bodies representing more specialized interests within the broad sector of agriculture, such as dairy producers.

Rather like the CBI, the union has a large national council, with the most influential members being the president and the general secretary. Below national level, the main unit of organization is the county branch, an often active and well-organized body, particularly in the large agricultural counties. Although farmers are traditionally strong supporters of the Conservative Party, the union nationally as well as at county level tends to adopt a strict political neutrality, though this is essentially of postwar origin. Before 1945 (the union was founded in 1908) it was more closely associated with the Conservative Party, despite formal assertions of nonpartisanship.[13] Once a body with substantial political clout, the NFU in recent years has had to adopt a more defensive stance against what it sees as government indifference or even hostility toward the interests of farmers and of the countryside.

There is thus a mass of sectional interest groups. The CBI and the TUC in particular serve as umbrella organizations for a vast range of groups and the coverage of each is not exhaustive. There are a large number of bodies that fall outside these particular groupings. Many professional bodies, for example, are not affiliated to the TUC. As we have already noted, most small businesses are not members of the CBI. Diversity is thus a feature of sectional interest groups.

Promotional Groups

Promotional groups are even more diverse than sectional interest groups in that they generally lack umbrella organizations to draw them together. They are notable for their growth in recent years and for their diversity. Most sectors of public policy have seen the growth of such groups.

We have already had cause to touch upon the nature and range of promotional groups. Many are created for altruistic purposes and have charitable status. There are more than 160,000 charities in the United Kingdom. Most are relatively small (almost half have an annual income of less than £10,000 [$16,400]) and do not concern themselves with seeking to influence public policy. However, the larger charities—there are just over 1,500 each with an annual income in excess of £5 million ($8.2m.)—are active in the policy arena. These include bodies concerned to improve the welfare of particular groups in society. The rubric includes animal as well as human welfare. Among the top 100 charities by income are bodies such as Oxfam (helping the homeless), Help the Aged, the National Society for the Prevention of Cruelty to Children (NSPCC), the Royal Society for the Prevention of Cruelty to Animals (RSPCA), and the Royal Society for the Protection of Birds (RSPB). In 2007–08, Oxfam had an income of

£78 million ($128.9m.) from trading, £107.4 million ($176.1m.) from institutional donors, and £105.7 million ($173.3m.) from supporters and the public. Though precluded by their charitable status from engaging in overtly political activities, they still take stands on public policy. Many have their own parliamentary officers; some hire political consultants (lobbyists). Though many charities have been founded in recent decades, some are long established. Some also have impressive membership figures. The RSPB, for example, founded in 1899, now has a membership of over 1 million. As noted in Chapter 4, this exceeds the combined membership of the three main political parties.

Other bodies, as we have noted, may be formed for ideological purposes and engage in overt political action; some may even engage in direct action. The bodies falling under this rubric are diverse and there is an overlap with the preceding category. Some bodies committed to animal welfare are overtly political bodies. Some confine their activities to working within the political system. Others take to the streets to make their voice heard. Of groups pressing for gay rights, the leading pressure group, Stonewall, utilizes traditional lobbying methods, while a much smaller fringe group, Outrage, adopts more confrontational tactics. Some groups combine public demonstrations with more traditional methods of leafleting and lobbying politicians.

One particular area of growth has been in the environmental field. The environmental group Greenpeace is now well established in the United Kingdom, as are a range of other, sometimes quite specific groups. These have included in recent years some direct action groups, including Reclaim the Streets, a group seeking to have streets used by pedestrians rather than motorists.

What emerges from this brief review is the diversity and the sheer extent of promotional groups in British politics. The numbers run into the thousands. Some, like the RSPB, have a large membership. Some have a handful of members. Increasingly, citizens are channeling their interests through organized groups. The postwar development of what Inglehart has termed *cognitive mobilization*[14]—citizens, through improved mass education and the mass media, being more aware of issues—has resulted in a greater interest and involvement in the political process, citizens forming groups to protect or further particular causes. Promotional groups are now a pervasive feature of the political landscape.

RELATIONS WITH GOVERNMENT

Various theoretical frameworks have been advanced to give shape to the relationship between groups and government. The two most longstanding have been those of *pluralism* and *corporatism*. More recently, the concept of *policy networks* has been developed to give shape to the complexity of the relationship.

Pluralism

The basic premise of the pluralist model is that the political system provides an essentially neutral process through which government acts as an arbiter between competing group demands. Within the political process, the essential element is the group, with individuals having the opportunity to join groups and then, through those groups, having some input into the making of public policy. Pluralists emphasize the extent and range of groups, their access to government, and the competition among them.[15] There is presumed to be a balance between groups, no one group enjoying supremacy, with the balance and institutionalized relationship between groups and government providing for stability in the political system and incremental policy making.

Corporatism

Corporatism has been subject to various definitions, but basically it entails a system in which government directs the activities of industry, which remains predominantly in private hands, through the representatives of a limited number of singular, compulsory, noncompetitive, hierarchically ordered, and functionally differentiated interest groups.[16] *Societal* corporatism exists where government tends to be but one participant in a complex of negotiations with such groups. Where government is dominant in the relationship, there exists a form of *state corporatism*.[17]

Policy Networks

Whereas pluralism stresses equality between groups and corporatism stresses hierarchy, with a small number of bodies coming together to determine policy, the policy network approach stresses the interaction of groups and policy makers and their dependence on one another for resources. Policy networks can take different forms: Rob Rhodes, for example, identifies five types, running along a continuum from integrated policy communities (stable, restricted membership) to loosely integrated issue networks (limited interdependence, large membership).[18] The emphasis is thus on complexity and interdependence.

Each of these approaches has its limitations. The pluralist approach fails to incorporate the impact of state institutions and ideology; the state is not necessarily a neutral arbiter and can (especially in a system with strong parties and single-party government, as in the United Kingdom) impose its will. Groups may be subordinate to the influence of political parties. Parties, as Richard Rose found, may not have a profound impact on economic indicators, but they do have *some* impact.[19] A party in office adopts a particular program and usually manages to implement most of it.[20] Corporatism has a fairly limited scope—it does not encompass the gamut of group activity. Each theory, as Martin Smith has noted, "has difficulty in dealing with the subtleties of the relationships between groups and government in particular policy areas. . . . They also fail to pay sufficient attention to the interests and resources of state actors."[21] The policy network approach is broad and has been subject to a range of variations;[22] it has also been criticized for having limited utility for examining different structures of governance.

Each approach, nonetheless, has some utility and can assist in making some sense of the relationship between groups and government in the United Kingdom and especially in giving some shape to that relationship over time. In terms of the relationship, three periods can be identified. The first period, up to the 1970s, was characterized by the institutionalization of the relationship between government and insider groups; by the development of particularly close relations between government and the peak organizations representing labor and business; and by the growth and political activity of outsider groups. At the level of high policy, the United Kingdom moved toward corporatism. At the level of intermediate policy, there was a move toward integrated policy communities. The process could thus be seen as essentially hierarchical and, to some degree, closed.

The second period, as we shall see, saw greater pluralism as the state resumed a more detached stance, especially at the level of high policy. Though not adopting the role of arbiter in determining high policy, especially economic and defense policy, the government became the target of a greater number of groups. Those groups also began to be brought within policy communities, outsider groups moving more toward insider status in terms of middle-level and, more especially, low-level policy. The move was thus from a closed to a more open process.

The third period has seen the greater fragmentation of power with the creation of elected assemblies in different parts of the United Kingdom. Organized interests now seek to influence public policy through a number of government bodies, and not simply through a single U.K. Government department. This greater fragmentation has been accompanied by some interdependence of groups and governmental bodies, the EU and devolved governments being fairly open to representations from groups. There has thus been a greater move toward policy networks. Though these may take different forms, the concept is nonetheless useful for characterizing the relationship that has developed between interest groups and different levels of government.

The Period up to 1979

INSIDER GROUPS: INSTITUTIONALIZATION As its responsibilities expanded, government came to have greater need of what groups could offer, and the groups, in turn, looked to government for the satisfaction of their demands. This relationship often necessitated frequent contact and increasingly became institutionalized. Groups not only were asked for advice on an informal or nonroutine basis, but also they became drawn into the processes of government by being invited to appoint representatives to serve on advisory bodies, tribunals, and committees of different sorts. This in itself is not a recent phenomenon. The National Health Insurance Act of 1924 provided for the functional representation of specific interests, such as the medical profession, on various committees appointed to administer the system of social insurance. Analogous provisions had appeared in the Trade Board acts of 1909 and 1918.

By the late 1950s, more than a hundred advisory bodies existed under statutory provision. The 1960s and 1970s witnessed the growth of bodies that comprised representatives of the CBI and the TUC as well as representatives of government. Examples of such bodies were the National Economic Development Council (the NEDC, known as "Neddy"), created in 1961 to provide a forum in which representatives of the three could meet to discuss the economy (and since disbanded); the Manpower Services Commission (since disbanded), to promote training and job creation schemes; the Health and Safety Commission, to help regulate and supervise safety and health at work; and the Advisory, Conciliation and Arbitration Service (known as ACAS), to help resolve industrial disputes. At the same time, various bodies at a lower level proliferated in number, to consider more specialized topics and to bring together representatives of the various core (as opposed to peak) groups. A report on such bodies in 1978 identified more than 1,560 advisory bodies and nearly 500 similar bodies with executive powers (to issue regulations, dispense funds, and carry out similar functions), such as the Manpower Services Commission.[23] Methods of appointment to these disparate bodies varied. In some cases there were statutory requirements to include representatives of particular groups, and in other cases the power was vested with the relevant minister, who could appoint people in a representative capacity (on behalf of a group) or in an individual capacity (drawn from but not officially representing a particular group). What is significant for our purposes is the number of such bodies and the extent to which they were staffed by, and indeed would be unable to function without, members of affected interest groups.

It is important to remember that such bodies constituted the formal, institutional embodiment of the close relationship between insider groups and government departments. Over and above these, there was regular contact between groups and departments through formal and informal meetings, sometimes through formal or informal social gatherings. At the level of regular contact, for example, the National Farmers Union and the then Ministry of Agriculture followed well-established procedures each year in discussing the annual price review. Each year, the two were in constant touch with one another, indeed "almost hourly contact" according to one study.[24] There was similar contact between other departments and groups within their sphere of responsibility.

Most middle- and virtually all low-level policies are made at departmental and subdepartmental levels. There are functional and legal, as well as cultural, reasons encouraging this practice. The range and extent of government policy making is such that the cabinet is able to deal with only a fraction of it. Legal powers are vested in individual ministers (not the cabinet), and for a proposal to be authoritative and enacted, it is often sufficient for a minister to give it formal approval. Furthermore, the political culture favors consensus within small policy communities of officials and group representatives. Disputes are neither sought nor encouraged. It is to the advantage of both group and civil servants to avoid dissent. Each needs the other, and disputes could jeopardize their relationship as well as pass the problem on for others to resolve. A desire to decide the issue for themselves impels civil servants and the groups to seek agreement. One of the characteristics of the British policy style, according to Jordan and Richardson, is that of "bureaucratic accommodation."[25]

A combination of this diversity and institutionalization has important implications for the nature of policy making in Britain, for it favors incrementalism. This has tended to create problems for any government seeking to impose a comprehensive new policy on both its own departments and affected groups. Departments or their various units have often become so closely associated with the groups with which they deal that they tend to represent the interests of the groups to the government rather than (or in addition to) representing the interests of government to the groups. This position, sometimes referred to as a form of "clientelism," results in departments speaking on behalf of different interests and often competing among themselves where those interests are not compatible. Thus, a government determined to cut public expenditure has the task of imposing cuts upon departments that are keen to resist them and that come up with plausible arguments for their own exemption, arguments that have the backing of the department's clientele groups. Similarly, cuts in other departments are resisted on analogous grounds, ministers competing to defend their own departmental budgets. Although a party manifesto might provide a government with its plan of action, achieving that plan is a task for which neither the manifesto nor control of a party majority in the House of Commons may be sufficient.

INSIDER GROUPS: TRIPARTISM   By the 1970s, the relationship between governments and groups was institutionalized. This was primarily the case in determining middle-level policy, primarily policy not at the heart of government policy, and low-level policy, that is, the detail for implementing policy. In the 1970s, it was also to become a feature of high-level policy making, with peak organizations being drawn in for discussions with the prime minister and other senior ministers to determine economic policy.

As we have seen, in the 1960s and 1970s, representatives of the CBI and the TUC were variously co-opted onto a range of bodies. In addition, negotiations with government, often at prime-ministerial level, were common; Labour Prime Minister Harold Wilson was keen to consult with the two peak organizations—in 1966, he told the House of Commons it was the government's duty to consult with them—and Conservative Prime Minister Edward Heath sought to arrange a voluntary prices-and-pay policy with both bodies in 1972. However, the relationship became a feature especially of the period from 1974 to 1979.

During this period, there was an especially close relationship between government and the trade unions. The government negotiated with the TUC a "social contract" that entailed the government's introducing various measures (on employment law, for example) favored by the unions, in return for which the unions moderated wage demands. The relationship that developed between government, and especially certain trade union leaders, was seen as an intimate one. By the end of the 1970s opinion polls demonstrated that the unions—and particular union leaders—were considered "too powerful." There were fears that other groups, as well as the public interest, were being excluded from the process; a pluralist system was being stifled by corporatist tendencies.

There was a close relationship at times between the government and the representatives of finance. The CBI, as we have seen, was variously integrated into formal bodies. On other occasions, its support was sought for particular policies. At times, various bodies were drawn together. The government had, in effect, to negotiate with the TUC, the International Monetary Fund, the CBI, the City of London, and (if not negotiate, at least take into account) the House of Commons to achieve the economic policy it wanted.

Various peak organizations were thus variously co-opted, at times on an institutionalized or semi-institutionalized level, into the process of making high-level policy. The nature and frequency of meetings at 10 Downing Street involving union representatives became popularized in the term "beer and sandwich" meetings, implying talks while beer and sandwiches were brought in to sustain the participants. Union as well as business leaders became used to being consulted by government.

OUTSIDER GROUPS: GREATER ACTIVITY   The growth and incorporation of insider groups was a particular feature of the period, especially the 1970s. Another was the growth and, by definition, nonincorporation of outsider groups. The growth of such groups we have touched upon already. The period between 1960 and 1979 was a notable period of pressure group formation.

Most outsider groups were, and remain, promotional groups. They fell into the outsider category largely for three reasons. The first reason was the fact that they generally lacked the political clout enjoyed by sectional interest groups. They usually lacked a monopoly of information and expertise, and certainly did not have information and expertise needed by government. As we have already noted, a feature of promotional groups is that there is no exclusive membership. They have few, if any, sanctions that they can employ against government if it proves unresponsive to their overtures. A second reason, specific to the period though not applicable to all groups, was the very newness of the groups. Ministers and officials were wary of groups that had not had an opportunity to establish their credentials. That tendency was likely to have been exacerbated if, in order to attract attention, the groups engaged in public demonstrations. The third reason, specific to a number of groups, was that some groups were ideologically unacceptable. There was little likelihood, for example, that the Ministry of Defence was going to accord insider status to the Campaign for Nuclear Disarmament. Indeed, given the causes promoted by some groups, a government may be keen to keep some of them at arm's length.

To achieve their goals, promotional groups, by virtue of their outsider status, often found themselves compelled to seek support outside the corridors of government departments. This often took the form of trying to attract support from Parliament, either directly or indirectly. Direct contact with

MPs took the form of letters or pamphlets sent to all MPs or, in the case of better organized groups, to MPs likely to be sympathetic to their cause and, increasingly, through lobbying of members by group supporters. Sympathetic MPs, some of whom held office in the groups (quite often as honorary vice presidents), variously arranged for delegations from a group to meet with other MPs or even a minister, or else they asked parliamentary questions or, in some cases, introduced private members' bills. Indirectly, groups sought to influence MPs through mass demonstrations, marches, public meetings, and press releases. In the absence of extremely large numbers or violence, attracting publicity by such means was an uphill struggle. The various means were not mutually exclusive. A campaign would often encompass a demonstration, a petition, or a campaign of writing letters to MPs.

The success of these groups varied considerably. The fact of outsider status did not necessarily doom a campaign to failure. It did mean, though, that the groups had to try much harder than insider groups to make their voice heard within government. Some groups achieved success through private members' legislation in the 1960s, when government was not unsympathetic but was not willing to commit itself publicly to introducing the measures. Several major measures of social reform—on divorce, abortion, homosexuality, the death penalty, and theater censorship—were enacted as private members' bills.[26] Such success, though, was exceptional. Some groups made some headway, achieving some action or concession. Others worked hard but often to little avail, at least in terms of government action.

Many of the features of British promotional groups, and indeed the causes pursued, are not dissimilar to those of U.S. promotional groups. Both benefited in this period from the development of television, which gave them more visual impact through their public demonstrations and lobbies. British groups, though, were—and remain—more limited than their U.S. counterparts by virtue of the strength of party. On an issue about which a party stance was taken, an MP could hide behind his or her party's position in responding to group pressure. It was, and it remains, an effective shield. Promotional groups present no significant threat to a sitting MP. They stand no chance of persuading electors to vote the MP out at the next election, because the party label will normally determine whether the MP stays or goes. Groups will have no leverage through campaign donations: Donations go to parties and, as we have seen, local campaign expenditure is strictly controlled. Occasionally, issues become divisive within parties—for example, capital punishment in the Conservative Party or abortion in the Labour Party—but rarely do they impinge upon an MP's chosen behavior or continuance as a party candidate.

This is not to argue that MPs did not align themselves with or were not persuaded by promotional groups. Many were associated with such groups and not infrequently served as active advocates of a group's cause. The point is that MPs were in a much stronger position than members of Congress to resist pressure from groups with which they—or their party—were not in sympathy. MPs did not need such groups and rarely could groups be considered a threat to their political survival.

This point is essential to understanding the distinction between insider and outsider groups. If government granted access to a group, it was an insider. If it denied access, it was an outsider. The strength of party made it difficult for a group to achieve access by alternative routes. The government had a supportive majority in the House of Commons. For outsider groups to have any influence on public policy, they need at least government acquiescence. In the United States, the barriers were not so sharp—party was not such a protective shield—and the distinction between insider and outsider status less relevant in explaining the genesis and development of public policy.

By the 1970s, interest groups were thus a major and integral part of the British political process. The period since the 1940s had seen a remarkable growth in the number of groups. The growth was especially marked in the period between 1960 and 1979. Of pressure groups and representative organizations listed in one directory published in 1979, more than 42 percent had come into existence since 1960.[27] Insider groups had a largely institutionalized relationship with government, not usually needing to seek publicity for their activities. Peak organizations enjoyed access at the highest levels of government. Outsider groups, by definition, lacked such access but were vigorous in promoting their cause. However, taking their cause to Parliament was generally viewed as an admission of failure and unlikely to admit of success in a body where the government dominated the proceedings.

From Tripartism to Pluralism: The Period of Conservative Government, 1979–97

Under the Conservative government of Margaret Thatcher, elected in 1979, there was a radical departure from past practice. The divorce from the past was not total. Indeed, we can identify two features of the period, one much commented upon, the other less noted. The first change was radical and much noticed. That was the attempt, at the level of high policy, to exclude groups from policy deliberations. As a result, peak organizations, especially the TUC, moved essentially from insider to outsider status. The second was less noticed. In seeking to influence middle- and low-level policy, outsider groups tended to make greater and more effective use of Parliament—and on occasion achieve some success. Peak organizations, pushed from insider status, also made greater use of Parliament. The consequence was a greater visibility for Parliament and a blurring of the distinction between insider and outsider groups. Lobbying by interest groups, whether insider or outsider, has become a feature of the political landscape.

HIGH POLICY: EXCLUSION   To achieve its neoliberal economic policy, the Thatcher government began to disengage itself from anything that smacked of corporatist relationships. The goal of a free-market economy was non-negotiable and corporatism distorted market forces. The government sought autonomy in policy making and, at the same time, wished to restrict bodies seen as employing restrictive practices. The trade unions were seen as a

particular target. The government introduced a number of legislative measures to reform the unions, limiting their capacity to strike and to impose
closed shops, as well as attempting to break up monopolistic practices in
other sectors.

By withdrawing from bipartite and tripartite relationships, the government removed an obstacle to the realization of goals by other groups. However, by virtue of its free-market orientation, it also became, especially at the
level of high policy or any policy that derived from its free market objective,
less responsive to demands made by those groups. The government did not
assume a position as independent arbiter, and certainly not at the level of economic policy making. In terms of economic policy, policy making was formulated by government and then imposed.

Groups thus faced the problem of how to make their voice heard by government in the making of high policy. As we shall see, they were still heard at
the lower levels, but at the upper levels they had notably less input than
before. The answer for many groups was, and remains, to engage in extensive, more open, and more professional lobbying—that is, directly and on
their own initiative, extolling their cases to decision makers. The years since
1979 have seen the growth of the professional lobbyist.

MEDIUM AND LOW-LEVEL POLICY: INCLUSION   One much neglected aspect of the
period since 1979 has been the extent to which, at the level at which government departments develop policy, groups retained insider status or acquired
insider status. Despite the arm's-length relationship established between
government and groups on high policy, there has been continuing contact
between departments and insider groups, and a willingness on the part of
departments to draw in more outsider groups. Departments continue to need
sectional interest groups for information. Ministers have continued to meet
with group representatives and to keep abreast of groups' activities and
thinking.[28] In consulting on proposed delegated legislation (usually detailed
proposals to give effect to particular provisions of Acts of Parliament),
departments have consulted widely, including groups that would previously
have been categorized as outsider groups. The inclusion of such groups
would appear in some cases to be the consequence of the groups having
established their credentials as serious organizations with advice that may be
helpful. Thus, for instance, Greenpeace—which would have been classed as
an outsider group in its early years—now appears on the list of groups sent
draft delegated legislation in its area of interest. So extensive nowadays is the
consultation with interested groups that there almost appears little relevance,
at least at this level, to the distinction between insider and outsider groups.[29]

The nature of this inclusion, though, should not be misunderstood. The
inclusion of groups did not necessarily mean that their advice was taken. Nor
did it mean that they were necessarily consulted about policy initiatives. For
groups to influence public policy, they may need to be proactive, especially if
they wish to see a new policy introduced. They may also need to take action
to get noticed if other groups are busy making a pitch to ministers. A greater

degree of consultation does not necessarily imply that all groups enjoy equal access. Some groups remain better regarded by government than others. Groups may still need, therefore, to lobby politicians. Indeed, that need has arguably been greater as a consequence of two of the developments we have identified. One is the growth in the number of groups. The more groups there are, the more each one has to work harder to get noticed. Furthermore, if groups taking an opposing view are created, the more one has to work to counter their activities. The second development was the stance taken by the Thatcher government toward peak groups. Though the practice of exclusion did not percolate down to all groups, it nonetheless generated the perception that the government was unreceptive to group pressure. Groups, whether insider or outsider, thus felt the need to lobby government to be heard and, to complement that, to lobby Parliament. No group wanted to be left out and therefore lobbying became a marked feature of British politics. It encompassed lobbying of both government and Parliament.

LOBBYING GOVERNMENT   Ministers and civil servants remain the principal targets of group lobbying.[30] Groups that are consulted but have not found their views accepted, and groups—often promotional groups—that are not consulted at all, will utilize in-house or professional lobbyists to make their case to the relevant minister or official. Many large companies now have their own in-house parliamentary or public affairs divisions, responsible for relations with government departments and Parliament. Others employ the services of independent political lobbyists, known formally as political consultants. Before 1979, there were hardly any firms of political consultants. By the mid-1990s, there were more than 40 such firms, the largest with about 30 or 40 employees, supplemented by a three-figure number of freelance consultants.

Most big companies and financial concerns now retain political consultants.[31] The practice of hiring consultants is not confined to commercial organizations. Lobbying firms are also used by sectional bodies such as the Bar as well as by a host of promotional groups, ranging from animal welfare organizations to bodies promoting the social sciences. The work of lobbyists has been supplemented by the appearance of a number of books and guides on lobbying;[32] among those producing such a guide is the CBI. The result has been a more crowded and proactive field of groups seeking to make their existence and their needs known to targeted ministers and officials. The task is facilitated by the fact that political consultancy firms frequently recruit staff from former civil servants and, in some cases, former ministers.[33]

LOBBYING PARLIAMENT   Lobbying government has added a new dimension to the relationship between groups and government departments. However, much more dramatic has been the growth in parliamentary lobbying. Parliament has always been a focus of groups seeking some change in the law, but for much of the twentieth century it was not regarded as the principal focus of those seeking change. Promotional groups variously used it, sometimes to effect (as with the social reform measures of the 1960s) but usually to no effect. Recognition of the limitations of lobbying Parliament resulted in many sectional groups not even bothering. They had their links with departments; in seeking to achieve some change in policy, those links were necessary and sufficient. The period since 1979 has seen a change in the perceptions, and consequently the practice, of such groups. They have made far greater use of Parliament than ever before.

A survey in 1986 of more than 250 organized groups, ranging from the CBI to small charities, found that one-fifth of them hired political consultants and, more significantly, three-quarters of them had regular or frequent contact with one or more MPs.[34] It is now common for groups to circulate briefing material to MPs and to have officers or lobbyists present during the committee proceedings on a bill. During the passage of one particular bill, more than 80 references were made by MPs on the committee to representations made by outside groups.[35] The MP's daily mailbag now bulges with material from pressure groups.[36] Though ministers and civil servants remain the principal target of group activity, Parliament constitutes an important and growing focus for such activity as well.

There are a number of reasons for this change in group behavior toward Parliament.[37] One, as we have seen, is that groups have looked elsewhere for other channels for getting their views heard by ministers and civil servants. However, Parliament itself has variously added to its own attractiveness. Greater behavioral independence has meant that MPs—and peers—may not only be willing but also more able than before to influence public policy (see Chapter 12). The creation of departmental select committees also has provided a focus for group lobbying. These committees determine their own agenda and, by concentrating on particular departments, act as magnets for groups seeking to influence those departments. The televising of proceedings has further added to the attractiveness of the institution for pressure groups seeking to put their case before government and the wider public.

Since 1979, lobbying has resulted in some notable instances of policy modification or even withdrawal. The extent of this influence is not amenable to precise quantification: Causal linkages between group lobbying and government action cannot usually be proved. Nonetheless, there have been some significant, and observable, examples of effective group pressure. In the 1980s, the most significant instance was the defeat of the Shops Bill, introduced to liberalize the law on Sunday trading. Pressure groups were active in lobbying both for and against the bill. A coalition of trade unions and religious groups, including the Church of England, lobbied against the bill and employed the services of a lobbying firm. Their campaign was stunningly effective: 72 Conservative MPs voted with Labour MPs against the bill, producing a notable defeat for the government.[38] Other instances are on a less dramatic scale, usually entailing persuading ministers to withdraw a particular provision, or support the insertion of a new one, in a particular bill.

A number of policy proposals implemented by the Labour government in 1997 may be seen to have their genesis in group pressure, including the policy of banning the private ownership of handguns[39] and a ban on foxhunting.

LOBBYING THE EUROPEAN UNION   Lobbying has not been confined to the U.K. government and Parliament. It also occurs at the level of the European Union. Though the United Kingdom became a member of the then EC in 1973 (see Chapter 9), it was only in the 1980s that organized interests began to see the value of lobbying at a supranational level. "The actual boom of lobbying in the EU began with the Single European Act (SEA) in 1986. The endorsement of the single market, the introduction of qualified majority voting for most measures concerning it, and the establishment of the so-called 1992 programme to complete single market legislation by 1992 triggered interest group lobbying of a new quality and quantity."[40] There was a new layer of policy making and one that companies began to realize had potentially major implications for how they operated. More and more firms and trade associations, as well as political lobbyists, began to set up offices in Brussels. The principal political consultancies in London established branches in Brussels.

The lobbying at a supranational level became more intense as the powers of the EC were extended by the treaty on European Union (the Maastricht Treaty, 1992), creating a three-pillar European Union. For many large organizations—commercial, consumer, and environmental—ensuring that their voices were heard in Brussels became as, and in many cases more, important than getting their cases heard in London.

Lobbying of the Directorates General of the European Commission became big business. The 2004 *European Public Affairs Directory* listed 2,081 representative offices.[41] The Directorates General were accessible bodies and consultation on proposals was usually extensive. At this level, the distinction between insider and outsider groups also appears rather blurred. There was a willingness to consider representations from any body with an interest in the subject under consideration.

For organized interests, the access points to the policy-making process thus became more numerous. Instead of simply establishing contacts with Whitehall (U.K. government departments) they now had to establish contacts at Westminster (the U.K. Parliament) and Brussels (the European Commission and committees of the European Parliament). Not only that, for some there was also another avenue for influencing public policy: The Strand, in London, home of the high court. If groups felt that a government department was acting beyond its legal powers, or in conflict with European law, it could take the case to court and, increasingly, groups did so. Seeking judicial review became, as we shall see, a feature of the period.

Groups thus had to lobby to get their voices heard. Increasingly, they had to compete with other groups to ensure that they were heard. Lobbying thus became the order of the day and it also became more extensive as organized interests entered the field to ensure their case did not go by default.

Policy Networks: Lobbying under Labour

Lobbying is thus extensive and visible—and has remained so under the Labour government elected in 1997. Ministers continue to adopt an inclusive policy—especially in determining the detail of policy implementation—and political consultancies continue to pitch for business. As we shall see, controversy over the close links between lobbyists and elected politicians has also continued to attract headlines and raise questions about the legitimacy of lobbying.

However, what has changed in the period since 1997 has been the further fragmentation of power. There are now new layers of government and thus additional sources of lobbying by organized interests. Interest groups have followed the flow of policy-making power. For groups keen to influence public policy, the sites of policy making have been extended to include Holyrood in Edinburgh (home of the Scottish executive), Cardiff (home of the Welsh executive), and, with the creation of a power-sharing executive in 2007, Stormont in Belfast (home of the Northern Ireland executive). They also include nine regional development agencies in England set up in 1999–2000 by government to encourage economic regeneration. The courts have also increased in significance as a consequence of the incorporation into British law of the European Convention on Human Rights.

The creation of a Scottish Parliament and a Welsh assembly has meant that groups with an interest in public policy in Scotland and Wales have to lobby members of the new executives and the elected bodies. The emphasis in both has tended to be one of inclusion, again eroding the distinction between insider and outsider groups. Many lobbying firms now have offices in different parts of the United Kingdom. Because of the powers devolved to Scotland (see Chapter 10), Edinburgh has been the most important site for such firms. Indeed, lobbying has been notable for its extent and its capacity to reach within the Scottish Parliament,[42] both through having access to cross-party groups[43] and acquiring parliamentary passes.[44] Some interest groups have also established offices in Cardiff. Lobbying in Stormont has not been as well developed, given that the assembly was suspended between 2002 and 2007, but has nonetheless become a feature: "the lobbyists are certainly picking up the scent of lucrative contracts now the Assembly is back in action."[45] The English regional development agencies also attract attention from interest groups keen to influence the disbursement of economic support.

These relationships have developed while those in the European Union have also expanded—in 2008 the European Commission estimated that there were around 15,000 lobbyists seeking to influence EU officials and members of the European Parliament[46]—and become more institutionalized. Policy networks, in different forms, are seen as helping give shape to the relationships that now exist between EU institutions and those groups seeking to influence policy outcomes. "Depending on the general policy type, networks exhibit more or less structural and membership stability. Unchanged, continuous policy communities seem to dominate distributive politics whilst more instable and open issue networks can be found in regulative politics."[47] As

Karr goes on to state, the policy network model "is better equipped to describe the EU reality than either corporatism or pluralism."[48]

The creation of the new assemblies and the incorporation into the British law of the ECHR will be considered in detail in later chapters, along with developments in the European Union. For the moment, it is sufficient to note them for the purpose of establishing the several points of access for groups seeking to influence the policy-making process. A single focus, the preserve largely of insider groups, has given way to several, and those points of access are open to a wide array of groups. There has been a move from a limited and closed system, one that included a corporatist element, to a much more open, pluralist system, with the development of an array of policy networks.

THE CURRENT DEBATE

Interest groups are a feature of a free society.[49] People join them for a variety of reasons. They may subscribe for the services they offer. They may belong as a condition of their professional activity. They may join in order to engage in a particular activity or as a means of integrating into the local community. They may belong in order to pursue a particular cause, be it for private benefit or for the public good.

Without interest groups—and political parties—there is not much that stands between the state and the individual. Groups, like parties, seek to aggregate and express opinions—they are efficient in that they save the individual from having to do all the work—and they pursue those opinions through seeking to influence government. They enable people to be involved in politics beyond the electoral arena. They "provide a linkage between the governed and government. Without such linkage, citizens might become alienated, and societal and democratic stability could be undermined."[50] The existence of interest groups may thus be seen as constituting a public good in itself.

Interest groups are entitled to express their views to government. In the United States, for example, the right to do so is constitutionally protected through the First Amendment right to petition government. Making representations to government and to the legislature in order to ensure their view is heard and, as appropriate, acted upon—in other words, lobbying—benefits not only those lobbying but also those being lobbied. Representations from interest groups provide policy makers with information they may not otherwise have. They provide parliamentarians with material with which they may question government. Parliamentarians—and parliamentary committees—may come to rely on interest groups as sources of briefing and data.

Lobbying by interest groups is an intrinsic and beneficial part of a political system. However, there are also problems associated with it. The system may be more pluralist than ever before, but it is not perfectly pluralist. Groups have to compete for access and some groups appear to achieve it more readily than others. The methods by which access appears to be gained have led to claims of "influence buying." Such claims have featured prominently in public debate, especially since 1994, leading to demands for a more regulated system of lobbying.

Groups that can afford lobbyists can achieve a degree of access to the political process that is likely to be denied to those without such resources. This criticism was fueled in the 1980s and early 1990s by the fact that many MPs were themselves political consultants, or were hired to advise consultants.[51] In addition, many civil servants were lured away to work for consultants (the Ministry of Defence, in particular, having a reputation as a "revolving door"),[52] thus ensuring that "insider" knowledge was available to clients who retained the consultants. These developments, according to *The Observer*, constituted "worryingly corrosive influences."[53]

The issue achieved especial prominence in 1994 when allegations were made of MPs accepting money for tabling parliamentary questions. In response, the prime minister established a special committee, the Committee on Standards in Public Life, to examine "current concerns" about standards of conduct of office holders and to make recommendations for changes that "might be required to ensure the highest standards of propriety in public life." In 1995, the committee came up with various recommendations for MPs.[54] After two heated debates, the House of Commons approved various changes, including the creation of a Parliamentary Commissioner for Standards, a new committee on standards, a code of conduct for MPs, a ban on paid advocacy, and the disclosure of income derived from service as an MP.

A consequence was a much clearer divide between lobbyists and MPs—the latter being on the receiving end of lobbying by the former, rather than themselves falling into the same category—and an official brought in from outside to report on and investigate claims of breaches of the code of conduct. Despite these changes, perceptions of influence buying, and of privileged access, persisted. One leading lobbying firm, implicated in influence buying, went out of business.[55] The issue returned after the election in 1997 of a Labour government, with various claims of cash being offered for access to ministers. It achieved especial prominence as a result of a decision to exempt Formula 1 motor racing from a ban on tobacco advertising following a £1 million ($1.64m.) donation to the Labour Party (and a meeting with Prime Minister Tony Blair) by the head of Formula 1 racing, Bernie Ecclestone. The outgoing chairman of the Committee on Standards in Public Life said in 2007: "My greatest regret has been the apparent failure to persuade the government to place high ethical standards at the heart of its thinking and, most importantly, behavior."[56] Nor were the newly elected assemblies in different parts of the United Kingdom immune from such controversy. Claims of conflicts of interest were leveled in Scotland and later in Northern Ireland against certain politicians and their relatives.

Parliament itself variously investigated the issue. The Select Committee on Members' Interests carried out an inquiry and reported in 1991. It recommended against having a register of lobbyists. The Public Administration Committee returned to the subject in 2008. As it recorded, "There has . . . been widespread public concern that some areas of government policy have effectively been captured at an early stage by interest groups, usually within industry, and that public consultations have been unbalanced in favour of these interests. Two prominent recent cases have concerned nuclear power and Heathrow airport."[57] One aspect of lobbying on behalf of nuclear power that it went on to record was the number of ex-MPs employed in support of the nuclear industry. After looking at regulatory practice in the United States, Canada, Australia, and Germany (as well as a voluntary system introduced for the European Parliament), the Committee went on to recommend the introduction of a register of lobbying activity. As it concluded: "Government needs to be open to outside interests and ideas. In recent years, it has become more open, in extended consultation, new sources of policy advice, and in greater movement of people in and out of government. All this brings benefits. Yet there are also risks, if the process is not carefully managed. The greatest risk is that some interests may acquire excessive influence, or are believed to have excessive influence, buttressing a public perception that government is not to be trusted."[58]

The negative publicity served to mask the value of lobbying. On balance, lobbyists tend to facilitate rather than impede greater pluralism in the system. A group with a good case to make needs to get that case heard by government. Lobbying makes that possible. The more lobbyists there are, the more crowded the field and the less easy it is for a single group to dominate. The growing availability of freelance lobbyists serves to enhance the pluralist ideal through allowing more and more groups to achieve some greater degree of access to officials and politicians. Groups may not achieve what they want, but they have at least made their voice heard. Politicians and civil servants are well able to recognize lobbying activities and to separate effective argument from weak argument, in whatever form it is presented. Parliamentarians tend to be wary of material presented in too lavish a form. Material of no relevance to them finds its way into the wastebasket. The value of representations from interest groups, especially those promoting particular causes, has not only been recognized but also encouraged by government. In the European Union, for example, some interest groups receive funding from the EU budget (including about 35 environmental groups);[59] in 2009, the U.K. government created a small fund to help charities mount campaigns.[60]

Lobbying by groups will nonetheless remain a point of controversy. Part of the problem derives from the activity being only partially observable; part derives from the fact that payment takes place for such activity. Given continuing criticism, some formal regulation of lobbyists—as recommended by the Public Administration Committee—may take place. However, lobbying is certain to continue as a growth industry. Whatever the ethics of lobbying, groups are not likely to want to be left behind in the rush to influence public policy.

CONCLUSION

Pressure groups in Britain are numerous and diverse. Insider groups enjoy a frequent and fairly well institutionalized relationship with government departments. For peak organizations, the relationship with government became especially close, and structured, in the 1960s and 1970s, when tripartism became a feature, or at least a partial feature, of policy making. Since then, the field of policy making has become open and crowded. A closed system has given way to a more pluralist one, marked by the development of a range of policy networks. Increasingly, in order to influence policy, groups have resorted to lobbying government, Parliament, the institutions of the European Union, the new assemblies in Scotland, Wales, and Northern Ireland, as well as having recourse to the courts (Chapter 14). By Capitol Hill standards, the development of lobbying is an extremely modest one, but it is growing and is likely to continue to do so.

NOTES

1. See G. Jordan, "Pressure Groups: Identifying the Target for Study," *Politics Review*, 18 (1), 2008, pp. 17–19.
2. J. H. Bimbaum, "The Road to Riches is Called K Street," *The Washington Post*, 22 June 2005.
3. W. Grant, *Pressure Groups, Politics and Democracy in Britain*, 2nd ed. (Harvester Wheatsheaf, 1995), p. 15.
4. See G. Jordan, "Pressure Groups: Identifying the Target for Study," *Politics Review*, 18 (1), 2008, pp. 17–19.
5. See Grant, p. 20.
6. R. M. Punnett, *British Government and Politics* (Heinemann, 1970 edition), p. 134.
7. R. T. McKenzie, "Parties, Pressure Groups and the British Political Process," *Political Quarterly*, 29 (1), 1958.
8. R. Klein, "Policy Making in the National Health Service," *Political Studies*, 22 (1), 1974, p. 6.
9. S. H. Beer, *Modern British Politics*, rev. ed. (Faber, 1969), p. 326.
10. See H. Grainger and A. Crowther, *Trade Union Membership 2006* (Department of Trade and Industry, 2007), http://www.berr.gov.uk/files/file39006.pdf
11. W. Grant and D. Marsh, *The CBI* (Hodder & Stoughton, 1977), p. 55.
12. CBI: Benefits of CBI membership (2009), http://www.cbi.org.uk
13. P. Self and H. Storing, "The Farmer and the State," in R. Kimber and J. Richardson (eds.), *Pressure Groups in Britain* (Dent, 1974), pp. 58–59.
14. R. Inglehart, *The Silent Revolution: Changing Values and Political Styles among Western Publics* (Princeton University Press, 1977).
15. The principal works on pluralism, now regarded as classics, are R. A. Dahl, *A Preface to Democratic Theory* (Chicago University Press, 1956); and R. A. Dahl, *Who Governs?* (Yale University Press, 1961). See also D. Truman, *The Governmental Process* (Knopf, 1962).
16. See A. Cawson, "Pluralism, Corporatism and the Role of the State," *Government and Opposition*, Spring 1978, p. 197.
17. P. C. Schmitter, "Still the Century of Corporatism?" *The Review of Politics*, 36 (1), 1974, pp. 85–131. See also R. Pahl and J. Winkler, "The Coming Corporatism," *New Society*, 10 October 1974, pp. 72–76.

18. R. A. W. Rhodes, *The National World of Local Government* (Allen & Unwin, 1986), Ch. 2.
19. R. Rose, *Do Parties Make a Difference?* 2nd ed. (Macmillan, 1984).
20. See R. I. Hofferbert and I. Budge, "The Party Mandate and the Westminster Model: Election Programmes and Government Spending in Britain, 1945–85," *British Journal of Political Science,* 22 (2), 1992, pp. 151–182.
21. M. J. Smith, *Pressure. Power and Policy* (Harvester Wheatsheaf, 1993), pp. 46–47.
22. See R. A. W. Rhodes, *Understanding Governance* (Open University Press, 1997), pp. 36–45.
23. *Report on Non-Departmental Public Bodies,* Cmnd. 7797 (Her Majesty's Stationery Office, 1980), p. 5.
24. G. K. Wilson, *Special Interests and Policy Making* (Wiley, 1977), quoted in Richardson and Jordan, p. 114.
25. G. Jordan and J. Richardson, "The British Style or the Logic of Negotiation?" in J. Richardson (ed.), *Policy Styles in Western Europe* (Allen & Unwin, 1982), p. 81.
26. See especially P. G. Richards, *Parliament and Conscience* (Allen & Unwin, 1970).
27. P. Shipley, *Directory of Pressure Groups and Representative Organisations* (Bowker, 1979).
28. See especially P. Norton, "Barons in a Shrinking Kingdom: Senior Ministers in British Government," in R. A. W. Rhodes (ed.), *Transforming British Government, Vol 2: Changing Roles and Relationships* (Macmillan, 2000), pp. 82–106.
29. See especially E. C. Page, "Insider and Outsider Groups: An Empirical Examination," unpublished manuscript, 1998.
30. M. Rush, "Parliament and Pressure Politics—An Overview," in M. Rush (ed.), *Parliament and Pressure Politics* (Clarendon Press, 1990), p. 272.
31. C. Grantham and C. Seymour-Ure, "Political Consultants," in Rush, *Parliament and Pressure Politics,* pp. 45–84.
32. As, for example, A. Dubbs, *Lobbying: An Insider's Guide to the Parliamentary Process* (Pluto Press, 1989); C. Miller, *Lobbying* (Blackwell, 1990); S. John, *The Persuaders* (Palgrave Macmillan, 2002); and L. Zetter, *Lobbying: The Art of Political Persuasion* (Harriman House, 2008).
33. See Grantham and Seymour-Ure, pp. 50–56, 58–59.
34. Rush, *Parliament and Pressure Politics.*
35. P. Norton, "Public Legislation," in Rush, *Parliament and Pressure Politics.*
36. See especially P. Norton, *Parliament in British Politics* (Palgrave Macmillan, 2005), Ch. 10.
37. See Norton, *Parliament in British Politics,* pp. 203–206.
38. See P. Regan, "The 1986 Shops Bill," *Parliamentary Affairs,* 41 (2), 1988; and A. C. S. Bown, "The Shops Bill," in Rush, *Parliament and Pressure Politics,* pp. 213–233.
39. Opposition to ownership of handguns was organized effectively by the Snowdrop Campaign, drawing on extensive public support following a massacre of children in a school in Dunblane, Scotland, by a deranged gunman.
40. K. Karr, *Democracy and Lobbying in the European Union* (Campus Verlag, 2007), p. 143.
41. Karr, p. 144.
42. See D. Miller, P. Schlesinger, and W. Dinan, "A Closed Scotland? Lobbying at Holyrood," in G. Hassan and C. Warhurst (eds.), *The Anatomy of the New Scotland: Power, Influence and Change* (Mainstream, 2002).

43. K. Nutt, "Money is Buying Influence in High Places," *The Sunday Times (Scotland)*, 29 January 2006.

44. P. Hutcheon, "Row as Lobbyists and Party Donors 'Access All Areas' with Holyrood," *The Sunday Herald*, 26 August 2007.

45. D. Miller, "Open Stormont? Lobbying Transparency for Northern Ireland," Spinwatch, 21 April 2008: http://www.spinwatch.org.uk/blogs-mainmenu-29/david-miller-unspun-mainmenu-31/4838-open-stormont-lobbying-transparency-for-northern-ireland

46. House of Lords, European Union Committee, *Initiation of EU Legislation*, 22nd Report, Session 2007–08, HL 150 (The Stationery Office, 2008), n33.

47. K. Karr, *Democracy and Lobbying in the European Union* (Campus Verlag, 2007), p. 130.

48. Karr, p. 154.

49. See G. Jordan and W. Maloney, *Interest Groups and Democracy* (Palgrave Macmillan, 2007).

50. W. Maloney, "Interest Groups in Britain," *Politics Review*, 16 (4), 2007, p. 28.

51. See M. Hollingsworth, *MPs for Hire* (Bloomsbury, 1991).

52. S. Berry, "Lobbyists: Techniques of the Political 'Insiders,'" *Parliamentary Affairs*, 45 (2), 1992, p. 229.

53. *The Observer*, 9 April 1989.

54. Committee on Standards in Public Life, *Volume 1: Report* (Her Majesty's Stationery Office, 1995).

55. See D. Leigh and E. Vulliamy, *Sleaze: The Corruption of Parliament* (Fourth Estate, 1997); I. Greer, *One Man's Word* (Andre Deutsch, 1997).

56. Sir Alistair Graham, 27 March 2007, quoted in. M. Bell, *The Truth that Sticks* (Icon Books, 2007), p. 3.

57. House of Commons, Select Committee on Public Administration, *Lobbying: Access and Influence in Whitehall*, 1st Report, Session 2008–09, Volume 1, HC 36-I (The Stationery Office, 2008), p. 10.

58. *Lobbying: Access and Influence in Whitehall*, p. 60.

59. House of Lords, European Union Committee, *Initiation of EU Legislation*, 22nd Report, Session 2007–08, HL 150 (The Stationery Office, 2008), para.112.

60. "Charity Plan 'Not Waste of Cash,'" *BBC News Online*, 8 April 2009, http://news.bbc.co.uk/1/hi/uk_politics/7989656.stm; and Cabinet Office, http://www.cabinetoffice.gov.uk/third_sector/news/news_releases/090408_charities.aspx

GOVERNMENTAL
DECISION MAKING

CHAPTER

8

The Executive
Government at the Center

The formal process of determining public policy in Britain is dominated by the executive. Once the executive has agreed on a measure, the assent of Parliament can usually be ensured. Parliament is essentially a policy-ratifying rather than a policy-making body. In the United States, by contrast, the executive enjoys no such dominance. The president cannot proceed on the assumption that any proposal he makes can be assured by the assent of Congress. The U.S. political system has been described as a "multiple-access" one. It also may be characterized as a "multiple-check" system. A proposal emanating from one branch of government can be checked—that is, negated—by another. A bill has to overcome a number of very real hurdles in Congress in order to become law. It may be pigeonholed in committee, it may fail to be scheduled by the House Rules Committee, and it may face a filibuster in the Senate. Congress has negating powers that it is prepared to and variously does use; Parliament has negating powers that it can but hardly ever does use. The executive in Britain can make assumptions about legislative support that few U.S. presidents would dare to make.

Viewed in terms of the Constitution and the relationships governed by conventions, the policy-making process in Britain may appear clear and effective. An executive is formed and proceeds to implement a party program with the support of a parliamentary majority. That has been a popular perception, in Britain itself as well as elsewhere. In practice, the process has proved to be more complex and constrained than this picture suggests. The Government has usually a majority in the House of Commons, but it faces an organized opposition. Unlike in the United States, the cabinet is challenged by an alternative, the "shadow cabinet." Government ministers are "shadowed" by members of the principal opposition party. The strength of a party may deliver a majority to the government, but the party system ensures that the government is subject, on a regular and organized basis, to critical scrutiny. The Government also has to work within an increasingly intricate political environment shaped by public expectations, judicial decisions, group pressures, party commitments, limited resources, the global economy, and a volatile milieu of international relations. The international constraints have become more pronounced as a consequence of membership in the European Union. Furthermore, to talk in terms of the executive as some homogeneous entity is misleading. Rather like the situation in the United States, government comprises a multitude of bodies, each with its own powers and responsibilities and pursuing its own interests rather than the interests of the government as a whole.

THE STRUCTURE

It is not only the environment external to the executive that is complex and not always (if ever) harmonious. The same may be said of the executive itself. It comprises a tangled web of bodies, powers, and relationships that, in practice, are not easy to discern. They confuse any attempt to delineate clearly how policy is formulated and where power lies within government. At the apex of government stands the cabinet, headed by the prime minister, and below that the individual government departments headed by ministers and staffed by civil servants. But even within the cabinet there exists a complex infrastructure and sometimes shifting relationships. As government has grown, it not only has become more complex but also has experienced problems of political accountability. There is a large body of civil servants. Recent years have seen the growth of semi-autonomous agencies within departments. At the edges of government, there are many nondepartmental public bodies. For the cabinet, itself diminishing in significance, maintaining control of the government body itself has become a formidable task.

In terms of the structure of the executive and the lines of responsibility to Parliament, the formal position is outlined in Figure 8.1. For the purposes of analysis, it is necessary to identify the essential features of the different elements of the executive. The main elements may be subsumed under the headings of the prime minister, the cabinet, ministers, departments, agencies, civil servants, and nondepartmental public bodies, a category encompassing "quangos" (quasi-autonomous national governmental organizations), and task forces. The powers, structure, and composition of each element and the relationships among them have become increasingly a matter of controversy.

The Prime Minister

The prime minister stands at the apex of the government. The position is a powerful and highly visible one. In the 1960s, there was a largely academic debate as to whether or not Britain had "prime-ministerial government." The debate widened in the 1970s and reached new heights in the eleven and a half years (1979–90) that Margaret Thatcher occupied No. 10 Downing Street (the prime minister's official residence). It resurfaced, with renewed vigor,

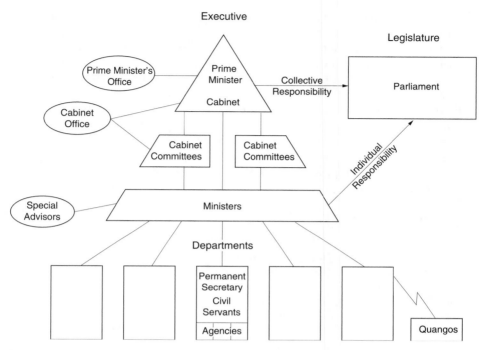

FIGURE 8.1

The structure of the executive and its relationship to the legislature

under the premierships of Tony Blair (1997–2007) and Gordon Brown (2007–). It is now common to find, in both academic literature and the press, accusations that Britain has acquired a "presidential" form of government.

In the sixteenth and seventeenth centuries, monarchs were often dependent on particular ministers. However, it was not until the eighteenth century that a recognizable first, or "prime," minister began to emerge. George I, the first of the Hanoverian kings, had little interest in British politics, spoke little or no English, and spent six months of each year on the Continent. He left the conduct of affairs entirely to the cabinet, his chosen group of ministers. "This," as Arthur Berriedale Keith observed, "led inevitably to the development of the office of Prime Minister; for, once the King was removed from the cabinet, the natural tendency was for some minister to take his place as a unifying influence."[1] The first minister to be considered—at least by historians—as prime minister was Sir Robert Walpole, from 1721 to 1742. The term itself had been used before, and Walpole himself disclaimed it. It came eventually into colloquial but not formal use. Not until the twentieth century was the position to be referred to in a statute. The official position held by most "prime" ministers was that of first lord of the treasury, a position that is still retained by holders of the office. Over time, however, the position of prime minister grew in recognition and in powers. The growth of party government acted as a particular spur to the growth of prime ministerial power. The nineteenth century, as we have seen (Chapter 3), witnessed a transfer of power from the monarch and later from Parliament to the cabinet, a cabinet headed—and chosen—by the prime minister.

The powers that inhere in the office of prime minister are considerable. They are also remarkable for the fact that they exist by convention and not by statute or common law. Prerogative powers, such as the appointment of ministers, reside in the monarch. Statutory powers are vested in individual ministers. The most powerful person in government is the one who wields no legal powers at all.

There are several powers that coalesce to make the prime minister the most powerful figure in the government. They are summarized in the list below.

PRIME-MINISTERIAL POWERS

1. Appoints, moves, and dismisses ministers
2. Dispenses patronage (honors—such as peerages and knighthoods—and various appointments to public office)
3. Chairs the cabinet
4. Determines the cabinet agenda
5. Appoints senior members of the civil service
6. Determines the date of general elections
7. Enjoys the mandate of an election victory
8. Represents the nation at international summits
9. Is a focus of media attention
10. Occupies an office once held by such great figures as Pitt, Gladstone, Disraeli, Lloyd George, and Churchill
11. Is party leader[2]

The best known as well as the most important of these powers are appointment and dismissal. The monarch formally appoints ministers, but by convention she does so on the advice of her prime minister. The reality of who does the choosing is well recognized. Announcements of ministerial appointments are made direct from Downing Street. The prime minister not only chooses who the ministers will be, he or she can also decide when they are no longer to be ministers. Ministerial reshuffles are used by prime ministers to make changes and bring new blood into the cabinet or the ranks of non-cabinet ministers. They are sometimes controversial, as in July 1962 when Harold Macmillan dismissed one-third of his cabinet and in July 1989 when Margaret Thatcher moved a very unwilling Sir Geoffrey Howe from the Foreign Office to the position of lord president of the council and leader of the House of Commons. The extent of prime ministerial patronage is considerable: There are now more than a hundred ministers, and all owe their positions to the prime minister. Nor does the patronage end with ministers. The prime minister historically has been able to choose new members of the House of Lords, decide other honors (such as the awarding of knighthoods), and appoint individuals to a range of public positions. Though some of the positions are now filled on the recommendation of other bodies, the formal power to advise the Queen (in effect, to decide) remains with the prime minister.

The power to appoint ministers is not unfettered. By convention, ministers must normally be drawn from Parliament and, by convention, predominantly from the House of Commons. (On very rare occasions, a ministerial post has been filled by someone outside Parliament.) Partisanship dictates that the ministers will be drawn from the prime minister's own party. It is also deemed politically prudent to ensure a reasonable balance of ministers, in terms of both geography—drawing ministers from different constituencies across the country—and the different wings of the party. There are also likely to be senior figures with considerable support among MPs whom the prime minister would find it difficult to exclude, not least because they could become dangerous critics from the back benches. Nonetheless, the extent of the balance is sometimes a little skewed—Edward Heath (1970–74) and Tony Blair (1997–2007) each faced accusations of selecting a personally loyal cabinet—and few are willing to challenge the prime minister's judgments. The appointing—and dismissal—power wielded by the prime minister serves to ensure loyalty on the part of ministers and of those MPs who would like to be ministers.

The power to choose ministers is important not only in ensuring ministerial loyalty to the prime minister; it is also a major tool in influencing the direction of public policy. As Maurice Kogan has observed, the authority to appoint, transfer, or dismiss enables the prime minister to allocate values and change or confirm an individual minister's policies.[3] Key supporters may be placed in strategic ministries. When Margaret Thatcher was prime minister, she ensured that supporters of her neoliberal economic policy occupied the economic ministries. Moving a minister or appointing a trusted confidant to a particular post may, for instance, signal a shift of emphasis to a more environmentally friendly, or a more business-orientated, agenda.

Power to determine the direction of policy is not confined to the blunt weapon of appointment and dismissal. It derives also from the prime minister's position as chairman of the cabinet. In the nineteenth century, John Morley described the prime minister as *primus inter pares* (first among equals) in the cabinet. In practice, the premier's position has always been much more than that. The prime minister determines when the cabinet will meet and what it will discuss. The prime minister sums up discussion. Very few prime ministers have resorted to taking votes in cabinet. The prime minister's summing up is therefore crucial. It is that which will determine what is recorded in the minutes. As chairman of the cabinet, the prime minister also determines the extent and composition of cabinet committees, appointed to save cabinet time by discussing and resolving issues before they go to full cabinet. As we shall see, the range of such committees is extensive.

The prime minister's control is not confined to the cabinet. It extends to the rest of Whitehall. The prime minister is minister for the civil service. The permanent head of the service reports directly to the prime minister. Power over the appointment of senior civil servants—primarily the permanent secretaries, the civil service heads of each department—rests with the prime minister, not with the ministers in whose departments they serve. If a minister wants to have a senior civil servant moved, as occasionally happens, the support of the prime minister is essential. It is also a potentially risky business; the prime minister might refuse and take the side of the civil servant.[4] Some premiers have taken an active interest in civil service appointments. Margaret Thatcher in particular intervened to ensure that a number of vacancies were filled by high-flying officials rather than by the person second in seniority. Tony Blair took an active interest in the management of the civil service and in ensuring that civil servants deliver on the government's promises, in so doing attracting claims that he was "politicizing" the civil service.

The prime minister can also determine the date of the general election (another prerogative power, where the sovereign takes the advice of her prime minister) and, if he leads his party to victory, has the added authority that derives from that victory. Credit tends to accrue to the person at the head of the winning campaign. Edward Heath was often seen as having won the 1970 general election for the Conservatives almost single-handedly, having led his party to an unexpected victory. A similar view was taken of Margaret Thatcher in her three consecutive election victories. By leading his party to its best-ever election victory in 1997, Tony Blair was claimed by commentators to be in an almost invincible position, many Labour members of parliament crediting their victory to his leadership.

As head of government, the prime minister represents the nation at major international summits, the foreign secretary (or, in economic summits, the chancellor of the exchequer) acting essentially in a supporting role. The more frequent such summits—and the number has increased substantially as a result of frequent meetings of the European Council, comprising the heads of government of the member states of the European Union—the greater the visibility of the prime minister on the international stage. As head of government, the prime minister also has considerable media visibility at home. He or she is a natural focus of media attention. The prime minister is a powerful political power—usually the most powerful political figure—and one who occupies an office once held by such towering figures as William Pitt (the elder, and the younger), William Gladstone, Benjamin Disraeli, David Lloyd George, and Winston Churchill. An aura attaches to the office, one now reinforced by security considerations: the prime minister has to be kept some distance from ordinary public contact. He or she travels with an escort—a very modest escort by U.S. standards, but an escort nonetheless.

The prime minister is thus a powerful political figure. However, there is one essential component of that power that has not yet been mentioned. The prime minister is also leader of his or her party. It is that leadership that is a necessary but not sufficient condition for becoming prime minister. (Electoral success provides the sufficient condition.) In office, the fact of being party leader gives the prime minister the capacity to call on party loyalty and also to utilize the machinery of the party organization. Historically, this has been particularly important on the Conservative side (see Chapter 6), with all party bodies being advisory to the leader and the leader appointing all the senior officers of the party. It has also become increasingly important in the Labour Party, Labour leaders since Neil Kinnock taking greater control of the party machinery. The confluence of party leadership and the premiership thus makes the prime minister a tremendously powerful figure. However, it does not render the prime minister all-powerful. The fact of being party leader is a double-edged weapon. The party, or that part of it that selects the leader, can withdraw its support, as Margaret Thatcher found to her cost in November 1990. Having lost the leadership of the Conservative Party, she resigned the premiership.

The prime minister has usually wielded the powers of the office with relatively limited institutional support. There is, formally, no prime minister's "department." The size of the prime minister's office has traditionally been small.[5] However, as chairman of the cabinet, the prime minister is serviced by the secretary to the cabinet (who is also usually head of the civil service) and the Cabinet Secretariat, which records and monitors cabinet decisions. A number of new units have also been created in the Cabinet Office since 1997 in order to increase central coordination. The prime minister also has the support of a number of advisors. That number is growing. Before the 1970s, prime ministers appointed advisors on an ad hoc basis. In 1970 the Central Policy Review Staff (CPRS), more popularly known as the "think tank," was established. Comprising a small number of political appointees and seconded civil servants, it provided wide-ranging policy advice to the cabinet and the prime minister. However, it was gradually overshadowed by a small body of advisors established to advise the prime minister—the No. 10 Policy Unit—and in 1983, the CPRS was disbanded. Under the premiership of Tony Blair, the No. 10 Policy Unit consisted of about a dozen politically committed specialists on particular subjects, offering party-oriented advice and working directly for the prime minister.[6] After the 2001 election, it was merged with the prime minister's private office to form a Policy Directorate. It is complemented by other bodies, including a Strategy Unit to provide strategy and policy advice and to support departments in developing strategies and policies. As a result of creating new units, and appointing more special advisers, the number of people working in Downing Street expanded substantially: Within two years of Tony Blair entering Downing Street, the number had increased by 50 percent.

The prime minister thus has an important—though still relatively small—body to offer advice independent of that coming from ministers and civil servants. It reinforces the prime minister's capacity to lead within government. The extent to which the prime minister chooses to lead, though, depends very much upon the occupant of the office.

Britain has had 21 prime ministers since the end of the nineteenth century (see Table 8.1). Their approach to the office has varied considerably. Some have been forceful wielders of power, others more emollient occupiers of the office. Some have been driven by a powerful ideological world view, others by the need to satisfy their egos. One useful way to analyze the people who have occupied No. 10 in the period since 1900 is to look at their purpose in seeking office. Utilizing this approach, it is possible to identify four prime ministerial types:[7]

TABLE 8.1

PRIME MINISTERS SINCE **1895**

Took Office	Prime Minister	Party
June 25, 1895	The third marquess of Salisbury	Unionist (Conservative)
July 12, 1902	Arthur James Balfour	Unionist (Conservative)
December 5, 1905	Sir Henry Campbell-Bannerman	Liberal
April 8, 1908	Herbert Henry Asquith	Liberal[1]
December 7, 1916	David Lloyd George	Liberal[2]
October 23, 1922	Andrew Bonar Law	Unionist (Conservative)
May 22, 1923	Stanley Baldwin	Unionist (Conservative)
January 22, 1924	J. Ramsay MacDonald	Labour
November 4, 1924	Stanley Baldwin	Conservative
June 5, 1929	J. Ramsay MacDonald	Labour
August 24, 1931	J. Ramsay MacDonald	National Labour[3]
June 7, 1935	Stanley Baldwin	Conservative[3]
May 28, 1937	Neville Chamberlain	Conservative[3]
May 10, 1940	Winston S. Churchill	Conservative[4]
May 23, 1945	Clement Attlee	Labour
October 26, 1951	Sir Winston Churchill	Conservative
April 6, 1955	Sir Anthony Eden	Conservative
January 10, 1957	Harold Macmillan	Conservative
October 19, 1963	Sir Alec Douglas-Home	Conservative
October 16, 1964	Harold Wilson	Labour
June 19, 1970	Edward Heath	Conservative
March 4, 1974	Harold Wilson	Labour
April 5, 1976	James Callaghan	Labour
May 4, 1979	Margaret Thatcher	Conservative
November 28, 1990	John Major	Conservative
May 2, 1997	Tony Blair	Labour
June 27, 2007	Gordon Brown	Labour

[1]Coalition from May 1915
[2]Coalition government
[3]National government
[4]Coalition government, May 1940–May 1945; national government, May–July 1945

Innovators. They seek power in order to achieve a future goal of their own creation and are prepared, if necessary, to bring their party kicking and screaming in their wake in order to achieve that goal.

Reformers. They seek power in order to achieve the implementation of a particular program, but one drawn up by the party rather than by the premier.

Egoists. They seek power for the sake of power; they are concerned with enjoying the here-and-now of office rather than with future goals, and they fight to keep power.

Balancers. They fall into two categories: those who seek power in order to achieve balance, within society and within party, and those who share the same goal but, rather than seeking power, have it thrust upon them, usually as compromise choices for leader; the latter may be described as conscripts in the office.

These four are ideal types. Some premiers have straddled categories. Others have changed over time: Winston Churchill was essentially an innovator as wartime prime minister but a balancer in peacetime. Purpose has also varied depending upon the context. Tony Blair was an innovator as Labour Party leader, forcing a radical change in the culture and organization of the party, but was probably closer to an egoist in his position as prime minister. Gordon Brown was seen as an innovator as chancellor of the exchequer but as an egoist once he had moved from No. 11 to No. 10 Downing Street. Nonetheless, the categories are useful for assessing and distinguishing prime ministers. Table 8.2 categorizes the prime ministers since Lord Salisbury. The past half-century has seen three power-seeking balancers (Macmillan, Callaghan, and Major), three

TABLE 8.2

TYPOLOGY OF PRIME MINISTERS

| | | | Balancers | |
| | | | --- | --- |
Innovators	Reformers	Egoists	Power-Seeking	Conscripts
Churchill (wartime)	Campbell-Bannerman	Lloyd George?	Salisbury	Bonar Law
		MacDonald?	Balfour?	Douglas-Home
Heath?	Asquith	Eden	Baldwin	
Thatcher	Chamberlain	Wilson	Churchill (peacetime)	
	Attlee	Heath?	Macmillan	
		Blair	Callaghan	
		Brown	Major	

Source: Developed from P. Norton, "Prime Ministerial Power," *Social Studies Review* 3 (3), 1988, p. 110.

egoists (Wilson, Blair, and Brown), a conscript balancer (Douglas-Home), an obvious innovator (Thatcher), and a premier who straddled the categories of innovator and egoist (Heath). The quest to occupy the office thus draws many different politicians. Which one actually reaches the top of what Disraeli described as "the greasy pole" will affect significantly how the powers of the office are used. Practices between premiers have varied considerably. Margaret Thatcher used to badger the cabinet and sometimes summed up discussions at the beginning! John Major allowed the cabinet to operate more as a relaxed seminar, with ministers questioning other ministers. Tony Blair kept his cabinet meetings as short as possible, with little of importance being discussed. Gordon Brown, in order to distinguish himself from his predecessor, moved the day of meeting and sought to give the meetings greater significance.

A particularly determined occupant of No. 10 is likely to achieve more, at least in the short term, than a less determined individual. Nonetheless, however determined the individual might be, wielding the powers of the office will not necessarily achieve the desired result. Prime ministerial power depends, in part, upon the skills of the individual in the office. He or she has to engage in "impression management." As Barbara Kellerman put it in the U.S. context, "the president must seem presidential."[8] Similarly, the prime minister must appear prime ministerial. The prime minister must not only look fit for the office but also has to have a feel for it, or in other words an intuitive grasp of how to deploy, or not deploy, the powers of the office. Some prime ministers have managed to mold a united cabinet, some have been able to judge what is or is not politically acceptable, some have been able to judge the parliamentary and the public mood and to capitalize on it, and some have proved good manipulators of other actors in the political system (the principal skill attributed to Major and, more notably, to his successor, Tony Blair). Few have managed to combine all such skills.

How the skills of the individual are deployed will help determine the extent to which the prime minister can influence the immediate political environment, encompassing not just the cabinet but also the rest of the executive, the legislature, and other proximate actors. In seeking to influence that immediate environment, the prime minister enjoys a position of superiority but not one of hegemony. The cabinet, individual ministers, civil servants, and the courts are not lacking in powers of their own to influence public policy in the United Kingdom.

Success also depends in part, and sometimes crucially, upon external circumstances over which the prime minister can have little or no control. A world recession, crop failure, or conflict in the Middle East can and do have major implications for the United Kingdom. So can decisions of the European Council, over which the prime minister does have a little more influence, but as one of 27 heads of the government. The future of the British prime minister may depend upon events well beyond Britain's shores and hence beyond her or his immediate political reach.

When a determined prime minister has been able to utilize skills effectively to achieve policy goals and when the external environment has proved helpful

TABLE 8.3

RATINGS OF TWENTIETH-CENTURY PRIME MINISTERS

Prime ministers ranked in order of success

1. Winston Churchill
2. David Lloyd George
3. Clement Attlee
4. Herbert Asquith
5. Margaret Thatcher
6. Harold Macmillan
7. Marquess of Salisbury
8. Stanley Baldwin
9. Sir Henry Campbell-Bannerman
10. Harold Wilson
11. Edward Heath
12. James Callaghan
13. Andrew Bonar Law
14. Ramsay MacDonald
15. Sir Alec Douglas-Home
16. Arthur Balfour
17. John Major
18. Neville Chamberlain
19. Sir Anthony Eden

Source: BBC *Westminster Hour* poll, broadcast December 26, 1999.

or benign, the consequence has generally been a prime minister judged as successful. A 1999 poll of historians and political scientists found that Winston Churchill was judged the greatest of twentieth-century prime ministers. Britain's other wartime leader, David Lloyd George, was judged second greatest. The egoist Sir Anthony Eden, who sent forces to try to take control of the Suez canal in 1956—and ran into powerful opposition from U.S. President Eisenhower—was deemed to be the least successful. Innovator Margaret Thatcher came fifth in the poll (see Table 8.3). Her successor, John Major, who presided over a divided party and led it to a disastrous election defeat in 1997, ranked near the bottom. Tony Blair, as the serving prime minister, was excluded from the poll.

The Cabinet

The cabinet is the collective decision-making body of the British government. It usually comprises just over 20 members (see Table 8.4), constituting the ministerial heads of all the principal government departments as well as a

TABLE 8.4

THE CABINET, APRIL 2009

Prime Minister, First Lord of the Treasury and Minister for the Civil Service	Rt Hon Gordon Brown MP
Chancellor of the Exchequer	Rt Hon Alistair Darling MP
Secretary of State for Foreign and Commonwealth Affairs	Rt Hon David Miliband MP
Secretary of State for Justice and Lord Chancellor	Rt Hon Jack Straw MP
Secretary of State for the Home Department	Rt Hon Jacqui Smith MP
Secretary of State for Health	Rt Hon Alan Johnson MP
Secretary of State for Business, Enterprise and Regulatory Reform	Rt Hon Lord Mandelson
Secretary of State for Environment, Food and Rural Affairs	Rt Hon Hilary Benn MP
Secretary of State for International Development	Rt Hon Douglas Alexander MP
Secretary of State for Defence	Rt Hon John Hutton MP
Leader of the House of Commons, Lord Privy Seal and Minister for Women and Equalities	Rt Hon Harriet Harman QC MP
Secretary of State for Communities and Local Government	Rt Hon Hazel Blears MP
Secretary of State for Transport	Rt Hon Geoff Hoon MP
Secretary of State for Children, Schools and Families	Rt Hon Ed Balls MP
Secretary of State for Energy and Climate Change	Rt Hon Edward Miliband MP
Secretary of State for Work and Pensions	Rt Hon James Purnell MP
Secretary of State for Northern Ireland	Rt Hon Shaun Woodward MP
Leader of the House of Lords and Lord President of the Council	Rt Hon Baroness Royall of Blaisdon
Secretary of State for Culture, Media and Sport	Rt Hon Andy Burnham MP
Secretary of State for Innovation, Universities and Skills	Rt Hon John Denham MP
Chief Secretary to the Treasury	Rt Hon Yvette Cooper MP
Secretary of State for Wales	Rt Hon Paul Murphy MP

(continued)

TABLE 8.4 (continued)	
Secretary of State for Scotland	Rt Hon Jim Murphy MP
Also attend Cabinet meetings:	
Parliamentary Secretary to the Treasury and Chief Whip	Rt Hon Nicholas Brown MP
Minister for the Cabinet Office and Chancellor of the Duchy of Lancaster	Rt Hon Liam Byrne MP
Minister of State for Housing	Rt Hon Margaret Beckett MP
Minister for Employment, Welfare Reform and London	Rt Hon Tony McNulty MP
Minister for Africa, Asia and the UN	Rt Hon Lord Malloch-Brown KCMG
Minister for Science	Rt Hon Lord Drayson
Minister for the Olympics and Paymaster General	Rt Hon Tessa Jowell MP
Attorney General	Rt Hon Baroness Scotland of Asthal QC
Minister of State for Europe	Rt Hon Caroline Flint MP
Minister for Children, Young People and Families	Rt Hon Beverley Hughes MP

number of ministers without departmental responsibilities (such as the president of the council and the lord privy seal, titles usually given to the ministers who serve as managerial leaders in the two houses of Parliament). By convention, as we have seen, its members are drawn from, and remain within, Parliament. All bar one or two will normally be drawn from the House of Commons. (The leader of the House of Lords is a member, plus one or occasionally two other peers.)[9] Most members have served a parliamentary apprenticeship, having moved up from the back benches to junior ministerial office and then to minister of state level before being considered for cabinet appointment. It is rare for cabinet ministers to be appointed from the ranks of back-benchers or from people outside the Commons. There have been rare exceptions: during the Second World War, for example, union leader Ernest Bevin was brought straight into government. In such cases, the normal practice is for the new minister to be created a peer or (less likely nowadays) to be found a safe seat to win in a by-election.

The cabinet, like the position of prime minister, developed in importance during the eighteenth and nineteenth centuries. However, as the monarch's principal body of advisors, it was not particularly efficient. It often had little to do; decisions were frequently leaked by waiters (it met for dinner at the home of one of its members); members sometimes slept during meetings; and there was no agenda. In the twentieth century, as the demands on the cabinet grew—public policy becoming both more extensive and more complex—it developed in terms of its political significance and its organization.

The second decade of the twentieth century witnessed a particular improvement in organization as well as an authoritative clarification of what its role was. In 1916 the Cabinet Secretariat came into being, responsible for circulating agenda, papers, and minutes and for monitoring the implementation of cabinet decisions. Previously, implementation had been very much dependent on the memories of ministers, some of whom forgot what had been decided. In 1918, the Machinery of Government Committee delineated the functions of the cabinet to be (1) the final determination of the policy to be submitted to Parliament, (2) the supreme control of the national executive in accordance with the policy prescribed by Parliament, and (3) the continuous coordination and delimitation of the authorities of the several departments of state. This delineation remains extant. It has not been superseded, but what has changed has been the cabinet's mode of fulfilling its functions. As the functions became more onerous for a single body meeting once or twice a week, it developed a complex infrastructure. Consequently, there are two vehicles through which the cabinet now operates: cabinet committees and the full cabinet.

Cabinet committees have burgeoned, particularly since 1945. They are formed from the ministers relevant to the area covered by the committee as well as some ministers free of departmental responsibilities. The committees' creation, membership, and chairmanship are determined by the prime minister. They are serviced by the Cabinet Secretariat, which, among other things, provides briefing papers for those who chair them.

Until the premiership of Margaret Thatcher, the committees were shrouded in secrecy. No details were given about them: officially, they did not exist. Mrs. Thatcher broke with tradition to admit their existence and named four standing committees. Her successor, John Major, took the revelations one step further and authorized the publication of the names, membership, and terms of reference of all cabinet committees, and that practice has been continued. At the end of 2008, there were ten committees and 25 subcommittees (see Table 8.5)[10]. Each is usually referred to by coded initials. The committees are supplemented by various committees or sub-committees appointed on an ad hoc basis and known by the code MISC (miscellaneous). As can be seen from Table 8.5, in 2008 there were three ad hoc committees and one sub-committee. The number of ad hoc committees varies over time: there is now far less reliance on them than used to be the case. Prior to Tony Blair's premiership, it was common to appoint a large number; in the first six years of her premiership, for example, Margaret Thatcher appointed in total about 150 ad hoc committees—a large number, but fewer than the number created by her predecessors, and less than half the number formed by Clement Attlee during his six-year premiership.[11]

Committee membership ranges in number from 5 (the committees on the security and intelligence services and public services and public expenditure) to 28 (the committee on domestic affairs). (There is no fixed membership for the committee on civil contingencies: who attends will depend on the nature of the emergency being faced.) Sub-committee memberships range from 4 (the sub-committee on the panel for regulatory accountability) to 24 (the sub-committee

TABLE 8.5

CABINET COMMITTEES, NOVEMBER 2008

Name and Coded Initials	Chair
National Economic Council (NEC)	Prime Minister
Ministerial Committee on Domestic Affairs (DA)	Secretary of State for Justice
Sub-committee on borders and migration (DA(BM))	Home Secretary
Sub-committee on communities and equalities (DA(CE))	Health Secretary
Sub-committee on food (DA(F))	Environment Secretary
Sub-committee on families, children and young people (DA(FCY))	Schools Secretary
Sub-committee on health and wellbeing (DA(HW))	Secretary of State for Justice
Sub-committee on justice and crime (DA(JC)	Secretary of State for Justice
Sub-committee on local government and the regions (DA(LGR))	Welsh Secretary
Sub-committee on personal data security (DA(PDS))	Welsh Secretary
Sub-committee on public engagement and the delivery of services (DA(PED))	Secretary of State for Justice
Ministerial Committee on Life Chances (LC)	Prime Minister
Sub-committee on social exclusion (LC(SE))	Chancellor of Duchy of Lancaster
Sub-Committee on talent and enterprise (LC(TE))	Prime Minister
Ministerial Committee on Economic Development (ED)	Chancellor of the Exchequer
Sub-committee on environment and energy (ED(EE))	Chancellor of the Exchequer
Sub-committee on housing, planning and regeneration (ED(HPR))	Chancellor of the Exchequer
Sub-committee on Olympic and Paralympic Games (ED(OPG))	Chancellor of the Exchequer
Sub-committee on panel for regulatory accountability (ED(PRA))	Chief Secretary to the Treasury
Sub-committee on productivity, skills and employment (ED(PSE))	Chancellor of the Exchequer

(continued)

TABLE 8.5 (continued)

Name and Coded Initials	Chair
Sub-committee on science and innovation (ED(SI))	Minister of State for Science and Innovation
Ministerial Committee on the Constitution (CN)	Secretary of State for Justice
Ministerial Committee on National Security, International Relations and Development (NSID)	Prime Minister
Sub-committee on Europe (NSID(EU))	Foreign Secretary
Sub-committee on nuclear security (NSID(NS))	Prime Minister
Sub-committee on overseas and defence (NSID(OD))	Prime Minister
Sub-committee on Africa (NSID(OD)(A))	International Development Secretary
Sub-committee on trade (NSID(OD)(T))	International Development Secretary
Sub-committee on protective security and resilience (NSID(PSR))	Home Secretary
Sub-committee on tackling extremism (NSID(E))	Prime Minister
Ministerial Committee on Civil Contingencies (CCC)	Home Secretary
Ministerial Committee on the Security and Intelligence Services (CSI)	Prime Minister
Ministerial Committee on Legislation (L)	Leader of the House of Commons
Ministerial Committee on Public Services and Public Expenditure (PSX)	Chancellor of the Exchequer
Sub-committee on public sector pay (PSX(P))	Chancellor of the Exchequer
Ministerial Committee on pandemic influenza planning (MISC32)	Health Secretary
Ministerial Committee on the Post Office Network (MISC33)	Business Secretary
Ministerial Committee on Digital Inclusion (MISC34)	Welsh Secretary
Ministerial sub-committee on ageing (MISC35)	Minister of State for Work and Pensions

Source: Cabinet Office. *Ministerial Committees of the Cabinet: Composition and Terms of Reference,* November 2008.

on Europe). The committees comprise wholly or almost wholly cabinet ministers: one or two ministers of state serve on some of them. The subcommittees have memberships that are mostly dominated by cabinet ministers, though three (two permanent and one ad hoc) comprise overwhelmingly junior ministers; one ad hoc sub-committee is a mix of cabinet and junior ministers. In addition to the ministers appointed to them, there are some where other ministers and some public officials may be invited to attend: the Mayor of London, for example, may be invited to the sub committee on the Olympic and Paralymic Games (to be held in London in 2012); the Government's Chief Scientific Adviser to the sub-committee on science and innovation; and the chiefs of the defence staff, among others, to the committee on national security. As can be seen from Table 8.5, with the exception of the ad hoc committee on ageing, the committees and subcommittees are chaired by the prime minister or by another cabinet minister.

Decisions emanating from the committees have the same authority as full cabinet decisions, and since 1967, disputes within committees can be referred to the full cabinet only with the approval of the committee chair. When important issues are under discussion, it is usual for the designated members to attend, though on other occasions senior ministers can and do replace themselves with their junior ministers.[12] Richard Crossman, subsequently a cabinet minister himself, took the view that the committees detracted from the power of the cabinet,[13] though the more general view is that they serve as a useful complement to the cabinet, lightening its workload, clarifying issues for it, and allowing it to concentrate on the more central and general matters of government.

The full cabinet usually meets every Tuesday morning in the Cabinet Room at 10 Downing Street. (Until 2007, the meeting day was Thursday.) The government chief whip attends the meetings in order to tender advice; under Tony Blair, the chief whip was made a member of the cabinet, but Gordon Brown reverted to the practice of the chief whip attending but not being a full member. The chief whip is the minister responsible for ensuring the support of the parliamentary party in parliamentary votes and acts as a channel or communication between the cabinet and its parliamentary supporters. Other ministers may be invited to attend; under Brown, several attend (Table 8.4). The cabinet secretary (a civil servant) sits on the prime minister's right. The length of cabinet meetings varies. Under some prime ministers, meetings have lasted for one to three hours, with additional meetings if necessary. Under others, notably Tony Blair, they have been short affairs; it was not unusual for meetings under Blair to last less than an hour.

The cabinet remains important as the central forum for the resolution of disputes between departments, particularly in the allocation of public expenditure. Ministers usually defend their particular department, often supported on a reciprocal basis by ministers representing other spending departments. Much depends on the personalities involved, not least that of the prime minister. Some prime ministers tend to involve themselves in a wide range of items being brought forward by ministers, whereas others content themselves with concentrating on central issues of the economy and foreign affairs,

222 | CHAPTER 8   The Executive

leaving other departmental ministers to get on with their jobs unhindered. The process by which a cabinet determines a policy thus varies from prime minister to prime minister and, depending on changing political circumstance, may vary during the tenure of office of one prime minister. The cabinet remains a forum for the resolution of most major issues of public policy, but a number of those issues may effectively be resolved elsewhere, either in Downing Street, cabinet committee, or a meeting of senior ministers. Less central issues usually do not reach the cabinet at all.

As with the position of prime minister, no formal powers are vested in the cabinet: It exists and operates by convention. The most important convention, one that in part governs its behavior as well as its relationship to Parliament, is that of collective responsibility. This convention, which developed during the eighteenth and nineteenth centuries, prescribes that members of the cabinet accept responsibility collectively for decisions made by it. Ministers may argue in cabinet session, but once a decision has been made they are required to support that decision publicly. Any minister failing to support a cabinet decision in public once it had been announced would be expected to resign: Failure to do so would result in the prime minister requesting that minister's resignation.

The convention is deemed also to dictate the necessity for secrecy to attach to cabinet discussions. The authority of the cabinet and of particular ministers could be undermined if cabinet disputes were made public. Ministers publicly defending decisions with which they are known to have disagreed in cabinet session would weaken the cabinet in trying to ensure implementation of those decisions. A minister's authority and influence could be undermined if it were known that he or she was implementing a policy against which he or she had fought in the cabinet. Nonetheless, recent years have witnessed a weakening of this aspect of the collective responsibility convention, with ministers engaging in semipublic and, for all intents and purposes, public leaks and disagreements, and with some ex-ministers recording cabinet discussions in their memoirs. On two occasions in the Labour government of 1974–79, the convention was actually suspended in order to allow ministers to vote against government policy in the House of Commons. Both occasions concerned the issue of British membership in the EC, on which the cabinet members were bitterly divided. To avoid the possibility of resignations or the cabinet falling apart, the prime minister (Harold Wilson in 1975, James Callaghan in 1977) decided to suspend the convention. Although the convention remains extant, it is becoming a difficult one for prime ministers to enforce.

One other condition dictated by the convention of collective responsibility continues to be followed. A government defeat in the House of Commons on a motion of confidence necessitates the government's resigning or requesting a dissolution. On March 28, 1979, when the minority Labour government was defeated on a vote of confidence, the prime minister immediately went to Buckingham Palace to request a dissolution. This requirement stipulated by the convention is one about which it remains possible to generalize with confidence.

Ministers

When a prime minister forms an administration, he or she is called on to select not only the senior ministers to head the various departments of state, as well as senior ministers without portfolio, but also a host of junior ministers. In addition to a ministerial head, who is usually of secretary of state rank, each department normally has one and sometimes more ministers of state and one or more undersecretaries of state. The prime minister also appoints in each House a chief whip along with a deputy whip and other whips. The number of appointments has grown in the past half-century. In 1945, there were 76 ministers. By the end of the twentieth century, the number exceeded 100—there were 109 in January 2000—and has increased notably in the twenty-first century, especially under the premiership of Gordon Brown. By April 2009, Brown had appointed 126 (see Table 8.6). The increase was almost wholly in respect of junior ministers. There is no limit on the number of ministerial appointments that can be made. There is, however, a statutory limit on the number of ministerial salaries that can be paid; as a result, 12 ministers under Brown receive no ministerial salaries.

Of the ministers appointed, the most important are, as one would expect, those appointed to head the various departments (see Table 8.4). The significance of junior ministers tends to vary. In past decades, many parliamentary undersecretaries had little to do and often were regarded as constituting something of an insignificant life form within the departments. To some extent, that remains the case today for a number of undersecretaries, known in Whitehall circles under the acronym PUSS (parliamentary undersecretaries of state).[14] The influence of junior ministers within departments tends to depend on the ministerial head. There is a growing tendency for ministers to assign greater responsibility for certain functions to their ministers of state and undersecretaries; when junior ministers attend cabinet committees, they gain some knowledge of the workings of the higher echelons of government.

TABLE 8.6

NUMBER OF GOVERNMENT MINISTERS, APRIL 2009

Rank	House of Commons	House of Lords	Total
Cabinet ministers (including PM)	21	2	23
Ministers of state	26	5	31
Law officers	1	2	3
Undersecretaries of state/ Parliamentary secretaries	31	11	42
Whips (excluding chief whip in Commons)	18	9	27
TOTAL	97	29	126

Nonetheless, disputes between junior ministers and the chief civil servant, the permanent secretary, in a department can be resolved only by the ministerial head, and there remains a tendency for interested bodies to try to influence the senior minister even on matters delegated to junior ministers.

The heads of departments have tended to become even more important decision makers than they were hitherto. Indeed, there is a case for arguing that, far from having prime ministerial or cabinet government, Britain has a form of ministerial government. As demands on government have increased, only the most important matters have percolated up to the cabinet for resolution. Most important decisions affecting a department are made by the minister. The relationship between a minister and the House of Commons and between the minister and his or her department is governed by the convention of individual ministerial responsibility. The convention is important not only for determining who is responsible to whom (civil servants to minister, minister to Parliament), but also for determining who is responsible for what. The cabinet as a body has no legal powers; powers are vested in ministers. When government takes on new responsibilities by statute, powers to fulfill those responsibilities are granted to a minister. A statute will typically stipulate that "The Secretary of State shall have power to. . . ." According to Nevil Johnson, "the enduring effect of the doctrine of ministerial responsibility has been over the past century or so that powers have been vested in ministers and on a relentlessly increasing scale."[15]

Ministers, then, are very much at the heart of the government process. Major issues are resolved in the cabinet session or directly with the prime minister and other senior ministers. Other issues are usually but not always resolved at the departmental level. And when issues go to the cabinet, it is the minister who is responsible for the document or proposal. Major changes in policy are usually announced through the publication of a "white paper." Such policy documents have to go through the cabinet (discussed in cabinet committee and then presented to the full cabinet), but they are drawn up within departments on the minister's instructions.

Though heavily dependent on their civil servants for information and advice, ministers have an alternative channel of advice in the form of special advisors. Senior ministers each have at least one special advisor. (Some junior ministers also share an advisor.) The advisor is a political appointee—often a high-flying young party activist destined later for a parliamentary seat—who is given temporary civil service status for the period of the appointment. The advisors provide political advice, which civil servants are precluded from doing, and act as conduits for information and advice from party sources and outside bodies. Each is chosen by the minister and serves essentially at the minister's pleasure. Some are political all-rounders and may follow a particular minister from one post to another; a few have more specialized knowledge. The number of political advisers increased with the return of a Labour Government in 1997.

Nonetheless, ministers operate under a number of significant constraints. Because of parliamentary, constituency, and various public duties, the time they have to devote to their jobs is limited. Special advisors, despite an increase in their numbers, are often as much overloaded with work as their ministers. Ministers have little time to get to know a department before moving on to another post. It is rare for a minister to serve in the same post for the lifetime of a Parliament. In the decades before 1945, the average tenure of a senior minister was four years. In the latter half of the century, the average tenure was approximately two years. As one former cabinet minister put it: "Normally, you're the minister for buttons one day, and secretary of state for string the next. . . . And the first morning, you have to do an interview with Brian Redhead [a radio interviewer] on string, and be an expert!"[16]

Given these limitations, and the sheer volume of business, ministers rely substantially on their civil servants. Many decisions have to be delegated to officials to make in the minister's name. Even matters that do come before ministers may be heavily weighted by the advice of officials and by the manner in which the issue is brought to the minister's attention. Such decisions also have to be taken within the context of limited resources. The minister has to battle with treasury ministers to try to get as big a slice of the government cake as possible. Given economic restraints, it is rarely likely to be enough to meet a department's self-determined needs.

The extent to which a minister is able to achieve desired results is dependent in part on the individual holding the office. As with prime ministers, it is possible to discern particular types of senior ministers. Five types of ministers can be identified:[17]

> *Commanders.* They have clear goals they wish to achieve, goals determined by their own personal philosophies, derived from experience or personal reflection.
> *Ideologues.* They seek to achieve particular goals determined by an existing political philosophy.
> *Managers.* They are more concerned with the here and now of political life, of ensuring the efficient running of their departments, implementing existing policies, and variously serving as brokers between competing demands.
> *Agents.* They seek to carry out the desired policy goals of other political actors, such as the prime minister or the civil servants within the department.
> *Team Players.* They are wary of making decisions on their own, preferring to take an issue to the cabinet for collective deliberation or, more informally, seeking the advice and confirmation of a team of trusted confidants.

Though commentators have variously argued that ministers have tended to be agents—carrying out uncritically the wishes of the prime minister—or that, under the Thatcher government, ideologues tended to dominate in cabinet, research by this writer has found that commanders and managers tend to be the most prevalent types to serve in the cabinet.[18] This view was also taken of most ministers in the Blair cabinet by the prime minister's parliamentary private secretary, who sat in on Cabinet meetings: most, he told a fellow MP, were "managerial types—capable, efficient, but without an ideological anchor."[19] Ministers will variously adopt the status of agents (a minister may straddle more than one category, depending in large part on the office held), but this will tend to be on particular issues on which they have no fixed view themselves and are prepared to follow the established departmental line.

Whether ministers are successful in achieving their goals will also depend, as with the prime minister, on their political skills as well as on the wider political environment. Their performance in Parliament—where oratorical skills are at a premium—as well as relationships with colleagues, with members of the parliamentary party, with the media, and with the party in the country can be important in helping them, or hindering them from achieving their policy goals and, indeed, their ambitions for higher office.

Departments

Ministers are appointed to head departments. The way these departments are structured and the responsibilities vested in them can affect the nature of policy making. Departments adopt particular processes. They acquire particular traditions and a distinctive ethos. "Departments matter. They lead lives of their own. As Shirley Williams put it, they have banners to defend on which the departmental traditions and orthodoxy are emblazoned like fading regimental colours in a cathedral—and these are defended against all-comers whether they be pressure-groups, select committees, international organizations or other ministries."[20]

The structure of departments, however, is not static. Structures and responsibilities change. There is no statutory framework: The structure is determined by the prime minister. The number of major departments has fluctuated over the past century, ranging from 18 in 1914 to a high of 30 in 1951.[21] Since then, the number has been reduced with the amalgamation of a number of departments. These have included, for example, the Ministry of Defence (formed in 1964 from the three departments covering the armed services) and the Foreign and Commonwealth Office (formed in 1968 from the Foreign and the Commonwealth Offices). Some "super" departments have variously been created in order to generate the capacity to manage larger resource-consuming programs and to reduce the need for interdepartmental compromise, allowing a single strategy to be pursued within one ministry. In 1997, for example, a massive Department of the Environment, Transport, and the Regions was created, headed by the Deputy Prime Minister, John Prescott. However, just as large departments have their attractions, so too does the splitting off from a large department of a new one. It allows for a more clearly defined administration of a particular responsibility and signals the importance the government attaches to the issue. These have included, for example, the Welsh Office and the Northern Ireland Department. Transport has variously been part of a larger department and at other times a free-standing department. It was later hived off, for example, from the super department headed by John Prescott and now constitutes a single department. There was a major restructuring of departments when Gordon Brown became prime minister, with some new departments being created. The formation of the Department of Energy and Climate Change, for example, signaled the importance the prime minister attached to environmental issues. The more frequent the changes, though, the more confusion among affected groups as to who exercises responsibility in a particular sector. The more new departments are created, the greater the pressure from groups for further departments to be formed in order to recognize the importance of their area of interest.

Changes in the number and responsibilities of departments are thus frequent. Departments vary considerably in their range of responsibilities and their size. At the end of 2008, there were 487,000 full-time equivalent civil servants. Of these, 72 percent work in the four largest departments: the Department of Work and Pensions (accounting for 21.8 percent of civil servants), Her Majesty's Revenue and Customs (17.7 percent), the Department of Justice (17.1 percent), and the Ministry of Defence (15.8 percent). Size, though, does not necessarily correlate with influence. The Foreign and Commonwealth Office, for example, has a relatively small number of civil servants—fewer than 10,000—but great political clout and a complex departmental infrastructure.

Each department is normally divided into functional areas. Each unit is headed by a civil servant who typically now has a functional title such as director general (they were previously known as assistant undersecretaries of state). They operate under the civil service head of the department, known as the permanent secretary. He (rarely she) is in effect the chief executive officer of the department and answers directly to the minister. A department may have anything from 3 to 16 functional units headed by a director general. In the Ministry of Justice, for example, the functional units are: access to justice; democracy, constitution, and law; finance and commercial; corporate performance; criminal justice group; and corporate human resources.

Despite a basic similarity in structure, departments vary considerably in size and functional organization. They are complex organizations. That complexity is now greater as a result of the creation of executive agencies.

Agencies

In 1988, following a report from an efficiency unit set up by the prime minister, the government decided that to the greatest extent possible the executive functions of departments (as distinct from the function of advising ministers) should be carried out by operationally distinct agencies, each with clearly defined tasks and managerial responsibility for carrying out those tasks.

Various sections within departments were identified as suitable for agency status. The initial list was a modest one, both in terms of numbers and responsibilities. The first agency created was the Vehicles Inspectorate, followed by bodies such as Her Majesty's Stationery Office. By early 1990, only 12 agencies, employing just over 10,000 staff, had been created. However, the program then gathered pace and by the middle of 1992, there were 75 agencies, with a staff exceeding 300,000—more than half the total number of civil servants. By the start of the twenty-first century, more than three-quarters of all civil servants were working in agencies and that has remained the case. Most departments have some agencies. In some cases, a department is responsible for only one or two: the Department for Culture, Media and Sport, for example, has only the Royal Parks Agency. Others cover several: The Ministry of Defence, for example, has 13, ranging from the Defence Analytical Services Agency through to the UK Hydrographic Office.

The agencies are essentially semi-autonomous bodies within the government. Each has a tailor-made framework document, setting out its aims and objectives, relationships with ministers and Parliament, and the regimes under which it will work. Performance targets are published. Each is headed by a chief executive, who is also the accounting officer. In other words, the chief executive—not the permanent secretary in the department—is accountable for how money is spent. Chief executives are typically recruited by open competition and a number drawn from outside the civil service. They nonetheless remain accountable to ministers, who are then answerable to Parliament for the work of the agencies.

Agencies thus form a considerable component of government departments (see Figure 8.1). They exercise important managerial functions, though remaining a formal part of government departments. The nature of their accountability to ministers and to Parliament, despite the wording of framework agreements, remains ambiguous.[22] Breaking away some measure of executive power does not necessarily march hand in hand with removing political responsibility. The creation of executive agencies has thus created fragmentation in structures and some ambiguity in lines of accountability.

Civil Service

Ministers stand at the political apex of the government. They head departments that are staffed by a body of permanent public employees, known collectively as the civil service. At the turn of the nineteenth century, there were a little more than 50,000 non-industrial civil servants. The number grew and reached a peacetime peak of 571,000 in 1977. The number then declined and was 479,000 in 1999. The number then increased again, reaching 538,000 in 2004 before cut backs reduced the number. By the end of 2008, as already noted, there were 487,000. (The figure does not include employees of nationalized industries or local government or members of the judiciary or the armed forces.) They serve to provide ministers with advice and to carry out their decisions and to administer the business of government.

The relationship between civil servants and ministers is governed by the principle of individual ministerial responsibility. The minister alone is answerable to Parliament for the department and its activities. The civil service head of each department—the permanent secretary—is answerable to the minister for the work of the civil servants within the department and serves usually as the minister's principal advisor. The convention of ministerial responsibility provides a cloak of anonymity to departmental activities. The advice a minister receives from officials and the manner of its formulation are kept from the public gaze. Knowledge of what goes on in a department, certainly at the higher levels, may be made available only by the minister or by officials acting on the minister's instructions.

Most civil servants carry out the routine tasks of government. About half are engaged in providing services to the public, such as issuing benefits and pensions. The rest carry out service-wide or internal departmental support functions. As we have seen, most are now employed in executive agencies. The number involved in advising ministers is small. The most-senior civil servants have, since 1996, formed "the senior civil service" (SCS). Posts are evaluated by each department to establish their level of responsibility, and pay is determined by each department within certain set salary bands. There are 4,700 civil servants in the SCS —occupying what used to be the posts of assistant secretaries (equivalent to the U.S. posts of bureau chiefs) upwards— and 31,900 in the next most-senior grades (Grades 6 and 7). The SCS comprises what are sometimes referred to as the "Whitehall mandarins," the civil servants who advise ministers, prepare briefing papers for them, and ensure that their decisions are carried out.

These senior officials take great care to brief incoming ministers. During each general election campaign, they study the party manifestos. The moment a new government is returned, they are ready with advice on how to implement its program. Where there is no established policy, officials look to the relevant minister to "take a view"—that is, make a decision. According to a study by Bruce Headey, civil servants prefer ministers who are capable of making decisions, of winning cabinet battles, and of defending their departments from parliamentary criticism.[23] Ministers, for their part, look for officials who will provide them with expert advice, a range of options from which to choose, and the loyal implementation of ministerial objectives and policies. In practice, neither ministers nor officials always get what they want, but the formal relationship between the two is well established.

Ministers are political appointees in office so long as the prime minister wishes them so to be and as long as their party remains in power. Civil servants are permanent public officials and as such required to be nonpartisan in the performance of their duties. They remain in post regardless of the outcome of general elections. They answer to ministers as ministers and not as party politicians. They help draft speeches given by the minister acting in a formal ministerial capacity—for example, addressing the House of Commons or a particular body that has invited the minister to speak in a ministerial capacity. They do not assist ministers with purely partisan speeches. Civil servants, for example, do not accompany ministers to party conferences nor to party engagements. Civil servants do not draft replies to letters from members of the public that raise party points. A letter about official policy will receive a reply written by civil servants. A letter asking why the minister's party has or has not done something will be drafted by the minister's special advisor.

Ministers reach office through established party and parliamentary routes. Civil servants reach their positions through open, competitive examination. There is a special recruitment procedure for the senior ranks of the service involving written examinations and an appearance before a final selection board. Competition for places is intense, and those recruited through this procedure tend to be drawn from an intellectual and social elite. Those successful tend to have the highest educational qualifications. They are also mostly male (though the number of women is increasing—up from approximately 13 percent in 1996 to 33 percent in 2008) and white (only 3.6 percent are drawn from ethnic backgrounds). They also tend to be drawn disproportionately from public school and Oxbridge graduates, despite attempts to widen the intake.[24] Recruitment also tends to favor generalists over specialists; that is, there is a tendency to select graduates in the arts and humanities rather than those in the pure or applied sciences. Relatively few science graduates apply, and the percentage being successful is small.[25]

Once an applicant is in the service, most training has tended to be on the job. Senior civil servants are geared to assisting ministers in the formulation and implementation of policy; traditionally, they have had little—often no—training as managers, even though they have extensive responsibilities for personnel and finance.[26] As one senior civil servant put it in 1987, "the golden route to the top" had been through policy, not management.[27] Recent years have seen various changes designed to inject a greater managerial element.

The 1980s saw the introduction of the Financial Management Initiative (FMI), designed to utilize management information systems and a range of financial management techniques. One of the principal reasons for the government's decision in 1988 to create executive agencies was to improve management within the civil service, creating a new team of identifiable managers separate from the permanent secretary, who previously was the general manager of a whole department. The Blair government introduced various units designed to improve coordination and management. These included in 2001 the creation of a Prime Minister's Delivery Unit and an Office of Public Service Reform, designed to help deliver a *Modernising Government* agenda. A new reform program, entitled *Civil Service Reform*, was launched in 2004. The intention was to create a more corporate identity and inject greater managerial efficiency into the service. A civil service management board (CSMB) was established, a national school of government created (incorporating the former civil service college) to provide training (for ministers as well as civil servants), and the old "specialist" and "generalist" labels replaced by three new categories: policy/expert analyst, operational delivery, and corporate services. Performance partnership agreements (PPAs) were introduced to provide an agreed view of what a department needed to do to cope with the challenges it faced and the priority actions it needed to pursue.[28] Each PPA was between the cabinet secretary, as head of the civil service, and the permanent secretary.

However, given the time it takes for civil servants to reach the top of their profession, senior civil servants remain, in most cases, generalists drawn from a particular social background. The similarity in social and educational background has produced a body of public servants that is relatively homogeneous. There is regular contact between senior officials, not only in an official capacity—the various interdepartmental committees and the meetings necessary to prepare material for ministers—but also socially: Senior civil servants are often members of the same London clubs and will sometimes wine and dine together. This homogeneity, and their permanence in office, is often seen as giving civil servants a common and a relatively long-term perspective on policy—relative, that is, to politicians—geared to what one permanent secretary referred to as "the common ground."[29] Civil servants carry out the wishes of their ministers but will be influenced by civil service and departmental norms and their perceptions of that common ground.

Though the homogeneity of the senior civil service is breaking down as greater openness and new methods of recruitment take effect, and civil servants see themselves as being on the defensive in the face of pressure from government to improve performance, the senior civil service remains at the heart of British government.

Nondepartmental Public Bodies

Nondepartmental public bodies are what in U.S. terminology would be referred to as an offline governmental agency (for example, the Environmental Protection Agency). They are public bodies set up either by administrative act or by statute to carry out various executive actions or to operate in an advisory capacity on a particular subject. Advisory bodies are usually formed to provide government with advice that it cannot get from within its own ranks. Such bodies will normally comprise representatives or appointees of interested groups (see Chapter 7). Bodies with executive powers are often formed in order to establish an arm's length relationship between government and a particular concern.

Two types of bodies can be grouped under this heading. The first are permanent bodies created to establish an arm's length relationship with government. They are often referred to as "quangos," though the term itself is subject to confusion, being treated by some as an acronym for quasi-autonomous *national* governmental organizations and by others as an acronym for quasi-autonomous *non*-governmental organizations. They are established to fulfill tasks that, for reasons of efficiency or for ensuring political neutrality, are deemed best fulfilled by a body other than government itself. Whereas the creation of government agencies represents a separation of functions *within* a department, quangos represent a separation of functions *from* a department. Quangos may be associated with a particular department but are not part of that department.

A number of quangos—nondepartmental public bodies—are long-standing.[30] The number increased considerably in the twentieth century and in two periods in particular: in the decades after the Second World War and again after 1968. The growth of government and the welfare state after 1945 spurred the creation of a wide range of nondepartmental public bodies. A report in 1968—the Report of the Fulton Committee on the Civil Service—raised the possibility of adding to their number through the splitting off of autonomous units from departments. The concept of separating functions found favor with the then Labour government and with the governments—first Conservative, then Labour—of the 1970s. Despite party differences, successive administrations were influenced by a prevailing managerialism—that services could be more efficiently provided through a managerial restructuring of government.

Among major nondepartmental public bodies created in the 1970s were the Manpower Services Commission; the Health and Safety Commission; and the Advisory, Conciliation, and Arbitration Service (ACAS). A report in 1980 identified the existence of more than 2,000 such bodies: 489 executive bodies and 1,561 advisory bodies.[31] The former were responsible for spending almost £5,800 million (about $9,000 million) in 1978 and had a staff of about 217,000.

Support for quangos came to an end with the return of a Conservative government under Margaret Thatcher in 1979. They were seen as unaccountable, interventionist, a drain on the public purse, and—when acting in a quasi-judicial capacity—a threat to the rule of law. The government initiated a "quango cull" and within three years more than 440 nondepartmental public bodies had been abolished, with more than 100 scheduled for extinction. As far as possible, remaining quangos were put under the aegis of a particular department, with ministers having responsibility for their efficient and effective operation.

Quangos, though, still remain a significant feature of public activity. Government has not been able to do without them. For various purposes, executive and advisory tasks need to be carried out by bodies that enjoy some degree of independence of ministers and civil servants. The number in existence remains a four-figure one, and ministers continue to announce the setting up of such bodies. Their number includes bodies as diverse as the Arts Council for England, the Environment Agency, and the Unrelated Live Transplant Regulatory Authority. Many of these are executive bodies and are responsible for the allocation of considerable sums of public money.

Whereas quangos, as such, are not seen as being in favor with government as a species of institution, there is another form of nondepartmental public body that is in favor. This is the "task force." Task forces are advisory bodies appointed to offer help to deal with a particular problem. They go under a variety of titles—task forces, reviews, working groups, and expert committees—and differ from quangos only inasmuch as they are essentially temporary bodies (they are disbanded once the problem has been addressed) and are viewed as existing to assist government in dealing with particular problems rather than being established at arm's length to government. Task forces have a long pedigree, but they have grown remarkably in number since 1997. According to government figures, in April 1999 there were 148 review groups and task forces in existence. However, one study identified 295 task forces and similar bodies as having been created in the first 18 months of

Labour government.[32] The disparity in numbers is because of the absence of an agreed definition. They remain a notable feature of the political landscape. They include, for example, an organized crime task force, a national task force on violence, an ethnic minority employment task force, a task force on child protection, a healthcare industries task force, and a youth taskforce. What is clear is that the government is keen to establish small bodies of experts and advisors in order to address particular problems; experts are, in effect, co-opted in the governmental process on a temporary basis.

THE CURRENT DEBATE

The bodies that form the executive in the United Kingdom are thus several— and greater in number than before—and the relationships among them, and between each of them and the citizen, complex. The range and complexity of those bodies have given rise to considerable debate, not least about the location of power in government. There are four separate approaches that have emerged. These have sought to locate the crucial decision-making power as resting with the prime minister (the presidential model), senior ministers (the baronial model), civil servants (the bureaucratic model), and with a combination of the different elements of government (power dependency). Each retains its proponents.

The Presidential Model

This thesis contends that power is concentrated at the center, with few, if any, significant checks on that power. Power has become more concentrated in the hands of government and, within government itself, in the hands of the prime minister. A number of writers, as we have noted, have claimed that Britain now has a form of "prime-ministerial government." The concentration of power in the hands of the prime minister, according to former Labour Cabinet minister Tony Benn, has gone too far "and amounts to a system of personal rule in the very heart of our parliamentary democracy."[33] This claim has been reformulated in two ways since the 1970s. In 1976, Lord Hailsham coined the term "elective dictatorship" to describe the centralization of power.[34] More recently, academic Michael Foley has been among various commentators to allege that Britain is acquiring a "presidential" form of government.[35] At the heart of this thesis is the contention that though the prime minister is not directly elected by the people, he acts as if he was. As a consequence, he distances himself from cabinet, parliament, and the party organization, assuming a detached role as the populist leader of the nation.[36]

Longevity in office, large parliamentary majorities, and a radical program of public policy derived from the prime minister's particular philosophy combined, in the eyes of many critics, to render Margaret Thatcher's premiership an exemplar of "presidentialism." She appointed supporters to head the key economic ministries, used bullying tactics in the cabinet—tactics described by one cabinet minister as "Stalinist"—in order to get her way, and used her powers to "handbag" any institution, including the civil service, that got in her way. (The concept of "handbagging" derives from the observation of one Conservative MP that Mrs Thatcher could not see an institution "without hitting it with her handbag.")[37] "Her conduct of meetings," recalled one senior minister, "became increasingly authoritarian."[38] In the wake of her third election victory in 1987, she was seen by many, including some within her own party, as politically invulnerable, capable of achieving what amounted to a system of one-woman rule. Texts analyzing the creation of "the strong state" grew in number, claiming that traditional safeguards were being eroded as more and more power became concentrated in the Thatcher government.[39]

The argument that Britain was experiencing a "presidential" form of government reemerged with renewed vigor when Tony Blair entered Downing Street in 1997. Under his premiership, the size of the prime minister's staff increased, more units were created inside No. 10, and cabinet meetings were kept to a minimum, each lasting—as we have already seen—less than an hour in duration. Blair operated in isolation from his party and from his own government, his background ensuring that he had little grounding in either.[40] He took decisions unilaterally or in conjunction with a few trusted colleagues. "The real deals are done elsewhere [than in cabinet], usually in the Prime Minister's study with only three or four people sitting around: and, as often as not, with only two."[41] According to J. H. Grainger, Blair was in the mold of Weber's ideal type of independent political leader, a monocrat. "Policy stems from or is endorsed by the free decision of the inner-determined, value-driven, subjective leader."[42] He was driven by his own set of beliefs, not by those set by his party or parliament. Blair's successor, Gordon Brown, though stressing the need to restore powers to parliament—and indeed grant it powers it had not previously exercised—maintained power in Downing Street. "In its first month, the Brown Government demonstrated considerable continuity, in its style of politics and government, with Blair's. This was particularly marked in its approach to the government of England: old habits die hard."[43] Brown was prone to unilateral decision making in the mold of his predecessor. He was, according to one former cabinet minister, "totally, totally uncollegiate."[44]

10 Downing Street is thus now seen, according to this approach, as the essential powerhouse of British government, the prime minister's advisers crammed into every available space. The cabinet, dominated by the prime minister's supporters, is no longer seen as a significant decision-making body. Key decisions are taken by the prime minister, either alone or in consultation with senior ministers or advisers, what was characterized, following a critical report (the Butler report) on how the decision to invade Iraq was taken,[45] as "sofa government." "A 'creeping bilateralism' long present, is increasingly the name of the Whitehall game, one empowering the prime minister and a clique at the expense of the collective authority of cabinet. Ministers are often limited by their departmental function; not so the prime minister."[46] The prime minister stands detached from government, from Parliament, and from his own party.

This thesis, though, does not go unchallenged. It is countered by the claim that the position of the prime minister relative to the cabinet and, most important of all, relative to the wider political environment has not changed as significantly as critics claim. The prime minister has always been powerful, but that power has not been exclusive or constant.[47]

The cabinet, meeting once or twice a week, is not a body geared to extensive debate and reflection. Much has been left to the prime minister and individual ministers. It was ever thus.[48] Instances of strong prime ministerial leadership are to be found as much in the nineteenth century as in the late twentieth and early twenty-first. Being powerful, though, is not the same as being all-powerful. The cabinet acts as a deterrent, a brake on prime ministers, however strong they may appear or want to be. Margaret Thatcher and Tony Blair faced cabinet revolts. When Margaret Thatcher could not muster support for her views, "she could then become unbelievably discursive . . . generally going round in circles and getting nowhere. . . . Broadcasting and education were two cases in point."[49] Indeed, her tactics in cabinet were essentially evidence of prime ministerial weakness, not strength. Ministers had to be browbeaten because their support could not be taken for granted. Most of her predecessors—even Churchill in wartime—had faced similar difficulties.

The demands on the prime minister's time are extensive. An increasing amount of time has to be spent abroad, not least at EU summits.[50] Tony Blair was frequently abroad, often for discussions in the United States with President George W. Bush. Gordon Brown has frequently had to travel to meet other leaders to discuss the state of the global economy. The resources at the prime minister's disposal in No. 10 are limited. Individual ministers have a far greater range of advisers and civil servants. The bolstering of resources in No. 10 by Tony Blair was the product of prime ministerial weakness, reflecting his inability to impose his will on the rest of government. Government is structured on the basis of departments. Blair expressed his frustration at what he called "departmentalitis,"[51] his frustration leading to his demands for civil service reform. Many policy decisions, especially at the level of medium- and micro-policy making, have to be left to individual ministers. The prime minister has limited time and resources to keep abreast of all aspects of government. He also has a limited inclination to do so. Few premiers are policy polymaths. They tend to focus on a limited number of policy areas, usually high policy (affecting the economic well-being and security of the nation). In other sectors, senior ministers are left to get on with their jobs.

Furthermore, the prime minister has a more crowded political environment to cope with. There has been a notable fragmentation of power in recent decades.[52] Interests are more organized than before. Policy-making competence in various sectors has passed increasingly to the institutions of the European Union. Margaret Thatcher sometimes found herself isolated in the European Council; Tony Blair had a similar experience. The European Union has taken up more time of the prime minister as the capacity to affect outcomes has declined. Power has been devolved to elected assemblies in different parts of the United Kingdom. Some of the established institutions, notably the courts, have become more active. Prime ministers have had to use more extensively the weapons in their prime-ministerial armory simply to keep pace with the changes in the wider environment.[53]

The Baronial Model

This thesis recognizes that ministers remain powerful figures, not necessarily collectively but rather individually. The basis for it has been outlined in the section on ministers. Statutory powers are vested not in the prime minister or cabinet but in individual ministers. Indeed, as we have seen, powers have been vested in ministers on an increasingly grand scale. The introduction of large regulatory measures results in more and more order-making powers being given to the relevant minister. Formal powers rest in ministers and, given that most ministers are ideologues, commanders, or managers, are frequently exercised by ministers acting on their own volition.

Indeed, such is the power exercised by ministers that the baronial model has been developed to identify their position within the British government.[54] The model stipulates that senior ministers are akin to medieval barons. They have their own territory (the policy sector covered by their department), their own courts (ministries), and courtiers (junior ministers, parliamentary private secretaries, and advisers). They hold a formal position of power and have their own armies (civil servants). They are formally the tenants-in-chief of the king (the prime minister) but are able to use their power bases to carve out an independent position. They build alliances with other barons and with influential figures at court. The power bases of some barons put them in a particularly powerful position, making it difficult for the monarch to move against them. Under the premiership of Tony Blair, for example, a number of senior ministers—most notably the Chancellor of the Exchequer Gordon Brown—were seen as occupying unassailable positions. Brown was an effective political operator with supporters in the House of Commons, in government, and in the party organization. When ministers are in powerful positions, the prime minister may seek to undermine them through arranging for off-the-record press briefings against them. Various ministers complained about this during the premiership of John Major and more recently under the premierships of Tony Blair and Gordon Brown; Blair and Brown had a tense relationship and variously briefed against one another.[55] Such skirmishes reflect the difficulties that a prime minister has in moving against his own "barons." Blair could not remove his most powerful baron.

The greater the responsibilities of the government, the less able the prime minister is to keep abreast of everything that is happening in the government. Senior ministers are left to get on with their particular jobs. Indeed, they are often largely left to determine the jobs for themselves.[56] One cabinet minister appointed by Tony Blair was asked who she wanted as a junior minister, and they discussed the new structure of the (revised) department; "I was then whisked off to my new department, where senior officials had gathered."[57] Another discussed "briefly," for about half an hour, the key issues to be faced in the key field of education.[58] Once appointed, it is up to the ministers to work up the key policies in their particular domains. They thus have considerable scope to carve out their own policy preferences.

Despite perceptions of a powerful premier, journalists variously employ the term barons to refer to the position of ministers. Tony Blair strengthened his body of advisers to try to counter the range of advisers at the disposal of senior ministers. The Government is still structured on the basis of departments, and those departments are headed by senior ministers. The baronial model is a highly plausible one.

This model, though, also has its critics. The analogy with medieval barons, it is argued, is too pat. Senior ministers, other than the chancellor of the exchequer, are not able to levy taxes, though they are able to exercise considerable power over those within their territory. They can be removed from office by the prime minister. The back benches of the House of Commons are littered with ex-ministers. Furthermore, ministers, just like the prime minister, are under increasing pressures. They occupy a political environment that is increasingly crowded and a policy space over which they exercise less and less unilateral power. They too are constrained by the effects of membership in the European Union; this is especially the case with particular ministers such as the minister of agriculture. They are also constrained by a more active judiciary and by the devolution of power to elected assemblies in Scotland and Wales. The secretaries of state for Scotland and Wales now have little to do. Ministers may not quite resemble medieval barons and, even if they do, they are operating in a shrinking kingdom.

The Bureaucratic Model

For some critics, the problem of government is not to be found with the prime minister and ministers generally. They are, after all, the leaders of a party elected to office. Rather, the problem is seen as being with the nonelected part of the executive: the civil service.

Senior civil servants are seen by critics as having the means to ensure the outcomes they want. Furthermore, those outcomes are criticized for contributing to Britain's poor economic performance. The background of civil servants has produced a body of generalists, with no particular knowledge or understanding of the problems faced by British industry and commerce. Rather, they are guided by some amorphous notion of "common ground"—which, for critics, means the common interest of senior civil servants.

Ministers come and go, but senior officials remain in place. Battles lost by civil servants under one minister can be fought again under another. A new government provides particular scope to refight old battles. By tradition, incoming ministers do not see the papers of their predecessors. This provides senior civil servants with an almost clean ministerial canvas on which to try their persuasive brushwork. During a minister's tenure, officials have various means for influencing outcomes. Ministers look to their permanent secretaries for knowledge of how their departments work. They look to officials for advice and briefing documents. They look to the civil servants in their private offices to control the flow of paperwork that reaches their desks and also to control their diaries.

Officials thus have the opportunity, should they choose to exercise it, to skew advice in favor of a particular course of action. They can swamp a minister with an excess of paperwork to obscure the importance of a particular document. They can submit important documents at the last minute to prevent time for reflection and outside advice. They can schedule so many meetings that the minister has little time to devote to particular issues. And, if these techniques fail to work, they can brief their counterparts in other departments, engage in some degree of misinterpretation of the minister's wishes, or simply stall until a new minister takes over. "Oh, he won't be here in another year or so" is a phrase that has been heard from the lips of civil servants, including in the hearing of this writer. And adding to their influence in recent years has been British membership in the European Union. Not only has membership entailed increased demands on ministers' time, especially in attending meetings of the Council of Ministers, but it also has given a greater role to bureaucrats. Most of the documents discussed by the council are prepared by officials: Contact between civil servants in the member states and officials in the European Commission is extensive. The dispersal of power also makes it increasingly difficult for the government to monitor the implementation of policy, especially that which is carried out through EU officials in Brussels.[59]

For ministers, there is thus the problem of ensuring that they have control of their departments. A capable and determined minister will normally enjoy mastery of the department. Even so, that mastery will usually extend only to important issues drawn to the minister's attention or to specific policy goals set by the minister. Other matters, of necessity, will be dealt with at lower levels. If there is a problem with senior officials—"some ministers," as Pyper notes, "operate in an atmosphere of almost continuous tension and conflict with their officials"[60]—then, as we have seen, the minister lacks the power to remove those officials. The matter has to be resolved by the prime minister, and it may not necessarily be resolved in the minister's favor. Less forceful, energetic, or intelligent ministers may find themselves guided by the papers and recommendations put before them by officials.

Compounding the problem is the homogeneity of senior officials. Insofar as they seek to influence decisions, they do so in support of what they see as the national interest—or "common ground"—but which critics claim as more the common interests of senior civil servants, the "national interest" often being synonymous with departmental or general civil service interests. The shared background and continuing social contact of officials reinforce both their shared perception of what is needed to maintain the common ground and their influence in order to effect the desired outcome. For critics, outcomes are as bad as the means by which they are arrived at, reflecting the self-assured but limited views of a social elite that has no experience of life beyond public school, Oxbridge, and the corridors of Whitehall.

The bureaucratic model has found favor among politicians on the left and right. Many of the left have tended to see the civil service as an inherently conservative body, likely to stifle the radical ambitions of a Socialist government. Margaret Thatcher, a Conservative premier with a radical policy, also tended to see the civil service as an impediment to change. She brought to the premiership a strong animosity toward the civil service, born of her neoliberal philosophy and of her own ministerial experience in the early 1970s: She had experienced poor relations with officials when she was education secretary. As one permanent secretary told Peter Hennessy, "She doesn't think clever chaps like us should be here at all. We should be outside, making profits."[61] And, as we have seen, Tony Blair saw the civil service as an impediment to the delivery of his government's reform agenda. One of his cabinet colleagues characterized the civil service as "an island within an island, a government within a government."[62]

However, this thesis is also challenged. The civil service, it is pointed out, is not quite the monolithic entity it is sometimes made out to be. Departmental ethos and attitudes differ. Some departments are fairly open in their dealings with parliamentarians, researchers, and journalists; others, such as the Ministry of Defence, tend toward excessive secrecy. Insofar as there is a civil service ethos, it is one that compels compliance with ministers' wishes. The relationship between ministers and officials is often more congenial and collegial than it is conflictual. John Prescott, deputy prime minister under Tony Blair, recorded that he "had great respect for all the civil servants I ever worked with and it made me a great admirer of the Civil Service."[63] Civil servants may argue a point in preliminary discussions, but once ministers have decided they then carry out whatever has been decided. "In my view," recorded one member of Margaret Thatcher's cabinet, "a good cabinet minister can always get what he or she wants out of the Civil Service."[64] This view was echoed by other ministers who served in government from 1979 to 1997; indeed, it appeared to constitute the prevailing view. Far from keeping officials at arm's length, some ministers drew more civil servants into meetings to discuss proposals. Civil servants may not always like the substance of what a minister decides, but—as Bruce Headey found in a seminal study of minister–civil service relations—they do like ministers capable of making decisions.[65] And, once the decision is made, they implement it. One energetic junior minister recalled the occasion when she summoned officials to discuss a big event she was organizing to promote health education. "I realized then just how disciplined some civil servants are when faced with a pesky minister with 'ideas.' It must have taken a lot of effort for the one who had to run the thing to keep saying 'Yes, Minister,' but bless her cotton socks, she did it."[66]

Furthermore, the changes that have taken place in civil service recruitment and organization have meant that civil servants feel more under threat than in control of the affairs of the government. Most civil servants are now working in agencies, senior jobs are increasingly being opened up to external candidates, and departments are being set targets to

meet. Every permanent secretary is now signed up to a performance
partnership agreement. Claims of the politicization of the civil service
were fueled during the Blair government, especially as a result of the
centralization of media relations in Downing Street and by the departure
of many departmental press officers (career civil servants). The result was
a growing demand for a civil service act to protect the independence of the
civil service. The perceptions of civil servants that underpinned criticism
in the late twentieth century no longer have the force they did. When he
was president, Gerald Ford declared that the presidency "was not so
much imperial as imperiled." By the beginning of the twenty-first century,
some civil servants could be forgiven for expressing a similar view about
the civil service.

The Power Dependency Model

The power dependency model has been advanced by R. A. W. Rhodes.[67]
Though developed to cover principally center–local relations, it is relevant
for the relationships between the different bodies of government at
national level. It contends that any organization is dependent upon other
organizations for resources and that in order to achieve their goals, organizations have to exchange resources. In short, no body can operate as an
exclusive entity. It depends on others to achieve outcomes just as other
bodies may have to rely on it to assist them to achieve what they want to
achieve. The prime minister has his own resources but is dependent on
senior ministers and on civil servants to get what he wants. Ministers have
to acquire allies in cabinet committees to ensure that their proposals are
accepted. Civil servants need ministers to win battles in cabinet and with
the treasury. Though the prime minister and senior ministers may have
formal powers, they need more than these powers to ensure they get the
outcomes they desire. Indeed, this approach is not dissimilar to Richard
Neustadt's thesis of presidential power: For a president to get his way, he
has to persuade others that what he wants is in their interests as well.[68]
Formal powers are but one of the weapons in the arsenal needed to achieve
particular outcomes. Professional reputation and popular support are other
important weapons.

The power dependency thesis offers a complex and less hierarchical
model than that advanced by the presidential model. It suggests that prime
minister, ministers, and civil servants have an interactive and mutually
dependent relationship. That mutual dependence was well drawn out by
Headey in his study of minister–civil servant relationships and has been
reiterated in recent studies: "The centre," wrote David Richards in 2007,
"is . . . dependent on departments as much as departments are dependent
on the centre, and ministers are dependent on civil servants as much as civil
servants are dependent on ministers."[69] Even Tony Blair, said Richards,
eventually "recognized the need to work with and not against this age-old
institution [the civil service]."[70]

The model can be widened. Ministers may be dependent on outside bodies for assistance in achieving the implementation of policy decisions. Departments may be dependent on sectional interest groups for information, advice, and cooperation. Interest groups may be dependent on ministers making decisions favorable to their interests. Ministers may build a parliamentary support base in order to ease the passage of contentious measures. MPs may support a minister in order to build goodwill for when they need the minister to make a decision favorable to their constituencies.

This model is highly plausible. It views the government as a complex network rather than a set of fairly disparate and discrete entities. However, it is not immune from criticism. It does not necessarily help explain who is principally responsible for determining a particular outcome. Extensive empirical study is necessary to discover that. It does not help explain outcomes that result from unilateral actions of the prime minister or ministers, nor outcomes achieved by actors adopting a confrontational rather than an alliance-building stance. As various ministers recorded, Margaret Thatcher was not noted for building alliances in the cabinet. The statutory powers vested in ministers means that, in many cases, they can (and do) act unilaterally. Certain ministers have built reputations for making decisions without reference to anyone else. One notable example was the Chancellor of the Exchequer from 1997 to 2007, Gordon Brown.

Nor does it necessarily explain shifts in power relationships. A prime minister may be powerful one moment, able to unilaterally determine the outcomes of public policy, and on other occasions may be dependent on political allies to rally round to ensure a particular preference is achieved. What, in the context of the U.S. presidency, James Barber characterized as the "power situation"[71] may move decisively against the prime minister. As the political columnist, Peter Riddell, observed in 2006, "Tony Blair's authority has waxed and waned since May 1997, strong at first, then weaker after the Iraq war."[72] Gordon Brown appeared all-powerful following his elevation to the premiership in 2007, yet within sixteen months was seen as politically vulnerable, some Labour MPs calling on him to step down from the premiership. As Michael Foley noted, "Brown's leadership attracted complaints about his poor-decision making, his inability to connect with the public in terms of presentational appeal and direct communication, his apparent lack of guiding vision and defining theme, and his weak credentials in respect to the opinion polls and claims of a public mandate."[73] Yet, as Foley goes on to note, "by the end of the year [2008], Brown's ratings increased as he launched initiatives in Britain and beyond to tackle the credit crunch and recession." In short, power dependency will vary as circumstances change. The model should be seen as dynamic and the relationships it posits as variable rather than fixed. Power within the executive is both varied and variable.

The power dependency model points to the complexity of governmental decision making. The criticisms of the model suggest that the reality of decision making is even more complex than the model suggests.

CONCLUSION

What is clear from our analysis is that it is misleading to refer to "the executive" as a monolithic body. It consists of a sophisticated and complex infrastructure, with relationships that are neither static nor easy to discern. There is no one part of the executive that can be identified clearly and unambiguously as the body for the making of public policy.

In so far as generalization is possible, one can identify a continuous and significant flow of advice and policy recommendations between officials and ministers, with the policy-making process resembling—insofar as a coherent shape can be ascribed to it—a pyramid, as shown in Figure 8.1. Policy is formulated and agreed on at different levels. What may be termed high policy (such as economic policy) is usually made at the level of prime minister and cabinet; medium-level policy (a new initiative on transport safety or school examinations, for example) at the ministerial level within departments; and low-level, or day-to-day incremental, policy at the civil service level, often in consultation with those representatives of outside groups who, together, form policy communities (Chapter 7). This last category probably accounts for the bulk of public policy or, perhaps more accurately, policy adjustments.[74]

Even this threefold delineation must be treated with caution. The boundaries are far from clear-cut. Contact between ministers and officials is extensive and continuous and, as posited by the power dependence model, few decisions are taken in isolation. The more important, and the more extensive, the policy the greater the involvement of all elements of government. On other occasions, important issues may, for reasons of time or security, have to be decided quickly or secretly by a few ministers. Minor issues may suddenly achieve public prominence and move up the decision-making ladder. Some decisions may, in effect, move down the ladder as a consequence of a lazy or not overly bright minister deferring to officials. The extent to which this happens, given the secrecy that still attaches to the process of government, is difficult to determine. All that one can say with confidence is that the process may resemble a pyramid, but that pyramid may become misshapen.

Furthermore, the structure and processes of government are not static. Not only are they variously modified—sometimes radically—but also they remain the subject of demands for further change. As we have seen (Chapter 3), some of the explanations offered for Britain's poor economic performance are political—most notably, in the context of this chapter, the concentration of power in the central government and, within that government, in the hands of the prime minister. Others have identified problems within that central government in terms of the civil service and the processes employed for determining public policy. The nub of the argument can be simply put. For critics of the existing political system, that system has not served the country well. For defenders, it constitutes a system that is, despite its complexity, adaptable and continues to ensure the effective delivery of public policy.

NOTES

1. A. B. Keith, *The British Cabinet System,* 2nd ed. by N. H. Gibbs (Stevens & Sons, 1952), p. 14.
2. Derived from B. Donoughue, *Prime Minister* (Jonathan Cape, 1987); and A. King, "The British Prime Ministership in the Age of the Career Politician," in G. W. Jones (ed.), *West European Prime Ministers* (Frank Cass, 1991).
3. M. Kogan, *The Politics of Education* (Penguin, 1971), p. 35.
4. There have been various instances recorded of ministers failing to get their way. Barbara Castle and Tony Benn both encountered problems in trying to get prime ministerial support in battles with senior officials in their departments (Castle when transport minister, 1965–68, and Benn as industry secretary, 1974–75, and energy secretary, 1975–79). Ministers appear to have had more success under more recent prime ministers.
5. See especially G. W. Jones, "The Prime Minister's Aides," in A. King (ed.), *The British Prime Minister,* 2nd ed. (Macmillan, 1985), pp. 72–95.
6. Prior to the Blair premiership, the Policy Unit comprised a mix of political appointees and individuals seconded from the civil service and outside organizations.
7. P. Norton, "Prime Ministerial Power," *Social Studies Review* 3 (3), 1988, p. 110; see also P. Norton, "Prime Ministerial Power: A Framework for Analysis," *Teaching Politics* 16 (3), 1987, pp. 325–345.
8. B. Kellerman, *The Political Presidency* (Oxford University Press, 1984), p. 37.
9. When the Lord Chancellor was a member of the Lords, he too was a member of the Cabinet. In recent years, the Government Chief Whip has sometimes been made a member of the Cabinet (or, more frequently, invited to attend.) On occasions, a senior departmental minister is drawn from the Lords (as with Lord Mandelson as business secretary in 2008), but such occasions are now rare.
10. Cabinet Office. *Ministerial Committees of the Cabinet: Composition and Terms of Reference,* November 2008: http://www.cabinetoffice.gov.uk/media/cabinetoffice/secretariats/assets/cabinet_committee_081103.pdf
11. P. Madgwick, *British Government: The Central Executive Territory* (Philip Allan, 1991), pp. 73–74.
12. J. Barnett, *Inside the Treasury* (Andre Deutsch, 1982), p. 27.
13. R. Crossman, "Introduction" to W. Bagehot, *The English Constitution* (Fontana, 1963 edition).
14. For insights into the life and limited impact of a junior minister, see the memoirs of Chris Mullin, who twice served as a junior minister under Tony Blair: C. Mullin, *A View from the Foothills* (Profile Books, 2009).
15. N. Johnson, *In Search of the Constitution* (Methuen, 1980), p. 84.
16. "The Typhoon Hits Hong Kong," *Sunday Times Magazine,* 30 August, 1992, p. 21.
17. P. Norton, "Barons in a Shrinking Kingdom? Senior Ministers in British Government," in R. A. W. Rhodes (ed.), *Transforming British Government,* Vol. 2: Changing Roles and Relationships (Macmillan, 2000).
18. P. Norton, "Barons in a Shrinking Kingdom?"
19. Bruce Grocott, quoted in C. Mullin, *A View from the Foothills* (Profile Books, 2009), p. 526.
20. P. Hennessy, *Whitehall* (Secker & Warburg, 1989), p. 380.
21. See Sir R. Clarke, "The Machinery of Government," in W. Thornhill (ed.), *The Modernization of British Government* (Pitman, 1975), p. 65.

22. T. Butcher, "Improving Civil Service Management: The Next Steps Programme," *Talking Politics* 3 (3), 1991, pp. 110–115; P. Norton, "Getting the Balance Right," *The House Magazine* 18 (585), 8 March, 1993, p. 16.

23. B. Headey, *British Cabinet Ministers* (George Allen & Unwin, 1974).

24. See R. Pyper, *The Evolving Civil Service* (Longman, 1991), p. 98; G. Drewry and T. Butcher, *The Civil Service Today* (Blackwell, 1988), pp. 71–72.

25. Drewry and Butcher, Table 3.9, p. 71.

26. See Hennessy; J. Garrett, *Managing the Civil Service* (Heinemann, 1980).

27. Quoted in Butcher, p. 111.

28. The agreements published in 2005 can be read at: http://www.civilservice.gov.uk/ improving_services/performance_partnership/view_the_performance_partner-ship_agreements/index.asp

29. Sir Anthony Part, speaking on an Independent Television program, "World in Action," 7 January 1980.

30. See P. Holland, *The Governance of Quangos* (Adam Smith Institute, 1981), pp. 10–12.

31. *Report on Non-Departmental Public Bodies,* Cmnd. 7797 (Her Majesty's Stationery Office, 1980).

32. A. Barker, I. Byrne, and A. Veal, *Ruling by Task Force* (Politico's, 1999). See also the debate on Task Forces in the House of Lords, February 23, 2000, *HL Deb.* Vol. 610, cols. 234–270. In the debate, the minister of state at the Cabinet Office said there were 46 task forces and 270 ad hoc reviews and advisory groups. See also *Reinforcing Standards: Sixth Report of the Committee on Standards in Public Life,* Vol. 1: Report, Cm 4557-I (The Stationery Office, 2000), pp. 123–124.

33. T. Benn, "The Case for a Constitutional Premiership," *Parliamentary Affairs* 33 (1), 1980, p. 7.

34. Lord Hailsham, *Elective Dictatorship* (BBC, 1976).

35. M. Foley. *The Rise of the British Presidency* (Manchester University Press, 1993). See also P. Norton, "The Presidentialization of British Politics," *Government and Opposition,* 38 (2), 2003, pp. 274–278; R. Heffernan and P. Webb, "The British Prime Minister: Much More Than 'First Among Equals,'" in T. Poguntke and P. Webb (eds.), *The Presidentialization of Politics* (Oxford University Press, 2005), pp. 26–62; and M. Foley, "The Presidential Controversy in Britain," *Politics Review,* 18 (3), 2009, pp. 20–22.

36. For an invaluable summary of these characteristics, see G. P. Thomas, *Prime Minister and Cabinet Today* (Manchester University Press, 1998), pp. 77–80.

37. J. Critchley, *Westminster Blues* (Futura, 1986), p. 126.

38. N. Lawson, *The View from No. 11* (Bantam, 1992), p. 128.

39. As, for example, A. Gamble, *The Free Economy and the Strong State* (Macmillan, 1988); C. Graham and T. Prosser (eds.), *Waiving the Rules* (Open University Press, 1988); and P. McAuslan and M. J. McEldowney (eds.), *Law, Legitimacy and the Constitution* (Sweet & Maxwell, 1985).

40. P. Norton, "Tony Blair and the Office of Prime Minister," in M. Beech and S. D. Lee (eds.), *Ten Years of New Labour* (Palgrave Macmillan, 2008), pp. 89–102.

41. J. Naughtie, *The Rivals* (The Fourth Estate, 2001), p. 104. See also A. Seldon, "The Blair legacy," *Politics Review,* 17 (4), 2008, pp. 6–7.

42. J. H. Grainger, *Tony Blair and the Ideal Type* (Imprint Academic, 2005), p. 38.

43. S D. Lee, *Best for Britain? The Politics and Legacy of Gordon Brown* (Oneworld Publications, 2007), pp. 236–237.

44. Charles Clarke, quoted in T. Bower, *Gordon Brown: Prime Minister* (Harper Perennial, 2007), p. 509.

45. *Review of Intelligence on Weapons of Mass Destruction. Chairman: The Rt Hon. Lord Butler of Brockwell KG GCB CVO* (the Butler Report), HC 898 (The Stationery Office, 2004), paragraphs 605–11.
46. R. Heffernan and P. Webb, "The British Prime Minister: Much More Than 'First Among Equals,'" in T. Poguntke and P. Webb (eds.), *The Presidentialization of Politics* (Oxford University Press, 2005), p. 40.
47. P. Riddell, "Tony Blair: prime minister or president?" *Politics Review*, 15 (3), 2006, pp. 30–33.
48. Norton, "Prime Ministerial Power," p. 114.
49. Lawson, p. 128.
50. P. Madgwick, *British Government: The Central Executive Territory* (Philip Allan, 1991), p. 142.
51. P. Webster and J. Sherman, "Straw Chosen to Relaunch the New Deal Message," *The Times*, 23 January 1998.
52. J. Greenaway, S. Smith, and J. Street, *Deciding Factors in British Politics* (Routledge, 1992), pp. 236–238; P. Norton, "In Defence of the Constitution," in P. Norton (ed.), *New Directions in British Politics?* (Edward Elgar, 1991), pp. 153–160.
53. P. Norton, "Governing Alone," *Parliamentary Affairs*, 56 (4), 2003, pp. 543–559.
54. P. Norton, "The New Barons? Senior Ministers in British Government," *Goldsmiths College Public Policy Paper* (Goldsmiths College, 1998); Norton, "Barons in a Shrinking Kingdom?"
55. See, for example, J. Naughtie, *The Rivals* (The Fourth Estate, 2001); F. Beckett and D. Hencke, *The Blairs and Their Court* (Aurum, 2004); A. Campbell, *The Blair Years* (Hutchinson, 2007).
56. P. Norton, "Barons in a Shrinking Kingdom? Senior Ministers in British Government," in R. A. W. Rhodes (ed.), *Transforming British Government*, Vol. 2: Changing Roles and Relationships (Macmillan, 2000).
57. C. Short, *An Honourable Deception?* (The Free Press, 2004), p. 56.
58. D. Blunkett, *The Blunkett Tapes* (Bloomsbury, 2006), p. 7.
59. Greenaway, Smith, and Street, p. 237.
60. Pyper, p. 43.
61. Hennessy, p. 592.
62. Blunkett, p. 352.
63. J. Prescott, *Prezza* (Headline Review, 2008), p. 216.
64. N. Ridley, *My Style of Government* (Fontana, 1992), p. 41.
65. Headey, *British Cabinet Ministers*.
66. E. Currie, *Life Lines* (Sidgwick & Jackson, 1989), p. 161.
67. R. A. W. Rhodes, *Control and Power in Centre-Local Government Relationships* (Gower, 1981); R. A. W. Rhodes, *Understanding Governance* (Open University Press, 1997), pp. 36–40. See also D. Richards, "New Labour and Whitehall," *Politics Review*, 16 (3), 2007, pp. 20–23.
68. R. E. Neustadt, *Presidential Power* (Free Press, 1990 edition).
69. D. Richards, "New Labour and Whitehall," *Politics Review*, 16 (3), 2007, p. 22.
70. Richards, "New Labour and Whitehall," p. 23.
71. J. D. Barber, *The Presidential Character*, 4th ed. (Prentice-Hall, 1992), p. 6.
72. P. Riddell, "Tony Blair: Prime Minister or President?" *Politics Review*, 15 (3), 2006, pp. 33.
73. M. Foley, "The Presidential Controversy in Britain," *Politics Review*, 18 (3), 2009, p. 22.
74. See especially Greenaway, Smith, and Street, Ch. 10.

CHAPTER

9

The European Union
Government above the Center

Prior to the 1970s, the United Kingdom had entered into various treaty obligations with other nations. It was a founding member of the United Nations Organization. It had joined the North Atlantic Treaty Organization (NATO). It signed, though at the time did not incorporate into domestic law, the European Convention on Human Rights. It participated in the various rounds of the General Agreement on Trade and Tariffs (GATT) to reduce barriers to free trade. At no time, though, did it hand over to a supranational body the power to make regulations that were to be applied directly within the United Kingdom and form part of the law of the land.

This situation was to change on January 1, 1973. On that date the United Kingdom became a member of the European Community (EC). Forty-two volumes of legislation promulgated by institutions of the EC were incorporated into British law. Under the provisions of the 1972 European Communities Act, future legislation emanating from the Community was to be incorporated as well. Further treaties led to an expansion of the Community, both geographically (more countries became members) and in terms of responsibilities. Under the terms of the Treaty on European Union (TEU), which took effect in 1993, a European Union was formed. The Union comprised three "pillars"—the EC, cooperation in foreign and security policy, and cooperation in dealing with justice and foreign affairs. Under the Lisbon Treaty, which took effect on December 1, 2009, the pillared system was replaced by a consolidated body with legal personality.

The United Kingdom is thus a member of a body that is expanding, both quantitatively and qualitatively, and one for which the United States has no equivalent. Though the United States is now part of the North American Free Trade Agreement (NAFTA), there is no supranational body in North America able to make law that can be imposed in the United States against the wishes of the president and Congress, and no supranational body interpreting that body of law. In this respect, the United States is not unusual. It is the member states of the European Union that are in a unique situation.

FROM COMMUNITY TO UNION

The EC, formally comprised three bodies: the European Steel and Coal Community, the European Atomic Energy Community (Euratom), and the European Economic Community (the EEC). The Steel and Coal Community, formed in 1951 under the Treaty of Paris, placed iron, steel, and coal production in member countries under a common authority. Euratom and the EEC were created under the Treaty of Rome and came into being on January 1, 1958. Euratom was designed to help create a civil nuclear industry in Europe. The EEC formed a common market for goods within the community of member states. The three bodies were merged in 1967 to form the European Communities, known by the singular term, the European Community.

Britain declined to join the individual bodies when they were first formed. The Labour government in 1951 found the supranational control of the Steel and Coal Community to be unacceptable. The succeeding Conservative government was not initially attracted by the concept of the EEC. The economic and political arguments for joining, which weighed heavily with the member states, did not carry great weight with British politicians. Britain was still seen as a world power. It was enjoying a period of prosperity. It had strong political and trading links with the Commonwealth. It had a "special relationship" with the United States. It had stood alone successfully during the Second World War. Lacking the experience of German occupation and the need to recreate a polity, Britain was not subject to the psychological appeal of a united Europe, so strong on the continental mainland.[1] Neither main political party was strongly attracted to the idea of a union with such an essentially foreign body. The Conservatives still hankered after the idea of empire, something that had died as a result of the war (Britain could no longer afford to maintain an empire and the principle of self-determination had taken root) and something for which the Commonwealth now served as a kind of a substitute. Labour politicians viewed with distrust the creation of a body that they saw as inherently antisocialist, designed to shore up the capitalist edifice of Western Europe and frustrate any future socialist policies that a Labour government in Britain would seek to implement. It was one of the few issues on which the leader of the Labour Party, Hugh Gaitskell, found himself in agreement with left-wingers within his own party.

The attitude of the British government toward the EEC, at both a ministerial and official level, was to undergo significant change in 1960. Britain's economic problems had become more apparent. Growth rates compared poorly with those of the six member states of the EEC (France, Germany, Italy, Holland, Belgium, and Luxembourg). There was a growing realization that having lost an empire, Britain had gained a Commonwealth. That Commonwealth, however, was not proving as amenable to British leadership as many Conservatives had hoped, nor was it proving to be the source of trade and materials that had been expected. Even the special relationship with the United States was undergoing a period of strain. The "special" appeared to be seeping out of the relationship. Some anti-Americanism lingered in Conservative ranks following the insistence of the White House that Britain abort its operation to occupy the Suez Canal zone in 1956, a distrust still not wholly dispelled. The sudden cancellation by the U.S. administration in 1960 of the Blue Streak, a missile that Britain had ordered and intended to employ as the major element of its nuclear defense policy, awakened British politicians to the fact that in the Atlantic partnership, Britain was very much the junior partner. The U.S. administration itself began to pay more attention to the EEC, and President John F. Kennedy made clear to his friend and distant relative, Prime Minister Harold Macmillan,[2] "that a British decision to join the Six would be welcome."[3] The option became one that had an increasing attraction to Britain.

Politically, the EEC was seen as a vehicle through which Britain could once again play a leading role on the world stage. Economically, it would provide a tariff-free market of 180 million people, it would provide the advantages of economy of scale, and it was assumed that it would encourage greater efficiency in British industry through more vigorous competition. Political and economic advantages were seen as inextricably linked. Economic strength was necessary to underpin the maintenance of political authority.[4] "If we are to meet the challenge of Communism," Macmillan wrote to Kennedy, "[we must show] that our modern society—the new form of capitalism—can run in a way that makes the fullest use of our resources and results in a steady expansion of our economic strength."[5] On July 31, 1961, he announced to the House of Commons that Britain was applying for membership.

The first application for membership was vetoed in January 1963 by the French president, General Charles de Gaulle. He viewed British motives with suspicion, believing that Britain could serve as a vehicle for the United States to establish its dominance within the EEC. A second application was lodged in 1967, this time by the Labour government of Harold Wilson.[6] Agreement to open negotiations was reached eventually in 1969. Negotiations began under the newly returned Conservative government of Edward Heath in 1970. Relations between the British and French governments on the issue were now more amicable, de Gaulle having resigned the presidency in 1969, and no French veto was imposed. Negotiations were completed in 1971 and the British government recommended entry on the terms achieved. On October 28, 1971, following a six-day debate, the House of Commons gave its approval to the principle of membership on the terms negotiated. The vote was 356 in favor, 244 against. Both parties were badly divided. Of Labour members of Parliament, 69 voted with the Conservative government in favor of entry and a further 20 abstained from voting. Of Conservatives, 39 voted with the Labour opposition against entry, and 2 abstained. It was the most divisive vote of the Parliament.

At the beginning of 1972, the Treaty of Accession was signed, and the European Communities bill, to give legal effect to British membership, was given a second reading on February 17. To ensure its passage, Prime Minister

Heath made the vote one of confidence. Despite that, the majority for the bill was a slim one of only eight, Labour MPs largely uniting against the bill and being joined by some Conservatives. The bill faced sustained opposition from Labour members and a number of dissident Conservatives, but it completed its remaining stages without amendment and was given a third reading on July 13.[7] The United Kingdom, as we have noted, duly became a member of the EC on January 1 the following year.

Britain's membership in the EC has been anything but uneventful. Following the return of a Labour government in 1974, the terms of membership were renegotiated and the renegotiated terms put to—and approved by—the electorate in 1975 in Britain's first (and still only) nationwide referendum. In the referendum, 17,378,581 people voted to remain in the EC on the terms negotiated; 8,470,073 voted no. Many commentators interpreted the result as putting Britain's membership beyond further dispute. However, it did not stop conflict taking place over Britain's role within the Community. After the return of a Conservative government in 1979, Prime Minister Margaret Thatcher argued that Britain's financial contribution to the EC was too high and pressed for a reduction. After several heated meetings with other EC heads of government, agreement was reached in 1984, with the United Kingdom receiving refunds on previous years' payments and with a new system to operate in the future. In 1986 the Thatcher government agreed to the terms of a new treaty, known as the Single European Act (SEA). This strengthened the institutions of the EC in measures designed to achieve a single market. However, the effects of the treaty were seen by opponents as weakening the member states. This appeared to be a view that Thatcher herself came to share. In 1988, she made a speech signaling her opposition to developments within the Community and to monetary union within the Community. She defined a role for the EC that was at odds with that envisaged by leaders of other member states. She was committed to achieving a single market but opposed to any moves designed to create a supranational government that could impose its will on member states. Her "so far and no further" stance left her often in a minority of one at EC summits and badly split the Conservative Party.

Thatcher's unwillingness to modify her negative stance was a contributory factor in her loss of the party leadership in 1990 (see Chapter 6). Her successor, John Major, adopted a more emollient approach and had some success in negotiations on a new Community treaty, the TEU, more commonly known as the Maastricht Treaty, in 1991. The bill to give effect to the treaty in British law proved difficult (opponents were spurred to mount a spirited campaign against the bill following the rejection of the treaty in a referendum in Denmark),[8] but it was eventually passed. The issue, however, divided the Conservative Party and Major had to contend with a vocal and determined section of his party that opposed further European integration and, in particular, opposed U.K. membership in a single European currency. Major had negotiated an "opt out" (or, as Major put it, an "opt in") provision for the United Kingdom as part of the Maastricht treaty: The United

Kingdom was not committed to joining a single currency, but could opt to join it if it wished. The stance of the Major government was one of "negotiate and decide" (popularly portrayed as "wait and see") but some Conservatives wanted him to rule out any prospect of British participation. In the run-up to the general election in 1997, a large number of Conservative candidates departed from the party line and expressed their opposition to membership in a single currency.

The election saw the return of a Labour government and a different stance to the issue of European integration. The Labour Party had moved from vehement opposition to membership in the EC—in its 1983 manifesto it had advocated withdrawal from the Community—to a position where, by 1997, it was seen as the more "Euro friendly" of the two parties. It favored a positive engagement in the European Union. Under Prime Minister Tony Blair, the government was involved in negotiating and gaining parliamentary approval for the Amsterdam treaty and the Nice treaties (discussed later). Ministers sought to portray a more positive approach to EU affairs than that taken by their Conservative predecessors. "The differences became more pronounced after 1997 as the Conservatives adopted a more Eurosceptic position. [Conservative leader] Hague promised to oppose British participation in the single currency for two Parliaments (that is, for up to ten years), though he did not rule out entry for all time as a matter of principle. Blair and the chancellor, Gordon Brown, signaled that Britain would join the euro, but only when five economic conditions had been met."[9] Blair achieved good personal relationships with some of the other European leaders and he pressed for a more market-oriented approach by the European Union as well as for some structural changes.[10] "Blair remained throughout his premiership utterly sincere about his intention to make Britain a leading nation in the European Union and at the heart of the debate about its future."[11] Nonetheless, the United Kingdom continued to be seen as a skeptical member of the Union—willing to say "no" when other leading member states were in agreement—and the issue of European integration and, especially, participation in a single currency remained very much on the political agenda. The government made clear that the United Kingdom would only join the single currency after a referendum. Brown, as chancellor, pursued the case for greater competitiveness and the need for the European Union to follow a British agenda, rather than for Britain to follow an EU agenda. Speaking to the CBI, "Brown provided his audience with an agenda on how the newly expanded EU should converge with the 'British model' of stability and enterprise."[12] He pursued this approach when he became prime minister, extolling the virtues of Anglo-American capitalism over the more statist EU approach.[13] Despite this, Labour continued to be seen as less hostile to the European Union than the Conservative Party, whose leaders continued to be drawn from the dominant Eurosceptic wing of the party. In the 2001 general election, Conservative leader William Hague put the issue at the forefront of his campaign. There was thus a divide between the parties, but both made clear that they were opposed to any conception of a European super-state. There was seen to be little political mileage in being overly enthusiastic for greater European integration.

British membership in the EC, now the European Union, has had major constitutional, economic, and political implications. The issue of "Europe" has always been a contentious one. It divides both main political parties and it is an issue that has variously dominated the political agenda.

Constitutional Implications

As we have already had cause to note (Chapter 4), membership in the EC added a new dimension to the British constitution. Under the provisions of the European Communities Act, existing EC law was to have general and binding applicability in the United Kingdom, as was all subsequent law promulgated by the Communities. Section 2(1) of the act gives the force of law in the United Kingdom to "rights, powers, liabilities, obligations, and restrictions from time to time created or arising by or under the Treaties." In other words, EC law passed in the future would not require assent by Parliament: It was already given under the terms of the 1972 Act. "Membership has meant, therefore, that Parliament's approval is no longer a prerequisite of changes to the law."[14] Section 2(4) provides that directly applicable EC law should prevail over conflicting provisions of domestic legislation. The effects of membership and the provisions of the act were several. Membership introduced two new decision-making bodies into the ambit of the British polity: the Council of Ministers and the Commission. It restricted the role and influence of Parliament in matters that came within the competence of the Communities. It injected a new judicial dimension to the constitution. Disputes concerning the treaties or legislation made under them were to be treated by the British courts as matters of law, with provision for their referral to the European Court of Justice (ECJ). And it allowed for British representation in the European Parliament, albeit until 1987 a body with very limited powers.

The constitutional implications were a matter of controversy at the time Britain joined the EC. Equally controversial were the implications of subsequent treaties. The *SEA* took effect in 1987. The provisions necessary to give effect to it in British law were enacted by the 1986 European Communities (Amendment) Act. The SEA was introduced in order to facilitate the achievement of a single market: Though that was the goal of the EEC, it had proved difficult to achieve. The SEA created a shift in power relationships *within* the institutions of the EC as well as *between* the institutions of the EC and the member states. Under the SEA, the European Parliament not only was designated as a parliament (its formal title previously was the European Assembly) but also was given a more powerful role in the EC lawmaking process. Previously its role was solely advisory. To allow for the approval of the measures necessary to achieve the single market, provision for the Council of Ministers to determine issues by qualified majority voting (QMV) was extended. Under QMV, each member state has a number of votes, the number varying according to the size of the country, and a set number of votes is necessary to approve a proposal. QMV replaced the usual practice of agreeing measures on the basis of unanimity. The use of QMV made it possible for measures to be passed despite the opposition of a small number of member states. By the end of the decade, British ministers had sometimes found themselves out-voted under this procedure.

The *TEU* (the Maastricht Treaty), negotiated in 1991, signed in 1992 and taking effect in 1993, established the European Union and established economic and monetary union as an objective of the Community. It also enhanced the powers of the European Parliament through introducing a new co-decision procedure. Under the procedure, the parliament cannot force the Council of Ministers to adopt a measure but it can block a measure. The treaty also embodied the principle of subsidiarity, stating that in areas outside its exclusive competence, the Community "shall take action ... only and in so far as the objectives of the proposed action cannot be sufficiently achieved by the Member States." Britain interpreted this as limiting the centralizing tendencies of the EC. Others took a different view, seeing it as a legitimation of the Community extending its reach. Opponents pointed out that it would still be at the level of the Community that the decisions would be made as to what should fall within the scope of subsidiarity.

The *Amsterdam Treaty*, which took effect in 1999, further strengthened the position of the European Parliament by making more treaty provisions subject to the co-decision procedure. This is now the procedure more used than any other. The treaty also further extended the policy-making competence of the Community. Provision for QMV was also extended, including to some areas under the second pillar (foreign and security policy) of the Union. The Commission also acquired new rights in respect of immigration and asylum policy.

The *Nice Treaty*, which was signed in 2001 and took effect in 2003, implemented changes to the structure of the Union, especially in respect of the size and composition of the commission, the weighting of votes in the Council of Ministers, and the extension of QMV. The changes were seen as necessary to make institutional adjustments to facilitate enlargement of the Union. (Ten new states joined in 2004, two more joined in 2007.) The treaty also extended the powers of the European Parliament, though not to the extent it wanted. The treaty was viewed as a temporary expedient until more wide-ranging reforms could be achieved. These reforms were embodied in a *Constitutional Treaty for Europe,* designed to clarify the purposes and powers of the European Union—it brought all the existing treaties into one document—and to establish the European Union as a legal entity in international affairs. It created an EU minister for foreign affairs, enhanced judicial cooperation in criminal matters, strengthened the position of the commission president, and sought to strengthen the European Parliament through making most legislative decisions subject to the co-decision procedure. It also provided the formal capacity for a state to secede from the Union and sought to strengthen the role of national parliaments in the EU law-making process. In the event, the treaty was never enacted: It was signed by the member states in 2004 but was blocked the following year by electors in France and the

Netherlands voting "no" in referendums. As a result, a new treaty—the *Lisbon Treaty*—was negotiated: It was designed to be distinguishable from the Constitutional Treaty in that it did not have the status of a constitution, though most of the novel provisions of the Constitutional Treaty were retained. This treaty fell foul of a referendum in Ireland in 2008. However, the following year another referendum was held and a "yes" vote achieved. The treaty as already noted, came into force in 2009.

The effect of the treaties to date has been to create a powerful supranational decision-making entity with fundamental implications for the constitution of the United Kingdom. Membership in the European Union constitutes an important part now of the British constitution, but it is a part that does fit well with other basic tenets. As we have seen, it serves to undermine, though formally not destroy, the doctrine of parliamentary sovereignty. Law can be promulgated by the institutions of the EU and that law has effect in the United Kingdom, even though the British minister may have voted against it in the Council of Ministers. If British law conflicts with the provisions of European law, the courts are to give precedence to the latter. In the *Factortame* case in 1990–91, the ECJ held that British courts could, in effect, suspend acts of Parliament that appeared to breach European law, until such time as a final judgment was made. In the *EOC* case in 1994 the courts struck down a provision of British law as being contrary to EC law. The position of the courts is further strengthened as the policy-making competence of the European Union is extended. It is also strengthened by moves to create new rights within the European Union.

The British Parliament, like other national parliaments, has a limited role in the EU law-making process. Parliament remains important when new treaties are negotiated: Member states have to give their approval through their usual constitutional procedures. Parliament has to approve bills to give effect to treaty changes. However, it has no power to block or amend legislation made under the treaties. Prior to the implementation of the Lisbon Treaty, all that Parliament could do to affect measures promulgated by the institutions of the European Union was to consider draft documents to be submitted to the Council of Ministers and to influence the relevant minister prior to meetings of the Council of Ministers. The Lisbon Treaty makes provision for a specified number of national parliaments to require the Council to reconsider a proposal if they consider it to fall foul of the principle of subsidiarity. The U.K. Parliament could thus join with others to influence the Council, but the provision is not expected to have a significant impact. The grounds for action are narrow (it does not cover whether measures are proportionate, for example) and not all national parliaments are geared to scrutinizing EU proposals in depth. Both houses of Parliament have committees to undertake scrutiny of EU documents.[15] The scrutiny they undertake is generally regarded as good, not least compared with that undertaken by most other national parliaments, but they serve essentially as advisory bodies in the process.

Economic Implications

The economic attractions for joining the EC were, as we have seen, a major influence in Britain's applying for membership. The Community offered, in trading terms, a "common market" (the popular name for the EEC), one which has assumed increasing significance for the British economy. Enlargement—there are now 27 member states—has resulted in a market of 490 million consumers.

Before membership, most U.K. trade was with countries outside the EC. Since joining, British exports to the EC increased and trade grew faster with EC states than it did with the rest of the world. In 1973, 36 percent of U.K. trade was with EC countries; in 2000, the figure was 58 percent. Exports to EU countries have continued to account for most of U.K. exports, though the rate of growth has since been outstripped by that to non-EU countries. (The position is similar in relation to imports.) Between 2001 and 2008, the annual growth rate in exports to EU countries was 2.62 percent. To non-EU countries, the annual growth rate was 4.48 percent. In 2008, exports to EU countries amounted to £139,239 million and to non-EU countries £108,110 million.

Britain also receives money from what are known as the European Union's *structural* and *cohesion funds*, designed to support the poorer parts of the European Union and to help develop infrastructure (especially in the transport sector) within the European Union. The two principal structural funds are the European regional development fund (ERDF), designed to promote economic and social cohesion within the European Union through reducing imbalances between regions and social groups, and the European social fund (ESF), designed to deliver the European Union's employment policy. The cohesion fund, which came into force in 1994, provides support for projects on the environment and transport networks in member states with a GDP below 90 percent of the EU average. The structural funds have a budget of 277 billion euros ($393.3b.) for 2007–13 and the cohesion fund 70 billion euros ($99.4b.) for the same period. The bulk of the cohesion fund goes to the new member states in central and eastern European. However, the United Kingdom receives 9.4 billion euros ($13.3b.) from the structural funds 2007–13 budget to assist with development and regeneration. Of this, 2.6 billion euros ($3.7b.) are being spent on the United Kingdom's poorest regions, 6.2 billion euros ($8.8b.) are being devoted to enhancing competitiveness and employment in other regions, and 0.6 billion euros ($0.85b.) are being spent on cross-border and trans-national cooperation activities. In Wales, for example, a total of 74 projects had received funding by March 2009, involving a commitment of £626 million ($1,026.6m.) of EU funds.

More controversial is the *common agricultural policy* (CAP). In 2006, this accounted for more than 45 percent of the EU budget. It constitutes a system of agricultural subsidies—ensuring support for farmers if prices fall below a certain level—and programs designed to facilitate rural development. It has been the subject of controversy in the United Kingdom since it has favored price supports rather than cheap food, thus working to the benefit of countries with large farming communities. France is the largest beneficiary in cash terms, and Greece and Ireland in terms of per capita income. The United Kingdom has a small, highly efficient farming sector, and in 2006 received 9 percent of the CAP budget, compared to 20 percent received by France. The policy has also worked against non-EU countries through creating high tariff barriers. Recent years have seen various reforms to the policy. In 2003, a scheme was introduced to break the link between farm aid and production of particular crops, and to introduce requirements to comply with certain environmental, animal welfare, and food safety standards. In 2008, it was agreed that more of the funds devoted to milk subsidies should be diverted to rural development and that eventually milk subsidies should be scrapped. The cost of the CAP, which has been falling for some years, is designed to reduce over time and by 2013 to be half of its traditional level.

The EU also administers a number of other funds and programs, such as one to provide assistance with energy research and development, and it also encompasses the European Investment Bank. Created under the Treaty of Rome, the bank operates on a nonprofit basis to grant loans and guarantees that facilitate the financing of new investment and projects concerned with modernization. It is now the largest international financing institution in the world. There is also now the European Central Bank (ECB), which was appointed in 1998 to oversee monetary policy once a single European currency was in place. The single currency—the euro—was brought into being on January 1, 1999. (Coins and notes were issued in 2002.) Eleven member states were deemed to have met the criteria necessary to participate. The exchange rates of the currencies of these states were irrevocably locked on that date. Since then, five other member states have met the criteria and joined the "eurozone."

The single currency proved highly controversial in the United Kingdom. Those who were already skeptical of British membership of the European Union attacked it as undermining Britain's capacity to decide its own fate. They pointed out that when in 1990 Britain had joined the European exchange rate mechanism (ERM)—linking the value of the pound to other European currencies—it had proved disastrous. Membership had not saved the pound from an attack by currency speculators in 1992 and the United Kingdom had to withdraw from the ERM. The skeptics argued that British membership had not delivered the economic benefits claimed for it. The cost of imports from the European Union far exceeds the value of exports and in the late 1990s exports to the rest of the world increased while trade with EU states actually declined. The largest single investor in the United Kingdom remained the United States (just as the United Kingdom remained the largest single investor in the States). Joining a single currency, they argued, would lead to harmonized taxation throughout the European Union, which would drive up the tax burden in the United Kingdom. It would also drive up borrowing costs, undermine the competitiveness of the City of London as the world's leading financial marketplace, create a major burden in funding pensions (other major EU countries having "unfunded" pensions), and lead to instability in the nation's trading relationship with the rest of the world. Supporters of joining the single currency argued that it would bring stability through ensuring a stable marketplace within the European Union. It would also likely result in a fall in interest rates and inflation. It would get rid of exchange rate transaction costs and make Britain an attractive location for foreign investors. Lower interest rates, it was claimed, would increase competitiveness and reduce unemployment. Opponents pointed out that during the period that Britain was in the ERM, unemployment doubled.

As we have seen, the Labour government after 1997 adopted a not dissimilar stance to that of its Conservative predecessor. It was committed to joining when the conditions appeared right. It was generally accepted that it would be some time for Britain to meet the necessary "convergence" criteria for joining, the British economy operating on a different cycle from that of other member states. As a consequence, the United Kingdom has not exercised its power to "opt in" to the single currency. As we shall see, the issue remains a highly divisive one in British politics.

Political Implications

British membership in the Community has had political implications in terms of U.K. domestic politics. It remains a contentious issue. However, it has wider political implications—that is, in terms of the member states acting together as a political power bloc. That, as we have seen, was one of the motivations for Britain joining the Community. For Britain, the prospect of EC member states acting together looked increasingly attractive as other avenues for maintaining a world status (the Commonwealth, the "special relationship" with the United States) receded in significance. In the event, the United Kingdom has supported moves toward creating the mechanisms for greater cooperation but has sometimes clashed with other member states in reaching decisions through those procedures. There has been a difference of conception as to the role of the European Union.

Various theories have been developed to explain the move toward European integration. The classical debate has been between *neo-functionalism*[16] and *inter-governmentalism*.[17] The former views integration as a product of pressure from societal forces and with integration in one area leading to pressure for integration in other areas (spillover), resulting in the creation of supranational institutions. The latter approach views integration as the result of self-interest on the part of states; nations participate because they judge that they gain more than they lose, but will continue to be driven by their particular interests. Other theories have been developed,[18] but these remain the two basic approaches.

These are theories designed to explain the moves toward integration. However, they are also useful in seeking to explain differences in attitudes toward further integration. Proponents of greater European integration, and those responsible for creating the initial European Communities, are often viewed as adopting a top-down, essentially elitist, approach, favoring spillover from one area to another and the creation of supranational institutions.

Neo-functionalism to some extent helps identify their particular approach. The approach of the U.K. government, on the other hand, has tended to favor an inter-governmental approach, supporting integration in so far as it facilitates a single trading market, but favoring an inter-governmental approach in other areas of public policy. It has been especially wary of moves (as it sees it) to encroach on areas that it believes should be reserved to the nation state. As prime minister, John Major fought during negotiations over the Maastricht Treaty to ensure that the United Kingdom retained the power to "opt out" from policies in certain areas (such as the social chapter) and Prime Minister Tony Blair set out various "red lines" during negotiations over the Lisbon Treaty: In essence, lines beyond which the U.K. government would not be prepared to go. In both cases, the U.K. government achieved its desired goals, brandishing the results as a success for the United Kingdom.

In taking an intergovernmentalist approach, the U.K. government is not alone. Other member states privilege the position of the state. However, the United Kingdom is seen as being somewhat isolated because of a notable difference in approach to the European Union's goal (embodied in the Treaty of Rome) of "ever closer union." In Chapter 2, we noted the approach to problem solving in the United Kingdom compared with some other European countries. Whereas the English adopt an empirical approach, the continental approach tends to be rationalist. In the context of EU policy making, this is reflected in the principal member states favoring rather broad formulations, while Britain favors more precise measures with the mechanism for implementation and achievement clearly laid out. This produces some disparity both in decision making and in implementation. Britain will prove difficult at times in policy making, sometimes to the exasperation of other member states, but prove very good in implementing measures once they are agreed. Other countries, such as Italy and France, will move quickly to agree to measures which they subsequently treat as essentially aspirational, implementing them how and when they think appropriate, if at all. By the end of 1999, not all measures necessary to achieve a single market had been implemented by member states. The best implementation rates were achieved by the United Kingdom and Denmark, the two countries regarded as the most "Euro-skeptic" within the European Union.

Successive British governments have faced the conundrum of wanting to be seen as a key player in the European Union—necessary in order to achieve outcomes favorable to the United Kingdom—while at the same time not wishing to be seen as overly supportive, given the history and culture of the United Kingdom. There is a general, though not universal, recognition of the value of EU cooperation, yet also a wariness of moves that may jeopardize the country's independence and its desire to be seen as player on the world stage in its own right and not solely as part of the European Union. The United Kingdom has tended to be especially keen to maintain an inter-governmental approach in relation to foreign policy and certain aspects of domestic policy.

This ambiguity on the part of the U.K. government—being in the European Union, yet wanting to protect Britain's capacity as an independent global actor—has led to some tension at times with other member states. British ministers have not been afraid to argue their case in the Council of Ministers. As a result, Britain has acquired a reputation within the European Union as "an awkward partner."[19] Though, as we have seen, relations appeared to improve under the Labour government elected in 1997, the perception remains, with ministers sometimes opposing proposals brought forward by the Commission. As we have touched upon, Prime Minister Gordon Brown has been as keen as his predecessor, Tony Blair, to push the Anglo-American approach to economic policy. "Atlanticism will continue to take precedence over European integration in British foreign policy. The Anglo-American model of capitalism will continue to enjoy supremacy, both moral and political, over the inflexible continental European rival."[20] Brown made some headway in pursuing this approach, though following the global economic crisis of 2008, some other European leaders, such as French president Nicolas Sarkozy, took a very different view as to the utility of this approach.

The perception of the United Kingdom as an awkward partner is, in many respects, misleading. The United Kingdom is often in agreement with other member states. On occasion, it is used as a surrogate by other member states, their representatives asking British ministers to voice their opposition for them. Nonetheless, the perception is widespread within the European Union and it shapes attitudes toward the United Kingdom. Domestic conflict about Britain's role in the European Union continues to fuel the perception.

INSTITUTIONS OF THE EUROPEAN UNION

The main bodies of the European Union are the European Council, the Council of Ministers, the Commission, the European Parliament, and the Committee of Permanent Representatives. There are also various other judicial and advisory bodies.

The *European Council*, more commonly known as the "European Summit," comprises the heads of government of the member states, the foreign ministers or equivalent from each member state, and the president and vice-president of the European Commission. Though already a regular feature, it was not until the SEA that it was given treaty status. The Lisbon Treaty established it formally as an EU institution and created the fixed-term post of President. It meets up to four times a year. It is the most powerful body within the European Union in terms of high policy: "it sets broad policy guidelines for the EU, resolves disputes between member states, agrees reforms of the treaties and steers EU foreign policy. It is the key institution in making decisions about the EU's future, about the powers of the institutions and policy areas in which the EU should be involved."[21]

The *Council of Ministers*—formally titled the Council of the European Union—comprises the ministers from the member states whose portfolios cover the subject under discussion. Thus a proposal covering agriculture will be considered by the council comprising agriculture ministers. (In practice, it would be more appropriate to refer to *councils* of ministers.) The demands made of the Council vary according to the subject. The Council of Foreign Ministers and the Council of Finance Ministers meet more often than do the others. The Council has to agree to any measure in order for it to become law. It combines legislative with non-legislative functions and prior to the expansion of the powers of the European Parliament it was the sole legislative body. The Council seeks to proceed on the basis of consensus and tacit agreement. Even before the passage of the SEA, various matters could be resolved through QMV. Some measures are subject to simple majority voting or to unanimity. Under the so-called Luxembourg compromise of 1966, a country may veto legislation if "very important interests" (in effect, vital national interests) are involved. However, this is a highly contentious provision, with no clear agreement on what is actually entailed. It is not clear that the Luxembourg compromise could now be invoked.

The Council of Ministers has limited powers to initiate measures. Rather it discusses and agrees to measures placed before it. The body principally responsible for initiating measures is the *Commission*. This constitutes the executive body of the European Union. It has a staff of about 15,000 and is headed by a College of Commissioners. Since 2004, there has been one commissioner drawn from each member state (prior to then, the larger countries each had two) though the number will start to reduce, on a rotation basis, after 2009. Though each member state nominates a commissioner, every commissioner takes an oath not to seek to represent national interests. The commission is headed by a commission president. The president is chosen by the heads of state in the European Council and is then subject to approval by the European Parliament. The commissioners meet once a week to adopt proposals, finalize policy papers, and make other decisions required of the commission.

The commission serves a five-year term and is responsible for initiating most policy proposals as well as for ensuring that the provisions of the treaties are complied with. It is also responsible for implementing policy decisions. It operates through 23 directorates-general and 15 specialist departments. Each commissioner has responsibility for one or more directorates-general. The directorates-general undertake widespread consultation before coming forward with a proposal for the commissioners. There is extensive contact with firms and other organizations affected by EU decision making and many bodies have offices in Brussels, where the commission is based. Lobbying of the commission by outside organizations is, as we have seen (Chapter 7), well developed.

The members of the commission are frequently people who have held high political office in their home country. In the case of the United Kingdom, commissioners have included former Labour leader Neil Kinnock and former Cabinet ministers such as Leon Brittan, Chris Patten, and Peter Mandelson. However, the commission was hit by controversy in 1999. In December 1998 a commission official, Paul van Buitenen, made allegations of fraud and mismanagement within the European Union. The same month the European Parliament refused to approve the European Union's accounts for 1996. The accusations led to an investigation by a special team of investigators. They issued a damning report, naming a number of commissioners for failing to exercise proper control and, in the case of the commission president, for allowing "a state within a state" to develop. Some commissioners were accused of favoritism in making appointments. Following publication of the report, the entire commission resigned, though some were then kept on to complete their terms. Since then, the commission has avoided such controversy and been seen as more of an effective and collegial body under its president, José Manuel Barrosa (2004–).

Until the passage of the SEA, the *European Parliament* was an advisory body in dealing with EC legislation. It did have two formal, but rather blunt, powers: One was to reject the budget, which it did employ (and continues to), and the other was to force the resignation of the commission *en bloc* (something it was to threaten in 1999). In the legislative process, though, it was called upon only to offer an opinion on a proposal emanating from the commission. That opinion was then passed on to the Council of Ministers to consider. The parliament could have some effect by failing to offer an opinion, but when it did offer one there was no obligation on the council to accept it.

The position of the parliament was strengthened by the SEA and by succeeding treaties. The SEA designated the parliament as a parliament (though it had previously styled itself the European Parliament, its formal title was the European Assembly) and it introduced the cooperation procedure. This gave the parliament a more significant role in certain types of legislation, principally that aimed at achieving a single market. A "second reading" was introduced. If the parliament amended or rejected the position taken by the council after the first reading (the traditional procedure), the commission reexamined and resubmitted the proposal. The council could then only amend, reject, or reinstate a proposal rejected by the parliament by unanimity.

The Maastricht Treaty introduced a new and more powerful procedure, the co-decision procedure. If the council and parliament could not agree after two readings, a conciliation committee was formed; if no agreement was reached, the council version prevailed unless the parliament voted it down. The co-decision procedure thus gave the parliament the capacity to block a measure. It was also given additional power under the assent procedure: Under this, the consent of the parliament is necessary for treaties bringing new members into the Union. The Amsterdam Treaty further strengthened the position of the parliament. Under the Maastricht Treaty, the co-decision procedure only applied to a small number of legislative proposals. Under the Amsterdam Treaty, it was extended to cover most of the areas previously covered by the cooperation procedure. It became the most common procedure. The cooperation procedure was retained largely for single market measures. The original procedure, the opinion of the parliament being sought, still applied for proposals in the agriculture sector. The Nice Treaty gave the parliament the legal powers to challenge acts of other EU institutions before the ECJ.

The parliament has thus become a significant political actor in the European Union. It has moved from constituting a legislature with little or no policy affect to one where it borders on constituting a policy-making legislature.[22] It has proved willing to exercise its powers and to press for more. It wants to be able to initiate proposals as well as to have its powers extended to cover all areas of EU responsibility. Though it seeks to cooperate with national parliaments, it is wary of moves that would involve national parliaments encroaching on its areas of responsibility. Some national politicians have argued the case for a second chamber within the parliament, with members drawn from the parliaments of the member states: The European Parliament has been a vigorous opponent of the proposal. It tends to see itself as a form of first chamber, with the Council of Ministers being a second chamber; the commission is the executive.[23]

The other principal body in the process is the *Committee of Permanent Representatives*, known as COREPER. This has the responsibility for preparing the work of the Council of Ministers and for carrying out tasks assigned to the council. As the name implies, it comprises official representatives (classified as ambassadors) from the member states, each assisted by a staff of diplomats and officials seconded (released from regular duty and temporarily assigned elsewhere) from the national civil service. COREPER studies a proposal on behalf of the council, isolating any problems associated with it. If the committee reaches agreement, it is usual for the council to adopt the proposal without further discussion.

These bodies are supplemented by a number of advisory bodies with members drawn from different organizations within the member states. The *Economic and Social Committee*, based in Brussels, offers opinions on commission proposals as well as on broader issues affecting society. The members are drawn from workers, employers, and consumers' organizations. The United Kingdom has 24 members on the 344-member body. The *Committee of the Regions,* on which the United Kingdom also has 24 members out of 344, was established under the Maastricht Treaty. It comprises members drawn from regional and local authorities. Members are appointed by national governments for four-year terms. There is now a legal obligation for the Committee to be consulted on various matters that concern the regions. There is also a large number of committees appointed to oversee and advise on the implementation of policy, the operation of these committees collectively being known as *comitology*.[24]

There are a number of other bodies standing outside the normal decision-making process. The ECJ, based in Luxembourg, ensures that European law is observed in the interpretation and application of the treaties, and this court can itself interpret European law. Its judgments are binding on member states and enforceable through the national courts. It has 27 members, one drawn from each member state, each serving for six-year terms. There is also now a *Court of First Instance* to help reduce the burden on the court in a limited number of areas, as well as *Civil Service Tribunal* to deal with cases brought by officials employed by EU institutions. Given that the ECJ has responsibility for determining, when cases are brought, whether member states have fulfilled their obligations under the treaties, it is an immensely powerful body, with a capacity to shape the relationship between the European Union and the member states—not dissimilar to the role played by the U.S. Supreme Court in the early decades of the United States.

The *Court of Auditors* exists to exercise a watchdog function on the European Union's financial practices. Its reports are usually "qualified," meaning that it is not satisfied with all the accounting practices. The *European Ombudsman* investigates allegations of "maladministration" leveled against an EU institution by an EU citizen. The Ombudsman has wide-ranging powers of inquiry and can, in certain cases, require the production of all documentation that he requires. He may also draw cases to the attention of the European Parliament.

The European Union thus has a range of powerful institutions. The structure of decision making within the European Union is unusual, indeed unique. It bears no relationship to existing political systems. Whereas most countries of Western Europe are used to a parliamentary form of government—with the executive being chosen through elections to the legislature—there is no equivalent procedure in the European Union. Nor do the institutions of the European Union bear any relationship to a presidential system of government. The executive within the European Union—the commission—is an appointed and not an elected body. This, coupled with the fact that the European Parliament had, prior to the Maastricht Treaty, very limited powers—and still lacks the power to initiate measures—and has attracted a low turnout in elections, has led to claims that there is within the institutions of the European Union a "democratic deficit."

ELECTIONS TO THE EUROPEAN PARLIAMENT

The European Parliament, as we have seen, is an increasingly powerful body. It is also a peripatetic body. It works principally through 20 standing committees and these meet in Brussels. However, it holds most of its plenary sessions in Strasbourg, France. Its secretariat is located in Luxembourg, though many staff are based in Brussels. (The secretariat has a staff of over 5,000, over a third being employed to deal with translation.) Three weeks are given over to committee meetings, followed by one week for plenary meetings. Each month, a mass of papers and other material is moved from Brussels to Strasbourg to be ready for the plenary session.

The parliament has grown in number with the accession of new members. Following the accession of Romania and Bulgaria in 2007, the number was 785. It was reduced for the 2009 elections to 736. Before 1979, the members were appointed from the members of the national parliaments of the member states. Direct election was introduced in 1979. The parliament is elected for a five-year term. There have thus been seven elections to the parliament (1979, 1984, 1989, 1994, 1999, 2004, and 2009). The number of

TABLE 9.1

NUMBER OF MEPs ELECTED FROM THE UNITED KINGDOM

Party	Election						
	1979	1984	1989	1994	1999	2004	2009
Conservative	60	45	32	18	36	27	25
Labour	17	32	45	62	29	19	13
Liberal Democrat	0	0	0	2	10	12	11
Scottish National	1	1	1	2	2	2	2
Plaid Cymru	0	0	0	0	2	1	1
UK Independence	0	0	0	0	3	12	13
Green	0	0	0	0	2	2	2
Democratic Unionist*	1	1	1	1	1	1	1
SDLP*	1	1	1	1	1	0	0
Ulster Unionist*	1	1	1	1	1	1	1**
Sinn Féin*	0	0	0	0	0	1	1
British National Party	0	0	0	0	0	0	2
TOTAL	81	81	81	87	87	78	72

*MEPs elected from Northern Ireland under the STV.
**Following an alliance between the UUs and the Conservatives, the UU candidate in 2009 stood as a Ulster Conservatives and Unionists candidate and sits with the Conservatives.

MEPs elected from the United Kingdom has varied as a result of changes in the size of the Parliament. In 2004, it was 78, reduced in 2009 to 72. Though there have been attempts to create pan-European political movements, the elections are essentially fought in each country by national parties. Indeed, the issues that dominate at European elections tend to be national rather than European, the elections being used as a means of passing opinion on the national government.

In the first two elections to the European Parliament, the Conservative Party did especially well, benefiting from the fact that the party was doing well in the opinion polls. In 1989 and 1994 it suffered a reversal in its fortunes: Having held 60 seats in 1979, it was reduced to 18 in 1994 (see Table 9.1). The Labour Party became the dominant party, achieving the election of 45 members (MEPs) in 1989 and 62 in 1994, its members playing a leading role within the Socialist Group in the parliament.

In the 1999 elections, a new method of election was used. From 1979 to 1994, the nation had been divided into single-member constituencies and the first-past-the-post method of election employed. (The exception was Northern Ireland where, because of the particular problems of the province, the three members were elected under the STV system.) The European Union was committed toward finding a uniform system of election, and the new Labour government elected in 1997 introduced a bill to provide for the use of a regional list system of elections. This was employed in 1999. Each region was allocated a set number of members, and voters went to the polls to vote for a particular party rather than for individual candidates. The results of the election were disastrous for the Labour Party, giving the Conservative party a boost at a time when it was still notably lagging behind Labour in the opinion polls. The Conservatives won 36 seats (a gain of 18), while Labour's representation went down from 62 to 29. It was Labour's worst result since 1979.

Both main parties have witnessed an erosion of support at the expense of third parties. In 2004, the Liberal Democrats and the UKIP each won 12 seats, an increase of ten seats for UKIP. In 2009, the far-right BNP won two seats. In 1979, the two main parties held 77 out of 81 seats. In 2009, they held only 38 seats out of 72. The position was especially bad for the Labour Party, holding 13 seats, the same number as achieved by the UKIP.

The elections have also been characterized by a low turnout (Table 9.2). In most elections, approximately two-thirds of U.K. electors have stayed at home: In 1999, more than three-quarters did so. The turnout increased in 2004, when the EU elections were held on the same day as local government elections and voting by postal ballot was utilized in four regions. Even so, most electors still stayed away from the polls. The figure declined to 34.7 percent in 2009. Though most other EU countries achieve a higher turnout (boosted in part by some countries, such as Belgium, having compulsory voting), there has been an EU-wide downward trend. In 1999, for the first time, more electors failed to vote than went to the polling booths: The turnout was just over 49 percent. The figure fell further in 2004 (a turnout of 45.47 percent) and in 2009 it was only 43 percent. Somewhat counter-intuitively, as the powers of the European Parliament have increased, the interest in it among citizens appears to have decreased.

TABLE 9.2

TURNOUT IN EUROPEAN PARLIAMENT ELECTIONS

Year	U.K. turnout (%)	EU average (%)
1979	32.2	63.0
1984	32.6	61.0
1989	36.2	58.5
1994	36.4	56.8
1999	24.0	49.8
2004	38.4	45.6
2009	34.7	43.0

Source: www.elections2009-results.eu/en/turnout_en.html

Within the parliament, Labour MEPs sit as part of the Party of European Socialists and Conservative MEPs have traditionally sat as part of the center-right Group of European People's Party and European Democrats (EPP-ED)—the largest grouping within the parliament—though the relationship has not been an easy one: The group comprises essentially Christian Democratic parties, who are supporters of greater European integration. In 2009, Conservative leader David Cameron withdrew Conservative MEPs from the group and, with allies from seven other countries (notably Poland and the Czech Republic) formed a new group, the European Conservatives and Reformists, with 55 MEPs.[25]

THE CURRENT DEBATE

The issue of European integration has been notable for the divisions it has created in British politics. Neither of the main parties has maintained a consistent stance on the issue and neither has ever been united in its stance. The issue has been identified as the "fault line" of British politics, with the capacity to split parties asunder. Sometimes the issue has receded in political prominence, but has variously been at the center of British politics.

The Labour Party was initially opposed to British membership in the EC, then moved to support membership in the 1960s. In the early 1970s it opposed membership on the terms negotiated and then supported membership after it won office in 1974 and had an opportunity to renegotiate the terms. In the early 1980s, with a leftward shift in the party, it swung heavily against membership. Under the leadership of Neil Kinnock, John Smith, and Tony Blair it moved toward embracing membership and the benefits that it was perceived to bring. Many trade unions also shifted their position. Having previously been hostile or skeptical, they began to see the EC as a means of achieving economic and social rights for workers. By the time of the 1997 election, Labour had established itself as a "Euro-friendly" party. The party's election manifesto declared that, though it was opposed to a European federal super-state, it would offer leadership in Europe. That has remained its position.

The Conservative Party was initially hostile to membership, but—as we have seen—shifted its position in the early 1960s. It was under a Conservative prime minister, Edward Heath, that the United Kingdom became a member of the EC. Heath remained committed to the concept of European integration. His successor as Conservative leader, Margaret Thatcher, campaigned for a "yes" vote in the 1975 referendum but, after becoming prime minister in 1979, adopted an increasingly skeptical position. In 1988, she launched a sharp attack on further moves toward European integration. In a speech to the College of Europe in Bruges, she attacked the idea of a supranational government capable of imposing its will on the member states. "We have not successfully rolled back the frontiers of the state in Britain," she declared, "only to see them re-imposed at a European level, with a European super-state exercising a new dominance from Brussels."[26] Her strident stance attracted the support of many Conservatives but it dismayed others. Her attack on the European Commission at the dispatch box of the House of Commons in 1990 sparked her deputy prime minister to resign. That resignation was to trigger a train of events resulting in Thatcher's loss of the party leadership (see Chapter 6). Her successor tried to keep the divided wings of the party together, but it proved a difficult task. Achieving passage of the European Communities (Amendment) Bill in 1992—to give effect to provisions of the Maastricht Treaty—proved difficult, the bill being passed in the summer of 1993, a year after it was intended to be passed. The party was badly divided on the issue of a single currency and entered the 1997 election as a divided party. After the election, the new party leader, William Hague, took a more Euro-skeptic stance—in the 1999 European Parliament elections, he adopted the slogan of "In Europe, not run by Europe"—and that stance has been maintained by his successors as party leader. The party committed itself to a referendum on the Constitutional Treaty and called for one on the Lisbon treaty.

There are essentially four groupings within the Conservative Party that can be identified on the issue of Europe. It is possible to refine the categorization even further, but this fourfold typology is sufficient to indicate the nature, and intensity, of the debate. There are similar groupings in the Labour Party, but it is the divisions within Conservative ranks that have attracted the most attention. The first category is that of the *anti-Europeans*. These are people who opposed British membership in the EC and continue to oppose it. The main objection has tended to be on constitutional grounds: They oppose the loss of sovereignty that comes with membership. They have also argued that it does not bring great economic gains either and that Britain would be well able to survive outside the European Union. The second category is the *Euro-skeptics*. These are people who support membership for the purposes of achieving a single market. However, their goal is the removal of trade barriers. They are opposed to any moves toward political union and the creation of a supranational government. They argue that the EU has moved beyond the initial aims of a common market. Since the 1980s—especially since Margaret Thatcher's 1988 Bruges speech—they have joined with anti-Europeans to oppose further moves toward European integration. The third category is that of *Euro-agnostics*. These are people who have no ingrained ideological stance on the issue but are driven by what they see as being in the interests of the nation, and the party, at any particular time. In the late 1980s, they tended to turn against Margaret Thatcher, believing her stance was harming British interests. In the 1990s, they moved toward a more hostile stance, especially on the issue of a single currency. The fourth and final category is the *Europhiles*. These are people who have a principled commitment to European integration and favor moves toward economic and monetary union. They campaign for Britain to enter the single currency.

In the early 1970s, the anti-Europeans were a small minority in the party. Since then, they have been joined in their opposition to further integration—

and especially in their opposition to a single currency—by the Euro-skeptics and the Euro-agnostics. Only the Europhiles continue to press for further integration, and they constitute a minority—about one-fifth—of the parliamentary party.[27] The Europhiles have the advantage of including some well-known political figures, but they have receded in number and only a handful—notably former chancellor of the exchequer Kenneth Clarke—remain in the House of Commons. Some politicians previously classed as Europhiles have expressed their opposition to the U.K. joining a single currency.

On the Labour benches, the Euro-agnostics generally side with the Europhiles in supporting the leadership's position, though with the Europhiles preferring a more positive stance (especially on the issue of the single currency). However, the number of Euro-skeptics and anti-Europeans is such as to limit the government in its approach. They have tended to keep a low profile relative to Conservative Euro-skeptics, but have been prepared to indicate their opposition when issues such as the single currency have come on to the political agenda.

Given the divided nature of both parties, the leaders of each have sought to reduce the political significance of the issue. One of the devices they have employed to achieve this has been to promise a referendum in the event of a government decision to recommend entry into the eurozone. This, coupled with the fact that the United Kingdom has not met the convergence criteria, has tended to take some of the heat out of the issue. Nonetheless, there remain important and contending pressures on the issue of European integration. On the one side, Europhiles press for further integration. On the side of the Euro-skeptics, there is pressure in the other direction; some anti-Europeans press for British withdrawal from the Union.

Europhiles have pressed for U.K. membership of the single currency and campaigned in favor of the Constitutional Treaty and the Lisbon Treaty. When the euro came into existence, various bodies were set up to advocate British membership. Supporters in both parties came together with various business figures to make the case: They joined established bodies, such as the European Movement. The CBI expressed some support for joining, but it did not campaign and there were known to be divisions among its members on the issue. The British Chambers of Commerce also expressed support, but again, did not campaign on the issue. A new campaign was launched early in 2009 to press the case for membership. "In the calamitous circumstances of manifest economic disaster, it is difficult to believe that British membership of the euro could be other than the inevitable consequence of this new situation," wrote Brendan Donnelly, the director of the Federal Trust.[28]

When the Constitutional Treaty was being debated, Europhiles made the case for ratification and argued this should be achieved through Parliament—the same as with previous treaties—and not through a referendum. This has also been the argument that they deployed in respect of the Lisbon Treaty. After Tony Blair had accepted the case for a referendum on the Constitutional Treaty, they supported the Government's stance when the Lisbon Treaty was negotiated: Namely, that it was not the same as the Constitutional

Treaty and therefore there was no need and no commitment for a referendum on the treaty.

Euro-skeptics have argued vigorously, both against a single currency and against ratification of the Constitutional Treaty and then the Lisbon Treaty. Various established Euro-skeptical bodies (such as the Bruges Group and the European Foundation) opposed the single currency and were joined by several new organizations. Some politicians, previously regarded as supporters of European integration, formed "New Europe": This supported British membership in the European Union but opposed monetary union. Opposition to, or disquiet about, membership in a single currency was also voiced by the Institute of Directors and the Federation of Small Businesses. The global economic crisis of 2008 and 2009 was seen as making the case for staying out of the single currency, enabling the United Kingdom to maintain its independence in determining its economic policies. It was not tied in to policies determined by France and Germany.

Opponents have generally been able to call in aid popular opinion. Opinion polls have shown a majority of respondents opposed to membership of the single currency: In May 2003, for example, a Populus poll for the *Sun* newspaper found that 63 percent of respondents would vote against a single currency; only 31 percent would vote in favor. The same poll found that an overwhelming majority supported a referendum on any treaty designed to give extra powers to the European Union and that, in any referendum on whether the United Kingdom should sign up to a European constitution giving extra powers to the European Union, 57 percent would vote against and only 31 percent would vote in favor. It was results such as this that were believed to make the government wary of signing up to a single currency and relieved when the Constitutional Treaty was lost in referendums in France and the Netherlands, thus making a referendum unnecessary in the United Kingdom. Fears of losing a referendum on the Lisbon Treaty were also believed to have induced the government not to endorse a referendum.

Whereas there was pressure to move the United Kingdom in the direction of further integration, Euro-skeptics and anti-Europeans were pressing for the government to move in the other direction. Some went so far as to press for the United Kingdom to withdraw from membership. They argued that, like many other independent countries, the United Kingdom would be able to survive on its own. Indeed, they argued that the moves toward globalization in trade rendered organizations like the European Union less relevant. They favored cooperation among independent nation states, rather than imposition through a supranational body that created significant tariff barriers. Europhiles argued the case for the benefits of membership. Former Tory deputy prime minister, Michael Heseltine, at the launch of Britain in Europe in October 1999, declared: "Whether we like it or not, what happens in Europe is inseparable from what happens to our own trade, employment, investment, and industry."[29]

Whereas Europhiles have not been able to persuade popular opinion to support moves toward greater integration, Euro-skeptics and anti-Europeans have not been able to sway the public to support moves to leave the European Union. Though public opinion in the 1970s tended to favor leaving the EC, the mood changed in the 1980s, with majorities supporting continued membership. The gap narrowed in the 1990s, but in the twenty-first century there appears popular support for the United Kingdom remaining in the European Union. The 2003 Populus poll, for example, found that in a referendum on whether the United Kingdom should leave or stay in the European Union, 54 percent of respondents would vote to stay in and 31 percent would vote to leave. Though opponents of the European Union may take some comfort from the fact that almost one in three respondents would vote to leave the European Union, the gap is much wider than it was in the 1990s. Nonetheless, the level of support has enabled the UKIP to gain seats in the European Parliament and employ it as a platform for making the case for British withdrawal.

The debate over "Europe" thus remains hotly contested, though the debate is notable more for its breadth than its depth. Members of the public tend to have a view on issues such as a single currency, but in the twenty-first century the issue of European integration is not one that ranks among their political priorities. The government for its part has had to walk a tightrope, playing a part as a full member of the European Union while having to keep a wary eye on public opinion at home.

NOTES

1. See A. King, *Britain Says Yes* (American Enterprise Institute, 1977), pp. 2–7.
2. The nephew of Macmillan's wife had married John Kennedy's sister Kathleen.
3. M. Camps, *Britain and the European Community 1955–1963* (Oxford University Press, 1964), p. 336.
4. See the comments of E. Heath, *Our Community* (Conservative Political Centre, 1977), p. 4.
5. H. Macmillan, *Pointing the Way* (Macmillan, 1972), p. 310.
6. On the first two applications, see R. J. Lieber, *British Politics and European Unity* (University of California Press, 1970); and U. Kitzinger, *The Second Try* (Pergamon, 1968).
7. See P. Norton, *Dissension in the House of Commons 1945–1974* (Macmillan, 1975), pp. 395–398; and U. Kitzinger, *Diplomacy and Persuasion* (Thames and Hudson, 1973), Ch. 13 and Appendix 1.
8. The treaty was later approved in a second Danish referendum.
9. P. Lynch, "British politics and Europe," *Politics Review,* 13 (4), 2004, p. 18.
10. A. Seldon, *Blair* (The Free Press, 2004), pp. 329–330.
11. Seldon, *Blair,* p. 328.
12. S. D. Lee, *Best for Britain? The Politics and Legacy of Gordon Brown* (Oneworld Publications, 2007), p. 201.
13. Lee, *Best for Britain?* p. 210.
14. A. Page, "Balancing Supremacy: EU Membership and the Constitution," in P. Giddings and G. Drewry (eds.), *Britain in the European Union* (Palgrave Macmillan, 2005), p. 40.
15. See P. Birkinshaw, *European Public Law* (Butterworths, 2003), Ch. 7; P. Giddings and G. Drewry (eds.), *Britain in the European Union* (Palgrave Macmillan, 2004);

P Norton, *Parliament in British Politics* (Palgrave Macmillan, 2005), Ch. 7; and R Rogers and R Walters, *How Parliament Works*, 6th ed. (Pearson/Longman, 2006), Ch 12.

16. C. S. Jensen, "Neo-functionalism," in M. Cini (ed.), *European Union Politics* (Oxford University Press, 2003), pp. 80–92.
17. M. Cini, "Intergovernmentalism," in M. Cini (ed.), *European Union Politics* (Oxford University Press, 2003), pp. 93–108.
18. See B. Rosamond, "New Theories of European Integration," in M. Cini (ed.), *European Union Politics* (Oxford University Press, 2003), pp. 109–27.
19. See S. George, *An Awkward Partner* (Oxford University Press, 1990).
20. S. D. Lee, *Best for Britain? The Politics and Legacy of Gordon Brown* (Oneworld Publications, 2007), p. 210.
21. R. Whitaker and P. Lynch, "Where does power lie in the European Union?" *Politics Review*, 18 (4), 2009, p. 10.
22. D. Judge and D. Earnshaw, *The European Parliament*, 2nd ed. (Palgrave Macmillan, 2008), p. 66.
23. See P. Norton, "How Many Bicameral Legislatures Are There?" *The Journal of Legislative Studies*, Vol. 10(4), 2004, pp. 6–7.
24. See R. Corbett, F. Jacobs, and M. Shackleton, *The European Parliament*, 7th ed. (John Harper, 2007), pp. 293–303.
25. The number was reduced by one shortly after the group was formed, when the whip was withdrawn from one Conservative MEP who contested (and won) a place as a Vice-President of the Parliament, standing against the official candidate of the group.
26. M. Thatcher, *Britain and Europe* (Conservative Political Centre, 1988), p. 4. This pamphlet constitutes the text of Thatcher's speech.
27. See P. Norton, "The Conservative Party: 'In Office but not in Power,'" in A. King (ed.), *New Labour Triumphs: Britain at the Polls* (Chatham House, 1998), p. 94.
28. B. Donnelly, "Europe and Its Policies," 16 January 2009: http://en.schumansquare.eu/screens/blogPage/viewBlog/sw_viewBlog.php?idTheme=6&idContribution=427.
29. *The Guardian*, 15 October 1999.

CHAPTER

10

The New Assemblies
Government beyond the Center

The United States is a federal nation. As such, autonomous and constitutionally protected powers are vested in both federal and state government. Article 1, section 8, of the Constitution enumerates the powers of Congress. The tenth amendment stipulates that powers not delegated to the United States by the Constitution, nor prohibited by it to the states, "are reserved to the States respectively, or to the people." The Constitution thus prescribes and protects two layers of government. Below those two levels there is a third: local government.

The position in the United Kingdom stands in marked contrast to that in the United States. Recent years have seen some notable changes in subnational government, with elected assemblies being created in Scotland, Wales, and Northern Ireland. However, the new structure differs from that of the United States in three ways.

First, as we have seen in Chapter 4, the United Kingdom remains formally a unitary state. The unitary state has sometimes been described as a union state, a number of countries having been brought together under a single crown and parliament. However, it is a unitary state in that state power resides at the center. The Queen-in-Parliament is the constitutionally supreme organ of power. New layers of government are created by an act of Parliament and can be removed by an act of Parliament. Thus, for example, Northern Ireland had a Parliament at Stormont, just outside Belfast, for fifty years, from 1922 to 1972. That parliament was established by an act of Parliament and, as we shall see, it was suspended and later abolished by an act of Parliament.

Second, the devolution of powers to elected assemblies in different parts of the United Kingdom has been termed asymmetrical devolution. The devolved bodies that have been created are not equal in terms of the powers vested in them. Not all parts of the United Kingdom have elected assemblies. Elected assemblies have been established in the least populated parts. The bulk of the population live, as we have seen in Chapter 1, in England. There is no elected assembly for England. Although some governmental bodies operate at a regional level in England, there are no elected assemblies in the English regions.

Third, the method of election employed for the elected assemblies differs from that used for elections in the United States and for elections to the House of Commons. The changes that have taken place in the United Kingdom have meant that the framework of government at the beginning of the twenty-first century differs markedly from that which existed throughout the twentieth century. However, it has not moved very much in the direction of the form of government that exists in the United States. As we shall see, there are some in the United Kingdom who would like it to do so.

The devolution of power to Scotland and Wales differs from that to Northern Ireland, which—as we have mentioned—has recent experience of its own parliament, and so deserves separate consideration. The history in each case is important for explaining the creation of the new assemblies. Given that some governmental bodies operate at a regional level in England—and there is pressure for the creation of elected assemblies in the English regions—we shall look briefly at regional government in England.

SCOTLAND AND WALES

Electors in Scotland went to the polls in May 1999 to elect the members of a Scottish parliament, a parliament with legislative and tax-raising powers. On the same day, electors in Wales went to the polls to elect members of a Welsh assembly, a body with power to determine the allocation of the Welsh budget. The last time that Scotland had a parliament was nearly three hundred years before. It ceased to exist when the Act of Union was agreed, the Scottish and English parliaments being superseded by a single British Parliament. The Welsh had never previously had an assembly. Pressure for the creation of both bodies built up in the last four decades of the century and culminated in referendums in Scotland and Wales in 1997 and the passage in 1998 of the Scotland Act and the Government of Wales Act.

Demands for Devolution

The demands for some form of "home rule" for Scotland and Wales were not confined to the latter decades of the twentieth century. The Liberal Party advocated the more radical proposal of federalism during most of its history.[1] Some form of home rule for Scotland and Wales had been advocated by the Scottish National(SNP) and Plaid Cymru (PC) parties, respectively, since their formation earlier in the twentieth century, but the main achievement of the two parties prior to the 1960s was simply to have survived. This situation was to change in the 1960s, when each party won one seat at a parliamentary by-election and also made gains in local elections. The apparent growing strength of nationalist sentiment was sufficient to encourage the Labour government to establish a Royal Commission on the Constitution; announced in 1968, it was appointed in 1969 and reported in 1973. It recommended some form of devolved government. By this time there had also emerged what A. H. Birch referred to as the "eruptive factor,"[2] North Sea oil. The SNP was able to play on the argument that the location of the offshore oil fields meant the oil was Scotland's as much as anyone's and that revenue from it would be sufficient to make a Scottish government viable. By playing on the expectation of a rising middle class in Scotland, whose expectations had been left unfulfilled by the Westminster government, the SNP began to make electoral inroads into the strength of both main parties. By playing on the cultural fears of the Welsh people, the PC had some impact in Wales. In the February 1974 general election, the SNP won 7 of the 71 Scottish seats and the PC won 2 of the 36 Welsh seats. In the October general election, the SNP increased the number of seats won to 11 and the PC to 3. Of the SNP's 11 seats, 9 were won from the Conservatives but the party had come second in 35 out of 41 Labour-held seats. In total number of votes received, it was the second largest party in Scotland.

The Labour government that was returned to office in 1974 saw the prospect of the SNP developing into the dominant party in Scotland and, in so doing, ruining Labour's chances of winning future elections (both Scotland and Wales constitute important electoral bases for the party; see Chapter 5). To respond to the nationalist challenge, the government put forward proposals for a form of devolved government in both Scotland and Wales. However, the proposals ran into opposition from the Conservative Party. Many Labour members also found them unpalatable. A number were opposed to devolution, seeing it as a step on the road to eventual independence. Some MPs from the north of England disliked devolution because they felt it would effectively discriminate against regions that were not to have similar assemblies. Given the opposition to its proposals, the government agreed that the devolution proposals would be submitted to referendums in Scotland and Wales. MPs carried amendments, against the government's wishes, stipulating that 40 percent of eligible voters had to vote "yes" in each referendum for devolution to take place.

The referendums in Scotland and Wales were held on March 1, 1979, and were preceded by vigorous campaigns in the two countries. In Wales, it appeared that the prospect of devolved government aroused suspicion among non–Welsh-speaking inhabitants—the majority—and was not gaining overwhelming support. In Scotland, some opponents feared devolution would constitute the thin end of the wedge, leading to an eventual breakup of the United Kingdom; supporters argued that it was necessary in order to maintain the unity of the kingdom. On March 1, 950,330 voters in Wales voted "no" to the devolution proposals; only 243,048 voted "yes." In Scotland, the result was a close one: 1,230,937 people voted "yes," and 1,153,502 voted "no." Although a slight majority of those who voted had opted for the devolution proposals, the number voting "yes" did not constitute 40 percent of all eligible voters. As a consequence, the Cabinet decided not to proceed with devolution, a decision that precipitated Nationalist MPs withdrawing their support from the government. This loss of Nationalist support deprived the government of a majority in a vote of confidence on March 28, 1979. The result was a general election and the return of a Conservative government. In the new Parliament, the government introduced the relevant motions for the repeal of the two acts and both motions were carried.

In the wake of the 1979 general election, it looked as though devolution was no longer an important issue on the political agenda. The SNP won only two seats in the election, as did PC. The new government was not keen to pursue the issue—Prime Minister Margaret Thatcher being a notable opponent of devolution—and other issues came to the fore. However, from the early 1980s onward, the subject began to reemerge as a feature of debate. Initially, much of the running was made by the Liberal Party and then the newly formed SDP, but the Labour Party, which had maintained a commitment to some form of devolution throughout the decade, also committed itself to support ten regional assemblies in England as well as assemblies in Scotland and Wales. The official Conservative policy remained opposed to devolution, Prime Minister John Major being just as firm an opponent as his predecessor. The government emphasized the importance of the union and pursued a limited political initiative in the context of that union: In 1993, it strengthened the position of the Scottish Office and a number of parliamentary bodies responsible for Scottish affairs.

The calls for some form of devolution continued to be heard, especially in Scotland. When EC leaders met for a summit in Edinburgh in December 1992, more than 25,000 people marched through the streets to demonstrate in support of Scottish home rule. Much was made of the fact that Scotland was governed by a Conservative government, even though a majority of MPs elected from Scotland were Labour MPs. The same case was made in Wales. In the 1997 general election, all main parties except for the Conservative Party supported devolution. In its election manifesto, the Labour Party declared that "we will meet the demand for decentralisation of power to Scotland and Wales, once established in referendums." As soon as possible after the election, it declared legislation would be introduced to provide for referendums. The party proposed a Scottish parliament with law-making powers—taking control of those matters controlled by the Scottish Office (the government department for Scotland)—and limited powers to vary rates of taxation. The Welsh assembly would not have powers to enact primary legislation nor to vary tax rates. Instead, it would have powers of secondary legislation (order-making powers granted by act of Parliament) and have control of functions carried out by the Welsh Office (the government department for Wales). Once the proposals had been approved in the referendums, bills would be brought forward to establish the new bodies.

The Labour Party won the 1997 general election by a decisive margin and promptly introduced legislation to provide for referendums. There were no threshold requirements: A simple majority was to suffice. The referendums were held in September 1997. Voters in Scotland had two questions to answer, whether they agreed with the proposal for a Scottish parliament, and if they supported having a parliament with tax varying powers. Voters in Wales were asked whether they agreed or not with the government's proposals for a Welsh assembly.

The arguments advanced in favor of devolution centered on both consent and effectiveness. Decisions taken in Scotland and Wales by elected government, it was argued, would be more efficient and effective because of a better appreciation of the area—its needs as well as its resources—and additionally would enhance consent by being closer to the people. Power would be removed from a distant government at Westminster and given—restored, in the Scottish case—to the people. Devolving governmental responsibilities would also serve to reduce pressure on central government and on Parliament. Both government and people, it was felt, would benefit.

Against this, Conservatives, as well as some Labour MPs, expressed the fear that devolution could lead to a breakup of the United Kingdom. They also opposed it on the grounds that it would introduce another expensive and unnecessary layer of government and that it would exacerbate economic inequality between the regions. Economically, it was argued, wealthy regions would fight to retain as much of their wealth as possible. Among the poorer parts of the United Kingdom to suffer would be Scotland and Wales; their small populations and limited resources made them economically dependent on the rest of the United Kingdom. The argument, in short, was that more government was not necessarily better government.

The "yes" campaign made most of the running in both countries, especially in Scotland. On September 11, voters in Scotland voted decisively—albeit in a turnout lower than in general elections—in favor of a Scottish parliament and in favor of a parliament with tax-varying powers. The voters in Wales went to the polls on September 18. As the figures in Table 10.1 reveal, the result in the province—where the turnout was only 50 percent—was not so decisive. By a majority of a 6,721 (0.6 percent of the poll), they

TABLE 10.1

REFERENDUM RESULTS: SCOTLAND AND WALES, 1997

Scotland	A Scottish Parliament	Tax-varying powers
Agree	1,775,045 (74.3%)	1,512,889 (63.5%)
Disagree	614,400 (25.7%)	870,263 (36.5%)
Turnout: 60.4%		
Wales	**A Welsh Assembly**	
Yes	559,419 (50.3%)	
No	552,698 (49.7%)	
Turnout: 50%		

voted for the assembly. There was a notable regional divide. Counties in the eastern half of Wales showed majorities voting against and counties in the western half had majorities voting in favor.

Following the "yes" vote in both referendums, the government introduced legislation to set up a Scottish parliament and a Welsh assembly. The Scotland Act and the Government of Wales Act were enacted in 1998. The former provided for an elected Parliament in Scotland and the latter for an elected assembly in Wales, with elections to take place to both bodies in 1999.

The Scottish Parliament

The parliament has power to legislate on all matters other than those that are explicitly reserved to the U.K. Parliament. Under Schedule 5 of the Scotland Act, the principal reserved matters are the Constitution (a rare reference in statute, given that—as we have seen—there is no codified document), foreign affairs, defense, the civil service, financial and economic matters, national security, immigration and nationality, trade and industry (covering such matters as competition and consumer protection), broadcasting, energy (nuclear energy, coal, gas and oil), social security, and employment. Although social policy as such is not a reserved matter, particular social issues are reserved to the U.K. Parliament, notably abortion and the misuse of drugs. By virtue of the doctrine of parliamentary sovereignty, the U.K. Parliament has the power to legislate on any matters that fall within the competence of the Scottish Parliament, but the convention has developed that the U.K. Parliament will only do so with the consent of the Scottish Parliament.

In practice, this means that the Scottish Parliament can legislate on a wide range of issues. They include the environment, education, health, agriculture, local government, the police, housing, planning, economic development, tourism, the courts, criminal justice and most aspects of the criminal and civil law, and some aspects of transport. The parliament also has the power to vary the standard rate of income tax by 3 pence in the pound. In addition, various matters that are reserved have been devolved to the Scottish Parliament to administer. This is known as executive devolution.

The parliament is elected for a fixed four-year term. Elections take place on the first Thursday in May every four years, though there are circumstances in which an election can take place at another time. The parliament has 129 members, 73 elected for individual constituencies on the first-past-the-post method of election and 56 additional members drawn on a proportional basis from party lists drawn up for each of eight larger regions. In the elections to the parliament, each elector is able to cast two votes: one for a constituency Member of the Scottish Parliament (MSP) and one for the party of their choice.

Once the parliament is elected, a Scottish executive is formed. The head of the executive is the first minister—in effect, a prime minister for Scotland—and the first minister nominates other ministers and junior ministers. (Two law officers—the lord advocate and the solicitor general for Scotland—

also serve as members.) The first minister is formally appointed by the queen, but the nomination has to be approved by the parliament. The first minister's nominees for other ministerial offices also have to be approved by the parliament before they are submitted to the queen. The ministers forming the executive operate on the basis of collective responsibility. They work, like the U.K. government, through departments (see Chapter 8). Where there are some subjects that cut across departmental responsibilities, cabinet committees are formed. Ministers are serviced by the civil service, in essence the civil servants that were previously employed in the Scottish Office.

The first election to the parliament took place on May 6, 1999. Labour emerged as the largest single party, but it failed to gain an absolute majority. The outcome of the election meant that Labour either had to form a minority government or else form a coalition with another party. In the event, it pursued the option of a coalition with the Liberal Democratic Party. After some intense negotiations, a coalition was formed and various policies agreed on. Labour held the post of first minister and the Liberal Democrats the post of the deputy first minister. The new government enacted various policies that were notably different to those enacted in England and Wales, including the abolition of university tuition fees and a less restrictive freedom of information act. In the first parliament, 60 acts were passed. In the 2003 elections, both coalition parties lost seats—the main gainers being third parties, notably the Scottish Greens and the Scottish Socialist Party (Table 10.2)—but retained a sufficient number of seats to maintain a majority. The coalition thus remained in office. However, the SNP subsequently gained in popularity—Labour suffered from accusations of poor leadership and was overshadowed by a resurgent SNP under Alex Salmond, a former leader who had returned

TABLE 10.2

ELECTIONS TO THE SCOTTISH PARLIAMENT

Party	Seats won		
	1999	2003	2007
Labour	56	50	46
SNP	35	27	47
Conservative	18	18	17
Liberal	17	17	16
Scottish Socialist	1	6	0
Independent Labour	1	0	0
Green	1	7	2
Scottish Senior Citizens Unity	0	1	0
Independents	0	3	0
Margo MacDonald	0	0	1
Total:	*129*	*129*	*129*

to take the helm. In the 2007 elections, the SNP won one more seat than Labour. Even Labour and the Liberal Democrats combined could not command an absolute majority. Labour was perceived as having "lost" and the SNP formed a minority administration. Scotland thus acquired a new government—one under a party that devolution had been designed to undermine. The SNP, though, was seen as the beneficiary of the unpopularity of the Labour government in London rather than having won on the basis of support for Scottish independence. One survey after the election found that almost one-third of SNP voters did not favor independence.[3] As a minority administration, the SNP could not in any event take steps to implement a policy opposed by the other parties. The global economic crisis in 2008 and 2009 was also seen to undermine the case for independence. The financial collapse of Iceland—often held up as a small independent country that Scotland could emulate—raised doubts about Scotland's capacity to cope with a similar crisis. Nonetheless, forming an administration gave the SNP governmental responsibility, a high public profile, and the opportunity to challenge Labour for the mantle of the dominant party in Scotland.

The Parliament established a regular routine,[4] the chamber sitting on Wednesday afternoons and all day Thursday, but with extensive use being made of committees, with each committee meeting weekly or fortnightly.[5] The committees are listed in Table 10.3. There are two principal types. Mandatory

TABLE 10.3

COMMITTEES IN THE SCOTTISH PARLIAMENT 2009

Mandatory committees

[remits sets out in standing orders]

Equal opportunities

European and external affairs

Finance

Public Audit

Public petitions

Standards, procedures and public appointments

Subordinate legislation

Subject committees

[remits based on the responsibilities of the executive]

Economy, energy and tourism

Education, lifelong learning and culture

Health and sport

Justice

Local government and communities

Rural affairs and environment

Transport, infrastructure and climate change

committees are established at the start of each session and their terms of reference are determined by parliamentary rules. Subject committees are usually established at the start of a session and cover topics falling within the responsibility of the executive. The Parliament may also establish temporary committees to consider particular issues. Each committee usually has between 5 and 15 members, reflecting the party balance in the chamber. The chamber approves who shall sit in the committees. MSPs who are not members of a committee are entitled to attend and can take part in public proceedings but not vote. The committees have the power to summon evidence and a great deal of time is spent taking oral evidence from witnesses, including members of the executive. Committees undertake inquiries as well as examine bills. In the first decade of the Parliament's existence, the committees conducted more than 250 inquiries. They not only examine bills introduced by the executive but may also initiate bills of their own. In practice, most time is taken up considering executive bills. The Parliament also has a public petitions committee to consider petitions submitted by individuals or groups. The committee can refer petitions to other committees for further consideration. In the first decade of its operation, more than 1,000 petitions were submitted.

Many of the features of the parliament were designed to establish a new style of politics within the United Kingdom, moving away from the adversary politics that characterized the Westminster parliament. The electoral system facilitated multiparty competition, of the sort seen in continental European countries, and the chamber was shaped in a semi-circle. (The parliament was initially housed in a temporary venue before moving to a purpose-built site at Holyrood, opposite Holyrood House, the Queen's official residence in Edinburgh.) The focus on committees was also designed to move away from the emphasis on party conflict in the chamber seen in Westminster. In the event, though the parliament operates in many areas very differently from the Westminster parliament, the politics of the institution are still marked by party conflict. Many of the politicians who established the Scottish Parliament were rooted in Westminster politics (all bar one of the first ministers have served as MPs at Westminster) and the deep animosity between the Labour Party and the SNP has fuelled notable partisan conflicts.

The National Assembly for Wales

When it was created, the Welsh assembly had no powers to make primary legislation or to vary rates of taxation. What it did, in effect, was to take over powers previously vested in the cabinet minister responsible for Wales (the secretary of state for Wales). The assembly had the power to "develop and implement policy" in a number of areas, including agriculture, culture, economic development, education, the environment, housing, social services, and transport. Though it could not enact primary legislation, it could exercise the power—previously vested in the secretary of state for Wales—to promulgate secondary legislation, that is, orders permitted to be made under a parent act of Parliament.

The limited powers vested in the assembly led to calls for more powers to be transferred to it from Westminster. The assembly wanted to be more like the Scottish Parliament. Though unwilling to concede powers to it on a par with those vested in the Scottish Parliament, the U.K. government did achieve passage of the Government of Wales Act 2006 designed to achieve some measure of rolling devolution. Under the Act, the U.K. Parliament may approve orders (legislative competence orders) that allow for legislative powers to be given to the assembly in relation to specified matters which fall within fields in which assembly ministers are able to exercise executive functions. The act also contains provisions for legislative power to be transferred to the assembly (similar to the position in Scotland) following approval by a referendum in Wales. Though various orders have been approved transferring various legislative powers, the provision for a referendum has not been triggered. The assembly thus continues to extend its powers on a sporadic basis, subject to the approval of Parliament at Westminster. The 2006 Act also separated the assembly from the Welsh executive: under the original Government of Wales Act they had formed a body corporate, a situation that proved essentially unworkable.

The assembly usually meets in plenary session on Tuesdays and Wednesdays and makes use of both subject and legislative committees. There are two official languages, English and Welsh, with simultaneous translation being provided. Like the Scottish Parliament, the assembly sits for a fixed four-year term. It has 60 members, elected by the same method (the additional member system) as members of the Scottish Parliament. Forty members of the assembly are elected for individual constituencies by the first-past-the-post method of election and 20 additional members are drawn on a proportional basis from party lists drawn up in four regions. The assembly scrutinizes the actions of the Welsh Assembly Government. Under the 2006 Government of Wales Act, a first minister, up to 12 ministers and deputy ministers, and a counsel general may be appointed. The government is assisted by a civil service, essentially the civil service that previously worked in the Welsh Office, the department headed by the secretary of state for Wales.

In the first elections to the assembly in 1999, Labour emerged as the largest single party. However, despite Wales being seen as a post-war Labour stronghold, it failed to achieve an absolute majority (see Table 10.4). It sought initially to govern as a minority administration but in 2000 joined with the Liberal Democrats to form a coalition. In the 2003 elections, Labour won 30 out of the 60 seats and, when the presiding officer and deputy presiding officer were nominated from other parties, this enabled it to govern as a majority administration. However, it slipped into minority status in 2005 when one of its members left the party. In the 2007 election, the party lost support: it was not good in promoting its message and was overshadowed by the performance of the Welsh National Party, PC, and the Conservatives.[6] It lost seats. Initially it looked as if the three opposition parties (Conservatives, PC, the Liberal Democrats) would form a coalition—they negotiated a joint

TABLE 10.4

ELECTIONS TO THE NATIONAL ASSEMBLY FOR WALES

Number of seats won

Party	1999	2003	2007
Labour	28	30	26
Plaid Cymru	17	12	15
Conservatives	9	11	12
Liberal Democrats	6	6	6
Others	0	1	1

accord, the *All Wales Accord*—but this eventually floundered because of splits in the ranks of the Liberal Democrats. Eventually, a coalition was formed between Labour and its historical rival, Plaid Cymru. Labour held out the possibility of a referendum on the creation of a Welsh parliament. There thus came into being what has been dubbed a red-green coalition. Whereas Labour in Scotland has witnessed several changes of leader, the Welsh administration was led from 2001 to 2009 by the same person, Rhodri Morgan, a former member of the Westminster parliament.

There remains pressure for further change to the constitutional arrangements in Wales, but with no agreement on any one option. A survey in 2008 commissioned by the Welsh assembly found that just under 40 percent favored a parliament for Wales (up from 18 percent in 1997), just over 30 percent preferred to retain an assembly, 15 percent did not want devolution (down from 37 percent in 1997), and 10 percent favored independence (compared with 13 percent in 1997).[7] The assembly and the government also favored having a stronger role, with more powers devolved from Westminster to Cardiff.

NORTHERN IRELAND

The demands for a new form of government in Northern Ireland have borne little relationship to the demands for devolution in Scotland and Wales. The debate about the future of the province is longstanding: it has existed ever since Northern Ireland came into being. The last four decades of the twentieth century were marked by violence and by the persistence of those engaged in the debate adopting mutually exclusive positions. However, by the end of the 1990s, a political solution was being pursued. After long and tortuous negotiations—conducted against a background of mistrust and continuing conflict—a new, cross-party power-sharing government, drawing together the two parties seen as being at the two extremes of the political spectrum, was formed in 2007. The creation of the new government marked a new era in the history of Northern Ireland.

Background

The history of Ireland has been a depressing and troubled one extending over many centuries and marked by bitter conflict between the English and the Irish and, within Ireland, between indigenous Catholic Irish and Protestant Scottish Presbyterian settlers. The Irish uprising in 1916 forced the U.K. government to recognize Irish demands for self-determination. In 1920 the Westminster Parliament passed the Government of Ireland Act, which provided for home rule in the country and created two parliaments: one for the six northern counties, part of the region of Ulster, and one for the remaining 26 counties. The provisions for the southern counties were stillborn. The continuing troubles in the country resulted in the Treaty of Ireland of 1922, which realized the Irish Free State. Ireland was partitioned and the provisions of the 1920 act applied in the new province of Northern Ireland. A bicameral parliament was established at Stormont, from which an executive was drawn. The new government of the province exercised a number of devolved powers and, in exercising those powers, was not much hindered by the Westminster government. British politicians were not keen to be drawn again into the bog of Irish politics.

The province of Northern Ireland was created at the forceful behest of the Protestant community of the North. Largely derived from Scottish Presbyterian stock, it had no wish to be engulfed within a Catholic Irish state. Within the new province, it was dominant. It was not, though, the only community within the province: one-third of the population was Catholic. The religious divide between the two communities was reinforced by social, economic, and educational differences as well as by centuries of ingrained animosity. Catholic children were educated in Catholic schools, were taught Irish history, played Gaelic games, and lived in Catholic communities. Protestant children were taught British history, played non-Gaelic games, lived in Protestant communities, and were taught to regard Catholics as threatening to the existence of the province. Catholics, in turn, looked on Protestants as being gravely in error. The divisions ran deep. The Protestants continued proudly to celebrate the victory of Protestant William of Orange in the Battle of the Boyne in 1690. Indeed, in the new province the anniversary of the victory was made a public holiday.

Northern Ireland after 1922 became for all intents and purposes a one-party province. The Unionists Party, representing the Protestants, regularly won two-thirds of the seats at Stormont (there was little alternation of seats from one party to the other) and formed the government, enjoying uninterrupted power. Despite occasional violence by the self-styled Irish Republican Army (the IRA), which wanted a united Ireland and was prepared to engage in terrorist activities to achieve it, the Stormont government enjoyed sufficient coercive powers to impose its will and did so in a manner that favored the Protestants. Catholics were discriminated against in the allocation of houses and jobs and were forced to live in an environment where they felt themselves to be second-class citizens. There was little they could do within the existing political structure, a position analogous to that faced by African Americans in the deep south of the United States.

"The Troubles"

The position in the province was to change in the latter half of the 1960s. A new, relatively liberal Unionist Prime Minister, Terence O'Neill, sought better relations with the Republic of Ireland, a move that caused consternation in the more traditional ranks of his party. On the Catholic side, the steps taken by the O'Neill government were seen as being too little and too late. A civil rights movement sprang up in the province, inspired by the experience of the United States. The Civil Rights Association was formed in 1967 and was joined the following year by a more revolutionary organization, the People's Democracy. They organized demonstrations and marches. These resulted in a vigorous reaction from the police force, the Royal Ulster Constabulary, as well as from various Protestant groups. Clashes between protesters and their opponents erupted into civil disorder that the police and their auxiliary forces, the so-called B-Specials (despised in the Catholic community), were unable to contain. In August 1969, at the request of the Northern Ireland cabinet, the Westminster government sent troops to the province to maintain order. In return for such action, the government insisted on phasing out the B-Specials and introducing full civil rights for Roman Catholics. Ensuring that the latter demand was complied with was another matter.

The arrival of troops was initially welcomed by Catholics in the province. However, the use of troops to support the civil authorities—in other words, the Protestant government and the police—and the search of Catholic areas for arms produced a rapid dissipation of that support. A "shooting war" broke out between the IRA and the British army in February 1971. In August the British government decided to intern without trial suspected IRA leaders. Instead of lessening the violence, the action appeared to exacerbate it: internment aroused greater sympathy for the IRA cause among the Catholic community, and the interned leaders were replaced by more extreme followers. At the same time, tension increased between the Stormont and Westminster governments, the former contending that the latter was not doing enough to counter the activities of the IRA. The Stormont government even made a request for troops in the province to be put under its control. The request was denied.

Violence in the province became more marked toward the end of 1971, with more than a hundred explosions a month. In the first two months of 1972, 49 people were killed and another 257 injured as a result of bombings and gunshots. In an attempt to break the deadlock in the province, the Conservative government at Westminster decided to pursue some form of political initiative. The government's proposals included periodic plebiscites on the issue of the border, a start to the phasing out of internment, and the transfer of responsibility for law and order from Stormont to London. The last proposal proved unacceptable to the Northern Ireland cabinet, which made clear that it would resign if the proposal was implemented. In consequence, Prime Minister Edward Heath informed the House of Commons on March 24, 1972, that the British government was left with no alternative but to assume full and direct responsibility for the administration of Northern Ireland until such time as a political solution to the problem of the province could be achieved. To give effect to the government's decision, the Northern Ireland (Temporary Provisions) Bill was quickly passed by Parliament, enjoying the support of the Labour opposition as well as of the Liberals. The new act suspended the Stormont parliament and transferred its powers to the Westminster government. A new Northern Ireland Office was established under a secretary of state.

Attempts to Achieve a Solution

The task of succeeding Northern Ireland secretaries was twofold: to try to maintain security within the province, doing so in a way that would not alienate either community (the Protestant community by not doing enough, the Catholic by doing too much), and at the same time to seek a political solution that was acceptable to both. Various political initiatives were attempted since 1972, each usually failing to mobilize the cross-community support necessary to sustain it.

The first attempt to reach a solution—a power-sharing elected assembly in 1974—was destroyed by a province-wide strike organized by the Protestant Ulster Workers Council. The new Labour government in London was unwilling to use its coercive powers to try to break the strike. The executive resigned. It had lasted four months. An elected constitutional convention in 1975 failed to break the deadlock: the Unionist-dominated body issued a report favoring a Stormont-type cabinet government—that is, a reversion to government by the majority party, unhindered by any form of power sharing—which was rejected by the government. A reconvened convention failed to reach agreement. A conference convened at the beginning of 1980 was boycotted by the Ulster Unionist Party. A proposal to create an advisory council of elected officials drawn from the province, to fulfill advisory and reporting functions until such time as a more durable settlement could be reached, was stillborn. It was overshadowed by hunger strikes of IRA prisoners in the Maze prison (demanding various concessions, including the reintroduction of "political status") and by a recommendation from former Prime Minister James Callaghan that the province develop into a "broadly independent State." In 1982 an attempt was made to introduce a form of "rolling devolution." This involved the election of a 78-member assembly under a system of proportional representation. The concept of rolling devolution allowed the assembly to propose at any time the transfer of executive responsibilities for any particular department to its own jurisdiction. The ultimate objective was full devolution, but to be achieved at a pace made possible by the assembly itself. In practice, the assembly proved short-lived. The elections to it, in October 1982, provided a publicity coup for Sinn Féin, the political wing of the Provisional IRA: it garnered one-tenth of the first-preference votes cast and saw five of its candidates elected. SDLP as well as Sinn Féin candidates elected to the assembly boycotted its sittings. Only Unionists attended. In March 1986 they decided not to fulfill the assembly's statutory functions in protest of the Anglo-Irish Agreement. Three months later the government decided to disband the assembly; like its predecessors, it had fallen foul of the lack of consensus it was designed to counter.

The Anglo-Irish Agreement

The Anglo-Irish Agreement was the product of the discussions that had taken place under the aegis of the Anglo-Irish Intergovernmental Council. Signed at Hillsborough Castle in Northern Ireland on November 15, 1985, by the British Prime Minister, Margaret Thatcher, and the *Taoiseach* (prime minister) of the Irish Republic, Dr. Garret Fitzgerald, the agreement had three essential elements. Under Article 1, both governments recognized that "any change in the status of Northern Ireland would only come about with the consent of the majority of the people of Northern Ireland." This was the first time the Irish government had given legal recognition to Northern Ireland's right to self-determination. The British government hoped this part of the agreement would help make the whole document acceptable to the Unionists. The second element was embodied in Articles 2–8, which established the Intergovernmental Conference, chaired by the secretary of state for Northern Ireland and the foreign minister of the republic. Through the conference, the republic was enabled to raise issues on the administration of the province that were of particular concern to the minority community. The committee was an advisory one, with a small secretariat. It became a particular target for Unionist opposition. The third element, covered by Articles 6, 7, and 9, provided for greater cross-border cooperation on security matters, and security became a subject regularly discussed at meetings of the conference. The agreement also dealt with a number of other topics, including the creation of an Anglo-Irish parliamentary body, and this came into being in February 1989.

The first and third elements of the agreement proved insufficient to make it acceptable to the Unionist parties. To them, the Intergovernmental Conference allowed a foreign government the opportunity to interfere in the affairs of the province and constituted a "thin end of the wedge," the first step toward forcing the province into a united Ireland. In protest, all 15 Unionist MPs in the province resigned their seats in December 1985, fighting by-elections as a means of demonstrating popular opposition to the agreement. The move was a partial success: one Unionist failed to achieve reelection; the rest were returned. Their next step was to refuse to fulfill the statutory functions of the Northern Ireland assembly, in effect signing the assembly's death warrant. Their actions failed to dent the government's resolve to persist with the agreement.

Five years after the signing of the agreement, the British government could point to a notable increase in cross-border coordination on security matters. It was also able to claim that the number of deaths and injuries each year attributable to the security position in the province was running well below that of the 1970s. Unionists could point to the fact that the biggest decline predated the agreement taking effect. There was greater contact between the British and Irish governments, with the Irish government agreeing to make some changes to its extradition policy, a contentious issue on which the British government had been pressing for reform for some years. On the British side, various measures had been introduced to meet some of the fears and demands of the nationalist community: an independent commission for complaints against the police, a fair employment act, the extension of the franchise for council elections, and the removal of special protection for the Union flag. Relative to the previous initiatives, the agreement—in terms of substance and longevity—constituted the most successful initiative taken by the British government since the imposition of direct rule.

Despite the Anglo-Irish Agreement—or, in the view of some of its opponents, because of it—the situation in the province remained tense. Ninety-three people were killed in 1988, the same number as in the previous year. The government sought to go beyond, and build on, the agreement in order to reach a political solution.

By the end of the 1980s, the IRA was losing support in the nationalist community, not least because of some of the killings it carried out, including 11 people killed by bombs in a Remembrance Day ceremony and a little girl who was shot. The new Secretary of State for Northern Ireland, Peter Brooke, signaled a willingness to talk and discussions took place between the various parties in 1991 and 1992 before finally ending in November 1992 without reaching overall agreement. However, the government continued discussions, mostly on a bilateral basis, with the Northern Ireland parties and separately with the Irish government on matters of mutual interest, including constitutional issues, under the auspices of the Anglo-Irish Intergovernmental Conference. Discussion between the British and Irish governments was to bear fruit in 1993 with the Downing Street Declaration.

The Downing Street Declaration

The joint declaration on December 15, 1993, known as the Downing Street Declaration, made clear that the consent of a majority of the people in Northern Ireland was required before any constitutional change could come about. The two governments agreed that, following a cessation of violence, democratically mandated parties that had established a commitment to exclusively peaceful methods, and that had shown that they would abide permanently by the democratic process, would be free to participate fully in democratic politics and to join in dialogue in due course between the governments and the political parties on the way ahead.

The text reiterated Northern Ireland's statutory constitutional guarantee and reaffirmed that the British government would uphold the democratic wish of a greater number of the people of Northern Ireland on the issue of whether they preferred to support the Union or a sovereign united Ireland. On this basis the British government reiterated that it had no selfish strategic or economic interest in Northern Ireland and that, were a majority in Northern Ireland to wish it, the government would introduce legislation to bring about a united Ireland. For their part the Irish government accepted that it would be wrong to attempt to impose a united Ireland in the absence of the freely given consent of a majority of the people of Northern Ireland. The Irish government also confirmed that in the event of an overall settlement, they would put forward and support proposals for change in the Irish Constitution, which would fully reflect the principle of consent in Northern Ireland.

The Downing Street Declaration helped create a new political situation, with some notable consequences. In August 1994, the IRA announced a "complete cessation of military operations." This was followed in October by a cease-fire by the loyalist paramilitary bodies. The British government proceeded to enter into talks with the different parties. Both governments launched the Twin Track Initiative in November 1995, the aim of which was to create the conditions necessary for substantive talks to begin early 1996. The initiative established an international body to examine the decommissioning of illegal arms and to undertake preparatory talks designed to establish, if possible, the basis for all-party negotiations. Former U.S. Senator George Mitchell was invited to chair the body. The International Body published its report on January 24, 1996. It concluded that the paramilitaries would not decommission any arms prior to all-party negotiations; set out six principles to which it said all parties should adhere, including a commitment to the fundamental principles of democracy and nonviolence; set out guidelines on decommissioning; and suggested a number of confidence-building measures including, if it were broadly acceptable, an elective process, to take negotiations forward.

The British government accepted the report but the peace process suffered a setback the following month, when the IRA ended its cease-fire and exploded a bomb in Canary Wharf, in London's Docklands, causing massive damage and resulting in two fatalities. The two governments decided to move ahead with all-party negotiations, following a broadly elective process, but with Sinn Féin's participation dependent on an unequivocal restoration of the IRA cease-fire and all parties agreeing to the Mitchell principles of democracy and nonviolence. Elections were held on May 30, 1996, and ten parties were elected to take part in initial negotiations and in a new deliberative Northern Ireland Forum. Multiparty talks opened in June but with Sinn Féin—one of the ten parties—excluded. Time was taken up with agreeing how to proceed before the focus moved to decommissioning of arms. No conclusion was reached. The new forum was also convened, but Sinn Féin, which was eligible to sit, declined to do so, and the SDLP withdrew from participation.

The Good Friday Agreement

The 1997 general election intervened. The new Labour government announced its intention that substantive negotiations should begin in September 1997, with a view to reaching a conclusion by May 1998, when the final outcome would be put to the people of Ireland, north and south, for approval in concurrent referendums. On July 19, 1997, the IRA announced an unequivocal restoration of the cease-fire. After six weeks, the government decided that the cease-fire met the conditions it had set and admitted Sinn Féin to the negotiations. Sinn Féin affirmed its commitment to the Mitchell principles. The two governments also announced the creation of an Independent International Commission on Decommissioning,

All-party negotiations took place from October 1997 through to April 1998. At various points, they looked under threat because of incidents of sectarian violence. However, agreement was reached on April 10, 1998. The agreement—dubbed the Good Friday Agreement—replaced the Anglo-Irish Agreement and was based on the three strands that had formed the basis of the talks. The first, dealing with the arrangements for the governance of Northern Ireland, resulted in a proposal for an 108-member Northern Ireland assembly, elected by STV. It would have responsibility for all legislative and executive matters within the domain of the existing six Northern Ireland government departments. Safeguards were built in to ensure that all sections of the community could participate. There would be an executive committee, with a first minister and a deputy first minister.

The second, dealing with the whole of Ireland, proposed the creation of a North-South Ministerial Council to bring together those with executive responsibilities in Northern Ireland and the Irish government "to develop consultation, co-operation and action within the island of Ireland—including through implementation on an all-island and cross-border basis—on matters of mutual interest within the competences of the Administrations, North and South." Among areas identified for cooperation were agriculture (animal and plant health), education (teacher qualifications and exchanges), transport (strategic planning), environmental protection, tourism, inland fisheries, and urban and rural development.

The third, dealing with relations between Britain and Ireland, proposed a British-Irish Council—dubbed the Council of the Isles—"to promote the harmonious and mutually beneficial development of the totality of relationships among the peoples of these islands." It was to comprise representatives of the British and Irish governments, devolved institutions in Northern Ireland, Scotland, and Wales, as well as the Isle of Man and the Channel Islands. It also proposed a British-Irish Intergovernmental Conference, which would subsume the Anglo-Irish Intergovernmental Council and the Intergovernmental Conference established under the 1985 Anglo-Irish Agreement. The conference would bring together the British and Irish governments "to promote bilateral co-operation at all levels on all matters of mutual interest within the competences of both governments."

The agreement also included sections on rights, safeguards, and equality of opportunity. It reaffirmed the commitment to "the total disarmament of all paramilitary organizations," the intention being to achieve decommissioning within two years of the agreement being endorsed in a referendum. Both governments also agreed to put in place mechanisms for an accelerated program for the release of prisoners—affiliated to organizations maintaining an unequivocal cease-fire—convicted of certain specified offenses. Both governments would sign a new British-Irish Agreement, replacing the 1985 Anglo-Irish Agreement.

The agreement also identified the timetable for progress. A referendum was to be held in both Northern Ireland and the Republic on May 22, 1998, and, if majorities supported the agreement, elections to the Northern Ireland assembly would take place on June 25. This program was maintained. On May 22, people both north and south of the border endorsed the Good Friday Agreement by massive majorities (Table 10.5). One exit poll showed that support was most pronounced in Northern Ireland among Catholic voters: 96 percent voted "yes." Though most Protestant voters voted in favor, the percentage was not so overwhelming: 55 percent voted in favor, and 45 percent voted against.

Resolving the Conflict

Following the Good Friday agreement, an assembly was elected—dominated by Unionists in different guises—and a power-sharing executive formed under the leader of the UUs, David Trimble, with an SDLP member as deputy first minister. A member of Sinn Féin—Martin McGuinness—was appointed as minister for education, the first occasion that Sinn Féin had accepted a role in the governing of the province. The new executive got under way, though with some internal conflict—the two Democratic Unionist ministers vowing not to attend executive meetings with Sinn Féin ministers present until the IRA decommissioned weapons—and some uncertainty as to whether the IRA would deliver on the promise to decommission. In the event, a failure to make progress on the decommissioning of arms—and claims of the IRA running a spying operation in the Northern Ireland office—resulted in the assembly twice being suspended, the second occasion being in 2002. Direct rule was resumed while the British and Irish governments sought a new settlement for the province. Fresh elections to the assembly were held in 2003. The DUP and Sinn Féin were the principal beneficiaries: the DUP emerged as the largest party, with 30 seats, and Sinn Féin won 24, coming second in terms of the share of the vote. The formerly dominant UUs won 27 seats and the SDLP 18. Substantive talks between the parties took place toward the end of

TABLE 10.5

RESULTS OF THE REFERENDUM ON THE GOOD FRIDAY AGREEMENT, 1998

	Yes	No
Northern Ireland Turnout: 80.9%	676,966 (71.1%)	274,879 (28.9%)
Republic of Ireland Turnout: 66.5%	1,401,919 (94.4%)	83,141 (5.6%)

2004, but there was a failure to reach agreement after the DUP insisted on photographic evidence that IRA arms had been decommissioned. The IRA said it was no longer prepared to go ahead with the final stage of decommissioning. However, progress was made toward the end of 2005 when the head of the independent decommissioning body announced his organization was satisfied that all the IRA's arms were now beyond use. In 2006, the British and Irish prime ministers unveiled plans for restoring devolution in the province. These included Sinn Féin accepting the police service of Northern Ireland and for the DUP to accept republicans in a power-sharing administration. The premiers announced the end of November 2006 as the deadline for reaching agreement. In October, the parties met at St Andrews in Scotland to discuss the proposals for restoring devolution. The government achieved approval from Parliament for extending the deadline for reaching agreement. It called for elections in the province on March 7 and for agreement on a power-sharing agreement to be reached by March 26. If no agreement was reached, the assembly would be dissolved and there would be a move toward greater British-Irish collaboration. The government also held out various incentives to reach a deal, including more financial aid to the province; the Irish government also indicated it would provide some support.

In the assembly elections on March 7, the DUP emerged as the largest party with 36 seats; Sinn Féin came second with 28, followed by the UUs with 18 and the SDLP with 16. The Alliance gained seven seats. "Sinn Féin has been rewarded by the nationalist electorate for its increased moderation in ending the IRA campaign and creating a participatory republican politics. The DUP has been rewarded by the unionist electorate for intra-bloc 'outbidding' of its unionist rival—appearing as the stouter defender of ethnic bloc interests—in opposing some of the conditions of the Good Friday Agreement and pressing for greater clarity from republicans in terms of support for state institutions."[8]

On 26 March, agreement was reached by the DUP and Sinn Féin to enter into a power-sharing government, with Ian Paisley as first minister and Martin McGuinness as deputy first minister. The agreement was generally hailed as historic, the two parties at the extremes of Northern Ireland politics—one committed to preserving the integrity of Northern Ireland as part of the United Kingdom and the other committed to the province becoming part of a united Ireland—coming together to pursue a peaceful resolution of policy issues in the province. The contrast with the position in preceding decades was stark.

In addition to the first minister and deputy first minister, there are ten departmental ministers. Under the provisions for creating an executive, ministerial posts are allocated in relation to party strength, with the parties determining who will fill "their" ministerial slots. Five posts, including of first minister, are filled by the DUP, four by Sinn Féin, two by the UUs, and one by the SDLP. There is no doctrine of collective ministerial responsibility. Each minister exercises powers in relation to their portfolio and is scrutinized by an assembly committee chaired by someone from a different party to that of the minister. Within the assembly, some legislation has to be approved by majorities within each "ethnic" bloc (parallel consent) or with at least some support from both ethnic blocs and an overall majority (weighted majority voting). The assembly began holding regular plenary sessions on a Monday and Tuesday, with other days being given over to committee work.[9]

In 2008, Ian Paisley was succeeded as DUP leader, and hence as first minister, by Peter Robinson. He and Martin McGuinness came together to promote economic development in the province—they both met President Barack Obama in Washington D. C. in March 2009—and ministers proved active in their particular areas. However, there was little agreement reached on issues collectively. Even so, the very fact that there was a power-sharing administration (or rather a government with power dispersed among the parties), with peace in the province, produced a situation that was believed to herald a new era for Northern Ireland. After decades when it looked unlikely that consensus could be reached on any one of several constitutional options,[10] agreement was achieved. For most of the time, the principal opposition to an agreement had come from Sinn Féin, in its capacity as the political wing of the IRA, and the unionists, especially the Democratic Unionists, intent on avoiding any move toward a united Ireland and any initiative involving a role for the Irish government. Attempts at reaching a political solution were attacked by Sinn Féin as not going far enough and by the Democratic Unionists as going too far. Eventually, Sinn Féin realized that it was losing support and that it could not realize its goals through armed struggle: a political solution was necessary. For the Democratic Unionists, power-sharing offered the prospect of ensuring that the province was governed by a Northern Ireland administration and not on the basis of involvement by the Irish government. Given the growing size of the Catholic population in Northern Ireland—with the prospect of the Catholic population in due course outnumbering the Protestant—there was also a case for reaching agreement and showing that there was a case for the province retaining its integrity as a self-governing province. There was thus an incentive for both sides to put aside their differences and work together.

REGIONAL GOVERNMENT IN ENGLAND

Scotland, Wales, and Northern Ireland now have devolved assemblies. This contrasts with England, which has no parliament nor, with the exception of Greater London, any elected regional assemblies. Greater London was seen to some extent as being on a par with the different parts of the United Kingdom and, following a referendum, an elected Mayor and Assembly were brought into being in 2000. Outside Greater London, there is no regional government. The Labour Party, in its 1997 election manifesto, promised "in time" to introduce legislation to allow people, region by region, to decide in a referendum whether they wanted directly elected regional government. The closeness of the result in the Welsh referendum in 1997 came as something of a surprise to ministers and appeared to discourage them from moving quickly to introduce the legislation. Eventually, the government published a White Paper in 2002, expanding on the government's proposals: referendums were to be held on a rolling basis, with the first being held in regions where support for regional assemblies was thought to be strongest. Three referendums were scheduled, but this was then scaled down to one. This was held in the North-East in 2004. In the event, there was an overwhelming "no" vote, with 78 percent of those voting opposing the proposal. The result essentially killed off moves toward regional devolution. No further referendums were scheduled.

Though there are no elected tiers of government at the regional level in England, there are a number of nonelected governmental or quasi-governmental bodies. Various factors have contributed to governmental functions being fulfilled at a regional level. Among the more important pressures have been administrative convenience, the need to involve more local authorities, technical advantages, the desire to dissociate central government from certain decision-making activities, and pressure from groups and professional bodies seeking some degree of regional autonomy in their sphere of activity.[11] Recent years have seen the number of government or public bodies operating at such a level decrease, the consequence of the Conservative government's privatization policy. A number of public utilities, which previously had an extensive regional organization (the regional water authorities being the most extensive), are no longer in the public sector. However, regional government has acquired a new significance with the creation of regional development agencies (RDAs).

Eight government departments have some organization at the regional level, either as an integral part of the department or as part of a service for which the department is responsible. The Prison Department in the Home Office, for example, has a regional organization. Within the Justice Department, courts are organized on a circuit—that is, regional—basis (see Chapter 14). Apart from government departments, a number of other public bodies also have a regional organization. The NHS, for example, operates at two levels, the district and regional level. Regional health authorities (RHAs) have responsibility for regional planning, resource allocation, major capital building work, and certain specialized hospital services that are more appropriately administered on a regional basis. (Various private companies, such as utilities, are also organized on a regional level.) There is thus some regional aspect to government in England. This has been extended by the creation of RDAs.

The Regional Development Agencies Act, enacted in 1998, established an RDA in each of nine regions. Each agency is designed as a small body—with 8 to 15 members drawn from the region and being business-led—with responsibility for furthering economic development and regeneration; promoting business efficiency, investment, and competitiveness; promoting the development and application of skills; and promoting sustainable development. Each RDA has power to develop its own approach. Each brings together various regeneration programs previously vested in a number of bodies, including government regional offices. Each is expected to force partnerships with other bodies in the region.

The RDAs are financed mostly from public funds. They have the status of nondepartmental public bodies and are answerable to ministers and to Parliament. However, provision is also made for the RDAs to be scrutinized by regional interests. Voluntary regional chambers were envisaged, drawing on regional interests and local councils, and under the act, power is given to the relevant minister to designate a chamber as the body to constitute the focus for consultation about the work of the RDA. These voluntary chambers were seen as a substitute for elected regional government and, indeed, as potential stepping stones to elected regional assemblies. Various such chambers, or assemblies, were created but they were abolished in 2009.

There is thus a layer of government operating at a regional level in England. The value of a regional tier is both managerial and economic. Membership of the European Union adds a further spur, creating opportunities for regions to seek funds from the different EU funding agencies (see Chapter 9). However, the regional structures that do exist vary in size and authority. The regions differ in size, both spatially and demographically. They also differ in terms of their definition. There is no agreement on what constitutes the regions of England. Some parts of the country have a clear regional identity; others do not. This, as we shall see, has some political significance.

THE CURRENT DEBATE

Devolution was described by the Secretary of State for Wales at the time of its implementation as "a process, not an event." The creation of the elected assemblies in Scotland, Wales, and Northern Ireland has not provided a settled constitutional solution but rather led to pressure for further change. There are three sets of pressures at work. There is pressure for more powers to be devolved to Wales and Scotland. Within England, there are many who believe that devolution has been to the detriment of England. They favor an English parliament and, in some cases, independence for the different parts of the United Kingdom. Just as the SNP favors independence for Scotland, there are now some people south of the border who support independence for England. There is also pressure as a result of tension between the different administrations. The party that dominates in Westminster is no longer the dominant party in Holyrood. There is no incentive built into the devolution settlement to generate a U.K.-wide approach to issues.

Pressure for more powers to be devolved has been a feature of Welsh politics since the inception of the National Assembly for Wales. The Assembly established a commission (the Richard Commission) which reported in 2004 and favored legislative powers being devolved, similar to the situation in Scotland. As we have seen, the Government of Wales Act 2006 provided for some degree of rolling devolution and created powers for full legislative devolution following a referendum. However, the U.K. Government has shown no desire to utilize the provision for holding a referendum. An All-Wales Convention was established in 2008 to encourage debate on achieving legislative devolution. A survey in 2009 found that 52 percent of people questioned in Wales would favor full-law making powers for the assembly; only 21 percent favored the status quo.[12] In Scotland, the SNP has pressed the case for independence and favors a referendum on the issue. In its 2007 White Paper, *Choosing Scotland's Future,* it emphasized its support for independence but also indicated a willingness to accept more radical devolution as an interim step to achieving independence. The other parties at Holyrood agreed in 2007 to establish a Commission on Scottish Devolution. It was appointed in 2008 to "recommend any changes to the present constitutional arrangements that would enable the Scottish Parliament to serve the people of Scotland better, improve the financial accountability of the Scottish Parliament, and continue to secure the position of Scotland within the United Kingdom." Whereas the SNP wanted to achieve independence from the United Kingdom, the other parties were seeking changes that would embed devolution within the United Kingdom. The situation in Northern Ireland is distinctive, with agreement between the parties being necessary for more powers to be exercised by the Stormont administration. As we have noted, there have been problems in achieving agreement. There also remains some tension within Northern Ireland, with some occasional acts of violence by republican splinter groups, such as the Real IRA, that have not accepted a political solution in the province.

The situation in Scotland and Wales also has major implications for England. It has created some degree of resentment both in respect of funding and law making. Under what it known as the Barnett formula, public funds are distributed in a way that favors those in Scotland, Wales, and Northern Ireland. Under the formula, the per capita distribution of public expenditure which can be identified as benefiting a particular country is greater in the devolved parts of the United Kingdom than in England. In 2006–07, if the U.K.-wide per capita average was 100 percent, the expenditure in England would be 97 percent and in Scotland 117 percent. This perceived discrimination against England fueled resentment within England, though successive governments were reluctant to change the formula because of the difficulty of achieving a consensus on what should succeed it.

Political controversy centered on what became known as the "West Lothian question." This was named after the constituency of the Labour MP, Tam Dalyell, who asked the question How could it be right that MPs from Scotland sitting in the U.K. Parliament could vote on matters that applied only to England when MPs sitting for English seats could not vote on matters that applied only to Scotland? MPs from Scotland could vote, for example, on bills dealing with transport in England, but English MPs could not vote on bills dealing with transport in Scotland, because that was a devolved subject. One partial solution that was implemented was a reduction in the number of Scottish seats in the U.K. Parliament. The number was reduced from 72 to 59. That, though, merely corrected for a recent historical disparity where the electoral quota (the average size of a constituency in terms of the number of electors) in Scotland was notably lower than that for England. The change that was implemented merely brought the electoral quota in Scotland into line with that in England. Another solution, variously advanced by Conservative leaders, is that bills that deal solely with English matters should be voted on only by English MPs. In 2007, Conservative leader David Cameron said a future Conservative government would seek to ban MPs from Scotland voting on issues that affected only England.

A more radical solution is that England should also have its own elected parliament, leaving the Westminster Parliament to deal with U.K.-wide matters such as defense and the currency. This, it was argued, would ensure equity, ensuring that England was on a par with the other parts of the United Kingdom. The English, declared one Conservative MP, "must be free to run their own country without interference from north of the border."[13] It would serve to produce, in effect, a federal structure. Various organizations have been formed to make the case for an English parliament, including the Campaign for an English Parliament (CEP). Its strategy is "to assemble the most powerful coalition of expert and public opinion possible with a view to securing an English referendum on the question of establishing a Parliament for the residents of England."[14] It has been able to claim some popular support. An Ipsos/MORI poll in June 2006 found that more than a quarter of those questioned favored a law-making English parliament. When the existence of parliaments in Scotland and Wales were factored in, the proportion rose to 44 percent.[15]

Other politicians, especially in the Labour and Liberal Democrat parties, continue to favor a regional solution, with elected assemblies in the different parts of England. Though government enthusiasm waned in the wake of the referendum in the North-East in 2004, it remains the preferred solution. This, it is argued, would be equitable, given that—in population terms—English regions would be more comparable in size to Scotland and Wales than would be the case if there was a single English parliament.

The arguments for an English parliament or elected regional assemblies are variously challenged. The objection to an English parliament is practical and political. It raises practical problems because of the population size of England. It would be a skewed form of federalism, with one parliament representing over 80 percent of the population of the United Kingdom. Fears are also expressed that it might increase the pressure for a breakup of the kingdom, encouraging the different parts to think in terms of independence. According to supporters of the union, the United Kingdom provides for strength in numbers: the whole is greater than the sum of the parts. Disaggregate the different parts of the kingdom and you weaken it immeasurably.

The problems with the proposal for elected regional assemblies are not only a perceived lack of popular support but also that there is not always a clear regional identity in parts of England. Though some regions have fairly clear boundaries and a regional identity (such as Yorkshire, a county big enough to constitute a region), in others it is difficult to discern obvious regions. The "southeast" of England is not a natural region in terms of economic activity or in terms of the perception of residents. It would also constitute a doughnut shape, circling Greater London. Creating artificial regions, it was argued, would encourage local animosity, rather in the way that creating new counties in 1974 had encountered strong local opposition.

The other tension within the existing framework is between the different parts of the United Kingdom. Devolution was able to bed in initially, not least because those responsible for it were drawn from Westminster. Many of the leaders of the devolved bodies were former MPs, thus facilitating cordial relations with ministers in London. It was also facilitated by the fact that one party was dominant in London, Holyrood, and Cardiff. That party domination ended in 2007. More politicians were elected to devolved bodies who had no experience of Westminster. There was greater potential for conflict between the administrations. This was exacerbated by the fact that there was no framework for addressing systematically U.K.-wide questions. As Charlie Jeffery has noted, the purpose of the union of the United Kingdom is unclear in its post-devolution form. "Because devolution is *asymmetrical*, establishing different relationships of each nation to the centre, the devolved administrations have no particular incentive to think UK-wide."[16] There is no incentive to come together to work in the interests of the United Kingdom as a whole.

CONCLUSION

The closing years of the twentieth century saw a remarkable change in the constitutional landscape of the United Kingdom. For most of the century, there was no elected tier of government in Britain between the national government and local government. At the end of the first decade of the twenty-first century, there were elected administrations in Scotland, Wales, and Northern Ireland, as well as in Greater London.

However, there was nothing uniform about the devolution of powers to these new bodies. Though an assembly was elected in Greater London, England had no parliament or regional elected government. The United Kingdom, as we have noted, acquired what was termed asymmetrical devolution. Pressure for change remained a feature of the political landscape, some bodies pressing for measures they believed would strengthen the union, others pressing for dismantling the union and allowing each part to become independent. There were tensions within and between the different administrations. As Jeffery has noted: "The continued absence of a systematic approach to the territorial government of the UK, and the existence of various forums for discussion of one or other nation's concerns point to a continuation of the centrifugal dynamic of the UK's strangely disconnected union."[17] Devolution may have addressed some problems, but its implementation has created others, leaving the future of the United Kingdom a continuing issue on the political agenda.

NOTES

1. David Steel refers to the commitment to such a policy as stemming from Gladstone's pamphlet of 1886 that argued for a reform of government consistent with the aspirations of the individual nations in Great Britain. D. Steel, "Federalism," in N. MacCormick (ed.), *The Scottish Debate* (Oxford University Press, 1970), p. 81.
2. A. H. Birch, *Integration and Disintegration in the British Isles* (Allen & Unwin, 1977).
3. D. Denver, "Scottish Parliament elections," *Politics Review,* 17 (1), 2007, p. 21.
4. On the parliament, see its website http://www.scottish.parliament.uk/corporate/index.htm
5. See Scottish Parliament, *The Work of Committees in the Scottish Parliament,* http://www.scottish.parliament.uk/vli/committees/documents/WOC-Eng.pdf
6. See H. Bradbury, "Welsh Assembly elections," *Politics Review,* 17 (2), 2007, p. 14.
7. National Assembly for Wales: Public Attitudes 2008, http://www.assemblywales.org/abthome/abt-commission/about_us-public_attitudes_2008.htm
8. J. Tonge, "The Return of Devolved Power-Sharing to Northern Ireland," *Politics Review,* 17 (2), 2007, p. 10.
9. On the work of the assembly, see its website http://www.niassembly.gov.uk/
10. See P. Norton, *The Constitution in Flux* (Martin Robertson, 1982), pp. 191–212.
11. See B. W. Hogwood, "Introduction," in B. W. Hogwood and M. Keating (eds.), *Regional Government in England* (Oxford University Press, 1982), pp. 10–12.
12. *BBC News Online,* 26 February 2009.
13. T. Gorman, *A Parliament for England* (Cheltenham: This England Books, 1999), p. 14.
14. Campaign for an English Parliament, http://www.thecep.org.uk/wordpress/
15. http://www.ipsos-mori.com/researchpublications/researcharchive/poll.aspx?oItemId=290
16. C. Jeffery, "Devolution: A Fractured Project," *Politics Review,* 14 (4), 2005, p. 17.
17. C. Jeffery, "Devolution and the UK: What's Wrong with the Status Quo?" *Politics Review,* 18 (4), 2009, 16.

11

Local Government
Government below the Center

L ocal government is a well-established feature of political life in Britain. The same can be said of local government in the United States. How-ever, where Britain differs from the United States is in terms of the history and status of local government as well as in changes made to the structures of local councils. Those changes have sometimes been motivated by the need to achieve greater administrative efficiency. Others have been motivated by a political impetus to limit the powers or actions of local government. Such changes demonstrate the extent to which local government in Britain is very much subordinate to Parliament. Though there is a fairly pervasive commitment to the principle of local governance, the form that such governance takes is determined by acts of Parliament. Recent decades have been notable for the number of acts passed that are changing the shape of local government in the United Kingdom.

THE CHANGING STRUCTURE OF LOCAL GOVERNMENT

There were local communities with leaders in Anglo-Saxon times. Counties and boroughs existed when the first parliament was summoned in the thirteenth century. From around the fifteenth century, three types of civil authority were well established: the parish (based on the church parish), responsible for law and order and for the poor; the borough, essentially a town granted a royal charter and enjoying certain privileges, including the right to self-admin-istration; and the shire (county), responsible for some degree of general oversight and administration.[1] Industrialization created pressures on local government, making it difficult for existing structures to cope with the scale of urban development and attendant problems of disease and crime. The response was initially piecemeal, but there was a major reform in 1880. This created a uniform two-tier system of local government. The first tier consisted of county boroughs, exercising control over all local government services within their boundaries, and county councils, each exercising control over certain local government services within the county (other than in county boroughs within their borders). Below the county councils was the second tier: municipal boroughs, urban districts, and rural districts, each exercising limited functions. Within rural districts, there was an additional layer of local government in the form of parish councils, each exercising very limited functions.

As demands on government grew further in the twentieth century—especially in the decades following the Second World War—and the responsibilities of local government expanded, there was pressure for further reform. After a period of little change, local government witnessed a period of significant change, and continues to do so. The last four decades of the twentieth century saw several major reforms.

Local government in Greater London was reformed in the 1960s: A Greater London Council (GLC) was created to deal with issues such as planning, roads, overspill housing, and other needs affecting the whole of the Greater London area. Responsibility for most local authority housing, and certain other services, was retained by the 32 borough councils within the GLC area.

Local government in the rest of England, and in Wales, was reorganized in 1974. The 1972 Local Government Act, which took effect in 1974, created a new two-tier system. It established 47 county councils, each with responsibility for education, transport, most highways, planning housing, personal social services, libraries, police, fire service, garbage disposal, and consumer protection. Below them a second tier of more than 300 district councils was created, each with responsibility for town planning, environmental health, building and housing management, and various registration and licensing functions. The act also created new local government structures in highly urbanized areas: Six separate metropolitan counties were created and, below them, 36 metropolitan districts. The metropolitan counties had the same responsibilities as county councils, except for education, personal social services, and libraries, which passed to the metropolitan districts. The metropolitan counties and districts also shared responsibility for certain amenities, such as parks, museums, and airports. Below the two tiers, provision for parish councils was retained.

In Scotland, under the provisions of the 1973 Local Government (Scotland) Act, a two-tier division was also created, between regional and district councils. Nine regional councils were established, but because of the concentration of population in the western lowlands of Scotland, one region—Strathclyde—contained more than half of the country's population.

The reorganization was designed to create a system of local government to last for the foreseeable future. It failed to live up to expectations. The spending and actions of some local councils also generated political controversy. The result has been frequent and piecemeal changes.

The reorganization proved costly and did little to enhance consent for government: There was little apparent increase in citizens' awareness of local authority responsibilities. Attempts to achieve an efficient managerial structure also encountered problems, councils variously reverting to old styles of management (committees based on established service, for example) rather than maintaining a new style (committees based on expenditure functions). Certain features of the reorganization created resentment. Inhabitants of counties that had been dismembered or abolished were often vehement in their vocal opposition to the changes. So too were former councilors and other citizens in the boroughs that were reduced to parish council status. Within some of the new counties, a number of boroughs resented and continue to resent the dominance of larger cities. Local government thus achieved no settled state.

Since then, there have been further significant reforms. These have covered structures and functions. The shape of local government has changed. So too has its responsibilities.

Reforms under a Conservative Government

Change was a significant feature under the Conservative government elected in 1979. The government clashed with many local authorities, especially the Labour-controlled GLC and metropolitan counties. The government wanted to limit public spending, and local government expenditure was one of the major features of public spending that exceeded government targets. In 1983–84, for example, GLC spending exceeded grant-related expenditure (the amount government considered it should spend) by 81 percent. The need to limit public spending was accorded priority over the commitment to the principle of local autonomy, and various measures were introduced to limit the spending of local councils. However, the GLC and many other Labour-controlled councils also constituted an additional thorn in the government's flesh as a result of campaigns that they waged on particular political issues. The GLC, under its leader Ken Livingstone, supported campaigns on a wide range of issues—usually opposed to government policy—and funded organizations (such as feminist and gay groups) that the government regarded as inappropriate recipients of public funds. By 1983, because of the government's annoyance at such activities, it promised to introduce a bill to abolish the GLC and the six metropolitan councils. The commitment was embodied in the party's 1983 election manifesto and was carried through two years later in the 1985 Local Government Act. The GLC and the metropolitan councils ceased to exist on March 31, 1986. The functions of the metropolitan councils were dispersed to metropolitan boroughs and to joint authorities to run police, fire, and passenger transport services. The functions of the GLC were given to the 32 London boroughs. As we shall see, the Conservative government also introduced a raft of measures to change the powers and responsibilities of local government.

The absence of an authority to cover the whole of London proved unpopular with opposition parties and with many London residents. The bifurcation of responsibilities between county and district councils created by the 1972 act continued to cause resentment and some confusion. Some of the new counties created by the 1972 act remained unpopular with residents. A number of cities resented having no more than district council status. This sense of dissatisfaction influenced the political parties. Both the Conservative and Labour parties committed themselves to a further reform of local government, and in 1992 the Conservative government achieved passage of a new Local Government Act. The act created a new local government commission to review local government structures and boundaries. As a result of the Commission's work, various county councils were abolished and replaced by a number of unitary authorities (all the functions of local government being vested in a single authority). The outcome was the creation of 46 new unitary authorities. "The result was to be a patchwork. Local government in England would now be characterized by the term 'hybridity'.... This did not look to be a particularly stable mix."[2] In Scotland and Wales, the position was very different. Instead of an extensive review, the government imposed a new uniform system of unitary authorities in each country. Scotland had 32 unitary authorities and Wales 22.

The government also sought to limit the powers and functions of local government. State schools were given the opportunity to opt out of local authority control (though only a small proportion chose to do so). The role of local government in the health service and in the oversight of certain bodies, such as the police, was reduced. The domain of local councils was also constricted by the government's policy of allowing the tenants of council housing (public housing) to buy their houses. In the late 1980s the government also began to place an emphasis on making local government services more competitive, the aim being to increase efficiency and secure greater value for money. Competitive bidding was encouraged and, indeed, increasingly required by law. Under this system, local government services are put out to tender and private firms are able to compete for the contract. The purpose of these various changes was to end the role of councils as "universal providers." Local councils were meant to become "enabling authorities," buying services rather than providing the services themselves through their own workforce.

The overall effect of these changes was to limit the role and powers of local government. The changes also had political consequences. As we shall, a new method of financing local government, the" poll tax," proved massively unpopular. The limitations imposed on local councils also proved unpopular, in that they were seen as an attack on local democracy. Whereas the government had effectively demonized certain Labour-controlled councils in the early 1980s—characterizing them as "loony left councils"—the demonization failed to have much impact in the 1990s, public sympathy flowing now in favor of local government, rather than against it.

Reforms under a Labour Government

The Labour government returned in 1997 was committed to devolution and to reform of the system of government for London. Devolution (see Chapter 10) is important in this context in that it resulted in the new Scottish parliament being given responsibility for local government. The parliament has since reformed local government, including the introduction of a new electoral system (the single transferable vote).

In its election manifesto, the Labour Party also promised—subject to a referendum of voters in London—to establish an elected mayor and strategic authority for the capital. The referendum was held on May 7, 1998, and—as can be seen from Table 11.1—produced a massive "yes" vote, albeit on a small turnout. The Greater London Authority Act was passed in 1999, with elections for the mayor and the 25-member authority taking place in 2000.

The Government also achieved passage of the Local Government Act 2000. This required councils to move to an executive-based system, utilizing one of three possible systems: a directly elected mayor, an executive comprising the council leader and a cabinet (broadly similar to government at the national level), or a council manager and mayor (based on the system adopted in some areas of the United States). Smaller district councils were given the option of a modified committee system. In practice, the overwhelmingly majority of local authorities opted for the mayor and cabinet system. Some councils held referendums on whether to have an elected mayor, but fewer than twenty resulted in a "yes" vote. The structure in most councils is thus to have a council leader (normally the leader of the largest party) and a cabinet (composed of members of the majority party or of parties forming a coalition), with other councilors serving on scrutiny committees to keep a check on what the executive is doing. The use of scrutiny committees is designed to ensure that party leaders are subject to more regular review than was the case under the previous system.

Further structural changes took place in 2009. The government had invited local authorities in England, in areas where there was the two-tier (county-district) structure, to submit their own consensus-based proposals for creating unitary authorities. Five counties became unitary authorities and in two counties the powers of the county councils were absorbed into a reduced number of district councils.

The government also made changes to the functions of local government, but without reversing the basic changes made by its Conservative predecessor. It removed the requirement to put services out to tender, but instead required

TABLE 11.1		
REFERENDUM RESULT IN LONDON, 1998		
I agree that there should be a London-wide assembly and a directly elected mayor:		
Yes	1,230,715	72.0%
No	478,413	28.0%
Majority	752,302	44.0%
Electorate: 5,014,567		
Turnout: 34.1%		

councils to obtain "best value." It encouraged innovation and also partnership with other local bodies. It introduced Local Public Service Agreements, to provide for local authorities to sign up to national programs of improved public service provision. In the second term of the Blair government, the emphasis shifted to what was termed "new localism," with councils drawing up plans in conjunction with other local providers, in order to meet the social, economic, and environmental needs of the local community, and then to enter into an agreement with central government to support the delivery of local as well as national targets. Greater freedom was also given to local bodies, such as NHS foundation trusts, schools (not least in the form of academies—see Chapter 1), and various housing bodies independent of local government. Councils were encouraged to join with other local bodies (such as the police, health authority, local businesses) to form Local Strategic Partnerships (LSPs). This was followed by an emphasis on community governance, the government advocating more powers being devolved with local authorities to neighborhood or parish bodies. In practice, the approach taken by the government did not always deliver the outcomes it sought. "Partnerships often proved complex to administer and, in the case of some regeneration projects, could actually inhibit effective delivery."[3] The government also sought to involve local people more in local decisions and, under a measure enacted in 2009, to ensure councils responded to local petitions.

The Changing Face of Local Government

By the first decade of the twenty-first century, the structure and responsibilities of local government were thus very different to what they had been for most of the twentieth-century. There were five principal features that distinguished local government from what it had been for the first seven decades of the twentieth-century.

First, a standard pattern of local government has given way to a patchwork quilt of local authorities. Some parts of England have two-tiers of local government, in others there is a single tier, either in a metropolitan district or a unitary authority (see Figure 1.1). Confusingly, district councils and unitary authorities go by different names, such as borough councils, city councils, and district councils. Some councils have a directly elected mayor, though most do not. Some small councils have structures that derive from the older committee system.

Second, whereas the old structure was based on a clear tiered system, the preference on the part of central government has been to move to a unitary system. Though the main change occurred under a Conservative government, it has been continued by a Labour government. However, this has not always been welcomed in the areas concerned, and some counties have resisted moves to create a single-tier structure.

Third, there has been a notable shift of power from local councils to the centre. The Thatcher government was widely criticized for limiting the powers of locally elected councils. Though there have been changes under a

Two-Tier

COUNTY COUNCILS
[responsible for education, social services, transport, strategic planning, fire services, consumer protection, refuse disposal, smallholdings, libraries]

DISTRICT COUNCILS
[responsible for local planning, housing, local highways, building regulation, environmental health, refuse collection]

Single Tier

METROPOLITAN COUNCILS
[covering large areas and exercising all the powers listed above of county and district councils]

UNITARY AUTHORITIES
[covering smaller areas and exercising all the powers listed above of county and district councils]

Some functions, such as fire, police, and public transport, may be exercised in some areas by joint boards, with representatives drawn from each of the councils in the area concerned.

FIGURE 11.1
Local government in England

Labour government, there has been no significant reversal of the basic relationship between the centre and the local authorities. The lack of power on the part of local authorities is variously offered as a reason for low turnouts in local government elections. As we shall see, the main political parties recognize that this situation is not popular, with widespread support for some restoration of powers to local councils.

Fourth, and related, there has been a shift of power not only vertically (upward to central government) but also horizontally (that is, sideways to unelected bodies). The councils "have lost many of their former functions to the private sector or appointed single-service agencies: primary healthcare and hospitals, the 'utilities' (water supply, gas, electricity), further education, employment services, and so on."[4] It is estimated that there are something like 5,000 of these bodies, forming what one parliamentary committee referred to as "the local quango state." Though many of these bodies are designed to be responsive to those who use them, they are not elected and are not directly answerable to the local councils. Rather, the councils are expected to act in partnership with them. Where councils retain responsibility for particular services, they are expected to achieve value for money, which may entail buying in services from private suppliers rather than delivering the services through their own workforce.

Fifth, whereas the structure of local government for much of the previous century was known and largely unchanging, there is now no steady state. As we have touched upon, succeeding governments have made changes to the structures and functions of local government. The Labour government of Tony Blair and Gordon Brown not only made changes, but variously proposed more. Ideas for change were embodied in a number of policy documents and white papers.

Ideas for change also emanate from various think tanks, such as the New Local Government Network (NLGN), founded in 1996 and "the primary advocate of New Localism,"[5] as well as from local government itself through the Local Government Association (LGA). Bills affecting local government are a regular feature of the legislative process. In 2009, for example, the Local Democracy, Economic Development and Construction Act was enacted in order to provide, among other things, for greater involvement of people in the processes of local authorities, and creating powers for councils to cooperate in promoting economic development. All main parties continue to advocate change.

Various academics have developed different models of local government, but, as the foregoing suggests, none has been embraced wholeheartedly by British government. One leading scholar, R. A. W. Rhodes, identified, at the beginning of the 1990s, four scenarios for local government: *centralization* (power being concentrated at the center); *the contract authority* (local government contracting with others for the provision of services); *community government* (a revival of the preeminence of local government as the institution of government beyond Whitehall); and *differentiation* (an extension of institutional fragmentation).[6] Rhodes himself inclined most to the differentiation scenario, despite the pressures—as we have seen—under Conservative governments to achieve some element of centralization as well as the creation of the enabling, or contract, authority. The chapter in which Rhodes summarized his approaches was entitled "Now Nobody Understands the System: The Changing Face of Local Government." The position that he sketched then remains largely the case today. Despite various changes, differentiation—continuing institutional fragmentation—remains the most plausible description of local government.

ELECTIONS AND MEMBERS

There are approximately 20,000 councilors. They are elected for four-year terms, with no limit on the number of terms one can serve. Not only is there a patchwork of local councils in England, there is also a patchwork of elections. County, London borough, some unitary, and shire district councils (and all parish councils) have whole council elections every four years. In each of the three years between the county council elections, all metropolitan districts, some unitary authorities, and some shire districts elect a third of their members.

The franchise to vote in local elections is essentially the same as that for national elections: citizens aged 18 or over who are resident in the area on the qualifying date. (Members of the House of Lords, who cannot vote in elections to the House of Commons, can vote in local elections.) Candidates in local elections must be citizens aged 18 or over (the age was lowered from 21 in 2006) and be resident in the local authority area or have resided in premises in the area for the preceding 12 months or, in that 12 months, have had their principal place of work in that area. No one may be elected to a council of which he or she is an employee. This prohibition was extended in 1988 by an act prohibiting senior council officials from being elected as councilors in any authority.

Election procedure is essentially the same as that for national elections. (In 1979 and 1997 the two actually coincided, with a general election taking place the same day as local elections.) The first-past-the-post electoral system is employed for all local elections, with the exception of directly elected mayors, where the supplementary vote (SV) is employed, and the Greater London Assembly, elected using the additional member system (AMS). Although elections are fought ostensibly on local issues, candidates now usually stand under a party label, a tendency that increased in postwar years and was given added impetus by the reorganization of the 1970s. Party has become the most important variable influencing the voting behavior of those electors who bother to cast a vote (turnout, as in local elections in the United States, is low, about 40 percent of eligible voters and declining); local elections are viewed as an annual opportunity to pass judgment on the incumbent national government. Once a party has an absolute majority of seats on a council, it takes control. The leader of the council is the person who exercises power. If no party achieves an absolute majority, the result is either an attempt at minority government by the largest single party or shared control by two of the parties. The party in government nationally is expected to lose council seats during the midterm of a Parliament; a net gain of seats by the governing party is hailed as a considerable victory. The Conservative Party suffered badly in the 1990s; the Labour Party suffered badly in its third term, especially under the leadership of Gordon Brown.

Although councilors are elected on party labels and usually operate within coherent party groupings, with elected officers and whips, they behave differently depending on local circumstances. Given that the needs and demands of communities vary, local parties temper their responses accordingly. The councilors themselves tend to be disproportionately white, male, and middle-age. A census of councilors carried out in 2008 by the LGA revealed that 96.6 percent of councilors were white (no change from 1997), almost 70 percent were male (down from over 92 percent in 1997), and the average age was 59 (up from 55 in 1997).[7] Attracting young candidates is a particular problem. In 2008, only 13.1 percent of councilors were aged under 45 years, down from 18.4 percent in 1997. They are also likely to be drawn from non-manual occupations, with an increasing number having a university education. Since 1972, councils have been empowered to pay members attendance allowances. No salaries are paid, though the attendance allowance can sometimes be the equivalent of a small wage, amounting in the case of some councils to £10,000 ($16,400) a year or more. Council leaders and cabinet members are paid additional sums, as are various other office holders, such as committee chairs.

What motivates individuals to seek election to local councils is not at all clear. Some appear to see it as a stepping-stone to higher things (a number are subsequently selected as parliamentary candidates); some do it out of a desire to further the aims of their party; some do it out of a sense of civic responsi-bility (to be found also in the performance of a wide range of other local activities, such as serving on the local magistrates' bench and doing voluntary social work); some do it to enhance their status in the community; and some do it for the simple reason that they were inveigled into running by friends or local party activists. Because of the number of councilors to be elected and the level of public indifference toward local government, local parties fre-quently have difficulty recruiting candidates to contest elections. About 80 percent of candidates in local elections are selected from a shortlist of one. Though most councilors would recommend their roles to others, 30 percent give up after their first term.

Councilors estimate that they spend on average just over 20 hours a week on council work or political business. Most of the time is given over to the plenary and committee meetings of the council.

Some councilors also devote themselves to activities that are beyond the law. Corruption has been an occasional problem in local government. There have been various high-profile scandals. Some cases have involved councilors who are serving on particular committees, such as planning committees, accepting bribes from contractors in return for approving contracts. Other cases have involved councilors submitting false expense claims or using coun-cil funds to go on trips that are not strictly necessary to fulfilling their official duties. Some councilors have also operated at a level that is not strictly illegal but is not necessarily regarded as legitimate by electors, such as receiving free tickets for particular events.

Two explanations have been offered for the level of corruption identified in local government. One is the fact that the decision-making structure of local government means that a small number of local, identifiable individuals make important decisions: They are visible and accessible to local firms and companies. (This contrasts with members of Parliament who, individually, have little scope to influence important decisions.) The other is the fact that many local councils are dominated by one party. This dominance, it is argued, facilitates an arrogance of power on the part of those in the majority party. There is a tendency to believe that they can do what they want or get away with misusing funds.

Allegations of corruption are investigated by the police. Allegations of maladministration (the term is not formally defined, but means, essentially, a failure to observe due process) are investigated by a public official known as the Local Government Ombudsman.[8] (There are separate ombudsmen for England, Scotland, Wales, and Northern Ireland.) Complaints may be made directly to the ombudsman by citizens. The ombudsman has powers of inves-tigation and can recommend remedies in cases where maladministration is held to have occurred. There are no formal powers of enforcement,[9] though if a local authority continues to refuse to comply with a recommendation for redress, the ombudsman can require it to publicize the reasons for its failure to comply. In 2007–08, the ombudsman received 17,628 complaints (down slightly on the number received in the previous year); just under 5,000 were referred to councils where they had not an opportunity to investigate the complaint. The ombudsman made almost 11,000 decisions, with nearly 3,000 complaints leading to local settlements.

Whereas complains about maladministration relate to councils, complaints about councilors failing to comply with the local government code of conduct are considered by a local standards committee or, if considered sufficiently serious, referred to the Standards Board for England.[10] The Standards Board was established by an Act of Parliament passed in 1999. Initially, complaints about councilors were sent direct to the Standards Board but from 2008 they go to a local standards committee. The Standards Board, now styled Standards for England, provides guidance to local committees as well as monitoring their performance. In 2007–08, 3,547 allegations were considered by the Board, with 14 percent being referred for investigation. The Board can decide to suspend or disqualify councilors for serious breaches of the code, though the occasions on which they do so are rare.

In recent years, some of the most high-profile complaints attracting media attention have not been related to individual conduct but rather the inability of councils to exercise effective oversight of council departments. Some cases of inadequate supervision by social services departments—resulting in some cases in deaths where children judged at risk have been left with violent parents—have led to investigations and recommendations for improvements in co-ordination within local government and between services.

POWERS AND FINANCE

Local government delivers major public services and employs a substantial workforce. Almost 2 million people are employed by local authorities. Just over a quarter of all public spending is done by local government. Of the service expenditure by local councils, about 40 percent is spent on education. Personal social services account for another 18 percent.

Local authorities thus constitute significant economic units. Councils are significant and integral parts of the way in which the United Kingdom is governed. However, they enjoy no constitutionally protected powers and can exercise only those powers vested in them by law. Their scope for branching out into areas of activity for which they have no specific statutory authority is limited: Under the 1972 Local Government Act, they could levy up to a 2p (pence) rate for generally whatever purpose they wished; under the 1988 Local Government and Housing Act, this amount was replaced by a per-adult limit (£5 [$8] per adult, for example, in the case of London boroughs and metropolitan district councils). Beyond that, they are limited by what Acts of Parliament say they can do. Unlike many local authorities in other European countries, they lack a "power of general competence." In addition to having to work within statutorily defined limits, councils are also constrained within the confines of powers held and policies pursued by national government.

Ministers have various statutory powers to make orders as well as to issue circulars to local authorities giving guidance on the implementation of government policy.

The limitations upon local government are considerable and these, as we have seen, were extended during the period of Conservative government from 1979 to 1997. During that period, more than 50 acts of Parliament were passed affecting local government. Various spending restrictions were imposed and the domain of local government control constricted. Further reforms were carried out by the succeeding Labour government. Local government is thus restrained by central control, more so than before. Central government retains powers to restrict, or cap, increases in the tax (council tax) that local authorities can levy. Local government is also dependent on central government for much of its spending.

Local authorities derive their revenue from three principal sources: a central government grant, a local tax (council tax), and a tax levied on local businesses. Some income also derives from services provided by the authority. Approximately half of all income derives from central government. Since 1993, the proportion accounted for by central government grants has ranged from 49 percent to 57 percent. In 2008–09, the revenue expenditure of local government in England was just over £98billion ($157billion). Government grants accounted for 53 percent, council tax 25 percent, and business rates 21 percent.[11] Local councils may also borrow as well as invest. A number of local councils were badly affected by the credit crunch in 2008–09, having invested part of their reserves in Icelandic banks that were overwhelmed in the crisis.

Though the local tax accounts for only a small proportion of local government income, it has proved to be the most controversial of the three sources. Until 1990, it took the form of an annual tax on real estate, based on a notional property value; each house had a rateable value and the local authority determined how much to levy each year. Known as "the rates," the system was replaced at the end of the 1980s, and has had two successors.

The Conservative government returned in 1979 took the view that the rating system was inherently unfair; a single person in a house paid the same rate as did a large family living next door, the former helping subsidize the services consumed by the latter. It decided to replace the rates with a community charge, immediately dubbed the "poll tax," levied on individuals rather than on property. Because everyone (with very few exceptions) would pay all or part of the new tax, the government argued that it would increase local accountability—because everyone would have a vested interest in how the council spent their money.

The new tax was brought in first in Scotland in 1989, and in England and Wales the following year. It was accompanied by a uniform business rate (UBR), set centrally by government, replacing the business rate that had been set by councils and that had varied significantly from one authority to another. The new tax proved extraordinarily unpopular, its introduction sparking mass demonstrations and London's worst riot in recent decades. It was one of the contributory factors to Margaret Thatcher's loss of the leadership of the Conservative Party (see Chapter 6): She had seen it as the flagship of her legislative program and was not prepared to contemplate its demise.[12] She was replaced by a leader who was willing to let it die, and in 1992 a new measure was approved by Parliament, replacing the poll tax with a "council tax."

This new tax is based on actual property values (grouped into seven bands, a house falling in the top band paying the highest level of tax), but with a reduction for people living alone. It came into effect on April 1, 1993. Though regarded as fairer than the poll tax, it remains a subject of controversy. It is a regressive tax: It takes up about 14 percent of the income of the poorest 10 percent of households, as against 3 percent for those in the richest 10 percent. A report on local government finance (the Lyons report), published in 2007, recommended that new valuation bands be introduced for those in the lowest-value properties, with those in the higher bands paying more.

THE CURRENT DEBATE

As we saw in Chapter 10, devolution of power to the elected assemblies in Scotland, Wales, and Northern Ireland has generated political debate. So too has local government. In large part, this stems from the various changes of recent decades. There is a debate about the future of local government as well as how to revitalize local involvement, not least through elections. The two are not unrelated, in that the reduction of local government powers in recent decades has often been offered as a reason for low and declining turnout in local elections.

Turnout in local government elections has traditionally been low but in recent decades has witnessed a further decline. Britain shares with the United States the worst turnouts in local elections in the western world. In most countries in western Europe, turnout in local elections ranges from 60 percent upward. In Britain and the United States, a turnout of 40 percent is nowadays considered good. In recent years, the turnout in Britain has been below 40 percent (except in 1997, when the local elections took place at the same time as the parliamentary elections). In 1999, it reached an all-time low. Turnout was less than 29 percent. In some council areas, less than a quarter of voters bother to go to the polls. In some individual wards, the turnout is sometimes well below the 20 percent level. There is thus seen to be a crisis in terms of local democracy. This has been exacerbated by various high-profile crises in some local councils, not least in the provision of services.

Some proposals for change have focused on structures and voting processes. As we have seen, local government was reorganized under the terms of the Local Government Act 2000: Most local councils now employ the executive (leader and cabinet) system. There has also been a continuing move to unitary (that is, single tier) authorities. A Government White Paper published in 2006, *Strong and Prosperous Communities,* stressed the need for greater engagement with local residents as well as indicating different systems that local councils could choose to adopt, including a directly elected executive (as opposed to a directly elected mayor or a leader elected by councilors). At the end of 2007, a report examining the incentives and barriers to serving on councils was published. The following year, in July 2008, the Government published another White Paper, *Communities in Control: Real People, Real Power,* detailing proposals for empowering local communities. The Local Democracy, Economic Development and Construction Act 2009 imposed a duty on local authorities to promote understanding of their functions and their democratic arrangements: It also required them to provide facilities for people to submit petitions electronically and to respond to petitions that met certain criteria. It also imposed a duty to involve representatives of interested persons in the exercise of their functions.

Various other proposals, designed to encourage greater participation in government elections, have included changing the method of election, employing all-postal voting, changing the voting day from a Thursday to a Sunday, allowing voting by telephone, and placing polling booths in places like supermarkets. A number of changes have been piloted. Various experiments were carried out in a number of local authority areas in the local elections in May 2000. All-postal ballots appeared to make a difference to turnout. Other schemes, such as allowing voters to vote on earlier days or to vote in supermarkets, had no appreciable impact. Electors may now opt to vote by post, without giving a reason, and an ICM survey of the 2008 local elections found that 27 percent of voters had voted by post.[13] However, the same survey also found that voters attached greater priority to the security of the ballot than they did to the convenience of voting. It also found that among non-voters the reason given by the largest single number for not voting was lack of time (20 percent). Only 5 percent offered as a reason the fact that "local councils can't do much."

Despite this particular finding, demands for restoring powers to local government remain a popular feature of political discourse. All main political parties tend to embrace the need to enhance local democracy and to strengthen local councils. As we have seen, various changes have been enacted under a Labour government. In 2009, Conservative leader David Cameron announced a "power to local communities" initiative, including empowering local residents to trigger referendums on council tax rises and other measures, remove the power of central government to cap spending, allowing councils to have more money from council tax receipts from new homes and from tax receipts from new businesses. "Over the last century," declared Cameron, "Britain has become one of the most centralized countries in the developed world as more and more power has been sucked to Westminster... When one-size-fits-all-solutions are dispensed from the centre, it's not surprising that they very often fail all-shape-all-size local communities."[14] It was part of a decentralization program, designed to move the focus from a top-down approach to one where local communities decide policy.

The problem for achieving coherent change in respect of local government is that national government is unwilling or unable to embrace a consistent approach. As we have seen, Rhodes has identified four different models of local government. Though political parties tend to embrace community government, not least when in opposition, they are reluctant to give up too many powers when in government. Centralization has tended to be to the fore and, in order to try to achieve greater efficiency, the contract authority model has also been utilized. There are thus conflicting pressures, generating the patchwork quilt of local government structures, relationships, and responsibilities that we have detailed. Local government remains a central feature of the political system. "Flawed as it is, our elected local government, with its democratic base and even restricted discretion, is one of the most precious safeguards we have against absolute power."[15] Despite its continuing importance, its embrace by national government and by electors tends to be at the intellectual and emotional level rather than the practical. National government is reluctant to confer new, autonomous powers on local councils and electors display little enthusiasm for voting for them.

NOTES

1. T. Byrne, *Local Government in Britain* (Penguin Books, 1981), p. 26.
2. K. Young and N. Rao, *Local Government since 1945* (Blackwell, 1997), p. 217.
3. T. Travers, "Local Government," in A. Seldon (ed.), *Blair's Britain 1997–2007* (Cambridge University Press, 2007), p. 67.
4. C. Game, "Local Government Matters," *Politics Review,* 14 (3), 2005, p. 30.
5. New Local Government Network (NLGN), http://www.nlgn.org.uk/public/about-nlgn/
6. R. A. W. Rhodes, "Now Nobody Understands the System: The Changing Face of Local Government," in P. Norton (ed.), *New Directions in British Politics* (Edward Elgar, 1991), pp. 83–112.
7. Improvement and Development Agency (IDeA), Press Release, 14 January 2009. http://www.idea.gov.uk/idk/core/page.do?pageId=9281215
8. See http://www.lgo.org.uk
9. Though in Northern Ireland a complainant can seek a court order for an appropriate remedy where a grievance is upheld by the ombudsman.
10. See http://www.standardsforengland.gov.uk/
11. Department for Communities and Local Government, *Local Government Finance Key Facts: England,* November 2008.
12. See P. Norton, "The Conservative Party from Thatcher to Major," in A. King (ed.), *Britain at the Polls 1992* (Chatham House, 1993), pp. 43–45.
13. ICM, *Local Elections 2008: Summary Report* (ICM, 2008), p. 7
14. *The Guardian,* 17 February 2009.
15. C. Game, "Local Government Matters," *Politics Review,* 14 (3), 2005, p. 31.

SCRUTINY AND LEGITIMATION

12

Parliament
Commons and Lords

The United States has a bicameral legislature. In legislative matters, each house is the equal of the other.[1] Both houses are chosen by popular vote, albeit by differently defined constituencies. They are elected separately from the executive, and members of the two houses are precluded by the Constitution from holding any civil office under the authority of the United States. Congress displays the characteristics of what Michael Mezey has aptly termed an "active" legislature: Its policy-making power is strong and it enjoys popular support as a legitimate political institution.[2] Each house is master of its own timetable and proceedings.

In their behavior, not least in their voting behavior, senators and members of the House of Representatives are influenced by party, more so in recent years than previously.[3] Nonetheless, though party is an important influence, it is not an exclusive one. Members of Congress are responsive to other influences. There is a high re-election rate not necessarily because of the party label but because of the benefits that the members are able to channel to their states or districts. Although the initiative in policy making has passed largely to the executive, Congress remains an important part of the process. As Michael Foley and John Owens have noted, there was a seesawing of power between president and Congress in the nineteenth century. "Although the power of the president was augmented exponentially in the twentieth century—notably during and after Franklin Roosevelt's presidency (1933–45)—the period has witnessed a similar see-sawing in the pre-eminence and power of the two branches."[4] The past century has witnessed various periods when Congress has overshadowed the president or fought for control of the political agenda.

The United Kingdom also has a bicameral legislature, but there the similarity ends. Of the two houses, only one—the House of Commons—is popularly elected. Members of the upper house, the House of Lords, are not elected: Until 1999, most members served by virtue of having inherited their seats. The two houses are no longer equal: The House of Commons as the elected chamber enjoys preeminence and can enforce its legislative will over the upper house under the provisions of the 1911 and 1949 Parliament Acts (see Chapter 3). The executive, or rather the political apex of the executive (i.e., ministers), is drawn from Parliament—there is no separate election—and its members remain within Parliament. The executive dominates both the business program (deciding what will be debated and when) and the voting of Parliament, party serving as the means of that domination. Party cohesion is a feature of voting in the House of Commons. (The same is largely true of the House of Lords, though fewer votes take place there.) Party is the determining influence in the election of an MP and it is normally the determining influence in the member's parliamentary behavior. Parliament exhibits the features of what Mezey has termed a "reactive" legislature: It enjoys popular support as a legitimate political institution but enjoys only modest power, if that, in policy making. Discussion of "the decline of Parliament" has been a characteristic feature of political discourse in Britain for many years.[5] MPs have on occasion been known to look with envy across the Atlantic at the power and influence of their U.S. counterparts.

The reasons for executive dominance of the legislature in Britain have been sketched already (Chapter 3). For part of the nineteenth century, Parliament exhibited the characteristics of an "active" legislature. The period was historically atypical. The 1832 Reform Act helped lessen the grip of the aristocracy and of the ministry on the House of Commons (seats were less easy to buy, given the size of the new electorate), allowing MPs greater freedom in their parliamentary behavior. Debates in the House could influence opinion and the outcome of votes was not a foregone conclusion. This period was short-lived. The 1867 Reform Act and later acts created a much larger and more demanding electorate. With the passage of the 1884 Representation of the People Act, most working men were enfranchised. Electors were now too numerous to be bribed, at least by individual candidates. The result was that "organized corruption was gradually replaced by party organization,"[6] as one observer puts it, and both main existing parties were developed from small cadre parties to form mass-membership and complex organizations. Party organization made possible contact with the electors. To stimulate voting, candidates had to promise something to electors, and electoral promises could be met only if parties displayed sufficient cohesion in parliamentary organization to ensure their enactment.

Institutional and environmental factors combined to ensure that the pressures generated by the changed electoral conditions resulted in a House of Commons with low policy influence. Competition for the all-or-nothing spoils of a general election victory, the single-member constituency with a plurality method of election, and a largely homogeneous population (relative to many other countries) would appear to have encouraged, if not always produced, a basic two-party as opposed to a multiparty system. One party was normally returned with an overall parliamentary majority. Given that the government was drawn from and remained within Parliament, the electoral fortunes of MPs depended primarily on the success or failure of that government. Government was dependent on the voting support of its parliamentary majority both for the passage of its promised measures and for its own continuance in office. Failure of government supporters to vote against a motion expressing "no confidence" in the government or, conversely, not to vote for an important measure that the government declared a "matter of confidence" would result in a dissolution. Within the House of Commons, party cohesion quickly became the norm.

Internal party pressures also encouraged MPs' willingness to defer to government. A member was chosen as a party candidate by the local party and was dependent on it for re-nomination as well as for campaign support. Assuming local party loyalty to the party leadership (an assumption that usually but not always could be made), local parties were unlikely to take kindly to any consistent dissent from "their" members. The norms of the constitution and of party structures also encouraged acquiescence. There were no career channels in Parliament alternative to those of government office, and a place in government was dependent on the prime minister, the *party* leader. Achieving a leadership position in the House meant, in effect, becoming a minister.

The nature of government decision making as well as the increasing responsibilities assumed by government also had the effect of moving policy making farther from the floor of the House. The conventions of collective and individual ministerial responsibility helped provide a protective cloak for decision making within the cabinet and within departments. Only the conclusions of discussions could be revealed. Furthermore, as government responsibilities expanded and became more dependent on the cooperation of outside groups (see Chapter 7), government measures came increasingly to be the product of negotiation between departments and interest groups, who then presented those measures to Parliament as packages already agreed on. As the demands on government grew, these "packages" increased in extent and complexity. The House of Commons was called on primarily to approve measures drawn up elsewhere and for which it lacked adequate time, resources, and knowledge to submit to sustained and informed debate.

Parliament thus came to occupy what was recognized as a back seat in policy making. This is not to say that it ceased to be an important political body. As we shall see, institutions are not neutral in their effect. The government remained dependent on Parliament for its support, and both houses continued to provide significant forums of debate and scrutiny. Nelson Polsby has distinguished between transformative legislatures (enjoying an independent capacity, frequently exercised, to mold and transform proposals into law) and arena legislatures (providing a formal arena in which significant political forces could be expressed).[7] The British Parliament can most appropriately be described as having moved from being temporarily a transformative legislature in the second third of the nineteenth century to an arena legislature in the twentieth. The U.S. Congress, by contrast, has remained a transformative legislature.

THE HOUSE OF COMMONS

The events of the nineteenth century that served to consolidate power in the executive served also to ensure the dominance of the House of Commons within the triumvirate of monarch, Lords, and Commons. The Commons constitutes the only body of the three that is popularly elected. Indeed, its dominance has become such that there is a tendency for many to treat "House of Commons" and "Parliament" as almost synonymous terms. The attention accorded it by the media and outside observers is far more extensive than that accorded the House of Lords.

Members

The House of Commons has a much larger membership than its U.S. equivalent. It has 646 members, each elected to serve a particular constituency (see Chapter 5). The size of the House has varied, ranging from a twentieth-century high of 707 members (from 1918 to 1922, subsequently reduced because of the loss of most Irish seats) to a low of 615 (from 1922 to 1945). After 1945, the size of the House increased gradually as a result of the recommendations of the Boundary Commissions and reached a peak of 659 members in the period from 1997 to 2005, when a reduction in the number of seats in Scotland resulted in the current size. As a result of boundary changes in England, the number of seats in the House elected in 2010 will rise to 650.

There is no formal limit on the number of terms an MP can serve. The average length of service in the British Parliament is much longer than that in other Western legislatures. As can be seen from Table 12.1, in the early 1990s the average length of service of a British MP was twenty years. This compared with just over eleven years for a U.S. senator and twelve years for a member of the House. The figure is an average. Some MPs serve for only one or two terms, leaving the House usually as a result of electoral defeat: The 1997 general election produced a large number of electoral casualties. Of members sitting in the House at the beginning of 2009, the average length of service was 13.4 years. Some members (as in the U.S. Congress, especially the Senate) serve for several decades. It is not uncommon for MPs representing safe seats to sit in the House for thirty years or more. Sir Winston Churchill sat in the House for a total of sixty-two years.[8] The MP with the longest continuous service in the House is given the courtesy title of "Father of the House." In 2009, the Father of the House, Alan Williams, had first been elected in 1964, though another MP (Sir Peter Tapsell), with discontinuous service, had first been elected in 1959.

The House elects one of its members as speaker. The speaker is normally though not always drawn from the majority party in the House,[9] though once in office may serve in succeeding Parliaments despite a change of government. The speaker, once elected, disclaims any party affiliation and serves as an independent presiding officer. Though she or he enjoys important powers of discipline and some business management, much of the speaker's activity is governed by precedent, most of it embodied in the handbook of parliamentary

TABLE 12.1

THE AVERAGE LENGTH OF LEGISLATIVE SERVICE, 1994

Country	Average length of service (years)
Canada	6.5
France	7
Denmark	7.8
Germany	8.2
Israel	11
United States (Senate)	11.1
United States (House)	12.2
New Zealand	13.1
Japan	15
United Kingdom	20

Source: A. Somit and A. Roemmele, "The Victorious Legislative Incumbent as a Threat to Democracy: A Nine Nation Study," *American Political Science Association: Legislative Studies Section Newsletter*, Vol. 18 (2), 1995.

practice, known as *Erskine May* (after the clerk in the nineteenth century responsible for its initial compilation); the speaker is also advised by the clerks, the full-time officers of the House of Commons. Three other members of the House are chosen to serve as deputy speakers. The deputy speakers retain their party labels, but—like the speaker—they serve as impartial officers of the House and do not normally take part in votes.

Members of Parliament are predominantly white, male, and middle class. In recent years they have become less white and male, though more middle class. Non-white MPs have occasionally been elected to the House, but none was elected between 1929 and 1987. In 1987, four non-white MPs were elected; in 2005, the number was fifteen (13 Labour and 2 Conservative). Women were first permitted to sit in 1918, but in subsequent elections only a handful were elected. In the 1983 general election, for example, only 23 were elected. It was not until 1997 that the number reached three-figures: In that election, 120 were elected to the House. The number fell to 118 in 2001 but increased to 128 in 2005. Most female MPs are Labour (98 in 2005), a consequence of the party utilizing all-women shortlists in order to select candidates in some seats. Some female MPs have occupied leadership positions: Margaret Thatcher was the first female prime minister (1979–90) and Betty Boothroyd the first female speaker (1992–2000). Paul Boateng became the first non-white cabinet minister in 2002.

Since 1945, MPs have become notably more middle class. Before the Second World War, and for a little time thereafter, the Parliamentary Labour Party (PLP) boasted a significant proportion of MPs from working-class backgrounds, often miners; the Conservative ranks were swelled by members

TABLE 12.2

THE EDUCATIONAL BACKGROUND OF MPs, 2005

Type of education	Conservative	Labour	Liberal Democrat
Secondary	7	38	4
Secondary + poly/college	16	86	6
Secondary + university	57	168	28
Public school	4	1	0
Pub sch + poly/college	11	4	3
Pub sch + university	103	58	21
Total	198	355	62
Oxford University	49	40	11
Cambridge University	37	18	8
Other universities	74	168	30
All universities	160	226	49
Eton	15	1	1
Harrow	—	—	—
Winchester	1	—	—
Other public schools	102	62	23
All "public" (i.e., private) schools	118	63	24

Source: Derived from B. Criddle, "MPs and Candidates," in D. Kavanagh and D. Butler (eds.), *The British General Election of 2005* (Palgrave Macmillan, 2005), Table 10.5, p. 164.

of aristocratic families and very wealthy industrialists. As parliamentary work has become more demanding, and as salaries and resources have improved, more members drawn from the professions and from academia have entered the House. Today most MPs have university degrees and enter the House after a spell in business or the professions. Tables 12.2 and 12.3 show the backgrounds of members returned to the House in 2005. An increasing number are drawn from careers in the political world, such as party researchers, parliamentary officers for pressure groups, and political lobbyists. Some are drawn from jobs that have been pursued as a temporary expedient, essentially to provide a base while pursuing election to the House of Commons. Labour MPs in 2005 "were increasingly drawn from the ranks of professional politicians, who dominated the new intake."[10] Such politicians have been characterized by Anthony King as "career politicians"—people who live for politics.[11] Career politicians have always existed in British politics, but they have grown in number in recent decades. They enter Parliament as soon as they can and pursue careers as parliamentarians. Critics contend that such MPs have little knowledge of the world outside the political domain; their defenders point out that they enter the House well versed in the ways of government and hence are in a good position to influence government on behalf of their constituents.

Members of Parliament are more numerous than members of the U.S. House of Representatives. There is also another notable difference. MPs, compared with their U.S. (and indeed many Western) counterparts, have generally been underpaid and under-resourced. The payment of salaries to MPs is a twentieth-century phenomenon—first introduced in 1912, when the princely sum of £400 ($656) was paid annually—and has generally lagged behind legislative salaries elsewhere and behind salaries of middle-level managers in the United Kingdom. Even in 1964 an MP enjoyed a salary of only £3,250 (just over $5,300). Apart from their salaries, MPs were provided with free travel between the constituency and London. They were provided with little else. Most MPs had no offices (they had to make do with school-type lockers) and for research and information were dependent on the facilities of the Commons' Library, a body with limited staff. There were no secretarial or research allowances. A number of MPs could not afford to hire secretaries and some replied to constituents' letters in longhand.

Conditions have notably changed since. Acquisition and conversion of various buildings close to the Palace of Westminster—coupled with the building of a large new office block, named Portcullis House—has meant that every MP has an office. Some of the offices are spacious and well equipped. Some are small and relatively barren. The more fortunate MPs have secretaries in adjoining offices. (Because MPs' offices are allocated by the party whips and secretarial offices allocated by the Sergeant at Arms' Office—an administrative department of the House—a Member's office can sometimes be some distance from the secretary's office; in some cases, they are in separate buildings.) A secretarial allowance—of £500 ($820) —was introduced in 1969 and has since been increased to cover research as well as secretarial support: By 2009 each MP was provided with a staffing allowance (of around £100,000 [$164,000]) for the employment of up to 3.5 staff; there is an increasing tendency for MPs to have one or more staff (such as a secretary or caseworker) based in the constituency. Library facilities have also been expanded, in terms of personnel and resources. There is also extensive provision of Internet and communication technology (ICT) resources through a dedicated ICT department serving both Houses.

An MP's annual salary has variously been increased decade by decade. By 2009, it was £64,766 ($106,200). Allowances have also been introduced to cover the cost of living away from one's main residence: It was £187.50 ($307) when first introduced in 1971, but by April 2009 had reached £24,222 ($39,724); for MPs representing seats in the capital there is a London supplement. These allowances attracted little attention until 2009 when unauthorized publication of the details of claims made by Members created a major political crisis. Some MPs were revealed to be claiming allowances for property mortgages that had already been paid off or for items not essential to the upkeep of a property (such as cleaning out a moat); some kept switching the designation of their main home when selling property (sales of second

TABLE 12.3

THE OCCUPATIONAL BACKGROUND OF MPs, 2005

Occupation	Conservative	Labour	Liberal Democrat
Professions			
Barrister	22	10	2
Solicitor	18	18	2
Doctor/dentist/optician	3	1	2
Architect/surveyor	4	1	2
Civil/chartered engineer	1	4	—
Accountant	5	3	2
Civil servant/local govt.	3	22	3
Armed services	13	1	—
Teachers			
University	—	16	3
Polytechnic/college	—	25	—
School	6	32	9
Other consultancies	1	1	—
Scientific/research	—	7	—
Total	76	141	25
	(38%)	(40%)	(40%)
Business			
Company director	23	4	6
Company executive	41	6	7
Commerce/insurance	7	1	3
Management/clerical	1	11	2
General business	3	3	—
Total	75	25	18
	(38%)	(7%)	(29%)
Miscellaneous			
Misc. white collar	4	70	4
Politician/pol. organizer	20	60	7
Publisher/journalist	14	24	5
Farmer	6	—	2
Housewife	1	—	—
Student	—	—	—
Total	45	154	18
	(23%)	(43%)	(29%)
Manual workers			
Miner	1	10	—
Skilled worker	—	20	1
Semi/unskilled worker	1	5	—
Total	2	35	1
	(1%)	(10%)	(2%)
Grand Total	198	355	62

Source: Derived from B. Criddle, "MPs and Candidates," in D. Kavanagh and D. Butler (eds.), *The British General Election of 2005* (Palgrave Macmillan, 2005), Table 10.6, p. 165.

homes were subject to a capital gains tax). Though treating such allowances as a salary top-up still left British MPs trailing behind some of their continental (and U.S.) counterparts, the controversy generated by the nature of the claims led to a number of MPs announcing they would not be seeking re-election as well as to the resignation of the speaker (Michael Martin), who had been seen as an obstacle to the publication of MPs' expenses and to a reform of the system. Rules on allowances were tightened up and wider changes proposed to bolster confidence in the political process.

MPs representing the governing party are generally regarded as aspirants for ministerial office. If one becomes a minister, one is able to exercise political power. One also enjoys the pay and perks of ministerial office. Ministers are paid separate ministerial salaries, enjoy the trappings of office (chauffeur-driven car, ministerial offices, and staff) and, as MPs, continue to receive their parliamentary salary and allowance. At the end of 2008, Cabinet ministers sitting in the House of Commons were each entitled to £141,866 ($232,660) a year, a figure that included their parliamentary salaries (the prime minister had a higher salary; cabinet ministers in the House of Lords had lower ones). Ministers of state received £104,050 ($170,600) and junior ministers £94,228 ($154,500), again with ministers in the Lords—and thus with no constituency responsibilities—receiving less.

The other notable difference between members of the House of Commons and members of the House of Representatives is that already touched upon at the beginning of this chapter: voting behavior. Members of the House of Representatives, as we have noted, are influenced by several sources. Party is important but not always the most important. With MPs, party is the dominant influence. If the parties issue a whip—in other words, declare a party line on an issue—then MPs will vote loyally with their party. In recent years, party voting has shown an increase in the U.S. Congress but, by international standards, party voting remains weak. In the years after 1970, party voting in the House of Commons was less pronounced than in previous decades. MPs proved more willing to vote against their own side on more occasions, in greater numbers and with more effect. However, the change was relative. Party cohesion remained a notable characteristic of voting in the House and it continues to do so. Even the most rebellious MPs vote with their party in more than 90 percent of all votes. The gap between the House of Representatives and the House of Commons in voting behavior is not as wide as it once was, but the remarkable feature is not the narrowing of the gap but simply the fact that it remains a gulf.

Functions

The Commons, like other legislatures, is a multifunctional body: That is, it fulfills a variety of tasks in addition to the defining task of legislatures (that of giving assent). The most important functions of the Commons are those of providing the personnel of government, of legitimation, of debate, and of scrutinizing and influencing government. The list is not exhaustive, nor are the functions mutually exclusive.

Parliament provides the personnel of government—that is, ministers; by convention, most ministers, including the prime minister, are drawn from the Commons. This function is largely a passive one in that the House itself does not do the choosing. The outcome of a general election determines which party will form the government, and the prime minister chooses who will fill which ministerial posts. Even so, the institution is important because membership is a prerequisite for appointment to office. In the United States, there are multiple routes to the top: The president can draw members of his administration from a wide range of positions. They do not have to be drawn from the Senate or the House. In the United Kingdom, the prime minister has a small pool from which to draw. Parliament holds a virtual monopoly on the supply of politicians for ministerial office. Furthermore, the House provides an important arena in which ministerial aspirants can demonstrate their political abilities. It also constitutes an important testing ground for ministers once they are appointed. Ministers remain members of the House. They have to cope with the demands of a sometimes rowdy chamber and of supporters who may be less than happy with ministers' performances at the Commons' dispatch box. A poor performance may hamper, on occasion even destroy, a ministerial career.

Legitimation is fundamental to the existence of Parliament. It constitutes the core defining function of the institution and is the oldest function of the House of Commons. Government requires the formal assent of Parliament both for the passage of legislation and for the grant of money. Given the government's control of a parliamentary majority, such assent is normally forthcoming. The giving of this assent, however much it may be taken for granted, fulfills an important symbolic role. It constitutes the elected assembly giving the seal of approval on behalf of the citizenry. Furthermore, it is important because the House retains the power to deny that assent. It may hardly ever use the power, but the option to do so remains. Parliament also provides what has been termed latent legitimation for government. By meeting regularly and uninterruptedly, by subjecting public policy to debate and questioning, and by being seen to do so, Parliament serves to legitimize the government. Citizens know that Parliament is there, carrying out tasks on their behalf.

The function that is the most obvious manifestation of an arena legislature is that of debate. Parliamentary debate forms a central mechanism for scrutinizing and attempting to influence government, but serves also as an important safety valve. The House provides an authoritative forum in which different and often conflicting views in society can be given expression. The most structured expression is through political parties, but MPs can also use the chamber to raise the concerns of other groups in society and to express the specific views of constituents. The power of the House to debate was established early in its history. The capacity of members to debate has been developed over several centuries. As an arena legislature, the emphasis has been on debate in the chamber. Debate takes place in public session and with ministers present to hear and respond to what is said. It also takes place according to extensive and well-established rules.

The House itself is not the government, but government is drawn from it and remains answerable to it. The House is thus uniquely placed to subject government to scrutiny, and to seek to influence it, on behalf of the citizenry. The means of scrutiny and influence are varied. They can be divided into those used for legislation and those employed for executive actions.

Legislation

Legislation is subject to a well-defined procedure once it has been submitted for parliamentary approval (see Table 12.4). First reading constitutes the formal introduction of a bill. At this stage, it is not debated. Indeed, it does not even exist in printed form. Once formally introduced, it is printed and set down for its second reading. Compared with the analogous procedure in the U.S. Congress, the second reading is distinct in two significant respects. First, it is the government that determines when the debate will take place. (With the exception of 20 "opposition days," and certain days given over to debates on reports, private business, private members' bills, and motions, the government has control of the parliamentary timetable.) The cabinet approves legislation to be placed before Parliament and a cabinet committee (the Legislation Committee—see Chapter 8) decides the program for the forthcoming session. Second, the debate in plenary session precedes the committee stage. On second reading, the principle of the bill is debated and approved. Only after it has received its second reading is it referred to a committee for consideration of its specific provisions.

Second reading debates follow a set pattern. With a government bill, a minister makes a speech outlining and justifying the bill. A member of the shadow cabinet then makes a speech in response, outlining the stance of the opposition. There will then usually be a speech from the relevant spokesperson on the Liberal Democrat benches. There then follows a series of speeches by back-benchers, alternating between the two sides of the House. Technically, members are called to speak by catching the speaker's eye, though in practice they will have notified the speaker in advance and will have received some indication as to whether or not they will be called. Speeches are usually prepared in advance and so those taking part usually offer set-piece presentations. To call it a "debate" is thus somewhat misleading. Also, in practice, there are often few MPs present to engage in debate. Attendance falls following the speeches from the front benches. In some debates a back-bencher may be speaking to only a handful of MPs in the chamber. More members tend to come in toward the end of the debate, with closing speeches made from the two front benches—the front-benchers responding to the points made during the debate. The question ("That the Bill be read a second time") is then put and, if some members shout "No," a vote takes place. All votes are roll-call votes with members going into voting lobbies on either side of the chamber. As long as a government has an overall majority, the House will almost always vote for the bill. During the whole of the twentieth century, there were only three occasions when a

TABLE 12.4

LEGISLATIVE STAGES IN PARLIAMENT

Stage	Where taken	Comments
First reading	On the floor of the house	Formal introduction; no debate
Second reading	On the floor of the house*	Debate on the principle
[Money resolution: Commons]	On the floor of the house	
Committee	In public bill committee in the Commons unless house votes otherwise (certain bills taken on the floor of the house); on the floor of the house or in grand committee in the Lords.	Considered clause by clause; amendments may be made.
Report	On the floor of the house**	Bill reported back to house; amendments may be made.
Third reading	On the floor of the house	Final approval; no amendments possible in the Commons
Lords (or Commons)	On the floor of the house amendments	Consideration of amendments made by other house

*In the Commons, non-contentious bills may be referred to a committee.
** If a bill is taken in committee of the whole House and no amendments are made, there is no report stage.
Source: Derived from P. Norton, *Parliament in British Politics* (Palgrave Macmillan, 2005), pp. 82–83.

government lost a bill on second reading and only on one of those occasions did a government have an overall parliamentary majority.

At committee stage, bills are considered usually by public bills committees. Before 2007, they were considered by what were known as standing committees—despite their name they had no permanent membership (it changed for each bill) and were not empowered to take evidence. Public bill committees, like their predecessors, have no permanent membership but are empowered to take evidence. A committee will be appointed to consider a specific bill and then, having completed its deliberations, ceases to exist in that form. Each committee has a membership of between 16 and 50 members, usually now 16 members for all but the largest and most contentious bills. They meet to take evidence from witnesses and then discuss the bill clause by clause and to consider amendments to each clause. In practice, the ability to amend and influence the content of measures is circumscribed. Once the House has approved the principle of the measure, a committee cannot make any changes that run counter to the principle embodied in the bill. The greatest constraints, however, are political. The format adopted at committee meetings is an adversarial one: Government MPs sit on one side, opposition MPs on the other. Debate is usually along party lines, as is voting. The result is that the amendments that are carried are almost always those introduced by ministers. (One or more ministers from the relevant department are always appointed to the committee.) Because most bills discussed by committees are introduced by the government, the main purpose of introducing government amendments is to correct drafting errors, improve the wording, or, more substantially, to meet points made by outside groups or meet points made by MPs that the government finds acceptable.

Public bill committees thus differ considerably from their U.S. counterparts. They are temporary, they are presided over by an impartial chairman (an MP drawn from a body of MPs appointed for their ability to chair such meetings), and they are confined in their deliberations solely to the content of bills. They have no power to undertake inquiries or to discuss anything other than the bill before them. The government's majority on a committee is in proportion to its majority in the house as a whole. Hence, as long as it has a majority in the House, it is assured a majority on such committees. The result is that bills usually emerge from committees relatively unscathed. Unlike U.S. congressional committees, public bill committees are not a burial ground for bills. Rather, they serve as temporary transit points in their passage.

Once a public bill committee has completed its deliberations, a bill is then returned to the House for the report stage, during which the House may make further amendments. This stage is not dissimilar to the committee stage and the government may use it to introduce amendments that it had not been able to introduce in committee (for example, to meet points raised in committee but for which it had not had time to formulate a precise amendment). The outcome of votes on amendments is the same as in committee. Government amendments are normally carried. Amendments introduced by private members are usually defeated, unless they find favor with the government. The acceptance rate is similar to that in committee.[12]

Each bill considered in a public bill committee goes through a report stage. Certain important bills, such as those introducing constitutional change (for example, reform of the House of Lords), have their committee stage on the floor of the house. If they emerge from this stage without amendment, there is no report stage: They proceed immediately to third reading. At third reading, the House gives its final approval to a measure. Debate at this stage is usually shorter than on second reading (it may be dispensed with altogether), and it must be confined to the content of the bill. Suggestions for amendments are out of order.

Once the House has approved third reading, the bill is sent to the House of Lords. (The exceptions, of course, are any bills that originate in the Lords.) If the Lords make any amendments, these are then sent to the Commons. The House debates these amendments, usually on a motion to agree or disagree with them. If the House disagrees with a Lords amendment, this fact—along with the reasons for the disagreement—is communicated to the upper house. The House of Lords then usually concurs with the Commons and does not press its amendment. Once a bill has passed both houses, it is sent for the Royal Assent.

Government bills dominate the legislative timetable. This is hardly surprising given the onus placed on government to initiate measures and the fact that the government controls the timetable. Between 20 and 60 government bills are introduced and passed each year (see Table 12.5). In recent decades, the number of government bills has not increased markedly, but the length of the bills has. Bills are longer and more complex than before and so require substantial parliamentary time.

Opportunities for private members to introduce bills of their own are limited. Certain Fridays each session (usually ten) are set aside to discuss private members' bills. So limited is the time available and so great the number of members wishing to introduce bills that a ballot is held each parliamentary session (that is, each year), and the resulting 20 top members have priority in introducing bills. In practice, only about the first six whose names are drawn will stand much chance of achieving a full debate for their bills, and even then there is no guarantee of the bills being passed. The opportunities available for a substantial or contested bill to get through all its stages during private members' time on Fridays are small. Such a bill will normally need more

TABLE 12.5

Bills introduced 2003–08

Session	Government*		Private members'**	
	Passed	Failed	Passed	Failed
2003–04	33	0	7	99
2004–05***	21	12	0	62
2005–06	56	1	3	137
2006–07	31	0	3	117
2007–08	29	0	3	110
Total	170	13	16	525

*Excludes bills carried over from one session to the next.

**The number of private members' bills includes bills introduced in the House of Lords but never brought to the Commons.

***Various government bills dropped because of general election.

Source: Calculated from House of Commons, Sessional Information Digests 2003–08 (The Stationery Office).

time than is available and will be dependent on government's finding time in its own timetable. The government is thus in a position to determine the fate of most private members' bills. It can deny such bills the necessary time to complete the required legislative stages or it can persuade its supporters to defeat them in a parliamentary vote. As a result, private members' bills often cover matters that are not politically contentious and are unlikely to arouse the opposition of government.[13] Until recent years, a fairly high number of such uncontentious bills, usually involving little or no debate, have been passed; 87 in the 1992–97 Parliament, for example. However, in recent years, the number has fallen. Rather than the number of successful bills being in double figures each year, it is now in single figures (see Table 12.5). A further important constraint is that such bills cannot make a charge on the public revenue. Only ministers can introduce bills that make such a charge.

Hence, the scope for legislative initiative by private members is limited but not nonexistent. Occasionally, a private member may introduce a bill on an important issue toward which the government is sympathetic and for which it is prepared to find time. This was the case especially in the 1960s, when a number of major social measures—reforming the laws on abortion, divorce, homosexuality, and the death penalty—were enacted through private members' legislation. The government left it up to the House, providing time where necessary in order for members to reach decisions. However, the period was exceptional. Since then, governments have been reluctant to find time for such bills. Rather, private members' bills are introduced as a way of raising issues. Debate on a bill allows for different views to be aired: It may even influence the government to introduce a bill of its own. If back-benchers are keen to achieve a change in the law on an important social issue, they are more likely now to move an amendment to a government bill than introduce a private member's bill.[14]

The number of days the House spends in session each year is shown in Table 12.6. About one-third of its time is taken up with debate on government bills. Less than 5 percent of its time is spent discussing private members' bills. Most of the rest of the time is given over to scrutinizing, in one form or another, the actions of government.

Executive Actions

Ministers and civil servants spend most of their time pursuing and administering policies and programs for which legislative authority has already been given or for which authority is not necessary (for example, policies pursued under prerogative powers). Hence, the formal approval of Parliament is not required. Nonetheless, the House of Commons subjects such actions to scrutiny. Various devices are employed for this purpose, principally parliamentary questions, debates, select committees, early day motions (EDM), and—outside the formal procedures—correspondence and private party meetings.

PARLIAMENTARY QUESTIONS   Question Time is a feature of the House of Commons for which there is no parallel in the Congress of the United States. It

TABLE 12.6

HOUSE OF COMMONS: SITTINGS AND PARLIAMENTARY QUESTIONS, 2003–08

	Parliamentary Session				
	2003–04	2004–05	2005–06	2006–07	2007–08
Number of days sitting	157	65	208	146	165
Number of hours sitting	1,215	535	1,572	1,118	1,306
Average length of sitting day	7hrs 44min	8hrs 14min	7hrs 33min	7hrs 40min	7hrs 55min
Parliamentary questions: Oral*	3,687	1,438	5,353	3,736	5,151
Written**	54,875	22,292	95,041	57,825	73,357

*Questions appearing on the Order Paper for oral answer
** Questions appearing on the Order Paper for written answer (ordinary or for a named day)
Note: The 2004–05 session was a short one because of the calling of a general election; the succeeding session was a long one.
Source: Figures derived from House of Commons, Sessional Information Digests 2003–08 (The Stationery Office).

has its origins in the eighteenth century and it entails the regular appearance of ministers, including the head of government, in the House to answer questions submitted by MPs who are not ministers. (The rough equivalent in the U.S. Congress would be for cabinet secretaries and the president to appear regularly on the floor of the House or Senate to answer questions; such sessions taking place several times a week.) Question Time in the House of Commons takes place each parliamentary sitting day, Monday to Thursday. (There is no Question Time when the House sits on a Friday.) On the first two days of the week it begins shortly after 2:30 P.M. and concludes promptly at 3:30 P.M. On Wednesday it begins shortly after the House sits at 11:30 A.M. and concludes at 12:30 P.M. On Thursdays, it begins shortly after 10:30 A.M. and concludes at 11:30 A.M. It is subject to well-defined procedures.[15] Ministers answer questions on a rota (rotation) basis, each principal minister coming up on the rota every four weeks. The prime minister has a regular slot, answering questions for 30 minutes from noon to 12:30 P.M. on a Wednesday.[16]

Questions are submitted (or "tabled") by MPs at least three days in advance. As the number exceeds the time available, there is a random selection (or shuffle)—initially done manually but now done by computer—to determine the order. Only those highly placed in the shuffle are printed on the daily Order Paper (see Figure 12.1). The House rarely gets through more than a dozen questions, if that, in the time available.

At Question Time, the MP whose question has come to the top in the shuffle rises and says, "Number One, Mr. Speaker." The minister then rises to answer the question. Ministers come armed with relevant information or responses compiled by their civil servants or special advisors and normally give prepared answers to the questions submitted three days before. Once the answer has been given, the speaker will then call on the MP who asked the question to put a supplementary, or follow-up, question. It is at the speaker's discretion as to how many supplementaries are allowed. If a member of the opposition front bench rises to put a supplementary, he or she enjoys priority over back-benchers. Having allowed one or more supplementaries—and rarely more than three or four—the speaker then calls the MP in whose name the second question stands. The MP rises, says, "Number Two, Mr Speaker," and the process is repeated. Questions that appear on the Order Paper but are not reached receive instead written answers that appear in *Hansard,* the official report of proceedings.

The last 15 minutes (for those departments with a 60-minute question time) or 10 minutes (for those with a 40-minute question time) are now given over to "topical questions": During this period, MPs can ask questions, without having given advance notice, on any subject relating to the department's responsibilities.

MPs also have the option of submitting questions for written answer. These are more numerous than questions tabled for an oral answer at Question Time: In a typical session, more than 50,000—sometimes considerably more—will be tabled (see Table 12.6). The answers, along with the questions, are published in *Hansard.* Written questions are popular as a means of eliciting statistics and other material that cannot easily be given in oral form. Oral questions, by contrast, are used to elicit statements and comments on government policy and matters that MPs think might embarrass (or, if the MP is on the government side, help) government or generate favorable attention back in the constituencies.[17] Prime minister's Question Time has become a particular vehicle for the partisan clash between the parties, and especially between the prime minister and the leader of the opposition. Because the prime minister has no departmental responsibilities, questions have to be general—or "open"—in nature. The most common is to ask the prime minister to list his engagements for the day (see Figure 12.1), thus leaving MPs free to raise almost any issue in supplementary questions. Through this technique, opposition MPs try to catch the prime minister out by asking difficult questions which he may not be anticipating.

DEBATES   As we have seen, debate is central to the House of Commons. Various types of debate are held on the floor of the House of Commons. The most important can be classified as general debates, held to discuss particular government policies. They start once any business after Question Time, such as ministerial statements, is concluded. A half-day debate will usually last up to three-and-a-half hours and a full-day debate up to six-and-a-half. Such debates take place on motions tabled by the government (for example, on motions to approve particular policies or to take note of particular

Oral Questions to the Secretary of State for International Development

*1 Mrs Anne McGuire (Stirling):   What assessment he has made of the effect of the global economic downturn on Ukraine's need for development aid from his Department.   (28179)

*2 Mr Mark Harper (Forest of Dean):   What steps he is taking to assess the effectiveness of his Department's programmes in Afghanistan.   (281791)

*3 Sandra Osborne (Ayr, Carrick and Cumnock):   What assistance his Department has provided to improve the humanitarian situation in North West Pakistan in the last 12 months.   (281794)

*4 Malcolm Bruce (Gordon):   What progress has been made on implementing the development agenda from the G20 London communiqué.   (281795)

*5 Mr Gordon Prentice (Pendle):   What recent steps his Department has taken to support projects to increase literacy amongst girls in Pakistan.   (281796)

*6 Mr Alistair Carmichael (Orkney and Shetland);   What recent assessment he has made of the humanitarian situation in Gaza; and if he will make a statement.   (281797)

*7 Mr Tom Clarke (Coatbridge, Chryston and Bellshill):   What steps his Department is taking together with international partners to ensure the direct delivery of aid to internally displaced persons in the autonomous tribal areas of northern Pakistan.   (281798)

*8 Alison Seabeck (Plymouth, Devonport):   What funding his Department has provided to fair-trade initiatives in the latest period for which figures are available.   (281799)

*9 Jim Sheridan (Paisley and Renfrewshire North):   What his latest assessment is of the humanitarian situation in Gaza: and if he will make a statement.   (281800)

*10 Jeremy Corbyn (Islington North):   What aid his Department provides to people from Western Sahara top refugee camps in Algeria.   (281801)

*11 Tom Brake (Carshalton & Wallington):   What his most recent assessment is of the humanitarian situation in camps for internally displaced persons in Sri Lanka; and if he will make a statement.   (281802)

*12 Rosie Cooper (West Lancashire):   What his latest assessment is of the effectiveness of his Department's projects to support economic development in the Palestinian West Bank.   (281803)

*13 Mr Andy Reed (Loughborough):   What recent assessment he has made of the contribution of faith organisations to his Department's work with civil society in developing nations.   (281804)

At 12 noon

Oral Questions to the Prime Minister

Unless otherwise indicated the Members listed below will ask a Question without notice.

*Q1 Patrick Hall (Bedford):   If he will list his official engagements for Wednesday 24 June.   (281805)

*Q2 Mr Jim Cunningham (Coventry South): (281806)

*Q3 Dr Ashok Kumar (Middlesbrough South & East Cleveland): (281808)

*Q4 Mr Tom Clarke (Coatbridge, Chryston and Belshill): (281809)

*Q5 Martin Salter (Reading West): (281810)

*Q6 Barry Gardiner (Brent North): (281811)

*Q7 Mr Mark Harper (Forest of Dean): (281812)

*Q8 Jim Dobbin (Heywood & Middleton): (281813)

*Q9 Mr Phil Willis (Harrogate & Knaresborough): (281814)

*Q10 Linda Gilroy (Plymouth, Sutton): (281815)

*Q11 Mr David Crausby (Bolton North East): (281816)

FIGURE 12.1
Questions on the House of Commons Order Paper

documents) or, on 20 "opposition days," by opposition parties (the official opposition decides the topic on 17 days, the third largest party—presently the Liberal Democrats—on the other three days). General debates are also held at the beginning of the parliamentary session on the Debate on the Address. Following the Queen's Speech opening the new session, in which government policy for the year is announced, a five-day debate is held. Formally, it takes place on an address to the queen, thanking her for her gracious speech, but in practice it covers particular government policies. One day, for example, is normally given over to a discussion of foreign affairs.

The other main type of debate is the adjournment debate. In practice, there are two forms of adjournment debate. One is the same essentially as a general debate; the only difference is that no substantive motion is before the house. Instead, a motion to adjourn is put down as a way of allowing debate to range freely on a topic for which the government has no specific policy or action that it wishes to be approved. In short, it is a useful means of sounding out the opinion of the House. At the end of the debate, the motion is usually rejected ("negatived") without a vote, thus enabling further business to be considered. The other type of adjournment debate is known as the half-hour adjournment debate and is held at the end of each day's sitting. These debates allow an MP, chosen usually after a ballot, to raise an issue, usually of constituency interest, for about 15 minutes, and allow the relevant minister (invariably a junior minister) about 15 minutes to respond to the points made. After exactly 30 minutes have elapsed, the House is automatically adjourned. These short debates take up little time but are extremely popular with back-bench MPs, allowing them to raise constituency problems or important but nonparty issues (for example, problems such as gambling, drug misuse, or the transferability of pensions). MPs raising the issues normally give ministers advance information of the points they intend to raise, thus allowing for a full reply to be prepared.

There are one or two other forms of debate. A recent innovation is the "topical debate." Introduced in 2007, it provides for a debate each week, for up to 90 minutes, on a "specified matter of regional, national or international importance." The topics are selected (on a Monday for debate on the Thursday) by the Leader of the House from suggestions put forward by members. In the 2007–08 session, topics included climate change, policing in London, drug strategy, anti-Semitism, and knife crime. Three days a year are also designated Estimates Days, formally to discuss selected financial estimates by government departments but in practice to discuss reports published by select committees (discussed later). All these debates are regularly scheduled debates. There is also provision for emergency debates. A member can ask leave to move the adjournment of the House "for the purpose of discussing a specific and important matter that should have urgent consideration." If the MP can convince the speaker that the matter (1) deserves urgent attention, (2) falls within the responsibility of government, and (3) cannot be raised quickly by another procedure, then the debate may be granted. If the debate is granted, it takes place the next day (or the following Monday if granted on a Thursday) or, if the speaker considers that the urgency of the matter justifies it, that same evening. In practice, the speaker tends to dislike the interruptions to scheduled business caused by such debates, and few are granted: Anything between none and four a session. They nonetheless constitute a useful safety valve, allowing members to discuss an important topic on occasion that the government had not proposed to bring before the House.

Of these various types of debate, general debates take up the most time. At least 10 percent of the House's time is usually taken up with debates on government motions. The format of such debates is similar to that of second reading debates. A government minister moves the motion; a member of the opposition front bench responds; then back-bench MPs speak, called alternately from each side of the House. In practice, as with second reading debates, any "debate" thus takes place among very few members. Most speeches are delivered from prepared notes and often have little relevance to the speeches that have preceded them. Nonetheless, any member wishing to have a speech printed in *Hansard* has to be present, catch the speaker's eye, and deliver it. There is no procedure in debate analogous to the American practice that allows for material to be inserted in the official record without it having been presented verbally in the chamber.

The opportunity for debate has also been extended beyond the chamber. In 1999, the House approved what are called "meetings in Westminster Hall." A large meeting room (the Grand Committee Room, just off Westminster Hall) is used, in effect, as a parallel chamber. Meetings are held there at set times on three days of the week to discuss noncontentious issues. Meetings can be held while the House itself is sitting and every MP is entitled to attend. The meeting room itself differs from the chamber in that the seating is arranged in a semicircular fashion, with desks rather than continuous benches, and with the chair sitting on a raised dais. As such, it resembles more the U.S. Senate than the British House of Commons. It is used in order to extend the opportunities for MPs to raise issues of concern. Tuesday and Wednesday sittings, for example, take the form of several short adjournment debates. Like the half-hour adjournment debates at the end of each sitting in the chamber, they are useful in that each debate receives a response from a minister. Like the half-hour adjournment debates, they receive little if any publicity and attract only a few MPs, but nonetheless are popular with members. Thursday sittings provide an opportunity to debate reports from select committees.

SELECT COMMITTEES Away from the floor of the House, the most important device employed for the scrutiny of the executive is that of select committees. Select committees are appointed to consider particular matters referred to them by the House. They have no responsibility for the formal scrutiny and approval of bills (that is the function of the separate public bill committees, unlike the procedure in the U.S. Congress, where the two responsibilities are combined in standing committees). They can be divided into two types: Domestic and investigative. Domestic committees deal with matters internal to the House, such as procedure, privileges, and administration. Investigative committees consider issues of public policy and the conduct of government. Our primary concern here is with investigative select committees. Such committees have been variously utilized in past centuries, but not on any consistent or comprehensive basis. Over the past two centuries, only two investigative committees have existed as important committees for any length of time. One is the Public Accounts Committee, first appointed in 1861 to ensure that public expenditure was properly incurred for the purpose for which it had been voted. Over time the committee has interpreted more widely its terms of references, conducting value-for-money exercises and investigating possible negligence. The committee has developed a reputation as a thorough and authoritative body, its recommendations resulting in government action to implement them or to provide a reasoned response to them. Traditionally, the committee is chaired by an opposition MP. The other important committee was the Estimates Committee. Unlike the Public Accounts Committee, it no longer exists. It was first appointed in 1912 and, after being suspended from 1914 to 1921, existed until 1971. It was appointed to look at the annual estimates and to consider ways in which policies could be carried out more cost-efficiently. It was not supposed to consider the merits of policies, but after 1945 began to venture into areas that could not be described as solely administrative. However, it was hampered by limited resources both in staff and in terms of the information presented to it by government. In 1971 it was replaced by a larger committee, the Expenditure Committee, itself divided into functional subcommittees. This committee disappeared in 1979, when a new system of committees was introduced.

The Select Committee on Nationalized Industries was formed in 1955 and a number of similar committees formed in the latter half of the 1960s. These later committees were disparate in the range of areas covered and vulnerable to government displeasure: One—a committee on agriculture—was wound up after encountering Foreign Office opposition to an inquiry it wanted to carry out in Brussels. In 1978, a Commons procedure committee recommended that if Commons scrutiny of the executive was to be effective, a new committee system was necessary, created on a systematic and permanent basis. Pressure for the creation of such a committee system built up within the house, and in 1979 the new Conservative leader of the house, Norman St. John-Stevas, brought forward motions for the appointment of the recommended committees. By 248 votes to 12, the House approved the creation of such committees to "examine the expenditure, administration, and policy of the principal Government Departments and associated public bodies." Twelve committees were agreed upon, though a further two—covering Scottish and Welsh affairs— were added shortly afterward. There have been some variations in numbers since, largely as a consequence of changes in government departments. At the beginning of 2009, there were 19 committees (Table 12.7). They are generally referred to as departmental select committees, thus distinguishing them from other investigative select committees of the House, such as the European Scrutiny Committee (looking at EU documents), the Environmental Audit Committee (looking at the extent to which government policies contribute

TABLE 12.7

HOUSE OF COMMONS: DEPARTMENTAL SELECT COMMITTEES, JUNE 2009

Committee	Number of members	Chairman
Business and Enterprise	11	Peter Luff (Con.)
Children, Schools and Families	14	Barry Sheerman (Lab.)
Communities and Local Government	11	Dr Phyllis Starkey (Lab.)
Culture, Media and Sports	11	John Whittingdale (Con.)
Defence	14	Rt Hon. James Arbuthnot (Con.)
Energy and Climate Change	14	Elliot Morley (Lab.)
Environment, Food and Rural Affairs	14	Rt Hon. Michael Jack (Con.)
Foreign Affairs	14	Mike Gapes (Lab.)
Health	14	Rt Hon. Kevin Barron (Lab.)
Home Affairs	11	Rt Hon. Keith Vaz (Lab.)
Innovation, Universities, Science and Skills	14	Phil Willis (Lib Dem.)
International Development	11	Rt Hon. Malcolm Bruce (Lib Dem.)
Justice	14	Rt Hon. Alan Beith (Lib Dem.)
Northern Ireland Affairs	13	Sir Patrick Cormack (Con.)
Scottish Affairs	11	Mohammad Sarwar (Lab.)
Transport	11	Louise Ellman (Lab.)
Treasury	14	Rt. Hon. John McFall (Lab.)
Welsh Affairs	11	Dr Hywel Francis (Lab.)
Work and Pensions	11	Terry Rooney (Lab.)

Con. = Conservative, Lab. = Labour, Lib. Dem. = Liberal Democrat

toward environmental protection), the Public Administration Committee (examining the civil service and reports from the ombudsman), and the Public Accounts Committee. They are also distinguishable from a new series of select committees—regional select committees—created in 2009.

The departmental select committees have faced a number of problems. They each have between 11 and 14 members and usually meet once a week for 90 minutes to two hours. Of necessity, each has to be selective in its choice of topics for investigation and in deciding whether to opt for short- or long-term studies, and whether to focus on policy, estimates, or administration (few have opted for estimates).[18] They have limited resources: Usually one or two full-time clerks each, secretarial support, and, in some cases, one or two specialist assistants (graduates with specialist knowledge, appointed usually on a fixed-term contract), with some specialist advisors drawn from outside institutions and paid on a daily basis. The committees have the formal power to "send for persons, papers and records" (in effect, to summon oral and written evidence), but that is of limited use in ensuring the attendance of ministers and other parliamentarians. (An order to attend, if ignored, can be enforced only by a resolution of the House, which is unlikely to be forthcoming against the wishes of government.) In practice, ministers do usually attend as requested: The real challenge is getting them to answer questions fully. Civil servants attend on behalf of their ministers and cannot express personal opinions or reveal any internal advice given to ministers. The relationship of the committees to the floor of the house is limited. There are very limited opportunities on the floor of the House for reports to be debated, though the opportunities have increased over time, not least as a result of utilizing sittings in Westminster Hall. Other reports may be mentioned ("tagged") on the Order Paper when a relevant debate occurs and occasionally there may be a special debate on a particular report, but there is no automatic procedure under which a committee can ensure its report is considered by the House. And, ultimately, the government may choose to ignore the recommendations of the committees. Though the government is committed to publishing a response to each report within two months (a target not always met), it is not committed to taking any further action on them.

Yet, despite these limitations, the committees have proved to be major improvements on their predecessors. They are more extensive and thorough in their scrutiny and have operated as identifiable and often cohesive units. Unlike most public bill committees, there is demand to join them, especially the more high-profile ones. They have proved to be prolific: Several hundred committee reports (usually between 300 and 400) are usually issued in each Parliament. Examples of reports issued by other committees are listed in Table 12.8. They have attracted more extensive media attention than their predecessors and they have become significant targets for representations from outside groups, something that never happened before. By their evidence-taking—and most committee sessions are used to take evidence from ministers, civil servants, or representatives of outside bodies—they have served to obtain information that otherwise would not be on the public record and also have served to inform debate. By taking evidence from outside bodies, they have provided the House with additional or alternative advice to that offered by government. They also have provided groups with an authoritative forum in which to make their views known and get them on the public record. They have sometimes served to have some influence on public policy. That impact has varied from committee to committee and is not amenable to precise quantification (government will not always give committees credit for a particular proposal) but there is some evidence of modest influence.[19] Reports may also serve a useful agenda-setting role, bringing an issue to the attention of ministers,[20] as well as providing some reinforcement for ministers in arguing a case for a particular policy.

TABLE 12.8

Select committee reports, session 2007–08: Foreign affairs and Home affairs

Committee	Substantive Reports
Foreign Affairs	Foreign and Commonwealth Office Annual Report 2006–07
	Global Security: Russia
	Foreign Policy Aspects of the Lisbon Treaty
	The Work of the Committee in 2007
	Global Security: Iran
	Proposed Appointment of the Rt Hon. Jack McConnell MSP as High Commissioner to Malawi
	Overseas Territories
	Scrutiny of Arms Export Controls
	Human Rights Annual Report 2007
	Global Security: Japan and Korea
Home affairs	The Government's Counter-Terrorism Proposals
	Bulgarian and Romanian Accession to the EU: Twelve months On
	Security Industries Authority: Licensing of Applicants
	Work of the Committee in 2007
	A Surveillance Society?
	Domestic Violence, Forced Marriage and "Honour"-Based Violence
	Policing in the 21st Century

Source: House of Commons, *Sessional Information Digest 2007–08* (The Stationery Office, 2008).

EARLY DAY MOTIONS EDMs are motions put down by members, technically for debate "on an early day." In practice, there is no time available to debate them. Rather, given that they are published, they serve as a means of expressing a written opinion. They constitute a form of notice board (sometimes less elegantly described as parliamentary graffiti). Members can and do add their signatures to such motions and the number of names a motion attracts serves as some indication of opinion within the House. A large number of signatures may occasionally influence the government to take action or may seriously embarrass it. Such occasions, though, are rare. The impact of EDMs is limited by the large number submitted and by the range of topics covered. In the 2007–08 session, for example, 2,727 were published. Some are essentially flippant or congratulatory (for example, congratulating some prominent figure or local body, such as a football team, on a recent achievement), whereas others express opinions on important issues of policy. Members are free to submit and to sign as many motions as they like. Some rarely do so; others have a reputation for signing every motion with which they have some sympathy. As a result, the significance of such motions is effectively diluted.

CORRESPONDENCE   Members do not rely solely on formal procedures. They can and do write to ministers, normally to elicit information and to convey the grievances, demands, and opinions of constituents and of different interests. Letter writing is an extensive activity, with between 10,000 and 20,000 letters a month being written by MPs to those of their number who are ministers. When a constituent writes to an MP, the MP will normally pass the letter on to the minister, requesting a response; there are printed cards available for the MP to use. A letter from an MP receives priority within a government department. A letter from a member of the public normally receives a reply from a civil servant. A letter from an MP must by convention be replied to by a minister. An MP's letter thus ensures that the particular issue reaches the minister's desk. In replying, ministers are not subject to the same time and partisan constraints that apply on the floor of the House. A detailed response can be and often is given, and this is then sent by the MP to the constituent. As we shall see, in writing to ministers, MPs are acting as important links between citizens and ministers. It is also a time-consuming activity.

PRIVATE PARTY MEETINGS   Both the Conservative and Labour parliamentary parties have their own party infrastructure. Each have plenary sessions: The PLP and the Conservative 1922 Committee (so named because it was initially formed by MPs first elected in 1922) meet each week. The Conservatives also used to have an extensive series of back-bench committees, but the reduction in the party's parliamentary ranks after 1997 meant that it was difficult to sustain them and they were replaced in the 2001 Parliament by a more modest arrangement. A policy group was created, meeting regularly but with different policy topics being considered at each meeting. The PLP developed a series of back-bench groups which tended to be less influential than their Conservative counterparts. However, following the return of the Labour Party to power in 1997, Labour groups have tended to be more active than before; they were helped by a change in the rules of the PLP imposing a greater duty on front-benchers to consult with the committees. Some ministers have reputations for being very good at consulting the relevant committee.

    The advantage of party meetings are that they are held in private, thus providing an opportunity for plain speaking between back-benchers and front-benchers. The party leader will variously address the parliamentary party and, at times of political crisis, the meetings can have a major impact on the leader or on party policy. A leader or other front-benchers may occasionally have to plead the case for a policy—or even their career—at a meeting of the PLP or the 1922 Committee. Various Conservative cabinet ministers have been effectively forced to resign by the 1922 Committee and in 2003 Conservative leader Iain Duncan Smith appealed, unsuccessfully, to Conservative MPs at a meeting of the committee not to vote him out as leader.

These, then, constitute the primary devices available to MPs to debate and scrutinize the actions of government. Most such devices are long-standing ones, though used more often in recent years than they were previously. Others are of recent origin. Together, they demonstrate that the relationship between Parliament and government is highly institutionalized. However, there is another vital relationship: that between Parliament and citizen.

LINKS WITH THE CITIZEN

MPs are elected, like members of the House of Representatives, in single-member districts (constituencies). The link with a local area has existed ever since the thirteenth century, when leading figures from the shires and then boroughs were summoned to the king's council (Chapter 3). The constituency role of the MP has grown in significance since the growth of a mass electorate in the nineteenth century. Constituents have come to expect their MP to be active on their behalf, fulfilling a range of functions, both in the constituency (such as being a local dignitary, seeing constituents with problems) and at Westminster (pursuing constituents' grievances and the interests of the constituency, acting as a safety valve for the expression of views, adding their voice to issues pursued by local groups).[21] Some of these functions have become more significant over the past half-century, though perhaps the most notable change has been the extent to which constituents now make contact with MPs in order to fulfill these functions. MPs have responded by devoting more of their time to constituency work.[22]

The growth of the welfare state in the latter half of the twentieth century meant that there was greater likelihood of citizens having some grievance against a public body. The expansion of mass education and the growth of the mass media contributed to a greater awareness of the political system and the availability of the local MP. Parliament itself has become more visible to electors, not least as a result of television coverage (cameras were allowed to cover proceedings in the Commons in 1989) and a greater use of the Internet: Considerable resources are now invested in the Parliament website (www.parliament.uk). MPs themselves have been increasingly keen to contact constituents in order to raise their profile. Traditional means of contact (leafleting, press releases, local meetings) have been complemented by the use of new technology.[23] Most MPs have websites and some write blogs and use social networking sites such as Facebook. Citizens thus have a greater awareness of Parliament and contact MPs on an ever increasing scale. One survey in late 2008 found that almost one person in ten had contacted an MP in the past two to three years.[24]

The form of contact varies. Virtually all MPs hold what are known as constituency "surgeries": publicly advertised meetings when constituents can come along and discuss issues in some detail. The average MP will hold at least two surgeries a month. In constituencies that are geographically large, an MP will often hold surgeries in different parts of the constituency. Such surgeries can, on rare occasions, be dangerous (early in 2000, an MP was attacked by a sword-wielding constituent and the MP's assistant was killed)[25] and, more pervasively, generate a significant volume of casework. However, the most significant and most time-consuming aspect of the MP–constituency link is through correspondence. Constituents write to their MPs and they do so on an increasing scale. In the mid-1950s, an MP may receive a dozen or so letters a week. By 2009, some were receiving several hundred a week. More than 4 million items of mail now flow into the Palace of Westminster each year; about 80 percent of these go to MPs and the rest to peers. E-mail correspondence now adds considerably to the burden. Most of those who write to the MP usually want an explanation or confirmation that something is in hand.[26]

Constituency correspondence takes priority in an MP's office. There is a parliamentary convention that an MP must reply to a letter written personally by a constituent. MPs reply not only because they feel that they have to but because they want to. Constituency work generates job satisfaction (by getting something done for a constituent—even if it is only obtaining an authoritative reply from a minister—an MP tends to feel something has been achieved) and is also increasingly seen as a means of bolstering support. Electors vote for a party but there is some evidence that MPs can attract a limited "personal" vote.[27] By working hard in the constituency, an MP may prevent supporters from peeling off and voting for another party. This may make a difference in some highly marginal seats. For most MPs it will not make any difference to the outcome, but the perception that it might do so motivates them to work hard in the constituency.[28]

MPs pursue constituency casework through a variety of means. They may table a question or they may even raise the matter in a daily adjournment debate. However, the most common means of pursuing casework is through correspondence with ministers. Writing to ministers following receipt of constituents' letters is also a time-efficient process of communication for MPs; it is a task undertaken at a time convenient to them, or at least less inconvenient than other means—such as questions for oral answer—that require their presence at a particular place at a particular time. If a minister's reply proves unsatisfactory to the member, then these other devices may be used. It is also a private means of communication, allowing the minister to reply without feeling the need to be defensive.

Evidence suggests that contact with MPs produces a positive evaluation on the part of constituents.[29] It also appears to contribute to a general perception that the local MP is doing a good job. When asked if the local MP was doing a good job, various surveys have found that roughly twice as many respondents gave a positive than a negative response, and the figures remained unchanged while evaluations of the House of Commons itself declined.[30] The reputation of MPs did, though, suffer as a result of the revelation in 2009 of Members' claims for additional costs for maintaining second homes: Some MPs, as we have noted, announced their decision to step down at the next election, while others suffered from criticism in their constituencies. One survey found that 76 percent of those questioned did not trust MPs to tell the truth. However, the role of the constituency MP lessened the impact: The figure was 44 percent for the local MP.[31]

The MP's role has thus changed over the years and the MP is now far more constituency active. MPs are also more active because of the work of interest groups. Citizens come together in groups to defend their interests and to promote particular causes (Chapter 7). Such groups have variously lobbied MPs to take action on their behalf, but the primary focus of such activity has been government. Though government remains the focus of group activity, interest groups have increasingly made use of Parliament in recent years. Government after 1979 appeared to adopt an arm's length relationship to interest groups (Chapter 7). The existence of more and more groups created a more competitive environment. Parliament also looked more attractive because of the creation of departmental select committees. MPs also appeared more willing to express their own views more than they previously did.[32] Groups started developing contacts with MPs and, as we have seen (Chapter 7), groups now inundate MPs with briefing material and requests to take action. Groups may also seek meetings with members as well as arranging mass lobbies and demonstrations. As we noted in Chapter 7, the use of professional lobbyists—little known before 1979—is now common. MPs pursue issues when legislation is going through—briefings from groups inform members as to problems with bills and amendments that may prove helpful—as well as raising issues on the floor of the House. The sheer range of organized interests means that MPs have a broad range of views to consider and party provides a protective shield. MPs are beholden to their parties and not to special interests. They can choose to take up an issue prompted by an interest group if they wish—and are especially likely to if there is a constituency connection—but they have the choice. The activities of interest groups are not likely to affect their chances of re-election. Representations from interest groups help MPs to be better informed about issues, and not dependent on government, and to pursue issues they believe have merit. Contact with MPs has generally elicited a positive evaluation by the groups.[33]

The work of MPs on behalf of citizens, either as individual constituents or drawn together in groups, is increasingly extensive and time-consuming. However, it has generated three problems. One has been the workload for MPs. There is an opportunity cost to dealing with all the correspondence they receive. By devoting so much time to constituency work, there is the danger that they may not have the time to fulfill their collective functions (such as scrutinizing legislation) effectively.[34] Members may have to forego attendance at committee meetings (or fail to do the preparatory work for such meetings) or listening to debates in the chamber. Though absence from the chamber may be a consequence of fulfilling constituency work, the image of empty green benches has an adverse effect on public perceptions of the House.

The second is that by working on behalf of interest groups, MPs have at times appeared to face a conflict of interests, putting the interests of a group (especially one that may be paying them a fee) ahead of the interests of their constituents. There was a particular controversy caused in 1994 by the "cash for questions" scandal, resulting—as we have seen in Chapter 7—in the creation of the Committee on Standards in Public Life and the acceptance of various recommendations made by that committee. As a result, MPs are now subject to a code of conduct for MPs; they are prohibited from advocating in the House any cause for which they receive payment; and they have to comply with extensive rules on the disclosure of interests and outside income derived from their position as MPs. A Parliamentary Commissioner for Standards exists in order to advise on the rules and to investigate allegations of any breaches of the rules. He reports to a committee of the House, the Committee on Standards and Privileges. Various MPs have fallen foul of the rules on disclosure, including leading figures of both main parties, and have been reprimanded or have apologized to the House. In more extreme cases, members have been suspended from service in the House for short periods.

The third problem has been that in order to fulfill their constituency roles, MPs are expected to maintain two homes. Before the 1960s, MPs often did not live in their constituencies, instead living in London and paying occasional visits to the constituency. Since then, local parties have increasingly expected the local MP to have a home in or near the constituency. To enable Members to maintain two homes, an additional cost allowance was introduced in 1971. As we have seen, this increased from just over £187 in 1971 to more than £24,000 in 2009. The amounts claimed were treated as confidential until the enactment of the Freedom of Information Act. When the figures for the amounts claimed were published, they attracted controversy, but nothing on the scale witnessed in 2009 when the detailed claims (what had been claimed for, rather than simply the total amount) were acquired by a national newspaper. Some MPs had claimed for items not deemed essential for maintaining a second home; some claims were deemed extravagant (such as a claim for a duck island) or even fraudulent (claiming to pay interest on mortgages that had already been paid). The controversy, as already noted, led to the resignation of the speaker. There was also a tightening of the rules governing allowances and an inquiry by the Committee on Standards in Public Life. The controversy undermined public confidence in MPs and the institution of which they were members.

THE HOUSE OF LORDS

The House of Lords is unusual in three respects and unique in a fourth. It is unusual in that it is a second chamber. Most countries have unicameral rather than bicameral legislatures. However, it is not unusual among Western legislatures, where second chambers tend to be the norm rather than the exception. It is unusual also in the size of its membership. Prior to a reform in

1999, it had just over 1,200 members. (There is no fixed number for membership.) Though this did not render it unique, it did render it exceptional among Western legislatures. Even after reform, it retains a large membership: 666 members at the end of November 1999, a number that had increased by 2009 to just over 730. It is unusual also in that it has a wholly appointed membership. Citizens do not elect any members of the second chamber. Though unusual in this respect, it is not alone. There are some other second chambers that are wholly appointed, most notably the Canadian senate. However, it is unique in that it has had a membership based predominantly on the principle of inheritance. Until 1999, the majority of members of the House of Lords—known as peers—served by virtue of having inherited their positions. Most members were hereditary peers.

The House has its origins in the court of Anglo-Saxon kings and their Norman successors. The king summoned to court his leading churchmen and his chief barons (who were the great landholders). The tradition developed of summoning the heir on the death of a baron and so the practice of an hereditary membership developed. From the time of the restoration, the hereditary peers outnumbered the churchmen. In the nineteenth century, the number of churchmen—known formally as the Lords Spiritual—was fixed at 26.

Though the principle that the House of Commons should initiate tax-raising measures was conceded in the fifteenth century, in other respects the two Houses were equal. However, the House of Lords was gradually forced to accept a subordinate position in its relationship with the House of Commons in the nineteenth and early twentieth centuries. The reason for this is clear. It was well stated by the Earl of Shaftesbury during debates on the 1867 Reform Bill. "So long as the other House of Parliament was elected upon a restricted principle," he declared, "I can understand that it would submit to a check from a House such as this. But in the presence of this great democratic power and the advance of this great democratic wave it passes my comprehension to understand how an hereditary House like this can hold its own."[35] Although not altogether swept away by this "great democratic wave," the House was at least to be swamped by it. It could not maintain a claim to equal status with the elected House, a house elected on an ever-widening franchise.

It is clear that the House of Lords cannot sustain a claim to being a representative chamber. Peers represent no one but themselves: Their writs of summons are personal. No member serves by virtue of popular election. It has thus had to accept a position as a subordinate chamber. It has undergone various reforms in order to adapt it to the changed circumstances. In the first half of the twentieth century, there were reforms to limit its powers. In the second half of the century, there were reforms to change its composition.

The changes to its powers were brought about by the Parliament Acts of 1911 and 1949. The 1911 Act stipulated that the House could delay a non-money bill for no more than two parliamentary sessions (in effect, two years) and could not delay a money bill (one certified by the speaker as dealing exclusively with money) at all. A money bill becomes law one month after being sent to the Lords, regardless of whether the House passes it or not. The 1949 Act reduced the delaying power from two sessions to one session. The House thus has the power to delay a bill for no more than one year.

The changes to its composition took place through three acts: the 1958 Life Peerages Act, the 1963 Peerages Act, and the 1999 House of Lords Act. The 1958 act introduced life peerages: These were peerages that, as the name suggests, were to exist only for the lifetime of the holder. They were introduced to try and strengthen the House by bringing in new people, especially those who found the principle of the hereditary peerage unacceptable. The creation of life peerages, rather than hereditary peerages, very quickly became the norm. Between 1964 and 1999, only three hereditary peerages were created. By the mid-1990s, the proportion of hereditary peers to life peers was approximately 2:1. However, life peers were, relative to their numbers, disproportionately active, both in the chamber and in the committee work of the House.[36] The introduction of life peerages, coupled with a new willingness on the part of peers from the late 1960s onward to fulfill the functions ascribed to the House,[37] had a notable impact on the activity of the House. It met for more days, had longer sittings than before, and witnessed a notable rise in attendance. The rise in attendance has been steady, decade by decade. By the 1990s the average daily attendance exceeded 400, representing about one-third of the membership.

The 1963 Peerages Act provided the means for hereditary peers to renounce their inherited titles. Though peers did not have to attend the House of Lords (and many did not do so, either for reasons of infirmity or because they were busy doing other things) they could not give up their titles. This was a problem to some peers, and more especially to their heirs, if they wanted to be elected to the House of Commons: Members of the House of Lords could not be elected to the Commons. The 1963 Act enabled Tony Benn, a Labour MP who had succeeded to his father's peerage, to return to the Commons; it also allowed the Earl of Home to accept the position of prime minister—he renounced his title and was elected to the Commons.

The 1999 Act was, historically, the most significant. Introduced in 1999 by the Labour government of Tony Blair, it sought to remove all hereditary peers from membership of the House of Lords. An amendment accepted during the passage of the Bill allowed 92 to remain. The Bill became the House of Lords Act in November 1999. Under its provisions, the House was thus transformed from one predominantly of hereditary peers to one of life peers. It constituted a change, in the eyes of some, from an aristocratic House to a meritocratic House, life peers being appointed because of their particular experience or expertise.

The removal of most hereditary peers had relatively little effect on attendance. The average daily attendance in recent years (see Table 12.9) has exceeded 400, representing more than one-half of the membership. The House also sits for about the same number of days as the Commons, though in the past has sometimes sat for more days because of the pressure

TABLE 12.9

Activity of the House of Lords, 2002–08

	Sittings of the Lords (by session)					
	2002–03	2003–04	2004–05*	2005–06	2006–07	2007–08
Sitting days	174	157	63	206	142	164
Average length of sitting (hrs./mins.)	7:15	6:58	7:17	6:39	6:31	6:46
Average daily attendance	362	368	388	403	415	413

*Short session because of a general election

Source: House of Lords, *The Work of the House of Lords* (House of Lords Information Office, 2009), pp. 34–35.

of business; it is likely to do so in the future in the event of a heavy legislative session. Like the House of Commons, it represents one of the busiest legislative chambers in the world.

The 1999 Act had a notable political consequence. The Conservative Party enjoyed disproportionate support among hereditary peers and had done so since the end of the eighteenth century. The removal of hereditary peers from the House of Lords was sought not only because of the fact that they were hereditary but also because they produced a political imbalance in the membership of the House of Lords. The removal of most hereditary peers reduced the Conservative strength in the House, though still leaving it as the largest single party. Since 1999, more Labour peers have been created, resulting in Labour becoming the largest single party in the House. More cross-bench (that is, independent) peers have also been created. This, combined with various deaths of Conservative peers, resulted in the Conservatives receding by 2009 to form the third largest grouping in the House (see Table 12.10). As can be seen from Table 12.10, no party has 30 percent of the membership of the House. This ensures that the government does not take the House for granted. Ministers have to persuade other parties, or the cross-bench peers, to support the government in order to get its measures through. This tends to have the effect of generating a less partisan environment than that of the House of Commons.

The House of Lords has thus changed dramatically in recent years. It remains a nonelected chamber, though the removal of most hereditary peers in 1999 was seen as making it a more legitimate chamber, and as such a more confident House, for fulfilling its functions.[38] It is a House nonetheless that is clearly subordinate to the elected chamber and, as such, it seeks to fulfill functions that complement, rather than challenge, the work of the first chamber.

TABLE 12.10

THE CHANGING PARTY COMPOSITION OF THE HOUSE OF LORDS, 1999–2009

	Number of peers		
Affiliation	January 1, 1999	March 1, 2000	May 1, 2009
Conservative	473	232	196
Labour	168	182	214
Liberal Democrat	67	54	72
Cross-bench	322	161	202

Cross-bench peers are independent peers who do not sit as members of the parties in the House. The numbers exclude the 26 Lords Spiritual (two archbishops and 24 bishops who sit in the House) and certain other peers classed as non-affiliated (for example, holders of particular offices, such as the Lord Speaker) who are not part of any formal grouping in the House.

Membership and Function

What, then, is the nature of the membership and what functions does the House perform?

MEMBERS   The members of the House of Lords tend to be male, middle or upper class, and middle and old aged. Because life peerages tend to be awarded to people who have achieved some distinction in life, they are usually conferred on people who are in their fifties or older. It is relatively rare but not unknown for life peerages to be conferred on people who are still in their thirties. Because peerages are for life, the House has a number of elderly members, pushing up the average age of the membership. The average age of the House in 2009 was 69. By the nature of the institution, members tend to be middle or upper class. When hereditary peers dominated, it had a much more upper-class flavor, many hereditary peers owning large estates. Life peerages have enabled people from modest backgrounds to enter the House. The membership tends to be male and white, though the number of women and members from ethnic backgrounds has increased notably. Women (who were first admitted to the House in 1958) comprise less than 20 percent of the membership, though they now often occupy leadership positions: In 2009, both the leader of the house (like three of her four immediate predecessors) and the first elected speaker of the House were women. The House has several peers drawn from different ethnic backgrounds as well as member of different nationalities; Commonwealth citizens can be created peers and several have been elevated to the peerage. The House also has some members who are disabled and wheelchair-bound. In the breadth of background of members, it has a somewhat broader spread of members than the House of Commons.

Members tend to be drawn from a range of professions and from people who have served in the House of Commons and in government office. The House has a reputation for the expertise that it is able to draw on when a particular subject is debated. A debate on medical ethics, for example, will attract peers who are leaders in the field of medicine and some of the nation's leading ethicists. A debate on higher education is likely to attract peers who are professors, heads of university colleges, former secretaries of state for education, members of university councils, university chancellors, and some who may have had responsibility for chairing funding or research councils. The nature of the House—best described as a full-time House of part-time members—is such that it has some members who are current experts, that is, still practicing in a professional capacity. One does not necessarily have to give up an existing job in order to become a member of the House of Lords. Some peers hold full-time posts, sometimes a considerable distance from London, while also attending the House.

Given that service in the House is not regarded as a full-time occupation, peers are entitled only to allowances to enable them to attend the House. (Peers who are ministers are paid salaries as are certain officers of the House, as well as the leader of the opposition and the opposition chief whip.) In mid-2009, peers could claim a daily attendance allowance of £86.50 (just under $142), an office cost allowance (for secretarial and research support) of £75 ($123), an overnight accommodation allowance of just over £174 (just over $285), and traveling expenses. Members have to attend the House in order to claim the allowances; officials of the House keep a note of who is present in the chamber each day.

FUNCTIONS Given that it is not an elected body and that it occupies a subordinate position in relation to the House of Commons, what functions are performed by the House? It provides some of the personnel of government. As we have seen in Chapter 8 (Table 8.6), almost 30 ministers are drawn from the House of Lords. Most are junior ministers or whips. (In the Lords, unlike the Commons, whips serve also as spokespersons for departments.) There is an advantage to the government in having some ministers in the House of Lords. It enables the government to defend itself in the House. It also produces ministers who have no constituency responsibilities and therefore who can spend more time in their departments than ministers who, as MPs, have constituency responsibilities. It also enables the prime minister to draw into the ranks of ministers people who have not sought elective office: Someone can be appointed a minister at the same time as a peerage is conferred on that person. Prime Minister Gordon Brown has made several such appointments, as did his predecessor, Tony Blair.

The other functions may be subsumed under the broad rubric of scrutiny and influence (of legislation and of executive actions), of providing a forum for public debate, and, formally, of legitimation. The House previously had also a unique judicial function: Until 2009, it constituted the highest domestic court of appeal, a function exercised by a judicial committee of specially appointed law lords. In October 2009, the function transferred to a new supreme court (Chapter 14).

These may be identified as the main functions of the House. Of them, one—that of legitimation—has been circumscribed both by the provisions of the Parliaments acts and by the acceptance by peers of their politically sub-ordinate status. Recognizing their undemocratic nature, members of the Lords have refrained from seeking to challenge the House of Commons. There have been occasional periods of bad feeling between the two houses, notably in the period of Labour government from 1974 to 1979 and, to some extent, since 1997, but the upper house rarely seeks to press an amendment—let alone delay a measure—when it is clear that the Commons is not prepared to support it. Under what is known as the Salisbury convention (first advanced by the Conservative leader in the Lords in 1945), the official opposition in the Lords does not force a vote on the second reading of any bill promised in the government's election manifesto. A government is usually ensured of the upper house approving (or rather, not opposing) the principle of any measure it proposes.

Given the Lords' reluctance to challenge the government on the principle of measures, the House concentrates instead on scrutinizing the specific provisions of such measures. Bills pass through the same legislative stages as in the Commons, though committee stage of a number of bills is sometimes taken on the floor of the House rather than in grand committee. In engaging in detailed legislative scrutiny, the House not only has the advantage of the experience and expertise of its members but also various procedural opportunities denied the House of Commons. In the Commons, the government can and variously does timetable the discussion of bills; given that the timetables (known as program motions) can be tight, the House may run out of time to discuss particular parts of a bill. In the Lords, there is no provision for program motions: The House considers bills for as long as members wish to discuss them. If the business is not completed within the time allocated, more time has to be found. In the Commons, there is not time to discuss all the amendments submitted by MPs, so the occupant of the chair selects which will be discussed. In the Lords, every amendment put down is discussed. Any peer can thus ensure that a particular proposal to change a bill is considered; MPs do not have that facility. The Lords also will consider amendments at the third reading of a Bill, thus providing an additional stage to discuss amendments that is denied the Commons. Adding to the leverage of the House is the fact that the government is in a minority in the House and is therefore vulnerable in the event of a vote: It can, and does, lose votes in the House, usually on amendments to legislation. In the 2005–06 session, for example, it was defeated 62 times, in 2006–07 45 times, and in 2007–08 29 times.

Consideration of a bill in the Lords thus allows for discussion of many provisions that may not have been debated fully in the Commons, for what may be termed technical scrutiny (ensuring that the specifics of a measure make sense and that they are correctly drafted), and for the introduction of further amendments. Of amendments made to bills during their passage through the House, most are introduced by the government, though frequently in response to prompting or amendments tabled by other members of the House. Each year, usually between 1,000 and 4,000 amendments are secured to government bills in the Lords, the overwhelming majority proving acceptable to the Commons (not surprisingly, given that they have been accepted by ministers in the Lords). Whereas the Commons is seen as the body that determines the ends of legislation, the Lords concentrates on the means, engaging in detailed and sometimes tedious scrutiny that MPs may not have the time or the political will to undertake.

Under the rubric of scrutiny of legislation may now be included scrutiny of draft legislation emanating from the European Union (see Chapter 10). It is a function shared with the House of Commons, but one that the Lords is generally credited with fulfilling especially effectively. The function is fulfilled primarily through the Select Committee on the European Union and its seven subcommittees. The subcommittees cover different subjects (sub-committee E, for example, deals with law and institutions, sub-committee F with home affairs) and make greater use than does the Commons of specialist advisors and outside witnesses. Each subcommittee comprises two or more members of the main committee and about ten co-opted members, appointed because of their expertise in the area. The result is that each week during parliamentary sittings, there are usually more than 70 members of the House engaged in the detailed scrutiny of EU legislation. Whereas the Commons committee goes for breadth in coverage, the Lords committee opts for depth, looking at selected proposals in some detail.[39] The nature of the inquiries, coupled with the expertise of the members, means usually that reports are detailed and authoritative, and are generally acknowledged as such, including by those working in the institutions of the European Union. The EU committee, like its counterpart in the Commons, makes use of what is known as the scrutiny reserve: The U.K. Government will not normally agree to a proposal in the Council of Ministers until it has cleared scrutiny by the two Houses. The reputation of the House for its work in EU legislation is now well established and widely recognized.[40]

Apart from scrutinizing bills introduced by government (and draft EU legislation), the House seeks also to scrutinize the actions of the executive. The procedures available to do this are similar to those employed in the Commons: debates and questions. The House spends about one-fifth of its time on general debates, though not all are confined to discussion of government actions and policy. The procedure for asking questions differs somewhat from Commons procedure. At the start of the day's business, only four oral questions may be asked (see Figure 12.2), though supplementary questions are permitted. Question time is a maximum of 30 minutes, which means that there is roughly 7 or 8 minutes for each question. This provides time for several supplementary questions, more than is possible on a single question in the Commons. There is also provision for what is known as a question for short debate (QSD, previously known as an "unstarred question"). This is held either during what is known as the dinner hour (between approximately 7:30 and 8:30 P.M., providing a break from the day's other proceedings) or at the conclusion of the day's business: If held during the dinner hour it lasts a maximum of 60 minutes and if the last business of the day it has 90 minutes. QSDs are questions (previously submitted, like all questions) on which a

- **Lord Pannick.** To ask Her Majesty's Government what is their assessment of the arrangements for the transfer of judicial functions from the Appellate Committee of the House of Lords to the United Kingdom Supreme Court.
- **Baroness Cox.** To ask Her Majesty's Government what is their response to developments in Sudan with regard to the comprehensive peace agreement and the provision of humanitarian assistance.
- **Lord Naseby.** To ask Her Majesty's Government what is their assessment of the number of unauthorised colleges and the number of false students in the United Kingdom.
- **Lord Grocott.** To ask Her Majesty's Government whether they will publish a response to the report of the Association of Train Operating Companies, *Connecting Communities: Expanding Access to the Rail Network.*

FIGURE 12.2

Questions on the House of Lords Order Paper, July 20, 2009

short debate may take place before a minister replies. Again, the time allows for several peers to contribute. As in the Commons, written questions may also be put down, and the answers are published in the Lords' *Hansard,* though peers are less prone to use this device than MPs. (MPs generally utilize questions for partisan purposes and send answers to their local newspapers:[41] Peers are less partisan in behavior and have no constituency to impress.) In the Lords, unlike the Commons, all questions are addressed to Her Majesty's government and not to individual ministers.

The House, like the Commons, is also becoming more specialized through the use of committees. There are a number of what may be termed domestic committees, covering the internal administration of the house and its privileges, and a growing number of investigative committees. It addition to the EU Committee, it has sessional (i.e., permanent) committees on science and technology, the constitution, economic affairs, communications, the merits of statutory instruments, and on delegated powers and deregulation. The delegated powers committee looks at bills after they are introduced to examine the powers to be delegated to ministers and reports on whether the delegation is appropriate or not: Its recommendations are normally acted on by governments. The House also appoints ad hoc committees for inquiries into different subjects. In recent years, the House has appointed committees to consider the role of regulators, international organizations, and the Barnett formula (see Chapter 9). It has also on occasion formed a joint committee with the Commons to consider issues of common concern. Since 2001, the joint committee on human rights has been a particularly important and high-profile body.

The other main function that may be ascribed to the Lords is that of providing a forum for debate of important public issues. A similar function, of course, may be ascribed to the Commons. The difference between the two is that the House of Lords allows somewhat greater scope for the discussion of important topics that are not the subject of contention between parties. Thursdays in particular are given over to general debates (usually two on each Thursday up to the Whitsun recess) and peers initiate debates on a wide range of subjects, usually those on which they have some specialized knowledge. These debates are complemented during the week by the more frequent questions for short debate.

Possibly the most significant role played by the House in acting as a forum of debate is as a safety valve. By avoiding replication of the party debate in the Commons, it allows for the occasional public debate on topics that might otherwise not receive an airing in an authoritative public forum. For some outside interests, making their voices heard through such a forum is all that they desire. The House of Lords has achieved a reputation for discussing on occasion important social issues and for helping ease onto the political agenda topics that might otherwise have been kept off. In recent years, for example, it has proved a valuable forum for those seeking to achieve change on issues as diverse as constitutional reform, assisted dying, and conditions in prisons.

The nature of scrutiny and debate in the Lords means that it attracts considerable interest from interest groups. Peers do not have constituents, so they do not receive the same volume of mail as MPs. Nonetheless, their mailbag can be considerable as a result of individuals and interest groups writing in order to try to have some input into a particular debate or consideration of a particular bill. Peers have greater opportunities than MPs to speak. (Peers sign up to speak in scheduled debates and a speakers' list is published in advance. All peers who have put their names down are listed and speak in the order listed. Whereas a back-bench MP only gets to make an average of four substantial speeches in the House each year, an active peer can make as many speeches in as many weeks.) Not surprisingly, therefore, lobbyists see the House of Lords as an important supplementary channel—and sometimes not so supplementary—to that of the Commons for getting an issue raised and onto the political agenda. It is quite common before or during committee stage of a bill for peers to receive briefings from bodies that have a particular interest in the bill. Given the expertise of peers in particular areas, and the fact that the government is not necessarily assured a majority in the event of a vote, ministers are usually prepared to engage in a discussion with peers and can be persuaded to accept amendments that improve the content of a bill. As a result, the House of Lords can sometimes be a more worthwhile focus of attention for interest groups than the House of Commons.

PARLIAMENTARY REFORM

In historical perspective, debate on parliamentary reform has tended to be more intense—and to generate the introduction of more measures of reform—when focused on the House of Lords. In recent years, however, both houses have become targets of radical proposals for change. Debate, though, has usually focused on one or other House rather than on reform of the institution as a whole. There has also been a notable difference in terms of the type of debate: Reform of the Commons is generally discussed in terms of powers (primarily in relation to the executive); reform of the Lords is discussed in terms of composition.

The House of Commons

In the House of Commons, the government is subject to sustained scrutiny by virtue of facing a body formally styled as the opposition. The procedures of the House are largely geared to the existence of two principal bodies: the government and the opposition. The official opposition is a concept well understood in Westminster systems of government.[42] The opposition has various formal rights and is seen as the main, but not exclusive, mechanism for challenging government. The House largely operates on the principle that the government is entitled to get its business but the opposition is entitled to be heard.

Many critics of the House, however, have argued that enabling the opposition to be heard, though important, is not sufficient in enabling the House to fulfill effectively its functions. They believe that the government is able to get its way too easily, listening to but usually ignoring the opposition. Though the opposition has the weapon of publicity, it usually lacks the political clout to constrain government. A majority of MPs sitting in the House are there usually in order to support the government, yet are members of an institution that is designed to subject that very same government to critical scrutiny. In the event of a clash between the interests of party and of the House of Commons, self-interest has usually dictated that members follow the party line.

This critical perspective has led to calls for reform. The reform proposals generally fall into two broad camps. One camp advocates radical reform—in effect, reform external to Parliament—in order to bring about a new role for the House of Commons within the nation's constitutional arrangements. For these reformers, changes to the structures and procedures of the House are essentially inadequate: They are seen as no more than tinkering with the problem and will not be sufficient to limit a powerful government secure in a majority in the House of Commons. They believe that the House needs to be transformed from a largely ineffective policy-influencing, or reactive, legislature into a policy-making, or active, legislature.[43] This, they argue, necessitates constitutional reform. The principal change advocated is that of electoral reform. Over the past thirty years, various academics and politicians have pushed the case for a system of proportional representation, arguing that under PR no one party is likely to achieve a majority of seats, thus necessitating coalition governments, and consensual decision-making, of the sort seen in many countries in continental Europe. The House of Commons would continue to provide most of the personnel of government, to subject government to (more effective) scrutiny and influence, and to legitimate the government and its measures. The most significant difference would be that the House itself would have a greater claim to legitimacy in fulfilling those functions and would be able to constrain government more effectively than the present House of Commons. As we have seen in Chapter 5, the issue has become a significant feature of political debate, especially following the election of a Labour government in May 1997. A few reformers have also advocated more fundamental reform in the shape of a formal separation of powers, with the executive elected separately from the legislature.

Pressure for radical reform has become more prominent, but it has not totally eclipsed continuing demands for internal reform. This constitutes the other approach to reform. This is premised on the belief that changes within the House can enable it to fulfill more effectively the functions ascribed to it. Various reform agenda have been advanced by bodies outside Parliament, such as the educational charity the Hansard Society, and by committees within Parliament, such as the Modernisation Committee of the House of Commons and the Constitution Committee of the House of Lords.[44] Proponents argue that internal changes are both achievable and effective. They point to the experience of the departmental select committees and the televising of proceedings as demonstrating the usefulness of change within the institution. They are also able to point to more recent changes: These include the development of pre-legislative scrutiny (some bills being considered in draft by parliamentary committees before their formal introduction to Parliament), the move from standing committees to evidence-taking public bill committees for the committee stages of bills, and the acceptance of government in 2008 of the case for post-legislative scrutiny; most Acts of Parliament are now to be reviewed three to five years after enactment to determine if they have achieved their goals, with the reviews to be submitted to the relevant departmental select committees in the Commons.

They also point out that there has also been a greater willingness of MPs, not least on the government side of the House, to challenge government. If change is to be achieved, then an attitudinal change on the part of MPs is necessary:[45] Since the 1970s, MPs have shown a greater willingness to vote against their own side, on occasion resulting in a defeat for government. Though such defeats are rare, no prime minister since 1970 has escaped one or more defeats in the House of Commons. In 2009, for example, the government of Gordon Brown was defeated when it resisted extending the right of abode in the United Kingdom to former Gurkha soldiers. Recent years have seen unprecedented dissent by government back-benchers.[46]

Reformers thus make the case for further change. Critics argue that it is an uphill, if not impossible, struggle. Power continues to be concentrated in Downing Street (see Chapter 8) and the government uses program motions to push bills through the Commons with little time for effective scrutiny. Despite the rare defeat, government whips continue to ensure that the government gets its way, including on issues on which there is widespread dissent within the ranks of the governing party. Some commentators (including some MPs) concede that the House of Lords is more effective than the House of Commons in challenging government and preventing unpopular provisions being enacted. Nonetheless, internal reformers point out that change is both possible and able to strengthen the Commons in fulfilling its functions. They therefore press for more changes within the House, including a strengthening of select committees, providing more time for public bill committees, and transferring some prerogative powers exercised by government to Parliament. Some of these calls have been accepted by both government and opposition. In 2009, the government introduced a bill (the Constitutional Reform and Governance Bill) to transfer powers of treaty ratification to Parliament and also agreed that by convention Parliament should have to approve decisions to commit armed forces to action abroad (the war-making power). Also in 2009, opposition leader David Cameron called for a strengthening of the House, including allowing MPs free votes in public bill committees, reducing the number of MPs (designed to make the House more efficient), and even raised the possibility of introducing fixed-term parliaments. There has also tended to be a general acceptance of the need to strengthen the relationship between the House and the citizen, providing for greater transparency in proceedings, and enabling people to be able to see and understand bills more effectively than at present.

There is thus a continuing debate as to how the House of Commons can be strengthened in fulfilling its functions. Some reformers press for radical reform, others continue to favor strengthening the House of Commons from within. Achieving change continues to be a significant challenge, especially in the face of government secure in a parliamentary majority.

The House of Lords

Though reform of the House of Commons is an important issue, it has often been overshadowed by debate about what to do with the House of Lords. The House has rarely been free of proposals for reform. As we have seen, various reforms have been enacted, the most recent being the removal of most hereditary peers from membership of the House in 1999. The 1999 reform was seen as an interim measure. The Labour government made clear that it wished to remove hereditary peers as the first stage of a two-stage reform process. In stage two, it wanted to make the House, according to its 1997 election manifesto, "more democratic and representative." At the beginning of 1999, under pressure from the opposition (which claimed the government did not want to have a "stage two" reform), it appointed a Royal Commission on the Reform of the House of Lords to advise on what form the second stage should take. The commission, chaired by a Conservative peer, Lord Wakeham, reported in January 2000.[47] The report received a critical press. Some critics attacked it for not going far enough. Some parliamentarians claimed that it went too far. In the event, no action was taken. Since then, the government has published various white papers on Lords reform (the most recent in 2008),[48] advocating a partially or largely elected House, and a joint committee of the two Houses has been appointed to consider reform. In 2003, both Houses voted on seven options for reform (ranging from all-elected to all-appointed): In the Commons, none of the options was carried; in the Lords, there was an overwhelming majority in support of an all-appointed House and against all the other options. In 2007, both Houses were again invited to vote on the issue. The Lords repeated its votes of 2003. In the Commons, there was a majority for an 80 percent elected House and for a wholly elected House. The government followed this with its 2008 white paper. However, the government accepted that no legislation would be possible before the next Parliament and, despite the votes in the Commons, there appeared to be no clear political will to take any immediate action. Though opposition leader David Cameron supported an elected House, he made it clear it would not be a priority for a future Conservative government.

The future of the House of Lords thus remains a topic of political debate. There is no clear agreement on what form it should take in the future. Indeed, four separate approaches to reform can be identified. These can be termed the four R's: retain, reform, replace, and remove altogether.[49]

RETAIN   This approach favors retaining a wholly appointed chamber. It accepts the need to introduce procedures to prevent excessive political patronage but argues that appointment allows the House to retain its existing strengths. That is, it is a House of expertise and experience, with members able to offer informed advice in a way that would not be possible with an elected chamber, which would produce a body of career politicians similar to the Commons. An appointed chamber ensures that the primacy of the elected first chamber is maintained and, as such, maintains what has been termed core accountability within the political system.[50] Electors know who to call to account for public policy, policy determined by a government elected through the House of Commons. As such, it is claimed to be the most democratic option if democracy is defined as the translation of the popular will into legislative outputs. The chamber continues to fulfill functions complementary to the first chamber, rather than competing with it. The existing House, it is argued, adds value to the political process, and that should be retained.

REFORM   This approach involves taking the existing House and modifying it rather than replacing with a completely new chamber. It seeks to retain some of the strengths of the existing House while conferring some element of electoral legitimacy. This was the approach favored by the Royal Commission. Other bodies also have advocated a part-elected chamber, though the proportion to be elected varies. Supporters argue that this approach offers the best of both worlds: It combines the expertise of appointed members while bolstering its authority through an element of election. Critics claim that it produces the worst of both worlds, creating a two-tier membership and the potential for conflict between the two tiers.

REPLACE   This approach wants to do away with the existing House and replace it with a new chamber.[51] Most advocates of this approach want to have a wholly or almost wholly elected chamber. Advocates claim that this would give the chamber the legitimacy it presently lacks and enable it to challenge the first chamber—hence, in effect, the government. This would limit an overly powerful government. It is also claimed to be the most democratic option if democracy is defined in terms of election. Opponents argue that it would introduce the potential for gridlock and deal-making within the political process and, in effect, rid the system of its accountability. In the event of conflict producing undesirable outcomes, whom do the electors hold account-able? And what value is there in having a second chamber of career politi-cians, essentially replicating the first chamber? Some advocates of a new second chamber do not want an elected House but instead want a functional chamber: that is, one composed of representatives of different groups in soci-ety. This has little support and critics point that it is difficult to achieve (how to decide which groups should have representation?) as well as undesirable, giving a position of power to special interests.

REMOVE ALTOGETHER   This approach favors getting rid of the House of Lords and not replacing it with anything. Unicameral legislatures, as we have noted, are common, so why should not the United Kingdom follow suit? Advocates claim that the only reason the House of Lords continues to exist is because of the inad-equacies of the House of Commons. If the House of Commons was reformed effectively, there would be no need to have a second chamber. The purpose of a second chamber, it is claimed, is contestable. If the second chamber simply agrees with the first chamber, it is superfluous. If it conflicts with it, it is objectionable. This approach has some advocates but is not widely held. There is little evidence that the Commons could cope with the increased burden that would be imposed on it; critics point out that it has difficulty coping with its current workload. It also is not in a position to review effectively its own work. As a result, there is general though not universal support for retaining a second chamber.

There is no consensus favoring any particular approach to reforming the House of Lords. There are various supporters of retaining a wholly appointed House, and they are to be found in both houses of Parliament. The "reform" approach is favored by the Royal Commission and, until 2007, by the Labour government. The "replace" approach is favored by some senior fig-ures in both Houses and, after the 2007 votes in the Commons, by the gov-ernment. There are some supporters of a functional chamber and of a unicameral legislature (and some writers who favor selection by lot) but they are in a notable minority. What Lord Wakeham has called "the center of gravity" on the issue appears uncertain as well as shifting. The issue has yet to be resolved. The absence of a consensus may mean that the "retain" option wins by default. The present House of Lords is seen as an interim House. However, the House of Lords following the passage of the 1911 Par-liament Act was seen as an interim House: The preface to the Act envisaged a move toward an elected chamber. The "interim" House lasted for nearly ninety years. The present "interim" chamber may be also a long-term one.

THE POWER OF PARLIAMENT

Debate about parliamentary reform has proceeded largely on the basis that Parliament has lost power. However, there is dispute as to the nature of par-liamentary power. The concept is usually not defined. From at least one per-spective, Parliament is a powerful institution. It is possible to identify three views of power,[52] each providing a different perspective on the capacity of Parliament to affect outcomes of public policy:[53] the decision-making (pluralist), non-decision making (elitist), and institutional views.

THE DECISION-MAKING, OR PLURALIST, VIEW   is the one commonly adopted by observers of the political system. (The same applies in the United States.) This focuses on observable decision-making: It is concerned with how issues are resolved once they are on the political agenda. Those who are able to achieve a desired outcome are exercising power. It can take two forms: coercive or persuasive. The former occurs when those responsible for outcomes believe they have no realistic choice in reaching a decision; the latter occurs when there is a choice. In terms of the legislature, for example, it has a coercive capacity in being able to say "no" definitively to a measure placed before it; it has a persuasive capacity in that members may, by dint of argument or threat of defeat, induce ministers to adopt a course other than the one they intended, but which they could continue to pursue had they so chosen.

It is from this perspective that Parliament is generally viewed and found wanting. As we have seen, it is common to bemoan the "decline" of Parliament. It has been a feature of the literature on legislative studies since the late nineteenth century.[54] There is a perception that Parliament is not able to affect outcomes, with a determined government being able to achieve the result it wishes. The growth of party is seen as the means through which government has become all powerful, with Parliament able to exercise little or no constraint on what it is doing. The discussion on reform takes place essentially within this pluralist framework. The approach, though, neglects the other views of power: Even within its own confines, it tends to be limited, with observers focusing on the coercive capacity of Parliament—and its reluctance (especially within the Commons) to employ it—and giving less attention to the persuasive capacity of members. Change to public policy has variously been achieved by members persuading ministers to adopt a different approach, sometimes utilizing the private avenues of discussion, such as party meetings and correspondence.

THE NON-DECISION MAKING (OR ELITIST) VIEW   is more concerned with agenda-setting rather than with how issues are resolved once they are on the agenda. It focuses on how issues are kept off the agenda. There may be shared attitudes among those who control access to the political agenda that keep certain matters off the agenda. However, in the context of Parliament, the relevance here is in the context of anticipated reaction. Ministers may decide not to proceed with a measure because they anticipate that it may prove unpopular with the parliamentary party—and attract unwelcome publicity—or even because they fear that it may be defeated. The problem with this view of power is that it is difficult to determine empirically the extent to which measures are not proceeded with (non-decision making) because of anticipated reaction. Sometimes there is evidence of non-decision making, but it is difficult to prove a causal relationship between a minister declining to proceed with a proposal and the hostile attitude of MPs: A minister may use anticipated reaction as an excuse, but it may not be the reason for not bringing a measure forward. There is difficulty in knowing the full extent of non-decision making, since ministers may determine not to proceed without any formal record being kept, and in some cases not give any significant thought to a proposal if the parliamentary response is expected to be overwhelmingly hostile.

There have been some cases where ministers are known to have decided not to proceed with a measure because of anticipated reaction in the Commons or Lords. There is thus some evidence of non-decision making. We do not have the basis for knowing whether the known cases exhaust the occasions of non-decision making, but even some instances provide an additional dimension to our understanding of Parliament's capacity to affect outcomes. It may have a greater impact than is apparent from the record. It may not have much capacity to affect outcomes once a measure is on the political agenda, but it may have some impact on whether or not an issue comes onto the agenda at all.

THE INSTITUTIONAL VIEW is the one that provides a marked contrast to the pluralist view. This view focuses not on decision making but rather the framework within which decisions are made. It is premised on the assumption that institutions are not neutral in their effect. In the United Kingdom, for a measure to become an Act of Parliament—that is, become the law of the land and be enforced by the courts and other agencies—it has to go through Parliament. As we have seen, there is a highly institutionalized process for dealing with legislation: Bills have to go through several stages in both Houses. There are stipulated gaps between each stage. Bills are considered by the two Houses consecutively and not concurrently. There is only a limited amount of time in each parliamentary session. Most bills not passed by the end of a session fall. And there is no alternative to the parliamentary process: There is popular acceptance of its legitimacy as the means for giving the seal of approval to measures of public policy if they are to be binding. Government cannot by-pass the process.

This institutional framework imposes a major constraint on government.[55] It has to limit the number of bills it brings forward. Every year, departments put forward more bills than there is time to get through Parliament. As a result, the cabinet has to be selective in determining which bills to bring forward. Under this view, the power of Parliament is to be found in the bills never brought forward than in those that are presented to Parliament. The most important question posed by the leader of the House of Commons when discussing in the cabinet's legislation committee whether a bill should be introduced is not "do we have the votes to get it through?" but rather "do we have the time?"

Though a government secure in a parliamentary majority could seek to change the rules, it can usually only do so at the margins. The rules themselves are extensive—*Erskine May,* the authoritative handbook of parliamentary procedure, runs to more than one-thousand pages—and government ministers are often not expert on those procedures: They rely on the guidance of clerks, who are independent of government, in each House. There are also dangers in seeking to upset what has been termed the equilibrium of legitimacy between government and opposition. "Each accepts the legitimacy of the other in what it seeks to do. If either side upsets the equilibrium, it delegitimizes their role and threatens to destabilize the parliamentary process and what they gain from it."[56] Governments are also constrained by the realization that not only is the opposition the alternative government but also that they are the alternative opposition. One day they could be on the benches opposite and needing to utilize the tools available to the opposition.

Parliament is thus, from this perspective, a powerful institution. Government needs Parliament: It cannot survive without it. A democratic regime rests on the existence of an elected assent-giving body. That is why legislatures are pervasive, even if, from a pluralist perspective, they appear to have little capacity to affect outcomes. Parliament may be limited in being able to affect outcomes once issues are on the political agenda—though the full extent to which it is able to do so is not known, and reformers are seeking to enhance its capacity to affect outcomes—but it remains an essential body, its highly institutionalized practices and procedures constraining government in what it can achieve. The Palace of Westminster is an iconic building. What goes on within it is also important in the determination of public policy in the United Kingdom.

NOTES

1. However, under Article 1, section 7(1), of the U.S. Constitution, all revenue-raising bills must originate in the House of Representatives.
2. M. Mezey, *Comparative Legislatures* (Duke University Press, 1979), Ch. 2.
3. See R. Fleischer, J. R. Bond, and J. E. Owens, "A Reassessment of Party Voting in the U.S. House," paper presented at the 65th Annual Meeting of the Midwest Political Science Association, Chicago IL, April 12–15, 2007, and the *Washington Post's* US Congress Votes Database, http://projects.washingtonpost.com/congress/
4. M. Foley and J. E. Owens *Congress and the Presidency* (Manchester University Press, 1996), p. 3.
5. The perception of decline was popularized by the scholar-statesman Lord Bryce in the 1920s. See P. Norton (ed.), *Legislatures* (Oxford University Press, 1990), Ch. 3. Bryce was British ambassador to the United States 1907–13.
6. R. H. S. Crossman, "Introduction," to W. Bagehot, *The English Constitution* (Fontana, 1963 edition), p. 39.
7. N. Polsby, "Legislatures," in F. I. Greenstein and N. Polsby (eds.), *Handbook of Political Science*, Vol. 5 (Addison-Wesley, 1975). See also Norton, *Legislatures*, Ch. 7.
8. Churchill sat in the House from 1900 to 1964, with a break between 1922 and 1924. He was Father of the House from 1959 to 1964.
9. The House departed from the practice in 1992 when, under a Conservative government, it elected Labour MP Betty Boothroyd as Speaker. She became the first woman speaker. It also departed from it in 2009 when a Conservative MP, John Bercow, was elected during a period of Labour government.
10. B. Criddle, "MPs and Candidates," in D. Kavanagh and D. Butler (eds.), *The British General Election of 2005* (Palgrave Macmillan, 2005), p. 166.

11. A. King, "The Rise of the Career Politician in Britain—And Its Consequences," *British Journal of Political Science,* Vol. 11, 1981, pp. 249–285. See also P. Riddell, *Honest Opportunism* (Hamish Hamilton, 1993).

12. See P. Norton, "Legislation," in M. Rush (ed.), *Parliament and Pressure Politics* (Oxford University Press, 1990), pp. 186–188.

13. See D. Marsh and M. Read, *Private Members' Bills* (Cambridge University Press, 1987).

14. See P. Cowley (ed.), *Conscience and Parliament* (Frank Cass, 1998).

15. See R. Rogers and R. Walters, *How Parliament Works,* 6th ed. (Longman, 2006), pp. 311–337.

16. This half-hour slot was introduced in May 1997. Before then, the prime minister answered questions in two 15-minute slots each week, one on Tuesday and the other on Thursday.

17. See P. Norton, "Questions and the Role of Parliament," in M. Franklin and P. Norton (eds.), *Parliamentary Questions* (Oxford University Press, 1993), pp. 194–207.

18. See D. Judge, *Parliament and Industry* (Dartmouth, 1990), pp. 176–184.

19. A. Hindmoor, P. Larkin, and A. Kennon, "Assessing the Influence of Select Committees in the UK: The Education and Skills Committee, 1997–2005," *The Journal of Legislative Studies,* Vol. 15 (1), 2009, pp. 71–89.

20. There is evidence that committees maximize their influence when they examine topics that are new to the political agenda. See D. Hawes, *Power on the Back Benches?* (S.A.U.S., 1993).

21. P. Norton, "The Growth of the Constituency Role of the MP," *Parliamentary Affairs,* 47 (4), 1994, pp. 705–720.

22. See P. Norton, *Parliament in British Politics* (Palgrave Macmillan, 2005), Ch. 9.

23. See P. Norton, "Four Models of Political Representation: British MPs and the Use of ICT," *The Journal of Legislative Studies,* 13 (3), 2007, pp. 354–369.

24. Hansard Society, *Audit of Political Engagement 6: The 2009 Report* (The Hansard Society, 2009), p. 23.

25. In 1981 an Ulster Unionist MP was shot dead by a terrorist while conducting a constituency "surgery." While physical attacks on MPs are very rare, many MPs are normally accompanied by a councilor or assistant, partly to take notes or assist in dealing with a case, but also as a form of security.

26. R. Rawlings, "The MP's Complaint Service," *Modern Law Review,* 53, 1990, p. 44.

27. See especially P. Norton and D. Wood, *Back from Westminster* (University Press of Kentucky, 1993).

28. See P. Norton, *Parliament in British Politics,* Ch. 9.

29. Norton, *Parliament in British Politics,* pp. 156–157.

30. Ibid., Table 9.3, p. 192.

31. BBC News Online, 2 June 2009, http://news.bbc.co.uk/1/hi/uk_politics/8078159.stm.

32. Norton, *Parliament in British Politics,* Ch. 10.

33. M. Rush (ed.), *Parliament and Pressure Politics* (Oxford University Press, 1990), pp. 282, 285.

34. See Norton and Wood, *Back from Westminster,* Ch. 3.

35. *Parliamentary Debates (Hansard),* Vol. 188, cols. 1925–6 (1867).

36. See N. Baldwin, "The House of Lords: Behavioural Changes," in P. Norton (ed.), *Parliament in the 1980s* (Blackwell, 1985), pp. 96–113; C. Grantham and C. M.

Hodgson, "The House of Lords: Structural Changes," in Norton, *Parliament in the 1980s*, pp. 114–135.

37. Baldwin, "The House of Lords: Behavioural Changes," pp. 96–113.

38. See M. Russell and M. Scaria, "Why Does the Government Get Defeated in the House of Lords? The Lords, the Party System and British Politics," *British Politics*, 2 (3), 2007, pp. 299–322.

39. See P. Norton, "The United Kingdom: Political Conflict, Parliamentary Scrutiny," in P. Norton (ed.), *National Parliaments and the European Union* (Frank Cass, 1996), pp. 92–109.

40. See D. Shell, "The House of Lords and the European Community, 1990–91," in P. Giddings and G. Drewry (eds.), *Westminster and Europe* (Macmillan, 1996), pp. 159–190; and P. Norton, "National Parliaments and the European Union," *Managerial Law*, 45 (5/6), 2003, pp. 5–25.

41. See M. Franklin and P. Norton, "Questions and Members," in Franklin and Norton, *Parliamentary Questions*, pp. 104–122.

42. See A. Kaiser, "Parliamentary Opposition in Westminster Democracies: Britain, Canada, Australia and New Zealand," *The Journal of Legislative Studies*, 14 (1/2), 2008, pp. 20–45.

43. On the concepts, see Mezey, *Comparative Legislatures*, and P. Norton, "Parliament and Policy in Britain: The House of Commons as a Policy Influencer," in P. Norton (ed.), *Legislatures* (Oxford University Press, 1990), pp. 177–180.

44. See, for example, Constitution Committee, House of Lords, *Parliament and the Legislative Process*, 14th report of Session 2003–04, HL Paper 173-I (The Stationery Office, 2004); and Select Committee on the Modernisation of the House of Commons, *The Legislative Process*, First report of Session 2005–06, HC 1097 (The Stationery Office, 2006).

45. See especially P. Norton, "The Norton View," in D. Judge (ed.), *The Politics of Parliamentary Reform* (Heinemann Education, 1983).

46. See, for example, P. Cowley, *Revolts and Rebellions* (Politico's, 2002); P. Cowley, *The Rebels* (Politico's, 2005); and P. Cowley and M. Stuart, *Browned Off? Dissension amongst the Parliamentary Labour Party, 2007–2008: A Data Handbook* (Nottingham University Politics Department, 2008).

47. Royal Commission on the Reform of the House of Lords, *A House for the Future*, Cm 4534 (The Stationery Office, 2000).

48. Ministry of Justice, *An Elected Second Chamber: Further Reform of the House of Lords*, Cm 7438 (The Stationery Office, 2008).

49. Derived from P. Norton, *The Constitution in Flux* (Martin Robertson, 1982), Ch. 6.

50. See P. Norton, "Adding Value? The Role of Second Chambers," *Asia Pacific Law Review*, 15 (1), 2007, pp. 3–18.

51. See I. Richard and D. Welfare, *Unfinished Business* (Vintage, 1999).

52. S. Lukes, *Power: A Radical View*, 2nd ed. (Palgrave Macmillan, 2005).

53. See Norton, *Parliament in British Politics*, Ch. 1.

54. See note 5.

55. See P. Norton, "Playing by the Rules: The Constraining Hand of Parliamentary Procedure," *The Journal of Legislative Studies*, 7 (3), 2001, pp. 13–33.

56. Norton, "Playing by the Rules," p. 28.

CHAPTER

13

The Monarchy
Above the Fray?

In the United States, the head of state is the president. In the United Kingdom, the head of state is the monarch. Both fulfill certain formal duties associated with the position. Beyond that there is little similarity between the two. In terms of history, determination of incumbency, powers, and current responsibilities, the U.S. presidency and the British monarchy have virtually nothing in common. The president is both head of state and political head of the administration. He operates directly and personally at the heart of the political decision-making process. The monarch, as head of state, stands above political decision making. In political terms, he or she serves not to decide but primarily to perform a symbolic role. The president serves by virtue of election; the monarch reigns by virtue of birth.

The monarchy is the oldest secular institution in Britain. It predates Parliament by some four centuries and the law courts by three centuries. The present monarch is able to trace her descent from King Egbert, who united England under his rule in A.D. 829. The continuity of the institution has been broken only once, during the period of military rule by Oliver Cromwell in the seventeenth century. There have been various interruptions in the direct line of succession, but the hereditary principle has been preserved since at least the eleventh century. The succession itself is governed by certain principles of common law and by statute. The throne descends to the eldest son or, in the absence of a son, the eldest daughter. By the Act of Settlement of 1701, affirmed by the Treaty of Union in 1707, the Crown was to descend to the heirs of the granddaughter of James I, Princess Sophia; this line has been confirmed by later acts.

For several centuries, there was no separation of powers: Executive, legislative, and judicial powers were exercised by the king. With the growth of Parliament (and its power of the purse) as well as the courts, the direct exercise of these functions progressively declined. As we have seen (Chapter 3), the conflict between king and Parliament in the seventeenth century resulted in the Settlement of 1688–89 and the establishment of what was essentially a limited constitutional monarchy. The monarch nonetheless remained at the head of government, in practice as well as formally. Those responsible for the Bill of Rights of 1689 wanted "a real, working, governing king, a king with a policy,"[1] albeit a king governing with the consent of Parliament. The centrality of the monarch to governing was to decline in the eighteenth century with the king's increasing dependence on his ministers. During this century, one can see the divorce of the positions of head of state and political head of government, previously united in the person of the king. The former remained with the king, the latter in practice became vested in his chief minister. The withdrawal of the monarch largely but by no means exclusively from active participation in political life was to be a marked feature of the succeeding century. Queen Victoria's reign (1837–1901) marked the transition from a monarch still active in political life to one fulfilling primarily a formal role, part of what Walter Bagehot in *The English Constitution* had identified as the "dignified" part of the Constitution.[2] The twentieth century realized the move to a politically neutral monarchy, standing well removed from the partisan fray of party government.

The years since 1688 have witnessed various landmarks on this path toward a neutral monarchy divorced from active partisan decision making. The last occasion on which a monarch vetoed a piece of legislation was when Queen Anne refused her assent to a Scottish Militia Bill in 1707, the last time a monarch dismissed a ministry was in 1834, and the last occasion on which the monarch clearly exercised a personal choice in the selection of a prime minister was Queen Victoria's summoning Lord Rosebery in 1894. (Monarchs have on occasion subsequently had to exercise a choice in the selection of prime ministers but, as we shall see, have acted under advice.) The last monarch to attempt to veto cabinet appointments, with some measure of success, was Queen Victoria. She was also the last monarch to be instrumental in pushing successfully for the enactment of particular legislation: On at least two occasions she virtually initiated legislation, the 1874 Public Worship Regulation Act and the 1876 Royal Titles Act.[3] She may also be described as the last monarch to indulge, albeit within a limited circle, in partisan expression. Initially a Whig, she became for all intents and purposes a vehement Conservative; she clearly adored her Conservative prime minister, Benjamin Disraeli, and made little secret of her utter disdain for the Liberal leader, William Gladstone. Partisan expression declined significantly under her successors. Indeed, according to Frank Hardie, this was a notable feature of the first half of the twentieth century: "Since 1901 the trend toward a real political neutrality, not merely a matter of appearances, has been steady, reign by reign."[4]

The result of these developments has been that monarchs have come to occupy a position in which they are called on to fulfill two primary tasks. One is to represent the unity of the nation. The other is to carry out certain political functions on the advice of ministers. The weakness of the monarch in being able to exercise independent decisions in the latter task has ensured the strength of the monarchy in fulfilling the first.

The Crown in Britain is the symbol of supreme executive authority. It serves essentially as a substitute for the concept of the state, a concept not well developed in Britain and one that has not made an impact on the national consciousness. The monarch is the person on whom the Crown is constitutionally conferred. Various public duties are carried out in the name of the Crown (for example, public prosecutions) and, as the person in whom the Crown vests, the monarch's name attaches to both government and the armed forces. The armed services are Her Majesty's Services. Her Majesty is commander in chief. People go to war to fight for "queen and country." The government is Her Majesty's government, ministers are Her Majesty's ministers. Even the opposition in Parliament is titled Her Majesty's Loyal Opposition. Postage stamps and coins bear the monarch's image. (British postage stamps are unique: The monarch's head substitutes for the name of the nation.) The monarch personifies what for Americans is represented by the Stars and Stripes.

In order that the Queen may embody the unity of the nation, it is imperative that she not only abstain from partisan activity but also be seen to abstain, indeed be seen to transcend political activity. The political functions she performs, such as the appointment of the prime minister, the appointment of ministers, the dispensing of honors, and the assent of legislation, are governed by convention. She acts on the advice of her ministers and is recognized as so acting. When the Queen's Speech is read from the throne on the opening of Parliament, the speech is handed to the queen by the lord chancellor and subsequently handed back to him, signifying that it is the government's responsibility. Government is carried on in the name of the monarch and not by the monarch.

The formal exercise of political functions by the monarch serves a useful purpose. It provides a sense of duty for government (fulfilling duties as Her Majesty's ministers is a reminder that they are in office to perform a service to the nation) and it provides a significant sense of continuity. Governments may come and governments may go, but the Queen continues to reign. When Queen Elizabeth II ascended to the throne in 1952, Winston Churchill was prime minister. She has been served by 11 different prime ministers (see Table 8.1). By being the person to whom prime ministers submit their resignations and who summons the new premier, the monarch gives a sense of continuity, one that arguably could not be provided by any other form of head of state in a free society.

The continuity provided by the monarch has another and, from the perspective of government, very useful aspect. Each prime minister has a regular audience with the Queen, usually at least once a week when the sovereign is in London; under a practice initiated by Harold Macmillan, the prime minister sends in advance a list of points he or she would like to raise. The Queen receives the minutes of cabinet meetings and cabinet committee meetings. She also receives copies of important Foreign and Commonwealth Office documents. According to her various prime ministers, she is an assiduous reader of all such papers. Apart from more than fifty years' experience of meeting with her prime ministers, the Queen is also head of the Commonwealth and has traveled extensively, building personal links with other heads of state.

This experience she can and does bring to bear in her meetings with the prime minister, doing so in a nonpartisan context (raising issues in the form of questions) and in an environment where the prime minister does not have to deal with an opponent or political rival. The audience provides the premier with a unique opportunity, as Sir Ian Gilmour expressed it, "to explain decisions and policies to a disinterested observer in the fullest privacy."[5] Successive prime ministers have attested to the value of such meetings. According to Harold Macmillan, "the Queen was a great support, because she is the one person you can talk to."[6] Labour prime ministers Harold Wilson, James Callaghan, and Tony Blair expressed similar views. Speaking at the time of the Queen's golden wedding anniversary in November 1997, Tony Blair said that he enjoyed his weekly audience with the Queen not simply because of her experience, but because she was an "extraordinarily shrewd and perceptive observer of the world. Her advice is worth having."[7] The only two prime ministers with whom relationships have reputedly been a little cool have been, ironically—given Conservative support for the monarchy—Conservatives Edward Heath and Margaret Thatcher; the Queen, according to some reports, was distressed at the strains that Mrs. Thatcher's refusal to endorse sanctions against South Africa was placing on the Commonwealth. The Queen attaches much importance to her role as head of the Commonwealth.

Prime ministers have reason also to be grateful to the monarch for the fulfillment of various formal duties. In the United States, the president as head of state has to fulfill a number of time-consuming tasks, including receiving new ambassadors, presenting medals, and attending a number of formal nonpolitical functions. The president is not trained to carry out these tasks and the time given over to them is at the expense of time that could be used for running the administration. In Britain, the symbolic tasks are carried out by the monarch or, in some cases, by other members of the royal family. The physical distinction between head of state and head of government allows for ceremonial duties to be carried out by someone schooled for the task and eliminates the conflicting time demands faced by any political leader who is also head of state.

By being scrupulously neutral in performing her duties, the Queen is able to fulfill her task of representing the unity of the nation. The hereditary principle in this context is a benefit rather than a hindrance. It helps provide a monarch prepared for the task, one free of the partisan implications that can inhere in the election of a head of state. A hereditary monarchy, as a number of observers have pointed out, serves also to prevent the growth of competing dynastic families. By fulfilling her duties in the way that she does, the Queen serves also to overcome any perceptions of incompatibility between a hereditary monarchy and a presumed democratic society. Indeed, there are those who see the monarch as fulfilling an essential role to protect democratic institutions.[8] In the unlikely event of an attempt to impose military or otherwise nondemocratic government, the monarch would be the most effective barrier to its realization. A monarch, as Gilmour observed, can engage the affections and loyalty of the armed forces more readily than can a president.[9] Almost paradoxically, the monarchy serves as a backstop, an ultimate safeguard, to protect those political institutions that have superseded it as the governing force in the United Kingdom.

The importance of these various functions has been confirmed by the public. A 1988 Gallup poll found that more than 80 percent of respondents judged the uniting, or figurehead, functions of the Queen, and her immediate family, to be very or quite important. Eighty-two percent attached importance to uniting the people "despite their political, economic and class differences" and more than 90 percent attached importance to representing the United Kingdom at home and abroad. More than 70 percent attached importance to maintaining the political neutrality of the armed forces.

What may be termed the core functions of the monarch thus enjoy widespread recognition. The Gallup poll also found other functions widely ascribed to the queen and her family. Recent years have witnessed a growing debate about the royal family. There has been relatively little debate about the core functions. The extent to which members of the royal family have fulfilled the other functions has been a matter of considerable comment.

THE CURRENT DEBATE

Over most of the past century, the monarchy has not been a major topic of public debate. During the Second World War (1939–45), the king (George VI) and his family proved especially popular, remaining in Buckingham Palace (which was partially bombed) and visiting bomb-damaged areas of the country. His successor, his daughter Elizabeth II, achieved particular popularity in the 1960s and 1970s, initiating royal "walkabouts" (talking and shaking hands with people in the street) and opening up the activities of the monarchy to the public gaze, relative to past and sometimes obsessive secrecy. The twenty-fifth anniversary of the Queen's accession to the throne in 1977 was marked by widespread public events throughout the country. So too was the Queen's fiftieth anniversary—the golden jubilee—in 2002. In that year, satisfaction with the way the Queen was doing her job reached a ten-year high. Almost 80 percent of those questioned in an Ipsos MORI poll said they would be celebrating the golden jubilee.[10] More than 1 million people thronged the Mall in central London on the day of the principal celebrations. As we shall, there remains popular support both for the Queen and the institution of the monarchy.

However, there have been occasions when the monarchy has been the subject of controversy and critical comment. There was two periods especially in the twentieth century. The first and most significant occasion was in 1936 when the new king, Edward VIII, wanted to marry an American divorcee, Wallis Simpson. The marriage was opposed by the British government and by the Archbishop of Canterbury. The problem was not that Mrs. Simpson was an American but that she was divorced (and had remarried). The king was the supreme governor of the Church of England and in the eyes of the church Mrs. Simpson was still married to her first husband. The king had to choose between the throne and Mrs. Simpson. He chose the latter and abdicated. The abdication crisis caused political controversy—some politicians, such as Winston Churchill (then out of office), backing the king's desire to marry and stay on the throne, others seeing Edward's actions as irresponsible and a threat to the institution of the monarchy. Support for the institution was largely restored by his brother, the Duke of York, who succeeded him, becoming George VI.

The second significant period of controversy was that of the 1990s. Both 1992 and 1997 proved particularly difficult years for the Queen and her family, with questions being raised about the behavior of members of the royal family as well as of the cost of the institution. The period witnessed the divorce of the heir to the throne and later the death of his popular former wife, Diana, Princess of Wales. As we shall see, the critical nature of the debate raised some doubt about the long-term future of the institution. Though public confidence in the monarchy was restored at the start of the twenty-first century, public concern about the monarchy under the Queen's heir, Prince Charles, remained a feature of debate. There are also continuing concerns about some aspects of the monarchy itself, not directly related to who is on the throne.

The main areas of debate concerning the monarchy can be subsumed under three heads: (1) the monarch's exercise of certain political powers not clearly governed by convention, (2) the cost and activity of members of the royal family, and (3) the future of the monarchy. The first is a continuing but not prominent one, and has been overshadowed since the early 1990s by the second and third.

The Exercise of Political Powers

A great many powers are vested in the crown. Prerogative powers include the declaration of war, treaty ratification, the conferring of honors, the summoning, prorogation, and dissolution of Parliament, and granting pardons. However, these are powers *vested in* the crown but not powers *exercised by* the monarch. They are exercised by ministers in the name of the crown. (In 2009, the government sought to transfer some of the powers to Parliament.) The monarch has no involvement. When war was declared in 1939, for example, the announcement was made by the prime minister, not the king. Announcements of new peerages are made from 10 Downing Street and not from Buckingham Palace. The formality is maintained but the political reality is widely understood, thus ensuring that there is popular recognition that the monarch is not exercising any independent power. None of this is stipulated by statute. It is governed by convention.

Conventions, though, do not cover all possible eventualities. Convention ensures that most actions of the monarch are predictable, but certain important powers remain vested in the monarch that on occasion may require a choice among alternative options, a choice not clearly dictated by convention. The most obvious and important power involved here is that of choosing a prime minister.

It is a convention of the Constitution that the monarch will select as prime minister someone who is capable of ensuring a majority in the House of Commons. In practice, this usually creates no problems. If a party obtains an overall majority in a general election, the Queen summons the leader of that party. But what happens if there is no party leader to be summoned or if no party is returned with an overall majority at a general election? The first possibility no longer faces the Queen, though until recently it did. Until 1965, the Conservative Party had no formal mechanism for choosing a leader. The leader was expected to "emerge" following soundings of one sort or another within the party. In the event of a Conservative prime minister's retiring with no successor immediately apparent, or with different contenders for the succession, the choice was left to the monarch. In 1957 the Queen was faced with summoning someone to succeed Sir Anthony Eden as prime minister. After consulting with senior statesmen, she sent for Harold Macmillan instead of, as many assumed she would, R. A. Butler. In 1963 she was confronted with the difficult task of appointing a prime minister in succession to Macmillan. After taking the advice of her outgoing prime minister, she summoned Lord Home (or Sir Alec Douglas-Home, as he quickly became after renouncing his peerage in order to seek a seat in the House of Commons). The choice was a controversial one and, though the decision was essentially that of Macmillan, it embroiled the Crown in political controversy. The prospect of any repetition was avoided when the Conservative Party in 1965 introduced a procedure for the election of the party leader. The party was thus in a position to elect a leader and avoid the Queen's having to make a selection on its behalf.

The second possibility, a party having no overall majority, is a real one. The outcomes of a number of general elections, most notably and most recently that of 1992, have been far from certain. What should the Queen do in the event of no party having an overall majority? Usually the position does not entail her having to make a decision. The outgoing prime minister formally remains in office until resigning and may therefore seek to strike a deal with a third party (as Edward Heath attempted to do, unsuccessfully, with the Liberals in February 1974). But what if the prime minister is unacceptable to the third party but another leader—drawn from the same party—might be? Does the Queen summon that leader or does she summon the leader of the opposition? In such a situation she would be saddled, as David Watt put it, "with a highly controversial and thankless responsibility."[11] It is one she would almost certainly prefer to do without.

One other power that has produced a similar debate is the power to dissolve Parliament. The usual practice is for the prime minister to recommend a dissolution to the Queen and for Her Majesty to accede to that request. There is some doubt, though, as to whether it is a convention for the monarch to accede automatically to that request. In the event of a government losing its parliamentary majority through defections or a major party split, and the prime minister's preference for dissolution rather than forming a coalition with a third party is opposed by the Cabinet, would the Queen be justified in withholding her consent to a dissolution? If the prime minister wanted a dissolution following a major defeat in the Commons, but his cabinet colleagues did not,[12] what should the Queen do? Lord Blake, a constitutional historian, argued that in such or similar circumstances the Queen would not be obliged to grant dissolution.[13] When the Tribune Group, a left-wing body of Labour MPs, argued in 1974 that the prime minister had an absolute right to determine the date of the election, a senior minister responded, "Constitutional lawyers of the highest authority are of the clear opinion that the Sovereign is not in all circumstances bound to grant a Prime Minister's request for a dissolution."[14] The problem is one of determining the circumstances that would justify the Queen's denying dissolution, and whether, whatever the circumstances, such an action could be taken without seriously damaging the queen's reputation for being above the partisan fray. "For the monarch," wrote Kingsley Martin, "the only safe rule is always to follow the Premier's advice."[15] If that rule was accepted as a convention, it would ensure that the Queen's actions were predictable, putting her beyond claims of partisanship. However, the problem presently is the absence of agreement that such a rule exists.

One alternative, advocated by former Labour cabinet minister Tony Benn is for the power of dissolution (indeed, all prerogative powers) to be transferred to the speaker of the House of Commons. This, Benn notes, would avoid the monarch being drawn into the heart of political debate, transferring instead the power to someone who "knows the Commons intimately and is therefore specially qualified to reach a judgment about the appropriate moment for granting a dissolution and who is most likely to command a majority."[16] The case was reiterated in a Fabian pamphlet in 1996, written by a Labour parliamentary candidate, and in a pamphlet from the left-wing think tank *Demos* in 1998.[17] There is also evidence of some popular support for the proposal. A MORI poll in August 1998 found that 49 percent thought the powers should be removed, against 45 percent who thought they should be retained. The difficulty with the proposal is that it would not solve the problem but rather transfer it. As we saw in Chapter 12, the speaker is a neutral figure, and to exercise the power of dissolution would draw the speaker into "the heart of political debate." The speaker is no keener to jeopardize his claim to being above the partisan fray than is the queen.

There thus remain certain circumstances in which the monarch may be called on to exercise a choice. Such circumstances could, and almost certainly would, draw the monarch into political controversy. Such circumstances are, though, exceptional.

The Cost and Activity of Members of the Royal Family

The crown vests in the monarch and there are certain tasks that only the monarch can perform. However, many public duties of the monarch can be, and are, performed on her behalf by members of her family. Members of the royal family can be deputed to represent the queen abroad and at various state functions. They will also often be invited themselves to perform public duties, such as opening a factory or hospital or acting as patron of a charity.

The work of members of the royal family has generally been seen in a positive light. There have been few criticisms of the Queen. Her mother, Queen Elizabeth the Queen Mother (widow of George VI) who died in 2002 at the age of 101, was also very popular: She continued to fulfill public engagements up to and beyond her 100th birthday. However, the conduct of other members of the royal family has come in for criticism. In the early 1990s, the activities of various "royals" led to public criticism of the amount of public money spent on the royal family. This criticism reached a peak in 1992. In the latter half of the 1990s, the activities of members of the royal family (including, on this occasion, the Queen herself) led to accusations of detachment from the rest of the country. This criticism reached a peak in 1997.

The costs incurred in fulfilling public duties by the queen and most other members of the royal family were met from the Civil List, that is, money voted by Parliament to cover the official expenses of the monarchy. For the queen, this covered such items as staff costs and the cost of state dinners and other functions.[18] For other members of the royal family, lesser sums were provided to cover staff and related expenses. (The exception was the Prince of Wales, whose income derived, and continues to derive, from the duchy of Cornwall.)[19] In 1990, to avoid an annual public debate on the amount to be paid through the Civil List, agreement was reached between the Queen and the government that the size of the list should be set at £7.9 million a year (just under $13m.) for a decade (for the current position, see Figure 13.1). When other costs were included that were not covered by the Civil List but paid instead by government departments, such as the maintenance costs of royal castles (more than £25 million—$41m.—in 1990–1991) and of the royal yacht Britannia (£9 million—$14.8m.), the annual public expenditure on the monarchy was estimated to be almost £60 million (£98.4m.).[20]

Three criticisms of such spending had been expressed for a number of years. The first was that the Civil List was large in absolute terms. The 1990 settlement marked a significant increase on previous years, designed to take account of inflation in future years. Even in 1988, 40 percent of respondents in a Gallup poll expressed the view that the monarchy cost "too much."[21] The second was that the country did not get particularly good value for the money from certain members of the royal family, especially junior members. A 1989 MORI poll found that senior members, such as the Queen, the Prince of Wales (Prince Charles), and the Princess Royal (Princess Anne) were judged to be hard working and cost-effective. However, when asked which two or three members of the royal family represented the worst value for the money to the British taxpayer, 37 percent identified Sarah, Duchess of York, and 23 percent identified her husband, Prince Andrew; they were followed by the Queen's sister, Princess Margaret, and the Queen's youngest son, Prince Edward.[22] Many critics tended to view such "hangers on," as they were often described, as serving no useful purpose. Third, there was criticism of the fact that the Queen received money from the Civil List despite enjoying a large

The Civil List is the sum provided by Parliament to meet the official expenses of The Queen's Household so that Her Majesty can fulfill her role as Head of State and Head of the Commonwealth. It is not in any sense "pay" for The Queen.

The Civil List dates back to the Restoration of the Monarchy in 1660, but the current system was created on the accession of George III in 1760, when it was decided that the whole cost of civil government should be provided by Parliament in return for the surrender of the hereditary revenues (principally the net surplus of the Crown Estate) by the King for the duration of the reign. Revenue from the Crown Estate amounted to £200 million ($328m.) in 2006–07 and this was paid to the Treasury.

About 70 per cent of Civil List expenditure goes to pay the salaries of staff working directly for The Queen. Their duties include dealing with State papers, organising public engagements and arranging meetings and receptions undertaken by The Queen. The Civil List also meets the costs of functions such as the Royal Garden Parties (Her Majesty entertains over 48,000 people each year) and official entertainment during State Visits.

The Civil List is set by Parliament as a fixed annual amount of £7.9 million (<$13m.) for a period of up to 10 years. (The current cycle ends in 2010.) Any surplus achieved in any one year is invested and kept in reserve and used to meet any excess expenditure in later years.

The budget for each year's projected net Civil List spending is reviewed by the Treasury, which audits the accounts and verifies that the Household's financial management is in line with best practice. Details of expenditure are published.

Source: Derived from the British Monarchy website, http://www.royal.gov.uk/TheRoyalHousehold/ Royalfinances/Sourcesoffunding/TheCivilList.aspx

FIGURE 13.1
The Civil List.

personal fortune—a fortune on which she paid no tax. The Queen is reputed to be one of the richest women in the world. (Her wealth has been estimated by some publications, including *Fortune* magazine, as running into several billion pounds, though this figure includes national treasures held in perpetuity on the nation's behalf by the monarch, such as the crown jewels, and which she is not at liberty to sell; her real personal, and disposable, wealth is believed to be closer to £100 million ($164m.) though even this figure was described by the Lord Chamberlain in 1993 as "grossly over-stated.") When income tax was introduced in the nineteenth century, Queen Victoria volunteered to pay tax and did so; in the twentieth century, the tax liability was whittled down and George VI reached agreement with the government to remove any tax burden from his successors. Various calls were made, not least by left-wing MPs critical of the institution of monarchy, for the queen to be subject to income tax.

These criticisms became more prominent in the latter half of the 1980s, in large part because of the antics of several younger—and newer—royals, such as the Duchess of York, who was portrayed as enjoying frequent sojourns in expensive ski resorts in preference to fulfilling mundane public duties at home, and at the end of the decade because of the increases in the Civil List at a time of recession. However, they were to reach a new level of intensity—eventually invoking action by the Queen—in 1992.

Criticism of the royal family became pronounced—generating intense, and often highly critical, media coverage—as a result of several independent developments. The first was the separation of the Duke and Duchess of York and the subsequent publication of photographs showing a topless Duchess in intimate proximity to a Texan friend, described as her "financial advisor," with her children present. The second was speculation about the state of the marriage of the Prince and Princess of Wales. The speculation was fueled by publication of a book about the Princess of Wales that portrayed her as the vulnerable wife in a difficult royal environment, not helped by a largely intolerant and distant husband.[23] The Princess was variously alleged to have allowed, even encouraged, friends to talk to the author in order to put out her side of the story. Some of the Prince's friends later retaliated, seeking to put out his side of the story. Media attention became intense following the release of a tape of an intercepted telephone conversation held some time previously between the Princess of Wales and a male admirer, referred to on the tape as "Squidgy."

Then came a separate development that appears to have been crucial in making 1992 what the Queen was to describe as an *annus horribilis* (a horrible year, translated by one tabloid headline writer as "a bum year"). On November 20, St. George's Hall of Windsor Castle was destroyed by fire. The national heritage secretary announced that the government would meet the cost of repairs—believed to be at least £50 million ($82m.)—as the castle was uninsured. The public response was strongly negative. Out of 30,283 callers to a television program, 95 percent said the taxpayer should not have to pay the entire bill. A Harris poll found three out of four respondents believing that ways should be found to cut the cost of the royal family. The normally loyal *Daily Mail* asked: "Why should a populace, many of whom have had to make huge sacrifices during this most bitter recession, have to pay the total bill when the Queen, who pays no taxes, contributes next to nothing?"[24] Six days after the fire at Windsor Castle, the prime minister announced in the House of Commons that the Queen "some months ago" had initiated discussions on changing her tax-free status and removing all members of the royal family, except herself, the Duke of Edinburgh, and the Queen Mother, from the Civil List. The announcement served to meet much of the immediate criticism. The Queen also announced that Buckingham Palace would be opened to the public and that income from doing so would be used to pay for the restoration of St. George's Hall.

Though criticism of the cost of the royal family peaked in 1992, the personal relationships of members of the royal family continued to attract media attention and were to produce a crisis of their own in 1997. The separation of the Prince and Princess of Wales was announced by the prime minister in December 1992. Unlike the separation of the Duke and Duchess of York, this separation raised a number of constitutional questions. In announcing it to the House of Commons, the prime minister emphasized that the separation as such had no constitutional implications. The Prince remained heir to the throne and would in due course become king, and there was no reason, said the prime minister, "why the Princess of Wales should not be crowned Queen," a statement that—according to *The Economist*—attracted "a murmur of disbelief."[25] Though the prime minister's statement was correct in constitutional terms, "the thought of them kneeling together before the Archbishop of Canterbury at the sacred moment of coronation now seems wildly implausible."[26] A survey in December 1992 found that 65 percent of those questioned thought it would be wrong for the Princess to become queen if the couple were still separated.[27] The issue became academic when, apparently on the prompting of the queen, the couple decided to divorce. The divorce took effect in 1996.

The status and role of the Princess of Wales became a matter of public debate. (Upon her divorce she lost the prefix of "her royal highness" and became simply "Diana, Princess of Wales.") Her relationships became a matter of media interest, as did those of the Prince of Wales. In a television interview, the Prince admitted he had committed adultery while being married. (It transpired that he had a mistress, Camilla Parker-Bowles, who—at the time—was also married.) In a later interview, the Princess made a similar admission, though saying that it happened after it was clear that the marriage was over. The Princess promoted various high-profile causes (such as banning the use of land mines) but also withdrew for a time from public activity. She was seen as a tragic figure and achieved something of an iconic status. In August 1997, she was killed in a car accident in Paris. She immediately became greater in death than in life. (Some commentators saw parallels with the death of President John F. Kennedy in 1963. As with Kennedy's death, many people remember exactly what they were doing when they first heard the news of what had happened.) There was an immediate and intense outpouring of popular grief, which was not confined to the United Kingdom.

Her death also resulted in a public relations fiasco for the royal family. The Prince of Wales went to Paris to collect the body of his former wife, but the Queen and other leading members of the royal family remained at Balmoral Castle, the royal holiday home in Scotland. The failure to return to London attracted intensely critical comments in the media. So too did the fact that the flag was not flown at half-staff at Buckingham Palace. (Because the Queen was not in residence there was no flag flown, so all that people saw was a bare flagpole.) There was a public perception that the royal family was detached from what was going on and was not sharing, or certainly not leading, the national grief. This had a serious negative impact on public perceptions of the monarchy. By the time the Queen returned to London, and made a televised address, the damage had been done. The funeral of the Princess of Wales was the occasion for unprecedented scenes of grief and a funeral oration in Westminster Abbey from the Princess's brother, the Earl Spencer, which was interpreted as an attack on the royal family. It was a low point for the monarchy.

The royal family has since recovered from those low points of the 1990s. The royal finances are better organized and also open. The Civil List (Figure 13.1) continues to fund the expenses of the Queen and Prince Philip. The annual figure of £7.9 million was renewed in 2000 and runs to 2010. (The Queen in 2009 requested an increase in order to meet rising costs.) Other expenditure is now met by grants-in-aid: a property grant-in-aid to cover the cost of maintenance of royal palaces and a travel grant-in-aid to cover transportation costs on official duties. These three sources amounted in total in 2007–08 to £40 million ($65.6m.), up from £38 million ($62.3m.) in 2006–07. Annual accounts are published and efficiency savings have been made in recent years. In the period from 2001 to 2008, expenditure reduced in real terms by 3.1 percent. A "Way Ahead" group has been formed, comprising the leading members of the royal family (principally the Queen, her husband Prince Philip, and the Prince of Wales) and senior officials, to discuss how to modernize the monarchy and adapt to changing conditions. One of the outcomes of such discussions has been a more visible and "popular" schedule for the Queen, visiting people in their homes, visiting a supermarket, and travelling on the underground. She and other leading members of the royal family continue to undertake an extensive range of public duties.

Prince Charles also appears to have recouped some of the popularity lost as a result of his divorce and popular disapproval of his relationship with Camilla Parker-Bowles. In 2005, the couple married in a civil ceremony in Windsor and, in order to assuage public opinion, it was decided that Parker-Bowles would use the title of Duchess of Cornwall rather than Princess of Wales (given its popular association with the late Diana, Princess of Wales). It was also announced that when Charles became king she would not take the usual title of Queen Consort. Though a proportion of the public have expressed a preference for the throne to pass on the demise of the Queen to Charles' elder son, Prince William,[28] Prince Charles has attracted support for his extensive charitable activities (the Prince's Trust which he established is one the leading youth charities in the United Kingdom, having helped over 500,000 young people since 1976)[29] and for the way he has brought up his two sons. In an Ipsos MORI poll in April 2006, 52 percent of respondents said they thought Charles would make a good king, against 28 percent who thought he would make a bad king.[30]

Although criticisms continue to be expressed of the cost of the monarchy and suggestions for greater efficiency made—in 2009, for example, the Public Accounts Committee of the House of Commons suggested Buckingham Palace be open to the public more often in order to pay for repairs to royal buildings—they are not on the scale of earlier decades. The activities of the Queen, Prince Charles, and other members of the royal family also appear to have stemmed much of the criticism leveled at the monarchy. However, the criticisms of recent years appear to have fueled skepticism about the long-term future of the institution.

The Future of the Monarchy

The continued existence of the monarchy has been challenged by various politicians and writers. The institution has been attacked as anachronistic and undemocratic, a bastion of privilege and conservatism unsuited to the late twentieth century, and certainly unsuited to the twenty-first century. Some Labour MPs have variously put the case for abolition, as have writers Tom Nairn in *The Enchanted Glass* (1988), Edgar Wilson in *The Myth of the*

British Monarchy (1989), and Alistair Gray and Adam Tomkins in *How We Should Rules Ourselves* (2005). There is an interest group, Republic, which campaigns for an elected head of state (www.republic.org.uk). In 1994, the influential weekly magazine, *The Economist,* came out in favor of abolishing the monarchy. In 2009, the left-wing magazine, *The New Statesman,* devoted an issue to making the case for getting rid of it.

To Wilson, the various arguments put forward to support the monarchy are essentially myths, generated to justify the existing order. Far from being neutral, he contends that the institution is arbitrary "and exercises a pernicious influence."[31] To Republic, the monarchy is "a drag on our democratic processes," and the royal family comprises people who are "snobbish, elitist and utterly out of touch with the rest of the country."[32] To *The New Statesman,* the monarchy "sits like a spider at the centre of a web of wealth and privilege in one of the richest countries in one of the richest regions of the world. Its continued existence gives legitimacy to the deeply unequal way in which British society is structured." [33] Such critics believe the functions fulfilled by the queen as head of state could equally well be carried out by an appointed or an elected president. A number of Labour MPs have expressed support for a presidential system, albeit one based on the German rather than the U.S. model: that is, with a head of state (the president) separate from the head of government. Most countries have a nonhereditary head of state. So, they ask, why not Britain?

Supporters of the monarchy have defended it on the grounds that the monarch fulfills functions that could not be carried out as well (or at all) by an elected or nominated head of state. An elected head of state, it is argued, could not perform the uniting task as well as the queen—in part because election would be potentially divisive and in part because he or she would not have been prepared for the office in the way that an heir to the throne is prepared. The queen stands above political activity in a way that others are unlikely to emulate, and her experience would be difficult to match, especially by presidents serving for fixed terms of office. For defenders, the pageantry of the office is a positive rather than a negative aspect of its existence, contributing both to a sense of pride in the nation and—at a more materialistic level—acting as a powerful incentive to tourists to visit Britain. According to Prime Minister Harold Macmillan, who took a romanticized view of the monarchy, replacing the queen with a president would be disastrous. He expressed himself in characteristic style:

> Imagine if at this moment, instead of the Queen, we had a gentleman in evening clothes, ill-made, probably from Moss Bros., with a white tie, going about everywhere, who had been elected by some deal made between the extreme Right and the extreme Left! Then we would all wait for the next one, another little man, who is it going to be? "Give it to 'X,' you know he's been such a bad Chancellor of the Exchequer, instead of getting rid of him, let's make him the next President," Can you imagine it? I mean, it doesn't make sense, that would be the final destruction of colour and life and the sense of the past in this country, wouldn't it?[34]

Critics would respond that Macmillan's analysis has not necessarily been borne out by experience elsewhere. The response of supporters of the monarchy would doubtless be that the monarchy attracts attention not only at home but also abroad, in a way than an elected president would not. In 2002, Gallup recorded that in the preceding fifty-four years, in its annual survey of the American public's most admired man and woman, no woman has been placed in the top ten more often than Queen Elizabeth.[35]

Defenders of the monarchy have also contended that it is efficient. By general consent, the Queen is hard working and fulfills her duties well. In 2006, 85 percent of those questioned in an Ipsos MORI expressed satisfaction with the way the Queen was doing her job. Only 8 percent were dissatisfied.[36] The issue of cost has now been addressed, even if not to everyone's satisfaction, and there is now greater transparency and efficiency in the royal finances. Supporters also point out that many of the costs attributed to the monarchy—such as the maintenance of national monuments—were costs that would have to be borne by the public purse regardless of whether one had a monarch or not. They have also contended that, on balance, the nation makes a profit out of the monarchy. Since the 1760s, as noted in Figure 13.1, each monarch has surrendered income from Crown lands in return for a Civil List. Income from crown lands exceeds the amount of public money spent on the monarchy. When this is coupled with the benefits derived from tourism and from the trade accruing from foreign tours—members of the royal family drumming up trade in a way an elected head of state could not—then the nation benefits financially from the monarch and the activity of members of the royal family.[37] Critics retort that the money from crown lands is now effectively public money anyway, that tourists would still come to Britain (the national monuments would still exist), and that trade does not necessarily follow the crown. The prime minister and other senior ministers can do a good job drumming up trade and are in a stronger position to offer government-backed incentives.

The controversies surrounding the royal family in recent years, and especially in 1992 and 1997, have served to dent but not to destroy support for the monarchy. Critics made some headway but did not carry the majority with them. The early 1990s saw an increase in the number of people favoring the abolition of the monarchy. Before 1992, less than 15 percent of people questioned wanted to get rid of the monarchy. At the end of 1992, the figure stood at 24 percent. That, however, was a high point in support for abolition. The majority of respondents favor retaining the monarchy. Given a choice between monarchy and a republic, more than 70 percent of respondents in Ipsos MORI polls usually opt for the monarchy (Table 13.1). There was a decline in support in 2005 (the year Charles married Camilla Parker-Bowles) but otherwise support has been reasonably consistent. Gallup polls have tended to find an even lower proportion of Britons favoring abolition of the monarchy.[38]

The figures, though, mask some skepticism about the future of the monarchy. Since the 1980s, there has been a notable increase in the proportion of the population that is doubtful about the long-term future of the

TABLE 13.1

ATTITUDES TOWARD THE MONARCHY

Q. If there were a referendum on the issue, would you favor Britain becoming a republic or remaining a monarchy? (Percentage)*

	April 1993	Dec. 1994	Sep. 1997	Nov. 1998	June 1999	May 2002	Apr. 2005	Apr. 2006
Republic	18	20	18	18	16	19	22	18
Monarchy	69	71	73	73	74	74	65	72
Don't know	14	9	9	9	10	7	13	10

* The question sometimes omits "If there were a referendum on the issue."
Source: Derived from MORI, British Public Opinion, and www.ipsos-mori.com

monarchy. Even many who support it think that it will not exist in fifty years' time. In 1992, for the first time more people thought that the monarchy would not exist in fifty years' time than thought it would (42 to 36 percent). That skepticism was maintained throughout the 1990s, but receded somewhat in the year of the Queen's golden jubilee (Table 13.2). In 2006, the number believing the monarchy would exist in fifty years' time was basically the same as the number believing it would not exist. The picture, though, is in stark contrast to the position in 1990. Also, more than half of those questioned believed the monarchy would not exist in one hundred years. Only 24 percent believed it would.

The debate about the future of the monarchy thus shows a mixed picture. Most people want the monarchy to continue but many are doubtful that it will survive for more than a few decades. The royal family has moved to bolster its position. The Queen retains public support. Prince Charles has also

TABLE 13.2

ATTITUDES TOWARD SURVIVAL OF THE MONARCHY

Q. Looking to the future, do you think that Britain will or will not have a monarchy in fifty years? (Percentage)

	Jan. 1990	Feb. 1991	Dec. 1992	Feb. 1996	Sept. 1996	Nov. 1998	May 2002	Apr. 2006
Will	69	55	36	33	30	33	44	41
Will not	11	21	42	43	45	42	33	40
Don't know	20	23	22	24	25	25	23	19

Source: Derived from MORI, British Public Opinion, and www.ipsos-mori.com

regained much of the support he lost in the early 1990s and following the death of Diana, Princess of Wales. Also bolstering the position of the monarchy is the fact that Prince Charles' heir, Prince William (elder son of Charles and Diana, born in 1982), who will succeed to the throne on the death of Charles, enjoys great popular support.

CONCLUSION

The queen fulfills the task of representing the unity of the nation as well as carrying out certain political tasks largely but not wholly governed by convention. Her role as a political actor is circumscribed, necessarily so in order for her to fulfill her unifying role, and any real choice she is called on to exercise is the product of circumstance and unclear conventions and not of any personal desire on her part. She carries out her duties assiduously and continues to maintain the support of the population. Recent years, however, have been problematic. At times, she has not been particularly well served by members of her family, and the funding of the monarchy (and, more especially, members of the royal family) has proved controversial. Survey data reveal something of a change in mood toward the monarchy but not a collapse of support. Support is generally consistent but not certain. The challenge for the monarchy is one of adapting, something that it has shown itself capable of doing, especially under Queen Elizabeth. Despite the problems of recent years, it is not in danger of imminent demise. Whether it does exist in fifty years' time depends on how well it adapts.

NOTES

1. F. W. Maitland, *Constitutional History of England*, quoted in H. V. Wiseman (ed.), *Parliament and the Executive* (Routledge and Kegan Paul, 1966), p. 5.
2. W. Bagehot, *The English Constitution* (first published 1867; Fontana, 1963 edition), p. 61.
3. F. Hardie, *The Political Influence of the British Monarchy 1868–1952* (Batsford, 1970).
4. Hardie, p. 188.
5. I. Gilmour, *The Body Politic*, rev. ed. (Hutchinson, 1970), p. 317.
6. A. Horne, *Macmillan*, Vol. II: 1957–1986 (Macmillan, 1989), p. 168.
7. Tony Blair, quoted in *The Times*, 21 November 1997.
8. See V. Bogdanor, *The Monarchy and the Constitution* (Oxford University Press, 1995).
9. Gilmour, p. 313.
10. Ipsos MORI, "Britain's Latest Views on the Monarchy," May 2002, http://www.ipsos-mori.com/content/britains-latest-views-on-the-monarchy.ashx
11. D. Watt, "If the Queen Has to Choose, Who Will It Be?" *The Times*, 11 December 1981.
12. The constitutional position in the event of such a scenario was raised in late 1992 after the prime minister's aides signaled that the prime minister might make a

particular vote on the Maastricht bill (see Chapter 9) a vote of confidence, thus necessitating a dissolution or the resignation of the government in the event of the vote being lost. This course of action was reported not to enjoy the support of his cabinet colleagues. In the event, the vote was not made one of confidence, though it was believed the prime minister himself would resign if the vote was lost. The government won the vote with a majority of 3.

13. Lord Blake, *The Office of Prime Minister* (Oxford University Press, 1975), pp. 60–61.
14. E. Short, quoted in Blake, p. 60.
15. K. Martin, *The Crown and the Establishment* (Penguin, 1963).
16. *New Socialist*, August 1982, reported in *The Daily Telegraph*, 27 August 1982.
17. P. Richards, *Long to Reign Over Us?* (Fabian Society, 1996); T. Hames and M. Leonard, *Modernising the Monarchy* (Demos, 1998).
18. Private expenditure as sovereign, such as gifts to visiting dignitaries, is met from the Privy Purse (the income from the duchy of Lancaster), and personal expenditure as an individual, such as wedding or Christmas gifts, is met from the queen's personal wealth.
19. Prince Charles, among other titles, is Duke of Cornwall, and the duchy encompasses a number of revenue-generating estates.
20. "Should One Pay Tax?" *The Economist*, 25 January 1992, p. 36.
21. *Gallup Political Index*, Report No. 341, January 1989, p. 10.
22. MORI, *British Public Opinion*, February 1989, p. 5.
23. A. Morton, *Diana: Her True Story* (Simon & Schuster, 1992).
24. *The Daily Mail*, 24 November 1992. For a summary of the chronology, see "Seven Days That Shook the Crown," *The Sunday Times*, 29 November 1992, p. 11.
25. "Admitting the Obvious," *The Economist*, 12 December 1992, p. 25
26. Ibid., p. 25.
27. "Royal Survey," *The Sunday Telegraph*, 13 December 1992, p. 2.
28. Thirty-nine percent expressed such a preference in a Populus poll in 2006. J. Stinson, "On Queen's 80th, Britons Ask: Is Monarchy Licked?", *USA Today*, 3 May 2006, http://www.usatoday.com/news/world/2006-04-20-royals-cover_x.htm
29. See http://www.princes-trust.org.uk/default.aspx
30. Monarchy Poll, March 2006 http://www.ipsos-mori.com/researchpublications/researcharchive/poll.aspx?oItemId=115&view=wide,
31. E. Wilson, *The Myth of the British Monarchy* (Journeyman/Republic, 1989), p. 178.
32. http://www.republic.org.uk/monarchy/index.php
33. "There Can Be No Constitutional Renewal While a Monarch Sits on the Throne," *The New Statesman*, 13 July 2009, p. 4.
34. Quoted in A. Horne, *Macmillan*, Vol. II: 1957–1986 (Macmillan, 1989), pp. 170–171.
35. D. K. Carlson, "Queen Elizabeth: 50 Years of Public Opinion," Gallup News Service, 6 February 2002 , http://www.gallup.com/poll/5299/Queen-Elizabeth-Years-Public-Opinion.aspx
36. Ipsos MORI poll, April 2006, http://www.ipsos-mori.com/researchpublications/researcharchive/poll.aspx?oItemId=378
37. See P. Norton, "The Case Against Abolition," *Social Studies Review*, 4 (3), 1989, p. 122.
38. D. K. Carlson, "Queen Elizabeth: 50 Years of Public Opinion," Gallup News Service, 6 February 2002, http://www.gallup.com/poll/5299/Queen-Elizabeth-Years-Public-Opinion.aspx

PART

V

ENFORCEMENT AND FEEDBACK

CHAPTER

14

Enforcement
The Courts and the Police

The U.S. Supreme Court, as one American expert observed, is neither a court nor a political agency, "it is inseparably both."[1] This special status derives from the court's power of constitutional interpretation, a power effectively read into the Constitution by Chief Justice John Marshall in his opinion in *Marbury v. Madison* in 1803. "It is emphatically the province and duty of the judicial department," declared Marshall, "to say what the law is." The Constitution amounts to a paramount law and, in the event of the ordinary law conflicting with it, the Court must resolve the conflict: "This is of the very essence of judicial duty."[2]

The chief justice's reasoning did not go unquestioned.[3] Nonetheless, acceptance of the Court as the arbiter of constitutional disputes was underpinned by the philosophy inherent in U.S. society[4] and has been reinforced by reasons of practicality (somebody has to perform the task) and of history (the judiciary has, in effect, always performed it). When Richard Nixon's attorney, James St. Clair, sought to argue in the case of *United States v. Nixon* (1974) that the president should interpret his own powers under the Constitution, he was more than one and a half centuries too late in advancing such an argument. Acceptance of the Court's power of constitutional interpretation was too well established to be overthrown. The Court remains the judicial arbiter of a document that is inherently political and one that by its own declaration constitutes the supreme law of the land—hence the Court's dual and inseparable roles.

The position of the British judiciary in the political process has, for most of its history, differed from that of its U.S. counterpart. There are two principal reasons for this. For one thing, there are inherent difficulties in seeking to interpret a constitution whose boundaries are not clearly delineated. For another, the judiciary has labored under the self-imposed doctrine of parliamentary sovereignty. Under this doctrine, the courts have no power to declare unconstitutional an act of Parliament. If the judicial interpretation of an act conflicts with the intentions of Parliament, a new act may be passed making explicit Parliament's wishes. The courts are duty-bound to enforce the new act. Under the doctrine, the last word rests with Parliament.

These difficulties serve to explain why the U.S. Supreme Court (indeed, the U.S. judiciary, given that any court can declare an act unconstitutional) may be deemed to form part of the political decision-making process in the United States, whereas the judiciary would not normally be considered to form part of that process in Britain. Nonetheless, such differences should not be overstated. A number of caveats need to be added to the distinctions that have just been drawn.

On the U.S. side, it is important to record that the Supreme Court will decide a case on the basis of constitutional interpretation only when it cannot be resolved by statutory interpretation.[5] The Court itself seeks to avoid political questions that it deems nonjusticiable. Nor is it free of constraints imposed by other bodies. Congress can limit, and on occasion has limited, the Court's appellate jurisdiction. The Court is dependent on the executive for the enforcement of its decisions. Although it may seek to give a lead to, or restrain the actions of, president or Congress, it will rarely beat a path too far ahead or too far behind what is politically acceptable. And in practice it has rarely struck down federal legislation. Although the power to strike down a measure serves as "an omnipresent and potentially omnipotent check upon the legislative branches of government," it is a power that, as Henry Abraham observed, "courts are understandably loathe to invoke."[6]

On the British side, the courts retain the power of statutory—and common law—interpretation and can determine, in any case brought before them, whether the purported exercise of a power is authorized by law. As a result, the executive actions of ministers and administrative authorities can, when challenged, come within their purview. The determination of the courts in such cases can always be overridden by a new act of Parliament authorizing that which the courts have struck down, but by having to determine such cases the courts are brought into the political limelight. This relative prominence has been especially evident in recent years, with a significant increase in the number of such cases.

Furthermore, the British constitution has acquired a new judicial dimension. British entry into the EC, now the European Union, gave a new role to the courts. As we have seen (Chapters 4 and 9), the 1972 European Communities Act provided that, in the event of a conflict between European and U.K. laws, the courts were to give precedence to the European law. Courts can strike down a measure of British law as being inconsistent with European law. This judicial dimension has been enlarged as a consequence of the devolution of powers to elected assemblies in different parts of the United Kingdom (Chapter 10) and the incorporation of most provisions of the European Convention on Human Rights (ECHR) into British law. Under devolution, the powers conferred on the newly elected assemblies have to be interpreted, and that interpretation will shape the relationship between the assemblies and the Westminster Parliament. The role falls to the courts. The courts also have to determine if British law falls foul of the ECHR. In the event of a conflict, the courts can issue a declaration of incompatibility. In effect, though not formally, the treaties establishing the EC and the ECHR constitute forms of "higher law."

Given this, the difference between British and American courts is not as extensive as it once was. Nonetheless, the courts in the United States remain far more powerful than their English counterparts. Parliament, for example, is not legally obliged to act when a court issue a declaration of incompatibility under the 1998 Human Rights Act. Parliament can pass new legislation determining the powers of the assemblies in Scotland, Wales, and Northern Ireland. Though some social issues are now the subject of litigation through the courts, the scale is not yet on a par with that of the United States. Social issues, such as abortion, are resolved in the United Kingdom through the parliamentary and not the judicial process.

Given the longstanding differences between the two systems, especially prior to British membership in the EC, the judiciary has not figured prominently in studies of British politics. Following Britain's membership in the EC and, now, the incorporation of the ECHR into British law, the courts have begun to acquire a political significance. Politicians have begun to look at courts in a new light.

THE JUDICIAL SYSTEM

The administration of justice is one of the prerogatives of the Crown, but it is a prerogative that has long been exercisable only through duly appointed courts and judges. The basic organizational division within the court system is that between criminal and civil. There is no such distinction in the court system of the United States. A simplified outline of the court system in England and Wales is provided in Figure 14.1. (Scotland and Northern Ireland each have different systems.) The Court of Appeal, the Crown Court, and the High Court together constitute what are now termed the Senior Courts of England and Wales.[7] At the apex of the structure sits a new Supreme Court.

Criminal Cases

Minor criminal cases are tried summarily in *magistrates' courts*. The courts are local courts, presided over in most cases by unpaid lay magistrates (of which there are just under 30,000)[8] or by legally qualified, full-time magistrates known as district judges (magistrates' courts), of which there are about 130. The courts have the power to levy fines and, depending on the offense, impose a prison sentence not exceeding six months. District judges sit alone. Lay magistrates sit in a bench, which can be between two and seven in number but is almost always three. They are advised by a legally qualified clerk of the court. Cases dealt with by them cover such matters as driving offenses,

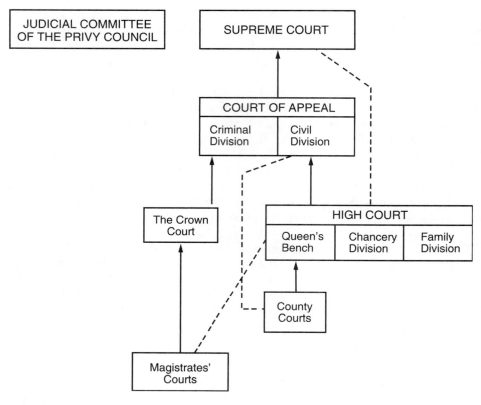

FIGURE 14.1

The court system in England and Wales
Note: Appeals are possible to higher courts as shown by arrows, usually through the immediate superior court or, in certain cases (shown by dotted lines), through another route. Tribunals and specialist courts are omitted.

assault charges, and public order offenses (for example, breach of the peace, causing an affray). District judges deal with the more complex or sensitive cases, such as those involving extradition or serious fraud. The courts also have limited civil jurisdiction and have semi-administrative functions in the licensing of public houses, betting shops, and clubs.

For many years, magistrates' courts were linked closely with the police. Until 1952, magistrates' courts in London were known as police courts and were often attached to police stations. Until 1986, the decision whether to prosecute—and the prosecution itself—was taken by the police. Since then, responsibility for the review and prosecution of all criminal cases instituted by police forces in England and Wales has rested, with certain exceptions, with the Crown Prosecution Service (CPS), headed by the director of public prosecutions (the DPP) who is usually a senior barrister. (In Scotland, responsibility for prosecution rests with the Crown Office and the Procurator Fiscal Service.) Members of the CPS are lawyers, but since the inception of the service, difficulties have been experienced in recruiting a sufficient number of well-qualified staff; private practice has tended to be more lucrative.

About 95 percent of all criminal cases are dealt with by magistrates' courts. The largest single number of cases tried is motoring offenses. Appeals from magistrates' courts are possible to the Crown Court or, in certain cases, to the High Court (to the Queen's Bench Division, for example, on points of law), though appeals are rare; less than 1 percent of those convicted in magistrates' courts appeal against conviction or sentence.

Serious criminal cases—known as indictable offenses—are tried before a jury or in some cases by a judge alone in the *Crown Court*. Over 100,000 people a year are committed for trial in the Crown Court. There are 77 Crown Court centers in England and Wales. Cases are heard either by a High Court judge (a senior judge who will normally preside over the most serious cases), a circuit judge, or a recorder. High Court and circuit judges are full-time, salaried judges; recorders are part-time and salaried, and when not presiding at court pursue their normal legal practice. All are legally qualified, drawn from the ranks of barristers or solicitors (discussed later). There are just over 100 High Court judges, 650 circuit judges, and just over 1,300 recorders.

Appeals from the Crown Court may be taken on a point of law to the Queen's Bench Division of the High Court but usually are taken to the criminal division of the *Court of Appeal*. Fewer than 10 percent of those convicted appeal. Appeals against conviction are possible on points of law (as of right) and on a question of fact (with the leave of the trial judge or Court of Appeal). Appeals against sentence, if not a sentence fixed by law, are also possible with the leave of the Appeal Court. Most appeals are against the sentence rather than the conviction. The Appeal Court may quash a conviction or uphold it. It can also vary the sentence imposed by the lower court. Since 1989 the power has existed (and been used) for the attorney general to refer to the court those sentences that appear to the prosecuting authorities to be unduly lenient. The Court of Appeal comprises the lord chief justice, the master of the rolls, and 37 Lords Justices. It is divided into two divisions: the criminal division, presided over by the lord chief justice, and the civil division, presided over by the master of the rolls; three members of the court normally sit to hear a case.

From the Court of Appeal, an appeal to the *Supreme Court* is possible if the court certifies that a point of law of general public importance is involved and it appears to the court or the Supreme Court that the point ought to be considered by the highest court of appeal. The Supreme Court was created in 2009, replacing the appellate committee of the House of Lords as the highest court of appeal. It comprises 12 Justices, all legally qualified and usually drawn from the ranks of the justices of the Court of Appeal. It is a U.K. body, legally separate from the courts of England and Wales as it also serves as the Supreme Court of Scotland and Northern Ireland.

Civil Cases

In civil proceedings, minor cases involving small sums of money are heard by *county courts*. These are presided over by circuit judges. More important cases go to the *High Court*. The High Court is divided into three divisions (Figure 14.1): the Queen's Bench Division and the Administrative Court, covering mainly matters of common law; the Chancery Division, dealing mainly with equity cases; and the Family Division, for cases of divorce and custody. Each division is headed by a senior judge. There are then, as we have noted, just over 100 High Court judges: They are known as puisne (pronounced *puny*) judges. In civil cases judges normally sit alone, though a divisional court of two or more judges may be formed, especially in the Queen's Bench Division, which has important responsibilities in the issuing of writs of habeas corpus and injunctions. Like other senior judicial posts, puisne judges are appointed from among eminent lawyers of long standing.

Appeals from county courts in bankruptcy cases are heard by a divisional court of the Chancery division. Various appeals from magistrates' courts may also go to the High Court. For example, appeals on points of law may be taken from a magistrate's court to a divisional court of the Queen's Bench Division.

Appeals from county courts (those not going to the High Court) and from the High Court go to the civil division of the Court of Appeal—presided over by the master of the rolls—and from there may go to the Supreme Court. In exceptional cases—on a point of law of exceptional difficulty calling for a reconsideration of a binding precedent—an appeal may go directly (with the leave of the Supreme Court) from the High Court to the Supreme Court. In the instance of European law, as we have seen, any case that reaches the Supreme Court must, under the provisions of the 1972 European Communities Act, be referred to the ECJ for a definitive ruling.

Finally, there is a judicial body that stands separate from the rest of the court structure. This is the *Judicial Committee of the Privy Council*. This committee was set up in 1833 to decide appeals from colonial, ecclesiastical, and admiralty courts. With the decline in Britain's colonial responsibilities, the committee receded in significance. Until recently, it had such a limited role—deciding occasional appeals from dependent territories—that it rarely figured in discussions of the judicial structure. It briefly acquired a new significance as a consequence of devolution. Under the provisions of the Government of Wales Act and the Scotland Act, what are termed "devolution issues" (determining whether a function is exercisable by the devolved body, whether powers have been exceeded, whether statutory obligations have not been fulfilled, and if there is a conflict with the ECHR) could be referred to the Judicial Committee of the Privy Council. However, this function was lost on the creation of the Supreme Court in 2009. Members of the Judicial Committee up to 2009 were usually law lords, that is, members of the appellate committee of the House of Lords. Since then, the members have been drawn from Justices of the Supreme Court as well as some others who have held high judicial office. A case is normally heard by a bench of three to five judges. The committee still hears some cases on appeal from a small number of Commonwealth countries.

The Judiciary

Magistrates' courts, with the exception of those presided over by district judges, are staffed by lay magistrates known as justices of the peace. These magistrates are not legally qualified, though they do receive some basic training; they usually are prominent local citizens. Any citizen can recommend the name of an individual for appointment as a magistrate, though in practice recommendations tend to come from local political parties and civic bodies.

Above the level of magistrates are the legally qualified judges, who are drawn from the ranks of the legal profession. Lawyers in Britain are divided into solicitors and barristers; there is no equivalent distinction in the United States. (There are also far fewer lawyers per capita in Britain than in the United States.)[9] A solicitor is a lawyer who undertakes ordinary legal business for clients. A barrister gives expert legal advice to solicitors and their clients and conducts cases in court. There is statutory provision as to how long one must have served as a solicitor or barrister before being eligible for appointment as a judge. Usually, judges are drawn from the ranks of barristers and have generally been in legal practice for longer than the minimum period required. In recent years, the ranks of judges have also been open to solicitors, though they remain a minority of the lawyers appointed to the bench. (Of recorders in 2009, for example, 1,196 were barristers and 109 were solicitors.) Those appointed are regarded as the outstanding members of their profession. The status of a judge is superior to that of a judge in the United States. Elevation to judicial office is regarded as a step up the professional ladder, something to be sought after, rather than a position one settles for if unable to establish oneself as a leading corporate lawyer.

Although judges are recruited from the ranks of well-qualified lawyers and are usually appointed or promoted on the basis of legal merit, their appointment was, until recently, made by members of the executive branch. Formally, all judges are appointed by the Crown. Prior to 2006, senior judicial appointments above the level of puisne judges were, by convention, made by the Crown on the advice of the prime minister. Other judicial appointments were made by the Crown on the advice of the lord chancellor. Though those appointed were leading and well-qualified lawyers, the Government decided there was a case for strengthening judicial independence by putting the selection process in the hands of an independent judicial appointments commission (JAC). The commission was established by the Constitutional Reform Act 2005 and started work in 2006. It selects and makes recommendations to the lord chancellor. Formally, the lord chancellor can reject a recommendation but is required to provide his reasons to the commission. Since the JAC began its work, no recommendation has been rejected. It is rare (though not unknown) for judicial appointments to be the subject of political controversy. Such appointments are not subject to any form of formal parliamentary approval.

The creation of the JAC was designed to reinforce the independence of the judiciary. It reinforces other protections that already exist in statute, common law, parliamentary rules, and an acceptance by government that the rule of law requires abstention from interference with the conduct of litigation. Judges of senior courts cannot be removed except for misbehavior in office and upon an address by both Houses of Parliament to the Crown, and their salaries are fixed by statute in order to avoid annual debate. They serve in office until they reach the age of 70 years (65 in the case of recorders) though there is provision for an extension in certain cases until the age of 75. They enjoy immunity from civil proceedings for anything said or done while acting in a judicial capacity. Judges of lower courts are also immune if acting within their jurisdiction.

By custom, questions are not asked in either house of Parliament about the conduct of courts in particular cases, reference may not be made in debate to matters awaiting or under adjudication before the courts (*sub judice* rules also prevent media comment on pending cases), and reflections may not be cast in debate upon the character or motives of a judge. Judges are not eligible for election to the House of Commons, and under the provisions of the Constitutional Reform 2005 ceased to be eligible to sit in the House of Lords following the creation of the Supreme Court in 2009. Two authors have suggested that another fact that promotes judicial independence is that judges "are all drawn from the bar after successful careers as barristers, a profession which tends to foster self-confidence and independence of mind."[10] Also, service as a judge is not usually seen as a stepping-stone to other things. One makes a career in the law, a career in which one's standing with colleagues and superiors is important and is essentially independent of partisan implications.

The degree to which judicial independence has been maintained is reflected in the fact that since judges of superior courts were accorded security of tenure under the Act of Settlement of 1701, only one senior judge has been removed from office—an Irish judge in 1830. He was found to have misappropriated money belonging to litigants and to have ceased to perform his judicial duties many years previously! Those presiding over lower courts, such as magistrates' courts, may be removed for various offenses and on occasion a magistrate has been removed for misconduct.

Although, as we shall see, the judiciary has not been free of criticism, the principle of judicial independence is a feature of the British Constitution and, in interpreting and applying the law, judges are generally more skilled and better regarded than their U.S. counterparts (especially those who serve in the state courts) and maintain probably a greater degree of judicial decorum in the proceedings before them. The rules and ethics of the legal profession also prevent much of the degrading touting for business by lawyers that is a feature of some U.S. courts.

Nonetheless, some of the problems experienced by the American judicial system find a pale—sometimes not so pale—reflection in Britain. Plea bargaining, as it exists in the United States, does not formally exist in the United Kingdom though, in practice, judges do take into account cooperation by a suspect before conviction. There is a process of "discounting" sentences for those who save the time of a court by pleading guilty. There are delays in bringing defendants to trial. Although there are various schemes, including a publicly funded community legal service, the cost of legal advice and various legal services is a problem for many citizens. The top lawyers, who may earn £1million ($1.64m.) or more a year, are available only to the very wealthy. As legal costs have soared, eligibility for legal aid has declined. For the average citizen in Britain, as in the United States, going to court is an expensive business.

A Developing Constitutional Role

Most of the work of the courts does not impinge on government. However, recent decades have seen the courts acquire a new significance in the political process. They are now, as we indicated earlier, closer to their U.S. counterparts. There are three phases that can be identified: (1) greater judicial activism, (2) membership of the European Community, and (3) constitutional reforms since 1997: devolution, the Human Rights Act, and the creation of a Supreme Court.

GREATER JUDICIAL ACTIVISM   This dates from the 1960s. The courts apply the law. This involves interpreting acts of Parliament. Acts of Parliament confer powers, on an ever increasing scale, on ministers. (An act, for example, may confer power on a minister to regulate a particular scheme or activity, or to lay down standards for a particular body.) The courts on occasion have to determine whether ministers have acted within the powers granted them by statute. The courts can strike down ministers' actions as being *ultra vires* (that is, beyond the powers granted). Undertaking this exercise is known as judicial review. This terminology should not be confused with judicial review in the United States: Judicial review there refers to constitutional interpretation. In the United Kingdom, judicial review is a form of statutory interpretation. The courts are not questioning or challenging acts of Parliament, but interpreting them to determine whether ministers have acted within their terms.

Prior to the 1960s the courts were largely deferential to government and few cases of judicial review resulted in the actions of ministers being declared *ultra vires*. The situation changed in the 1960s. In a number of celebrated cases, the courts found against ministers. In one case, the House of Lords, in its judicial capacity, not only considered why, but also how, a ministerial decision was made. Activism on the part of the courts became a feature of succeeding decades. More challenges were made to ministerial decisions. At the beginning of the 1980s, there were about 500 applications a year for leave to apply for judicial review. By 1990, the figure exceeded 2,000. In 1998 it was 4,539. In 2007 it reached 6,690.[11] Though most applications fail (only 21 percent were granted leave to apply in 2007 and of the 338 substantive applications disposed of, only 162 were allowed) and more applications are against local authorities than ministers, ministers nonetheless have sometimes fallen foul of an activist judiciary. Successive Conservative home secretaries in the 1990s encountered problems with the courts. In 1993 the House of Lords (then still the highest court of appeal) held that a former secretary, Kenneth Baker, acting in his ministerial capacity, was in contempt of court for failing to comply with a court order in an asylum case. Baker's successor, Michael Howard, was found in a number of cases to have acted beyond his powers. In 1995, for example, the House of Lords ruled that a criminal injuries compensation scheme he had introduced was unlawful. Indeed, Howard's period of office was characterized by particular tension between the executive and the judiciary. Howard's Labour successors have also fallen foul of the courts. In 1999, the House of Lords declared unlawful Jack Straw's decision to ban journalists investigating miscarriages of justice from interviewing prisoners. The Appeal Court found against him when he attempted to return three asylum seekers to France or Germany. In more recent years, as we shall see, the tension has increased as a consequence of judicial interpretation under the Human Rights Act 1998.

MEMBERSHIP OF THE EUROPEAN COMMUNITY   In exercising their existing common law powers, the courts thus came to acquire greater political visibility. This visibility became greater as a consequence of British membership in the EC, now the European Union. As we have seen (Chapter 4), new powers were vested in the courts. The courts were responsible for interpreting EC law and for resolving any disputes between EC and U.K. law. The full implications of these powers were only fully grasped in the 1990s. In the *Factortame* case in 1990–91, the ECJ held that national courts could grant interim relief (*Factortame I*), in effect enabling the courts to set aside a decision of Parliament, and that the 1988 Merchant Shipping Act contravened provisions of European law (*Factortame II*). U.K. courts could thus disapply national law that contravened EC law. In the case of *R. v. Secretary of State for Employment, ex parte the Equal Opportunities Commission* (the *Ex Parte EOC* case) in 1994, the House of Lords held that certain provisions of the 1978 Employment Protection (Consolidation) Act were unlawful as they were incompatible with EC law. By virtue of British membership in the EC, the courts thus acquired a new power: They could strike down acts of Parliament, something they had not been able to do since the Glorious Revolution of 1688.

CONSTITUTIONAL REFORMS SINCE 1997: DEVOLUTION, THE HUMAN RIGHTS ACT, AND THE CREATION OF THE SUPREME COURT   The third phase occurred with the election of a Labour government in 1997. It brought in measures that had the effect of further strengthening the role of the courts. Devolution to elected assemblies in different parts of the United Kingdom was achieved through various acts of Parliament. Those acts had to be interpreted and each was, in effect, a form of constitution for the particular part of the United Kingdom that it covered. The courts had the task of interpretation. The way in which the courts interpret the acts will determine the power of the different devolved assemblies. The importance of this power was noted in respect of Scotland by two authors: "The courts are inevitably faced with a grave responsibility: the way in which they interpret the SA [Scotland Act] may be a significant factor in deciding whether devolution proves to be the reform which cements the union, or whether it is the first step towards its dissolution."[12]

This important responsibility was not the only one conferred on the courts. Under the terms of the Human Rights Act 1998, most provisions of the ECHR are incorporated into British law. Under the Act, as we have noted already (Chapter 4), the courts can consider whether a measure or action by a public authority is in breach of the Convention. If it finds that it is, it can issue a declaration of incompatibility. It is then for Parliament to change the law to ensure that it complies with the Convention. This new power is a major one, far more important than it may appear to be under the terms of the 1998 Act. The courts, in effect, apply a "higher law" document—the ECHR—and certify cases where U.K. law falls foul of that document. So important was this change that judges had to be specially trained in dealing with ECHR cases. To give time for the training to be completed, the principal provisions were not brought into effect until 2000: The main provisions took effect on October 2, 2000. The number of cases that have been brought alleging a breach of convention rights has been small: Between 2003 and 2007, the number of human rights cases to reach the House of Lords totaled 63 out of a total of 279 cases considered by the court.[13] However, there have been some notably high profile, and politically contentious, cases. The most controversial have been in the field of anti-terrorism legislation. In 2004, in the *Bellmarsh* case, the House of Lords held that powers in Part 4 of the Anti-Terrorism, Crime and Security Act 2001 breached convention rights. The Government brought in a new measure, the Prevention of Terrorism Act 2005, to try to meet the judgment of the court, but provisions of this Act, concerning control orders, were also deemed by a divisional court and then the Court of Appeal to breach convention rights.[14] Each of the judicial decisions were attacked by ministers—one minister in response to the *Bellmarsh* case said that the judges were "simply wrong"—and Prime Minister Tony Blair indicated that the government would if necessary amend the Human Rights Act in order to enable it to combat terrorism. The lord chief justice spoke up in defense of the courts—judges, he pointed out, were doing their job of applying the law passed by Parliament. The judges had not changed: It was the law that had changed. A review of the Act was initiated; in the light of that, the prime minister accepted that it would not be possible to amend it. The Act thus thrust the courts into a new level of political visibility and demonstrated a capacity for conflict between the courts and government.

The other major constitutional change affecting the judiciary was the creation of a new Supreme Court. Until 2009, the highest court of appeal was the House of Lords. Formally, this meant the whole House, but in practice cases were considered by the appellate committee of the House. This comprised 12 lords specially appointed for the purpose—law lords, formally known as Lords of Appeal in Ordinary—and certain other lords who had held high judicial office. The law lords were senior lawyers, usually drawn from the ranks of Appeal Court judges, and usually recognized as being outstanding judicial figures. Cases were considered usually by a panel of five law lords, hearings being held in a committee room in the Palace of Westminster. Though law lords were members of the House of Lords, they normally declined to take part in any proceedings on legislation or other matters that could potentially come before them in a judicial capacity or that might compromise their judicial independence.

In 2003 the Government announced plans to replace the House of Lords in its judicial capacity with a dedicated Supreme Court. The announcement was unexpected and controversial. Six law lords were opposed to the move, as were many other members of the Lords. They argued that the existing system was recognized to deliver justice and there was no compelling argument for change. The government argued that in a modern liberal democracy there needed to be a clear separation between the legislature and the courts and that people did not understand the distinction between the House of Lords in its legislative capacity and the House in its judicial capacity. It achieved passage of the Constitutional Reform Act 2005. This transferred the position of head of the judiciary from the lord chancellor (a political appointee) to the lord chief justice (a judge) and also provided for the creation of a Supreme Court. This came into being in October 2009, once the building designed for it (formerly Middlesex Guildhall, in Parliament Square opposite the Palace of Westminster) was ready.

The creation of the Supreme Court involved primarily a physical move rather than any creation of new judicial powers. The Supreme Court exercises the same powers as those previously exercised by the House of Lords. Its members were also essentially the same as those who served in the Lords as law lords. Law lords at the time of the transfer became Justices of the Supreme Court. The first Justice to be appointed who had not served as a law lord was Lord Clarke of Stone-cum-Ebony, a former master of the rolls.

A combination of these developments has created a new and significant judicial dimension to the British constitution. Though the creation of the Supreme Court involved no new powers, it nonetheless gave the highest court of appeal a far greater visibility. It came into being at a time when the courts were more active than before, not least because of new roles given them by constitutional changes. It also came after the courts had acquired greater scope to examine parliamentary proceedings.[15] There was thus the potential for clashes with both Parliament and government. As we have seen, this potential has variously been realized.

This judicial dimension to the constitution had been lacking for nearly three hundred years following the Glorious Revolution. Though British judges do not have the constitutional role held by American judges, they have moved far more in their direction. It is a position that, as we have seen (Chapter 4), does not fit well with the traditional British constitution.

THE POLICE FORCE

The British police force has been regarded for many years as a paragon among police forces. In recent decades it has undergone major changes. It has also become a topic of public debate. Like police forces elsewhere, it has been criticized for not tackling high rates of crime and a fear of crime. It has also had to face accusations of corruption in certain forces and of strained relations with particular elements of the community.

In the United Kingdom there are 52 police forces (43 in England and Wales, 8 in Scotland, and 1—the Police Service of Northern Ireland—in Northern Ireland), each responsible for law enforcement in its area. Outside the London metropolis each force is under the direction of a chief constable. The metropolitan police force, with its headquarters in New Scotland Yard, is under the control of a commissioner. (There is a separate City of London force.) Within each police force, areas are broken down into divisions, each headed by a superintendent. Each division is then broken down into a series of local stations, each headed usually by an inspector. Below inspectors are sergeants and police constables (PCs). Within each force there are various specialist departments, such as the traffic division, drugs squads, firearms units, fraud squads, and air support units.

The number of police officers has grown over the past century and by 2009 there were more than 145,500 police officers in England and Wales—about 1 for every 400 people, roughly the same ratio as in the United States. Nearly three-quarters of all police officers in England and Wales are police constables. In addition to the regular police officers, there is also the special constabulary, comprising approximately 14,000 unpaid volunteers who spend a few hours each week helping their local force. They are trained, wear police uniforms, and have the same powers as regular police officers. A recent innovation is the introduction of Police Community Support Officers (PCSOs). They go out on routine patrol—providing some level of public reassurance—but have neither the same level of training as police officers nor the same powers. They can issue fixed-penalty notices for anti-social behavior, for example, but cannot stop and search individuals. By 2009, there were over 16,000 PCSOs.

The police force relies for its effectiveness on the consent and the cooperation of the community. As far as possible, the police have sought to operate as a part of the local community. Police officers live in the community they serve (that is, they live in local houses rather than in barracks), they have limited but original powers, and for many years they patrolled their allotted beats on foot. Patrolling is now done more frequently by car. Remarkable in American terms is the fact that, with certain exceptions (such as officers providing diplomatic protection), they are not regularly armed. PCs on beat patrol used to carry only a truncheon (a wooden baton) and whistle, though now they usually have a long baton (similar to the U.S. nightstick), a small spray canister of CS gas (a stinging, debilitating gas), and a radio. In the event of an armed incident, teams of specially trained armed officers are dispatched, though the first officers on the scene are usually unarmed. Although in some parts of the community the police have always been treated with suspicion, popular trust in the police has been a feature of recent British history. This was especially the case in the quarter-century from 1945 to 1970. The local policeman was portrayed, including on some popular television programs, as a kindly figure, walking the beat, ready to pass the time of day with residents, and obligingly telling children the time or seeing them safely across the road.

It has also been a nonpolitical force in that it has been kept largely at one remove from direct government control. (Only the Special Branch, which carries out arrests on behalf of the intelligence services, could be described as fulfilling a political role.)[16] The fear of a national police force under government control has prevented the creation of such a force. Each force is accountable to a Police Authority. (There is also a separate Police Authority for the British Transport Police.) In Northern Ireland, the authority is called the Policing Board. Each authority comprises local councilors and independent members (at least one of whom must be a magistrate).[17] Each authority sets the strategic direction for the force as well as holding the budget and determining the appointment of the chief constable and senior officers.

A chief constable, the head of each force, has to submit an annual report to his authority, and the authority can require him to supply a report on any topic, other than on the operational deployment of his force (or anything that could be against the public interest, as confirmed by the home secretary). Funding of the police is through grants from central government and from local authorities. This funding provides, or could provide, both the home secretary and the police authorities with leverage in seeking to ensure police accountability. In practice, chief constables have tended to achieve autonomy in their activities, local authorities being more concerned with the provision of funds than the policies for which those funds are intended.

Pitted against the fear of centralized government control has been the desire for greater operational efficiency. Problems arising from the existence of too many autonomous police forces (such as the 40,000 police forces that exist in the United States) have encouraged the amalgamation of forces, reducing the number in England and Wales from a little under 200 in the 1920s to the present 43. There have been calls for the number to be reduced even further.

Perceptions of the police as a local, unarmed, well-trained force (all officers undergo a standard training) that is free of political direction, combined with a crime rate relatively low by international standards (especially when compared with the United States), helped produce the positive view of the police held at home and abroad, particularly in the 1950s and, to a lesser extent, the 1960s.

Since the latter half of the 1960s, the public attitude toward the police has undergone some change. In part, this is attributable to certain changes in the police force itself. From being the local constable on the beat with nothing more than a whistle to summon assistance, the police officer was transferred to driving a car (known as a panda car because of its appearance) and was equipped with a personal radio. As a result of being in a car, the police officer had less direct contact with the local citizenry. By having a personal radio he or she was able to summon the assistance of colleagues; there was less need to appeal to local citizens or pursue a diplomatic approach in handling quarrelsome characters. There also emerged a new breed of professional chief constables, more self-assertive and imposing their own views on policing. More recently, the equipment worn by police officers, especially in dealing with riots and other serious incidents, has tended to make them look distant and intimidating. Whereas a police constable has been seen tradition-ally as a citizen in uniform, police officers tackling serious incidents appear quasi-military and threatening.

Public attitudes toward the police force also have been affected adversely by three other features. In combination, they have generated what has amounted at times to a crisis of confidence in the police, especially among certain sections of the population. Those developments are a fear of crime, corruption, and poor relationship with certain communities.

Crime and the Fear of Crime

Crime in the United Kingdom increased over the twentieth century. Before the 1920s, the police recorded fewer than 100,000 offenses each year in England and Wales. In 1950, the figure was 500,000 and by 1999 it was 5.2 million. These constitute offenses reported to the police; the actual level of crime is accepted to be much higher. (Offenses such as rape, even though witnessing an increase in the number reported, are widely accepted to be significantly underreported.) In 1998, new methods of reporting offenses were introduced. If someone breaks into five cars in a parking lot, it is now recorded as five separate offenses; under the previous method of recording crime, it would have been treated as a single incident. The increase in crime in 1999 was a "real" increase in that the 1998 figures were based on the new, rather than the old method, of recording offenses.

As crime increased, the percentage of offenses cleared up by the police (that is, offenses resulting in an arrest) decreased. In 1971, 45 percent of indictable offenses reported to the police were classified as cleared up. In 1990, the clear-up rate—though not precisely comparable with 1971 because of some changes in accounting practices—was 32 percent. In 1996 the figure was 26 percent, in 1997 it was 28 percent. The lowest clear-up rate was for burglary, where only one in every four reported offenses resulted in an arrest. Furthermore, the clear-up rate decreased as police resources—in personnel and equipment—increased significantly.

Recent years have seen a fall in the crime rate, both in terms of crime reported to the police and in crime admitted by respondents in the British Crime Survey (BCS) but not necessarily reported to the police. In 2007–08, BCS crime fell by 10 percent and reported crime by 9 percent. Violent crime was down by 12 percent and the risk of being a victim of crime fell from 24 percent to 22 percent, the lowest level since the BCS was begun in 1981.

Despite the decrease, public concern has remained. Crime remains a seri-ous issue both in absolute and relative terms. Though historically the United Kingdom has been a middle-ranking Western country in terms of crime rates, it now is among the leaders in western Europe in the incidence of common crime (along with Ireland, the Netherlands and Denmark).[18] There are two particular dimensions to crime in the United Kingdom that affect the police force. The first is the fear of crime and the second is the belief that the police are not doing enough to tackle it.

In recent years, there has been little correlation between trends in crime rates and perceptions of an increase in crime. Though crime rates have been falling, the perception that crime is increasing has been a constant of surveys over the past decade. In 2007–08, about two-thirds of people believed that crime had increased over the past two years.[19] As a Government White Paper on policing summarized the problem: "Tackling crime is the most important issue for the public and we know that the public remain unconvinced that crime has gone down and are understandably alarmed by the few, but high profile, incidences of serious crime and the wider problems. If crime falls but people do not have the confidence that this is happening in their neighbourhoods, their quality of life is affected and the benefits of reduced crime are not realized. This matters because it undermines our efforts to engage the community through crime reporting, intelligence gathering and community engagement activities."[20]

Despite a marked increase in police funding, there remains a perception that the police are not highly efficient in dealing with crime. A 2005 survey of 18 European countries found improved ratings in police performance, except in the United Kingdom, Netherlands, and France.[21] Surveys have shown a decrease in confidence in the way that the police handle crime. A MORI poll in April 2000 found that only 50 percent of those questioned were very or fairly confident that, if they dialed the police in an emergency, they would arrive within 10 minutes.[22] The same poll found decreasing levels of satisfaction among respondents as to the way their area was policed. In 1981, 75 percent of those questioned were very or fairly satisfied with the way their area was policed. The level of satisfaction decreased in succeeding years. In 1992 and 1993 only 51 percent were satisfied. Levels of satisfaction increased as the 1990s progressed, but then fell back again in 2000. In April 2000, 53 percent were satisfied.[23] The figure fell but was back to 53 percent in 2008.[24]

The police have come under particular pressure to mount higher-profile policing of certain areas, not least inner city areas plagued by drug problems and gang conflict. Rural dwellers are also increasingly feeling under threat, even though crime levels remain lower in rural than in urban areas. The issue attracted national prominence in 2000. An eccentric farmer who lived in an isolated farmhouse in Essex and had shot dead a burglar and wounded another was convicted of murder. He was automatically given a sentence of life imprisonment. The case sparked a national controversy about levels of policing in rural areas. In a MORI poll, conducted shortly after the case, 75 percent of those questioned said that their sympathy was entirely or mainly with the farmer. (Only 4 percent said mainly or entirely with the burglar.) Only 18 percent strongly agreed or tended to agree with the statement that the sentence on the farmer was the right one for the crime. Some 96 percent of respondents strongly agreed or tended to agree with the statement that people should have the right to defend their own property.

The government has made various attempts to increase police efficiency and restore public trust. These have included a series of efficiency audits, an opening up of police performance to public scrutiny (requiring forces to publish such details as response times), and put an emphasis on returning police officers to beat patrols. Though beat patrols have little effect on crime rates, they are important for reassuring local residents. A number of police forces have also undertaken their own initiatives in an attempt to increase efficiency and public confidence, ranging from local customer surveys to transferring officers from cars to bicycles (the latter, where tried, apparently proving quite effective in silent detection and mobility). However, improving efficiency and public confidence are not always compatible goals. Some police forces have closed some police stations and reduced the number staffed on a round-the-clock basis, an action that has rarely proved popular with local citizens. This was seen by many as underpinning the response to the case of the Essex farmer, many believing that the police were unable to provide effective protection for people living in isolated areas.

Corruption

Corruption has been a problem especially, though not exclusively, in the metropolitan police force. In a five-year period in the 1970s, the commissioner removed more than 450 officers and in 1976 there was the biggest trial involving detectives seen since 1877. Recent decades have witnessed a number of highly publicized cases of alleged corruption. Most cases have involved individual officers, for example disclosing confidential information, but some have involved teams or internally networked corruption. Several cases involving officers from the West Midlands force resulted in the chief constable of the West Midlands in 1989 removing from operational duty every member of his 53-member criminal investigation department, having earlier wound up its serious crime squad following allegations of evidence having been fabricated. In the early 1990s, members of the South East Regional Crime Squad were found to be protecting a drug dealer in return for evidence against other drug dealers as well as stealing cash during raids. Various cases have involved officers tipping-off suspects about raids. According to one study, "There are the cases where they've already got the kettle on when the police arrive."[25] In other cases, accusations have been made of officers rewriting notes after the event and of officers misusing corporate credit cards: In 2009, one Metropolitan police officer was charged with misconduct in public office and 48 cases regarding use of corporate credit cards had been referred to the Independent Police Complaints Commission (IPCC).

Though cases of corruption are rare, they undermine public confidence in the police. Various changes have been implemented to take on the problem of corruption and dishonesty. The 1984 Police and Criminal Evidence Act requires the recording of all interviews. Most of the major cases involving fabricated evidence predated the act. However, in one case in 1989, the lord chief justice quashed a conviction after declaring that the officers in the case had shown "a lamentable attitude" to the codes of practice laid down by the act. In 2004, a new body, the IPCC, replacing a Police Complaints Authority, was created to oversee complaints made against the police. The IPCC investigates serious cases, notably where deaths involving police officers occur, such as in police custody, in road accidents with police vehicles, or where someone is shot by police officers. It also considers appeals where complainants are not satisfied with how the police have dealt with their complaint. In 2007/08, 28,963 complaints were recorded by police forces in England and Wales (involving in some cases multiple allegations). The IPCC dealt with 4,171 appeals; of 3,592 appeals deemed to be valid, 28 percent were upheld.[26] Various steps have thus been taken to address accusations of police corruption, including creating a body designed to inject greater independence and transparency into the process. Ironically, corruption appears less of a problem than it was at a time when public trust in the police was much higher. Cases of corruption, however rare, taint the reputation of the police.

Poor Relationship with Certain Communities

The police have also attracted criticism because of alleged bias or aggressiveness in dealing with certain communities. Britain experienced a number of riots in the 1980s and early 1990s in a number of urban areas. One of the reasons given for riots in some areas was the attitude taken by the police toward the local black community. There were allegations of racism on the part of some police officers and of a heavy-handed approach in dealing with black suspects. More pervasively, police officers are often seen by black youths as picking on them whenever offenses are committed and sometimes when no offense has been committed. Various other groups in society have also alleged bias against the police, including "new age" travelers and homosexuals. Some police forces, especially the metropolitan police force, have been criticized for targeting and harassing the gay community.

Attempts have been made to address these problems. The 1984 Police and Criminal Evidence Act requires the police to obtain the views of local people about the policing of their area; most areas now have police-community consultative groups. The police have also attempted to recruit more Asian and Afro-Caribbean officers to their ranks, albeit with very limited success; less than 4 percent of officers are drawn from ethnic communities, few of them in senior positions. Retention is a problem: Twice as many recruits from ethnic minorities drop out in their first six months compared with their white counterparts. Police officers receive training in race and community relations as part of their probationary service. Various attempts have been made to tackle discrimination against gays. Some forces now have liaison officers to work with the gay community.

Such moves, however, have tended to be outweighed by allegations of harassment and of racial bias and insensitivity. The police have been accused of failing to recognize racial motivation in various cases and of failing to pursue vigorously crimes against members of ethnic minorities. The murder of a young black teenager, Stephen Lawrence, by white assailants in London in 1993 led to major criticism of the police. Claims that they were incompetent and racist led to various internal investigations and to a public inquiry chaired by a former judge, Sir William Macpherson. The report of the

Macpherson inquiry was published in 1999. It was an extensive document. It concluded: "There is no doubt but that there were fundamental errors. The investigation was marred by a combination of professional incompetence, institutional racism and a failure of leadership by senior officers."[27] The Commissioner of the Metropolitan Police accepted that there was institutional racism in his force.

There was also other evidence of dissatisfaction with police handling of cases involving racial minorities. The BCS of 1996 found that victims reporting crime thought to be racially motivated were less satisfied with the police responses than those reporting other crimes. In one incident, two black youths being attacked by white youths were arrested by police officers, even though closed-circuit cameras showed that the black youths were the victims. In another case, police failed to treat the death of a young black, who died after being found covered in flames, as a racially motivated murder; they initially claimed that the youth had set himself alight. A number of blacks died while being held in police custody. Though police in various areas built up good relationships with different ethnic and other bodies, the work was overshadowed by such high-profile incidents. Negative perceptions of the police may also explain why many racially motivated crimes are not reported to the police. The BCS found that only 45 percent of racially motivated crimes were reported.

These criticisms of the police have undermined support for the police force. As Sir William Macpherson noted in his report, "The public and the Police Services of the United Kingdom are justifiably proud of the tradition of an unarmed police service which polices with the consent of the public," but he went on to say that "at present the confidence and trust of the minority ethnic communities is at a low ebb." Black and Asian youths continue to be subject disproportionately to being stopped and searched by the police. Various senior police officers who are black or Asian have been investigated and on occasion charged with disciplinary or criminal offenses. In 2008, the Black Police Association urged a recruitment boycott of the Metropolitan Police on the grounds that there existed within the force "a hostile atmosphere where racism is allowed to spread." (The Association itself was the subject of an investigation by the IPCC for its poor management and possible misconduct.)[28] In 2009, the Runnymede Trust, a charitable research body, and the Equalities and Human Rights Commission published reports critical of how the police dealt with ethnic communities. The Commission found that black and Asian police officers felt disadvantaged by "old-fashioned working practices"; the Runnymede Trust said that the police force, despite attempts to tackle the issue, was still institutionally racist. Some police forces, it claimed, were still "dragging their feet" when it came to recording and reporting racist crimes. Ten years after the Macpherson report, it said, "there is still significant progress to be made—notably in relation to the career experiences of black and minority ethnic officers and the disproportionate use of stop and search procedures against Black groups."

As we have seen, there is a widespread concern about crime and the capacity of the police to deal with it. Even so, there is still some trust in police officers. Police officers who risk their lives in tackling suspects or rescuing people are widely admired. The public generally share the frustration of police officers with the amount of time tied up with paperwork and office routine. Most people trust police officers to tell the truth. The percentage of people trusting them to tell the truth has not changed much over the past quarter-century. During the period, around 60 percent of those questioned have trusted them to tell the truth. In 1999, the figure was 61 percent; in 2007 it was 59 percent.[29] However, the percentages trusting doctors, teachers, and professors to tell the truth are much higher. There is also some recognition that the police are being left to tackle jobs that should be tackled in conjunction with the community. For the police in the twenty-first century, there is a problem of morale, trying to do a difficult job in difficult circumstances and at a time when they are criticized for being inefficient and racist.

THE CURRENT DEBATE

In recent decades, various criticisms have been leveled at the courts and at the police. We have touched already on criticisms made of the police force. The whole criminal justice system at times has come under attack. The criticisms that have been made are several. Discussion revolves around the background, interests, and recruitment of judges; the conduct of the courts and the police in certain cases, resulting in various miscarriages of justice; and demands for the courts to be given greater powers, not least through an entrenched bill of rights.

Background and Recruitment of Judges

Though judges are recruited on merit through a formal judicial appointments process, they remain overwhelmingly white, male, and middle or upper class. Of 153 senior judges in 1999, only 8 were women. Over the next decade, there was only a small increase. In 2009, of 164 senior judges, 15 were women. There is one female justice of the Supreme Court. Of 37 lord justices of appeal, only 3 are woman. Of the 164 senior judges, only 3 are drawn from ethnic backgrounds. The majority of senior judges went to "public" (i.e., private) schools (see Chapter 1)—among the most senior judges the proportion exceeds 80 percent—and the overwhelming majority went to Oxford or Cambridge Universities. Senior judges are almost wholly drawn from the ranks of barristers. Only four are drawn from the ranks of solicitors. Training to be a barrister is expensive and therefore tends to be more attractive to those with parents who can afford to support them.

Judges thus form part of a social elite. Their background has led to claims that they are out of touch with contemporary society. Though detachment may be an advantage, a lack of knowledge of everyday social life and interests may, in the eyes of critics, be a disadvantage. In one civil case involving Olympic sprinter Linford Christie, in which Christie—who wore a figure-hugging running outfit on the track—objected to references to his "lunch box" (the protrusion of his private parts through his running gear), the judge had to ask what a "lunch box" was. The male dominance of the bench has also led to claims of insensitivity in some cases involving women, not least in rape cases. The background of judges has also led to claims that they are biased toward the existing order—a point of relevance to the next section—and toward the government of the day. As one noted critic, J. A. G. Griffith put it, senior judges construe the public interest as favoring law and order and upholding the interests of the state.[30]

Various efforts have been made to make the judiciary more open, sensitive, and accountable.[31] Recent lord chief justices and masters of the roll have reformed some of the practices of the courts. Senior judges are more open; recent lord chief justices have been willing to give interviews. The lord chief justice now publishes an annual report. The new supreme court is also required to do so by the 2005 Constitutional Reform Act. The lord chief justice usually appears annually before the constitution committee of the House of Lords. Some efforts are being made to recruit more solicitors to the ranks of the judiciary. As we have seen, judges have been trained in how to handle cases involving the ECHR. Judges are now recruited through open competition by an independent JAC.

In some areas, though, progress has been notably slow. As we have seen, very few solicitors have made it to the bench. The increase in the number of women at senior levels has also been slow. It takes time to work one's way to the top of the judicial hierarchy. Women are more numerous at the lower levels: 27 percent of deputy district judges are female. Just over 4 percent of recorders, and 7 percent of deputy district judges (magistrates' courts), are drawn from ethnic minorities.

Criticism of judges has also been heightened, as we shall see, by various miscarriages of justice. However, judges continue to enjoy respect. Most people trust them to tell the truth. In 1999, 79 percent of respondents in one survey trusted them to tell the truth: In 2007, the figure was 78 percent. As with police officers, the percentage trusting them was lower than for doctors, teachers, and professors.[32] Lord Bingham, lord chief justice from 1996 to 2000 and after that the most senior law lord, also noted that, though judges were often portrayed as elderly, out of touch, upper class, and remote, whenever some serious issue arose, the cry went up "we need a judicial inquiry."[33] It is common for major public inquiries to be headed by serving or retired judges. There is thus, as Lord Bingham noted, an ambivalent public attitude toward judges. Many judges are also well aware of social problems and the nature of society. Some exploit modern technology, using laptops and using electronic databases to check sources.

Miscarriages of Justice

Confidence in the courts and the police has been dented in recent years by a number of highly publicized cases of miscarriages of justice.[34] The most prominent but not the only cases have involved individuals convicted of terrorist offenses, most notably the "Birmingham Six," convicted of pub bombings in Birmingham in 1974; the "Guildford Four," convicted in 1975 of bombings in Guildford; and the Maguire family, convicted of running an IRA bomb factory. In 1989 the Guildford Four were released, after spending fourteen years in jail, pending an inquiry into their original conviction, the DPP having found himself unable to argue in support of the convictions. In 1990 the Maguire case was referred to the Appeal Court after the home secretary received evidence that the convictions could not be upheld. In 1991 the Birmingham Six were released, after spending sixteen years in jail, when the Court of Appeal quashed their convictions. Another prominent case not related to terrorist offenses involved the conviction of several men for the murder of a newspaper delivery boy, Carl Bridgewater, who had disturbed a burglary at a remote farmhouse. The men were convicted in 1979. They were refused leave to appeal in 1981 and had an appeal turned down in 1987. The case was again referred to the Court of Appeal in 1996 and the men were released in 1997, eighteen years after they were convicted.

Most of the criticism in these cases was directed at the police and the evidence they presented at the original trials, the convictions being quashed on the grounds that the evidence was unsound or fabricated. However, the courts did not escape blame. The trial judges and others involved in the trials, including the Court of Appeal, were accused of being over-reliant on the good faith of key prosecution witnesses.[35] The Appeal Court came in for particular criticism for its apparent reluctance to even consider that there may have been miscarriages of justice. Nor did the civil courts escape censure. When the Birmingham Six had brought a claim for damages, in an attempt to establish police malpractice, the then master of the rolls, Lord Denning, delivered an *obiter dictum* "to the effect that exposure of injustice in individual cases was less important than preserving a façade of infallibility."[36] The observation made a particularly bad impression, especially when the real facts of the case started to emerge shortly afterward. By the 1990s, the façade of infallibility had disappeared.

The government sought to tackle many of the problems associated with the criminal justice system. In 1991 it established a Royal Commission, which reported in 1993. Its recommendations led to various changes. A Criminal Procedure and Investigations Act was enacted to make sure that the prosecution disclosed to the defense everything which could be relevant to their case. In 1997 a Criminal Cases Review Commission (CCRC) began work. It has 11 commissioners and about 100 staff. It investigates possible miscarriages of justice and decides whether convictions or sentences should be referred to the court of appeal. Though it has been criticized for being under-funded and under-staffed, with a backlog of cases, it has nonetheless had a high success rate in referring cases to the court of appeal which have then been quashed. By May 31, 2009, the Commission had investigated over 11,000 applications, with over 400 under review. It had referred 392 cases to the court of appeal, of which 277 had been quashed and 115 upheld.[37]

The situation has improved notably over the past quarter-century. Legislation designed to reduce the likelihood of miscarriages of justice, the creation of the CCRC, the existence of various voluntary campaigning bodies to identify miscarriages of justice, advances in medical technology (not least DNA), and changes in police personnel and practices have reduced the likelihood of any repetition of the miscarriages of justice of earlier decades. Nonetheless, as we have seen, there are still criticisms of both the courts and the police and cases continue to be referred to the CCRC, including some relatively recent cases. In May 2009, a leading civil rights lawyer claimed that there were as many miscarriage of justice victims behind bars as there had been in the 1980s.[38] The chair of the CCRC asked the CPC to review cases where DNA was involved to see if scientific evidence could be used to establish the innocence of prisoners. Various campaigns continued in respect of particular cases.[39]

A More Powerful Judiciary

Recent years, as we have seen, have witnessed tensions between the courts and the executive. Ministers have criticized judges for exceeding their remit and for making judge-made law. However, there are jurists who wish to protect and enhance the role of the courts. Judges are viewed as detached and important, able to protect individuals from unjust actions by the executive and other bodies. Lord Scarman in 1989 imputed to society a wish for judges to defend the liberties of the individual from arbitrary acts of government. "Let us keep in mind," he wrote, "that in a pluralist society many minorities have no real opportunity of acquiring political power and rely on the law's protection against oppression by the majority."[40] Whereas Parliament may be the medium through which popular will could be expressed, the courts were seen as protecting minorities and others from oppression by popular will or those acting in the name of the people.

A consequence, as we have seen, has been greater judicial activism. Judges have acquired a greater capacity to constrain public bodies. One of the most used means for doing so has been the incorporation of the ECHR into U.K. law through the Human Rights Act 1998. For many, this constitutes a bill of rights; some, though, press for such a bill to enjoy protection from possible political interference.

For many years prior to 1998, lawyers and some politicians argued the case for a bill of rights for the United Kingdom. Though formally the nation already has the Bill of Rights of 1689, which remains part of British law, that act asserted the supremacy of Parliament over the king. It was not a document principally embodying the rights of the citizen. Reformers wanted such a bill of rights to be introduced. The case for it was advanced in articles and pamphlets from the 1970s onward. The case for it gained a boost in the late 1980s, when Charter '88, a constitutional reform movement supported by some well-known figures on the Left, made a bill of rights a central feature of its manifesto.

Advocates argued that Parliament was no longer capable of resisting the encroachment of government on rights previously considered inviolate.

Britain, according to Lord Hailsham, labored under an "elective dictatorship." If the rights of the individual were to be protected, some new means of protection were necessary to supplement or replace those provided inadequately by Parliament. The answer was deemed to lay in a bill of rights that stipulated the rights of the individual, possibly a bill akin to that of the United States. Such a measure would then be subject to interpretation by the courts, which, if the bill enjoyed a degree of entrenchment, would be able to strike down conflicting measures as being contrary to its provisions. It is not axiomatic that the courts would enjoy such a power. Nonetheless, that was the clear intention of those who advocated the measure. They sought to put certain rights beyond the reach of government and place them into the care of the courts.

Advocacy of such a bill did not go unchallenged. A number of critics, especially on the Left, opposed it because it would be handing power to judges drawn from a particular background and with a narrow view of society. The courts construed the public interest as the interest of the government. Other critics of a bill of rights opposed it not on grounds of the background of judges, but simply on the grounds that they were judges. "The objection is to the very fact that it is judges *qua* judges that would be empowered to determine issues that are inherently political."[41] Power would, in effect, be transferred from an elected dictatorship to a nonelected dictatorship. It would introduce into the British polity a "democratic deficit."[42] "I should hate to rely upon the appointed judiciary rather than upon the elected members of a legislature for the rights of the people," declared an MP, perhaps not altogether disinterestedly.[43]

Advocates of a bill of rights achieved their most significant success, as we have seen, with the enactment of the Human Rights Act 1998. However, the Act has not satisfied all supporters of a bill of rights. The Act preserves the doctrine of parliamentary sovereignty. As we have seen, the courts cannot strike down a measure or an action as being contrary to the provisions of the ECHR. They can only issue declarations of incompatibility. It is up to Parliament to act on those declarations. It is not legally obliged to do so. Parliament may also amend the 1998 Act. It may pass a subsequent act stipulating that it shall not be subject to the provisions of the 1998 Act. Though it is unlikely to do so, there is no mechanism to prevent it doing so. Supporters of a bill of rights would thus like to see some form of protection introduced, to put the ECHR beyond the reach of a simple majority in the two Houses of Parliament. They want some form of entrenchment, providing that the provisions of the Act can be amended only by some extraordinary procedure. At a minimum, they would like to see the courts given the power to enforce the ECHR through striking down measures that are incompatible with it, rather than simply calling Parliament's attention to any incompatibility.

To an American weaned on an entrenched bill of rights interpreted by independent magistrates, opposition to an entrenched bill of rights on such grounds is difficult to comprehend. Britain, however, lacks those characteristics that have underpinned the American's acceptance of constitutional interpretation by the U.S. Supreme Court. The United Kingdom is not a federal state nor has it wholly embraced the principles articulated by John Locke (Chapter 2) that formed the bedrock of the first new nation. For Britons, an entrenched bill of rights is not something that enjoys universal support.

Pressure for some form of entrenchment adds to the tensions that have built up between the executive and the courts. Although the government has been responsible for such measures as the Human Rights Act, ministers have nonetheless criticized judges when they have found against the government. The creation of the new supreme court, in the eyes of some, enhances and may embolden the judges in standing up to the executive. Others fear it may leave the court isolated, no longer being housed in and enjoying the understanding of the House of Lords.[44] Moves toward an entrenched bill of rights would exacerbate the tensions already apparent.

CONCLUSION

The courts in Britain have acquired an increasingly important role in the United Kingdom. The British constitution has acquired a significant judicial dimension. Judges now play a far greater role in the political process. In terms of their constitutional role, they have moved nearer to their U.S. counterparts, though still not occupying the same powerful position. There are pressures for that role to be strengthened. At the level of criminal justice, the courts and the police have encountered criticisms for their handling of particular cases and for being detached from certain sections of society. Judges have been challenged for holding the views of a social elite, the police for having a "locker room" mentality. There have been various moves to address these criticisms and to ensure that the criminal justice system works effectively, efficiently, and fairly—and be seen to do so. The courts and the police still face pressure for further changes.

NOTES

1. J. J. Magee, "Constitutional Vagaries and American Judicial Review," *Hull Papers in Politics No. 10* (Hull University Politics Department, 1979).
2. C. J. Marshall, *Marbury v. Madison*, 5 U.S. (1 Cranch) 137 2L.Ed.60; H. W. Chase and C. R. Ducat, *Constitutional Interpretation* (West Publishing, 1974), p. 26.
3. See the cogent argument advanced by Justice Gibson in his dissenting opinion in *Eakin v. Raub*, 1825, Supreme Court of Pennsylvania, 12 S. & R. 330; Chase and Ducat, pp. 27–33.
4. See Ch. 2 and L. Hartz, *The Liberal Tradition in America* (Harcourt, Brace and World, 1955), especially Ch. 9.
5. Only a minority of cases are resolved by constitutional interpretation.
6. H. J. Abraham, *The Judicial Process*, 5th ed. (Oxford University Press, 1986), p. 293.
7. They were previously known collectively as the Supreme Court. The name was changed under the provisions of the Constitutional Reform Act 2005 in order to avoid confusion with the new Supreme Court of the United Kingdom that came into being in 2009.

8. There were 29,270 as of April 1, 2009.
9. Lawyers are more than twice as numerous, per capita in the United States than in the United Kingdom. Another difference is that in England barristers and solicitors (they take different examinations) are each subject to one set of national standards, whereas in the United States there are variations in the standards set by the 50 state bar associations.
10. T. C. Hartley and J. A. G. Griffith, *Government and the Law,* 2nd ed. (Weidenfeld & Nicolson, 1981), p. 181.
11. Ministry of Justice, *Judicial and Court Statistics 2007,* Cm 7467 (The Stationery Office, 2008), p. 16.
12. P. Craig and M. Walters, "The Courts, Devolution and Judicial Review," *Public Law,* Summer 1999, p. 303.
13. Ministry of Justice, *Judicial and Court Statistics 2007,* Cm 7467 (The Stationery Office, 2008), p. 21.
14. P. Norton, "The Constitution," in A. Seldon (ed.), *Blair's Britain 1997–2007* (Cambridge University Press, 2007), pp. 117–118.
15. See Lord Norton of Louth, "Parliament and the Courts," in N. D. J. Baldwin (ed.), *Parliament in the 21st Century* (Politico's, 2005), pp. 318–321.
16. In the Metropolitan Police, the Special Branch has become part of the Counter Terrorism Command.
17. The police authority for London differs from other authorities. The authority for the metropolis used to be the home secretary. With the introduction of a Greater London Authority in 2000, a new 23-member Police Authority was created.
18. J. Vsn Dijk, R. Mancgin, J. Van Kesteren, S. Nevala, and G. Hideg, *The Burden of Crime in the EU: A Comparative Analysis of the European Crime and Safety Survey* (EU ICS, 2005).
19. C. Kershaw, S. Nicholas, and A. Walker (eds.), *Crime in England and Wales 2007/08,* Home Office Statistical Bulletin, July 2008 (The Home Office, 2008), p. 10.
20. *From the Neighbourhood to the National: Policing Our Communities Together,* Cm 7448 (The Home Office, 2008), p. 10.
21. J. Vsn Dijk, R. Mancgin, J. Van Kesteren, S. Nevala, and G. Hideg, *The Burden of Crime in the EU: A Comparative Analysis of the European Crime and Safety Survey* (EU ICS, 2005).
22. MORI, *British Public Opinion,* 23 (4), May 2000, p. 6.
23. Ibid.
24. C. Kershaw, S. Nicholas, and A. Walker (eds.), *Crime in England and Wales 2007/08,* Home Office Statistical Bulletin, July 2008 (The Home Office, 2008).
25. J. Miller, *Police Corruption in England and Wales: An Assessment of Current Evidence,* Home Office Online Report 11/03 (The Home Office, 2003), p. 15.
26. *Police Complaints: Statistics for England and Wales 2007/08,* IPCC Research and Statistics Series: Paper 12 (IPCC, 2008), p. vi.
27. *Report of the Stephen Lawrence Inquiry* (The Stationery Office, 1999), Ch. 46.
28. *Commissioner's Report Following the IPCC Independent Investigation into Alleged Misconduct by Police Officers and Police Staff Working on Behalf of the National Black Police Association from 2003–2005* (Independent Police Complaints Commission, 2009). The report found poor management but no criminal conduct.
29. MORI, *British Public Opinion,* 22 (1), Jan–Feb. 1999, p. 3; Trust in Professions 2007 (Royal College of Physicians, 2007), p. 7.

30. J. A. G. Griffith, *The Politics of the Judiciary,* 5th ed. (Fontana, 1997).
31. See A. Le Sueur, "Judges in the Modern British Constitution," *Politics Review*, 18 (3), 2009, pp. 14–16.
32. MORI, *British Public Opinion*, 22 (1), Jan–Feb. 1999, p. 1; Trust in Professions 2007 (Royal College of Physicians, 2007), p. 7.
33. "Judges are Not Doddery and Remote," *The Times*, 29 July 1998, Features, p. 17.
34. See especially C. Walker and K. Starmer, *Miscarriages of Justice* (Blackstone Press, 1999).
35. See "Sins of Confession" (editorial), *The Times*, 26 November 1991.
36. C. Harlow, "The Legal System," in P. Catterall (ed.), *Contemporary Britain: An Annual Review* (Blackwell, 1991), p. 98.
37. Criminal Cases Review Commission, *Case Statistics,* Figures to 31 May 2009; for more recent case statistics go to the Case Library at http://www.ccrc.gov.uk/
38. D. Campbell, "DNA Search for Miscarriages of Justice," *The Guardian*, 5 May 2009.
39. See, for example, http://www.innocent.org.uk and http://www.mojuk.org.uk
40. Lord Scarman, "A Bill of Rights Could Become the Conscience of the Nation," *The Independent*, 9 June 1989.
41. P. Norton, "A Bill of Rights: The Case Against," *Talking Politics*, 5 (3), 1993, p. 149.
42. Ibid.
43. House of Commons Debates (Hansard), 6th series, Vol. 2, col. 1256.
44. See Lord Norton of Louth, "Parliament and the Courts," in N. D. J. Baldwin (ed.), *Parliament in the 21st Century* (Politico's, 2005), pp. 321–323.

15

Communication and Feedback
The Mass Media

Communication is an essential and integral part of any society. It is a necessary, if not always well used, tool of the politician's trade. To influence others, one must communicate. With the advent of a mass electorate, politicians have had to communicate with a large audience. In the eighteenth century, when affairs of state were the concern of an aristocratic elite, communication by word of mouth or by letter was often sufficient to reach those with political influence. In the nineteenth century, the newspaper became more important as a medium of communication, especially toward the end of the century. (The only other medium of mass communication, or at least one capable of reaching a large audience, was the political pamphlet.) In the twentieth century, newspapers remained important but were supplemented, in some cases supplanted, in the latter half of the century by radio and television. Increasingly other means of communication, notably the Internet, are assuming importance. It is now possible to reach a mass audience through a range of media.

Other forms of communicating by a single medium to a large number of people also exist. These include compact disks, films, and books. Although some of these have served as vehicles for political communication and, more especially, influence—there have been some books that have made a major contribution to thought and the organization of states—they are not means of communicating information on a continuous basis. In Britain, as in the United States, the primary mass media for communicating political information are television, radio, newspapers, and, increasingly, the Internet.

THE PRESS AND BROADCASTING IN BRITAIN

Despite an increase in the sophistication of mass communication, the sheer size and diversity of the United States has militated against the development of "national" newspapers. The number of daily newspapers with anything other than a geographically limited readership can be counted probably on the fingers of one hand. Even the titles of most of the exceptions—*The Washington Post, The New York Times, The Wall Street Journal*—imply specific parochial interests; *USA Today* stands alone in its explicitly national orientation. In Britain, by contrast, factors of geography and demography have tended to encourage the development of a national daily press. The country is geographically small, with most of the population living in England, the greatest concentration living in the nation's capital. Consequently, with some exceptions (such as the Scottish *Daily Record),* the leading mass-circulation newspapers are London-based and national (which often means London) in orientation. The newspaper emerged as a medium of political information and influence at the end of the nineteenth century and has remained an important medium since. Despite declining sales, Britons remain great newspaper readers.

The advent of "popular" newspapers, those designed to appeal (in both content and price) to artisans and the lower middle class, took place in the 1890s, a development made possible by advances in adult literacy and in printing technology. The first such newspaper was the *Daily Mail*, founded in 1896 by Alfred Harmsworth (later Lord Northcliffe). It was followed by the *Daily Express* in 1900, the *Daily Mirror* in 1903, and the *Daily Sketch* in 1908. They built up mass readerships not enjoyed by the more sedate and serious newspapers such as *The Times,* the doyen of influential newspapers founded in 1788; the *Morning Post* (merged with the *Daily Telegraph* in 1937); or the *Manchester Guardian*, one of the few significant newspapers with a regional orientation. The mass circulation of the new popular "dailies" attracted advertisers, and income from advertising came to constitute a (and in some cases, the) main form of revenue, thus allowing the publishers to keep down the cost of their papers. Harmsworth boasted that he was able to sell a one-penny paper for half a penny.[1] The newspapers themselves were largely in the hands of a few wealthy individuals, known in the early decades of the century as the "press barons." The Harmsworth family was especially influential (owning the *Mail*, the *Mirror* and, from 1908 to 1922, *The Times*), as was the Canadian Max Aitken (Lord Beaverbrook), who acquired control of the *Daily Express* in 1916. Although the papers were run as essentially commercial enterprises, proprietors were not averse to using their newspapers in attempts to influence political developments. In the early 1930s the Conservative leader, Stanley Baldwin, bitterly assailed the press barons for seeking to engineer his removal from the party leadership, uttering the memorable observation that they exercised "power without responsibility—the prerogative of the harlot through the ages." The attempt to oust Baldwin was one that many critics of the press would regard as the tip of a very sizable iceberg. Overt political partisanship remains a feature of British newspapers.

The first six decades of the twentieth century represented the highpoint of newspapers in the United Kingdom. By 1945 the circulation of the main daily newspapers had reached nearly 13 million. Throughout the 1950s it exceeded 16 million. Since then, circulation has declined. It dropped to below 15 million in the 1970s, to 13.5 million in 1998, and to just over 11 million in 2007. The data in Table 15.1 show that the trend continues to be one of decline. However, each copy of a newspaper is usually read by more than one person (and most households order only one daily paper). In 2006, nearly 22 million adults read at least one of the main national newspapers. However, this too represented a decline over previous decades: In 1992, the figure had been nearly 27 million. A similar decline in circulation and readership has been witnessed in the United States and Europe.[2]

Of the national newspapers currently available, there is in terms of numbers a relatively wide choice. Table 15.1 lists the principal national daily newspapers, along with their sales figures and ownership. There are in addition a variety of national Sunday newspapers, weekly magazines of news and current affairs (preeminent among them being *The Economist*), regional daily newspapers, and a host of local daily and weekly papers: Hardly any community is without its "local" publication. In total, there are over 100 daily newspapers. There are also about 1,300 regional and several thousand periodical publications. As with national newspapers, regional and local newspapers are also under pressure from declining circulations.

Until the 1980s, most national newspapers were edited and printed in Fleet Street, and the name of the street became synonymous with the national press. In the 1980s newspapers, taking advantage of new technology, began to move out, thereby weakening the influence of the traditionally powerful print unions. Led by the publications of News International, most newspapers relocated to the docklands of London. The last national newspaper left Fleet Street in 1989. The move reflected in part the needs of the press to be more efficient in the face of increasing competition. The decline in circulation has been a product of several pressures, not least competition from other media such as the television, the Internet, and free newspapers, and a related decline in advertising revenue. It has also been ascribed to changes in lifestyle. One study published in 2006 found that 36 percent of those who read a newspaper less frequently than before said that this was in part due to the fact that they did have as much time for newspapers as they did before.[3]

Although journalists may differ in their political beliefs, individual newspapers tend to adopt a particular though not always committed editorial position in support of a political party or general political persuasion. Traditionally, the party that has benefited most from editorial preferences has been the Conservative Party. The *Daily Telegraph* has generally been regarded as *the* Conservative newspaper and is widely read by Conservatives. During the 1970s and 1980s, the *Daily Telegraph, Daily Mail, Express*, and *The Sun* (originally a Labour supporter) also tended to fall firmly within the Conservative camp, though not always giving editorial support to specific Conservative policies. Of the serious press, both *The*

TABLE 15.1

NATIONAL NEWSPAPERS: CIRCULATION, DECEMBER 2008

Newspaper	December 2008	Circulation December 2007	% change	Owner
The Sun	2,899,310	2,985,672	−2.89	News International
Daily Mail	2,139,178	2,310,806	−7.43	Daily Mail and General Trust plc
Daily Mirror	1,346,916	1,494,114	−9.85	Trinity Mirror
Daily Telegraph	824,244	873,523	−5.64	Telegraph Group
Daily Express	728,296	744,539	−2.18	Northern and Shell plc
Daily Star	725,671	726,464	−0.11	Northern and Shell plc
The Times	600,962	615,313	−2.33	Times International
Financial Times	435,319	445,231	−2.23	Pearson plc
Daily Record	349,235	385,928	−9.51	Scottish Daily Record and Sunday Mail Ltd
Guardian	343,010	353,436	−2.95	The Scott Trust
Independent	200,242	228,400	−12.33	Independent Newspapers

Source: Audit Bureau of Circulations, National Daily Newspaper Circulation December 2008, The Guardian, 9 January 2009; D. Kavanagh and D. Butler, The British General Election of 2005 (Palgrave Macmillan, 2005), pp. 120–121.

Times and the Financial Times leaned toward the Conservative Party. The Mirror was the only mass circulation paper to support the Labour Party. The Guardian took a center-left stance, falling politically somewhere between Labour and the Liberal Democrats. The Independent sought to live up to its name. In any general election, the Conservative Party normally received the endorsement of most national newspapers. That support started to slip in the 1990s. In the 1992 general election, The Financial Times unexpectedly advised its readers to vote Labour. In the 1997 election, there was a massive hemorrhaging of Conservative support. The performance of the Conservative government, and some changes in ownership, produced a notable shift in favor of the Labour Party. In the election, no fewer than 11 out of 19 national papers endorsed the Labour Party, a level of support previously enjoyed by the Conservatives. Even the normally right-wing *The Sun* gave qualified support to Labour. Since then, the political allegiance of the press has been less predictable than in the past. In the 2001 and 2005 elections, half of the ten major national newspapers supported a Labour victory.[4] The *Daily Mail* and the *Daily Express* remain associated with the political right; the *Daily Telegraph* retains a Conservative readership, though under new ownership its editorial leaning is less certain. The *Mirror* continues to support the Labour Party and *The Guardian* retains its center-left stance. *The Sun* and *The Times*—part of News International (owned by Rupert Murdoch)—have tended to be sympathetic to the Labour government, though not to its policy of supporting European integration.

Critics have tended to ascribe the traditional Conservative bias of the press to the nature of ownership, newspapers being part and parcel of a capitalist system, with more and more newspapers coming within the control of fewer hands. The press in Britain is owned by a relatively few people. "The consolidation of media ownership adds to the risk of disproportionate influence. In the United Kingdom, the national newspaper industry is run by eight companies—one of which has over 35 percent of the national newspaper market."[5] Foremost among the present-day "press barons" is Rupert Murdoch, owner of News International, whose media empire includes the biggest-selling daily tabloid (*The Sun*), the biggest-selling Sunday tabloid (*News of the World*), and two quality papers (*The Times* and the *Sunday Times*). A similar concentration is to be found in other media, with a considerable overlap of ownership. By 2007, four publishers of regional and local newspapers had almost 70 percent of the market share. However, the stance of the newspapers in the 1997 general election suggests that support for the Conservatives is contingent. When the party was unable to demonstrate that it was a safe pair of hands in handling the economy, and the Labour Party appeared that it might be, the newspapers switched their allegiance. In short, the support is not necessarily for the Conservative Party as such, but rather for the values it embraces (procapitalist, free market). If another party appears to embrace those values, and appears better able to promote them, then owners may find the alternative acceptable and even more palatable.

Whereas newspapers, being owned by private concerns, are free to express their partisan preferences (and do so), the broadcast media are more constrained. Initially, the British Broadcasting Corporation (the BBC) enjoyed a monopoly on radio and television broadcasting. The BBC is a quasi-autonomous state corporation that came into being on January 1, 1927. (It succeeded an independent company, the British Broadcasting Company Ltd.) It was granted a license to broadcast under Royal Charter and it was and remains financed by a license fee levied originally on radio receivers (abolished in 1971) and subsequently, from 1946 onward, on television sets. The first scheduled public television service was started in 1936, though it was suspended during the Second World War. The 1950s witnessed the growth of television. More sets were purchased and more services became available.

In 1954 the BBC's monopoly was ended and the following year the first commercial independent television (ITV) channel began broadcasting. Television was well established in Britain by the 1960s; more than 10 million television licenses were issued in 1960. Succeeding decades have witnessed a massive expansion in broadcasting outlets. In the 1960s, a second BBC channel (BBC2) began broadcasting, catering more to minority tastes, especially in the arts and education. The BBC also began setting up local radio stations. In the 1970s independent local radio stations were authorized and began transmission. In the 1980s, a fourth television channel (Channel 4) began broadcasting, catering—like BBC2—to minority tastes, and breakfast television began. Cable television also became available (though attracting relatively few subscribers) and in 1989 the first satellite television channel—Sky television—began transmission; after a slow start, it began to attract subscribers—and, consequently, advertisers. A fifth terrestrial channel, Channel 5, was introduced in March 1997. In 1998, BBC Choice was launched, followed by Film Four, Sky Digital, ONdigital, ITV2, and BBC Knowledge. Since then, the revolution in digital broadcasting has meant that subscribers can now access television programs around the globe. (By 2012, analogue television in the United Kingdom will have been phased out and replaced by digital television.) By 2007, almost 90 percent of U.K. households had access to more channels than just the four main terrestrial channels.[6] Whereas in the 1950s, viewers had a choice between two channels, each broadcasting for only part of the day, nearly sixty years later they could, depending on their subscription basis, select from more than 200 channels, some delivering programs on a 24-hour basis. Those wanting 24-hour news programs could watch not only BBC News 24 and Sky News but also CNN, Fox News, Bloomberg, Al Jazeera International, Russia Today, and France 24.

Increased competition has meant that BBC and ITV no longer dominate the viewing figures. More people watch one or the other rather than any other broadcasting channel, but the figures have not only declined but continue to do so as the market becomes more competitive. In 1992, 75 percent of the viewing public watched BBC1 and ITV1. By 2000, the figure was 58 percent. By May 2009, *all* terrestrial television accounted for only 55 percent of the weekly viewing figures. BBC1, though, retained the largest single audience, taking almost one-fifth of the viewing figures, followed by ITV1 with almost the same figures (Table 15.2). The vast majority of satellite and cable channels struggled to achieve more than 0.3 percent of the viewing audience.[7]

In their coverage of politics, broadcasters are required, under the Communications Act 2003, to treat all major matters with due impartiality. The concept of equal time has been applied to the two main parties, though the growth of third parties (and of more fringe candidates in parliamentary by-elections) has created problems in determining the allocation of time for other parties. No paid political advertisements are permitted on radio and television, though the main public service broadcasters (BBC, ITV, Channels 4

TABLE 15.2

SHARE OF VIEWING AUDIENCE, 2009

Share of weekly viewing audience, May 2009

Channel	Share of audience (%)
BBC1	19.0
BBC2	6.5
ITV1	18.3
Channel 4/S4C	6.1
Channel 5	4.8
All terrestrial channels	*54.7*

Source: Broadcasters' Audience Research Board (BARB)

and 5) carry an agreed-upon number of party political broadcasts between general elections and party election broadcasts during elections. Any party fielding 50 or more candidates is entitled to a broadcast. The broadcasts are scripted and presented by the parties themselves, the broadcasting media transmitting them without comment. The public service broadcasters are also required to maintain a certain level of news output. The Communications Act provides power for the communications regulatory body Ofcom to set quotas for news output.

THE INTERNET

The development of the Internet has created both an opportunity and a challenge for the print and broadcast media. It has proved an opportunity in that the media are able to use the Internet as a medium for transmitting their own programs and stories. Newspapers can be read online. The BBC has developed an award-winning web page (BBC Online, http://news.bbc.co.uk/). It is a challenge in that it is an alternative attraction to the existing media. It is also a challenge in that it is unregulated. Whereas broadcast and print media, especially the former, are subject to various legal constraints, a mass of uncontrolled material can find its way—often from sites outside the United Kingdom—onto the Internet. Ultimately, the Internet may serve to render newspapers, in paper form, superfluous. The Internet offers access to a mass of data and opinion. People who were previously unable to disseminate their opinions now have a medium that enables them to do so.

The Internet offers an important means of communication for organizations that had been dependent on the broadcast and print media to get their views to a mass audience. For political parties, and for organs of the state, the Internet offers a highly efficient way of communicating with citizens. It also offers a means of communication free of an intermediary. The political parties have developed their websites, putting out information that television and radio may not have bothered to report or may have reported only partially. No. 10 Downing Street has its own website, as do the monarchy and government departments. The Downing Street website not only contains the latest announcements from No. 10, magazine features, and a policy forum, but also carries a regular broadcast from the prime minister. The monarchy website, like the Downing Street website, has tended to be at the forefront of website development and has proved extremely popular. Parliament also has its own website, though MPs have been somewhat slower than their counterparts in America to recognize the value of having their own web pages. Though the vast majority of MPs have websites, and some have their own blogs, the sites are utilized for imparting information rather than for interacting with constituents.[8]

It has also been utilized by individuals with a particular view to express. The use of blogs—enabling an individual to post comments and for others to respond—has become a feature of political discourse in the United Kingdom. A vibrant community of bloggers has developed, with some attracting regular national attention. Foremost among political bloggers at the end of the first decade of the twenty-first century were right-wing bloggers Guido Fawkes[9] and Iain Dale[10], each attracting viewing figures that matched some newspapers. Each occasionally broke political stories ahead of the mainstream media. In 2009, for example, Guido Fawkes broke a story that led to the resignation of one of Prime Minister Gordon Brown's closest aides.

The Internet is also a means for those who have been denied access to print and broadcast media to make their views known. These include groups whose activity is outlawed or deemed socially unacceptable. Hate groups of various kinds are able to post material on the Internet and to make contact with others who share their views. Contact through the Internet may also be used by groups to organize demonstrations and direct action.

The development of the Internet has been rapid and constitutes a major form of communication. Like newspapers and television, political communication only forms a small part of what it is about. Where it differs from the more traditional forms of communication is that it is unmediated, offering the individual or group the opportunity to disseminate material without the interference of a third party. Access to the Internet offers unrivalled opportunities to select and read material that was previously unavailable or not easily available.

However, despite the growing pervasiveness of the Internet, it still remains a limited means of acquiring political information. In 2006, only 6 percent of U.K. adults identified the Internet as their main source of news. The principal source remained television (65 percent), followed by newspapers (14 percent), and radio (11 percent).[11] "The traditional forms of news," concluded a House of Lords committee in 2007, "are likely to continue to be the most popular sources of news for the foreseeable future."[12] However, as we shall see, these traditional forms of news are devoting less space than before to news stories.

POLITICAL INFLUENCE

The mass media, by the content and method of their communicating or failing to communicate information, can exert tremendous political influence. Political evaluations and actions of politician and citizen are based on receipt of information. How that information is portrayed and transmitted can significantly affect both the evaluation and the action taken on the basis of that evaluation.

The political information transmitted by the mass media is, of necessity, limited. Newspapers do not have the space nor broadcasting media the air time to transmit comprehensive coverage of daily events (nationally or worldwide) of political significance. Nor do they have the inclination to do so. Although newspapers and the broadcasting media constitute the primary means of transmitting political information to a mass audience, they do not exist exclusively or indeed even primarily to fulfill such a function. Television and radio are essentially media of entertainment. Newspapers may make some claim, by virtue of the written word, to be more a medium of information, but the information transmitted is not usually on the subject of political behavior. Although the so-called quality, or "broadsheet," newspapers (*The Times, Financial Times, Daily Telegraph, Independent,* and *Guardian*) devote a significant proportion of space to reporting and commenting on political events, the mass readership, or "tabloid," newspapers do not.

Indeed, the trend has been away from covering political items to what publishers consider human-interest stories. In postwar decades, news coverage in the mass-circulation dailies has decreased significantly.[13] The tabloid newspapers have generally expanded human-interest content, entertainment features, sports, and home and family articles.[14] The greater the circulation war between papers, the greater the emphasis on these human-interest features, which constitute the most consistently read part of newspapers. One study found that in 1997 celebrity entertainment stories made up 17 percent of the news stories in the tabloid press, up from 6 percent in 1952.[15] The competition for a decreasing market has also produced competitions and greater emphasis on short items and color pictures.

Television has also seen some reduction in political coverage. Various current affairs programs disappeared in the 1990s and first decade of the twenty-first century or were reduced in length or transferred to late-night slots. By 1999, television was covering Parliament less than it was a decade previously, when the cameras were first allowed into the House of Commons. Budget cuts also meant that some news and current affairs programs had to cut down on carrying features that were expensive (such as outside broadcast reports) and concentrate instead on cheaper studio-based items. Regional companies also saw similar cutbacks. In 2007, ITV signaled its intention to further reduce its provision of regional TV news.

Nonetheless, the role of the mass media in transmitting political information remains of vital significance. Indeed, the significance of newspapers and television as media of communication has increased over the past century not only because of the size of the audiences but also because of the increase in sophistication of communication technology. Television, in particular, has been influential because of its immediacy. Not only can various happenings—a bomb blast, politicians arguing with one another—be portrayed visually and in sound, but they may also be transmitted live. Receiving information with such immediacy, and in such a form, can affect viewers' evaluations in a way not possible when this medium of communication did not exist. As Hedley Donovan queried once in *Time* magazine: "Could the Civil War have survived the 7 P.M. news? Could George Washington have held his command after a TV special on Valley Forge?"[16] Media coverage of the Vietnam War clearly affected the American public's perception of the wisdom, or lack of it, in such an action. In Britain, recognition of the implications of media coverage influenced the government in its actions and its control of information during the Falklands War in 1982. The government controlled the means of transmitting news from the Task Force to Britain, and facilities for the quick transmission of television pictures were not made available. To have shown on television during the conflict "pictures of the sort of realism that the Americans had during the Vietnamese war," to be seen by servicemen's families, would, in the words of one commanding officer, "have had a very serious effect" on troop morale.[17] Pictures of dead servicemen—or of captured officers being paraded by enemy forces—have greater emotional impact than a written report. Pictures of human suffering may engender a desire for action. Media coverage of particular events such as riots may extend beyond constituting an impartial recording of those events to being an alleged instigator of them. There have been accusations in some conflicts of skirmishes being staged, or of the presence of a camera crew inciting, unwittingly or otherwise, disorder. The activities of the media themselves may constitute political issues.

The way in which information is channeled, then, is not neutral in its effect. The mass media, in short, exert political influence. This influence may be primary, that is, affecting the recipient of the communication. It may be secondary, affecting a party independent of the communication process (e.g., a politician whose capacity to achieve a particular action is limited by public reaction to news of a certain event as, for instance, President George W. Bush and Prime Minister Tony Blair in respect of the Iraq war). The influence of the media may be seen as especially important in terms of *the legitimacy of the political system, the partisan support of electors*, and *the behavior of politicians*. The influence exerted in each case may be described as that of enhancing, of reinforcing, and of constraining, respectively.

The media fulfill a function of latent legitimation of the political—as well as the social and economic—system.[18] By operating within that system and accepting its norms, newspapers and television help to maintain its popular legitimacy. When a political crisis arises, journalists and TV reporters descend upon ministers and MPs for comment, hence accepting and reinforcing the legitimacy of those questioned to comment on the matter at hand. The media have studios in a building (known by its address—4 Millbank) just across the road from Parliament. What political leaders do in a public and often in a private capacity is considered newsworthy. The movements of Diana, Princess of Wales, attracted extensive media attention, not just in the United Kingdom. Though her activities were viewed on occasion as undermining the monarchy, her status derived from the very fact that she had been married to the Prince of Wales. Her death in a car accident in August 1997 was the occasion for a massive outpouring of grief. By according status to politicians and other occupants (or even the spouses of occupants) of public office and to the institutions they occupy and represent, the media serve to reinforce the legitimacy of such bodies. Where a body does not enjoy popular legitimacy, the media probably could not create it. Where it does exist, however, they can and do reinforce it by the very nature of their activities.

At times, certain media may also fulfill the more conscious role of overt legitimation. At times of national crisis, some newspapers consider it not only their duty but also that of their readers to support the national effort, and vigorously exhort their readers to provide such support. One example that has passed into folklore was that of a number of national newspapers, most notably *The Sun*, during the Falklands War in 1982. Reporting of the war was merged with vigorous, not to say crude, editorializing in support of the British effort, any critics being roundly condemned as unpatriotic. The broadcast media, by virtue of their charters, sought to take a more detached position.

On party political preferences, the media may be seen as having primarily a reinforcing effect. This is in line with the findings of various studies of the effect of mass communication. Persuasive mass communication, according to Klapper's classic study, tends to serve far more heavily in the interests of reinforcement and of minor change than of converting opinions.[19] As one analyst of the British media put it, "the media do more towards corroborating opinion than creating it."[20] There is a marked tendency for the recipients of communications to indulge in a process of selective exposure, perception, and retention. This phenomenon was borne out by Butler and Stokes's study in Britain on the effects of newspaper reading.[21] Most readers chose a newspaper whose partisan stance was in line with their own stance or, for young people, with that of their parents; when the children absorbed and accepted the preferences of their parents, they continued to read the same newspaper. In 2004, a majority of readers of the *Daily Telegraph* and the *Daily Mail* were Conservative supporters and the majority of the readers of the *Daily Mirror* were Labour supporters.[22] No newspaper had a fairly even spread of readers across the three main parties.

The effect of reading any given partisan newspaper was characterized by Butler and Stokes as "magnetic": "Readers who are already close to their paper's party will tend to be held close; those at some distance will tend to be pulled towards it."[23] A similar finding emerged from a study by Dunleavy and Husbands. In their analysis of media influence on voting in 1983, they found that the greater the exposure to Conservative newspapers, the greater the likelihood to vote Conservative. The relationship remained strong even when social class was controlled for. "Within all the class categories used the Conservative vote is some 30 percentage points lower among people primarily exposed to non-Tory messages than it is amongst readers of the Tory press, a high level of association that has few parallels amongst either social background or issue influences. The difference is even more marked when we compare the two extreme groups, those exposed to a predominantly Tory message and those receiving a predominantly non-Tory one; the differences in Conservative support range from 36 to 58 points."[24] The relationships they established were, they concluded, too close to be attributable solely or even mainly to partisan self-selection. Hence, according to their analysis, newspaper reading can have a political influence. The beneficiary of such influence has been, at least until 1997, the Conservative Party. Even so, the extent of the influence should not be exaggerated. As John Curtice and Holli Semetko pointed out in their analysis of the 1992 general election, "only 38 percent of the readers of the *Sun,* supposedly the most stridently pro-Conservative newspaper, voted Conservative."[25] And as Margaret Scammell and Martin Harrop argued in their study of the press in the 1997 general election, the impact of the press in changing votes was marginal. As they wrote, "the *Sun's* endorsement of Tony Blair was certainly remarkable evidence of the success of his political project, but like the rest of the press, the *Sun* was following opinion more than creating it."[26] The press may serve to reinforce opinions, perhaps even shape them over time, but has limited impact in getting readers to switch their allegiance.

Media coverage may serve to have a constraining effect on politicians' behavior. To achieve their aims, politicians must be able to communicate with others, at what may be described as the horizontal level (i.e., with fellow politicians, civil servants, and other policy makers) as well as the vertical (i.e., politician to the public). They must also at times ensure the noncommunication of material. Most politicians crave the attention of the media. Such attention enhances their legitimacy and provides them with the means to influence others. Political behavior may often be geared, in consequence, to the needs of television and newspapers. Press conferences and unofficial briefings are now *de rigueur*. Texts of speeches are given in advance of delivery to journalists and TV reporters. The clash between the Prime Minister and the Leader of the Opposition in Prime Minister's Question Time in the House of Commons is geared more for the television cameras than it is for the members in the chamber. Meetings are organized so as to present a good televisual effect and also timed to meet newspaper deadlines or to get onto the early television evening news. The Labour Party has been credited with bringing these techniques to a new level of sophistication.

The effect or presumed effect of the televising of particular politicians may even influence the careers of political leaders. A politician whose words in print may be persuasive may come across as hesitant and bumbling on television; he or she may not be photogenic. When the television cameras entered the House of Commons in 1989, Margaret Thatcher was judged to come across well on the screen, whereas her Labour rival, Neil Kinnock, came across as negative and hectoring. Between 1997 and 2005, Conservative leaders William Hague, Iain Duncan-Smith, and Michael Howard failed to achieve positive media presences; David Cameron, the Conservative leader since 2005, has been credited with having effective communication skills.[27] It is also common now for politicians to give more attention to how they appear. Margaret Thatcher had voice training. Leading politicians have "makeovers," their appearance (haircut, dress) being groomed by professional advisers. Politicians are thus constrained not only in how they behave in seeking to put across a particular message but also in how they look and how they present themselves before the television cameras.

The media may constrain or dictate the actions of politicians. Knowledge that one's activities may be observed and reported may deter a minister, for example, from engaging in a policy or particular action that is thought to be unpopular or likely to incur the wrath of one's colleagues or supporters. In military conflicts, policy makers are keen to achieve a quick military victory with as few casualties as possible. They are conscious that reports of heavy losses or a long, drawn-out, and indecisive campaign could have an effect on public morale similar to that of media coverage of the Vietnam War. Politicians may also be wary of taking action seen as helpful to groups that are the butt of media criticism. The *Daily Mail,* for example, is a scourge of certain groups, such as illegal immigrants. Civil servants and other public officials may decide not to pursue a particular line for fear that details may be leaked to the press and television. The effect of media reporting may thus limit the options that policy makers believe are open to them.

The media may also be more proactive in breaking news stories and affecting how politicians behave. In 2009, the *Daily Telegraph* published details of MPs' expenses (see Chapter 12): The story dominated the news for several weeks, increased the newspaper's circulation, led to the resignation of the speaker of the House of Commons, resulted in a number of MPs announcing that they would stand down at the next general election, and induced the Government to establish an external independent body to supervise MPs' expenses.

Thus despite their not seeking to act primarily as channels of political information and influence, the mass media in Britain constitute an integral part of the political process. Through reading newspapers and watching television (or listening to radio), citizens receive information that helps shape and reinforce their political attitudes and that, by its presentation, reinforces the legitimacy of the political system and may at times help modify their attitudes. By similarly reading newspapers and watching news and current affairs programs, politicians are aware of the material that is being communicated to the public. Their perceptions of the likely impact of this material may influence their behavior, even if the communication does not have the impact expected.

The media also serve to communicate information to political leaders on how particular policies and programs are being received. Investigative work by journalists or television researchers may present new public evidence on a particular issue. The reporting of evidence researched by others, the coverage of demonstrations, or the publication of opinion polls commissioned by the newspaper or program serve to inform both the public and political leaders of attitudes and responses to policies and the actions of policy makers. The Labour government in office since 1997 is known to employ focus groups to monitor reaction to its policies but it also pays close attention to opinion poll data.

The mass media, by which we mean radio, television, and newspapers, are thus significant. The Internet also has significance, but in a somewhat different way. It may have consequences similar to those of the mass media. As we have seen, established bodies such as the monarchy, government, and political parties can use it to make information available. However, it is also a subversive element in that anyone who can create a website can put information into the public domain. A range of bodies and indeed individuals exploit the opportunity to put their views on the Internet. Internet users may have difficulty finding and selecting material that is reliable. Whereas the mass media make, in effect, a choice for the reader or viewer (you shall have the opportunity to read or to see only this), the Internet user is effectively left to make a choice from an increasing mass of material. There is no mechanism by which the citizen's view of society is shaped by intermediaries. By accident or design, Internet users may come across views or material that shape their perceptions in a way that would not be possible through watching television or reading a newspaper. In practice, the most significant political consequence appears to be that it enables those who wish to access material previously unavailable (such as from extreme groups or political movements) to do so. The very fact of its dissemination may also give such groups, in the eyes of their supporters, a credence they previously lacked.

THE CURRENT DEBATE

The media serve to convey information. They also form part of contemporary political debate. There are four criticisms that are leveled against the media: That they *intrude unduly on privacy*, that *they are politically biased*, that *they manufacture news*, and that *they allow unsavory material to be broadcast or printed*.

Privacy

There is a potential conflict between the freedom of the press and the right to privacy. Achieving a balance between the two is not easy. The media are often accused of invading privacy. More recently, the press has criticized the courts for attempting to introduce a judge-made law of privacy, restricting the freedom of the press to report stories about prominent individuals.

The activities of the popular press in particular in obtaining stories have proved a cause of controversy. The harassment of individuals by journalists and television crews—camping outside their homes, constantly telephoning, pursuing them down the street whenever they venture out—has been a cause of serious complaint, ranging from pursuit of aged and innocent relatives of figures in the public eye to the engulfing of certain members of the royal family and those close to them. The pursuit of the Princess of Wales prior to her marriage and during her first pregnancy aroused the ire of Buckingham

Palace, as did speculation about the state of her marriage following publication of a book about the princess—*Diana: Her True Story*—in 1992. The Princess also sometimes complained about media intrusiveness following her divorce. She was trailed by photographers up to and including the time of her fatal accident in Paris in 1997. The use of money to elicit exclusive stories has similarly incurred public criticism, particularly in instances when it has been employed to obtain evidence from witnesses involved in pending court cases. It has been likewise with the practice of making up "interviews" from disparate quotations already on the public record and the publication of private or intrusive photographs.

Extensive criticism has also been generated by many of the stories that have resulted, the press having considerable license to criticize and abuse. The position has been exacerbated by the limited means available to those attacked by the press to achieve a redress of grievance. The only means available until recently have been to sue for libel or to report the matter to the Press Complaints Commission (or, in the case of television, to Ofcom.) Neither is considered a particularly effective course of action. For individuals, the cost of pursuing a case through the courts is, in most cases, financially prohibitive. (Legal aid is not available in such cases.) Only those with personal wealth are in a position to sustain a lengthy libel action.[28] Newspapers have the resources to defend themselves against any libel actions and in recent years have put up some vigorous defenses. Reporting cases to the Press Complaints Commission is a course of action available to all. The problem here is lack of powers available to the commission. A nonstatutory body established by the newspaper industry, it came into being in 1991, replacing the Press Council. It has a smaller membership than its predecessor and a stronger code of practice, and it can investigate and adjudicate on complaints against newspapers. Usually, only a small number require adjudication by the full commission: The rest are resolved prior to that stage. (In the six-month period from October 2008 to March 2009, there were 2,499 complaints: Only 26 required adjudication by the commission; 329 were already resolved or sufficient action had been offered to resolve the complaint, and the rest were either inadmissible or not pursued.)[29] If the commission upholds a complaint, the paper concerned is committed to publishing the commission's statement. However, such reports are not necessarily printed in a prominent position and are sometimes treated with contempt. Critics also point out that the code of practice it polices was drawn up by the newspapers and has no statutory force, and that 7 of the 16 members of the Commission are senior newspaper editors.

Various bodies over the years have called for greater protection for privacy, not least through a statutory right to privacy. An official report in 1990—the Calcutt report—said that if the press did not put its own house in order, then statutory restraints should be introduced. Though no dedicated privacy law was introduced, some protection has been provided by the Human Rights Act 1998 incorporating the ECHR into British law: Article 8 of the convention provides a right to "private and family life." Various high-profile cases brought under the Act have resulted in the courts finding against the media. One or the most notable cases was in 2008, when Max Mosley, president of the motor racing body, the FIA, won a case against the Sunday newspaper, the *News of the World,* which had revealed details of his private sex life. The judge in the case, Mr. Justice Eady, was attacked by Paul Dacre, editor of the *Daily Mail,* for that and other judgments he had made in privacy cases. Dacre claimed that the judge was using human rights law to curb press freedom to expose the moral shortcomings of those in high places. Others in the media claimed that a form of judge-made law was being created. A number of leading barristers defended the judge, contending that he was applying the law passed by Parliament and that he was always subject to review by higher courts. They also pointed out that there was a balance to be struck between freedom of expression and the right to privacy. As one solicitor put it, "The test is simply: is it private information that is in the public interest to know? Judges make decisions like this on the facts every day in the courts and in all areas of law."[30] The point is variously made that something that is of interest to the public does not mean that it is necessarily in the public interest for it to be published. Various newspapers have exhibited a tendency to give "public interest" a rather broad interpretation. In interpreting and applying the Human Rights Act, the courts have not drawn the line between freedom of expression and privacy at quite the same point.

Political Bias

There is controversy as to the political influence of the mass media. Fulfilling the function of latent legitimization has attracted criticism from left-wing bodies opposed to the existing political system. They see the media as buttressing opposition to change. Radical critics such as the Glasgow University Media Group have argued that rather than devoting space to the activities of the royal family or to interviewing MPs, television and newspapers should give greater coverage to the activities and the opinions of factory workers and the unemployed. Such criticism from the Left of the political spectrum is an enduring feature of debate, but on occasion criticism is leveled by government and other elements of the existing political system. Such criticism often stems from media coverage of bodies and activities that are opposed to the existing political order. For example, interviewing IRA leaders in Northern Ireland during the period of "the troubles," or interviewing Muslim clerics who advocate violence against the West, has sometimes generated a strong reaction from political leaders in Britain. The response of the media, especially the broadcasting media (which are most sensitive to criticisms from government sources), is that coverage does not imply approval and that to fail to report what is going on would constitute a form of censorship.

Criticism of the media function of legitimation has extended, more obviously, to its overt attempts to reinforce the legitimacy of particular institutions or of specific actions. Opponents of the monarchy decry the extent not only of coverage given the royal family by the media but also the editorializing and some degree of sycophancy in its support. When in April 2000 the

BBC revealed that it did not intend to provide live coverage of a parade in honor of the 100th birthday of Queen Elizabeth the Queen Mother, two tabloid newspapers attacked the BBC in lead front-page stories. And just as the media may be accused of indulging in overt attempts at legitimation, various media—especially certain newspapers—are accused also of seeking to deny the legitimacy of certain bodies and types of activity. Among groups portrayed as being in some respect not legitimate, not least by tabloid newspapers, are "new age" travelers, strikers, demonstrators, communists, homosexuals, and individuals dubbed "social security scroungers" who manage to obtain social security payments to which they are not entitled.

On occasion, the media have also come under pressure from the government of the day for failing to indulge in more overt approval of particular actions. This has been notable at times of national crisis, especially when British troops have been in action abroad: for example, during the Falklands War in 1982. Though some newspapers were enthusiastic in their support of the British action in the Falklands, some media—notably television—were accused of treating Argentinean news releases as being on a par with those of the British and of seeking to present in a neutral fashion both sides of the dispute. The BBC came in for special condemnation from Conservative MPs when a *Panorama* program devoted itself to a study of the Conservative critics of the action. Such programs were taken by some Conservatives as reinforcing their belief that the BBC was manned by left-wing sympathizers.

Less dramatically and more pervasively, the media also come under pressure from government to give favorable coverage to domestic government policy and the actions of ministers. Editors and reporters come under pressure to provide similar positive coverage for opposition parties and other political actors. However, the government of the day has the advantage of being what it is—the government. What it does is deemed newsworthy, more so than the activities of opposition parties. Increasingly, government is accused of indulging in "spin doctoring," that is, trying to give a particular slant to events that is favorable to its position. As soon as some news breaks, government press officers are busy phoning news editors to provide the government's particular interpretation of events. Alastair Campbell, the director of communications under Prime Minister Tony Blair, was a particular master of pressuring reporters and ensuring that the government's interpretation ("spin") dominated media coverage of a story. The government came in for considerable criticism following its election in 1997 for trying to politicize the government press service, with a number of career press officers in government departments being removed or resigning. Opposition parties have criticized both the coverage the government receives and the extent to which the stories, and the political agenda, are shaped by the spin doctoring of the Downing Street press office.

Political bias in the media thus takes different forms. There is a bias in favor of established institutions and a bias toward—and against—certain groups in society. There is some partisan bias, especially on the part of newspapers. Critics also ascribe some bias to the broadcast media, though the criticism sometimes comes from both Left and Right. The Left regard the broadcast media as inherently conservative. Many on the Right complain of an anti-Conservative bias in the BBC. There is also a perceived media bias in favor of the government of the day. That bias, according to Conservatives, was pronounced during the premiership of Tony Blair, at least until 2003. In that year, there was a clash between government and the BBC over the events leading up to the suicide of a scientist, Dr David Kelly, who was a source for a story broadcast on BBC radio alleging that the government had deliberately exaggerated claims in a dossier claiming that Iraq possessed weapons of mass destruction. The government's handling of Dr Kelly (allowing him to be publicly identified) and his subsequent suicide led to an inquiry chaired by a former law lord, Lord Hutton, which exonerated the government and criticized the BBC over its claims, resulting in the resignation of the chairman of the board of governors and the director-general. A later inquiry found that the government had indeed exaggerated the claims in its dossier.

The media gravitate toward the government as the source of important stories, and editors do not wish to lose their sources. The Blair government exploited that fact possibly more ruthlessly than any of its predecessors. However, a worsening economy and perceived bad decisions by Prime Minister Gordon Brown meant that Blair's successor was not able to exploit the media quite so effectively.

Creating News

Other criticisms of media influence have centered on the media's ability to set the agenda of political debate and on the extent to which events may be manufactured for the benefit of media coverage. The former is an important but possibly overstated point. By selecting certain materials and events to cover, newspapers and news programs can influence the agenda of political debate. However, for that debate to be sustained, the media have to find some apparently solid base on which to pursue it and it has to be considered a salient issue by those who participate in the debate. If an issue fails to elicit a response or, worse still, produces a counterproductive response (readers or viewers objecting to the line taken), then media coverage may be affected accordingly—that is, the issue may not be pursued or the editorial policy may be changed. In the case of newspapers, it is important to recall that their primary concern is to sell copies. Taking an unpopular political line that could jeopardize sales of the newspaper would be unlikely to find favor with the proprietors. Although the significance of the media in helping set the agenda of political debate is great, the preceding qualification is important. They rarely can help influence that debate by operating in a political vacuum.

The accusation that events are created for the benefit of media coverage is an important and contemporary one. Clearly, politicians and others, as we have seen, modify their actions to try to ensure media coverage. Where controversy arises is in the cases of violent demonstrations or specific acts of violence being carried out, allegedly, to attract media attention. By being present on the streets of Belfast during the time of "the troubles," or during riots in Trafalgar Square in London, television crews have been criticized for encouraging—not actively, but passively, by virtue of their presence waiting for something to happen—the stoning of troops or police by rioters. Again, it is important to stress that rioting is unlikely to take place merely for its own sake (so-called "copycat" rioting is rarely sustained), but had camera crews not been present, the incidents that occurred might not have been as extensive or as violent as they were. The problem for the media, primarily the broadcast media, is deciding what to do in such circumstances. Once rioting has begun, they can hardly ignore it. Yet, once present at the scene, they are open to claims that their presence served to instigate continued or renewed rioting. The problem was not helped by claims in the late 1990s that some skirmishes in overseas conflicts, such as Sierra Leone, were reenacted for the benefit of the cameras.

Accusations of creating stories, and criticisms of the means of obtaining stories, have contributed to a notable lack of trust in journalists. Though people tend to trust television newsreaders to tell the truth, no such trust is vested in journalists. An Ipsos MORI survey in 2007 found that journalists came bottom of the table of professions deemed to be trustworthy. Only 18 percent of those questioned thought that journalists could generally be trusted to tell the truth.[31] They ranked alongside politicians. The figure for television newsreaders was 61 percent.

Publishing Offensive Material

Though there are, as we have seen, some legal constraints on what may be printed or broadcast, editors have considerable freedom in deciding what to publish. What they publish sometimes attracts criticism for going beyond the bounds of what is socially and politically acceptable. Some material is deemed politically unacceptable, such as printing information about how to make a bomb or security arrangements for a public figure. In 2008, for instance, Ofcom considered a complaint that a satellite channel had glorified the terrorist activities of the Liberation Tigers of Tamil Eelam (LTTE), a proscribed terrorist organization, and that a radio show hosted by a left-wing MP, George Galloway, had been unduly biased against Israel.[32] Some material is deemed socially offensive. This tends to be the more extensive category. Such material does not fall foul of the objection that it invades privacy but rather that it is degrading and is offensive to the reader or viewer. Some newspapers publish pictures of seminude women, television channels occasionally screen programs with simulated violence or sex, and some media carry stories that are deemed offensive to particular groups in society. Sexually explicit material is available on video, and the Internet has created access to a range of unregulated material. Among the established mass media, *The Sun* newspaper has a longstanding reputation for its topless "page three girls." Channel 5 has acquired a reputation for screening programs portraying sex. The biggest contemporary concerns are whether or not there is a link between the portrayal of physical and sexual violence on the television or film screen and its occurrence in real life and with the impact of the Internet. Though research has rarely found proof of a causal link between violence on screen and in real life, some high-profile cases of murder, in which the assailant has watched a particular film, have fueled popular beliefs that there is such a link. Problems encountered with children being able to watch unsuitable programs on television are now writ large in terms of what they can access on the Internet.

CONCLUSION

The mass media in Britain play a significant, indeed vital, role in the political process. They serve to communicate information to a large audience. By virtue of the way in which they present that information, they can and do exert influence on attitudes toward the political system, on partisan support, on attitudes toward particular issues, and on politicians' behavior. They help set the agenda of political debate. Not only do they help communicate contemporary political debate, they are themselves in part the subject of that debate. They remain the subject of criticism, not least (but by no means exclusively) on grounds of political bias and their limited coverage of politics. Though constituting the primary means for communicating political information to a mass audience, the national newspapers and the broadcast media remain first and foremost intent on maintaining readership and viewing figures. To achieve a large audience, they are predominantly media of entertainment. Indeed, they are moving even further in that direction, facing accusations of a "dumbing down" of quality as they compete in a more fragmented and competitive marketplace. The most-watched television programs on a continuing basis remain soap operas: *Coronation Street,* on ITV (the longest running soap opera on British television), and *Eastenders,* the BBC's answer to *Coronation Street.* Other programs attracting high viewing figures are those with a competitive element and inviting viewers to vote for those competing: They include *The X Factor* (for music) and *Britain's Got Talent* (for variety acts). The winning acts can get more votes than a political party achieves in a general election. To the media, their output is meeting the demands of the market. To critics, they are pandering to the lowest common denominator.

NOTES

1. J. Whale, *The Press and the Media* (Fontana, 1977), p. 86.
2. Select Committee on Communication, House of Lords, *The Ownership of the News,* Vol. 1: Report, HL Paper 122-I, Session 2007–08 (The Stationery Office, 2008), p. 12.
3. S. Barnett, "Reasons to be Cheerful," *British Journalism Review,* Vol. 17 (1), 2006, pp. 7–14, cited in *The Ownership of the News,* p. 15.
4. M. Scammell and M. Harrop, "The Press: Still for Labour, Despite Blair," in D. Kavanagh and D. Butler, *The British General Election of 2005* (Palgrave Macmillan, 2005), pp. 120–121.
5. *The Ownership of the News,* p. 7.

6. Ibid., p. 23.
7. Broadcasters' Audience Research Board Ltd (BARB), Weekly Multi-Channel Viewing Summary, May 2009, http://www.barb.co.uk/report/weeklyViewingSummary
8. See P. Norton, "Four Models of Political Representation: British MPs and the Use of ICT," *The Journal of Legislative Studies,* Vol. 13 (3), 2007, pp. 354–369.
9. http://order-order.com/
10. http://www.iaindale.blogspot.com/
11. *The Ownership of the News,* p. 6.
12. Ibid.
13. C. Seymour-Ure, *The British Press and Broadcasting Since 1945* (Blackwell, 1991), pp. 129–133.
14. J. Curran and J. Seaton, *Power without Responsibility: The Press and Broadcasting in Britain,* 6th ed. (Routledge, 2003), pp. 92–93.
15. S. McLachlan and P. Golding, "Tabloidization in the British Press: A Quantitative Investigation into Changes in British Newspapers, 1952–1997," in C. Sparks and J. Tulloch (eds.), *Tabloid Tales* (Rowman and Littlefield, 2000), pp. 75–89, cited in *The Ownership of the News,* p. 18.
16. "Fluctuations on the Presidential Exchange," *Time,* 9 November 1981, p. 60.
17. *The Handling of Press and Public Information during the Falklands Conflict,* First Report from the Select Committee on Defence, Session 1981–82, HC 17-I (Her Majesty's Stationery Office, 1982), p. xiv.
18. See Curran and Seaton, p. 103.
19. J. Klapper, *The Effects of Mass Communication* (Free Press, 1960), pp. 15–18.
20. J. Whale, *The Politics of the Media* (Longman, 1977), p. 85.
21. D. Butler and D. Stokes, *Political Change in Britain* (Penguin, 1971), pp. 281–300.
22. M. Scammell and M. Harrop, "The Press: Still for Labour, Despite Blair," in D. Kavanagh and D. Butler, *The British General Election of 2005* (Palgrave Macmillan, 2005), p. 139.
23. Butler and Stokes, p. 291.
24. P. Dunleavy and C. T. Husbands, "Media Influences on Voting in 1983," in J. Anderson and A. Cochrane (eds.), *A State of Crisis* (Hodder & Stoughton, 1989) pp. 291–292.
25. J. Curtice and H. Semetko, "Does it Matter What the Papers Say?" in A. Heath, R. Jowell, and J. Curtice, with B. Taylor, *Labour's Last Chance: The 1992 Election and Beyond* (Dartmouth, 1994), p. 44.
26. M. Scammell and M. Harrop, "The Press," in D. Butler and D. Kavanagh, *The British General Election of 1997* (Macmillan, 1997), p. 184.
27. See P. Norton, "David Cameron and Tory Success: Architect or By-stander?" in S. Lee and M. Beech (eds.), *The Conservatives under David Cameron* (Palgrave Macmillan, 2009), pp. 31–43.
28. Among those who have done so are Elton John, the singer, successful in a major action against *The Sun,* settled out of court for a seven-figure sum. See Seymour-Ure, pp. 228–229.
29. Press Complaints Commission, Complaints Summary (October 2008–March 2009), http://www.pcc.org.uk/statistics/101112_05.html
30. F. Gibb, "QCs Defend Mr Justice Eady as Newspapers Accuse Him of Privacy Law Rulings," *The Times,* 11 November, 2008.
31. *Trust in Professions 2007* (Royal College of Physicians, 2007), p. 7.
32. Ofcom, *In Breach,* Broadcast Bulletins Issue number 136–22 June 2009. http:// www.ofcom.org.uk/tv/obb/prog_cb/obb136/

PART

VI

CONCLUSION

CHAPTER

16

Future Directions
The Polity under Challenge

The British polity has witnessed major changes in recent years. The constitutional and political landscape of Britain looks very different at the start of the twenty-first century from that which existed for most of the twentieth. It is impossible not to be struck by the extent of the change. Writing in 2002 of constitutional change in the period from 1970 to 2000, Robert Stevens said that it "provided a practical and psychological transformation" comparable to the constitutional revolution wrought in the period from 1640 to 1720.[1] There had been major changes to the nation's constitutional arrangements in the intervening years, but "they were essentially independent acts rather than part of a dramatic period of constitutional restructuring."[2] The "restructuring" of recent years has continued. The British constitution has been characterized as unsettled.[3] Professor Anthony King has described it as "a mess."[4] How then to give some shape to what has happened? And what for the future?

In so far as one can identify any shape to it, the British polity has been moving in a direction that will be familiar to American readers. Reformers have been pressing for a political system in which power is dispersed: dispersed among different branches of government—executive, legislative, and judicial—and dispersed among different levels of government. They have been pressing for a system in which the rights of citizens enjoy some degree of constitutional protection, those rights embodied in a formal, and judicially protected, document. They have, in recent years, achieved a measure of success. Indeed, Professor Vernon Bogdanor has written of a "new" British constitution, with checks and balances becoming a feature of the polity.[5] In American eyes, these developments may appear both unremarkable and unobjectionable. However, to many British eyes, they are anything but. The British polity has changed and is subject to demands for further change, but with no agreement on the constitution that is deemed most appropriate for the United Kingdom.

Political debate used to take place within a constitutional framework that was taken largely for granted. Now, the constitution is itself on the agenda of political debate. The debate is one that is hotly contested.

Let us first remind ourselves of the extent of change and then consider the arguments as to the direction that constitutional change should take. There are those who advocate further, and sometimes radical, change. There are others who make the case for existing constitutional arrangements. The British polity has been marked by significant continuity as well as change and there is a case for maintaining the strengths of the Westminster model of government.

THE EXTENT OF CHANGE

The extent of change is clear from the foregoing chapters. As we have seen in Chapter 4, there have been two principal waves of constitutional change. The first wave derives from Britain's membership in the European Union. Membership has had significant constitutional, economic, and political consequences (Chapter 9). Membership has served to undermine the core doctrine at the heart of the British constitution: that of parliamentary sovereignty. Subsequent treaties have served to effect further shifts in power between the institutions of the European Union and the member states. The second wave began in 1997, following the election of a Labour government. The new government introduced a raft of constitutional reform measures. Elected assemblies have been created in Scotland, Wales, and Northern Ireland (Chapter 10). London also now has an elected mayor and strategic authority. These changes followed referendums, no longer novel constitutional devices but still unusual ones. The new bodies have been elected by electoral systems that depart from the system used for British parliamentary elections. The Human Rights Act has incorporated most provisions of the ECHR into British law. Public authorities are now expected to comply with the provisions of the Convention. The incorporation of the Convention into British law, combined with membership in the European Union and the devolution of powers to the new assemblies, has introduced a new judicial dimension to the constitution (Chapter 14). The centrality of the courts has been exemplified by the creation of a Supreme Court. Though not introducing any significant new powers, the move from a committee of the House of Lords to a distinct body, occupying its own building (as in the United States, just across the road from the national legislature), gives the highest court in the land a new visibility.

There have also been what may be described as subsidiary waves, such as the creation of a regulatory state, beginning under a Conservative government and being continued by a Labour one.[6] Various public utilities, such as gas and electricity, have been transferred to the private sector. Regulators have been appointed in order to encourage competition and to protect the consumer. They have joined a large number of extant regulatory bodies. The regulators operate at arm's length from government. They thus add to the range of bodies exercising powers independent of Government and Parliament.

As we have seen in Chapter 4, this list is not exhaustive. Other free-standing measures have been enacted. These have included a change in the membership of the second chamber of Parliament as well as the enactment of a Freedom of Information Act. There have also been changes to the structures and powers of local government, with more in the offing.

The fact of change is clear. The changes have been described in the preceding chapters. As we have also seen, there have been notable changes in the social and political landscape. Our focus is the changing constitutional landscape. To put the change in context, we have to understand the demands for change. In so doing, we can give some shape to the current debate and a notable, and arguably dangerous, dichotomy: The debate has reached a new and intellectually coherent level, but one with which the main political parties have yet to engage. Various coherent approaches to constitutional change have been generated. Proponents of each stipulate a particular constitution they consider most appropriate for the United Kingdom. They have a particular goal. The Labour and Conservative Parties advocate or oppose particular changes, but neither has yet identified its goal in terms of constitutional change.

DEMANDS FOR CHANGE

Demands for constitutional change have developed over time. Indeed, four periods can be identified: The first was the period of a settled constitution; the second was one of largely inchoate demands for reform; the third was the emergence of intellectually coherent approaches to constitutional change; and the fourth was the emergence of a fundamental divide between traditional and liberal approaches, reflecting a basic philosophical conflict in constitutional discourse.

A Settled Polity

During the Second World War (1939–45) the nation's democratic institutions continued to operate. The outcome of the war appeared to confirm the legitimacy of those institutions. The nation's economy gradually recovered and the country began to enjoy some degree of relative economic growth (see Chapter 3). Governments were able to raise resources to meet commitments of public policy. Labour and Conservative governments were able to maintain full employment and a national health service.

As a result, the constitution was not a subject of much debate in the quarter-century after the end of the Second World War. The political system appeared to function well. Britain had an effective two-party system and only a small percentage of citizens failed to vote in elections. The Westminster model of government was rarely discussed, other than occasionally for the purpose of praise and for recommending its emulation elsewhere. It was variously exported to newly independent colonies. The constitution was admired by politicians on both the left and right of the political spectrum. Indeed, one of its notable adherents was left-wing academic Harold Laski, who, lecturing in 1950 on the subject of the House of Commons, declared: "On the House of Commons as an institution I would like to add this final word. With all the changes that have taken place in it during this last half century, I see no decline in its greatness, nor any ultimate danger that it should be by-passed in its fundamental purposes, above all in the most fundamental of its purposes, the duty to see that the conditions are maintained which protect the freedom of the ordinary citizen."[7] Such praise continued to be expressed in later years, and not just by Britons.[8] There was, in essence, a basic consensus on the acceptability of the fundamentals of the constitution. Those fundamentals were seen as appropriate for delineation in law texts, not the basis of debate in political science texts. Political debate took place within a settled constitutional framework. The constitution itself was not the subject of debate.

Demands for Change

The situation was to change in the 1960s and, more especially, the 1970s. As we have seen (Chapter 3), the country saw an economic downturn. It lagged behind its European neighbors. Northern Ireland witnessed the beginning of "the troubles" (see Chapter 10). Rising unemployment, slow growth and inflation (known as stagflation) became a feature of the 1970s. At one point the annual inflation rate topped 25 percent. There were two general elections in one year, neither producing a notably decisive outcome. The proportion of voters going to the polls declined, as did the proportion voting for either of the two main parties (Chapter 5). There was a growing perception that the political system was dysfunctional. In the view of an increasing number of critics, it was not sufficient to replace one party in government with another. The system itself was seen as part of the problem. There were various demands for constitutional reform.

Some politicians called for a new electoral system. Two new groups came into being: Conservative Action for Electoral Reform (CAER) and the Labour Study Group on Electoral Reform. Some politicians and lawyers argued the case for a Bill of Rights. Two prominent jurists—Lords Scarman and Hailsham—made high-profile speeches making the case for such a measure.[9] A number of Labour politicians attacked the House of Lords, arguing the case for reform or abolition. In 1977, the Labour Party conference approved a motion calling for "an efficient and single-chamber legislating body." Following the 1975 referendum on Britain's continued membership of the EC, there were calls for referendums on different issues, such as trade union reform, as well as for their regular use.[10]

These demands, however, were rather disparate. There was little experience of discussing the constitution as a constitution: The tradition of constitutional discourse, which has sometimes been a feature of the nation's history, had disappeared in the years after 1945. The reforms advocated were offered as responses to particular problems rather than deriving from a clear view of a particular type of constitution deemed most appropriate for the United Kingdom. They derived from a limited bottom-up approach to constitutional change: They were not integrated into intellectually coherent, or top-down, approaches to constitutional change.

Different Approaches to Constitutional Change

The situation was to change in the 1980s. As the decade wore on, it was possible to discern a number of emerging approaches to constitutional change. Seven approaches have been identified: These are shown in Figure 16.1. Each approach had its advocates.

High Tory

Believes that the conveniences of existing arrangements are preferable to the unknown. Argues that the constitution has evolved organically and cannot be improved by artificial change. It is opposed not only to major reforms—such as electoral reform and an elected second chamber—but also to minor changes to existing arrangements. Its stance on any proposed reform is thus predictable: It is against it.

Socialist

Believes that the political system should be geared to realizing the wishes of the people. This approach favors reform, but a particular type of reform. It seeks strong government, but a party-dominated strong government, with adherence to the principle of intraparty democracy and the concept of the mandate. It wants to shift power from the existing "top-down" form of control (government to people) to a "bottom-up" form (people to government), with party acting as the channel for the exercise of that control. It favors limiting the powers of the prime minister, sweeping away privileged positions (monarchy, unelected members of a second chamber), and the use of more elective processes, both for public offices as well as within the Labour Party. It wants, for example, the election of members of a Labour cabinet by Labour MPs. It is wary of, or opposed to, reforms that might prevent the return of a socialist government and the implementation of a socialist program. For government to carry through socialist policies, it has to be free of constitutional constraints that favor or are dominated by its opponents.

Marxist

Sees the restructuring of the political system as largely irrelevant, certainly in the long run, serving merely to delay the collapse of capitalist society. Government, any government, is forced to work in the interests of finance capital. Whatever the structures, government will be constrained by external elites, and those elites will themselves be forced to follow rather than determine events. The clash between the imperatives of capitalism and decreasing profit rates in the meso-economy determine what capitalists do. Political structures will be changed in order to facilitate the hegemonic position of capitalism. Constitutional reform, in consequence, is not advocated but rather taken as demonstrating tensions within the international capitalist economy.

FIGURE 16.1
Approaches to constitutional change

Group

Favors a consensual policy-making process, incorporating organized interests. Argues that an integrated process can facilitate a more stable economic system and therefore seeks the co-option of functional interests into the governmental process. Supporters of this approach have cited countries such as Germany as examples of what can be achieved. This approach, in its pure form, favors a functional second chamber as well as a right for organized interests to be consulted on policy proposals in their sector.

New Right

Believes in the superiority of the free market. State intervention in economic affairs is viewed as illegitimate and dangerous, distorting the natural forces of the market and denying the consumer the freedom to choose. The state should therefore withdraw from economic activity. This entails a contraction of the public sector, with state-owned industries being returned to the private sector. If institutions need reforming in order to facilitate the free market, then so be it: Under this approach, no institution is deemed sacrosanct.

Liberal

Derives from traditional liberal theory and emphasises the centrality of what Giovanni Sartori in *Democratic Theory* terms "the theory and practice of individual liberty, juridicial defence and the constitutional state." It views the individual as increasingly isolated in decision making, being pushed aside by powerful interests and divorced from a highly centralized governmental process that is dominated by a single party. The individual has no means of protection, hence the need for radical constitutional change. In its pure form, the approach embraces federalism, a system of proportional representation for parliamentary elections, an entrenched Bill of Rights, and an elected second chamber, with the new constitutional structure codified in a written constitution. These changes would shift power from government to the individual. The only reform about which it is ambivalent is the use of referendums, some adherents to this approach seeing the referendum as a device for oppression by the majority.

Traditional

Draws on Tory theory in its emphasis on the need for strong government and on Whig theory in stressing the importance of Parliament as the agent for setting the limits within which government may act. These emphases coalesce in the Westminster model of government, a model that is part descriptive (what is) and part prescriptive (what should be). Government, in this model, must be able to formulate a coherent program of public policy, with Parliament scrutinizing the actions and the program of government and providing the limits within which government may govern. This approach stresses the importance of the House of Commons as the deliberative body of the nation, citizens exhibiting a contingent deference to the deliberative wisdom of Parliament. The approach opposes any change that damages the basic features of the Westminster model but is not opposed to changes designed to strengthen the model.

FIGURE 16.1 (conitinued)

Source: Adapted from P. Norton, *The Constitution in Flux* (Blackwell, 1982) and P. Norton, "The Constitution." in B. Jones (ed.), *Politics UK,* 6th ed. (Pearson Education, 2007).

The *high-Tory* approach was not prominent but it had its supporters. In a debate in the House of Commons in 1981, Conservative MP Sir John Stokes drew attention "to the uniqueness of the British Constitution, which is not readily susceptible to analysis on continental models" and declared that, distinguished from other constitutions, "our constitution is the envy of the world."[11] The 1970s had seen some form of tripartite cooperation between government, business, and labor (Chapter 7) and advocates of the *group approach* wanted this to be taken further. The *socialist* and *Marxist* approaches were variously articulated in magazines and pamphlets and had some articulate supporters. The socialist approach had a particular influence in the Labour Party in the early 1980s. The party's manifesto in the 1983 general election was essentially a socialist manifesto, advocating—among other things—British withdrawal from the European Community (see Chapter 6).

The *new right* approach also came to the fore. There were various new-right think tanks coming up with new ideas and publishing pamphlets. The deputy director of the Institute of Economic Affairs—a long-established think tank—argued the case for a "free market written constitution." The approach found a high-profile supporter in the leader of the Conservative Party, Margaret Thatcher. Though she supported the basic constitutional framework—she was essentially an adherent to the traditional approach—her support for the free market nonetheless meant that she had no qualms about tackling vested interests that interfered with the operation of the market.

The *liberal approach* gained momentum in the 1970s and 1980s. It was supported by the Liberal Party and the successor Liberal Democrat Party but acquired new adherents as more people became critical of existing constitutional arrangements. In 1988, the tercentenary year of the Glorious Revolution of 1688, a new reform movement, Charter'88 was formed to draw together those who supported a new constitutional settlement for the United Kingdom. The organization, as its name implies, subscribed to a charter of reforms, at the heart of which was a written constitution, and invited supporters to sign up to the charter. By 1991 it had attracted 25,000 signatures. It published pamphlets and papers as well as organizing meetings: It attracted media attention, especially from one of the broadsheet newspapers, *The Guardian*.

The *traditional approach* favored the Westminster model of government and during this period was powerful, not so much through advocacy but through its adherents being in government. The approach attracted support especially, though not exclusively, from Conservatives, and the Conservative Party was in government. Some of the most articulate supporters of the traditional approach were seated around the Cabinet table.

The situation was to change in the 1990s. In the first half of the decade the debate started to polarize around two of the approaches. The high-Tory approach had never been too prominent and did not make any of the running in debate. Events in central and eastern Europe, coupled with the changes made to the Labour Party under the leadership of Neil Kinnock and John Smith (Chapter 6), undermined the prominence and the credibility of the

Socialist and Marxist approaches. The group approach had been overshadowed by the new-right approach and was further marginalized by the Labour Party moving toward an acceptance of the market economy. The new-right approach lost its icon when Margaret Thatcher lost the leadership of the Conservative Party in 1990. Though her successor, John Major, pursued her economic policies, he was—in terms of the constitution—committed to the traditional approach. The liberal and the traditional approaches were the beneficiaries of the changes. Some notable intellectuals on the left of the political spectrum, including the editor of the journal *Marxism Today*, threw their support behind Charter'88. High Tories made common cause with supporters of the traditional approach in opposing radical change.

The traditional approach also found supporters articulating the case for the Westminster model. Previously, it had been assumed that by engaging in debate with supporters of Charter'88 it would raise the profile of the reform movement: It was hoped that by ignoring the movement it would decline and disappear. When it was clear that this was not going to happen, traditionalists began to put their heads above the political parapet and argue their case. Among those doing so were Cabinet ministers such as foreign secretary Douglas Hurd and education secretary John Patten.[12] The Prime Minister, John Major, was also a powerful advocate of the traditional approach, arguing especially against devolution and in favor of the existing union. The period thus saw an important debate taking place on constitutional change. Debate was engaged between the liberal and traditional approaches.

A Fundamental Divide

The debate between the liberal and traditional approaches represents a basic philosophical split. For much of the twentieth century, both approaches were united in favoring the constitutional arrangements that existed. The liberal stance was premised on a consensual society, with various checks and balances existing within the political system, with some degree of limited government and with political rights being extended (female suffrage and with the 1949 Representation of the People Act being perceived as delivering on the principle of "one person, one vote"). However, the events of the 1960s and since have led the approach to become a distinct, radical approach to change, at odds with the traditional approach.

The divide reflects a basic disagreement as to what a constitution is designed to achieve. In Chapter 4, we were able to define a constitution. There is agreement on what a constitution is but not necessarily on what a constitution is *for*. Some view the constitution as primarily a mechanism for ensuring that the will of the majority prevails. Others view it as a mechanism of constraint, entrenching certain values which cannot be set aside by the potentially transient will of a majority of citizens or of a majority in the legislature. The distinction is sometimes characterized as one between *parliamentary government* (or what has been termed positive constitutionalism) and *constitutionalism* (sometimes characterized as negative constitutionalism). The divide between the two has been well summarized by Anthony Bradley, Katja Ziegler, and Denis Baranger. In a system of parliamentary government, they note that there are problems in guarding against the exercise or arbitrary power because a majority of the legislature provides the executive with the authority to govern and usually is supportive of what it is trying to achieve. They continue:

> Second, a related reason why parliamentary government is not the natural partner of constitutionalism is that the former is concerned primarily with the interests of *the majority*; the latter is concerned to a significant extent with protecting minorities and individuals against excessive or abusive exercise of power by (or in the assumed interests of) the majority, whether by the executive or the legislature acting separately or through a close relationship between the two. Accordingly, constitutionalism and parliamentary government are often seen as potential adversaries or rivals, rather than as natural allies.[13]

The two positions are not necessarily mutually exclusive in that in a liberal democracy there is an attempt to balance the two, but they can be identified as being at opposite ends of a spectrum. Indeed, if we create such a spectrum, we can locate the several approaches we have identified. In Figure 16.2, six of the seven approaches are shown, distinguishing between collective and individual approaches to decision making. As can be seen, the liberal and traditional approaches are at different ends of the spectrum. What, then, are the arguments advanced by the proponents of each of these two approaches?

THE LIBERAL APPROACH

The liberal approach stresses the centrality of the individual and limited government. Its advocates argue that the political system was able to meet its goals in the nineteenth century. The scope of public policy was essentially

Basic unit of society	NEGATIVE CONSTITUTIONALISM [rights based]			POSITIVE CONSTITUTIONALISM [popular will]	
Individual	*liberal* [political]	*new right* [economic]	**High Tory** [status quo] < >	*traditional* [Westminister model] [constrained by Parliament]	[direct democracy]
Collective		*Group* [constrained by tripartite structures]		*Socialist* [constrained by party]	

FIGURE 16.2
Approaches to constitutional change: an ideological spectrum

limited, primarily to the defense of the nation and the maintenance of the Queen's peace. There were various checks and balances in the system, not least with each House of Parliament enjoying powers to block measures of the other. The political rights of the individual were being extended, especially through reform of the franchise. The balance within the constitution prevented an electoral majority from oppressing minorities or individuals.[14] The concepts of limited government and of the rights of the individual were well established. Even in the First World War there was apparently opposition to providing armed escorts to merchant ships on the grounds that this interfered with the freedom of the captains to determine their own courses.

While such a situation pertained, the liberal approach was not a radical one. However, as we have seen, the situation changed in the last quarter of the twentieth century. There was the perception that individual liberties were under threat, not just from government but from other public bodies and private organizations. A government, secure in its parliamentary majority, was able to get whatever measure it wished enacted. In the 1960s and 1970s it listened to organized interests; after 1979, it was accused of not listening to any particular interests. In the formulation of public policy, individuals were ignored. Governments fought to bolster their position, pushing through whatever they wanted against the vocal opposition of their political opponents. Both parties sought to out-promise the other in general elections, the winner then committed to policies that might be expensive to fulfill.

Institutions were becoming divorced from citizens and increasingly unable to protect them and act in their interests. As institutions failed to deliver what was expected of them, so—as we noted in Chapter 2—trust in the effectiveness and equity of government began to decline. The less it was trusted, the less able it was to proceed on the basis of cooperation. Power became more centralized in order to enable government to get its way. The result, according to critics such as Samuel Beer, was a "collapse" in the civic culture. The empirical basis for this claim was to be found in the decline in voter turnout, in party membership, in popular support for a change in the system of government, and in perceptions of a centralization of power. Lord Hailsham in 1976 coined the phrase "elective dictatorship." This was taken by reformers as a fair characterization of the system of government. The "dictatorship" became more pronounced as the "elective" element diminished, with parties gaining power on a minority of votes. As we recorded in Chapter 2, various surveys showed that most people thought that the system of government needed "a great deal" of improvement or could be "improved quite a lot." In 1991, 63 percent gave those responses. In 1995 the figure had increased to 75 percent.

According to adherents of the liberal approach, the political system was thus dysfunctional. It needed fundamental reform in order to restore the centrality of the individual. The approach stressed decentralization of decision making. This would limit an overmighty government and allow greater opportunities for citizens to engage in decision making. Greater participation, it was argued, would help maintain consent for the political system as well as improve the quality of decision making: Decisions would be taken closer to those affected by the decisions. The approach also stresses the use of checks and balances in the political system: Power should be made to counteract power. Each institutional element of the system should be strengthened. In the legislature, this meant an elected second chamber. It also meant a powerful judiciary; the rights of the individual could be protected through a bill of rights, with those rights then being enforced through the courts. An entrenched bill of rights would put rights beyond the reach of simple majorities in the two Houses of Parliament. The approach also stresses the need for consensus, moving away from the hegemony (and hence the arrogance) of a single-party government. To this end, it seeks the end of an adversary system in which parties compete with one another for the all-or-nothing spoils of election victory.

The liberal approach thus embraces a new constitution for the United Kingdom. We have already outlined the measures it proposes. It favors decentralization through a devolution of powers or—in the pure form of the approach—federalism. It favors building up checks and balances through an elected second chamber and a more powerful judiciary. It wants to protect rights through an entrenched bill of rights. It believes that consensus will be encouraged through the use of a new electoral system for parliamentary elections. A new system, it argues, will deny any one party a majority of seats, thus forcing a coalition of parties to form the government. It wants the new constitution to be codified, that is, to be embodied in a written constitution. There have been various attempts to craft such a constitution.[15]

Advocates of the liberal approach support most of the changes introduced by the Labour government but they want to see the changes taken further. Supporters of the liberal approach want to abandon the Westminster model and for the government to introduce measures to give effect to a liberal constitution of a sort that is familiar to Americans. Indeed, it may seem strange to American eyes that there is opposition to introducing such a constitution. The opposition is powerful and, I believe, persuasive.

THE TRADITIONAL APPROACH

Those who support the traditional approach argue that the liberal approach derives from a false analysis and that it mistakes the real problems facing the nation. Further, it argues that the Westminster model of government has delivered benefits that cannot be matched by the liberal, or any other, model. The Westminster model is the most appropriate for the United Kingdom.

Those arguing that there has been a demise of the civic culture in Britain rely too heavily on data that will not bear the weight given them. Britain has not seen a collapse of attitudes and values from some golden age to a new dismal age. If there ever was anything approaching a "golden age" it was to be found in the quarter-century following the Second World War—certainly not before—and that period of stability and relative economic prosperity produced particularly high levels of pride in institutions, a pride tapped by Almond and Verba in *The Civic Culture*. Those heady and exceptional days may be past, but the basic orientations toward cooperation and problem solving are not. The civic culture remains intact. Britain is a pluralist society, more pluralist than ever before.[16] The culture remains essentially a deferential one, but that deference—as we have argued—is contingent and not certain. If government goes beyond what is acceptable, various mechanisms still exist to check it. That is allied with the empirical approach to problem solving and cooperation. If things appear to be going too far, then efforts are made to find a practical solution.

It is this empirical approach that is emphasized by the traditional approach to the constitution. There is an attachment to the basics of the existing system. If there is dissatisfaction, it tends not to be with the fundamentals of the system but rather with politicians, political parties, and recent changes to the system. There are notably high levels of trust in bodies such as the army and the police—running above the EU average; the level of trust in the legal system is also above the EU average.[17] The *Audit of Political Engagement 5* (2008) found that, on a range of issues, the highest level of dissatisfaction was with Scottish MPs being able to vote on English issues in the House of Commons and with how political parties are funded. The highest levels of satisfaction were with having a voting age of 18 years, letting the government decide the date of a general election, and how votes cast at a general election translate into seats in the House of Commons.[18] There was a notable decline in trust in politicians in 2009 following the revelations about the use of MPs' expenses, but the lack of trust was in the political class rather than the political system. Though the proportion of people believing the political system "needs a great deal of improvement" was greater at the end of 2008 than it was in 1973, it was lower than the figure for 1995.[19] The Hansard Society's annual Audits of Political Engagement, which began in 2004, do not suggest a dramatic change in recent years. A plurality of people tends to think the system could be improved "quite a lot"—the proportion has not changed significantly since 1991—but the Audit of Political Engagement 5 found that those who felt the political system as a whole needed improvement "are more likely to be satisfied than dissatisfied with how votes cast in a general election translate into seats in the Commons (33 percent compared to 22 percent), the minimum voting age (65 percent to 13 percent) and letting the government decide the date of a general election (34 percent to 27 percent)."[20] The highest level of dissatisfaction was recorded at a time of notably low levels of satisfaction in the government.[21] There is also a correlation between satisfaction and party support: As the 2009 report noted "Conservatives and Liberal Democrats are more likely to express dissatisfaction than Labour supporters across the board."[22]

Also, if there is a "decline" in the civic culture, then that is not apparent from citizen participation in public affairs (Chapter 2). Some forms of participation may not be indulged in by many citizens, but that is not evidence of a change from a previous era. The Audits of Political Engagement reflect no linear decline.[23] People tend to believe that voting in an election is the most effective way of having an impact on how the country is run: Over 70 percent expressed such a view in 2008; only 6 percent thought that it was not effective at all.[24] Over 50 percent thought that contacting a local councilor, MP or MEP was effective; only 9 percent thought that it was not effective at all. It is also notable that disillusionment, or a belief that politicians are untrustworthy, does not account for most of those who do not get involved in the political process. When people who said they would like to be involved in influencing decision making were asked what prevented them from getting involved, the largest proportion (40 percent) said lack of time.[25]

None of this is to argue that the United Kingdom does not face a number of social and economic problems. We have touched upon these in the preceding chapters. There are also political problems. There has been a decline in the membership of the political parties. People are devoting their energies to organized groups—often single-issue groups—rather than to the political parties. There are low levels of turnout in elections to local councils and to the European Parliament. Although traditionally exhibiting low levels of turnout, the electoral turnout among young people is a significant problem. However, where supporters of the traditional approach take issue with advocates of the liberal approach is in the explanation for these phenomena. They argue that the causes are not structural: They are not specific to the political institutions of the United Kingdom. A decline in party membership—and greater attachment to single-issue organized groups—is an international phenomenon. Low turnouts in local elections are not confined to Britain: A similar phenomenon exists in the United States, most voters staying at home in off-year elections. A low turnout across the European Union was a feature of the 2009 elections to the European Parliament. There are problems, but to ascribe them to a dysfunctional political system in the United Kingdom is misleading. So ascribing them detracts from attempts to identify the real cause of the problem.

The analysis of existing arrangements by advocates of the liberal approach is thus deemed to be flawed. The existing system is not a cause of the problems it identifies. Far from being part of the problem, traditionalists argue that the existing system remains, if anything, part of the solution. It offers a number of benefits that other systems cannot offer, and by moving away from it, one is likely to undermine rather than bolster support for the political system. The attributes of the system as a whole are not dissimilar to those ascribed to the electoral process (see Chapter 5). Fundamentally, the system delivers a high level of accountability to the electors, what has been termed core accountability.[26] Responsibility is not divided or lost among several bodies. There is one body—the party-in-government—that is responsible for measures of public policy. Electors therefore know whom to blame, or to praise, for public policy. If they disapprove, they have the option of getting rid of the party-in-government and replacing it with another. Too much emphasis in debate is placed on the "hiring" aspects of elections and not enough on the "firing" aspects. The essence of democracy, according to the late philosopher Sir Karl Popper, is the capacity of citizens to get rid of the body in power and to do so in a peaceful way:

> In *The Open Society and its Enemies* I suggested that an entirely new problem should be recognized as the fundamental problem of a rational political theory. The new problem, as distinct from the old "Who should rule?", can be formulated as follows: how is the state to be constituted so that bad rulers can be got rid of without bloodshed, without violence?[27]

The electoral system of the United Kingdom was, as Popper recognized, central to ensuring that citizens can remove a party from government. There is less potential than in continental systems, which employ forms of proportional representation, to stay in office through post-election bargaining despite a slump in electoral support. Furthermore, the system usually delivers a decisive method of election. A party can be swept out of office on election day, and on the following day a new prime minister and government are in place. There is no lengthy hiatus while parties haggle over who is to be in power. Unlike in the United States, there is no lengthy transitional period between election and taking office. There may be a change of party but there is continuity in government.

The problems associated with a new electoral system are to be found in the experience of Scotland and Wales. Under the form of AMS employed in Scotland and Wales, the elections have tended to produce no one party with an overall majority. Following the 2007 elections to the Scottish parliament, a minority SNP administration was formed, in other words, an administration for which only a minority of Scottish voters had cast their ballots. Following the elections to the National Assembly for Wales in the same year, a coalition was eventually formed comprising the nationalist party, Plaid Cymru and its historic opponent, the Labour Party—a coalition for which not one voter had formally cast a vote. Some electors had voted PC and some had voted Labour (see Chapter 10) but not one voter had voted for Plaid Cymru + Labour. The electoral legitimacy of the administration could not then be claimed to be greater than that of a government produced through elections to the House of Commons.

The experience of Scotland and Wales also points to the dangers of moving away from the centrality of an accountable party-in-government at Westminster. The more layers of elected government there are, the less accountable each one becomes. Electors are uncertain as to which layer of government is responsible for what, and if one layer of government cannot deliver because it is blocked by another, then there is the danger of a decline in support for the system of government. Some levels of government may also be undermined if electors fail to attach significance to them. There are problems with elections to local councils in the United Kingdom as well as elections to the European Parliament. One distinguished public servant, Lord Dahrendorf—a member of the House of Lords, but previously a government minister in Germany and European Commissioner—queried whether the European Parliament is any more legitimate under direct elections than it was when its members were appointed from national parliaments.

The existing system is also responsive. Ministers know that they may be turned out of office at the next election. They are therefore sensitive to public opinion and to shifts in that opinion. There is thus a closer link between electors and elected than is the case in many continental countries, where politicians can act without being unduly concerned by shifts in opinion, knowing that they are likely to be able to negotiate their way back into government after the next election. The system is also transparent. A party is elected to office on the basis of a program that it placed before the electors at the election, and that program provides the framework for action: Political parties have a good record in implementing election promises. The program is, above all, a published program; electors have a benchmark against which to assess government.

The existing system also provides representation at both a general and a particular level. The general is delivered through parties, the particular through the individual MP. The MP is the essential link between citizen and government. Constituency representation is an integral part of the existing political system and is reinforced by the political culture. For the purpose of expressing grievances and demands to government, contacting one's MP is the most popular form of personal action and—as we have noted—is judged to be effective. MPs serve as important safety valves as well as grievance chasers on behalf of citizens.[28] The essence of the relationship between MP and citizen has been well summarized by Ivor Crewe: "The further away the local Member is from the constituency . . . the less the public approve. People want to have their Member. . . . Familiarity appears to breed content."[29] However, the general representation acts as a constraint on an abuse of the relationship. Party provides a crucial shield for MPs, protecting them from undue influence by outside groups. The political system is not open to special interests in the way that it is in the United States.

The political system in the United Kingdom is essentially stable as well as effective and flexible. It is not necessarily more stable nor more effective than some other systems, but they are central features of the system. The attributes of the system are threatened by the reforms advocated by the liberal approach. A dispersal of power undermines core accountability. There is no one body that electors can hold to account for public policy. Giving power to the courts moves power from the people's elected representatives to unelected jurists: Political decisions are decided not by a political process but by a judicial process. Though there is an acceptance of political questions being resolved by judicial means in some other polities, including the United States, it is alien to the British political culture.

Democracy, like representation, is subject to different definitions. Some define it in terms of input legitimacy: that is, election. So defined, there is a case for dispersing power to different elected bodies. On that definition, the United States is a highly democratic polity. However, if democracy is defined in terms of output legitimacy—that is, translating popular will into legislative output—then the United States is far from democratic. There is often a mismatch between what most electors want and what Congress delivers. In the words of Hibbing and Theiss-Morse, writing in 1995, one would be "hard-pressed to design a Congress that less accurately reflected the process preferences of the people than the one we see in the mid-1990s."[30] On this definition, it is the United Kingdom that is democratic. The measures advocated by the liberal approach are designed to constrain (negative constitutionalism) rather than reinforce this democratic element.

The traditional approach thus emphasizes the accountability of the existing arrangements (a form of positive constitutionalism) and the fact that there is no popular support to move away from it. Though majorities can be found in surveys for particular items in the liberal reform agenda, there is no popular support for a new political system. Constitutional change is accorded no priority by electors and does not feature in the list of issues deemed to be the most important issues facing the nation. To traditionalists, advocates of the liberal approach offer a false prospectus and the more the United Kingdom moves in that direction the less the nation benefits.

PROBLEMS FOR THE PARTIES

There are thus powerful arguments advanced for and against change. How, then, do these arguments relate to the position of the political parties? The debate creates problems for both main parties.

During the 1990s, the Liberal Democrats were wedded to a new constitutional settlement for the United Kingdom. The Conservatives, the party in power, were wedded to the existing Westminster model of government. The Labour Party favored some change and in 1997 it was elected to power and began, as we have seen (Chapter 4), to implement measures of constitutional change. However, the changes that have taken place have not replaced the Westminster model of government with another. Instead, as we mentioned in Chapter 4, what Britain has is a modified Westminster model of government.

The Labour Party in the 1980s and 1990s moved away from the socialist approach to constitutional change. It embraced some of the liberal agenda. The more time the party spent as the "out" party in British politics, the more attractive some element of constitutional change began to appear. If the party could not prosper under the existing constitutional arrangements, perhaps the time had come to consider new constitutional arrangements? The party was also opposed to what it saw as the effects of a centralized and arrogant government. It began to advocate some change to the existing constitution. It was committed to devolution of powers to Scotland and Wales, not least because in Scotland the SNP was the chief challenger to its dominant position and it wanted to undermine the SNP's position. It began to advocate a charter of rights and many members began to see some merit in changing the electoral system for parliamentary elections. The party's manifesto in the 1992 general election moved the party in the direction of the liberal approach but fell short of embracing all the elements of that approach. Its manifesto in the 1997 general election was similar, though arguably not moving quite as far as the 1992 manifesto. The 1992 manifesto was the high point of Labour's advocacy of anything approaching the liberal approach. However, the closest the liberal approach came to realizing its goals was in 1997, when Labour was elected to power. As we have seen, some of the things it wanted were introduced by the Labour government.

However, the Labour Party has never fully embraced the liberal approach. Though it was the "out" party in British politics for eighteen years, from 1979 to 1997, it was nonetheless the alternative party of government. As the 1990s progressed, it became apparent that it was likely to become the "in" party. It was therefore wary of committing itself to measures that could limit in when it was in government. As we have seen, when returned to government, it introduced various measures of constitutional change, including devolution, the incorporation of the ECHR, and reforming the composition of the second chamber. What is equally important to note, though, is what the government did not do. It did not move to destroy the doctrine of parliamentary sovereignty. Parliament retains the powers to abolish or change the elected assemblies in the different parts of the United Kingdom. The courts cannot strike down acts of Parliament as being contrary to the ECHR. The government set up a commission on the voting system (Chapter 5) but did not move to hold a referendum on the voting system. Though it managed to remove most hereditary peers from membership of the House of Lords, it did not move to replace an unelected second chamber with an elected chamber (Chapter 12). Although projecting itself as being "Euro-friendly," the government was not prepared to commit itself to membership in a single European currency. The government was careful not to destroy its capacity to gets its way, ultimately, through utilizing its parliamentary majority.

The support of the Labour government for the liberal approach to the constitution was thus, at best, highly qualified support. It did not embrace the approach, it did not wholly discard the traditional approach, and it failed to generate an approach of its own. It was accused of adopting a stance that was essentially disparate and discrete, similar to that taken by people advocating constitutional change in the 1970s: They saw particular problems and addressed them, but failed to put them in any intellectually coherent approach to change. When challenged as to the government's approach, ministers remained silent. Eventually, however, in a debate in the House of Lords in 2002, the Lord Chancellor, Lord Irvine, asserted that the government proceeded "by way of pragmatism based on principle, without," he conceded, "the need for an all-embracing theory." The principles, he said, were, first, that the United Kingdom should remain a parliamentary democracy with the Westminster Parliament supreme and within that the Commons the dominant chamber; second, increase public engagement with democracy through "developing a mature democracy with different centres of power, where individuals enjoy greater rights and where government is carried out closer to the people"; and, third, "to devise a solution to each problem on its own terms."[31] These three principles have been likened to saying (a) that power will reside at the center, (b) power won't reside at the center, and (c) "we'll make it up as we go along."[32] They did not provide any guidance as to the type of constitution that the government wished to have in place in five or ten years. The constitution of the United Kingdom is being changed, but not according to any particular principle or goal. Hence, as we have seen, the country now has not a new constitution but a modified—critics claim a vandalized—Westminster model.

The nature of the change introduced by the Labour government creates problems for the political parties. In the case of the Labour Party, then, the problem is immediate: trying to identify a clear coherent approach. For the Conservative Party, the problem is prospective. It has been able to adopt a consistent stance in response to most of the measures of constitutional reform introduced by the Labour government: It has opposed them. However, it faces a problem when next in Government: The constitution will be different to that which it had been defending when last in office. When, then, should it do? It has three options.[33] First, it could adopt a *reactionary approach*, that is, support the *status quo ante* and seek to return the constitution to what it was before 1997. Second, it could adopt a *conservative approach* and seek to retain the constitution as it exists at the time it enters office. Though the constitution has undergone changes viewed as largely undesirable, nonetheless it still retains the recognizable features of the Westminster model. It may not be the ideal, but it is the real. Third, it could decide that the changes wrought under a Labour government have so disfigured the Westminster model that the only answer is to embrace a *radical approach*, perhaps even moving in the direction of the liberal approach. There are some Conservatives who admire the American system of government.

There is a recognition that it cannot go back to the situation as it existed before 1997. Conservative leader William Hague in 1998 accepted that devolution is a feature now of the British polity. However, the party has not addressed whether it wishes to embrace a conservative or radical approach. Some in the party have not altogether given up on a reactionary approach: Some favor repeal of the Human Rights Act. The party thus faces the prospect of entering office without having a clear stance on constitutional change.

For the Liberal Democrats, the problem is one of tempering principle with expediency. The party supports the liberal approach to the constitution. Intellectually and morally, it has no problem with that stance. However, it would also like to be in government. Recognizing that this may not be possible on its own, it is prepared to cooperate with another party. In 1996 it formed a joint consultation committee with the Labour Party.[34] In 1997, a cabinet committee, drawing together ministers and leading members of the party, was formed, though folded after a few years. There is the prospect that the party could hold the balance of power in a future Parliament in which no one party holds an absolute majority. Recognition of this fact is believed to have motivated Tony Blair in maintaining a dialogue with the Liberal Democrats. Recognition that there is no guarantee of a "hung" Parliament means that the Liberal Democrats cannot afford to be too demanding in their negotiations with the Labour Party. The dilemma they face is shown in respect to electoral reform. The party is deeply committed to a system of proportional representation and has variously claimed that a commitment to introduce it would be a precondition of any future pact with the Labour party. However, it has proved willing to modify its position, and in 2000 dialogue continued even though it was reported that party leaders had accepted that there would be no referendum on the electoral system before the next general election and the prime minister had decided against implementing the report of the commission on the voting system. The party leaves itself open to the accusation of abandoning its principles in favor of achieving some modicum of political power.

All three parties thus face difficulties in delineating their stance in relation to constitutional change. Those difficulties are especially acute in relation to the Conservative and Labour Parties. They have not engaged with the wider debate. The debate itself may also seem insular. There is a problem as to the capacity of government to determine outcomes given global developments. While constitutional reformers see problems in systemic terms, they tend to ignore what is going on in the wider world.

EXTERNAL CHALLENGES

The capacity of the United Kingdom to determine issues is under challenge, but less from internal pressures than from external developments. One of these is membership in the European Union. We have already discussed some of the implications (Chapter 9). The United Kingdom is in danger of acquiring what amounts to a written constitution through its membership in the European Union: The treaties establishing the European Communities and the European Union—embodied now in the Lisbon Treaty—form something of a "higher law." That higher law derives its authority from an act of Parliament. Formally, the doctrine of parliamentary sovereignty remains in place. Parliament could repeal the 1972 European Communities Act. The effect would be to take Britain out of the European Union, since the United Kingdom would no longer be able to fulfill its treaty commitments. However, such a withdrawal is unlikely. The United Kingdom thus has to address how to adapt its constitutional arrangements to membership in the European Union without allowing greater encroachment on its domestic policy-making arrangements.

The other external development is subsumed under the heading of globalization. A liberalization in capital markets has meant a global capital market. There has been something of a globalization in terms of communications and, to a lesser extent, in terms of trade. Governments have limited capacity to affect markets. The British government discovered that, to its cost, in 1992 when it was forced to withdraw from the European ERM and in 2008 in seeking to respond to the global "credit crunch." There is a certain inherent conflict in the stance taken by neoliberals in the United Kingdom. On the one hand, there is an embrace of the free market and hence globalization in trade and capital. On the other, neoliberals are at the forefront of opposition to the seepage of policy-making power from British government to the European Union, arguing the merits of decision making by the nation state. Yet a global market implies, indeed necessitates, some weakening of the nation state.[35] The nation state loses some of its capacity to determine outcomes; indeed, according to some critics, the nation state is beginning to crumble.[36] The inherent conflict in the neoliberal approach was exemplified by Margaret Thatcher when she was leader of the Conservative Party, and it was a feature of what was termed Thatcherism (see Chapter 6). The Labour Party has moved some way toward the Conservative approach: It has accepted the imperatives of a market approach and, although claiming a positive attitude toward European integration, has made clear its opposition to moves to create a United States of Europe. Under Tony Blair, the party embraced, or at least accepted, what has been termed "The Third Way," a position somewhere between capitalism and social democracy,[37] but the essence of the approach has not been fleshed out in detail. For the political parties in Britain, there is the challenge of coping with developments external to—though also encompassing—Britain's shores. The challenges are not peculiar to the United Kingdom.

CONCLUSION

At times of economic, social, or political difficulty, there has been a tendency—not confined to the United Kingdom—to look to constitutional change as a palliative or a means of dealing with the difficulty, of producing a system capable of being effective and resolving problems. At the time of the Depression in the 1930s, for example, the implications for the constitution were noted by Conservative leader Stanley Baldwin. "There is bound to be unrest," he said, "when more questions are being put than statesmen can answer. Within the House of Commons itself there is a growing sense of the need for overhauling the ship of state."[38] Disappointment with the working of representative government, he observed, was no new thing. "It recurs periodically and we are in one of the fermenting periods now. It may be uncomfortable but it is not surprising."[39]

The years after the Second World War in Britain witnessed a period of stability and—especially in the 1950s—relative economic prosperity, with little debate consequently about constitutional arrangements. As the economic condition of the nation worsened in the 1960s, calls for change in structures began to be heard. Those calls became more strident in the 1970s and 1980s. Various blueprints for constitutional reform, including a new constitution, were devised. Since then, much of the debate has focused on the liberal and traditionalist approaches. The nature of the debate is not unique in the context of British history. What is disputed is the extent to which change is necessary and how Britain should respond to wider changes in the global environment.

NOTES

1. R. Stevens, *The English Judges* (Hart Publishing, 2002), p. xiii.
2. Stevens, p. xiii.
3. P. Norton, "The Unsettled British Constitution," *Politics Review,* Vol. 16 (1), 2006, pp. 6–9.
4. A. King, *The British Constitution* (Oxford University Press, 2007), p. 345.
5. V. Bogdanor, *The New British Constitution* (Hart Publishing, 2009), Ch. 11.
6. See P. Norton, "Regulating the Regulatory State," *Parliamentary Affairs,* Vol. 57 (4), 2004, pp. 785–799.
7. H. J. Laski, *Reflections on the Constitution* (Manchester University Press, 1951), p. 92.
8. See Bogdanor, *The New British Constitution,* pp. 3–4.
9. L. Scarman, *English Law—The New Dimension* (Stevens, 1974); Lord Hailsham, *Elective Dictatorship* (BBC, 1976).
10. See V. Bogandor, *The People and the Party System* (Cambridge University Press, 1981).
11. *House of Commons Debates: Official Report (Hansard),* Vol. 2, col. 1213 [April 10, 1981].
12. See, for example, J. Patten, *Political Culture, Conservatism and Rolling Constitutional Change* (Conservative Political Centre, 1991).
13. A. W. Bradley, K. S. Ziegler, and D. Baranger, "Constitutionalism and the Role of Parliaments," in K. S. Ziegler, D. Baranger, and A. W. Bradley (eds.), *Constitutionalism and the Role of Parliaments* (Hart Publishing, 2007), p. 2.
14. P. Norton, *The Constitution in Flux* (Blackwell, 1982), p. 276.
15. See, for example, the Institute of Public Policy Research, *A Written Constitution for the United Kingdom* (Mansell, 1993) and C. Bryant (ed.), *Towards a New Constitutional Settlement* (The Smith Institute, 2007).
16. See P. Norton, "In Defence of the Constitution," in P. Norton (ed.), *New Directions in British Government?* (Edward Elgar, 1991), pp. 154–160.
17. *Eurobarometer 69,* Spring 2008, National Report: United Kingdom, p. 25.
18. Hansard Society/Ministry of Justice, *Audit of Political Engagement 5: The 2008 Report* (Hansard Society, 2008), p. 28.
19. Hansard Society/Ministry of Justice, *Audit of Political Engagement 6: The 2009 Report* (Hansard Society, 2009), p. 30.
20. Hansard Society/Ministry of Justice, *Audit of Political Engagement 5: The 2008 Report* (Hansard Society, 2008), p. 28.
21. Hansard Society/Ministry of Justice, *Audit of Political Engagement 6: The 2009 Report* (Hansard Society, 2009), pp. 30–31.
22. Hansard Society/Ministry of Justice, *Audit of Political Engagement 5: The 2008 Report* (Hansard Society, 2008), p. 29.
23. Hansard Society/Ministry of Justice, *Audit of Political Engagement 6: The 2009 Report* (Hansard Society, 2009), p. 27.
24. Ibid., p. 40.
25. Ibid., p. 38.
26. See P. Norton, "Adding Value? The Role of Second Chambers," *Asia Pacific Law Review,* Vol. 15(1), 2007, pp. 3–18.
27. Sir K. Popper, "The Open Society and its Enemies Revisited," *The Economist,* 23 April 1988.
28. See P. Norton, *Power to the People* (Conservative Policy Forum, 1998), p. 3.

29. I. Crewe, "Electoral Reform and the Local MP," in S. E. Finer (ed.), *Adversary Politics and Electoral Reform* (Wigram, 1975), p. 322.

30. J. R. Hibbing and E. Theiss-Morse, *Congress as Public Enemy* (Cambridge University Press, 1995), p. 161.

31. House of Lords: Official Report *(Hansard):* Vol. 642, col. 692 [18 December 2002].

32. P. Norton, "Tony Blair and the Constitution," *British Politics,* Vol. 2(2), 2007, pp. 269–281.

33. P. Norton, "The Constitution," in K. Hickson (ed.), *The Political Thought of the Conservative Party since 1945* (Palgrave Macmillan, 2005), pp. 93–112.

34. The committee agreed on a report on constitutional reform. *Report of the Joint Consultative Committee on Constitutional Reform* (1997).

35. See, for example, T. Banuri and J. B. Schor, *Financial Openness and National Autonomy* (Oxford University Press, 1992). I am grateful to D. J. Skelton, "'EMU and the Neo-Liberal Project': The Decapitation of Parliamentary Democracy," undergraduate dissertation, University of Hull, 2000, for this source and for the clarity with which it develops the point embodied in this paragraph.

36. K. Ohmae, *The End of the Nation State—The Rise of Regional Economies* (Free Press, 1995).

37. See A. Giddens, *The Third Way: The Renewal of Social Democracy* (Polity Press, 1998).

38. S. Baldwin, *The Torch of Freedom,* 4th ed. (Hodder & Stoughton, 1937), p. 50.

39. Ibid.

SELECT READING LIST

This is neither a bibliography of works used nor a comprehensive survey of available literature. Rather, it is a brief guide to the main works available for further study. Chapter endnotes provide a pointer to further reading for students whose intellectual appetite is not satiated by what follows.

PART I: INTRODUCTION

Social and economic data are provided by the Office for National Statistics (ONS). It publishes annually *Social Trends* (Palgrave Macmillan). The 2008 edition focuses on societal well-being. The 2009 edition includes a special article on households, families, and children. The ONS also makes a great deal of data available online at: http://www.statistics.gov.uk/default.asp There is also a Virtual Bookshelf: http://www.statistics.gov.uk/onlineproducts/default.asp

There is a valuable annual publication, *British Social Attitudes,* drawing on the British Social Attitudes Survey carried out by the National Centre for Social Research. The 2009 edition is Alison Park, John Curtice, Katarina Thomson, Miranda Phillips, and Elizabeth Clery (eds.), *British Social Attitudes: The 25th Report* (Sage Publications, 2009). Since 2004, there has been an annual audit of political engagement, based on public polling on a range of indicators of political engagement. The most recent is *Audit of Political Engagement 6: The 2009 Report* (Hansard Society/Ministry of Justice, 2009). There is also a useful survey of trends in Ben Marshall, Bobby Duffy, Julian Thompson, Sarah Castell, and Suzanne Hall, *Blair's Britain: The Social and Cultural Legacy* (Ipsos MORI, 2007). On what it means to be British, see the essays in Matthew D'Ancona (ed.), *Being British: The Search for Values That Bind a Nation* (Mainstream Publishing, 2009).

The history of Britain is treated in numerous works, including the 15-volume *Oxford History of England,* published by Oxford University Press. There is also a highly acclaimed political history, *The British Political Tradition,* by W. H. Greenleaf, published in three volumes: *Vol. 1: The Rise of Collectivism* (Longman, 1983), *Vol. 2: The Ideological Inheritance* (Longman, 1983), and *Vol. 3: A Much Governed Nation* (Longman, 1987). Other interpretative works include David Marquand, *Britain Since 1918: The Strange Career of British Democracy* (Weidenfeld & Nicolson, 2008) and Peter Kellner, *Democracy: 1,000 Years in Pursuit of British Liberty* (Mainstream Publishing, 2009).

For those new to British history looking for a single-volume work, there is Kenneth O. Morgan, *The Oxford History of Britain,* 3rd ed. (Oxford Paperbacks, 2001) and, for the history of Britain after 1945, Andrew Marr, *A History of Modern Britain* (Pan Books, 2009).

PART II: THE POLITICAL ENVIRONMENT

Vernon Bogdanor (ed.), *The British Constitution in the Twentieth Century* (Oxford University Press, 2003) seeks to provide a coherent interpretation of the constitution.

452

The most recent analyses of the constitution are Anthony King, *The British Constitution* (Oxford University Press, 2007) and Vernon Bogdanor, *The New British Constitution* (Hart Publishing, 2009). Also useful are Dawn Oliver, *Constitutional Reform in the UK* (Oxford University Press, 2003); Andrew McDonald (ed.), *Reinventing Britain: Constitutional Change under New Labour* (Politico's, 2007); Rodney Brazier, *Constitutional Reform*, 3rd ed. (Oxford University Press, 2008); and Robert Hazell (ed.), *Constitutional Futures Revisited: Britain's Constitution to 2020* (Palgrave Macmillan, 2008).

Election results, and details of candidates, are published after each general election in *The Times Guide to the House of Commons* (*The Times*). The standard works of analysis on British general elections are those published in the Nuffield election series, published after each election. The most recent edition is Dennis Kavanagh and David Butler, *The British General Election of 2005* (Palgrave Macmillan, 2005). Two other works also cover the 2005 election: Andrew Geddes and Jonathan Tonge (eds.), *Britain Decides: The UK General Election 2005* (Palgrave Macmillan, 2005) and John Bartle and Anthony King (eds.), *Britain at the Polls 2005* (CQ Press, 2006).

The electoral process is dealt with comprehensively in Robert Blackburn, *The Electoral System in Britain* (Macmillan, 1995). On hustings in British politics—in effect, the relationship between electors and candidates during a campaign—see Jon Lawrence, *Electing Our Masters: The Hustings in British Politics from Hogarth to Blair* (Oxford University Press, 2009). On electoral change, see Pippa Norris, *Electoral Change Since 1945* (Blackwell, 1997) and David Denver, *Elections and Voters in Britain* (Palgrave Macmillan, 2003). On the different electoral systems now in use in the United Kingdom, and their consequences, there is a valuable compendium produced by the Ministry of Justice, *Review of Voting Systems: The Experience of New Voting System in the United Kingdom Since 1997*, Cm 7304 (The Stationery Office, 2008). The report is also available online at: http://www.justice.gov.uk/publications/docs/voting-systems-review-full.pdf

The classic but now dated work on political parties is Robert McKenzie, *British Political Parties*, 2nd ed. (Heinemann, 1964). Recent introductory texts are Paul D. Webb, *The Modern British Party System* (Sage Publications, 2000) and Stephen J. Ingle, *The British Party System: An Introduction*, 4th ed. (Routledge, 2007).

On the history of the Conservative Party, see Robert Blake, *The Conservative Party from Peel to Major* (Arrow Books, 1997) and John Charmley, *A History of Conservative Politics Since 1830*, 2nd ed. (Palgrave Macmillan, 2008). An extensive treatment of the party's history, support, and organization is provided in Anthony Seldon and Stuart Ball (eds.), *Conservative Century* (Oxford University Press, 1994) and Philip Norton (ed.), *The Conservative Party* (Prentice Hall/Harvester Wheatsheaf, 1996). Paul Whiteley, Pat Seyd, and Jeremy Richardson, *True Blues* (Clarendon Press, 1994) provides a fascinating study of the party's membership and Kevin Hickson (ed.), *The Political Thought of the Conservative Party Since 1945* (Palgrave Macmillan, 2005) is good on the party's political thought. On the party under David Cameron, see Simon Lee and Matt Beech (eds.), *The Conservatives under David Cameron* (Palgrave Macmillan, 2009).

For a history of the Labour Party, see Alistair J. Reid and Henry Pelling, *A Short History of the Labour Party*, 12th ed. (Palgrave Macmillan, 2008) and Andrew Thorpe, *A History of the British Labour Party*, 3rd ed. (Palgrave Macmillan, 2008). On New Labour under Tony Blair, see Stephen Fielding (ed.), *The Labour Party: Continuity and Change in the Making of New Labour* (Palgrave Macmillan, 2002); Stephen Driver, *New Labour*, 2nd ed. (Polity Press, 2006); Anthony Seldon (ed.),

Blair's Britain, 1997–2007 (Cambridge University Press, 2007); and Matt Beech and Simon Lee (eds.), *Ten Years of New Labour* (Palgrave Macmillan, 2008). On Tony Blair, see Anthony Seldon, *Blair* (Simon & Schuster, 2004) and *Blair Unbound* (Simon & Shuster, 2007).

On the Liberal Party and its successor, see David Dutton, *A History of the Liberal Party in the Twentieth Century* (Palgrave Macmillan, 2004); Andrew Russell and Edward Fieldhouse, *Neither Right Nor Left? The Liberal Democrats and the Electorate: The Electoral Politics of the Liberal Democrats* (Manchester University Press, 2004); and Douglas Roy, *Liberals: A History of the Liberal and Liberal Democratic Parties* (Hambledon Continuum, 2005).

On the development of group influence in British politics, see the seminal works of Samuel H. Beer, *Modern British Politics* (Faber, 1965 edition; 3rd ed. 1982) and Keith Middlemass, *Politics in Industrial Society* (Andre Deutsch, 1979). On the contemporary role of pressure groups, see Wyn Grant, *Pressure Groups and British Politics* (Palgrave Macmillan, 2000), Bill Coxall, *Pressure Groups in British Politics* (Longman, 2001), and Duncan Watts, *Pressure Groups* (Edinburgh University Press, 2007). On lobbying, see the report of the Public Administration Committee of the House of Commons, *Lobbying: Access and Influence in Whitehall,* First Report of Session 2008–09, HC 36-I (The Stationery Office, 2008). The relationship of Parliament and pressure groups is explored in Chapter 2 of Philip Norton (ed.), *Parliaments and Pressure Groups in Western Europe* (Cass, 1998).

PART III: GOVERNMENTAL DECISION MAKING

There are various works looking at the policy process in the United Kingdom. Among the most recent are David Richards and Martin J. Smith, *Governance and Public Policy in the United Kingdom* (Oxford University Press, 2002) and Michael Hill, *The Public Policy Process* (Longman, 2009).

Though there are a great many works on individual prime ministers, works on the premiership as such are notable for their rarity. The most recent are Graham P. Thomas, *Prime Minister and Cabinet Today* (Manchester University Press, 1998) and Peter Hennessy, *The Prime Minister: The Office and Its Holders Since 1945* (Allen Lane, 2000). On the development of the office, see Robert Blake, *The Office of Prime Minister* (Oxford University Press, 1975) and on the role of the prime minister in a changing political environment, Richard Rose, *The Prime Minister in a Shrinking World* (Polity Press, 2001). On the support and advice available to the prime minister, see Dennis Kavanagh and Anthony Seldon, *The Powers Behind the Prime Minister* (HarperCollins, 1999). On the argument that there is a "presidential" premiership, see Michael Foley, *The Rise of the British Presidency* (Manchester University Press, 1993). There is also a chapter on the United Kingdom, by Richard Heffernan and Paul Webb, in Thomas Poguntke and Paul Webb (eds.), *The Presidentialization of Politics* (Oxford University Press, 2005). On Tony Blair and the premiership, see Philip Norton, "Tony Blair and the Office of Prime Minister," in Matt Beech and Simon Lee (eds.), *Ten Years of New Labour* (Palgrave Macmillan, 2008).

The classic work on the Cabinet is John P. Mackintosh, *The British Cabinet*, 3rd ed. (Stevens, 1977). More recent works covering the Cabinet include Martin Burch and Ian Holliday, *The British Cabinet System* (Prentice Hall/Harvester Wheatsheaf, 1996); Martin J. Smith, *The Core Executive in Britain* (Macmillan, 1999); and Anthony Seldon, "The Cabinet System," in Bogdanor, *The British Constitution in the Twentieth Century*. Revelations about the workings of cabinet and government departments are also provided by ministerial memoirs and diaries. Among the more recent are Robin Cook, *The Point of Departure* (Simon & Shuster, 2003); Clare Short, *An Honourable Deception?* (The Free Press, 2004); and David Blunkett, *The Blunkett Diaries* (Bloomsbury, 2006). Useful insights from a junior ministerial perspective are provided in Chris Mullin, *A View from the Foothills* (Profile Books, 2009). On Tony Blair as Prime Minister, see the two volumes by Anthony Seldon, *Blair* and *Blair Unbound*. See also John Rentoul, *Tony Blair: Prime Minister* (Little, Brown, 2001) and Alastair Campbell, *The Blair Years* (Hutchinson, 2007).

The civil service is explored exhaustively in Peter Hennessy, *Whitehall*, 2nd revised ed. (Pimlico, 2001). See also Edward Page and Bill Jenkins, *Policy Bureaucracy: Government with a Cast of Thousands* (Oxford University Press, 2005) and Vernon Bogdanor, "The Civil Service," in Bogdanor, *The British Constitution in the Twentieth Century*. On the relationship of civil servants to ministers and Parliament, see the report of the Public Administration Committee of the House of Commons, *Politics and Administration: Ministers and Civil Servants,* Third Report of Session 2006–07, HC 122-I (The Stationery Office, 2007). On the management framework governing changes to the civil service, see Andrew Massey and Robert Pyper, *New Public Management and Modernisation in Britain* (Palgrave Macmillan, 2005).

There are also now numerous publications on the politics and institutions of the European Union and on Britain's position in the European Union. On Britain in the European Union, see Philip Giddings and Gavin Drewry (eds.), *Britain in the European Union* (Palgrave Macmillsn, 2004). See also Stephen Wall, *A Stranger in Europe: Britain and the EU from Thatcher to Blair* (Oxford University Press, 2008) and, from a different perspective, Patrick Minford and Vidya Mahambare, *Should Britain Leave the EU* (Edward Elgar, 2005). On the institutions of the European Union, recent works include Neill Nugent, *The Government and Politics of the European Union,* 6th ed. (Palgrave Macmillan, 2006); John Peterson and Michael Shackleton, *The Institutions of the European Union,* 2nd ed. (Oxford University Press, 2006); and Elizabeth Blomberg, John Peterson, and Alexander Stubb, *The European Union: How Does It Work?* 2nd ed. (Oxford University Press, 2008). Useful recent works on the European Parliament are Simon Hix, Abdul G. Noury, and Gerard Roland, *Democratic Politics in the European Parliament* (Cambridge University Press, 2007) and David Judge and David Earnshaw, *The European Parliament*, 2nd ed. (Palgrave Macmillan, 2008). On lobbying in the European Union, see especially Karolina Karr, *Democracy and Lobbying in the European Union* (Campus Verlag, 2006).

On politics in the different parts of the United Kingdom, there are several useful works. On devolution, see Vernon Bogdanor, *Devolution*, revised ed. (Oxford Paperbacks, 2001) and Michael O'Neill, *Devolution and British Politics* (Longman, 2004). There is a regular volume, *The State of the Nations*, produced by the Constitution Unit at University College, London, examining developments in the different parts of the United Kingdom. The 2008 edition is Alan Trench (ed.), *The State of the Nations 2008* (Imprint Academic, 2008). On Scotland, Michael Keating, *The Government of Scotland* (Edinburgh University Press, 2005) is recommended. On Northern Ireland, see Joanne McEvoy, *The Politics of Northern Ireland* (Edinburgh University Press, 2008).

Useful texts on local government include David Wilson and Chris Game, *Local Government in the UK*, 4th ed. (Palgrave Macmillan, 2006) and John A. Chandler, *Local Government Today*, 4th ed. (Manchester University Press, 2009). See also Gerry Stoker, *Transforming Local Governance: From Thatcherism to New Labour* (Palgrave Macmillan, 2003) and Colin Copus, *Party Politics and Local Government* (Manchester University Press, 2004). Gerry Stoker and David Wilson (eds.), *British Local*

Governance in the 21st Century (Palgrave Macmillan, 2004) provides a useful compendium of essays.

PART IV: SCRUTINY AND LEGITIMATION

The principal introductory works on Parliament are P. Norton, *Parliament in British Politics* (Palgrave Macmillan, 2005); Michael Rush, *Parliament Today* (Manchester University Press, 2005); and Robert Rogers and Rhodri Walters, *How Parliament Works,* 6th ed. (Longman, 2006). Nicholas D. J. Baldwin (ed.), *Parliament in the 21st Century* (Politico's, 2005) offers a useful collection of essays.

Parliamentary questions are considered in Mark Franklin and Philip Norton (eds.), *Parliamentary Questions* (Oxford University Press, 1993) and in the report of the Public Administration Committee of the House of Commons, *Ministerial Accountability and Parliamentary Questions,* Fifth Report of Session 2004–05, HC 449-I (The Stationery Office, 2005). The relationship of Parliament to the European Union is covered in Giddings and Drewry, *Britain in the European Union.* The relationship between Parliament and the law is dealt with in Dawn Oliver and Gavin Drewry (eds.), *The Law and Parliament* (Butterworths, 1998). The constituency role of MPs is considered in Philip Norton and David M. Wood, *Back from Westminster* (University Press of Kentucky, 1993). How Parliament deals with "conscience" issues, such as abortion and homosexuality, is covered in Philip Cowley (ed.), *Conscience and Parliament* (Cass, 1998). The behavior of MPs is addressed in Philip Cowley, *Revolts and Rebellions* (Politico's, 2002) and *The Rebels* (Politico's, 2005). The regulation of parliamentary behavior is considered in Oonagh Gay and Patricia Leopold (eds.), *Conduct Unbecoming* (Politico's, 2004).

The most recent work on the House of Lords is Donald Shell, *The House of Lords* (Manchester University Press, 2007). There is also a useful anthropological study in Emma Crewe, *Lords of Parliament* (Manchester University Press, 2005). The House of Lords is put in comparative perspective in M. Russell, *Reforming the House of Lords: Lessons from Overseas* (Oxford University Press, 2000).

On parliamentary reform and the future of Parliament, the most recent academic works include Philip Giddings (ed.), *The Future of Parliament: Issues for a New Century* (Palgrave Macmillan, 2005) and Alexandra Kelso, *Parliamentary Reform at Westminster* (Manchester University Press, 2009).

There are many works dealing with the problems of the royal family but few good works putting the monarchy in a political context. The principal scholarly work is Vernon Bogdanor, *The Monarchy and the Constitution* (Oxford University Press, 1995). Ben Pimlott, *The Queen* (HarperCollins, 1996) provides an excellent biography of Queen Elizabeth II. There is also a useful chapter, "The Monarchy," by Rodney Brazier, in Bogdanor, *The British Constitution in the Twentieth Century.*

PART V: ENFORCEMENT AND FEEDBACK

There are several works, usually entitled *Constitutional and Administrative Law,* that provide introductions to the English (and sometimes the Scottish) legal system, as well as the broader constitutional context. Recent examples include John Alder, *Constitutional and Administrative Law,* 5th ed. (Palgrave Macmillan, 2005) and Anthony W. Bradley and Keith D. Ewing, *Constitutional and Administrative Law,* 14th ed. (Pearson Longman, 2007). There is a useful introduction to civil liberties in Richard Stone, *Textbook on Civil Liberties & Human Right,* 6th ed. (Oxford

University Press, 2006) and a useful chapter—David Feldman, "Civil Liberties"—in Bogdanor, *The British Constitution in the Twentieth Century*. European law is addressed in Patrick Birkinshaw, *European Public Law* (Butterworths, 2003).

On the role of judges, see Robert Stevens, *The English Judges* (Hart Publishing, 2002) and the chapter, "Government and the Judiciary," by the same author in Bogdanor, *The British Constitution in the Twentieth Century*. On the preparation for the creation of the Supreme Court, see Andrew le Sueur (ed.), *Building the UK's Supreme Court: National and Comparative Perspectives* (Oxford University Press, 2004). On the role of the police, see Robert Reiner, *The Politics of the Police*, 3rd ed. (Oxford University Press, 2000); Steve Savage, *Police Reform: Forces for Change* (Oxford University Press, 2007); and Michael Rowe (ed.), *Policy Beyond Macpherson: Issues in Policing, Race and Society* (Willan Publishing, 2007).

There is a growing volume of literature on the role and effect of the mass media. Among recent publications are James Curran and Janet Seaton, *Power Without Responsibility: The Press and Broadcasting in Britain*, 6th ed. (Routledge, 2003); James Curran and Michael Gurevitch, *Mass Media and Society*, 4th ed. (Hodder Education, 2005); Brian McNair, *News and Journalism in the UK*, 5th ed. (Routledge, 2005); and Mick Temple, *The British Press* (Open University Press, 2008).

PART VI: CONCLUSION

Much recent scholarship on the case for constitutional change and its consequences are to be found in journals, notably *Public Law, The Modern Law Review,* and *Parliamentary Affairs*. Studies are also variously published by the Constitution Unit at University College, London. (See its website at: http://www.ucl.ac.uk/constitution-unit/) Among recent publications addressing the case for constitutional change are *The Power Report: Power to the People* (Rowntree Foundation, 2006); Chris Bryant (ed.), *Towards a New Constitutional Settlement* (The Smith Institute, 2007); and, from the right, Douglas Carswell and Dan Hannam, *The Plan: Twelve Months to Renew Britain* (Douglas Carswell, 2008). See also Christopher Foster, *British Government in Crisis* (Hart Publishing, 2005).

Though pressure for constitutional change has tended to come from the left, various works critical of the contemporary polity have appeared in recent years from commentators on the right, a number adopting a polemical approach. A scholarly reflection on constitutional change is provided by the late Nevil Johnson in *Reshaping the Constitution* (Palgrave Macmillan, 2004). Examples of more polemical works are Peter Oborne, *The Art of Political Lying* (Free Press, 2005) and Peter Hitchens, *The British Compass: How British Politics Lost Its Way* (Continuum International Publishing, 2009), which argues for the reestablishment of adversarial politics in the United Kingdom. See also Eamonn Butler, *The Rotten State of Britain* (Gibson Square Books, 2009).

GLOSSARY

Back-bencher   A member of either house of Parliament who is neither a government minister nor a spokesperson for the opposition. The name derives from where the members sit: on the back benches.

Barrister   A specialist lawyer who appears on behalf of clients in superior courts and is retained through a solicitor.

Big Ben   The clock housed in the clock tower of the Palace of Westminster. (The clock tower itself is sometimes referred to, inaccurately, as Big Ben.) Various explanations have been offered as to why the clock is so named. Some ascribe it to the name of a popular boxer at the time it was installed, others to the first commissioner of works, Sir Benjamin Hall. A light shines above the clock tower whenever either House of Parliament is sitting at night.

Bill   A measure introduced into Parliament for enactment as law. It has to go through several stages. It remains a bill until such time as it receives the royal assent. At that point, it becomes an Act of Parliament.

"The bill"   A colloquial name for the police. See "bobby."

Black rod   The Gentleman Usher of the Black Rod is an official of the House of Lords who has responsibility for security and administration. He is commonly called "Black Rod" even though this refers formally to his baton of office. He summons the House of Commons to attend the House of Lords when the queen opens a new session of Parliament.

"Blairite"   Supporters within the Labour Party of party leader Tony Blair (1994–2007), generally associated with a more social market philosophy than traditional Labour supporters.

"Bobby"   Colloquial name for a policeman (not used much now) that was derived from the first name of the home secretary, Sir Robert Peel, who was responsible for the creation of the (metropolitan) police force in 1829. The police are also sometimes known by other colloquialisms, most notably nowadays "the bill" (now the title of a popular long-running TV police series), but also "the filth" and "pigs" (both rarely used nowadays).

"Brownite"   Supporters within the Labour Party of party leader Gordon Brown (2007–), usually associated with a more traditional, union-oriented approach than that associated with Brown's predecessor, Tony Blair.

Buckingham Palace   The official London residence of the queen. When the prime minister "goes to the palace" for an audience (i.e., meeting) with the queen, the reference is to Buckingham Palace.

By-election   The election to return an MP in a constituency in which a vacancy has occurred (usually because of the death or resignation of the incumbent). A vacancy can be filled only by means of an election. By agreement between the parties, the precise date of a by-election is usually determined by the party that previously held the seat. Like general elections, by-elections are traditionally held on a Thursday.

Cardiff Bay   An area of Cardiff that houses the National Assembly for Wales.

Chequers   The official country residence of the prime minister, located close to London, near Princes Risborough in Buckinghamshire. It was given to the nation by Lord Lee of Fareham in 1917.

Chief constable The professional head of each police force, except in London, where the metropolitan and City of London forces are each headed by a commissioner.

Chiltern Hundreds Technically, a member of the House of Commons cannot resign. To give up a seat in the House, a member has to apply for a nominal office of profit under the Crown which then disqualifies the member from remaining in the House. Traditionally, the two offices used for this purpose are that of the steward or bailiff of Her Majesty's Three Chiltern Hundreds of Stoke (known simply as the Chiltern Hundreds) or the steward of the manor of Northstead. To say that an MP "has applied for the Chiltern Hundreds" means that he or she is, in effect, resigning.

The City The City of London, occupying one square mile in the heart of London; it is the traditional home of the Bank of England, the stock exchange, and the nation's other financial institutions.

Clerk of the House of Commons The senior official in the House of Commons who advises the Speaker and other members of the House on procedure and who has responsibility for a large part of the administration of the House. The clerk is the corporate officer as well as the accounting officer for the House. He is supported by other clerks. When sitting at the Table in the House, he (never yet she) wears a black robe and a wig, as do other clerks sitting at the Table.

Clerk of the Parliaments The senior official in the House of Lords; he (never yet she) is the equivalent to the Clerk of the House of Commons. He is responsible also for the accuracy of the texts of acts of Parliament and is the custodian of the records of both Houses of Parliament.

Collective ministerial responsibility The answerability of all members of the government to Parliament for decisions made by the cabinet.

Commonwealth A voluntary association of independent states and territories. The Commonwealth evolved from the British Empire and exists now to provide cultural, sporting, and some political links among member states. The queen is head of the Commonwealth.

Constituency An electoral area equivalent in nature to a congressional district. Each is known by a geographical name (such as Nottingham South) rather than by number. Each constituency elects one MP.

Contest an election To stand for election.

Conventions of the Constitution Informal constitutional rules treated as binding by those to whom they are directed.

"Credit crunch" The term used to refer to the global economic recession that began in 2008 following the collapse of the sub-prime market in the United States.

Delegated legislation Orders made by ministers under the authority of an act of Parliament. They usually take the form of what are known as Statutory Instruments.

Devolution The devolving of powers from national government to subordinate assemblies.

Dispatch box The Table in each House of Parliament has two dispatch boxes on either side. These are used to store papers but are employed by speakers on the two front benches to rest their notes when addressing the House.

Dissolution The closing, or dissolving, of Parliament to prepare for a general election, that is, the election of a new Parliament.

Division lobbies The voting lobbies in the two houses of Parliament. When members vote (divide), they enter lobbies on the two sides of the chamber; the "aye" lobby is to the right of the presiding officer, the "no" lobby to the left. In the House of Commons, the terminology is "aye" or "no," in the House of Lords it is "content" or "not content."

Downing Street A small cul-de-sac off Whitehall housing three principal houses—numbers 10, 11, and 12. No. 10 is the official London residence of the prime minister and No. 11 the official London residence of the chancellor of the exchequer. No. 12 is also employed for government use. All three have interconnecting doors. No. 10 also has interconnecting doors to the cabinet office in Whitehall.

Elector A registered voter.

Empire The British Empire comprised countries under British sovereignty (though some were self-governing) and in 1918 it encompassed well over a quarter of the human race and more than a quarter of the world's land surface. It began to wither as various dominions gained independence. From the 1920s onward, it came to be called the British Commonwealth of Nations, now known simply as the Commonwealth.

Erskine May The manual of parliamentary procedure—"the parliamentary bible"—the full title of which is *Erskine May's Treatise on the Law, Privileges, Proceedings and Usage of Parliament.* Sir Thomas Erskine May was a nineteenth-century clerk of the House of Commons. The book is now in its 23rd edition, published in 2004; new editions are compiled by clerks under the direction of the clerk of the house. It is relied upon by parliamentarians but has no binding force.

Field a candidate To put up a candidate for election.

Fleet Street A street in central London, a continuation of the Strand (off Trafalgar Square), that traditionally has housed the main national newspapers. The name is still used to refer to the British press, even though no national newspapers are still based there; the last newspaper left in 1989. Most have relocated in the docklands area of east London.

Free votes Parliamentary votes in which parties have not formally requested their members to vote in a particular way.

Front-benchers The front bench on the government side of the House of Commons (known as the Treasury bench, and extending halfway down the chamber) is by custom reserved for ministers, and the equivalent bench on the opposition side of the house is reserved for spokespersons of the official opposition party. Hence, those who occupy them are known as front-benchers. Front benches also exist in the House of Lords.

General election The election of a new House of Commons.

Going to the country The calling of a general election; hence "the prime minister has decided to go to the country" means that the premier has requested a dissolution and the election of a new House of Commons.

Hack A colloquial name for a journalist.

Hansard The name given to the official report of the proceedings in both Houses of Parliament. The name derives from the early nineteenth century, when T. C. Hansard took over Cobbett's Parliamentary Debates. The business was sold in 1889 but the name of Hansard remained associated with the publication and, since 1943, *Hansard* has appeared on the cover of the official report.

Head of government Political head of the executive. In the United Kingdom, the prime minister.

Head of state Ceremonial leader of the nation. In the United Kingdom, the queen.

Holyrood A part of Edinburgh that houses the Scottish Parliament.

Hon (Honorable). The prefix is a courtesy title used by the children of barons and viscounts and by and the younger sons of earls. It is also used by certain office holders (such as judges of the High Court). Though MPs are referred to in the House of Commons as "honorable members," they are not entitled to the use of the prefix.

Individual ministerial responsibility The answerability of ministers to the Crown (formally) and to Parliament (politically) for their official actions and those of civil servants within their particular departments.

Law lords Judges who until 2009 were appointed to membership of the House of Lords to enable the House to fulfill its judicial function as the highest domestic court of appeal. The function was transferred to a Supreme Court in October 2009.

Lord chancellor A member of the Cabinet. The holder of the office used to be head of the judiciary and formally the presiding officer of the House of Lords (though this entailed the exercise of no significant powers), but both roles were removed under the Constitutional Reform Act 2005. Some duties still inhere in the office, though the post is now usually combined with that of Secretary of State for Justice. Since the 2005 Act, it has been possible for the post to be held by a member of either House. Previously, the holder always sat in the House of Lords.

Lord chief justice A senior, professional judge who heads the criminal division of the Court of Appeal and, since 2006, head of the judiciary.

Lord speaker The presiding officer of the House of Lords was traditionally the Lord chancellor, but this role was lost under the Constitutional Reform Act 2005. The House of Lords now elects a speaker. The first, Baroness Hayman, was elected in 2006. The speaker has no powers—the House is a self-regulating body—and the principal role is essentially an ambassadorial one, representing the House to the outside world. The holder also serves on various committees.

Manifesto A party's election platform, embodied in a written document.

Master of the rolls A senior, professional judge who presides over the Civil Division of the Court of Appeal.

Member of Parliament (MP) A member of the House of Commons. No such designation applies to members of the House of Lords, who are known by their titles.

Ministry A government department or the government collectively.

"New" Commonwealth countries A term employed to refer to Asian and African countries that were granted independence by Britain in and since the 1940s, thus distinguishing them from the "old" Commonwealth countries of Canada, Australia, and New Zealand.

New Labour The name applied to the Labour Party under the leadership of Tony Blair.

New Scotland Yard See "Scotland Yard."

Officials A reference usually, though not exclusively, to civil servants.

Old Bailey The name used to denote the Central Criminal Court in London, part of the Crown Court, where serious criminal trials are held. The name derives from the street name.

"Old Labour" A term used since the emergence of New Labour to denote Labour Party supporters who favor the party's previous more socialist-oriented approach.

Oxbridge The universities of Oxford and Cambridge.

Palace of Westminster The building, originally (and, formally, still) a royal palace, that houses Parliament. Strictly speaking, its correct title is the New Palace of Westminster. The Old Palace was largely destroyed by fire in 1834. In practice, the parliamentary estate extends beyond the Palace, encompassing now various nearby buildings.

Peer A member of the peerage (i.e., a lord). There are two types of peer: hereditary peers (who inherit their titles) and life peers (who hold their titles for their lifetime only).

Peerage A lordship. Though holders of peerages are known collectively as lords, there are five ranks: barons, viscounts, earls, marquesses, and dukes. Hereditary peers hold different ranks, but all life peers are created as barons.

Premier Alternative term used to refer to the prime minister.

Private members All MPs who are not ministers. The term is not synonymous with back-benchers, as opposition front-benchers are private members.

Public schools A term used, confusingly, to denote private schools. Schools in the public sector are usually referred to as state schools. Leading public schools include Eton and Harrow.

Quango Quasi-autonomous national government organization.

Rt. Hon (Right Honorable). This prefix—as, for example, the Rt Hon. Gordon Brown MP—denotes a member of the Privy Council. The council, historically, was an important advisory body to the Crown but is now largely ceremonial in nature. However, membership in the council is still important because members can receive state secrets. All members of the cabinet and other senior ministers, as well as some other holders of major public offices, are sworn in as members of the Privy Council. Once sworn, they remain members for life. Confusingly, all members of the House of Lords are also entitled to be styled "The Rt Hon," though few employ the prefix if they are not members of the Privy Council.

Scotland Yard The headquarters of the metropolitan police force, presently titled New Scotland Yard. The name derives from the location of the original headquarters—Scotland Yard, Westminster (just off Whitehall). It now occupies a modern building in Broadway, Westminster.

Serjeant at Arms Officer of the House of Commons with responsibilities for

security, enforcing the orders of the House, and some administration.

Solicitors Lawyers who deal with general legal issues and works in offices in towns and cities.

Speaker The presiding officer of the House of Commons, selected by the house from among its members. The speaker has the power to select members for debate (through "catching the speaker's eye"), to select amendments for debate, and to discipline members, though all within fairly well-defined limits and procedures. After election to the post, the speaker ceases to be a member of a political party (seeking reelection at a general election simply as "the speaker") and operates as a nonpartisan figure. Upon retirement, the speaker is traditionally offered a peerage.

Spin doctors Politicians and their aides who seek to give a particular interpretation ("spin") to a news story that is favorable to their position, often by phoning or seeing journalists in advance of the story breaking.

Stormont A part of Belfast that houses the Northern Ireland assembly.

Swing An average measure of the changes in the percentages of the vote received by the two major parties in successive elections.

Tabling a motion The act of submitting a motion for debate. This is a positive move—the start of a process—and should not be confused with the U.S. equivalent, which means to shelve a motion.

Thatcherism A term used to denote the philosophy espoused by Margaret Thatcher when she was leader of the Conservative Party (1975–90). It combines a neoliberal economic philosophy with an emphasis on maintaining social standards.

Third Way A philosophic approach associated in the United Kingdom with the sociologist Anthony (Lord) Giddens and adopted by Labour Prime Minister

Tony Blair and his supporters, denoting an acceptance of the market and democratic socialism.

Tory   A colloquial name for a member of the Conservative Party, deriving from the name of the party, the Tory Party, from which the Conservative Party evolved in the 1830s. The term also refers to a specific strand of thought within British conservatism.

Ulster   The northern nine counties of Ireland form the historic region of Ulster. However, the name Ulster is often used, especially by Unionists, to refer to the northern six counties that now constitute Northern Ireland.

Upper house   The House of Lords. (The House of Commons is the lower house, though it is rarely referred to as such.)

Vote of confidence   A formal motion expressing confidence (or no confidence) in the government, or a vote on a motion on which the government has declared that, if defeated, it will resign or request a dissolution. Such motions are normally discussed only in the House of Commons.

Wapping   An area in the docklands of London to which a number of national newspapers have relocated from Fleet Street.

Westminster   A district in London. The name is usually employed to refer to the Palace of Westminster, where the two houses of Parliament are located.

Westminster Hall   Part of the Palace of Westminster, the hall was originally a great hall of the king's palace and a place where justice was dispensed. It was built in the eleventh century and remodeled in the fourteenth century. It survived the fire of 1834 that destroyed the rest of the Palace of Westminster. King Charles I was tried in Westminster Hall. Today it is used occasionally for exhibitions and state events.

Whipped votes   Votes in Parliament in which the parties have requested their members to vote in a particular manner. Such requests are issued through a weekly written document known as the written whip. The request in the whip is given emphasis by underlining. The most important votes during which all party members are expected to be present and vote in unison are underlined three times. The term "three-line whip" derives from this practice. If there is a free vote (see above), there is no underlining.

Whips   Apart from the weekly written whip, there are members of each parliamentary party designated as whips. They act as channels of communication between party leaders and back-benchers, and largely as business managers. They are responsible for ensuring that party members know what business is being transacted and that they are present to vote when necessary and, on occasion, to speak when insufficient members have volunteered to take part in a debate. Contact between the whips' offices, especially the government and opposition chief whips, is known as contact "through the usual channels."

Whitehall   London street, between the Palace of Westminster and Trafalgar Square, traditionally housing government departments. The name is still employed to denote the environment occupied by ministers, and especially civil servants, even though most departments are now located elsewhere.

Whitehall Mandarins   The name employed on occasion to refer to the senior civil servants in government departments.

Woolsack   The seat on which the Speaker in the House of Lords (now the Lord Speaker, previously the Lord Chancellor) sits to preside over meetings of the House. It is stuffed with wool and was designed originally to show the importance of wool to the wealth of the nation.

INDEX

Ship To:

Caroline Hilferink-Lenaerts
9625 SWAN LAKE DR
Granite Bay, CA 95746607 USA RIVER GROVE, IL 60171

Ship From: TEXTBOOKSNOW-AMAZON
8950 W PALMER ST
RIVER GROVE, IL 60171

Return Information (cut and attach to the outside of return shipment)
TEXTBOOKSNOW-AMAZON   **Order #:** 104-1241976-3047432
8950 W PALMER ST
RIVER GROVE, IL 60171

(Attn: Returns)

D352261

Order #: 104-1241976-3047432

Date: 08/21/2012

SKU	Qty	Condition	Title	Price	Total
4406997U 1		Used	British Polity	$ 40.34	$ 40.34
			5 9780321216663 Refund Eligible Through= 9/24/2012		

Order #: 104-1241976-3047432

Sub Total	$	40.34
Shipping & Handling	$	3.99
Sales Tax	$	0.00
Order Total	**$**	**44.33**

Refund Policy: All items must be returned within 30 days of receipt. Pack your book securely, so it will arrive back to us in its original condition. To avoid delays, please use the return section and label provided with your original packing slip to identify your return. Be sure to include a return reason. For your protection, we suggest using a traceable, insured shipping service (UPS or Insured Parcel Post). We are not responsible for lost or damaged returns. Item(s) returned must be received in the original condition as sold and including all additional materials such as CDs, workbooks, etc. We will initiate a refund of your purchase price including applicable taxes within 5 business days of receipt. Shipping charges will not be refunded unless we have committed an error with your order. If there is an error with your order or the item is not received in the condition as purchased, please contact us immediately for return assistance.

Reason for Refund/Return:
Condition   Incorrect Item Received   Incorrect Item Ordered   Dropped Class   Purchased Elsewhere   Other
Contact Us: For customer service, email us at customerservice@textbooksNow.com.